A HISTORY
OF THE
TIMUCUA
INDIANS
AND
MISSIONS

The Ripley P. Bullen Series
Florida Museum of Natural History

JOHN H. HANN

Foreword by Jerald T. Milanich

A HISTORY
OF THE
TIMUCUA
INDIANS
AND
MISSIONS

University Press of Florida

Gainesville Tallahassee Tampa Boca Raton Pensacola Orlando Miami Jacksonville

01 00 99 98 97 96 6 5 4 3 2 1

Library of Congress Cataloging-in-Publication Data
Hann, John H.
   A history of the Timucua Indians and missions / John H. Hann: foreword
by Jerald T. Milanich.
                    p. cm. — (Ripley P. Bullen series)
   Includes bibliographical references (p.) and index.
   ISBN 0–8130–1424–7 (cloth: alk. paper)
   1. Timucua Indians. 2. Timucua Indians—Missions—History.
I. Title II. Series.
E99.T55H36 1996   95-32615
975.9′004975—dc20   CIP

The University Press of Florida is the scholarly publishing agency for the
State University System of Florida, comprised of Florida A & M University,
Florida Atlantic University, Florida International University, Florida State
University, University of Central Florida, University of Florida, University of
North Florida, University of South Florida, and University of West Florida.

University Press of Florida
15 Northwest 15th Street
Gainesville, FL 32611

To Nettie Lee Benson
for the lasting impression she made
on the members of her first
graduate history seminar

CONTENTS

List of Maps   viii
Foreword by Jerald T. Milanich   ix
Preface   xi
Native, Spanish, and French Names   xv

 1. The Timucua and Their Land   1
 2. The Timucua People at Contact   20
 3. First Contacts with Europeans   27
 4. The Timucua and Menéndez de Avilés   50
 5. Timucua Political Organization   73
 6. The Timucua's Material World   85
 7. Timucua Traditions and Customs   103
 8. The Timucua Language   122
 9. Beginnings of Missionization   137
10. The Advance of Missionization, 1609–1655   174
11. The Timucua Revolt of 1656   200
12. The Timucua Missions, 1657–1678   223
13. Timucua Demography   257
14. The Extinction of the Timucua Missions, 1680–1704   268
15. The Timucua's Last Years in Florida   296
16. Timucua Acculturation   325

Notes   329
Glossary   333
Abbreviations   338
Bibliography   339
Index   371

MAPS

1. Timucua Provinces and Their Neighbors   2
2. Timucua Missions and Sites to 1655   141
3. Coastal Freshwater Timucua Villages and Surruque   170
4. Timucua Missions in 1675   245
5. The Alonso Solana Map of 1683   270
6. Pilitiriba and the Mouth of the St. Johns River, 1703   272

FOREWORD

The Timucua Indians were among the native American groups who lived in Florida during the period of European colonization. Beginning in the 1580s the Timucua were organized into mission villages by Spanish Franciscan priests who brought Catholicism to the native people. Over the ensuing decades several generations of the Timucua were integrated into Spain's *La Florida* colony.

In this scholarly study John Hann of the Florida Bureau of Archaeological Research recounts the history of the Timucua and the mission system. Using archival materials from the colonial period he traces the interactions between native villagers and Spaniards well into the eighteenth century, documenting the demographic catastrophe that befell the Timucua, the result of disease epidemics, warfare, and a life of servitude. By the mid-1700s literally only a few handfuls of Timucua survived in Florida.

During the past decade Hann has written voluminously on the colonial period native populations of Florida. His translations and interpretations of many previously little known or little used documents have opened new vistas on the history of those people. This volume joins his previous books on the Florida Indians—the award-winning *Apalachee: The Land between the Rivers* and *Missions to the Calusa*, both published by the University Press of Florida (1988, 1991). Together the three establish Hann as one of the premier historians of colonial period native peoples in the Americas.

Thanks to John Hann the histories of the Apalachee, Calusa, Timucua, and other Indians of Spanish Florida now can be read by other scholars and by an interested public. As never before, we can understand the tremendous impact of the European presence on the native societies of Florida. Hann's scholarship is a legacy that will lead future generations to view our past in a new light.

Jerald T. Milanich
General Editor, Bullen Series

PREFACE

Three peoples—the Timucua-speakers, the Apalachee, and the Calusa—stand out as the most important of Florida's aboriginal inhabitants. Timucua-speakers were the most numerous among the three groups at contact and directly occupied more territory than any other native people in sixteenth-century Florida. They were the people with whom the first Spaniards and French had the most substantial contact and the only group among Florida's aboriginal peoples for whom there is an iconographic record. They are the only aboriginal people of Florida whose language has survived in literature of sufficient quality and quantity to permit significant study. Consequently, a considerable literature exists describing the Europeans' first contacts with the Timucua and presenting other aspects of their history and culture. But, to date, no general in-depth study of the Timucua of the historic era has appeared.

This work is designed to meet the need for such a general study. It grew out of my work at the San Luis Archaeological and Historic Site and the encouragement of Jerald Milanich that I provide a general overview of the Timucua's historic-era experience, similar to my work on the Apalachee. My study of the Timucua and their experience under the mission regime began in the hope that such a study of the Apalachee's most important Florida neighbors would improve our understanding of the Apalachee and their experience under the friars' tutelage. After embarking on that task, I held off putting pen to paper for several years on learning that Bruce Chappell, archivist of the P.K. Yonge Library of Florida History, had located the *residencia* for Governor Diego de Rebolledo, under whom the Timucua revolt of 1656 occurred. The library expected to obtain a microfilm copy of the document, which I hoped would shed new light on the revolt and possibly on the 40 years prior to it, when most of the western

Timucua missions, about which so little was known, were established. The microfilm never arrived because of the document's precarious state after being exposed to a fire. John E. Worth resolved the problem by going to Seville to look at the document as part of the research for his dissertation and by reproducing testimony about the revolt in an appendix to his dissertation. The documents that he published became a major source for my chapter on the revolt.

This work is principally historical in approach, but attention has been given to aspects of Timucua culture derived from archaeological research, particularly where archaeologists' conclusions appear to be in conflict with conclusions suggested by the documents. Jerald Milanich provided project reports he had written on Timucua ethnography and archaeology and an early draft of his contribution on the Timucua for an expected Southeastern volume of the *Handbook of North American Indians*. My book is based principally on a survey of the existing published literature on the Timucua and on substantial research in the copies of documents from Spanish archives held by the P.K. Yonge Library of Florida History at the University of Florida, and particularly those contained in the Stetson Collection, the library's residencia series, and its copy of the Jeannette Thurber Connor Collection. I have relied on Florida State University's Strozier Library for documents from the Woodbury Lowery Collection. A travel grant from the National Endowment for the Humanities permitted consultation of transcriptions of Spanish documents in the John Tate Lanning Collection at the Thomas Jefferson Library of the University of Missouri at St. Louis. The National Anthropological Archives of the National Museum of Natural History, Smithsonian Institution, made available photocopies of Fray Francisco de Pareja's two catechisms in Spanish and Timucua, published in 1612, and Fray Gregorio de Movilla's ritual for administering the sacraments to the Indians. Eugene Lyon provided access to several documents from the 1560s from his collection at the St. Augustine Foundation and lent a microfilm copy of the Fernando de Valdés Inquiry of 1602 for my translation of the same. Jane G. Landers provided censuses from the 1750s, and F. Wayne Childers made available translations of documents from the early 1700s that he had copied from the Newberry Library's Ayer Collection. Charles Hudson provided several pieces written by James T. Crawford. Elizabeth Alexander and Bruce Chappell unfailingly gave assistance at the P.K. Yonge Library.

Bonnie G. McEwan, at the San Luis site, graciously answered my questions on archaeological and anthropological matters and encouraged my work on the Timucua project. She provided a meticulous and in-valuable critique of a lengthy early draft of the manuscript, as did Jerald T. Milanich. Jeffrey M. Mitchem shed light on the border between Safety Harbor culture and that of the Alachua tradition. I am grateful for the encouragement and support I have received from George Percy and John Girvin, director and assistant director, respectively, of the Florida Division of Historical Resources, and from Jim Miller, chief of the Florida Bureau of Archaeological Research. I thank Charles Poe for his work on the book's maps and Jean Wilson for her dedication in performing the arduous task of preparing a clean computer copy from a very imperfect laser-scanned version of the typescript, to which accents and italics had to be added.

NATIVE, SPANISH, AND FRENCH NAMES

Seventeenth- and eighteenth-century Spaniards almost invariably used the spelling *Timuqua* when referring to the name of the people who are the subject of this book. But I have used the conventional modern spelling, *Timucua,* except where the name appears in the titles of seventeenth-century documents or in quotations from such Spanish documents. Spaniards were not so consistent in spelling many other native or Spanish names. The name of the western Timucua province of Yustaga is one to which Spaniards applied a variety of spellings such as Yustega and Ustaca. Where such divergences appear, I have chosen one used frequently as a standard spelling and have noted the existence of some of the variations when convenient. But when the variation appears in a quotation or document title, I have retained it. The native names for which such variations exist are too numerous to mention here.

In rendering Spanish names, I have followed modern usage on the whole, changing *b* to *v* and *ç* to *s* or *z* as the case demanded. I have not done so in the Bibliography, however, unless the name appears in two forms. I have modernized the spelling in that case to avoid the inconvenience of having the same author's name appear in separate places in the Bibliography. I have not changed the spelling of names such as Péres, Gómes, and Rodrígues or Gonzáles where such spelling could be an indicator of the Galician or Portuguese origin of the person concerned. I have followed the eccentricity of Anglo-American usage in rendering names such as de Soto and the familiar spelling of St. Augustine when that name is applied to the still-existing town that Pedro Menéndez de Avilés founded. I have accented names such as Santa Fé when they are applied to extinct missions but have omitted the accent when the name identifies the river in Florida that still bears the Santa Fé mission's name. Although Spaniards frequently rendered the mission's name as Fée, I will use Fé unless the former appears in a quotation or in a formal listing of the missions.

The divergent Spanish and French renderings of the same native names present a special problem. By and large their differing renditions of Timucua names resemble one another closely enough to be identifiable with one another. I have invariably adopted the conventional modern spelling, of *Saturiwa*, for the leader whom the French identified as Satouriona and the Spaniards as Saturiba or Saturiva. I have used the French spelling *Outina* generally for Saturiwa's Freshwater rival. But occasionally I have used the Spaniards' *Aotina* and *Hotina* to show that his village survived into the early seventeenth century. For the other major leaders of the 1560s, I have generally used the Spanish renditions—Potano, Tacatacuru, and Yustaga—but I have introduced the French variants on occasion. For the lesser chiefs I have followed the Spanish form.

Although the propriety of using the name *Utina* for the western Timucua province that Spaniards referred to usually as *Timucua Province* has been questioned recently, I have used Utina on occasion. Exclusive reliance on the name Timucua Province to denote Utina's territory is not satisfactory in some circumstances because Spaniards also used the name Timucua Province in the latter half of the seventeenth century to refer to a unit made up of Utina, Potano, and Yustaga. And there appears to be some justification based on Spanish usage for applying the term Utina to western Timucua territory. On at least one occasion a Spaniard referred to parts of the enlarged Timucua Province as "Upper" and "Lower" Utina.

In the citation of manuscripts such as letters in the Bibliography, I have omitted the place of origin when it was St. Augustine, as it was for the majority of the manuscripts cited.

1.

THE TIMUCUA
AND THEIR LAND

Florida's native peoples were among the first in North America to have contact with Europeans after Christopher Columbus's first voyages to the New World. Florida and the Florida Straits appeared on a map as early as 1502 (Sauer 1971:25). We do not know the identity of those first Europeans who gave mapmakers the information on Florida. They probably were Spanish slavers working in the Lucayos, then the Spaniards' name for the Bahamas and their native population. The Lucayos knew about Florida and various peoples who lived there. They allegedly called the peninsula Cautió because its people wore breechclouts woven from palm fiber. But a waggish Lucayo may have invented the name to end persistent questions from Spaniards who believed that the Lucayos would have a name for the entire peninsula, as did Europeans. Spaniards had found it impossible in the beginning to learn the name the Lucayos gave to Florida as a whole because the natives insisted on giving the name for each province (Herrera 1720:248).

The Lucayos probably mentioned one or more provinces inhabited by people we know as Timucua. It is not known what name, if any, the Lucayos or other neighbors of Timucua-speakers had for that people as a whole. The first Europeans to record their contacts with Timucua-speakers provided no general name for the various groups they met. Only after prolonged contact with them did Spaniards begin to call them Timucua, from the name they gave the language shared by the distinct provinces. Even then Spaniards generally reserved the name Timucua for a specific group or groups of Timucua-speakers in the hinterland west of the St. Johns River.

Coastal Timucua-speakers are likely to have been among the Europeans' early contacts because of the long stretch of coast they controlled and the relative density of their population compared with that of coastal peoples

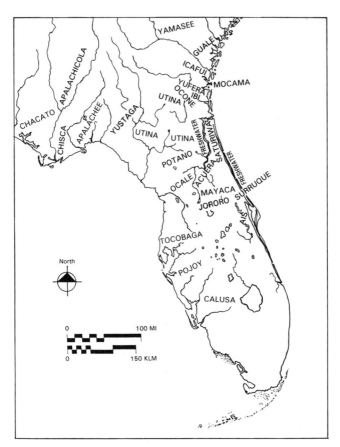

Timucua provinces and their neighbors

south of them. Europeans who approached the shores where there was a Timucua village close to the water could not have missed the pungent odor of roasting *cacina* leaves for the tea consumed daily or, in season, the sweet essence of parching maize. They would often have heard a *whomp, whomp, whomp* from the mortar-like hollowed-out logs used to convert maize kernels into flour. At times, billowing smoke from slow fires used to cure meats, fish, and fruits as mundane as palm berries would have caught the visitors' eyes.

Timucua Territory

Timucua-speakers occupied much of north Florida and parts of south Georgia when the first Europeans arrived. They were then the most numerous people by far in Florida proper (Dobyns 1983:204–8; Milanich and Fairbanks 1980:18). Their domain was the largest also, although scholars disagree about the boundaries of their territory along its southern frontier from coast to coast. Their territory began on the mid-Georgia coast just below the mouth of the Altamaha River and extended southward to a little beyond Daytona Beach at least. Scholars like Swanton (n.d.) and Milanich (1994b) extend it to Cape Canaveral to include the Surruque, a people tied to the Timucua-speakers' St. Johns archaeological tradition. But linguistically and politically, the Surruque may be more akin to the Ais just south of them than to the Timucua-speakers. The Timucua's territory in Georgia spread inland some distance beyond the Okefenokee Swamp, reaching at least as far as the lower Alapaha River, which shares its name with Arapaha, a Timucua village. (Seminoles or Mikasuki, whose languages lacked the letter *r*, probably transformed the *r* to *l*.) At some point in this Georgia hinterland, Timucua territory extended to the Altamaha itself at the Santa Isabel de Utinahica mission (Oré 1936:129–30). Spaniards' reference to the Altamaha as the river of Santa Isabel suggests that Utinahica was on that river (Córcoles y Martínez 1707b; Worth 1992a:76n.14, 77n.16).

Timucua territory reached westward across north Florida to the Aucilla River and southward into central Florida's lakes district to the Withlacoochee's northern bank below modern Ocala, coinciding roughly "with the lower end of the north-central Pine-oak zone" at the Marion-Lake county line (Milanich 1978:59). The Withlacoochee is also the northern boundary of the Safety Harbor culture area and the southern limit of the clearly Timucua Alachua tradition (Mitchem 1989b:571–72). Farther north, at least, Timucua territory reached to the Gulf at the mouth of the Suwannee (Worth 1992a:59–60). Based on the linguistic skills of Hernando de Soto's interpreter, Juan Ortiz, and Timucua place-names recorded for the Tampa Bay region, authorities include some of the bay's people among the Timucua speakers (Milanich 1978:60; Milanich and Hudson 1993:24; Swanton 1922:328–29, n.d.:1). But the Tocobaga of north Tampa Bay, whose village is the type-site for the Safety Harbor culture that dominates the bay area, spoke a language distinct from Timucua (D. de Leturiondo 1978:117–18; Méndez de Canzo 1601). And the bay's Uçita and Mocoso, where Ortiz acquired his native languages, spoke distinct tongues (Elvas 1933:1:61).

A similar uncertainty prevails about the Timucua's southern limits farther east, between the Oklawaha and St. Johns rivers. Some have identified the Mayaca and Jororo, two major peoples in that area, as probably

Timucua-speakers. However, a knowledgeable Spaniard identified them as speaking Mayaca (Ayala y Escobar 1717; Hann 1993a:111, 115–16). For another group, the Ayapaja, the evidence is somewhat contradictory. They have an obviously Timucua-sounding name, but they were linked with both the Jororo and the Acuera. When the Ayapaja first appeared during Governor Diego de Quiroga y Losada's term (1687–93), they were united with a band of heathen Acuera and the two groups apparently acknowledged the same chief. Three years later, however, some of the Ayapaja (under the name Aypaja) were living in the Jororo village of Atoyquime. Governor Quiroga's successor referred to Aypaja as a place of the province of Jororo (Hann l991a:6; 1993a:111–12, 115–16, 118, 132–133; Quiroga y Losada n.d. [1697]; Torres y Ayala 1697).

Two other groups generally identified today as Timucua-speakers are believed by most authorities to have lived isolated from the rest. They place one, the Ocone, in Georgia's Oconee Valley and the other, the Tawasa, in northern Alabama (Deagan 1978:90–91; Granberry 1989:29–30; Hann 1986a:382; Milanich and Fairbanks 1980:216). The Ocone in question are definitely Timucua-speakers, but their identification as an isolate is questionable as it is seemingly based on nothing more than their name's resemblance to that of the Hitchiti-speaking Ocone, for whom the river is probably named. John Worth's (1992a:60–62) interpretation of the evidence for the location of the Timucua-speaking Ocone has ruled out a north-central Georgia placement of them during the mission era, and nothing is known about them prior to that.

Despite the Timucua-speakers' numbers and extensive territory, they may not have been the most powerful of Florida's aboriginal peoples when the historic era began for them. In contrast to other important Florida peoples such as the Apalachee and Calusa, Timucua-speakers were divided into mutually hostile chiefdoms or allied groups of chiefdoms that dissipated their potentially overwhelming strength in wars with one another as well as with non-Timucua-speakers on their borders.

Distinct Provinces and Dialects

Scholars currently recognize 14 or 15 distinct tribes, which spoke possibly up to 11 different dialects of their common tongue. But the number of tribes may have been higher. Scholars classify the Timucua more broadly as belonging to eastern and western groupings, on the basis of their adaptations to different environments and manifestation of belonging to distinct ceramic traditions. Horticulture appears to have made a greater contribution to subsistence for the westerners as a whole than it did for the easterners, some of whom may have been largely or even exclusively fisher-hunter-gatherers.

Authorities place nine of the tribes, which Spaniards referred to as provinces, among the eastern Timucua. They are:

1. Mocama or Tacatacuru
2. Cascangue
3. Icafui or Icafi
4. Ibi or Yui
5. Yufera
6. Tucururu or Tucuru
7. Saturiwa
8. Agua Dulce or Freshwater
9. Acuera or Diminiyuti or Ibiniyuti

The Ocone probably should be included as a tenth eastern tribe. When first mentioned in 1602, they lived a three-day journey from the mouth of the St. Johns River and two days from San Pedro on Cumberland Island, probably on the eastern edge of the Okefenokee Swamp (Worth 1992a:156–57). At least some of the natives aggregated at a place called Lake of Ocone in the 1640s were fugitives from villages of the province of Utina and of other places. San Pedro may have been one of the other places. Reference to the fugitives as "aggregated" indicates that they joined a preexisting settlement (Ruíz de Salazar Vallecilla 1646; Worth 1992a:157). The Salamototo and Utinahica may have been additional distinct tribes, but not enough is known about them to permit a judgment.

Potano, Yustaga, Ocale, and Utina or Timucua are usually recognized as constituting the western division. Spaniards used the name Timucua for the province we know as Utina. They occasionally applied the name to Mocama as well early in the mission period. If the northern towns designated as Arapaha or Onatheaqua Province were distinct from Utina Province, they would constitute a fifth western province. Not enough is known about those northern peoples to characterize them as a distinct province.

Spaniards ceased to refer to Potano as a province as its population declined. It became part of Timucua Province. Spaniards also frequently viewed Yustaga as being part of Timucua Province for other reasons. But Yustaga retained its identity at times. A Spaniard even mentioned Yustaga in 1675 as an alternate name for Timucua Province, probably in recognition of the Yustaga's overwhelming predominance in the province's population by that date (Palacios [1675]). As early as 1601 a governor spoke of Timucua Province as bordering on Apalachee and, hence, as including

Yustaga. The same governor stated that Potano bordered on both Apalachee and Tocobaga, providing one of the pieces of evidence that Potano extended westward to the Gulf coastal lowlands (Méndez de Canzo 1601).

If they were Timucua, the Tawasa were the one definitely isolated tribe. Evidence for identifying them as Timucua is very tenuous, a 60-word vocabulary on the back of John Walker's version of the Lamhatty document. Until its discovery in 1929, John R. Swanton (1929:436, 446–47, 453) noted that "it was assumed, on the best of grounds, that the language of this tribe differed in no respect from standard Alabama, and this impression was actually strengthened by the discovery of the first Lamhatty manuscript and accompanying map." But, after studying the new vocabulary, Swanton felt compelled to revise his conclusions "at least in part and align Tawasa with the language or languages of the so-called Timuquanan stock of northern Florida." A question may be raised, however, whether the circumstances of the composition of the Lamhatty document justify such confidence in its reliability as a historical source. (For details on this question see Hann 1988b:96.)

Division of the Timucua-speakers by dialects generally parallels that by tribes or provinces, but there are exceptions: three dialects were shared by two or more provinces. The Cascangue/Icafui and the Ibi had a common dialect known as Itafi or Icafi. The Tacatacuru and Saturiwa spoke the same dialect usually referred to today as the Mocama and referred to at times erroneously as the Saltwater dialect. Authorities believe that Potano was shared by Potano and Yustaga and possibly by Ocale as well (Deagan 1978:92, table 1; Granberry 1989:37, table 3; Milanich and Sturtevant 1972:1). Most or all of the rest, the Yufera, Utina or Timucua, Freshwater, Acuera, Ocone, Tucururu, and possibly Tawasa, are dialects of the people so named by Spaniards. The Tucururu are a possible exception.

Julian Vinson (1885:xxi) observed that Fray Pareja identified 10 dialects, alluding in his grammar to the five dialects of "Timuqua, Agua Salada, Oconi, Yufera [and] Potano." Vinson noted that "in his other works, he speaks of those of Itafi, the Agua Fresca, Tucururu, Acuera, and of the Coast (Mocama en timucua)." Vinson's choice of *Côte,* or "Coast," to refer to the Mocama dialect appears to be based on Pareja's (1612b:60) reference to his parishioners' dialect in one of his first two catechisms. Pareja did not use the name Mocama but rather the expression "with the names of those from here of the maritime [dialect] (*con los nombres de los de aca de la maritima*)." Pareja's two references in his grammar to an Agua Salada or Saltwater dialect indicate that the dialect which he characterized as "Saltwater" was distinct from the "Maritime" dialect in which he wrote all of his works (Adam and Vinson 1886:88, 121). Pareja spelled Yufera variously as Iufera, Yufera, and Yufara in his grammar (Adam and Vinson 1886:47, 88, 124).

The vocabulary differences among the dialects that Pareja chose to record appear to be relatively few. In his grammar he noted only eight for Timucua Province's dialect, four for Potano, three for Yufera, two for Agua Salada, and one for Ocone (Adam and Vinson 1886:47, 88, 108, 111, 112, 119, 121, 124). In one of the catechisms Pareja (1612b:58, 60, 66) mentioned the Timucua and Potano dialects twice, and the Icafi, Agua Dulce, and Maritime (his own) dialects once each. A rapid scanning of Pareja's other two catechisms produced no evidence of his mentioning the dialects in them.

Little is known about the speakers of the Tucururu dialect except that they were characterized as "belonging to the southern coast along with the people of Santa Lucia de Acuera." Spaniards regarded Mocama as the most polished of the dialects (*lengua mas pulítica*) along with Timucua, the dialect for Utina Province. Pareja identified the Tucuru and the Acuera of the Santa Lucia mission as the people who spoke the most unpolished (*mas tosca*) dialect, with more differences from the Maritime standard in their words than the other dialects had. These differences arose in large part from the Tucururu and Acuera's contacts with people on the south coast who spoke a different language (Granberry 1989:35–38; A. López 1931:48). Possibly Tucururu was the dialect of a subgroup of the Acuera. The Acuera name was associated in 1616 with a mission named Avino (Oré 1936:126). Swanton (1922:323) mentioned a village named Tucuru in association with Avino, locating both of them 40 leagues inland, or four days' journey from St. Augustine.

Nothing is known about the identity of the people who spoke the Agua Salada dialect that Pareja mentioned. Granberry (1989:36) speculated that it was "spoken on undefined sections of the Florida Atlantic coast." Based on the two lexical forms from the Saltwater dialect that Pareja recorded and the ones that Pareja cited for other dialects, Granberry concluded that the Agua Salada dialect was more closely aligned with the western dialects of Potano and Timucua than with Mocama.

Uncertainty whether the tribes numbered 14 or 15 derives from authorities like Deagan (1978:89) who treat the Cascangue and Icafui as a single entity. Belief that they were separate provinces stemmed from a statement by a friar who worked among them: "This chiefdom and land of San Pedro has other villages toward the hinterland, which are its subjects and tributaries and very much neighbors to this island [Cumberland Is-

land], such as are Cascangue and eight villages that are called land of Ycafui."
But subsequently in the same document the friar implied that all of those
villages were part of Cascangue, observing that "the eight villages of
Cascangue, which are alluded to above as being catechized, would have
up to eleven hundred big and little Indians" (B. López 1602). The equally
knowledgeable Pareja (1602) gave the same impression in speaking of
Timucua provinces of mainland Georgia, mentioning only Cascangue in
this fashion: "Cascangue, which are seven villages subject to the chiefdom
of the village of San Pedro." Thus Cascangue and Icafui appear to be one
and the same.

Nonetheless, there conceivably was a fifteenth tribe, the Salamototo.
They first appeared under that name only in the 1650s and were identified
in the early eighteenth century as Timucua-speakers belonging to "the
Salamototo nation" (Díaz Vara Calderón 1675a; D. Leturiondo 1678; Primo
de Rivera 1717; Worth 1992a:300). It is more likely, however, that
Salamototo is an alternate name for one of the Timucua tribes from Georgia such as the Ocone or the Mocama or a subgroup of the same. In the
1640s a Spanish governor ordered removal southward of the Ocone to the
San Diego de Laca mission site to carry on the work of ferrying passengers
across the St. Johns River after that mission had become depopulated. It is
problematical whether the governor's orders were carried out in the 1640s.
A 1655 mission list still gave the mission's name as San Diego de Laca, and
that list had an Ocone mission 30 leagues from St. Augustine on an island.
Worth (1992a:300) noted that the name Salamototo was used for the river-
crossing village as early as the latter half of the 1650s when the governor
ordered a new road to that village opened. By 1675 San Diego de Laca had
clearly become San Diego de Salamototo. The Rollestown site, believed to
have been the site of the Laca and Salamototo missions, contains Georgia-
type ceramics similar to those of the Mocama, and, in an earlier stratum,
ceramics and features identified with the people of the St. Johns archaeological tradition which inhabited the region in the 1560s (Deagan 1978:106;
Hann 1989:186–87; Ruíz de Salazar Vallecilla 1646). In the early eighteenth century many Salamototo were living in Mocama villages, and in a
retrospective report in the 1730s a Spaniard identified Salamototo as a
town of the province of Mocama (Hann 1989:186–87; Worth 1995:184).

Location of the Tribes

The territory of some Timucua-speaking tribes in the sixteenth and seventeenth centuries is relatively well defined. There is little or no information

for others; at best, their territory is ill defined. The latter is true particularly for tribes of the Georgia mainland, who appeared infrequently in the documentation and whose territory has been little studied by archaeologists.

The boundaries of the western tribes as a group are the most clearly defined both in the era of Hernando de Soto and in the mission era of the seventeenth century. The main body of the Potano lived in what is today Alachua County. Recently some have argued that the Potano were confined to the Gainesville-Micanopy area and that the county's northernmost village complex, Cholupaha–Santa Fé de Toloco, belonged to the province of Utina, the rest of which lay north of the Santa Fe River (Johnson 1991:176–77; Milanich and Hudson 1993:172). Their arguments for extending Utina's border south of the river are open to question. The Potano's hunting and gathering probably took them eastward a considerable distance toward the St. Johns River and westward as well. The tribe's territory probably extended westward along the lower Suwannee to the river's mouth. Circumstantial evidence indicates that the short-lived early mission of Cofa at that river's mouth belonged to Potano Province. Two allusions to Potano and Apalachee being close to one another also support that thesis (Méndez de Canzo 1601; Pareja and Peñaranda 1607).

The Utina lived from the Santa Fe River northward into southern Georgia and westward through that territory to the Suwannee and Alapaha rivers. Utina's easternmost village appears to have been at Itchetucknee Springs. Utina's northern boundaries are less certain. A northern tier of Timucua villages in the south Georgia hinterland west of the Okefenokee Swamp may have constituted one or more distinct provinces. A soldier referred to Arapaha as a province in 1630, describing it as bordering on the east with the province of Santa Isabel (de Utinahica) and on the west with Apalachee (Worth 1992a:69). The Arapaha region's physical isolation from the settlements of southern Utina and the Arapaha region's failure to follow Utina's leader during the 1656 revolt lend credence to the idea of the region's autonomy at the very least. Too little is known about Utinahica to judge whether it merited the classification as a province that the soldier gave it. It was isolated from Utina Province, at 50 leagues' distance from Tarihica through a largely uninhabited district on a route that was described as a "shortcut" (Oré 1936:128–29).

Yustaga's east-west limits are clearly the Suwannee and the Aucilla rivers. The tribe's sphere of hunting and gathering extended southwestward toward the Gulf coast. The reference to Arapaha Province's bordering on Apalachee, if it is reliable, suggests that Yustaga did not extend far into Georgia.

The Ocale occupied a zone of north-central Florida south of Alachua County and north of the central Florida lakes region from west of the Ocala forest to the Withlacoochee River (Milanich 1978:69; Milanich and Hudson 1993:92–95, 98–102).

The territories of the Saturiwa and the Freshwater Timucua are the most clearly defined among the eastern Timucua. The Saturiwa lived along the lower St. Johns River and on adjacent coastal lands between the river and the coast as far south as St. Augustine. Authorities differ about the upriver reach of the Saturiwa domain. One extended it as far south as the Rollestown site (PU–64b) (Deagan 1978:106). Another restricts it to Jacksonville's limits along the river but extends it north along the coast to the St. Marys River (Milanich 1994b). Freshwater Timucua lived upriver from Saturiwa territory to the vicinity of Welatka at least and possibly as far as Lake George, and also on freshwater coastal inlets and lagoons south of St. Augustine down to Daytona Beach. Not long after establishment of St. Augustine, a Freshwater community (probably from the St. Johns River) established San Sebastian on the river of that name just back of St. Augustine. Some archaeologists extend the Freshwater hinterland as far south as Lake Harney opposite the Canaveral National Seashore, but it is unlikely that it reached upriver beyond Lake George (Deagan 1978:104, 108–9; Hann 1991b:164–68).

Tacatacuru or Mocama territory centered on Cumberland Island, where the province's head chief ruled. It reached southward in historic and late prehistoric times through the coastal islands to Fort George Island, embracing what Milanich (1994a:248) has called the St. Marys variant of the St. Johns region. Mocama extended northward to St. Simons Island, where John Tate Lanning (1935:203) tentatively placed San Buenaventura de Guadalquini, northernmost of the Mocama missions. Worth (1995: app. A, 195–96) has established St. Simons Island as the location of the Guadalquini mission. Tacatacuru is the name for the province that appears in the sixteenth-century documentation. It was the natives' name for the St. Marys River and for a small island just north of the mouth of the St. Johns, one-fourth of a league from Fort Caroline, where a band of Tacatacuru killed the Jesuit Father Pedro Martínez in 1566 (Alegre 1956:45–48; González de Barcia Carballido y Zúñiga 1951:130–31, 145; Hann 1990b:26–27; Vargas Ugarte 1935:61). Although the Guadalquini's tribal affiliation was not identified when they were first mentioned in 1580, their hostility to the Guale at that time suggests that they were Timucua even then (Ross 1923:274–79). Some authorities have identified them as Guale both then and later, despite seventeenth-century documentation identifying them as Timucua-speakers.

The domains of the tribes of the Georgia mainland opposite Tacatacuru territory are less clearly defined. Cascangue and Icafui are considered to have been the northernmost, probably occupying the coast opposite Jekyll Island south to the Satilla River. Fray Baltasar López (1602) described Cascangue and the villages of Icafui as neighbors of his San Pedro. They were close enough to permit him to visit them often to instruct their people. Several of the few allusions to Cascangue suggest that it was on the northern fringe of Timucua territory, possibly somewhat inland, and that there were two Cascangues, one Timucua and one Guale. A chief of Cascangue went to the Guale village of Talaje on the lower Altamaha River rather than to San Pedro to be confirmed in 1606 (Dávila 1606). The first Indian whom Spanish forces captured in the wake of the 1597 Guale revolt was a Guale whose chief was the deceased chief of Cascangue (Guale Indian 1597). A soldier and two friars stopped at Cascangue and Yufera on their way back from a 1597 expedition to Tama and Ocute (located probably in the Oconee Valley of north-central Georgia). In 1601 Florida's governor spoke globally of "the province of San Pedro, with all that of Cascangue and Yufera" as being 50 leagues from St. Augustine. The village of San Pedro was only 20 leagues from St. Augustine (Serrano y Sanz 1912:145, 162).

Yufera similarly lay inland from the coast. It was an independent chiefdom in 1604 but an ally of San Pedro's chief (Serrano y Sanz 1912:176). It was not mentioned by the friars in 1602 in their listing of places where people had been catechized. Deagan (1978:98) described Yufera as "inland from Cumberland Island south and west of the Cascangue bordering the Satilla, Cumberland, and St. Marys Rivers" and identified Yufera as the land of Queen Cubaconi, widow of King Hiocaia, whom the French visited in the 1560s. If Cubaconi was *cacica* of Yufera, Yufera could not have been far inland. René Laudonnière placed the land of King Hiocaia a mere 12 leagues from Fort Caroline at the mouth of the St. Johns River, roughly the same distance from the French fort as was San Pedro Mocama. Laudonnière situated Hiocaia's domain on a river the natives called Iracana, which is the Satilla. Both Frenchmen spoke of the region in superlatives as "the most fertile in maize (*mil*) that there is on all the coast and the most beautiful," "of an inexpressible fertility," and "as the place where the prettiest girls and women of the country are." Ribaut described the river as "divided into many large streams, which slice the country into large and

beautiful islands and excellent little prairies and meadows," with an in-
credible abundance of fish everywhere (Lussagnet 1958:20, 21, 135–36,
157).

The hinterland in this zone was more heavily settled than it was farther
north behind the Guale coast on the trail to Tama and Ocute in the Georgia piedmont. The travelers on the 1597 expedition to Tama and Ocute
reported that "they returned by another different road than they had gone
by [when setting out from Guale], very much better and more populated,
because there was no stretch of greater than two days without a settlement, and on the other there was a stretch of seven days [out of eight],
and the horse that the said friars brought with them came more content-
edly to Yufera and Cascangue" (Méndez de Canzo 1600b).

Ibi was another autonomous inland province in 1602, consisting of five
villages containing 700 to 800 people. On the basis of its 14-league distance from San Pedro, Ibi has been identified as "the farthest inland of the
southeastern Georgia, eastern Timucua tribes" (Deagan 1978:99; B. López
1602). While the Yufera spoke a dialect bearing their name, the Ibi shared
the Icafui or Itafi dialect of the other mainland tribe, the Cascangue (Deagan
1978:91; Granberry 1989:37).

The only indications of Tucururu's location are a passing remark that it,
like Santa Lucia de Acuera, "belonged to the southern coast" and Swanton's
(1922:323) observation that Tucuru was associated with Acuera's Avino
mission of 1616 (A. López 1931:48; Oré 1936:126). The expression "southern coast" obviously was used loosely, and it, like Acuera, seems to have
been a distance inland. Moving southward beyond Tucururu, one left the
domain of the Timucua-speakers. Inasmuch as the Acuera are identified as
eastern Timucua, the Tucururu's association with them and their placement on "the southern coast" seem to justify identification of the Tucururu
also as eastern Timucuan.

Although Acuera is better known than Tucururu, documentary and
archaeological information on it is still scant. Deagan (1978:111) observed
that the Acuera "probably occupied the area between the Oklawaha and
St. Johns Rivers" and that their "territory included the Oklawaha River
drainage and consisted mainly of pine/oak scrub forests, with numerous
springs and lakes." Milanich and Hudson (1993:74) placed the de Soto–era
village of Acuera "in the Lake Weir–Lake Griffin vicinity." Although Deagan
remarked that the extent of the Acuera's horticulture remains unknown,
de Soto was told that Acuera had plenty of maize (Milanich and Hudson
1993:72). He twice sent soldiers to Acuera from his base camp at Ocale to

gather provisions (Fernández de Oviedo y Valdés 1851:1,550). Avino, believed to be another name for Acuera, was mentioned early in the seventeenth century as a good agricultural region (Oré 1936:126; Swanton
1922:323). Acuera was spoken of on one occasion as bordering on Potano.

When the Tawasa first appeared in the historic record in the de Soto
era, they lived somewhere in northern Alabama under the name *Toasi*.
Authorities differ as to Toasi's exact location then. There is general agreement that they were living in the vicinity of Montgomery, Alabama, by
the 1680s. Because of the slight and dubious evidence that exists for the
Tawasa's Timucua identity, this work will henceforth ignore the Tawasa
except in the chapter on the Timucua language (Hann 1988b:92–103).

Timucua's Archaeological Traditions

Timucua-speakers at contact belonged to an undefined number of distinct
material cultural traditions, as one might expect of people who occupied
so extensive a territory with such a diversity of habitats. Only the provinces of the Saturiwa, Freshwater, Acuera, Tacatacuru, Potano, Ocale, and
Utina have been investigated sufficiently to permit identification of their
late prehistoric and early historic material culture.

The Saturiwa, Freshwater, and Acuera belong to the St. Johns cultural
tradition. Chalky paste with sponge spicules and check-stamping, when
decorated, characterize its ceramics. Burial mounds and shell middens are
characteristic. Their coastal shell heaps, composed mainly of oysters, are
among the largest such middens in the United States. The earliest historical sources from the 1560s indicate that they practiced horticulture, but
archaeologists of late have questioned the significance of horticulture in
the late prehistoric period and early historic period for the peoples living
from the St. Johns estuary northward to the St. Marys River region. It is
not clear whether coastal Freshwater Timucua south of St. Augustine practiced horticulture at all (Ashley 1994; Russo 1992:118–20; Milanich and
Fairbanks 1980:157–62). French sources state that at contact the Saturiwa
moved inland during winter for better hunting and for gathering acorns,
nuts, and wild fruit. Archaeologists have recently questioned the validity
of such a "transhuman settlement-subsistence pattern" for the St. Johns
estuary's inhabitants and for those living in similar environments along
the coast northward into southern Georgia (Ashley 1994).

The Potano and Ocale belong to the Alachua tradition, which was derived from Wilmington-related peoples from inland Georgia's Dougherty

Uplift who moved into Florida. Alachua ceramics have a heavy grit paste. The earlier Potano and Ocale ceramics were mostly cord-marked when decorated. Later, cob-marking prevailed. The Potano always located their villages on high ground close to lakes and ponds, often with sinkholes and small streams. Such bodies of water provided fish, eels, mussels, and turtles. Hunting was important, with the white-tailed deer the largest source of meat. They relied more on horticulture than did coastal Timucua. Only two burial mounds have been found and adequately excavated. They lacked grave goods except for two child burials that had shell beads. The acidic soil's destruction of skeletal material raises the possibility that other burial mounds have gone undetected because of the absence of grave goods with burials.

The Tacatacuru are the only coastal Timucua-speakers living north of the St. Johns River about whose archaeological tradition much is known. For their center on Cumberland Island, knowledge about their ceramics and shell middens is still based mainly on surface surveys. But recent intensive work in the southern portion of Tacatacuru territory has confirmed that their sites represent a transition zone in terms of ceramics, with many having a mixture of St. Johns ceramics and Savannah-derived ones or others typical of northern Georgia, with the Georgia type predominant. There is also hybridization of the two types with "e.g., some St. Johns ceramics . . . more sandy than chalky, and some Savannah wares are less gritty and contain sponge spicules (Russo 1992; Cordell 1993) [sic]" (Ashley 1994). This characteristic appears from the mouth of the St. Johns northward. This subarea has lately been given the name St. Marys region. The Tacatacuru disposed of their shells in small circular piles believed to be the product of individual housing sites, in contrast to the large communal middens of the St. Johns area. The smaller accumulations possibly reflect a more dispersed settlement pattern than the one prevailing along the St. Johns River. The sherd-tempered pottery is often cob-marked, but cord-marking also appears. The little that is known about the Timucua portion of the Georgia coastal mainland and its immediate hinterland suggests that their ceramics also were influenced by those of the upper Georgia coast (Deagan 1978:92, 100–101; Milanich 1994a:248–49; Milanich and Fairbanks 1980:170–79, 216).

The little work done in Yustaga Province has revealed nothing about its protohistoric ceramics. Its mission-era ceramics were part of the ubiquitous Leon–Jefferson complex found in mission-era Apalachee, which was strongly influenced by the Lamar complex of central Georgia in the vicinity of Macon (Milanich 1978:63–67). So strong is the resemblance that John F. Scarry (1985:222) proposed that Jefferson Ware be subsumed within Lamar Complicated Stamped.

Until the early 1990s the protohistoric and late prehistoric ceramics of Utina Province were as unknown as those of Yustaga. All that was known was that Leon–Jefferson Ware also was a characteristic of the few mission-era sites that had been located and explored to some degree. Work at the Fig Springs site in Itchetucknee State Park and a search for other places mentioned by de Soto's chroniclers produced data on the region's late prehistoric ceramics that have shown them to be similar to those of the Alachua tradition. That is what one would expect in view of eastern Utina's position between Potano and the Dougherty Uplift. However, the archaeologists who collected the data have emphasized relatively minor differences in launching new typologies under the names Indian Pond complex and Suwannee Valley series. Late prehistoric Utina ceramics were "tempered with moderate to large amounts of sand or grit" and marked with cobs, cords, and other materials. Advocates of the Indian Pond series maintain that the Alachua seriation does not work for Utina because of a low frequency of cob-marked sherds. A proponent of the Suwannee Valley series observed more tentatively that "although ceramics of the Alachua and Suwannee Valley series are more similar to one another than to any contemporaneous ceramic assemblages in adjacent regions they will remain typologically separate for the present time." For the mission-period complicated-stamped ceramics at Fig Springs formerly classified as Leon–Jefferson, a predominance of sherd-tempering has been used to argue for the unsuitability of Scarry's classification of such ceramics under the umbrella of the Lamar name (Johnson and Nelson 1990:48–62; Worth 1992b:188–93).

Problems of Timucua Nomenclature

Timucua nomenclature presents problems that require clarification. Most important of the problems is the use and significance of the name Timucua itself. Direct evidence for natives' use of the word is scant. Over time Spaniards came to use it variously to designate the common language shared by all the tribes identified today as Timucua-speakers, or all the people who spoke that language, or one of the distinct dialects and provinces of western Timucua (Utina), and then, as populations declined, a combination of Utina, Potano, and Yustaga. It is not known whether Timucua-speakers themselves ever applied the name globally to themselves in recognition of elements such as language that they shared.

The striking absence of the name *Timuqua* from early records contrasts sharply with early usage of *Apalache* to designate both that province and its people. Although Alvar Núñez Cabeza de Vaca traveled through part of western Timucua in 1528 in his trek from Tampa Bay to Apalachee, the Apalachee were the first people he identified by name. The de Soto chroniclers provided names for various subdivisions of the Timucua-speaking peoples. But despite de Soto's having traversed the length and breadth of western Timucua and having sent sorties into Acuera as well, his chroniclers never used the name Timucua to refer to any of those natives or their language. Laudonnière was the first European who heard the name and recorded the event. He reported that the Saltwater leader named Saturiwa applied the term to indicate that the principal Freshwater leader and that leader's people were the Saturiwa's ancient and inveterate enemies. Those *Thimagona* lived upriver to the south of Saturiwa's territory, a short distance west of the river "in the vicinity of Lake Grandin in northwestern Putnam County, near its boundary with Clay County," on a parallel with Picolata, where a Spanish mission trail crossed the river (Lussagnet 1958:93, 101; Milanich and Hudson 1993:189).

Spaniards made little if any use of the name Timucua before the 1590s. They began to use the name at that time for the province we know as Utina. The Spanish usage led archaeologists and historians to refer to that western Timucua province as *Utina* in a case of mistaken identity. They confused the Spaniards' "province of Timucua" of the 1590s and thereafter with the land of *Holata,* or Chief, Outina (or Aotina) of French and Spanish accounts from the 1560s. Holata Outina was the Freshwater leader whom Saturiwa referred to as "Thimagona." French linkage of the term *Thimagona* with that Chief Outina and later Spanish linkage of the name *Timucua* to another province located in a different area seem to have led scholars either to overlook indications that the French and Spanish applied the name Timucua to distinct provinces or to assume that the Outina-Thimagona of the 1560s had moved by the 1590s to the area of the Spaniards' "Timucua Province" (Hann 1990a:8–9).

No such move had occurred. At the time Spaniards used the name *Timucua* for the western Timucua province and its head chief's settlement, known later as the mission of San Martín de Ayacutu or Ayaocuto, the Freshwater village of the Chief Outina of the 1560s was still in existence at its 1560s location under the name *Nyaautina* (F. de Valdés 1602). Spaniards made scant use of the name *Utina* in referring to regions in western Timucua. A late-seventeenth-century document referred to an *Alta*, or "Upper," Utina without indicating where it was. With only that reference available, one might be tempted to assume that the term "Upper" was attached to Utina on that occasion to distinguish it from the more southerly, or "lower," village on the St. Johns River. That probably was not the case. A few years later another Spaniard alluded to "Upper Timucua" and "Lower Timucua" in a context that makes it clear that Yustaga was "Upper Timucua" and that "Lower Timucua" embraced Santa Fé and San Francisco Potano, two missions in Alachua County (Nieto de Carbajal 1707).

By at least the beginning of the seventeenth century, friars and governors were using the name Timucua in a wider sense, applying it to the language that was common to all the provinces and, possibly, to all the people who spoke the language. Fray López spoke in 1602 in this fashion of his work among the Tacatacuru: "I have been in this land for seventeen years . . . all of them among the Indians, and thus, because of knowing them from such great experience and from knowing the language of this province of Timuqua." His remark could be interpreted, of course, as applying the name either to the entire Timucua-speaking world or to his bailiwick alone. A day earlier Fray Pareja used the expression "language of Timuqua" similarly (B. López 1602; Pareja 1602). But in applying the name to the language in the titles of his various works, it is probable that Pareja (1612b) used the name in the broad sense to embrace all who spoke the language. Thus the earliest of his works bore the title *Catechism in the Castilian and Timuquan Languages in Which Is Contained What Can Be Taught to the Adults Who Are to Be Baptized*. Governor Pedro de Ybarra gave clearer evidence of using the name in a restrictive sense in 1604, identifying the San Pedro mission as "principal head of the language of Timuqua" (Serrano y Sanz 1912:171). In the same 1602 inquiry that evoked the two friars' letters cited above, soldiers who testified invariably reserved the name Timucua for the western province of Utina (F. de Valdés 1602). When speaking of the people, Spaniards in general seem to have continued to refer to them by tribal names such as Tacatacuru or Agua Dulce rather than generically as Timucua. As the seventeenth century wore on, the name was used almost exclusively for either Utina Province alone or the three western provinces of Utina, Yustaga, and Potano together (J. de Florencia 1695:196, 202, 205; Hann 1986a:104; D. de Leturiondo 1678:95, 122; San Antonio et al. 1657:11–12).

The usage of *Mocama* requires explanation as well. Scholars use it today to designate the dialect of the provinces of Saturiwa and Tacatacuru in which most of the extant writings in Timucua were composed (Deagan 1978:92; Granberry 1989:36; Milanich 1978:61, 62). It is not clear, however, whether Pareja or other speakers of the language used the term Mocama to describe that dialect. *Moca* means "sea" or "ocean" in Timucua (Granberry 1989:174). In the portions of Pareja's publications and letters that I have viewed, he never applied the term Mocama to identify a province or to refer to the San Pedro mission on Cumberland Island. He and his contemporaries referred to the mission simply as "San Pedro" and to the territory as "province of San Pedro" or "language (*lengua*) of San Pedro." In my experience, the earliest use of the name Mocama to refer to the people or the province occurred in a 1646 order by Florida's treasury officials (F. Menéndez Márquez and P. B. Horruytiner 1647c).

The name *Mocama,* misspelled Mocamo, was first applied to the San Pedro mission in a 1655 mission list that is a secondary source. Granberry (1989:35) correctly characterized the form Mocamo as a bogus one that has "inadvertently crept into the literature on Florida archaeology since the 1960s." That spelling had become so enshrined by the 1980s that the editor of a journal that published one of my articles insisted on changing my spelling from Mocama to the bogus one. When the name appears in Spanish documents from 1646 on, it is always spelled Mocama. The "ma" added to *moca* is the Timucua suffix "-ma." The name *Tacatacuru* used earlier for Mocama territory fell into disuse after the very early seventeenth century.

French use of the name *Onatheaqua* in the 1560s to designate a hinterland Timucua province has been another source of confusion. The French usage has led authorities to posit a shadowy fifth western Timucua tribe bearing that name despite the name's absence in a near 200-year span of Spanish documentation. More cautiously, Milanich (1978:60) suggested that as "later documents do not refer to such a tribe in north central Florida . . . it seems best to delete them from the list of Timucua tribes until there is more evidence concerning their existence." As the French made no mention of the western Timucua whom we know as Utina, a logical alternative solution is to identify the Onatheaqua of French sources with the modern Utina or with Arapaha if it was an autonomous province. The French sources' juxtaposition of *Onatheaqua* and *Houstaqua* (their name for Yustaga) suggests such an identification, as does the Le Moyne map's depiction of the two provinces vis-à-vis Apalachee and Potano. Laudonnière's mention of warfare between Potano and Onatheaqua points in the same direction (Bennett 1975:77; Lorant 1965:34–35). The authorities have over-looked the coincidence of Onatheaqua and Utina because of their mistaken identification of Chief Outina of the 1560s with the later mission province that Spaniards called "province of Timuqua."

2.

THE TIMUCUA PEOPLE AT CONTACT

The Timucua are unique among Florida's aboriginal peoples for the descriptions of their physical appearance and dress that exist, not to mention Theodore de Bry's illustrations based on the work of Jacques Le Moyne du Morgues. But the illustrations are not an unmixed blessing. Because only one of Le Moyne's drawings has survived, there is no indication how many of the details of de Bry's engravings were drawn from Le Moyne's work and how many derived from de Bry's imagination or from other sources. De Bry may have taken some details from depictions of Brazil's Indians with whom French adventurers and merchants had been in contact for half a century before the French arrived in Florida. Failure of a French Huguenot attempt at settlement at the site of present-day Rio de Janeiro in 1555 stimulated the attempt to establish such a settlement in Florida early in the 1560s by way of compensation (Buarque de Holanda 1963: 1:147–60).

Influence of the Brazilian experience is reflected occasionally even in the vocabulary of the Frenchmen who wrote about their experience in Florida. An example is Nicolas Le Challeux's use of *migan* (derived from the Tupi's *mingao*) to describe the Timucua's corn meal porridge (Lussagnet 1958:212, 212n.4).

Fortunately, in some instances René Laudonnière described in detail scenes that Le Moyne and de Bry chose to illustrate and those illustrations appear to be based on Laudonnière's text. Their captions reproduce Laudonnière's text almost word for word. Nonetheless, in using even those engravings one must keep in mind William C. Sturtevant's (1977:70) caution that "the artifacts and activities shown unfortunately cannot be taken as reliable representations of Timucuan life." There are numerous discrepancies between what the engravings portray and what archaeologists have found or what the French and Spanish accounts have described. After analyzing 34 of the 42 de Bry engravings, W. John Faupel (1992:160n.26, 178) concluded "that at least twelve have nothing to do with Le Moyne and have been composed by the engraver entirely from Laudonnière's text," while 13 "principally reflect Le Moyne's own work." Faupel felt that the other nine could have varying elements from both men. He omitted discussion of engravings 9, 18, 19, 21, 23, 28, 32, and 34 "because they could not be directly associated with any part of Laudonnière's text."

The People's Appearance

Laudonnière described the Saltwater Timucua whom the French met at the mouth of the St. Johns River as tawny or olive in color, large of body and well proportioned, without deformities, hawk-nosed, and of pleasant countenance (Lussagnet 1958:42). A friar accounted for the lack of deformities, observing that, during their heathen days, the tribe killed soon after birth any child born with a physical defect. He noted also that "as the land is cold, they are born white. But as they go about naked, although with their private parts covered, [and are] tanned with the sun, wind, and cold, they lose their white color and become swarthy (*trigueños*)" (Jesús 1630a:93). Le Challeux described the men as "neither flat-nosed nor big-lipped (*ne camus ne lippus*) and tending toward a reddish complexion, with a round flat face (*le visage rond et plain*), the eyes keen and sharp (*aspres et vigoreux*)." He noted that they "wore their hair very long and tucked up neatly around their head," remarking that this piling up of their hair served them as a quiver for their arrows when they went to war. He observed that "for adornment they have their skin tattooed in a bizarre pattern [and] that they have no clothing, the men no more than the women, but that the women gird themselves with a little covering (*un petit voile*) [made] from the skin of a deer (*Ciof*) or other animal, the knot being tied over the thigh on the left side in order to cover the more private part of their natural endowment" (Lussagnet 1958:211). Jean Ribaut (1927:71, 79–80) recorded that most men wore loincloths of well-cured deerskin painted ingeniously in diverse colors and that on the front of their bodies, arms, and thighs most bore cleverly designed tattoos in blue, red, and black, done so well that the best painter in Europe would not have been able to improve upon them. A remark by one of Laudonnière's soldiers that the men were "painted in black all over, in beautiful designs," suggests that black may have served in some cases as a background color or field for the designs (Bennett 1964:67). In contrast to those permanently etched designs, the painting on their faces was changed daily. Two hinterland chiefs of the 1560s, Onatheaqua and Houstaqua, painted their faces black in contrast to Freshwater Timucua chiefs like Molona, who painted theirs red (Lussagnet 1958:103). In his caption for plate 39, de Bry noted that chiefs and their wives painted the skin around their mouths blue (Lorant 1965:113).

The two French observers' remarks cited here, that men in general or most men wore tattoos, are a case in point where de Bry's engravings are misleading. De Bry showed only the chief and his wife bearing tattoos.

Jean Ribaut (1927:71, 79–80) described the men's hair as very black, worn hip-length, and trussed up high on the tops of their heads. Hair arrangement varied from day to day for leaders at least. On Ribaut's first encounter with the chief on the St. Johns River's south bank, the chief's hair was "trussed up with lace made of herbs, to the top of their heads." On the following day he "found them . . . trimmed with new pictures [paintings] upon their faces, and feathers upon their heads . . . and hair, which was trussed up of a height, a kind of hair of some wild beast dyed red, gathered and wrought together with great cunning and fashioned after the form of a diadem."[1]

One of the Indians wore a well-polished little round plate of red copper hanging at his neck on that occasion and it had a smaller plate of silver in the middle of it. The same Indian had a little plate of copper "at his ear," which Ribaut believed the Indian used to strip sweat from his body. Le Moyne described Chief Saturiwa's warriors as adorned with "feathers of different kinds, necklaces of a special sort of shell, bracelets made of fish teeth, belts of silver-colored balls, round and oblong, and pearly anklets." He noted that many of the men "wore round, flat plates of gold, silver, or brass, which hung upon their legs, tinkling like little bells." He characterized those adornments as "their riches" (Lorant 1965:38).

A Spaniard, possibly referring only to natives of the coast south of St. Augustine, whom he had observed in 1595, remarked that "all the Indians of this coast wear nothing more than a breechclout woven of palms, four fingers in width, with three strands extending out from it. Two of them encircle the waist and the other goes below. And each one ends in a tassel of the same palm, and all three together form a broom (escoba), which covers part of their buttocks" (G. García 1902:208–9).

Deerskin seems to have been more widely used for breechclouts, as it alone was noted by Laudonnière (Lussagnet 1958:42). A friar described dressed deerskin as the principal material for making breechclouts but noted that those who lacked deerskins made theirs from roots (Jesús 1630a:94–98). Bishop Gabriel Díaz Vara Calderón (1675a) described the material simply as "skin" (*piel*), observing that by the time of his visit some men also wore unlined coats made of a rough worsted serge (*guerguilla*) or a blanket (*frazada*).

Ribaut described the women on the river's north side as "well favored and modest," basing the judgment as to their modesty apparently on the women's disinclination to permit the Frenchmen to come close to them (Lussagnet 1958:10; Ribaut 1927:69–70). Laudonnière observed that the women were as agile as the men and big, of the same color, painted just like the men, and strong swimmers, capable of crossing a large river while holding an infant out of the water with one hand, and equally adept at climbing the highest trees. He attributed the darkening of their skin not only to their frequent exposure to the sun but also to their anointing of their skin with oil for a ceremony about which he was unable to learn anything (Lussagnet 1958:49). A friar observed that the women usually were smaller than the men but described both sexes as "corpulent . . . and of great strength" and "all of an excellent state of health (*de gentil disposicion*)." Women also wore their hair very long and well combed. But the friar noted that men were expected to sacrifice their long hair at baptism and thenceforth to wear it "cut and clipped (*trasquilado*) like the Spaniards" (Jesús 1630a:93, 98–99).

A factor that may have made men amenable to the friars' demands was the Timucua's custom of cutting their hair upon the death of a principal chief. Men and women cut off one-half of their hair on such occasions to demonstrate their devotion to the deceased chief (Lussagnet 1958:46). A friar noted that children from the common people were buried with a deceased principal chief in some provinces, while the rest of his subjects "offered a portion of their hair as a sign of sorrow . . . along with the most precious adornments that they have" (Jesús 1630a:99).

In contrast to the deerskin-clad women whom Le Challeux mentioned, most women probably wore garments made of Spanish moss. The deerskin-clad women likely belonged to the chiefly class. A Spaniard observed that women in southern Guale in 1595 dressed in Spanish moss except for the cacique's two wives. They were loaded down with deerskins placed one on top of the other. The Spaniard speculated that this excess was probably designed to set them apart, as one deerskin would have sufficed for clothing (G. García 1902:193, 194; Ribaut 1927:69). It is probable that most women of the chiefly class began to wear European fabrics with the onset of missionization. But ordinary women continued to rely on Spanish moss even late in the mission period. Cuba's bishop described the usual woman's garment in 1675 as like a skirt (*basquina*) that covered them from their throats to their feet, made of Spanish moss, which, he noted, the natives called *guano*. The predecessor of that Christian woman's garment was probably akin to the ones de Bry depicted, although fuller, either a skirt covering the body from waist to knees or a shawl-like garment draped over one shoulder and covering the torso diagonally (Lorant 1965:113, pl. 39). Timucua women appear to have been more pliant about altering their dress code than were those of Apalachee. As late as 1675 Cuba's bishop found 4,081 Apalachee women still wearing nothing more than a Spanish moss skirt that covered them only from waist to knees (Díaz Vara Calderón 1675a).[2] Without commenting on the length of the garment, a friar noted 45 years earlier that "the women weave certain coverings with which they cover themselves from an intertwined plant, which they call *guano.*" But he then mentioned an alternative garment that seems to resemble the short Apalachee skirt noted previously: "And where they do not have it [Spanish moss], they make another covering that covers them down to the knees" (Jesús 1630a:98).

As adornment, men and women wore ornaments, often made of shell, around their throats, upper arms, wrists, ankles, upper calves just below the knees, and suspended from belts around their waists (G. García 1902:194; Lorant 1965:63, pl. 14, 71, pl. 18, 103, pl. 34). A friar noted that shell was turned into money in some provinces. He observed that "each one manufactures it in his house in order to buy what is needed and [with] this they are accustomed to pay the tribute that the lord assigns them.[3] And from this same money the women wear (*traen*) their *arrecades*[4] and necklaces (*gargantillas*) as did the men in their heathen days" (Jesús 1630a:97). The friar's last remark indicates that men had to forgo use of such adornments when they became Christians. Both sexes pierced their earlobes to pass red-dyed, small oblong fish bladders through them. When the bladders were inflated they "shone like light-coloured carbuncles" (Lorant 1965:99, pl.32; Lowery 1911:2:61).

A special garment, worn by chiefs at least, consisted of a large deerskin dressed like chamois and painted in compartments in various and strange colors. Laudonnière's admiration of one possessed by Saturiwa was so obvious that the chief offered it to him as a gift. The Frenchman described it as artless yet so in conformity with the formal rules of art that not even the most exquisite painter would find anything in it to criticize (Lussagnet 1958:89).

The French noted the presence of large numbers of *berdaches*, whom they referred to as hermaphrodites. They were men who assumed the roles of women because they chose not to be warriors. Their status was odious and they were assigned the heaviest and most unpleasant tasks, such as carrying provisions for those who went to war, caring for those ill with contagious disease, and carrying the dead to the burial place. Tasks around the charnel house probably fell to them. They painted their faces and fluffed out their hair to make themselves as repulsive as possible. The French also observed that some Timucua were homosexuals (*sodomites*) (Lorant 1965:69, pl.17; Lussagnet 1958:44, 96, 139). The status of berdache, if not all the work that berdaches performed, is likely to have been suppressed once the Timucua became missionized or acknowledged Spanish sovereignty. Berdaches are not mentioned in Spanish documents, unlike homosexuals.

Social Stratification

Social stratification divided Timucua society into nobles and commoners. Chiefs usually achieved their position through inheritance, as did their four most important counselors. Although the distinction between nobles and commoners was sharp, the division was not rigid. Commoners with special talents as warriors or speakers could advance into the leadership class. Those who gave up children to be buried with a deceased principal chief gained noble status and the privileges it entailed. Chiefs could create particular lords who, as Fray Jesús (1630a:96) phrased it, "obey and recognize the one who created and gave them the status (*el ser*) and command that they hold." Chiefs may once have ruled as absolute lords, being regarded as semidivine, but they reached decisions in historic times only with the accord and advice of their counselors. Only in the creation of his particular lords and other such matters of favor was a chief free and absolute master in historic times. This stratification survived all the disruptions of native society introduced by the Spanish presence and demographic disaster.

In addition to participation in the decision-making process, exemptions from manual labor and from demeaning punishments such as whipping were two privileges of the noble class. Chiefs, and possibly others, collected tribute. The stratification is exemplified best in the community council house. Fray Jesús (1630a:94) observed that in it "they have its seats placed around with great order and arrangement, with the one belonging to the principal chief being the best and the highest. That no one is permitted to approach this one except with the great respect [and] fear that we are taught for approaching our sacred things. Those of the remaining leading men follow after this seat, without there being any confusion in it, while also having seats for the remaining common people, where they seat themselves without this order and arrangement." The chief's seat was elevated above the rest. Women were not ordinarily admitted to the council house except for functions such as dances or other similar assemblies unless a village had a chieftainness as its leader. Fray Jesús noted that, when the leader was a woman, "she sits alone on her seat (*barbacoa*) and the rest of the women separated from the men." The exclusion of women was not absolute, however, as women prepared the cacina, the native tea that was usually drunk only in the council house (D. de Leturiondo 1678:141; Lorant 1965:93, pl.29). A governor's attempt to ignore the leaders' exemption from manual labor in insisting that they carry their own provisions when he called the native militia to St. Augustine's defense provided the spark that ignited the Timucua revolt of 1656 (San Antonio et al. 1657:11, 12).

3.
FIRST CONTACTS
WITH EUROPEANS

Ponce de León, 1513, and Narváez, 1528

Popular writers have often identified Juan Ponce de León as the first European who landed in Timucua territory, placing the landing in the vicinity of St. Augustine. They based that supposition on the reading of 30 degrees and eight minutes latitude that Ponce de León's pilot gave for the ship's position when those on board sighted the Florida coast. Scholars have shown that the pilot's observations are off consistently by more than one degree, or 60-plus nautical miles, and that Ponce de León's first sighting of land was farther south than popular writers supposed. That has led investigators to identify the landfall as "perhaps near Ponce de León inlet, just north of New Smyrna Beach" or still farther south, below Cape Canaveral, which is beyond the Timucua's domain. Although mists enshroud the identity of the landfall, a possibility remains that Ponce de León landed in Timucua territory. Wherever he first sighted the coast, he sailed to the north briefly before turning south on the sixth day after his landfall. Sometime during that interval, he landed to take possession for the Crown and to gather information. The only extant source provides no other data about his activity during those five days (Herrera 1720:1:246; Peck 1992:143–47; Weddle 1985:41–42).

Pánfilo de Narváez did indeed pass through a portion of western Timucua territory. But beyond that scrap of information, Alvar Núñez Cabeza de Vaca's account of Narváez's trek from Tampa Bay to Apalachee is scarcely more informative about the people that the Spaniards encountered on that march than the account for Ponce de León. Of the Spaniards' experience in the unidentified Timucua territory, he recorded only their satisfaction on reaching Apalachee "both because of the length of the trail and because of the great need for provisions, because, although they found maize in some places through the land, they traveled for four or five days many times without finding it" (Fernández de Oviedo y Valdés 1851:I,584).

Hernando de Soto, 1539

Chroniclers of de Soto's violent passage through the heart of western Timucua provided the first substantial information on any of the Timucua-speakers. Those who extend the Timucua domain to Tampa Bay consider it probable that de Soto was in Timucua territory as soon as he landed (Milanich and Hudson 1993:70, 71, 124). Twenty to 30 leagues from de Soto's base camp on the north side of the Little Manatee River, part of his expedition entered the territory of a leader who bore the title *paracoxi* or *orriparacoxi*, used in the form *parucusi* by many Timucua leaders along the St. Johns River in the 1560s. That first appearance of the title does not necessarily mean that the paracoxi near Tampa Bay was a Timucua-speaker. Linguistically distinct groups often shared such leadership titles. Paracoxi collected tribute from a number of chiefs living along the lower east side of Tampa Bay well within the territory of the Safety Harbor culture centered on Tampa Bay. Jeffrey M. Mitchem and Dale L. Hutchinson have shown trade contact between inland peoples belonging to the Safety Harbor group and groups to the east and north of them as far away as the Altamaha River that would have acquainted them with such Timucua titles (Elvas 1933:46; Fernández de Oviedo y Valdés 1851:I,547–49; Hann 1992b:197–98; Lussagnet 1958:86–113 passim; Mitchem 1989a:317–36; 1989b:571–72; Mitchem and Hutchinson 1986:43–44). Paracoxi's village probably lay in the vicinity of Lake Butler southwest of Orlando (Milanich and Hudson 1993:84).

De Soto entered definite Timucua territory on crossing the Withlacoochee River into the province of Ocale. He found the first abundance of ripe (*seco,* or dry) maize there despite the small size of the province's main village, named Ocale or Etocale. The soldiers harvested enough maize to last them for three months. The famished Spaniards also found beans and little dogs, which they ate. Garcilaso de la Vega listed additionally "other grains, vegetables, and fruits such as prunes, raisins, nuts, and acorns" as having been found in the 600 dwellings he attributed to Ocale. In view of Luys Hernández de Biedma's description of Ocale as "small (*pequeño*)," Garcilaso's estimate of the village's size seems to be as unreliable as is much of the rest of his account of de Soto's passage through Timucua territory. Ocale's residents ground their maize in military-mortar-shaped or bowl-like vessels (*morterro ou gral*) made from a log with a heavy pestle (*mão*) that resembled a bar for closing a door (*tranca*) or a tough piece of wood (*ho mora*). The Gentleman of Elvas's description of that vessel conforms remarkably with the mortar a young Spaniard saw in Guale's Asao in 1595. Before reaching the village of Ocale, de Soto passed through one named Uqueten that was part of the province. In Ocale as mostly elsewhere in Timucua territory, the principal town of the district, its chief, and the province he headed all bore the same name, according to the perception of the Spaniards at least (Biedma 1857:48; Elvas 1932:32v., 1933:52–54; Fernández de Oviedo y Valdés 1851:I,550; G. García 1902:127; Varner and Varner 1951:121–23). The best current estimate places Ocale in southwest Marion County, although no site has been located there that is a likely prospect (Milanich and Hudson 1993:92–93, 94–95).

Ocale's inhabitants withdrew with their possessions before the Spaniards arrived. Garcilaso's statement that Ocale's chief returned after six days is suspect in view of the other chroniclers' failure to mention the event. They noted only skirmishing with the Ocale while soldiers were harvesting maize. One of two natives captured in such encounters told the Spaniards of a very large province named Apalachee seven days' journey farther on that had an abundance of maize. That intelligence prompted de Soto to move on with part of his force, leaving the rest encamped at Ocale until they should receive further orders from him (Elvas 1933:54; Fernández de Oviedo y Valdés 1851:I, 551). He had already left 100 of his men behind in the village of Mocoso with his ships (Clayton et al. 1993:1:62–65, 255–58).

De Soto's first day's travel brought him to a small village named Itara that belonged to the province of Potano. He reached Potano on the following day and Utinama on the third day. From there he proceeded to a town the Spaniards called Bad Peace for a deceit practiced by the Indians. He slept the next night at the village of Cholupaha. Its abundance of maize led the Spaniards to rename it Villafarta (Rich City), a name that might be rendered more colloquially as "Fat City." They also found an abundance there of small, wild, very flavorful dried chestnuts (*castañas pequeñas apiladas muy sabrosas, naturales castañas*),[1] which were probably chinquapins. The land had big chestnut trees as well, similar to ones the Spaniards were familiar with in their own country. The Spaniards crossed another river just beyond Cholupaha that could only be the Santa Fe (Elvas 1933:55–57; Fernández de Oviedo y Valdés 1851:I,551).

The most widely used translation of Rodrigo Ranjel's account (Bourne 1904:2:70) represents Cholupaha as a "fair-sized village." Oviedo's Span-

ish is *"bonico pueblo."* As *bonico* is a diminutive of *bueno,* a rendering of
"pretty" or "pleasant" is probably preferable to one overtly suggestive of
the size of the village.

De Soto could have followed either of two possible trails northward
from Ocale toward the Santa Fe River, which passed along the east and
west sides of Paynes Prairie. Either trail has village sites that could be the
Potano villages that de Soto visited. Jerald T. Milanich and Charles Hudson
(1993:136–38, 145–48) feel that the western trail or a combination of the
two routes is more likely the path de Soto followed. The western trail has
the densest distribution of Alachua-tradition sites and is the more direct
route, but its sites have not yielded any de Soto–era Spanish artifacts. The
southern part of the eastern trail has a greater density of sites and an excellent match for de Soto's village of Potano, namely the Richardson site
on the northwest shore of Orange Lake just north of Evinston. The site has
yielded both early sixteenth-century and seventeenth-century Spanish
ceramics and the lake location fits Potano of the 1560s as shown on the Le
Moyne map.

Documentary evidence from the beginning of the mission era firmly
establishes de Soto's presence in Potano Province. Fray Martín Prieto, who
founded the first missions in the province, met hostility initially from an
old chief of a village Prieto named Santa Ana, the chief having suffered at
de Soto's hands as a youth (Oré 1936:113). Potano is one of only four
place-names for Timucua mentioned in the de Soto chronicles that survived into the mission era.

The five villages de Soto visited correspond nicely with the five towns
Potano Province was said to have at the beginning of the seventeenth century, although the spatial arrangement in the early 1600s differed from
the one in de Soto's time. Traditionally, Cholupaha and its mission counterpart (Santa Fé) have been considered part of Potano. Their link with
Potano has been challenged recently because of the presence of Indian
Pond ceramics both at the Robinson Sinks cluster identified with Cholupaha
and at a site of the Santa Fé mission, rather than ceramics of the Alachua
complex found at Potano sites farther south. Santa Fé's and Cholupaha's
ceramic ties certainly raise questions about their status as part of Potano.
But the proponent of the Indian Pond complex admits that its ceramics as
a whole still strongly resemble Alachua ceramics (Johnson 1991:176–77;
Johnson and Nelson 1990:49–61). The ceramic ties with the Utina to the
north of the Santa Fe River are not conclusive evidence by themselves that
Cholupaha's and Santa Fé's tribal and political ties were with the Utina
rather than with the Potano, with whom they were more closely linked

geographically. Ceramics are not always secure indicators of linguistic ties or boundaries, let alone tribal or political divisions. Rivers are common markers for tribal boundaries, as are wider-than-usual uninhabited buffer zones; Cholupaha is on the same side of the river as the other four Potano villages. One day's journey or less separated all five towns from Itara to Cholupaha. But when de Soto crossed the river just beyond Cholupaha, he traveled through uninhabited lands for two days before reaching the next settlement, named Caliquen or Aguacaleyquen (Elvas 1932:33–34; Fernández de Oviedo y Valdés 1851:I,551). While the de Soto chronicles portray the towns north of the river as linked by ties of blood and alliance, they give no hint even of any such ties for Cholupaha. Consequently, the evidence is not sufficient to assign Cholupaha or Santa Fé unequivocally to either Potano or Utina, but it favors a Potano affiliation.

Evidence is strong for linking Cholupaha and a Santa Fé mission to the Robertson Sinks cluster. Kenneth Johnson's field surveys for the de Soto Trail project "located a crescent-shaped village area just north of the mounds' former location" that dates from the early contact period and could be Cholupaha. Johnson found the site of Santa Fé de Toloco mission just south of the contact-era village (Milanich and Hudson 1993:145).

The first village de Soto encountered north of the Santa Fe River (Caliquen) is believed to be the forerunner of the San Martín de Ayacutu mission at Itchetucknee Springs. After bridging and crossing a river that was close to Caliquen, he went to an unidentified "little settlement" to sleep. The river was the Itchetucknee, which began north of the springs in earlier times. He reached a village named Uriutina on the next day (a Friday). Heavy rain kept the Spaniards there until the following Monday morning. They reached the next settlement only on the following Friday. They passed from there to Napituca in one day despite encountering a very bad marsh. From Napituca they passed on to the Suwannee in one day. After crossing the river, de Soto passed through two unidentified little settlements and a very large one named Apalu or Hapaluya and then reached Usachile to sleep, all in one day. An extensive uninhabited buffer zone lay west of Usachile. After a day's travel westward, the Spaniards slept in a pine grove for the night, reaching Agile on the next day. Ranjel described this westernmost Yustaga outpost as "subject to Apalachee" (Elvas 1932:35, 38–39; Fernández de Oviedo y Valdés 1851:I,552, 553–54). A Spanish governor also listed the village as under Apalachee's jurisdiction a little over a century later (Hann 1986a:102). Among the villages listed here that the de Soto chroniclers mentioned by name, only the names Agile and Apalu reappeared in later documents. However, the Apalu mentioned later appears to be distinct from the Yustagan Apalu of de Soto's time.

Comparison of Garcilaso's account of the trek from Ocale to Apalachee reveals the untrustworthiness of the Inca's portrayal of much of western Timucua. He placed the river that was close to Cholupaha much farther south, close to Ocale. Garcilaso did not mention Potano Province or its villages. In the Inca's account, de Soto, after building a bridge to cross a nonexistent river just north of Ocale, passed through 16 leagues of an unpopulated but pleasant land to reach a village he named Ochile, first village of a large province to which the Inca gave the Apalachee name of Vitachuco. He also gave that name to the village the other chroniclers called Napituca. His account of the battles that occurred at his Vitachuco and his description of the two ponds in its environs leave no doubt that the Inca's Vitachuco is the Napituca of the other chroniclers. But his error may involve more than the simple exchange of the name Vitachuco for Napituca. He has evidently confused Napituca to some degree with Apalachee's Ivitachuco, for there is a void where Ivitachuco should have been in his description of de Soto's entry into Apalachee. This suggests that the Inca may have unwittingly imposed some of the Apalachee Ivitachuco's identity on Napituca. Consequently, except for data corroborated by the other chroniclers, there is little else in this section of the Inca's account that inspires confidence in knowing whether the Inca is talking about Utina's Napituca or Apalachee's Ivitachuco. This stricture applies particularly to his description of Vitachuco-Napituca as consisting of "two hundred large and strong houses, not to mention many other small ones that there were in the vicinity round about them like Suburbs" (Varner and Varner 1951:131–57, 161–68). These shortcomings of his work should be kept in mind when reading works on Florida in this era. Because the Inca's account is the most detailed one and the one that gives the most specific demographic data, it has often been cited uncritically as authoritative.

Similarly, clouds hang over the Inca's description of Yustaga's Osachile. Even though the name he gave the settlement closely resembles the Usachile and Veachile of the other chroniclers, his description of the town as a ceremonial center suggests that he may have confused it with some other place. Milanich and Hudson (1993:164) noted that there is no archaeological trace of any ceremonial mound complex having been built in western Timucua such as the one the Inca placed at his Osachile.

As the Spanish forces moved inland and then northward from Tampa Bay, they found steadily greater supplies of food and larger populations. The increase appears to have been especially significant north of the Santa

Fe River. Ranjel noted that de Soto, on seeing that the land was more populous and better provisioned, sent for the forces he had left behind at Ocale (Fernández de Oviedo y Valdés 1851:I,551–52). Milanich and Hudson (1993:157) attributed that decision to de Soto's concern over the precariousness of his military position in the face of "the great multitude of Indians" who confronted him at Caliquen. That undoubtedly was a factor. But, intelligence about Apalachee, which de Soto obtained upon his arrival at Caliquen, probably influenced his decision as well, as he made a firm decision to push on to Apalachee.

Resorting to psychological warfare, the Caliquen sought to sow dissension in Spanish ranks by telling the Spaniards of Narváez's dismay on reaching Apalachee and finding no trail or settlements beyond it, but only water in every direction, which made him abandon the enterprise in improvised boats. Many of de Soto's men urged their commander to turn back lest they suffer the fate of Narváez and most of his men (Elvas 1932:39).

In de Soto's time all the Timucua villages north of the Santa Fe River and west to Apalachee were united in an alliance between their two major chiefs, Caliquen and Usachile, who were said to be kinsmen. After de Soto reached Caliquen, one of his lieutenants captured 17 people, one of whom was a daughter of the chief. When Caliquen came in peace to secure his daughter's release, de Soto then detained the chief as well. De Soto took both prisoners with him on setting out from Caliquen with his reunited forces. Groups of Timucua came in peace to meet de Soto on the trail, begging him to release their chief and promising that Usachile was awaiting him farther on to offer him an alliance and assistance against the Timucua's great enemy, the Apalachee.

The natives lost patience eventually with de Soto's evasive and dilatory replies. The result was a confrontation at Napituca. Seven chiefs, who identified themselves as subjects of Usachile, assembled there with 400 warriors. Offering friendship and an alliance against Apalachee, the chiefs invited de Soto to come out with Caliquen to a large open field to parley. They hoped to surprise the Spaniards with forces concealed in nearby woods and thereby free Caliquen. Although de Soto was aware of the natives' plans, he agreed and went out to the field with only six soldiers, confident that his cavalry, concealed and at the ready, would more than neutralize the risk he was taking. De Soto had scarcely seated himself on the chair that he had brought along when he was surrounded by Indians advancing, armed with bows and arrows. The cavalry charged at once without waiting for the agreed-on trumpet signal, spearing 30 or 40 of the Indians. Nevertheless, the danger was real, as the Indians killed de Soto's horse from under him at the beginning of the melee. The Indians fought with great spirit for a time before fleeing and seeking refuge in the two large ponds nearby. The Spaniards were able to surround one of the ponds. All but a few of the leading men had surrendered by morning, providing de Soto with about 300 prisoners, including five or six chiefs. Chief Uriutina held out the longest, refusing to surrender until Indians from Usachile pulled him out by force. De Soto placed the captives in chains and distributed them to the soldiers as slaves.

But that did not end the captives' resistance. They made plans to rebel at the first opportunity that arose for one of them to seize hold of de Soto. When de Soto went walking among them later to become acquainted with the chiefs in the hope of winning them over to peace, one of the chiefs, whom he had ordered untied, immediately gave the governor so strong a blow that he bathed his teeth in blood. That assault sparked a general revolt in which the captives seized anything at hand, such as a pestle for grinding maize, to use as a weapon. After all of them had been killed or subdued, de Soto ordered the execution of all but the youngest. The captives were tied to posts, and Indians from the Tampa Bay region, whom de Soto had brought along as bearers, shot them with arrows (Elvas 1932:35–37; Fernández de Oviedo y Valdés 1851:I,552–53).

The Spaniards' passage must have been very disruptive in Utina Province, particularly in view of the deaths of important elements of the leadership cadre as well as of the warrior class in general. The impact in Yustaga was probably less severe. Elements from Usachile perished at Napituca. But, chastened by the slaughter there, most Yustagans abandoned their villages as de Soto approached. In forays from their base at Usachile, two of de Soto's captains captured about 100 men and women from the surrounding countryside. The Spaniards took a few more women at Agile when they surprised that village. All the native bearers from the Tampa Bay region, lacking clothing, perished from the cold of the Apalachee winter. Spaniards' confiscation of native food supplies along their line of march must have created near-famine conditions that took some toll on lives (Elvas 1932:38–39; Fernández de Oviedo y Valdés 1851:I,553–54).

Research for marking out the de Soto Trail has permitted a probable identification of some stops on the Spaniards' passage through Utina and Yustaga Provinces. The little settlement where they spent the first night after leaving Caliquen at Fig Springs was probably near Alligator Lake. Uriutina was probably near Indian Pond in westernmost Columbia County, within a site cluster that includes the McKeithen site. Lake Sampala probably was the location of Usachile and also the site of the later mission of

San Pedro de Potohiriba. Agile doubtless was close to the site of the later mission of San Miguel de Asile, as there are several late pre-Columbian sites near the mission site (Milanich and Hudson 1993:160–63, 165–66). (For more details on the entire de Soto route through Timucua territory, see Milanich and Hudson.)

Until arrival of the French Huguenots in the early 1560s no further contact is recorded between Europeans and the Timucua once de Soto brought the forces he had left at Tampa Bay to his winter camp at Apalachee's Anhayca. If the Timucua's contact with the forces of Narváez and de Soto unleashed any severe epidemics during or after those explorers' passage through their territory, there is no evidence of them in documentation from the renewal of European-Timucua contact in the 1560s. Neither the French nor the Spanish mention deserted villages such as the one de Soto found near Cofatichiqui or the shrunken populations Tristán de Luna encountered in 1559–60 in places farther north and west through which de Soto had passed. Even Henry F. Dobyns, while maintaining that the Native American way of life de Soto's men saw "had for the most part collapsed," conceded that, by the time of Jean Ribaut's arrival in 1562, "the Timucua chiefdoms and the Calusa of South Florida still functioned with something resembling the splendor and commodity abundance that they had known before 1539–42." Dobyns (1983:267, 271) concluded that "the functioning authoritarian political structure of the Timucua chiefdoms reported in the 1560s suggests that Florida's peoples may have suffered less depopulation during preceding decades than did inhabitants of chiefdoms elsewhere in the Southeast."

Jean Ribaut, 1562

Except for the Potano, eastern Timucuans bore the brunt of the Europeans' return to north Florida in the 1560s and for the rest of the century. Crowds of Saltwater Timucua lined the north and south shores of the St. Johns River on May 1, 1562, as boats from two French ships crossed the bar and proceeded upstream. Jean Ribaut, who commanded the ships, had come to Florida with 150 men to establish a Huguenot colony. He had reached the river's mouth late in the preceding day and anchored outside the bar.

An unidentified band hailing the French from the north shore was the first to attract Ribaut's attention. Surprisingly showing no fear of the strange newcomers, a brother of one of the chiefs sent an Indian out to show them the easiest place to land. When Ribaut rewarded the Indian with a few mirrors and trinkets, a native leader sent Ribaut a red leather belt he was wearing as a further sign of friendly intentions and of the desire to trade (Ribaut 1927:65–67). The Indians' desire for alliance with the Europeans and for the trade goods they brought overcame whatever negative feelings remained from their knowledge of de Soto's brutal passage through western Timucua a generation earlier.

It is likely that the chief and other Indians who were the first to greet Ribaut were from the village of Alimacani on Fort George Island. The village, not visible from the river, was probably located in the middle of the island, as was its successor, the mission village of San Juan del Puerto. In the 1690s, San Juan was about a mile from the landing place "through a kirt of wood into the Indian plantations" (Barrientos 1965:41; Dickinson 1981:66).

For a parley with the newcomers, the natives constructed two bowers of fragrant bay laurel (*laurier*) opposite one another, about 12 feet apart. This was the coastal Timucua's standard way of parleying with visitors and a practice maintained by the Creek two centuries later. As Ribaut (1927:68–70) observed, the chief sat "apart from the meaner sort" among his subjects, who showed great obedience to their leaders. When Ribaut sat down, he had to endure a long speech by the chief, of which he understood nothing. In an exchange of gifts that followed, the chief presented Ribaut with deerskins. The two sides communicated their mutual desires for friendship and alliance through sign language. The chief showed considerable displeasure when Ribaut desired to leave to visit the natives assembled on the southern shore. But, as parting gifts, the chief gave him an egret feather dyed red, a palm-fiber basket of fine workmanship, and a large hide that portrayed various wild animals with such realism that the animals almost appeared to be alive. The chief's Indians placed quantities of fish from nearby weirs into the Frenchmen's boats (Lussagnet 1958:51; Ribaut 1927:70).

Led by Chief Saturiwa and two of his sons, the south bank natives received Ribaut with friendliness equal to that shown by those on the north bank. But Saturiwa and his companions showed more caution, coming with bows and arrows in hand and without their women and children, in contrast to their rivals across the river. Saturiwa was paramount for about 30 villages along the lower St. Johns and in the land between the river and the sea as far south as St. Augustine. Before Ribaut landed, Saturiwa's subjects brought the French little baskets of maize and red and white mulberries, while some offered to carry the Frenchmen to shore. Ribaut recorded that Saturiwa and his companions were grave, with soldier-like bearing and boldness. When he informed the chief that the French would have to return to their ships for the night, the chief asked for his cup so that he might drink with them before their departure, even though it was his people's custom not to eat or drink anything between sunup and sundown (Lussagnet 1958:52, 87, 102; Ribaut 1927:71–72, 75). The source did not make clear whether the drink of which they partook was the natives' cacina or the Frenchmen's wine. If it were the latter, that might indicate that Saturiwa knew of the attractions of wine from an earlier unrecorded European voyage along that coast.

When the French revisited their new allies on the north shore the next day, its natives showered them with gifts of painted and unpainted deerskins, meal, little cakes, fresh water, rhubarb-like roots used to make a medicinal drink, little bags of red color (probably red ochre), and bits of some type of ore. On going to the south shore, the French found Saturiwa and his people waiting for them quietly with their faces painted differently than on the previous day and wearing feathers in their hair. Although the chief's sons received Ribaut graciously, Saturiwa initially maintained an austere reserve that led Ribaut to speculate that Saturiwa was displeased over the Frenchman's erection of a stone marker in his territory or because the French had again visited with the north shore's inhabitants first. But Saturiwa's reserve melted when Ribaut presented him with various gifts (Lussagnet 1958:15, 52–53; Ribaut 1927:79).

After only two days at the river's mouth, Ribaut sailed northward, stopping at various bays and their rivers between the St. Johns and the Savannah. At their first stop, the mouth of the St. Marys, the French saw their first Timucua village about three leagues into the estuary. They landed close to the village and inspected its houses. Although the natives were unhappy over this, they did not attempt to stop the French. As the French approached, the men simply cried out so that their wives and children might flee with their household goods. They would not accompany the French into the village until they saw that the French meant no harm. As the French were leaving, the Indians presented them with deerskins, fruit, and water. On an island farther north, possibly Cumberland Island, they met another Timucua chief as affable as all the others had been. That was probably their last stop in Timucua territory (Lussagnet 1958:53; Ribaut 1927:83–85, 86, 88). During the voyage, neither Ribaut nor the men he left behind when he returned to Europe had any further contact with Timucua-speakers.

Hernando Manrique de Rojas, 1564

Spaniards were the next Europeans to visit Timucua territory in May of 1564. In response to orders from his king, Cuba's governor dispatched Captain Hernando Manrique de Rojas to look for the stone columns the French had left and the fort they had built at Port Royal in southern South Carolina. If the two readings taken by his pilot were accurate, Manrique de Rojas made his first landing in the vicinity of Mosquito Inlet, probably the southern limit of Timucua territory. Spaniards then identified that section of the coast as the Ribera de la Cruz (Shore of the Cross). They found no sign of the French presence there in a village on the bank of a river that flowed into the harbor. The village is likely to have been one of the southernmost Freshwater settlements such as Caparaca or Cicale. The Spaniards failed to learn anything about the French from the natives because of the language barrier.

The Spaniards landed next at about 29 1/2 degrees latitude at another river eight or nine leagues to the north. The distance suggests that it was in the Tomoka Basin. If that is the case, the deserted Indian huts that they saw close to (*junto a*) the river's mouth on the arm on the north side are those identified by John Griffin and Hale Smith (1949:341) simply as habitations rather than the village of Nocoroco, which is on the south side of the basin.

Manrique de Rojas finally found signs of the French presence on landing within the mouth of the St. Johns River. However, he did not find the stone pillar there. He visited an unidentified village on an arm of the river that ran southward, such as does the Channel of San Pablo, where they encountered about 80 Indians. The Indians told them through sign language of the visit by three French ships, which had sailed away northward. Before the Spaniards landed again, they had passed beyond Timucua territory to a region whose chief held the unmistakably Muskogean title of "*micoo*" (Manrique de Rojas 1564; Mexía 1605d; Rouse 1951:266, 269–71; Wenhold 1959:45–51).

René de Laudonnière, 1564–1565

Timucua contact with the French resumed on June 22, 1564, when René de Laudonnière landed near the soon-to-be-established Spanish settlement of St. Augustine. He received a friendly reception from that area's Indians, probably inhabitants of Seloy, which Pedro Menéndez would appropriate as the first site for St. Augustine (Lussagnet 1958:53–54).

The Timucua's sustained contact with Europeans began with Laudonnière's arrival. For the 1560s at least, this contact produced a much more fruitful documentary record than the earlier episodic contacts. The French and Spanish accounts' greatest contribution is the light they focus on the political panorama of the world of the eastern Timucua in the 1560s.

The *paraousti,* or chief, who greeted Laudonnière at Matanzas Inlet was anxious that the French should trade with him and his people. The chief explained by signs that they wanted to give some presents to the French. Excusing himself from such offers tied to a long-term commitment, Laudonnière sailed north to the St. Johns River in search of a place to build a fort and village. He found Saturiwa waiting for him, shouting, "Antipola, Antipola," which he interpreted as meaning "brother" or "friend" or something similar. The chief was accompanied by women as well as men on this occasion. He soon suggested a visit to the stone marker that Ribaut had left. The French found it crowned with laurel, and little baskets of maize were placed at the foot of it. The natives kissed the stone with great reverence and asked the French to do the same. Aware of what would arouse French interest in a permanent alliance, Saturiwa had one of his sons present an ingot (*lingot*) of silver to Laudonnière. After that, Laudonnière returned to his ships for the night (Lorant 1965:32, 51, pl. 8; Lussagnet 1958:86–88).

The next morning he found Saturiwa awaiting him in the customary arbor, accompanied by 80 Indians and wearing the large decorated deer-skin mentioned earlier. When Laudonnière asked to be excused so that he might explore upriver a short distance, Saturiwa offered him the deerskin as a pledge for his promise to wait there until Laudonnière's return. On his return, Laudonnière asked the chief where the silver ingot had come from. When Laudonnière failed to grasp the chief's quick verbal response, the chief showed him "by obvious signs that all of it came from farther inland on the river some days journey from this place and he made us understand that they had taken all that they had by force of arms from the inhabitants of that place, whom they called 'Thimagona,' their most ancient and natural enemies" (Lussagnet 1958:87, 88, 93).

The preceding passage shows that the French were still relying on sign language at this stage, contrary to Le Moyne's assertion that one of Laudonnière's officers, François de la Caille, understood the natives' language because he had been there before with Ribaut (Lorant 1965:38). Le Moyne did not explain how la Caille had learned Timucua in the four or five days at most that Ribaut spent in Timucua territory in 1562.

Laudonnière, having perceived the emotion with which the chief uttered the name Thimagona and understanding what Saturiwa would like to hear, volunteered to accompany Saturiwa with all the French forces if Saturiwa should wish to fight the Thimagona. Hope of establishing such an alliance with the powerful newcomers had doubtless inspired the enthusiastically friendly reception the French received on their return. Elated, Saturiwa assured his new ally that he would make the expedition within a short time, once he had ground maize in sufficient quantity and commanded his people to ready their bows and an adequate number of arrows. He begged Laudonnière very warmly not to go back on his promise, pointing out that both their interests converged in this project, as Laudonnière would obtain a good quantity of gold and silver from a successful campaign (Lussagnet 1958:93). Saturiwa's concern was prescient. Considering the Thimagona's chief a more valuable ally in view of his control of access to stores of silver and gold, Laudonnière was soon to ally himself with the Thimagona in a campaign against another of the Thimagona's enemies, the Potano chief whom the French called Potavou.

On the next day the French sailed toward the St. Marys River, to which they had given the name Seine and then on to the Satilla, known to the French as the Somme. On landing to explore, they were received by a chief with whom Ribaut had formed an alliance in 1562. Although Laudonnière identified the chief only as one of the tallest and best-proportioned men possible, it is probable that he was Cumberland Island's Chief Tacatacuru, paramount for the region. The chief was accompanied by a beauteous wife and five daughters. The chief had his wife present Laudonnière with a number of little silver balls (*petites boulettes*), indicating that precious metals had spread widely among eastern Timucuan leaders. The chief presented Laudonnière his bow and arrows, as he had done with Ribaut. The latter gift signified confederation and perpetual alliance.

On returning to his ships, Laudonnière convoked a meeting of his people to decide where the new French settlement should be made. The abundance of maize in the vicinity of the St. Johns River and the inhabitants' possession of gold and silver induced them to select the mouth of the St. Johns River. They found a suitable site in short order on land belonging to Chief Saturiwa, whose village was its closest neighbor.

The chief watched their activity closely. Laudonnière supplied him liberally with merchandise to maintain his goodwill. Not long after the French began work on the fort, a number of Saturiwa's chiefs, in their turn, sought to impress Laudonnière with Saturiwa's power, claiming that he could muster an army many thousand strong. That news moved the French to hasten completion of their fort (Lorant 1965:37–38; Lussagnet 1958:93–98).

Saturiwa's Attack on the Thimagona

About two months after Laudonnière's arrival, Saturiwa informed him that his expedition against Paracousi Outina, leader of the Thimagona, was ready to depart. Laudonnière had allied with Outina by then in the belief that Outina was more powerful than Saturiwa and that his goodwill was needed for access to the source of the gold and silver Laudonnière had seen among the Timucua. He had established contact with the Thimagona as soon as he had completed his fort. Consequently, he offered lame excuses rather than soldiers, suggesting that Saturiwa defer the campaign for two moons' time, saying that he would then inform him about fulfilling the promise given earlier. Chagrined, Saturiwa went forward with the expedition because his own good faith was by then involved in doing so at once. He had readied the needed foodstuffs and assembled 10 other paracousis and more than 500 warriors who were to join him in the enterprise.

After ceremonies to invoke the sun-god's favor and after loading his equipment, Saturiwa proceeded upriver with such speed that he reached enemy territory two hours before sunset on the second day. He assembled his council after landing 8 or 10 leagues short of the enemy's villages. It was decided that five of the paracousis would go forward by water with one-half of the warriors, while Saturiwa took the rest overland through the woods as quietly as possible, joining up for a surprise attack on the village at daybreak. The strategy succeeded in that the attackers took an unspecified number of scalps along with 24 prisoners, who were sent off downriver. The warriors also withdrew at once to dugouts that awaited them.

Nature of Indian Warfare

Such short surprise raids by relatively small forces seem to have been the standard form of Indian warfare throughout Florida, rather than prolonged campaigns designed to vanquish an enemy completely, involving most or all of a chief's available warriors. Such a limited approach to war provoked the disgust of French auxiliaries who assisted Paracousi Outina later in an attack on another principal rival, Potavou. Once Potano's forces had been routed and a considerable number of them killed in a three-hour engagement, Outina insisted in breaking off the attack and returning home to celebrate the victory. He was not interested in pursuing the struggle to defeat the Potano decisively, as the French wanted to do in conformity with the European idea of what war was all about. Laudonnière noted that chiefs always made war by surprise attack, killing and scalping all the men they could, but sparing women and children, whom they retained permanently among themselves. Victorious chiefs assembled all their subjects on their return for three days and nights of merrymaking during which they danced and sang (Lorant 1965:42, 44; Lussagnet 1958:43, 107–10).

Laudonnière's Alliance with Paracousi Outina

When Saturiwa returned from his victorious raid, Laudonnière compounded his earlier affront to the chief in refusing to aid him against Outina. He forced Saturiwa to hand over to him the Thimagona captives that the expedition had taken. However much Saturiwa was angered by this imposition, his desire for a French alliance or his fear of French power was such that he continued friendly relations, sending gifts of food and promising the French that they would not want for food as long as they remained in his land. Laudonnière, in turn, sought to convince Saturiwa that it was in the chief's interest to make peace with Outina so that the chief might gain passage through Outina's territory to attack another old enemy named Oathaqua, who lived farther south in the area of Cape Canaveral.

The reliability of the statement that Oathaqua was Saturiwa's enemy is questionable. Elsewhere Mayaca was described as an ally of Saturiwa and it also seems to have been allied to Ais leaders such as Oathaqua (Lussagnet 1958:112). The sheer distance that separated the two chiefs, not to mention the hostile territory of Outina, which lay between their lands, would seem to have ruled out any mutual hostilities.

Prior to demanding that Saturiwa hand over his Thimagona captives, the French established friendly relations with some of Outina's vassal chiefs through an expedition upriver. They encountered three canoes of Thimagona about 20 leagues from the French fort. The French asked by signs if they had any gold or silver with them. The natives replied no, but said the metals could be had from a chief named Mayrra, who lived three days' journey to the south. Before returning to the fort, the Frenchmen left a soldier behind, who was to go to Mayrra. By the time a second expedition under Captain Thomas Le Vasseur headed upriver 15 days later, the soldier had collected five or six pounds of silver in barter with the natives. Le Vasseur found the soldier at the house of a chief named Molona, who identified himself and nine chiefs allied to him as among Outina's more than 40 vassal chiefs. The nine were Cadecha, Chilili, Eclavou, Euacappe, Calanay, Onachaquara, Omittaqua, Acuera, and Moquoso.

Molona entranced the French with fantastic tales about the wealth in precious metals held by those nine chiefs and by Chiefs Onatheaqua and Houstaqua of western Timucua. When Le Vasseur promised an alliance with Outina for a campaign against Onatheaqua and Houstaqua, Molona assured him that even the least of the chiefs whom he had named as allies would give such an expedition's leader a height of two feet of gold and silver, which they had already taken by conquest from those two chiefs (Lussagnet 1958:99–103). Although native leaders of central and south Florida had acquired gold and silver from shipwrecks through trade and tribute or as gifts, there is no evidence that the metals reached Freshwater Timucua, the Acuera, or the western Timucua in such quantity. Molona seems to have concocted his tales to win a French alliance for Outina and his supporters against an enemy closer at hand, the Potano. His stories achieved their purpose.

To cement French ties directly with Outina, Laudonnière returned the Thimagona captives to that chief by means of a small French force under Lord d'Arlac, whom he instructed to stay with Outina for a time. D'Arlac and Le Vasseur sailed with the captives around September 10, 1564. Outina welcomed them with a feast and asked them to stay for a time to join him in waging war against his enemy, Potano, who lived 25 leagues from Outina's village. When d'Arlac agreed, 200 natives and six Frenchmen took the village by surprise. When a musket shot felled the leader of the Potano defenders, the rest fled, permitting Outina's Indians to enter the village and take men, women, and children as prisoners. When d'Arlac returned to Fort Caroline about two weeks later, Outina sent Laudonnière gifts: some silver, a little bit of gold, painted skins, and other apparel, along with a thousand thanks and a promise that, if Laudonnière should need men for any enterprise of consequence, Outina would furnish him with 300 or more (Lussagnet 1958:114–16).

Subsequently Outina asked for 12 to 15 soldiers armed with harquebuses to assist him in attacking Potano again, promising that when Potano was defeated, he would conduct Laudonnière to the mountains where the treasures that the French sought were to be found. Laudonnière sent 30 men under Lieutenant d'Ottigny. Two days after their arrival, when provisions had been readied, Outina set out with the French and 300 warriors. By nightfall they had not yet covered half the distance to Potano. The natives broke into groups of six for the night's camp, scattered in a circle around the place where Outina bedded down. Each group built a campfire. The most trusted archers stood guard around the chief. On the second day a scouting party encountered three Potano fishermen on a pond about three leagues from Potano. The escape of two of the Potano prompted Outina to turn to his seer-shaman for advice. After performing his ceremonies, the shaman advised against continuing the expedition, warning that Potano would be waiting for them at a certain place with a full 2,000 warriors who would capture some of Outina's warriors. Only d'Ottigny's anger and contempt shamed Outina into going forward.

Allegedly, they encountered Potano at the place the shaman had foretold. After a three-hour battle in which many of Potano's warriors were killed, the rest abandoned the field. It was on this occasion that Outina, satisfied with that achievement, further angered the French by refusing to pursue and crush the enemy, as the French wished to do (Lussagnet 1958:138–41).

On returning to his village, Outina summoned 18 or 20 of his other vassal chiefs to attend the feasts and dances held to celebrate his victory. Despite his disgust with the native style of warfare, d'Ottigny left 12 of his men temporarily in Outina's village to help protect it from a Potano retaliatory attack.

Overlooking this developing French alliance with Outina, a number of Saturiwa's vassal chiefs visited Laudonnière after d'Ottigny's return to Fort Caroline. Bringing presents, they proposed that Laudonnière now take the Saturiwa as his allies and hold Outina in hatred (Lussagnet 1958:141).

Timucua Traders

As the spring of 1565 advanced and the expected resupply from France did not appear, the French began to experience hunger. By then the Indians were unable to provide them with much other than a few fish. Aware that they enjoyed a sellers' market, the Indians' hard bargaining soon exhausted the remaining French merchandise. The Indians met French objections to the prices with mockery, telling the French to eat the merchandise if they were not content with the Indians' prices. Even Laudonnière's appeals to Outina brought nothing other than 12 or 15 baskets of acorns and two of chinquapins, as Outina insisted that what maize he had left was meant for planting. But Outina held out the hope that if the French helped him against one of his disobedient vassals, the French might capture maize and acorns. The suggestion was a ruse. When the French arrived, Outina employed them against enemies who were not his vassals and who had no stores of food to be captured. This soured French relations with Outina (Lussagnet 1958:142–45).

The French Take Outina Hostage

Angered by the deception and prodded by hunger, the French seized Outina as a hostage, to be ransomed by his people in exchange for food. The tactic gained the French little food, eventually brought hostilities between Outina's warriors and the French, and set off a struggle for Outina's leadership position that undermined his value as a hostage. Despairing of freeing Outina, his people assembled in their council house to choose a new leader. Because of the importance of Laudonnière's description of this development and the potentially misleading free rendition given it in the Bennett translation, Laudonnière's text is presented here word for word in a literal rendering. "Then Outina's father-in-law lifted one of the King's little children (*petits enfans*) up onto the Royal seat (*le siege Royal*); and this done, that by a plurality of voice, homage was rendered to him by each one. This election was almost (*presque*) the cause of great troubles among them because the relative (*parent*) of one of the neighboring kings claimed the kingdom and in fact he already had a faction (*partie*) among its subjects. Nevertheless, this enterprise was not able to be executed, as he was checked by the common consent of the leaders and notified that the child (*enfant*) was more suited (*plus idoine*) to succeed his father than any other" (Lussagnet 1958:148).

Conceivably, the struggle for power indeed involved the elements that Laudonnière portrayed. But it is very possible that his Eurocentric views on succession distorted his identification of the elements involved. A chief's heir among the Timucua was normally his oldest nephew from his eldest sister. But in such troubled times the solution of installing one of Outina's children may have won support as a way of safeguarding Outina's rights in case he won his freedom. Such a solution may have appealed as well to the leader or leaders who would serve as regent for the young child.

Detention of Outina brought many offers from hostile neighbors to provide all the food the French needed if Laudonnière would put Outina to death. On two occasions Saturiwa sent seven or eight baskets of maize or acorns as a pledge of his sincerity, seeking to whet Laudonnière's appetite for such a deal. Laudonnière resisted trading Outina's life for food even in the face of demands from his soldiers that Outina be killed after they had made expeditions upriver inspired by false reports from Outina that maize had begun to ripen. Laudonnière contented himself with plundering the new crops when such reports proved to be true (Lussagnet 1958:148, 149–50, 152, 153, 154, 158).

Maize and other foodstuffs were freely given to the French in some places. When Laudonnière met Outina's sister at Enacaque, she received him hospitably and sent fish to the French. Laudonnière maintained good relations on the whole with the eight villages closest to his fort and with those north of the St. Johns River, who continued to supply foodstuffs occasionally. One exception was a French mission to Athore, when Casti and two sons of Emoloa killed two carpenters who stole some fresh maize while going through the fields on their way to Athore's village. Chief Hioacaia's widow appears to have been particularly generous. As the new season's crops were ripening, Laudonnière sent two boats to her village on the Satilla River, known to the natives as the Iracana. The French found a number of native leaders assembled there to enjoy themselves, as that place was reputed to have the prettiest women of the region. As the French were leaving, the cacica had their two boats filled with maize. With these supplies and others he had accumulated earlier, Laudonnière began to plan seriously to return to France because of the lack of resupply from there (Lussagnet 1958:149–51, 156–57, 158).

John Hawkins's Arrival, 1565

John Hawkins landed at the French settlement shortly thereafter on August 3, 1565, to resupply his ships with water. He provided Laudonnière with additional food and a ship. Laudonnière gave him the fort's artillery. Many Indians came to visit while Hawkins was there, asking Laudonnière if the visitor was "his brother." He replied yes, assuring them that because of the supply Hawkins had brought, he would no longer have to take food from them. Laudonnière reported that news of this change spread quickly through the land and that "ambassadors arrived from all sides, who asked to contract alliance with me in the name of . . . their Kings." Even some who had wished to make war on him declared themselves friends (Lussagnet 1958:159–60).

It is likely that Laudonnière released Outina at this time, for it served no purpose to hold him any longer. He expressed regret for the war with Outina's people that the French need for food had provoked. The last French foray to Outina's village resulted in a day-long battle as the French were returning to their boats on the St. Johns River. The Indians killed two Frenchmen and wounded 22 others (Lussagnet 1958:151–56). When Pedro Menéndez de Avilés arrived shortly thereafter, Outina and other Freshwater Timucua allied with him against the French.

When the Indians learned of Laudonnière's plans to return to France, they asked if he intended to come back to them and, if so, how soon. He promised to return within 10 moons with such power that he would be able to make them victorious over all their enemies. The natives asked him to leave his fort and associated structures intact and to give them one of his boats to use in making war on their enemies (Lussagnet 1958:163–64).

Jean Ribaut's Return, 1565

On August 28, 1565, just as Laudonnière prepared to abandon Florida, the long-awaited reinforcements arrived with Captain Jean Ribaut, who bore orders to supplant Laudonnière. Indians arrived from all parts during the next day to learn the identity of the latest newcomers. Those from nearby villages, some of whom recognized Ribaut from 1562, brought him many presents. Laudonnière identified "Kings Omoloa, Saranay, Alimacany, and Casti" as being among those who came to visit, bringing "many presents in accord with their custom." When Laudonnière told the natives that Ribaut was to take his place and that he was to leave, the leaders asked whether it was Ribaut's pleasure "to have the merchandise delivered to them that he was scheduled to give to them, [promising] that in a few days they would guide him to the mountains of Palacy" as they had promised Laudonnière. The natives told Ribaut that he would find red copper there. Laudonnière noted that the natives called it *Sieroa Pira,* meaning "red metal" (Lussagnet 1958:165, 170–71).

Arrival of Pedro Menéndez de Avilés, 1565

Pedro Menéndez de Avilés's fleet of six ships arrived off the mouth of the St. Johns River only a week after Ribaut's return. The Spaniard initiated the definitive phase of the Timucua's contact with Europeans and Africans, which would leave the Timucua well on their way to extinction just over a century later. The Spaniards' first move, after unsuccessfully chasing the fleeing French ships, was to land many of their supplies at Matanzas Inlet and to establish a fortified position from which to contest the French presence before the French ships could return with their complements of soldiers. The French ships had fled initially because all their soldiers were at Fort Caroline when the Spaniards appeared (López de Mendoza Grajales 1567:447–51; Lussagnet 1958:172–75; Menéndez de Avilés 1565a:76–79; Solís de Merás 1923:83–90).

Chief Emoloa informed the French at Fort Caroline that the "Spaniards had landed in great number and that they had seized the houses of Seloy, to the largest of which they had sent the Negroes whom they had brought for the work and that they were billeted [there] around which they had made many trenches" (Lussagnet 1958:172, 175). A Spanish source, López de Mendoza Grajales (1567:450–51), gives a different account, recording that the Spaniards were well received by the Indians where they landed and that the Indians "gave them a very large house belonging to a cacique, which is alongside the bank of a river." A ditch and a terreplein of earth and brush were made around the house. Beyond that, the records suggest that the chiefs in the vicinity of Fort Caroline did little to assist the French or even to alert them to Spanish moves during the first weeks after Menéndez de Avilés's arrival. Two Indian chiefs, described as brothers and great enemies of the French, who allegedly had been in Fort Caroline only six days before the Spaniards set out by land to assault it, served as guides on that march (López de Mendoza Grajales 1567:454; Solís de Merás 1923:95). Spanish sources do not give the names of any of the first Indians they encountered.

Menéndez de Avilés first sighted the coast near Cape Canaveral on the very day of Ribaut's arrival at the St. Johns River.[2] Having been told the French fort was between 28 and 29 degrees, Menéndez de Avilés sailed along the coast for several days, going as far north as 29 1/2 degrees. There he saw fires and Indians on the beach. When he landed 21 armed men, the Indians retreated toward the woods. But when one of the soldiers advanced alone and unarmed, carrying a few presents, the Indians received him well. They informed the Spaniards through signs that the French were farther north.[3]

Menéndez de Avilés's placement of this landing seven or eight leagues south of St. Augustine indicates that the Indians were coastal Freshwater Timucua, probably allies of Outina. The great display of both high- and low-grade gold the Spaniards saw among those Indians points in the same direction, confirming French reports about the gold to be found in Outina's domain and farther south. Menéndez de Avilés (1565a:83) observed that the Indians there wore the gold as ornaments hanging from their ears, lips, and arms.

After the same Indians had entertained the 21 Spaniards for a time, they asked to meet the armada's commander but declined an invitation to go out to the ship to do so. When Menéndez landed the following morning with 50 harquebusiers, the Indians put aside their bows and arrows and came toward him gesturing in the direction of the sky. He was favorably impressed by these first Florida natives whom he encountered, noting that they appeared to be "noble people." He told the king that he did not consent to any of his men taking any gold from those Indians, lest they become aware of the Spaniards' greed for it, although Indians gave one soldier an amount equivalent to a little more than 22 carats (*quilates*).[4] Menéndez distributed presents and sweets to the natives, leaving them very content. On heading north on September 4, he spotted Ribaut's four ships at anchor at two o'clock in the afternoon (López de Mendoza Grajales 1567:446–47; Menéndez de Avilés 1565a:76; Solís de Merás 1923:82–83).

4.

THE TIMUCUA
AND MENÉNDEZ DE AVILÉS

After Menéndez de Avilés's initial encounter with the French ships, he returned to St. Augustine harbor, which he had noted as he sailed northward on September 4. Indians gave a good reception to his first captains, who landed at Chief Seloy's village. When Menéndez disembarked on September 8 to take formal possession of the land for his monarch, many Indians were waiting there to greet him, encouraged by the reports of his earlier landing eight leagues south. He landed with many flags unfurled, amid a fanfare of trumpets and other instruments and salutes fired by his cannon. Menéndez remarked that the Indians in attendance included many leading men who "showed themselves to be our friends and it appeared to us they were enemies of the French." After mass he fed the Indians and dined himself. Sources do not indicate whether Chief Seloy was among those in attendance. The Indians in attendance informed Menéndez that many caciques were friends of the French (López de Mendoza Grajales 1567:450–51; Menéndez de Avilés 1565a:78; Solís de Merás 1923:88–89).

Speculating that a hurricane that struck soon thereafter would wreck Ribaut's fleet or carry it afar at the very least, leaving Fort Caroline undermanned, Menéndez de Avilés resolved to attack the fort under cover of the storm. When he set out for the attack, despite the Saturiwa chiefs' friendship with the French, none of them alerted Laudonnière to Menéndez's advance, permitting the Spaniards the advantage of complete surprise. Of course, the hurricane may have had something to do with that. Ten Frenchmen who escaped the massacre at the fort by seeking refuge with Saturiwa's caciques were later ransomed from them by Menéndez (López de Mendoza Grajales 1567:453–54; Menéndez de Avilés 1565b:85–87; Solís de Merás 1923:106).

The first evidence of the storm's destructiveness for the French ships at sea appeared on September 22, before Menéndez de Avilés's triumphant return to St. Augustine from Fort Caroline. Spanish sailors sent to the shore to fish found a Frenchman who had been part of the 16-man crew of a frigate Laudonnière had sent out to gather intelligence on what the Spaniards were doing. The storm had driven them ashore at the mouth of the Matanzas River, where five of the crewmen drowned. Indians attacked the survivors on the following morning, killing three of them with clubs. The one whom the Spaniards captured had taken cover in a pit. Ten Spaniards sent to refloat the frigate retreated when a large number of Indians advanced on them in a seemingly hostile manner. But when a group went out subsequently, the Indians recognized them as Spaniards and assisted them in refloating the vessel.

After Menéndez de Avilés's return to St. Augustine, Indians came from the south to inform him by signs of the first contingent of about 200 survivors from the wrecking of Ribaut's fleet during the hurricane. Matanzas Inlet, a narrow arm of the sea that swung inland, had stalled their progress northward. No Indians offered to ferry them across. That intelligence gave Menéndez the opportunity for the first of the two massacres of the French that led him to give the inlet its name commemorating the exploit. When a second group of survivors headed by Ribaut reached the same inlet, Indians again alerted Menéndez. The Indians' identity was not specified. They could have been Saltwater Timucua allied to Seloy, as the inlet was only four leagues from St. Augustine. Or they could have been Freshwater Timucua. Laudonnière's alienation of the latter by his imprisonment of Outina made them natural allies of the Spaniards. And Laudonnière's spurning of Seloy's overtures at his first landing in that chief's territory may have influenced him and other Saltwater Timucua in the vicinity of Seloy's village to welcome the Spaniards. It is worthy of note that Laudonnière made no mention of contact with Seloy after that first encounter.

The only recorded act of Indian assistance to the French immediately after Spanish capture of Fort Caroline was alerting Laudonnière and the others who escaped with him that the Spaniards were readying to capture the three ships on which the escapees had taken refuge. There may well have been other acts by the Saturiwa reflecting their alliance with the French that went unrecorded. Spaniards' repeated references from this time on to the Saturiwa's and the Tacatacuru's alliance with the French suggest, at the very least, that coolness characterized those Indians' relations with the Spaniards from the beginning, even if they were not overtly or consistently hostile.

Attitude of the Saltwater Timucua

Overall, the evidence about the attitude of Saturiwa and the other Saltwater Indians in the vicinity of St. Augustine and Fort Caroline toward the Spaniards is inconclusive or conflicting for the first months after the Spaniards' arrival. In a passing remark, Gonzalo Solís de Merás observed that Saturiwa's relations with the Spaniards had been very friendly. Bartolomé Barrientos, however, remarked twice that Saturiwa had always been a friend of the "Lutherans," the name Spaniards in Florida used invariably for the Calvinist Huguenots. Barrientos's judgment on this matter may have been colored by inveterate later acts of hostility by Saturiwa and his allies and subjects. Menéndez de Avilés's first letters, both before and after his attack on Fort Caroline, reflect his belief that the French had many friends among the Indians in the vicinity of Fort Caroline. Before its capture, he expected those Indians to assist the French when they attacked his camp at St. Augustine. Yet, Saturiwa's handing over of the French who sought refuge with his people suggests a degree of cooperation with the Spaniards in the early days rather than steadfast friendship with the French. The multitude of Indians recorded as having witnessed Menéndez de Avilés's solemn taking possession of the land suggests that it may have included more than Freshwater Timucua (Barrientos 1965:112, 133; Lussagnet 1958:86; Menéndez de Avilés 1565a, 1565b:76, 78, 83–84, 85, 86–87, 92, 102; Solís de Merás 1923:89, 95, 106, 109, 115, 159).

There is no record of Menéndez de Avilés himself having made any significant direct effort to win the alliance of Saturiwa or chiefs subject to or allied with him during the Spaniard's early months in Florida. His only recorded attempt to meet Saturiwa occurred in the spring of 1567, a full year and one-half after his arrival. By then he had already met the other major chieftains of coastal zones he was interested in: Tocobaga in Tampa Bay, Carlos on the southwest coast, Tequesta on Biscayne Bay, Ais on the Indian River, Tolomato and Guale on the north Georgia coast, and Escamacu and Orista near Santa Elena, not to mention the Freshwater Chief Hotina or Aotina (Spanish renderings of the French Outina) of the upper St. Johns River. Much as Menéndez de Avilés wanted friendly relations with Saturiwa and Tacatacuru, actions by his rebellious subordinates thoroughly antagonized Saturiwa long before the attempted meeting in 1567. Only a mutual aloofness on both sides during the first weeks after the Spanish arrival seems to account for Menéndez's not having met either of the two principal Saltwater leaders. Part of the problem, doubtless, was the surprisingly little time Menéndez spent at St. Augustine and San Mateo after the first month and one-half or so of his first stay in Florida. He devoted much of that time, of course, to elimination of the French threat represented by Fort Caroline and Ribaut's forces and to establishment of Spanish garrisons at St. Augustine and San Mateo.

Naming of the St. Johns River

The St. Johns River was known by a variety of names before the present name became permanently attached to it. The Timucua's name for it is not known. The French called it the river of May for their arrival on it, on May 1, 1562. When Menéndez de Avilés renamed Fort Caroline as Fort San Mateo because of having captured it on the feast day of the apostle Matthew, Spaniards transferred the name Mateo to the river on which the fort stood. After the disappearance of Fort San Mateo and the rise of the San Juan del Puerto mission in Alimacani's village at the end of the century, the river began to be known as the San Juan or St. Johns (Barrientos 1965:55, 77–90, 94, 96–106, 111–12, 115–21, 126–33; Menéndez de Avilés 1565b:87, 92, 102; Solís de Merás 1923:128, 139–51, 159, 167–79, 202, 204, 224–28, 230). Spaniards also referred to it at times as the river of Currents (*Corrientes*) during the seventeenth century (Díaz Vara Calderón 1675a) and as the river of Salamototo for the mission San Diego de Salamototo at the mission trail's principal crossing point on the river (Hann 1989:186–87).

Menéndez de Avilés's Indian Policy

Before Menéndez de Avilés eliminated the French, he envisioned a carrot-and-stick policy for dealing with Indians allied with the French. He planned to bring in horses to impress and intimidate the natives and to prevent them from maintaining contact with the French, as well as preventing the French from leaving the fort. He believed that when the Indians saw that the Spaniards were more powerful than the French, all the Indians would be friends of the Spaniards. On the other hand, he also insisted that the Indians were to be treated very well. He felt that food should not be taken from them under any circumstances but that the Spaniards should instead provide food when the Indians were lacking, in order to win their trust and friendship. His garrisons' chronic shortage of food ruled out any such idyllic situation. The Spanish forces' inability to cope with the tactics of Saturiwa's warriors in the field indicates that no significant number of horses reached Florida during the 1560s to implement the "stick" side of his policy (Menéndez de Avilés 1565a:78–81).

Menéndez de Avilés's (1565b:87) report to the king on October 15, 1565, in the wake of his capture of Fort Caroline, indicates that by then he had contact through subordinates with Indians allied with the French. One of those contacts was Ensign Rodrigo Troche at San Mateo, described at the time Saturiwa took him prisoner and ordered him killed as having been well acquainted with that Indian leader. Menéndez observed in his letter that "these French had many Indians as friends and they [the Indians] have shown great sorrow over their loss and especially for two or three teachers of their evil sect who were teaching the caciques and Indians. And they followed after them like the Apostles after Our Lord." He affirmed that he would do what he could to gain the goodwill of the Indians allied to the French and to avoid hostilities with them. He refused to please his Indian allies by assisting them in war against their enemies such as Saturiwa. Menéndez began the first of many long absences from Timucua territory shortly after writing that letter. Before he returned, relations between Saturiwa and the Spanish garrisons became much more openly hostile. Menéndez was forced to become involved in the wars against the Indians he had hoped to avoid.

Within 20 days of Menéndez de Avilés's killing of Ribaut and the men with him who were not Catholics, Indians brought him word of another large group of Frenchmen on the beach eight days' march to the south, who were building a fort and a ship there. Menéndez set out along the beach with 300 men on October 26, 1565. Three boats coasting the shore carried their supplies. On this occasion he spared the lives of all Frenchmen who surrendered to him, without regard to their religion, because the numbers of the French no longer represented a threat to their Spanish captors. After the successful conclusion of that expedition, Menéndez continued on to Cuba to procure badly needed supplies for his garrisons at St. Augustine and Fort San Mateo and for a new garrison he left among the Ais of the Indian River region (Solís de Merás 1923:124, 125–26, 127).

Saturiwa Turns Openly Hostile

Many months were to pass before Menéndez de Avilés returned to Timucua territory. When he sailed for Florida anew on February 10, 1566, his first destination was Calusa on Florida's southwest coast in the vicinity of the Caloosahatchee River. He returned to St. Augustine only on March 20,

after an absence of almost five months. Saturiwa's relations with the Spaniards had turned openly hostile by that time, largely because of actions
taken by the leaders of mutinous Spanish soldiers at San Mateo who mistreated the Indians and killed a number of them, including three unidentified prominent Indians. At St. Augustine, Menéndez de Avilés's brother's
requests for food from the Indians may also have strained relations. Nothing is known of the nature of those requests or the Indians' response.

When Menéndez returned to St. Augustine, the mutineers were still
near San Mateo on a supply ship they had commandeered. Thirty-five of
the mutineers reaffirmed their loyalty to him when he offered them am-
nesty. Further poisoning relations with the Indians, the mutineers landed
the newly loyal Spaniards at a place where they were sure to be killed by
the Indians. And, as Solís de Merás (1923:138–53, 159–60) noted, "in order that this might happen the more quickly, the mutineers stripped them
of their clothes, and robbing them of whatever they had, took them on
shore in a boat; and as they began to walk toward the fort, the Indians
sallied forth very fiercely and with their arrows killed them all." When San
Mateo's commander, unaware that the Indians had turned hostile, dispatched two of his men to St. Augustine to request reinforcements for his
depleted garrison, Indians captured them and brought them to Saturiwa,
who was well acquainted with one of them, the commander's ensign,
Rodrigo Troche. Saturiwa ordered that the breasts of both men be split
open and their hearts pulled out.

Menéndez left the trouble with the Saturiwa behind him at the beginning of April 1566, as he set off for a month and a half of establishing
relations with the Indians of Guale and the vicinity of Santa Elena. As he
returned southward toward mid-May, following waterways between the
islands and the mainland, Indians from the villages he passed along the
Georgia coast gave him an enthusiastic reception because of a reputation
he had gained in Guale as a rainmaker. It is likely that some of those villages were inhabited by Timucua. But on his arrival at San Mateo on May
15, 1566, Menéndez learned that the Saturiwa had escalated their hostilities. The fort's commander reported that all the Indians in the vicinity of
the two Spanish garrisons in Saturiwa territory were on the warpath, preventing the Spaniards from going out in search of shellfish and palmetto to
supplement their inadequate food supplies. Indians had killed two soldiers
at St. Augustine and destroyed the settlement by shooting fire-arrows at
the thatched roof of the powder magazine. A breeze spread the fire to the
rest of the village, burning many supplies.

The Indians' agility and arms were more than a match for the Spanish soldiers in the region's marshy terrain. In the time it took soldiers to reload their harquebuses, the Indians could approach them, fire four or five arrows, and then retreat and hit the ground the moment they saw the powder take fire. The Spaniards were not swift enough to overtake the Indians and the prevalence of tidal creeks and swamps also made pursuit difficult against naked Indians who were excellent swimmers, having only their bows and arrows to carry. The only tactic Spaniards found to have an impact was to cut down their planted fields, destroy their fish-weirs and stored supplies of food, burn their houses, and take their canoes. This forced the Indians to make peace or move farther away, where they were less of a menace. In reporting this problem, Solís de Merás (1923:164–79, 182–85) noted that the Indians had killed more than 100 Spanish soldiers during an unspecified period.

After destruction of the settlement on the site of Seloy's village, Menéndez de Avilés moved St. Augustine to a new location that offered better defense against the Indians and better control of the harbor against enemy vessels that might attempt to enter it. Menéndez had noted the need for such a move in his first report to the king.

The Moving of St. Augustine

Scholars have generally assumed that Menéndez moved St. Augustine to the location that the old city presently occupies. That may not be the case. In the wake of a particularly severe storm on September 22, 1599, which did much damage to the city, the king's factor for the treasury there suggested that it was advisable to move the city to "the other side of the channel and arm of the sea which is at the back of this one (*a las espaldas deste*) of St. Augustine," next to the mission village of San Sebastian, where the land was higher and thus stronger for defense purposes. The factor stated that Menéndez de Avilés had wanted to move the city to that site before his last visit to Spain but that, "because of the happenstance of his going to Spain, he put off doing so until his return." Death overtook him before he could return. In advocating a move to the San Sebastian site at the beginning of 1600, the factor argued that such a move would not be unprecedented. He noted that "when this land was conquered by the said adelantado Pedro Menéndez de Avilés, for many years it was said this presidio of St. Augustine the old was settled on the island that is in front of it and, because of the sea's having eaten away a great part of the island where the fort and village were, it was necessary to move it from this other side to where it is now, which is longer than this move that now needs to be made" (A. de las Alas 1600).

Menéndez headed for Havana again at the beginning of June to procure food for his beleaguered garrisons. He sailed for St. Augustine anew only on July 1, 1566, arriving in eight days. Saturiwa's Indians had killed more soldiers during Menéndez's absence, as hunger forced them to go out in search of shellfish and palmetto. The soldiers were safe from attack only if they went out in large groups. After attending to disposition of new forces that had arrived during his absence and providing directions for building a new fort at St. Augustine, Menéndez set out on a voyage up the St. Johns River to meet its principal caciques and learn whether the river provided a navigable route across the peninsula to the Gulf (Menéndez de Avilés 1565a; Solís de Merás 1923:192, 193, 194–95, 196–200).

Menéndez de Avilés's Visit with the Freshwater Chiefs

The Spaniards had more success in their dealings with the Freshwater Timucua than they were having at the time with Saturiwa and his Saltwater allies. On sailing from San Mateo, Menéndez de Avilés went directly to establish contact with the Freshwater paramount, Hotina. He sailed for 20 leagues and then walked overland from the river for five leagues to the chief's village.

Hotina received an advance party of six soldiers and a guide-interpreter very well but told them that, because he feared Menéndez, the latter should bring no more than 20 soldiers and should pray to his God for rain as he had done so successfully in Guale, as Hotina's maize fields had not seen a good rain for six months. Menéndez satisfied the latter request too well. A very hard rain began just as he reached the village. Hotina took refuge in the woods in great fear of a man who had such power with his God as to bring rain so quickly. He sent word from that sanctuary asking Menéndez to leave his territory, saying that he would consider him his elder brother and friend as long as Menéndez remained out of his territory and that he did not wish to fight with the Spaniards but that his Indians did. He professed concern that the Spaniards' continued presence could provoke trouble with his Indians. While agreeing to withdraw, Menéndez informed Hotina that he did not fear him or his men and that he was determined to proceed upriver through Hotina's territory. He instructed Hotina to notify his people in the villages along the river to remain in their homes without fear. Hotina was to warn them that, if they fled, Menéndez would make war on them by destroying their villages, canoes, and fish-weirs. Hotina complied and the villages at which Menéndez stopped gave him a good reception.

Menéndez de Avilés ascended the river about 50 leagues, two leagues farther than the French had gone, according to two guides Menéndez had with him, who had also served the French in that capacity. He had passed beyond Hotina's domain by then and entered that of a cacique whose name Solís de Merás rendered as Macoya. Macoya's village was probably the Mayaca mission of the early seventeenth century, believed to be a little south of Lake George. Menéndez found Macoya's village deserted. Although Macoya was a friend of Saturiwa, Menéndez ordered his men to do no harm in the village and sought to establish ties of friendship with Macoya and secure guides for exploration farther upriver. Menéndez went upriver a little farther before turning back because of the obvious hostility of Indians lining the banks. They presented a growing threat to his men, as the river narrowed drastically and the rowers for the first time encountered a swift current that slowed their progress. In an explicit warning, Macoya had threatened Menéndez with war if he did not turn back. Menéndez's guide and interpreter, presumably a Timucua, had been a slave of the cacique of Ais and, as such, had become acquainted with Macoya. The guide counseled Menéndez to turn back because the land was home to a large number of very warlike Indians and because the river remained narrow all the way to the lake of Maymi (Lake Okeechobee) (Barrientos 1965:115, 118; Solís de Merás 1923:202–5).

Menéndez went back downriver about seven or eight leagues to the village of Calabay, or Carabay, where some Indians were waiting for him. Its chief told Menéndez that Macoya had sent him to warn Menéndez that he should not go up that river. Calabay told Menéndez that he himself was taking Menéndez for an elder brother and would do what he commanded. He stated that he and his people wished to become Christians and asked Menéndez to give him a cross and six soldiers to teach them the new faith, as he had done in Guale. The repeated references natives made to Menéndez's recent visit to Guale show that news of such events spread with remarkable speed from the north Georgia coast to the upper St. Johns River despite the hostility between Saturiwa and Hotina. Calabay promised Menéndez that he would guide the six men up the river as far as Lake Maymi, explaining that Macoya would not object to so small a force. That promise suggests that Calabay had a pledge from Macoya to that effect.

Menéndez complied with Calabay's request, although with some misgivings because Calabay was both a vassal of Hotina and a friend of Saturiwa and Macoya. As Calabay was only 12 leagues from St. Augustine by land, however, the Spaniards could retaliate easily for any betrayal that harmed the soldiers. The soldiers did not reach Lake Maymi because Calabay soon returned them to St. Augustine, under threats from Saturiwa. On learning of the soldiers' presence, Saturiwa ordered Calabay to kill them or surrender them if he did not want Saturiwa as an enemy.

As Menéndez continued downriver, he received a warm reception in three or four other villages whose people were Hotina's vassals. He was still very anxious to meet Hotina because he had been told that this particular Indian was a young man of great understanding who commanded great influence over a wide area. Menéndez overcame Hotina's reluctance to meet with him in a second approach, threatening that he would otherwise consider him an enemy. When Menéndez appeared with the 20 soldiers Hotina had authorized earlier, the chief again took fright, asking him to reduce the number to two, while Hotina brought 300 warriors out of the more than 1,000 he was reputed to have at his disposal. Hotina and his men paid homage to Menéndez after their fashion. Hotina took him for his elder brother, to do what he commanded, and asked for a cross, six soldiers to instruct them in the new faith, and a trumpeter. Menéndez complied and the two parted as very good friends.

Spanish Relations with the Saltwater Timucua Worsen

Menéndez learned, on returning to San Mateo, that relations with Saturiwa had worsened as a result of new hostilities. Without authorization from San Mateo's commander, 12 harquebusiers had traveled two leagues to rob some houses belonging to Saturiwa. The Indians attacked, killing eight of them and badly wounding the other four, who escaped by hiding in a forest (Barrientos 1965:116, 118–19; Solís de Merás 1923:204–8). There is no report of a Spanish retaliation at that time.

Menéndez gave almost no attention to relations with the Timucua for the rest of 1566 and well into 1567. After only two days at San Mateo, he visited Santa Elena again and then Guale. When he came back from there, he spent only two more days at San Mateo before going on to St. Augustine to deal with problems there and to prepare for a naval expedition to the Caribbean to chase pirates. While at St. Augustine he learned of the mid-September killing of one of the first three Jesuits who came to Florida at Menéndez's special request to work among its natives.

The Jesuits had come from Havana on a Flemish ship without a pilot familiar with Florida's landmarks. After missing the entrance for St. Augustine, the ship sent a small boat ashore to ask the Indians the distance and direction to St. Augustine or Santa Elena. Shortly thereafter, a storm forced the ship out to sea and the Flemish crew insisted on returning to Cuba without attempting to rescue their stranded shipmates. Days later, Tacatacuru killed Father Pedro Martínez and several of the sailors stranded with him when they approached shore just north of the St. Johns River. The rest escaped in the boat and were discovered shortly thereafter by people from San Mateo. In retaliation for those deaths and for others, Captain Martín de Ochoa burned many villages, destroyed maize fields, and killed many Indians. In mid-October Menéndez painted a dire picture of relations with the Timucua, reporting that Indians came to besiege his men in the two forts regularly, shooting arrows at them, killing two or three each time, and wounding others. He was ready to leave for the Caribbean by the end of September, but contrary winds delayed his departure until October 20. He did not return to Timucua territory until spring of 1667 (Alegre 1956:45–48; Barrientos 1965:121–32; Hann l99la:287; Solís de Merás 1923:208–9, 211, 212, 213, 219, 232; Vargas Ugarte 1935:61; Zubillaga 1946:193–97).

By Menéndez's return to San Mateo, relations with Saturiwa had deteriorated further. San Mateo's commander, Gonzalo de Villaroel, had launched a campaign against the Indians in retaliation for Saturiwa's ongoing harassment of the fort. Spaniards killed an unspecified number of Saturiwa's caciques and subjects and captured 16 others, whom Villaroel was holding in chains. The captives included Chief Emoloa, a son of Emoloa, two heirs to chiefdoms, and two of Saturiwa's leading men. Villaroel informed Menéndez that Saturiwa was then mustering a large number of warriors to retaliate against the Spaniards and that Indians had killed all the fort's cattle.

A major battle occurred sometime in 1567 at the bar of Tacatacuru between Spaniards and natives of that region. A large number of Indians attacked three of Menéndez's principal lieutenants while they were taking a group of soldiers from San Mateo to Santa Elena. Pedro Menéndez Márques, one of the three, reported that the Spaniards had gone from San Mateo to the vicinity of Sarabay (most likely Sarabay Island between Ft. George Island and Amelia Island), stopping there to spend the night next to the village. On a trail in a little woods they encountered Moloa, Siquetoro, and the sons of Saturiwa, and they met them again four leagues farther on. When the Spaniards reached the bar of Tacatacuru (the mouth of the St. Marys River), Menéndez Márques reported that so great a multitude of

Indians attacked them that it was a miracle that they escaped by sailing out to sea (Lyon 1988; P. Menéndez Márquez 1568). Pedro Menéndez Márques and Esteban de las Alas later planned a retaliatory attack on the village of Tacatacuru in conjunction with a Guale force, but a series of misfortunes prevented the Spaniards from executing their design at the time agreed upon. Somewhat later Alas hired the frigate *Nuestra Señora del Pinar* to carry 150 soldiers northward to lay waste the lands of the Islands of Tacatacuru (Cumberland Island) and Caxon for their part in the earlier killing of Spaniards (E. de las Alas 1569a).

Menéndez de Avilés's Attempted Meeting with Saturiwa

As Menéndez de Avilés was about to return to Spain to seek resources directly from the Crown, he tried to reach an understanding with Saturiwa. He and Saturiwa had never met. Menéndez released one of the Indians imprisoned at San Mateo to tell Saturiwa that he greatly wished to talk with him the next morning at the point of the bar of San Mateo, two leagues from the fort. Saturiwa agreed to meet him and asked him to bring the other imprisoned Indians because he wished to see them.

Menéndez complied to the extent of bringing Emoloa and six other leading Indians with him. He went to the meeting by ship, as he was on his way to St. Augustine to settle matters there before his departure for Europe. On arriving at the bar, Menéndez found Saturiwa holding back quite a distance from the shore. He released one of the captives to tell Saturiwa to come to the shore, under a pledge that no harm would be done to him. In reply Saturiwa asked him to land Emoloa and the other captives as he wished to speak to them first. Menéndez did so but kept them shackled. He placed them in front of a brigantine with 20 harquebusiers at the ready, along with two demiculverins loaded with shot in case any of Saturiwa's Indians tried to carry the captives off on their backs. Saturiwa still did not come to the shore. Instead, he sent two of his leading Indians to speak with Emoloa. They shuttled between Saturiwa and Emoloa for more than two hours, until Menéndez learned that Saturiwa's intent was to free the captives and induce Menéndez to land so that a large number of warriors he had in ambush might kill him. A soldier heard the Indians discussing the plot among themselves. While feeding the Indians during their captivity, he had learned to understand their language to some degree, unknown to the Indians.

Menéndez then retrieved the captives, sending word to Saturiwa that he had always wished to be his friend and regretted that Saturiwa did not reciprocate. He informed him that henceforth he would be his enemy. Saturiwa replied in kind, informing Menéndez that, although he had told Spanish captains many times that he was Menéndez's friend, he had not meant it because he considered all Christians enemies, and that Menéndez "and his soldiers were hens and cowards; that they ought to land and fight with him and his Indians" (Barrientos 1965:132–33; Solís de Merás 1923:233–35).

Menéndez's Campaign against Saturiwa

Menéndez did not respond to Saturiwa's challenge at that moment. But before his departure for Spain, he launched a four-pronged attack aimed at killing or capturing Saturiwa. Menéndez himself led 60 or 70 soldiers on an all-night forced march of 10 leagues. None of the Spanish forces found Saturiwa, but they killed 30 Indians, burned a number of villages, pulled up their fields of maize, and did whatever other damage they could.

In a turnabout gesture of conciliation before leaving, however, Menéndez de Avilés released Emoloa and all but three of the other captives. He told Emoloa that he was taking the other three to Spain with him and that he would treat them well. But he warned those he was freeing that if Saturiwa made war on the Spaniards while he was away and if Emoloa and his Indians or the other leading Indians whom he was releasing helped Saturiwa, he would behead the three whom he was taking with him. Menéndez sailed for Spain from Santa Elena on May 18, 1567 (Barrientos 1965:133, 139–40; Solís de Merás 1923:236, 238).

Menéndez's Defensive Plan against the Timucua

Before leaving, the *adelantado* devised a defensive plan to cope with Salt-water Timucua hostility. He ordered the building of blockhouses as soon as possible at Palica, Soloy, Saturiwa's village, Alimacani, and at the original site of St. Augustine to overawe the unfriendly Indians or to force them to move if they would not keep the peace. Palica, an island close to the Matanzas River, five leagues south of St. Augustine, where cattle were to be kept, was to be protected from Indian marauders by the nightly unleashing of dogs trained to hunt the Indians. Two blockhouses were to be built on high ground on this island. One was to secure the island against the Indians by day. The other one, probably more a watchtower, was for scanning the sea for enemy ships. Both Palica and Soloy were to have 100-man garrisons. Menéndez ordered the building of the blockhouse at Alimacani on a height overlooking the chief's residence (Barrientos 1965:134–35).

It is not clear how many of the blockhouses were built. One known to have been built was in Alimacani's village. Another one, not called for in the adelantado's instructions, was built across the river from Alimacani's village so that the two together might control access to the river. It is unlikely that one was built in Saturiwa's village. It would have been a likely target for attack by Dominique de Gourgues had it existed in April 1568.

When he drew up his defensive plan, Menéndez also ordered the tracking down and killing of Chief Tacatacuru, whom he held responsible for the death of Father Martínez. Tacatacuru had also recently killed Captain Pedro de Larando and 10 soldiers. Until those incidents, Spaniards had maintained friendly relations with Tacatacuru. The chief had invited Larando and his soldiers to his residence under the cover of friendship and had them killed in their sleep. Tacatacuru had also killed a Guale chief because the chief had shown friendship for Menéndez de Avilés.

Menéndez ordered that no Indians, male or female, were ever to be allowed into the newly built blockhouses lest they gather intelligence that would facilitate a surprise assault. On the other hand, he warned his soldiers not to commit aggressions against the Indians, rather to treat them kindly and try to win them over with presents (Barrientos 1965:134–35; P. Menéndez Márquez 1568).

Saltwater-Mayaca Alliance against Hotina

Not much is known about details of Spanish-Timucua relations between Menéndez's departure and the arrival of Dominique de Gourgues's retaliatory French expedition in April of 1568. Eugene Lyon (1976:198) noted that tensions between the Spanish garrisons and Saturiwa and his allies reached a climax in the summer of 1567. A widespread native alliance formed against Chief Hotina's Freshwater Timucua, the one group with whom Menéndez had established friendly relations. Saturiwa joined with Indians of the Nocoroco-Mayaca area and the Potano to wage war upon Hotina. In contravention of the Menéndez policy of avoiding involvement in the natives' chronic internal conflicts, Spaniards were drawn into this struggle. As Lyon phrased it, "The enemies of the French had, perforce, become friends of the Spanish, and Indians who had allied with

Laudonnière were now firmly united against the Spaniards." It was an ironic twist, as the French had initially allied themselves actively with Chief Hotina for military action against Potano.

Spaniards went to Hotina's assistance in the latter part of July 1567. Captain Pedro de Andrada led 80 soldiers into the interior west of the St. Johns River to attack Potano. After that attack, the cowardice of a Spanish captain permitted the Potano to retaliate successfully for the destruction of their village. When a Potano force struck the Spaniards by surprise from the rear, the captain who was protecting the rear fled toward the vanguard on seeing the enemy approaching. Captain Andrada and many of his men were killed in a hail of arrows. Sources tallied the number killed variously as 19, 21, or more than 30 (Connor 1925:63; López de Mendoza Grajales 1567:330; Méndez de Canzo 1601; Menéndez 1584; Swanton 1922:336; Worth 1992a:27–28).

Arrival of Gourgues, 1568

When Dominique de Gourgues arrived bent on revenge for Menéndez's killing of so many of the soldiers of Laudonnière and Ribaut, the Saltwater Timucua's hatred for the Spaniards was still intense and searching for an outlet. On the last day of March 1568, a couple of weeks prior to Gourgues's arrival, 400 Timucua had attacked Fort San Mateo at dawn, forcing one side of the fortress and wounding several soldiers before withdrawing.

After passing close enough to shore opposite St. Augustine to receive a salute from its fort, Gourgues sailed on north for 15 leagues to the mouth of the Tacatacuru River (the St. Marys). Soon the shore was lined with warriors armed with bows and arrows, ready to prevent a landing. To identify himself and inform the Indians that he had come to renew the earlier French friendship, Gourgues sent a trumpeter ashore who had been in Florida with Laudonnière. On learning their identity, Saturiwa welcomed them with a fat deer and asked Gourgues to meet with him and his allied and subject chiefs the next morning to form an alliance against the Spaniards.

Saturiwa, Tacadacourou (Tacatacuru), Halmacanir (probably Alimacani), Athore, Haipaha (or Harpaha), Helmacope (or Helmacape), Heliocopile (or Helycopile), and Molona (or Moloua) were the chiefs identified as being present the next morning. Saturiwa went to meet the French when they came ashore. He made Gourgues sit at his right on a seat of mastic wood (*siege de bois de Lentisque*) covered with moss, purposely made similar to his own. Two of the eldest Indians there pulled up the brambles and other plants growing in front of the seats. When the space had been well cleared, they all sat down on the ground around the two principals. When Gourgues wished to speak first, Saturiwa forestalled him, speaking at length about the evils and outrages the Spaniards had inflicted on all of them and their wives and children since their killing of the Frenchmen. He asked the French to join them in avenging these crimes and those the French had suffered at Spanish hands, on the basis of the strong friendship Saturiwa and his allies had shown earlier toward the French. That was pleasant news to the French, who had arrived ignorant of the state of relations between Spaniards and Timucua at the mouth of the St. Johns. Gourgues then distributed presents such as daggers (*dagues*), knives (*cousteaux*), mirrors, axes, rings, small bells (*sonnettes*), and other objects Gourgues described as being trifles to Europeans but very precious to the native kings. Glass beads are likely to have been among those "trifles." On seeing Gourgues's generosity, Saturiwa asked that he give each of them a shirt, to be worn only on their solemn days and to be buried in when they died. In recompense, Saturiwa gave Gourgues two silver chains that hung from his neck. Each of the other chiefs gave Gourgues some deerskins dressed in the native fashion. The Indians then withdrew, dancing with joy, promising that they would return with a goodly number of armed warriors to join the French in their attacks on the Spaniards. Saturiwa delivered various hostages to Gourgues. They were Saturiwa's nephew, Olotocara (probably his heir), one of Saturiwa's sons, and Saturiwa's favorite wife, a young woman 18 years old. Olotocara was also to serve as a guide for the French scouting party that wished to reconnoiter the Spanish positions they planned to attack.

The French targets were the two blockhouses on either side of the St. Johns River, which guarded the entrance to it, and Fort San Mateo. The blockhouse on the river's north side was the one Menéndez de Avilés had ordered to be built at Alimacani's village overlooking the chief's house. Various Spaniards referred to the Alimacani blockhouse as "the house of Alimacani" (Alas 1569). It is probable that the word "house" (*casa*) that they used referred to the blockhouse as a distinct structure rather than to Chief Alimacani's house, although use of the chief's house for building the blockhouse cannot be ruled out. Spaniards generally used the native term *buhío* for the chief's house and the council house.

A Spaniard identified the first blockhouse that Gourgues attacked as "on the other side of the Island of Alimacani," noting that it held 60 soldiers. Another Spaniard said 34. A soldier manning a culverin repulsed the first two charges by the French and Indians. In the third charge, Olotocara leapt up on the gun platform and ran the soldier through with a pike before he could get off a third shot. For the attack on the second blockhouse, many of the Indians swam across the river, holding their bows and arrows out of the water with one hand. The soldiers at San Mateo abandoned their fort without much of a fight, many having slipped away before the French and Indians arrived before the fort (Gourgues 1964:60–63; Lussagnet 1958:188–96; Lyon 1976:199–200).

Fort San Pedro and Spanish Retaliation

The disaster at San Mateo and the blockhouses moved the Spaniards to punish the Indians who had aided the French and to build a strong outpost on the island of Tacatacuru as a barrier to any more such attacks from hostile communities in the vicinity of the mouth of the St. Marys River. Little is known about the building of the San Pedro fort other than that it had been built on Cumberland Island by early 1569. Captain Antonio de Prado (1569:291) described it as having been built "on the island of Tacatacoru about twenty leagues from St. Augustine" to protect communications between that city and Santa Elena. He listed it as one of four vital forts, the others being ones at Carlos, St. Augustine, and Santa Elena. He felt that the San Pedro fort needed 100 men because of the island's size, its natives' hostility, and the possibility that the French might carry out Gourgues's pledge to return to that island to build a fort. Fort San Pedro appears to have remained under something approaching a state of siege under its first commander. Indians killed many Spaniards who ventured out to fish, even when they were in sight of the fort.

The fort's second commander, Captain Juan Gutiérrez de Palomar (1571:4, 32–36), who was in charge from July 26, 1569, until August 13, 1570, claimed that he had brought an end to that state of affairs by waging war on the Tacatacuru so fiercely that they ultimately asked for peace. He claimed to have inflicted much damage and many deaths on them before that occurred. The campaign by Esteban de las Alas and Guale allies, originally planned for early 1569, which was mentioned earlier, may have coincided with Palomar's offensive. Under the peace settlement, the Indians handed over the little sons of four principal chiefs to be held as hostages to guarantee that the Indians would not kill any more Spaniards. Palomar forbade any Indian to carry a bow within half a league of the fort under penalty of death. The Indians were to provide provisions when Spaniards needed them and to assist the Spaniards against anyone who made war on them.

This momentary improvement of relations may even have extended to the Saturiwa. Something that occurred in 1570 led Spanish authorities to expect that Saturiwa as well as Tacatacuru would obey orders to entrust some of their children to the Jesuits to be educated in a school they were planning to open in Havana. When Father Juan Rogel and Father Antonio Sedeño abandoned the Santa Elena region, Sedeño was to stay in the St. Augustine area long enough to collect the children. But when the priests reached St. Augustine, they found the forts to be in such bad condition and saw so many signs that the Indians were on the warpath that they and Pedro Menéndez Márques, who was then in charge at St. Augustine, decided that it was not safe for Sedeño to remain there (Rogel 1570:307).

The apparent return to instability noted by Rogel late in 1570 may have resulted in part from Esteban de las Alas's removal of 23 of the San Pedro fort's soldiers and its commander, Gutiérrez de Palomar, in August of 1570 as part of a general reduction of forces in Florida ordered by the Crown. Only 28 soldiers remained at San Pedro under the new commander, Antonio Hernández. Soldiers who returned to Spain with las Alas described the fort as decrepit, adequate against the usual Indian attack but totally inadequate if the attackers were French or English pirates. The soldiers were poorly armed, powder in short supply, especially that for the harquebuses, and morale was low because of lack of adequate food and clothing. In August 1570, San Pedro had enough flour and maize to provide the soldiers a daily ration of one pound of flour or maize. They had no other food or wine. Soldiers who went out to fish risked their lives because of the danger of Indian attack. The latter comment suggests that Palomar's Draconian measures may not have been as totally effective as he claimed when he said that no soldier had been killed or wounded in such attacks while he was commander (Connor 1925:297, 301, 303, 311). Fort San Pedro appears to have been abandoned sometime before 1573. In testimony taken in Madrid early in 1573 about the state of affairs in Florida and the status of its forts, only the forts at Santa Elena and St. Augustine were mentioned as being in existence (Connor 1925:83, 86, 93, 97, 99).

Other Blockhouses

The blockhouse at Matanzas was completed before the end of 1569 and garrisoned with about 50 soldiers. The coastal Timucua south of Matanzas were hostile to the Spaniards and allies of the French at that time. To curb their hostility, Captain Antonio Prado recommended two more coastal blockhouses, one at the port of San Simón, known also as Mosquitos, 10 leagues south of the Matanzas blockhouse, and another at Nocoroco in the Tomoka Basin. He described Nocoroco as situated between two rivers, one that went to Matanzas and the other to Mosquitos (Connor 1925:291).

Impact of the Hostilities

Nothing is known about the attrition of the Timucua population that resulted from hostilities with the Spaniards. Similarly unknown is the impact of the intensified warfare between Freshwater Timucua loyal to Parucusi Hotina and Saturiwa and his allies or the demographic effect of Spanish destruction of native villages, plantings, fish-weirs, and other resources. The disruption of native life must have been considerable.

Peace between Saltwater Timucua and Spaniards

Little or nothing is known about the Saturiwa's or the Tacatacuru's relations with the Spaniards for much of the 1570s, and nothing is known about the death of either Saturiwa or Tacatacuru. Relations with most of the Saltwater Timucua seem to have remained hostile into the early 1570s at least, and the Mocama Gualequini gave French interlopers a friendly reception as late as 1580. In an April 1573 royal decree asking Menéndez de Avilés for information on his relations with the Indians, a Chief Tinicua, Chief Tacatacuru, and Chief Cazacolo were identified as still friends of the French. But that judgment probably was based on old information related to their part in the Gourgues attack. The decree identified Chiefs Chinica and Sarabay as friends of the Spaniards whose belongings Tinicua, Tacatacuru, and Cazacolo had taken during Gourgues's attack. Chinica and Sarabay had asked Menéndez de Avilés for help in recovering their belongings (Cedulario of Florida 1573).

Peaceful relations appear to have been established with most of the Saltwater Timucua by the time of the revolt of the Guale and Escamacu-Orista in 1576. No Timucua-speakers seem to have joined in that war against the Spaniards. But while Pedro Menéndez Márquez was rebuilding Santa Elena in the latter half of 1577, Spaniards' concern about the intentions of the Timucua was aroused by word of renewed French activity along the northern coasts. Menéndez Márquez worked feverishly to complete the new fort and then hastened to St. Augustine to secure his defenses there and to hold a friendly conclave with the nearby Timucua. He found the Indians around St. Augustine peaceful on his return from Santa Elena. He reported to the king in mid-1578 that the Indians were then more peaceful than they had ever been, remarking that, after his arrival in St. Augustine, the Indians there told him that Indians from Guale and the Santa Elena district had approached them to discuss forming an alliance. The Timucua informed them that they were at peace and did not want any strife. Nine months later he reported that the St. Augustine province's Indians' attachment to peace had intensified after seeing the war he had just waged against the Guale and Escamacu in which he had burned 19 villages. He expressed hope that the Timucua's peaceful coexistence with Spaniards would lead some day to their becoming Christians, lamenting that, at present, there was no discussing that with them. The Indians maintained flatly that they were not interested and preferred to remain with their ancestral religion. Occasionally adults conceded that, if their young people wished to become Christians, they might do so. But when Spaniards asked for the children so that they might teach them, the Indians would not give them up (P. Menéndez Márquez 1578:79, 81; 1579:225; Ross 1923:253–59). Among the early Saltwater chiefs who were initially allies of the French, Cazacolo alone was recorded as having lived long enough to have become a Christian when evangelization of the Mocama on Cumberland Island began in the latter half of the 1580s.

Renewed French Incursions

The first new French incursion involved a ship captained by Nicolas Strozzi that went aground. Its crew then built a fort and five houses within it on a river north of Santa Elena. Guale eventually took the fort by surprise, enslaving 100 or so Frenchmen who survived the attack. They were distributed among a number of Guale chiefs and the chief of Cosapoy. Those French captives were behind the Guale attempt (mentioned previously) to form an alliance of all the seaboard natives against the Spaniards. All but three who were in the hinterland were eventually surrendered to the Spaniards after the latter obtained those at Cosapoy in a successful attack on that village in 1579.

A French threat of alliance with the natives reappeared in 1580, as an undetermined number of French ships returned to Florida's and Georgia's coasts. Two appeared at San Mateo in July 1580. One left almost at once after taking on maize, fish, and venison. The other, under Captain Gil, tarried to trade with the Indians and to seek information on Strozzi's where-abouts. Informed of Gil's presence by an Indian courier, Menéndez Márques defeated him, killing him and most of his crew during the battle. At least five other ships and possibly as many as 20 were reported off Georgia's coast during July and August. Most of Georgia's Indians had little contact with those French vessels. But two that anchored at Guadalquini found a friendly reception there and from Tolomato's *mico*. Sapala's and Tupiqui's chiefs informed the Spaniards of their presence and of the Frenchmen's proposal of an alliance for a campaign against the Spaniards, promising that the Indians would receive all the spoils. Although 22 chiefs agreed to join, nothing came of it beyond the assembly of possibly 1,000 hostile na-tives on the outskirts of Santa Elena, who besieged it for about two weeks. Prompt moving of reinforcements to Santa Elena and diplomacy by Vicente Gonsálvez restored an uneasy peace before the end of 1580. The French did not reappear in the spring of 1581 as they had promised.

French overtures to the Guadalquini during this episode indicate that even at this date Guadalquini's inhabitants were Timucua rather than Guale. The Guadalquini were to organize a rebellion by the Guale and Escamacu to enlist them in the French-inspired campaign. In return the French prom-ised the Guadalquini that once the French and allied native forces had driven the Spaniards from Santa Elena, the French would then join the Guadalquini in attacking their traditional enemies, the Guale and Escamacu. The French would thereby be avenged on the Guale and Escamacu for handing over Strozzi and his men to the Spaniards and for the earlier at-tack on Strozzi's fort. As Paul Hoffman (1990:280–81) noted, "In that way both the French and the Guadalquini would settle their scores with their enemies." The sources do not indicate whether the Guadalquini involved any of their Tacatacuru brothers to the south in the conspiracy (Ross 1923:259–81).

Nothing definite is known about the mechanism by which the state of peaceful coexistence was achieved by the Spaniards. It is likely that the Spanish tactic of "fire and blood," involving surprise night attacks on vil-lages in retaliation for the Timucua's killing of Spaniards, convinced enough of the Indians of the desirability of peace to force the hands of leaders who had chosen war. The disappearance of leaders like Saturiwa and Tacatacuru may have facilitated the change. Guale and Escamacu-Orista hostilities with the Spaniards beginning in 1576 may have played a role, if Timucua hostility to the Guale was deeper than that toward the Spaniards. Pedro Menéndez Márques (1580:283) was able to report in early 1580 that all the coastal Indians between St. Augustine and Santa Elena were peaceful, although the brief disturbance in the north (mentioned previously) marred the peace briefly later that year. This peace opened the way for the first successful missions among the Timucua later in the 1580s.

First Christian Timucua

By the late 1570s a few individuals from the two Timucua villages closest to St. Augustine, Nombre de Dios to the north and San Sebastian to the south and west on the river of that name, had relinquished their attachment to their ancestral religion sufficiently to begin to become Christians. *Visitas* probably had been established in those villages by then. After Fray Alonso Reinoso's arrival in 1577 with a number of friars, their work at Nombre de Dios is alleged to have had such success that converts were soon attending mass regularly in St. Augustine. The *doctrina,* or mission, at Nombre de Dios appears to date from 1587, when the recently arrived Fray Alonso de Escobedo was assigned there (Geiger 1937:55; Hann 1990b:11; Shea 1886:151).

Don Pedro Márques, Freshwater chief of San Sebastian and Tocoy, established the San Sebastian settlement at an unspecified time prior to 1579 to be close to the Spaniards. Before then, presumably, he had lived on the St. Johns River in or near Tocoy. Early in the seventeenth century his successor and son, Gaspar Márques, recalled that in the time of Menéndez de Avilés his father had been among the first caciques who allied with the Spaniards and that during the Spaniards' wars with the natives, his father "always said that he was on the side of the Spaniards." This was, of course, a consequence of mutuality of interests. The Saltwater Timucua and Potano with whom the Spaniards warred were enemies of the Freshwater Timucua on the river who were allied with Parucusi Hotina. During the Spaniards' times of hunger don Pedro assisted them with food. He also served them as interpreter and guide. And he had participated in Pedro Menéndez Márques's attack on Captain Gil's ship in 1580 (Márques [1606]; Ross 1923:270–73).

Potano Remains Hostile

The Potano appear to have remained a problem for the Spaniards. Pedro Menéndez Márques dispatched a punitive expedition against them in 1584 in retaliation for unspecified offenses. One of the participants noted that the governor sent the expedition to explore the San Mateo River and to make war against the Potano, who were in rebellion and at war with the Spaniards (Baldés 1608). The Spaniards explored for 115 leagues upstream without finding any land good for Spanish purposes, only marsh and swamp, mudholes and quagmires. They found less than 300 Indians in a 51-league stretch, who subsisted almost entirely on fish from that river (Menéndez 1584). Gutierre de Miranda headed the 33-man expedition. Don Pedro Márques accompanied it and provided a number of Indian pack bearers. Miranda's force attacked the village of Potano successfully, killing 20 Indians, capturing others, burning the town, and destroying its maize fields. Potano's cacique survived the attack but found it prudent to relocate farther west, abandoning what is presumed to have been the Richardson site (Milanich and Hudson 1993:146). After 13 years of insecurity and fear of another such attack, Potano finally sought reconciliation with the Spaniards in 1597.

That year proved to be a watershed for Spanish relations with other Timucua groups such as the Acuera and the western Timucua people, whom Spaniards then referred to simply as "the Timuqua," the people known today as the Utina (Machado 1597; Márques [1606]; Worth 1992a:28–29).

5.

TIMUCUA POLITICAL ORGANIZATION

In matters of political organization the Timucua are among the best and least known of Florida's Indians who had substantial contact with Europeans. More is known about the organization of the Timucua world in the sixteenth century than is known about any other natives of Spanish Florida with the possible exception of the Guale. But that said, our knowledge of this aspect of Timucua life leaves much to be desired. The data are spotty geographically and temporally. Given the Timucua's dispersion over so wide an area of differing habitats and economies, as well as the minimal records from European contacts with many of the Timucua political subdivisions, it is impossible to generalize about their political organization. Various chiefdoms were autonomous; some were subject to leaders of other provinces to some degree; ties of alliance or confederacy appear to have bound other chiefdoms together. As Europeans provided most of the data and as much of the data comes from the relatively short-term observations by the French, a question arises as to how much their preconceptions about political authority colored their accounts. For data from the years after first contact, questions arise about how native political institutions and interrelations were influenced by that contact.

The de Soto chronicles provide most of the early data for the western hinterland. Sources from the 1560s provide most of the data for the eastern Timucua. The data are best for Saltwater and Freshwater chiefs living along the St. Johns River in that period, although data from the turn of the century shed light on the people of coastal Georgia. Documentation from the mid-seventeenth century provides our best knowledge of the western Timucua. About people on the northern and southern peripheries of the hinterland and the coastal Timucua south of St. Augustine, almost nothing is known.

A friar writing about the Timucua in general and the Guale in 1630 provided the best general description. He observed that their government, "although it does not have the perfection of ours, is very much in conformity with the natural law. They have their natural lords . . . [who] govern their republics as head with the assistance of counsellors, who also are such by birth and inheritance." With their counsels and accord, he determines and agrees on everything that is appropriate for the village and the common good except in matters of favor (*cosas de merced*), for which the cacique is free and absolute master by himself (Jesús 1630a:95–96). As the sway formerly exercised by provincial chiefs had largely disappeared by 1630, that friar had nothing to say about the authority of chiefs above the village level. But another friar alluding to the pre-Christian era noted that Utina Province's head chief had then been like an emperor and absolute lord and that when he challenged an order by a Spanish governor that ignored the privileged status of chiefs and leading men, many of the other chiefs and leading men from three provinces of western Timucua, "while being Christian . . . [still] recognized him as such an absolute lord" and followed him in revolt (Gómez de Engraba 1657a:127).

But, in that earlier era various factors probably restrained rulers from arbitrary use of their power. Above all, rulers were limited by the expectations of their subjects, which formed one of the pillars of the subjects' willingness to be ruled by those in power. A young sixteenth-century Calusa ruler described those limits well in resisting a Jesuit's pressure to abandon the cult of idols. The chief explained that he had been instructed during his childhood in all the things that a king was expected to know about the cult of the idols and that, if he were suddenly to forsake the worship of them at the beginning of his reign, his vassals and the other chiefs tributary to him or allied with him "would say that he was not a legitimate king as he did not know what kings are obliged to know; that for this reason he had forsaken the cult of the idols and had received the Christian law" (Rogel 1568:247–48).

Timucuan chiefs doubtless claimed a supernatural sanction for their authority, as did leaders of other native peoples in the Southeast. Even though the Timucua had religious specialists, chiefs also had religious functions and led or participated in many religious observances (Hann 1991a:224; Lorant 1965:58). What Judith Francis Zeitlin and Lillian Thomas (1992:298–99) said of Zapotec rulers probably applied to Timucua paramounts as well. "One of the ruler's primary responsibilities was to render proper service to the spiritual forces upon which the community depended. . . . In the secular sphere, he was responsible for the material well-being of his people."

The people's "traditional ideas about the ruler's duty to act for the good of the community" ordinarily restrained them from arbitrary action that would bring their fulfillment of that duty into question. The friar's comments in 1630 quoted previously and other sources suggest that in important matters a chief was expected to follow the consensus arrived at in his discussion with his counselors.

Chiefly Titles

Three chiefly titles, parucusi, holata, and utina, appear in the de Soto chronicles. Holata is a title that had wide currency throughout the Southeast. But among the Timucua and their Apalachee neighbors, it could mean "head chief," in contrast to general usage north of Florida, where it designated a lesser chief. The chiefly title utina is peculiarly Timucua. Except possibly for the single instance in the de Soto chronicles, parucusi also seems to be a peculiarly Timucua title. *Ano* may also have been a chiefly title meaning "lord" or "master," but there is no instance of its being applied to a particular ruler (Granberry 1989:158).

   The de Soto chroniclers applied the title parucusi in forms such as paracoxi and hurriparacuxi to a chief living 20 or 30 leagues inland from Tampa Bay who collected tribute from chiefs living on or close to the bay (Biedma 1857; Elvas 1933:46; Fernández de Oviedo y Valdés 1851:I, 549). One chronicler used holata in the form Itaraholata to refer to a Potano village that a second chronicler identified simply as Ytara. As places and their chiefs bore the same name in the perception of Spaniards, Itaraholata had the meaning "Lord" or "Chief" Itara. Chroniclers referred to another Potano village variously as Utinama and Utinamocharra. The "-ma" was a suffix also attached to holata to form *holatama* and to other titles such as *iniha*. Uriutina was also the name of a village in Utina Province. Uriutina probably had the sense of "war chief," as did hurriparacuxi (Granberry 1989:171, 229; Lorant 1965:11).

   Laudonnière's account of his second voyage is our main source for the usage of parucusi as a title for individuals. He presented the title in the forms *paracousi* and *paraousti*. He used the form paraousti first for the unidentified chief he met at Matanzas Inlet, observing that it meant "king and superior." He first used paracousi in telling of his initial encounter with Saturiwa. He noted that "the Paraousti took him by the hand . . . and told me that he was named Paracousi Satouriona, which means the same as King Satouriona. The children bear the same title of Paraousti." Laudonnière used the forms interchangeably as a title for specific chiefs and for speaking of chiefs in general (Lussagnet 1958:86, 87, 89, 90, 94, 104, 105, 110, 112, 113, 115, 116). The extent of Laudonnière's use of the two forms was lost in Charles E. Bennett's translation, as Bennett (1975:60, 61ff.) rendered both forms as "chief" after their initial appearance. Whether by accident or design, Laudonnière did not use either form for chiefs living north of the St. Johns River or for Chiefs Potano, Onatheaqua, and Houstaqua.

Spaniards never applied the title parucusi to a specific ruler after de Soto's time. Survival of the title is known only from Francisco Pareja's catechisms of 1612 and 1627. It appears in them as *ano parucusi holata yco* and *vtina parucusi holata,* respectively. Spaniards were almost as sparing in their use of holata as a title for specific chiefs. That practice contrasts sharply with their usage of *mico* and *mica* for Guale leaders. Pareja and the friar who translated Chief Manuel of Asile's letter employed holata as the equivalent of "cacique" when they were using "cacique" in a general sense (Ystasa 1651; Milanich and Sturtevant 1972:67). Literate chiefs signing their names provide most of the evidence for continued use of the title by specific chiefs. Chief Manuel signed his name "holata manuel ystaSa," and Chief Chamile signed his name "Lazaro Chamile Holatama" (Hann 1986b:106). One of the few instances of Spaniards using the title to address a chief occurred as late as 1706 in a letter the governor addressed to the chiefs of Santa Fé and San Francisco Potano (Córcoles y Martínez 1706c).

Based on post–de Soto documentation, *utina* appears to have been the least commonly used of the three titles. It was so little used, probably, in part because it signified an upper echelon chief. The title is reflected in the name of the Freshwater head chief of the 1560s—Outina, or Hotina, or Aotina—and in the name Nyaautina for another Freshwater chief in 1602. It was also part of the name of the mission village of Santa Isabel de Utinahica, meaning "village of the lord" (Granberry 1989:167; Lussagnet 1958:passim; Solís de Merás 1923:202, 203, 206; F. de Valdés 1602). Albert S. Gatschet's (1878:492) belief that *utinama* was one of the titles applied to upper-level chiefs is supported by an anecdote that Fray Gerónimo de Oré (1936:106–7) recorded. Using a report by Pareja, Oré noted that non-Christian Timucua were using Utinama to refer to the Christians' God. Oré observed that when non-Christians came daily to Christian towns to receive the blessing of the friar, the latter asked the Indians, "What are you looking for here?" They answered, "We came to see the church and your house and that of our relatives because they consider themselves related, provided they have the same names or lineage even if there is a difference of a hundred degrees." After a time they come and say, "Father, we have a house for you and a church; come and instruct us for the Christians have already told us it is of prime importance for us to go and see the *Utinama* who is in heaven above." That usage for utinama suggests that the chiefs who bore the title claimed a supernatural status or origin.

Iniha

Among the Timucua, as among many other horticulturists throughout the eastern Southeast, *iniha* (often spelled *inija* or *inihama*) was the title of the chief's second-in-command, responsible for seeing to it that essential public works were carried out. That function is expressed aptly in the term *mandador,* or order-giver, that Spaniards used most frequently in referring to the iniha except in Apalachee. A soldier made the connection clear in testifying that Apalachee's deputy-governor "broke the head of Bi Bentura, *enija* of the village of San Luis, who is order-giver (*mandador*), second person to the cacique" (Matheos 1686). The position was hereditary. Pareja (1612b:66) described the "*Ynihama* as coming from the same lineage as the head chief" and as the counselor closest to the chief.

Pareja seems to have been the earliest to refer to the Ynihama by that name, but Governor Pedro de Ibarra used the title mandador in his 1604 visitation record. Pareja reported that "when the Cacique does not wish to take the counsel of the *Ynihama,* he calls upon this second one (i.e., counselor), who is *Anacotima.*" In the same context Pareja observed that there was another counselor "who is accustomed to accompany the *Yniha,* who is the first branch of the Cacique, who is called *Yvitano.*"[1]

Pareja's (1612b:66) recording of the lineages that provided counselors for Timucuan head chiefs possibly indicates a collective iniha-ship that was similar to the *Enehau Ulgee,* which Benjamin Hawkins (1982:15) portrayed as occupying the mico's cabin on the left in the Creek square ground. The Enehau Ulgee were in charge of public works (like Spanish Florida's inihas) and the preparation of black drink. These counselors whom Pareja listed were, in descending order, the ynihama, two *anacotimas,* and the *asetama, yvitano, toponole, ybichara,* and *amalachini.* Milanich (1972:12) observed that "Pareja's description of the tribal political organization indicates a moiety system like the White and Tciloki moieties of the Creek (Swanton 1928) or the White and Red moieties of the Cherokee (Gilbert 1943). Each moiety had its own hierarchy of statuses, probably based both on inherited title and achieved status (as warriors). Among the Saturiwa

these moiety statuses were both ranked below the chief and his *inihama*."
Milanich listed the two anacotimas and the asetama as constituting the
first moiety and the other four plus the *ytorimitono* as comprising the second group, in descending order.[2] Because of their greater number, he believed that the latter group probably included the warrior statuses.

Among the Apalachee and Chacato, inihas had deputies known as
chacales. Spaniards even used *chacal* occasionally as though it were synonymous with iniha. We have no instance of any specific Timucuan official being identified as a chacal. But, Pareja's use of the term *chacalicarema*
shows that chacales existed among the Timucua (Milanich and Sturtevant
1972:69). The "-care" simply indicates the plural form of *chacal,* and the
"-ma" here and in many of these titles is a possession indicator (Granberry
1989:161, 173). Thus *utinama* has the sense of "my Lord" or "his lord."

As far as is known, Timucua had no specific term for paramount chief
as distinguished from other head chiefs. Pareja (1612b:65–66) indicated
that all three chiefly titles were used to designate head chiefs. "Head chiefs,
who have other chiefs [as] subjects are: *Ano parucusi holata yco,* 1. *olata aco,*
1. *vtinama."* The sources do not indicate any special title for underchiefs
either. For the St. Johns Valley Laudonnière used paracousi and paraousti
indiscriminately for the regional paramounts, Saturiwa and Outina, and
for the chiefs from that region whom he described as their subjects and
allies. He also gave Alimacani the title paracousi on the first occasion that
he mentioned him. He gave Tacatacuru no title at all on the one occasion
that he mentioned him (Lussagnet 1958:113, 157).

Nature of Head Chiefs' Power

Sources from the 1560s do not provide enough information on the ties
that bound subject and allied chiefs to the regional paramounts, Saturiwa
and Outina, to assess the origin and nature of their power over the others
or its solidity under stress. It is not clear whether their authority over subject chiefs was based on a de jure claim or de facto power. The chief of
Nyaautina, the presumed successor village for Outina of the 1560s, was no
longer head of the upriver Freshwater Timucua by the beginning of the
seventeenth century. The honor had passed to a chief and village named
Antonico (F. de Valdés 1602). Chief Calanay, a subject of Outina, was also
a friend of Saturiwa and on speaking terms at least with Chief Macoya,
both enemies of Outina (Solís de Merás 1923:206). Chief Tacatacuru's
position is murky for the 1560s beyond his being an ally of Saturiwa. By

the end of the century, San Pedro's chief, a successor to Tacatacuru, was a paramount chief with authority over some Georgia mainland chiefs and other chiefs as far south as San Juan del Puerto (B. López 1602; Pareja 1602). Alimacani, southernmost of the Tacatacuru chiefs, was a rival as well as an ally of Saturiwa. Such is the implication of his displeasure when Ribaut, on his first visit in 1562, crossed to the south bank to visit Saturiwa. For the eastern Timucua overall, it is not clear how much the paramount's position surpassed the status of first among equals.

Documentation from the mid-seventeenth century and earlier provides a clearer image for the two westernmost provinces. They each had a paramount who once wielded considerable authority. In de Soto's time Yustaga's Usachile seems to have been the paramount (Fernández de Oviedo y Valdés 1851:I, 551–53; Milanich and Hudson 1993:227). Laudonnière exalted the military power of Yustaga, noting that its king was so powerful that he could put 3,000 or 4,000 warriors in the field. But he gave the edge to Houstaqua's neighbor Onatheaqua (Lussagnet 1958:102, 137). Onatheaqua's likely successor by the end of the century was a chief whom Spaniards identified as head chief of Timucua (meaning the province of Utina) (Machado 1597). A decade later, a friar who knew that chief well referred to him as "the great cacique of Timucua who is greatly esteemed and feared in the whole land of Florida," noting that he had more than 20 places under his command (Oré 1936:114). He was the chief of the mission of San Martín de Ayacutu, the once "absolute lord" who led the 1656 revolt. At that time he had a number of important chiefs of major villages under him, who in their turn had lesser chiefs of other villages under them, parallel to the pattern for Apalachee. Spaniards called the midlevel chiefs "principal caciques." The lower-level chiefs headed settlements that were satellites of the principal chief's village (Hann 1986a:372, 374–75, 385–87; 1986b:passim).

The powers and importance of head chiefs and chiefs in general seem to have declined rapidly under Spanish rule and the disruption caused by epidemics of European-introduced diseases. A governor remarked in 1602, "In general the caciques are held in little consideration and are little respected by their Indians except in the making of the salute to them seated on their bench in the council house and in having preference in the handing out of what comes from the cookhouse and for the people whom he indicates. And in everything else they have little respect for him and less fear" (Méndez de Canzo 1602). His remarks, of course, would have applied then more to coastal chiefs than to ones of the hinterland. But only

15 years later friars spoke of Apalachee's chiefs in a similar vein (Hann 1988a:12).

Rival Chiefdoms and Alliances

French and Spanish sources from the 1560s present a fairly complete picture of a system of rival chiefdoms and alliances as a characteristic of the Timucua world at that time. At least five chiefdoms appear to have been major players, those of Saturiwa and Outina in the St. Johns Valley and Potano, Yustaga, and Onatheaqua from western Timucua. Conceivably, Tacatacuru was a sixth major player, but he is mentioned principally as an ally of Saturiwa. Saturiwa controlled chieftains directly, 10 of whom were spoken of as being his brothers. But that relationship may have been fictive rather than one of blood. His major rival, Outina, may have been more powerful, with 40 subject chiefs and allies who included the Acuera and Mocoso. Saturiwa, of course, had his Tacatacuru allies and other non-Timucua allies on the upper St. Johns beyond the domain of Outina. Potano was another major rival of Outina. The other western Timucua were probably more concerned about the Apalachee and Muskogean peoples of north-central Georgia. But Onatheaqua and Yustaga were also enemies of Outina. That suggests that they may have been allies of Potano. The Tacatacuru's major rivals were probably the Guale to their north.

The Intensity of the Rivalries

The intensity and bitterness of the interchiefdom rivalries and hostilities are reflected in a bizarre scapegoat ceremony that Laudonnière recorded. The ceremony was staged in the village of a Paracousi Molona, who was subject to Saturiwa. Whenever one of Molona's friends or allies returned from a sortie against the Thimagona without bringing back the heads (*testes*) of some of their enemies or prisoners, the chief caused the most beloved of his children to be wounded with the same weapons with which Thimagona had killed his ancestors, in order to recall the suffering and death those enemies had caused. In this instance the victim was struck twice in the ribs with a javelin, causing serious but apparently not fatal wounds. In renewing the wounds on a family member, the family mourned the earlier death again. A Frenchman (supposedly allied with the Saturiwa) triggered the ceremony on stopping at the village while returning from an expedition to Thimagona territory to establish good relations with Outina.

He reported duplicitously that he had wanted to slay the Thimagona on that expedition but had been foiled. For details on the ceremony see Bennett (1975:78ff.) or Lussagnet (1958:104–7).

The Saturiwa and Outina Confederations

French and Spanish sources identified a considerable number of the chiefs who belonged to the rival confederations or alliances headed by Saturiwa and Outina. The sources also provide data on the location of many of the villages, although the information is not always consistent. The Le Moyne map's placement of villages disagrees with written accounts in various instances and is obviously in error in at least some of them. Discrepancies occur as well between French and Spanish accounts. The most notable one involves the distance upriver to Outina's village from Fort Caroline. The Spanish source appears to be the more reliable of the two. Both sources agree more or less on the length of the overland trek from the river landing to the village, about five leagues. For details see Barrientos (1965:41, 102, 134, 135), Hakluyt (1964:60v., 61, 61v., 62), Lorant (1965:34–35), Lussagnet (1958:20n.3, 100, 101, 110, 113, 115, 131, 171n.1, 191, 243–45), Milanich and Hudson (1993:242–45), and Solís de Merás (1923:203, 206, 208). The following are the villages or provinces identified as belonging to the two confederations.

Saturiwa		*Outina*	
Palican	Alicamani	Molona	Mocoso
Seloy	Tacatacuru	Calabay	Omittaqua
Athore	Helicopile	Mayarca	Macoya
Sarabay	Haipaha	Patica	Coya
Casti	Helmocape	Chilili	Edelano
Molona	Carabayan	Onachaquara	Encaque
Emoloa	Soloy	Cadeca	Astina
Malica		Mayrra	Mathiaca
		Acquera	

Potano

Little is known about the power potential of Potano in the 1560s or about the authority of Chief Potano in the 1560s or earlier or later. The naming of the province for him suggests that he was the province's most important chief, at least. Five villages are mentioned for the province in de Soto's time and at the beginning of the mission era. There is no concrete indication of Potano's military strength except a prognostication by Outina's seer-shaman that Potano would be waiting for Outina with 2,000 warriors. It is not clear if the prediction had any foundation in reality. Outina then had only 300 warriors with him, and he brought only 200 on an earlier expedition against Potano. Potano's warriors stood up to Outina's 300 warriors and 30 Frenchmen with firearms for three hours until his severe losses at the hands of the French caused him to break off the fight and flee. Laudonnière maintained that Potano would have defeated Outina had it not been for the French presence.

Outina was capable of mounting a larger force than those he led against Potano. In Outina's people's conflict with the French, they attacked in successive waves of 200 to 300 warriors. For their attack on Outina, Saturiwa and 10 of his chiefs assembled slightly more than 500 warriors. When the Saltwater Timucua joined Gourgues for the attack on the Spaniards, Saturiwa had 500 to 600 warriors under his command, and the eight chiefs allied with him, who were mentioned, each had between 100 and 120 warriors (Lussagnet 1958:115–16, 139–40, 243–44).

Succession to Chiefdoms

Solid evidence indicates that succession to chieftainships and some other leadership positions followed the matrilineal pattern under which a deceased chief was succeeded by a nephew or niece, children of his eldest sister, rather than by his own son or daughter. Fray Alonso de Jesús (1630a:96) clearly affirmed the prevalence of succession through the female line, noting that hereditary succession extended to the first four of a chief's counselors. Matrilineal succession was still being followed in western provinces as late as 1695 (J. de Florencia 1695:198). In some of the coastal provinces matrilineal succession either was not followed or was quickly supplanted by the patrilineal model under European influence. When Laudonnière seized Chief Outina, the chief's people allegedly chose one of Outina's children as his successor. But Laudonnière may have misinterpreted the successor's relationship to Outina, influenced by his Eurocentric views. As early as 1593 a governor reported for the coastal area that, among the Christianized natives, sons of chiefs were demanding adoption of the Spaniards' patrilineal system (P. Menéndez Márquez 1593).

Two instances of such succession are known for this early period. Upon the death of don Pedro Márques, Freshwater chief of San Sebastian and

Tocoy, his son Gaspar Márques succeeded to the chieftainship. At Nombre de Dios, its first Christian cacica was succeeded by her daughter (Lussagnet 1958:148; María 1600; Márques [1606]). Those examples may simply reflect rapid acculturation of people who allied with the Spaniards early and lived in close contact with the Spanish community at St. Augustine, where they attended church during the first years after their conversion. If doña María at Nombre de Dios had already married the Spanish soldier Clemente Vernal by the time of her mother's death, that marriage would have heightened Spanish interest and pressure for following the Spanish model (F. de Valdés 1602).

Pareja (1612b:66–68) noted that specific clans provided chiefs and other officials. Head chiefs came from a clan called Honosonayo, or White Deer, lineage. He added that "in the Agua Dulce and province of Potano they called all these lineages of caciques *Qibiro ano,* lineage of Large Deer (*benado grande*)." He noted that chiefly phratries also included "*oyorano fiyo chuluquita oconi, oyolano.*" He listed as "common lineages of the common people: earth lineage or *vtihasomi enatiqi;* fish lineage or *cuiuhasomi*"; and noted as "descendants of this lineage, *cuiuhasomiaroqui, cuiuhasomiele,*" and as "relatives (*parie[n]tes*) of this lineage, *tucunubala, yrihibano, apichi.*" Swanton (1922:371) observed that *hasomi* meant "clan" (Milanich 1972:12).

Although the Timucua's political organization became subservient to Spanish demands once its leaders gave obedience to the governor and although paramounts lost much of their authority over time, the native hierarchy and its system of inherited offices seem to have remained largely intact. On the whole, Spaniards seem to have interfered with the system significantly only in cases of revolt. If there was interference, it is likely to have occurred among the Saltwater Timucua during the time they passed from hostility toward the Spaniards to acquiescence to their presence and then to Christianization. Unfortunately, there is no data on the circumstances under which those accommodations occurred.

In contrast to New Spain and other such territories, Spaniards did not impose their cabildo government on the native villages in Florida. The only Spanish term used in Florida to refer to native leaders was *gobernador,* or governor. When that title was applied to native rulers elsewhere, it usually indicated that the cabildo system had been introduced or was being introduced. Its introduction led gradually but inevitably to replacement of hereditary chiefs' rule by the rule of elected officeholders limited to one two-year term and subject to accountability in the form of the *residencia* (Zeitlin and Thomas 1992:289, 297).

Timucua leaders known to have been given the title "governor" ran their village under that title when the legitimate cacique or cacica was incapable of exercising the duties of the office because of age or infirmity. Those Timucua recorded as having been given the title were the legitimate heirs of the leader for whom they ruled. Typical is an instance recorded for Yustaga's San Matheo de Tolapatafi. During the 1695 visitation, village leaders reported that the lawful heir, Julian, "was governing because his aunt, who is the legitimate cacica, has not died and that, although she is incapacitated, he has preferred, nonetheless, not to take formal possession of the chieftainship until she dies because of the respect that he owes her." The visitor sanctioned the status quo, observing that the heir's interim rule had proved adequate to the village's needs. But he ordered that the official title of governor be issued to Julian "so that he may govern this village in virtue of it with legitimacy" (J. de Florencia 1695:198). Spanish introduction of the visitation process brought with it an element of accountability for native leaders.

6.
THE TIMUCUA'S
MATERIAL WORLD

Archaeological research has revealed that, in a number of regions in the course of the seventeenth century, the ceramics prevalent at contact or through the sixteenth century gave way in varying degrees to new or intrusive styles. (See chapter 1 for archaeological traditions in the various provinces at contact.) Several new ceramic styles appeared in western Timucua, but the Lamar-derived Leon-Jefferson was the dominant one overall. In eastern Timucua the traditional St. Johns ceramics gave way to Georgia-style San Marcos ceramics that archaeologists have usually interpreted as an indicator of Guale replacement of the aboriginal inhabitants, although documents often suggest otherwise.

On Utina and Yustaga sites associated with missions, Leon-Jefferson ceramics largely replaced the traditional ones in cases where the identity of the earlier ceramics is known. Not enough archaeological work has been done to provide an explanation for the change. For Yustaga, which has been little studied beyond surface collecting, there is no documentary indication of any influx of new peoples during the seventeenth century. On the contrary, Yustaga supplied people to revivify settlements in other regions. Documents establish a movement of peoples southward into Utina proper from the Arapaha region in the late 1650s. But the migrants do not seem to have remained long at the depopulated sites to which they had been coerced to move. The absence of leaders among the Utina and Yustaga bearing the distinctive title of mico associated with the Lamar heartland or the absence of a significant number of people speaking its Muskogean language seems to rule out an influx of Lamar peoples as the origin of the Leon-Jefferson complex in those regions.

Alachua-tradition ceramics continued dominant overall in Potano and Ocale, but significant quantities of non-Alachua ones began to appear during the seventeenth century. Archaeologists have interpreted the changes as indicating an influx of peoples from eastern Timucua, coastal Georgia, and Apalachee and/or Utina and Yustaga. Early in the century, the neighboring eastern Timucua provided the intrusive pottery. Leon-Jefferson ceramics began to appear by 1630. During the 1660–1700 period, 68 percent of ceramics at the Zetrouer site were San Marcos type. Archaeologists generally interpret them as representing a Guale influx, although there is no documentary evidence for their presence in Potano. Timucua from coastal Georgia, who also used San Marcos ceramics, seem a more likely source, in the absence of other evidence for the presence of Guale-speakers. Utina and Yustaga could account for the Leon-Jefferson ceramics. Apalachee seem to be ruled out. Documents place only a few in Potano, none of them women, the usual pottery-makers (Friars 1664; Hann 1986a:376–79, 383–85; 1986b:105; Milanich 1978:61–62, 75, 79; Worth 1992b:290–300).

Among the eastern Timucua, only Freshwater and Saltwater sites have been extensively studied archaeologically. The recent identification of the St. Marys region, extending south to the mouth of the St. Johns River, as a transition zone containing San Marcos and St. Johns ceramics and the identification of Saturiwa territory as falling within this transition zone have solved some of the problems arising from changes noted at St. Johns River sites characterized exclusively by St. Johns ceramics before the seventeenth century. This applies particularly to the Rollestown site, believed to be the location successively of San Diego de Laca and San Diego de Salamototo. There San Marcos ceramics overlie St. Johns ceramics. That site would now be considered as falling within Freshwater territory rather than belonging to Saturiwa territory. The later Salamototo occupants, identified repeatedly as Timucua-speakers, probably were migrants from Timucua territory in coastal Georgia rather than from Guale. On the other hand, the Tolomato mission, identified with the Wrights Landing site on the Guana River, is clearly identified as Guale. The predominance of San Marcos ceramics at San Juan del Puerto is probably attributable to the documented presence of Mocama at that site during all or most of the historic era through the seventeenth century and to its occupants' belonging to the St. Marys region variant. The origin of ceramic changes in both western and eastern Timucua needs more study (Ayala y Escobar 1717; Deagan 1978:92–93, 106; Hann 1989:186–87; D. de Leturiondo 1678:141).

Structures

At least eight distinct structures may have existed in or near pre-Christian settlements. They are houses of common Indians; the larger house of a chief; the council house or communal meeting place; the "house of food"; *barbacoas,* or private food-storage structures; burial structures, including charnel houses and the structure that served as final repository for the bones; and menstrual huts or postchildbirth huts. All the above are mentioned explicitly or implicitly. Another simpler structure is the barbacoa used for smoking and drying meat and other foods. Distinctive structures may have housed village leaders below the level of chief. Temples are another possibility, although they are not mentioned.

Le Challeux portrayed the coastal Timucua's houses as round and almost in the style of the dovecotes of France, erected with stout trees and covered with palm fronds (Lussagnet 1958:212). Ribaut described houses at the mouth of the St. Marys River as "properly constructed of pieces of wood placed vertically and generally covered with reed after the fashion of a tent" (Lussagnet 1958:18; Ribaut 1927:84). Fray Jesús (1630a:93–94) described the houses as made "with precision (*al juste*) and regularity (*forma*) with round logs because of the many and very strong winds; with no nails, covered with palm fronds; built so well that they last for many years, because, in being spherical, their shape forms a pyramidal figure. And thus the water flows down without penetrating the straw, which is placed all around and thickly (*esta ceñida puesta y tupida*)."

Individual dwellings lacked a window. The door opening was about 32 inches high and 16 in width. A frame of small reed bars about two feet off the ground (*armador de barillas de caña*), also called a barbacoa, served as seat and bed. A bearskin was its only cover (Díaz Vara Calderón 1675a; Ribaut 1927:84). A description of Guale houses at the mouth of the Altamaha in 1595 probably has some application for those of the neighboring coastal Timucua of Georgia. All were small, being meant simply for shelter, because the Indians had little to keep in them. Even the head chief's house was small, although undoubtedly larger than that of the ordinary Indian, as "it had three or four small rooms and differed from the rest in having something more in the way of provisions, but this amounted to no more than some maize and some Castilian hens" (G. García 1902:194).

Only for Saturiwa territory and Potano have archaeologists done enough research to describe the houses of ordinary Indians. The Saturiwa houses were oval to roughly circular with a long axis of about 21 feet (seven meters) and a short axis of about 19 1/2 feet (six meters). The wall posts were straight pine limbs nine to 10 inches (20 to 22 centimeters) in diameter, spaced two to nine feet apart. They were sharpened at the basal end and driven into the ground. Walls and roofs were covered with palm fronds. Archaeological evidence suggests a central fire pit 40 to 80 inches in diameter. Layers of ash and burned cultural debris filled the pits. Burned bone, oyster shells, and potsherds constituted much of the debris. No evidence was found of the benches that documents describe. There is no evidence of wall height (Deagan 1979:90, 95, 98). For Potano, excavations at the Richardson site, believed to have been occupied in the sixteenth century, suggested a village of 15 to 20 houses set about 75 feet apart. Portions of two houses excavated revealed them to be round, about 25 feet in diameter, with wall posts two or three feet apart. Bed platforms along the inside wall had smudge pits underneath them to ward off insects.

The Potano cooked food within the houses in bell-shaped pits, one to two feet in diameter and one to one and one-half feet deep. Deer, turtle, and fish comprised the largest portion of the diet, along with maize. Evidence also indicated consumption of alligator, mud eel, opossum, raccoon, rabbit, brown bear, skunk, squirrel, and cotton rat. Archaeologists recovered charred corn, palm berries, hickory nuts, and walnuts (Milanich 1972:21; personal communication 1994).

Several of de Bry's engravings depict villages in whole or in part and the structures they contained. One, entitled "A Fortified Village," depicts a compact settlement of about 50 houses surrounded by a stout palisade. Its caption states that Indians placed such fortified villages near a swift stream on a site made as level as possible. The chief's house stood in the center of the enclosure and was "somewhat sunken into the ground to avoid the heat of the sun and surrounded by the houses of the principal men." The roofs were only lightly thatched (Lorant 1965:95, pl.30, 101, pl.33, 113, pl.40).

Those engravings present problems that raise questions as to their accuracy. No text other than de Bry's caption mentions fortified villages, and limited excavations in eastern Timucua have not found any sign of palisaded villages. De Bry's compact settlement pattern is at odds with existing descriptions and allusions to villages. A Spanish governor at the end of the sixteenth century described the settlement pattern prevailing then as being very dispersed. "The settlements of the natives that there are in these provinces do not have cities or towns or organized villages (*pueblos avezindados*) [amounting to anything] more than that each cacique has a community house where the Indians come together to hold their dances and to drink a brew (*brevage*) of *Casina* . . . and they are all scattered about with their little houses (*casillas*) at intervals on the edges (*haldas*) of the woods [where] they hoe their little fields where they sow their maize and some vegetables for their sustenance" (Méndez de Canzo 1602). Ribaut's

(1927:84) mention of gardens in association with the houses in a village on the St. Marys River suggests that de Bry's village pattern is not typical, if it existed at all. Testimony by a Mocama native about the Guale attack on San Pedro in 1597 suggests that the native's planted fields were close to his house (A. López 1597). If a chief's or shaman's house were to be burned at his death in a village as compact as the ones de Bry depicted, the rest of the village would burn as well. De Bry's structures are a hodgepodge of round and rectangular houses. There is no other evidence, documentary or archaeological, for rectangular structures in Timucua territory. His village seems to lack a council house and definitely lacks the large plaza that was typical of villages in Timucua, Guale, and Apalachee. De Bry shows no *garitas,* or corncribs. One wonders where the coastal natives found the swift streams de Bry described along which to place their fortified villages, particularly along the placid lower St. Johns River, with which the French were most familiar.

The most impressive structure of each village throughout the core area of Spanish Florida was a large round one known as the council house, where the chief met with his counselors each morning to receive their salutes, discuss village business, and drink cacina. Rodrigo Ranjel was the first European to mention a Timucuan council house. He described one at Uriutina in Utina Province as very large (*un muy gran buhío*) with a large open space (*gran patio*) in the middle of it (Fernández de Oviedo y Valdés 1851:I, 552). Ribaut (1927:84) noted one at the mouth of the St. Marys River as a house that stood out from the rest, "very great, long and broad with seats round about made of reeds, trimly couched together, which serve them both for beds and seats . . . set on great round pillars painted with red, yellow, and blue." Laudonnière referred to it as "the great public house," observing that before the daily discussion of village affairs began in it, each of the leaders came before the chief in turn to salute him, beginning with the eldest. They made the salute by raising their two hands twice to the height of their face while saying, "ha, he, ya, ha, ha," to which the others responded, "ha, ha." After saluting, each sat down on one of the seats that circled the inside of the house's exterior wall (Lussagnet 1958:46). A young Spaniard who visited the council house at the San Pedro mission on Cumberland Island in 1595 described it as bigger than ones he had seen in Guale at the mouth of the Altamaha and, in contrast to the Guale structures, as "open at the top with a skylight (*claraboya*) such as can be made in a *jacal,*[1] round in shape and made of whole pine trees" (G. García 1902:199).

Fray Jesús (1630a:94–95), speaking of council houses of Timucua and

Guale in general, added additional details. He noted that they were "away from (*fuera de*) the private ones [houses]" and that this structure was the place where they assembled for their favorite pastimes "such as making bows and arrows, dressing deerskins, those things that are their arms and their clothes." He observed that there is room for everyone even should there be two thousand Indians. But, he remarked, when food or drink was being distributed there, "In no way are women alone (*mujeres solas*) found there; they eat with their family in their houses of conjugal cohabitation." Bishop Díaz Vara Calderón (1675a) noted that most council houses were capable of holding up to 2,000 and even 3,000 people. He described the seats as niches that served also as lodging for soldiers and travelers. The niches were doubtless the "painted cabins or compartments" that Jonathan Dickinson (1981:65–67) described as gracing the inside of the outer wall of the council house, or "war house," as he termed it, at one of the coastal missions he visited in the last years of the seventeenth century. Each cubicle was large enough for two people. Fires were prepared in front of those compartments in addition to the main fire at the center of the quadrangle under the skylight, around which the dances and other festivities were held.

The bishop's observations about the massive size of the council houses he saw, their roof openings, and the placement of the central fire have been borne out by data from the only mission-era council house excavated to date, the one at Apalachee's San Luis de Talimali. It also had an inner ring of benches around the perimeter of the quadrangle and cob-filled smudge pits under both circles of benches for pest control (Shapiro and Hann 1990:518–22; Shapiro and McEwan 1992:21–47, 63–68).

The council house symbolized the bond of community for villages where dwellings were often widely scattered. A governor remarked in 1602 that the coastal settlements amounted to nothing more than each chief's "having a community house where the Indians came together to hold their dances and assemblies and to drink a brew of cacina." He noted that consumption of cacina was restricted to the council house (Méndez de Canzo 1602). The chief, as proprietor of the council house, had an exclusive franchise, as it were, for distribution of cacina. That stricture still endured three-quarters of a century later. During the 1678 visitation, a cacica of Asilepaja, who was bedridden and then living at Salamototo, pleaded with the visitor for permission to prepare cacina in her house, noting that it was normally forbidden to prepare the beverage in a private dwelling. He granted her request but stipulated that the cacina thus prepared be served to her alone and that she was not to have anyone in the house on such occasions (D. de Leturiondo 1678:141). The implication seems to be that she was not to set up a court rivaling that of the village chief, as that would infringe on his monopoly.

Council houses appear to have been peculiarly the chief's property and a symbol of the allegiance owed him. An incident during the 1695 visitation at Guadalquini reflects the chief's proprietorship. The visitor reminded the inhabitants that the preceding governor had ordered them to move to the more secure island settlement of San Juan del Puerto and asked why they had not done so. The cacique replied that he had done his best to persuade his villagers to move, going so far as to build a council house for them at San Juan (Pueyo 1695:243; Shapiro and Hann 1990:516). Villagers were citizens, as it were, of a certain council house. A visitor to Guale and Mocama in 1677 characterized the council houses as places "where it is the custom to hold the assemblies and hearings [for those] who recognize they are united to the said council houses" (Antonio de Argüelles 1678:88). The same sense of citizenship in a council house is conveyed by a complaint by a Guale chief that, with slight cause, Indians from his council house were passing to another one. In response the visitor ordered that the Indians "should remain in their own state (*estado*)" (Antonio de Argüelles 1678:89).

Council house walls were covered with murals in some part of Timucua. At a place called Aramazaca on the hacienda of doña Luisa de los Angeles y Argüelles on the lower St. Johns River, Indians extracted "very fine and light powders of all colors which they use to make pigments." St. Augustine's pastor in the 1690s reported that they painted their council houses and churches with them, depicting their battles and histories with great naturalness (Hann 1986d:201). Neither Dickinson nor the pastor said anything more specific about the painting. Some of it may have been analogous to that alluded to by William Bartram and David I. Bushnell (1919:80). (For more detail see D. Bushnell, along with Shapiro and Hann 1990:512).

Laudonnière spoke of all of the maize harvested being brought to the "public house (*la maison publique*)," from whence it was distributed to each one according to his rank. The significance of his statement is not clear on several counts. Was his "public house" the council house or a structure distinct from it? Did this storage involve only maize the chief collected for distribution in times of emergency or did it include the entire harvest, as Laudonnière seemingly suggested? Suzanne Lussagnet (1958:48, 48n.2) observed, in a comment on the passage mentioning the "public house," that chiefs exacted labor from their subjects for cultivation of the chief's own fields and for community fields. Laudonnière's public maize-storage structure may have housed the harvest from such community fields. That is suggested by a citation Lussagnet made from Le Moyne, stating that such provisions stored under the chief's surveillance were to be distributed only in the case of absolute need. Thus it was a strategic reserve. Laudonnière alluded to such a reserve in remarking that, even when the French were very much in need, Saturiwa never dipped into his emergency supply to assist the French. Laudonnière's "public house" has a parallel of sorts in a community storage structure under the chief's surveillance that is mentioned for the late mission period for Apalachee and the coastal missions (J. de Florencia 1695:190, 244).

Fray Jesús (1630a:95) suggested just such a regular communal distribution of food, writing, "In some provinces the Indians eat only one time during the day. The drink that they call *cazina* which I have spoken of is made in this house of the food that is distributed for all the houses and in it alone." The friar's allusion to cacina identifies the structure as the council house, as other sources attest that normally cacina could be made and served only in the council house (D. de Leturiondo 1678:141; Méndez de Canzo 1602). The friar's remark at this time about women being required to eat at home implies that men took their one meal a day in the council house where food was distributed communally. The Saturiwa were one of the peoples who ate only once a day, after sundown (Ribaut 1927:75).

De Bry indicated existence of a separate structure (apart from the council house) that served as a communal food storage building. But his description of that structure is fraught with even more problems than were noted for his "Fortified Village" plate and its caption. The Indians allegedly gathered the food put into that structure twice a year from islands that produced it in abundance. The granaries were "low and roomy," built of stones and earth and thickly roofed with palm branches and a kind of soft earth. To preserve their contents better, the structures usually were placed in the shade of a river bluff or mountain to shelter them from the sun's heat (Lorant 1965:79, pl.22). The nature of de Bry's public granary is sharply at odds with what other more reliable sources reveal about the Indians' private storage buildings. They were elevated structures. No other source even suggests the Timucua's use of stone in their buildings. If they had built with stone, archaeologists would surely have found a trace of them before now. De Bry did not explain where Florida's natives found mountains with which to shade those structures. One could list other absurdities, but these suffice to suggest that de Bry or Le Moyne may have given free rein to his imagination in composing this portrait and its caption. These are but a sample of the misrepresentations that led Sturtevant (1977:70) to warn about the unreliability of many aspects of the de Bry engravings.

In mission times each house had its own food-storage structure, off to one side of the house, elevated, and supported on 12 beams (Díaz Vara Calderón 1675a). Elvas (1933:37v., 75) remarked on one at Napituca in Utina Province as a raised structure made of canes. He provided more details about one at Toalli, a little to the north of Apalachee in western Georgia. "They have *barbacoas* in which they keep their maize. This is a house raised up on four posts, timbered like a loft and the floor of canes." John Lawson described one in the Carolina hinterland in 1700 that had a feature that may well have been used in Florida. He noted that the laths of the structure were well daubed with clay inside and out, "which makes them tight, and fit to keep out the smallest insect" (Hudson 1990:110). The Timucua seem to have had some such means of insect-proofing their barbacoas, inasmuch as they were able to keep supplies of maize until well into the spring. Spaniards complained that they were unable to keep maize more than three or four months before it was eaten by weevils (*gorgoxo*) and grain moths (*palomylla*), which left nothing but chaff (F. de Valdés 1602:passim).

In addition to their dwellings in the village, the Timucua built single houses in corners of distant fields for the people who stayed there to protect the maize from birds and animals that threatened the harvest (Lussagnet 1958:89; F. de Valdés 1602:passim).

Another structure likely to have been found outside the village is a menstrual hut to which women withdrew during their periods and just after childbirth because of the taboos involving male contact with women during such times. There is no explicit evidence, documentary or archaeological, for their existence among the Timucua, but it is suggested by the requirement that women had to light "a separate fire" during their periods and just after childbirth (Milanich and Sturtevant 1972:25, 43). As Patricia Galloway (1991) has noted, little is known about such structures anywhere in the Southeast.

There is no mention of the Timucua having any temples for their worship of the sun and moon and other gods. None of the mounds in indisputably Timucua territory appear to be temple mounds. However, inclusion of Tampa Bay's Safety Harbor culture peoples within the Timucua-speakers' domain introduces an element that had temple mounds. In beginning the Christianization of Utina Province at Ayacutu, Fray Martín Prieto burned twelve images in the center of the plaza there but made no mention of their having been housed in any structure (Oré 1936:114–15). In depicting the Freshwater Timucua's offering to the sun of a deerskin stuffed with the choicest tubers that their land produced, de Bry showed the ceremony taking place outdoors (Lorant 1965:105, pl.35).

Subsistence

Most of the Timucua-speakers were relatively sedentary horticulturists. Horticulture provided a greater proportion of total subsistence among the inland peoples than it did for coastal tribes and those living along the St. Johns River. The latter two relied more heavily on fishing, hunting, and gathering of shellfish, nuts, acorns, and starchy roots. De Soto found a steadily greater abundance of food in the Timucua hinterland as he moved from south to north. Laudonnière remarked of the natives nearer the coast that they planted no more than was necessary for six months. They abandoned their villages for three or four months during the winter to live in the woods in little houses made of palm fronds, eating acorns (*gland*), fish, oysters, deer, turkeys, alligators, and other game (Lussagnet 1958:48–49). Either the maize supply was not so limited everywhere in the coastal region, or production increased under Spanish prodding. In 1595 Tacatacuru's San Pedro still had a supply of maize in April (G. García 1902:199).

Some of the Timucua may have been largely or completely fisher-hunter-gatherers. Some of the Ocone appear to have been solely fisher-hunter-gatherers, and the same may have been true of coastal Freshwater Timucua living south of St. Augustine. Speaking of the Indians of that coast in general in 1595, a Spaniard noted, "These Indians neither sow nor gather" (G. García 1902:209). A governor spoke in a similar vein in 1602 about Freshwater people living along the St. Johns River, namely, Tocoy, Antonico, and Mayaca. He described them as "a poor and miserable people who sustain themselves with nothing but fish and roots from the swamps and woods" and observed that, because of this, they had never paid tribute, unlike the Saltwater Timucua and Guale (Méndez de Canzo 1602). The importance of roots gathered in the wild for the Freshwater Timucua is highlighted by the offering to the sun mentioned in the preceding section. But some Freshwater Timucua, such as the people of Chief Outina, were planting maize in the 1560s (Lussagnet 1958:145–46, 149, 150, 151). Mayaca, living just south of Freshwater Timucua territory, were described in the 1680s as "being so wild (*tan indómito*) a nation and of no sense at all, who in no way want to make a village, nor even less plant for their sustenance, nor ever live in a determined place" (Ayeta 1691).

The French listed the crops the Saltwater Timucua grew around their houses as maize, beans, pumpkins, gourds, cucumbers, citrons, peas, and many other fruits and tubers with which they were not familiar. Laudonnière gave the Indian name of one of the roots as *hassez,* noting that the Indians made bread from it in time of need. It is undoubtedly the root Spaniards mentioned frequently as *ache,* to which they also had recourse when starchy foods were in short supply. It was gathered rather than planted (J. de Florencia 1695:208, 212; Hann 1986e:91–93; 1992a:461; Lussagnet 1958:40, 47; Ribaut 1927:73).

Allusions to the root place it clearly in an aquatic habitat of ponds, bogs, and marshes. Alonso de Leturiondo spoke thus of the plant's habitat and of the work required to extract it: "Removal of this root or tuber (*patata*) requires a lot of work because it grows in mudholes (*variales*) full of water, and the entire tuber has so many roots, like a horse's mane or like hair, that in order to pull it out of the ground some very strong levers (*espeques muy fuertes*) are needed on which one may expend his strength and throw the weight of his body in order to dislodge them" (Hann 1986d:202).

Leturiondo spoke from bitter experience. When a governor failed to repay maize the priest had lent him, the priest and a slave had to stalk out to the woods to search for ache. Leturiondo recorded that he had stomped about the swamps in water up to his knees pulling out ache. Although most of the Indian people were similarly engaged, he observed that the roots were not to be found for sale or borrowing because the work of extracting them and processing them was such that "those who go to extract them can do it only to sustain their households" (A. de Leturiondo 1697; A. Bushnell 1981:28, 79).

Traditionally, authorities have identified the root as *Zamia integrifolia,* source of the Seminoles' *Koonte tsahte,* or white coontie, and our arrowroot starch (Bennett 1975:9, 215n.7; Larson 1980:199–201; Lussagnet 1958:133n.3; Swanton 1946:282–83). Spanish and French accounts' placement of ache in an aquatic habitat rules out such an identification. Zamias are denizens of dry sandy hammocks, pinelands, Indian middens (Boyrie Moya et al. 1957:18–19; Long and Lakela 1971:109–10; Morton 1982:64), and even high pinelands in the Potanos' Alachua County (Harper 1914: 317).

Acorns, hickory nuts, chinquapins, blueberries, blackberries (*mûre*), and

mulberries were among the additional foodstuffs that Timucua gathered
(J. de Florencia 1695:208, 212; G. García 1902:200–1; Hann 1986d:201–2;
Lussagnet 1958:11; Ribaut 1927:21). The acorns were used as a source of
cooking oil and also for making bread (Hann 1986e:94). Alonso de
Leturiondo identified the acorns used specifically as bitter acorns and described their processing for making bread. After the husks were removed,
the acorns were ground in a hand mill. The meal was then buried in pits to
remove the bitterness and other harmful ingredients and left there for
eight days or more. When the purified meal was baked as small loaves,
Leturiondo attested the bread to be delicious (Hann 1986d:202). Possibly,
Spaniards had improved on the natives' processing techniques. In 1595 a
starving group of shipwrecked Spaniards found a Gualean variety of the
bread so sharp-tasting and bitter that they refused to eat it (G. García
1902:185, 191–92).

Hickory nuts also were a source of cooking oil. The flour left over from
the oil extraction was used in corn cakes and mixed with parched maize
meal to serve as a sort of K ration on the trail. The mixture was fortified
additionally with dried persimmons and blueberries. It was mixed with
water for consumption (Hann 1986d:200, 202).

The Timucua's usual drink other than water was a tea made from the
toasted leaves of the yaupon holly (*Ilex vomitoria*), a relative of the tree
used for *yerba mate* among natives of South America's Plata Basin. Consumption of cacina also had ceremonial functions. Indeed, Laudonnière's
account of cacina consumption, read in isolation from other sources, might
be interpreted to mean that its consumption was confined to ceremonial
occasions and restricted to the warrior element. Each morning after the
village leaders had discussed the day's business, the chief ordered the brew-
ing of cacina. Laudonnière noted that the Indians drank the tea very hot,
that it made them break out in a very heavy sweat, and that when the
sweating passed, they did not feel hunger or thirst for 24 hours. If he was
talking about the Saturiwa, this statement is at odds with the claim that
the Saturiwa neither ate nor drank anything before sundown. Something
more than yaupon holly may have been used for the ceremonial draft.
Challeux noted that "*cassinet* is made from a composite of herbs and looks
like the beer of our country." The chief was the first to drink in this ceremonial use, employing a vessel (*vase*) that held about a quart by Paris
measure. All the rest then drank from the same vessel, one after the other
(Lussagnet 1958:46, 212–13).

Other sources indicate that cacina's consumption was widespread. A

Spaniard noted that its use had been adopted by his countrymen in St. Augustine by 1595. He observed that "both Indians and Spaniards drink it in the morning and they say that it helps prevent the stone and that because of the drink there is no Indian who has it [the stone] because it makes them urinate a great deal" (G. García 1902:197). Cacina was still being widely used by Indians and Spaniards a century later (Hann 1986d:202).

To prepare the tea, leaves were toasted over a fire in jars (*hollas*). Then the leaves were crushed and water was poured over the resultant powder. After letting the tea boil for a time, the natives filtered it and drank it hot (Hann 1986d:202). The vessel the Guale used for toasting the leaves was identified as a *cosuela*, a round bowl wider than it is deep. Some of the jars associated with the preparation of the tea appear to have been of a standard size that was quite ample. A source used the term *tinaja* to describe a large vessel containing a reserve supply of liquid cacina. A tinaja is an amphora-shaped jar, much wider in the middle than in the mouth or the bottom, that needs to be set into a ring or to be imbedded in the ground. The imbibers at Guale's Asao drank the cacina from an array of prefilled half-gallon jars (*ollas de a dos asumbres*) (G. García 1902:196). Guale on Amelia Island complaining in 1695 of the amount of seafood the soldiers at Santa María required them to supply daily noted that this had to be in such abundance that the measure for oysters was the fill of a cacina jar (*olla cassinera*) (Pueyo 1695:235–36). The lightning whelk (*Busycon contrarium*) appears to have been favored by Timucua as a drinking cup for ceremonial consumption. It is the one archaeologists have found to be used most commonly for that purpose (Milanich 1979:85).

It is worthy of note, however, that shell drinking cups for cacina are little mentioned in documentary sources except Dickinson (1981:25) and de Bry. Dickinson recorded the St. Lucie Indians' use of a conch shell. Laudonnière used the general term *vase* (vessel) for the container used by the chief and his counselors and the equally neutral *hanap* (goblet or drinking bowl) for the vessel the Indians placed on the chief's grave (Basanier 1853:10). Although de Bry's captions for two plates showing shell drinking cups appear to be almost literal translations of Laudonnière's text, de Bry transformed Laudonnière's vase into *capace concha* (large clam shell). His engravings portrayed the cups erroneously as nautilus shells (Hulton 1977:II, pl. 121; Merrill 1979:48).

Le Challeux reported "roots, fruits, herbs, and fish of different types" as among the coastal people's food. He noted that the fish were very fat and that the Timucua extracted the fat to use in lieu of butter and sauce, a process they called *Boucane* in their language (Lussagnet 1958:212). He described the maize as seven feet tall with a thick bamboo-like stalk and grains as big (*gros*) as peas. "The ear (*espy*) a foot in length, its color is like that of new beeswax." The very small ears that archaeologists have found raise questions about the validity of his description. He noted that the Indians pounded the maize kernels to turn it into flour and then mixed the flour with water to prepare a "*Migan*," a porridge that resembled one made of rice in France (Lussagnet 1958:212). Spaniards referred to this thick gruel as *atole,* observing that it was the form in which maize was most commonly consumed. In Mexico and Cuba atole was a gruel made by boiling maize flour in water or milk. Small cakes also were made from the flour. They were a little smaller than *comales* (tortilla stones) and two fingers thick, and they cooked under the embers (G. García 1902:197).

Maize parched over a fire was another important form in which the grain was consumed. Because it kept very well, it was a preferred ration along with bread made with honey for those who were traveling, as on military expeditions. The meal was usually mixed with water when it was about to be consumed (Lussagnet 1958:45).

Speaking of the mission provinces in general, Bishop Díaz Vara Calderón (1675a) described the Indians' ordinary sustenance as a stew (*gachas*) made of maize with ashes and squash and kidney beans and, for those who were better off, some game or freshwater fish. The fish, of course, would have been salt water or estuarine for coastal peoples. *Gacha* today has the sense of a very watery porridge.

To prepare fields for a new crop, the maize stalks and the weeds that succeeded them were burned during December and January along with the undergrowth of the surrounding woods. The burning was the occasion for a communal hunt in which game such as deer, ducks, and rabbits feeding in the fields were killed by people surrounding them as the game fled from the flames. *Hurimelas* was the Timucua name for this fire hunt. It combined the words *huri,* meaning "to free or liberate," and *mela,* meaning "heat." When the fire abated, the Indians entered the newly open woods to search for bear and panther. The bishop used the name *ojeo* for that phase of the hunt, but it is not clear whether that word is Timucua.

Game caught during this hunt was brought to the principal chief so that he might distribute it and claim the skins that were his perquisite. All bear-skins belonged to the chief and possibly panther skins as well. Fray Jesús (1630a:91) commented that none of the land's common trees were damaged by this annual burning except for some resinous pines. Although burning improved browse for the game, the friar recorded that the Indians' principal intent in setting the fires was to catch many deer and other animals (Díaz Vara Calderón 1675a; Granberry 1989:169; Hann 1988b:192).

It was probably at this time that the Indians accumulated much of their strategic reserve of protein mentioned by de Bry. Le Moyne noted that the natives put in a store of meats, fish, and crocodiles at a certain time each year, to be used only in times of necessity. They preserved such food by drying and curing it with heat and smoke on wooden gratings set on four posts. Those reserves are portrayed by de Bry as including foods of vegetable origin. The Timucua never gave the French anything from those reserve supplies. Every Indian shared in them in accord with his rank. The chief had first choice and took whatever pleased him (Lorant 1965:81, 83, pl. 23, 24).

After arrival of the Spaniards in 1565, the Indians soon added European and African cultigens to their sources of food as well as European domesticates such as chickens and hogs. Chickens and hogs found acceptance very quickly, as did peaches and watermelon. A young shipwrecked Spaniard found chickens for sale by the Indians of the San Pedro mission of Cumberland Island and at Guale's Asao, which was beyond the mission frontier in 1595 when he was there (G. García 1902:195, 197). Exotic cultigens for which there is archaeological or documentary evidence include barley and wheat, chickpeas, European greens, various aromatic herbs, peas, sugarcane, garlic, lemons, watermelons, peaches, pears, medlars, figs, and pomegranates. Watermelon and other melons, cucumbers, pomegranates, peaches, European grapes, cabbages, lettuce, radishes, and sweet potatoes were introduced by 1602. It is not clear how quickly natives adopted all of these (Boniface 1971:123; Castilla 1740; Jesús 1630a:92; Hann 1986d:200–201; F. de Valdés 1602).

Agricultural Tools and Techniques

Timucua worked the soil with wooden spades and mattocks. The latter were hoe-like instruments described as like those used in France for digging around vines (*une mare ou houe large*). De Bry described the hoe as "made from fish bone fitted to wooden handles," noting that the natives used digging sticks to plant the seed. His implication that planting took place early in winter is at odds with accounts that place the burning of the fields in December and January. Furthermore, seed planted then would be likely to rot unless it was more durable than modern varieties (Lorant 1965:77, pl. 21; Lussagnet 1958:13, 48).

Fish Procurement

Fish-weirs were used widely along the coast and for a considerable distance up the coastal streams. Some were small, consisting simply of stakes driven into the ground. Larger ones were made of stakes and reed grass, "all driven into the ground and well tied together, placed in a line in the manner in which one would with a fishnet." Such weirs extended for the reach of a musket shot, or about 750 feet. When the tide went out, the fish concentrated within a small corral built in the deepest part between the two arms. A round cast net (*Tarraya*) was used to catch them there (G. García 1902:202–3). Ribaut (1927:70–71) described weirs at the mouth of the St. Johns River as made with large reeds so cleverly placed that they formed a maze "with many turns and crooks." Weirs at that river's mouth in the beginning of May 1562 provided trout, mullet, flounder, turbot, and many other species that were unfamiliar to the French (Lussagnet 1958:52).

A technique Dickinson (1981:13) recorded for the Ais of the Indian River area doubtless was used by coastal Timucua as well when schools of fish such as mullet came inshore. The Indians darted after the fish and impaled them by throwing a spear-like staff.

Transport

A canoe-like vessel known as a pirogue provided water transportation. Ribaut (1927:80–81) likened pirogues to floating troughs and their oars to shovels. Rowers plied the oars while standing upright. The canoes he saw held 15 or 20 people and moved very swiftly. With more precision, a Spaniard described the pirogues of 1595 as made from a single log of cypress or red cedar with nothing more done to the exterior than to remove the bark. He noted that the Indians hollowed them out with fire before they had iron tools. All the pirogues he saw appeared to have been made with iron tools. Paddles were two yards long, made from one piece of tough wood. They had a lance-like handle and a blade half a yard long and a little over five inches wide, all well worked (G. García 1902:206, 207). Natives improvised a raft-like vessel (*balsa*) at times for crossing rivers such as the St. Johns (Hann 1992a:461). Bishop Díaz Vara Calderón's party crossed that river in two canoes tied together (Palacios [1675]).

Weapons and Warfare

The Timucua's weapons included bows and arrows, javelins and spears, wooden clubs, stone hatchets, and fingernails. Bow and arrow appear to have been the weapon used most commonly for warfare and the hunt. The club and stone celt axe were important as symbols of elite warrior status (Van Horne 1993:107–8). Bow strings were made from skin or deer entrails. The Timucua used both flint and fish teeth for arrowheads, but archaeologists find ones of flint much more often. Both men and women wore their nails long. Men used their nails in close combat to rake the enemy's forehead and blind him with the flow of blood (Lorant 1965:61, 63, 64; Lussagnet 1958:42, 43).

Their aim in warfare was to strike a blow without suffering too many casualties and to bring back trophies to attest to the success of the raid. Participants who killed one of the enemy warriors gained status for that feat. The name *noroco,* indicating one of the warrior statuses among the Apalachee, appeared among the Timucua as well. A public defender for a heathen Acuera accused of murder argued diminished responsibility for his client on this account because it was the general rule "among the Indians, both heathen and Christian [that] their greatest exploit (*valentia*) [and] trophy is to kill their enemies to obtain the name of *noroco*" (Hann 1992a:467; Lorant 1965:65 pl. 15; Lussagnet 1958:43, 109–10).

Musical Instruments

The Timucua had at least several musical instruments. One was a small tambourine (*atavel*) that the Indians beat to accompany singing and dancing (Jesús 1630a:97). They possibly had two wind instruments. One was a species of panpipe or trumpet, made from a thick reed. The player blew into a hole at the top and the sound came out of an opening at the other end. Twenty such pipers accompanied Saturiwa on a visit to the French fort, making what Le Moyne described as the wildest sort of noise, without harmony or rhythm, each one "blowing with all his might as if to see who could blow the loudest" (Lorant 1965:39–40). The Utina had a possibly less cacophonous instrument described as a flute (*frautas* or *flauta*) (Elvas 1933:1:67; Fernández de Oviedo y Valdés 1851:I,552). The other two instruments were gourd rattles and a flat stone pounded with a club. The Saturiwa used them to accompany a shamanistic ceremony held after a victorious raid on an enemy village (Lorant 1965:67 pl. 16).

Friars attested to the Timucua's love for music, which led them to participate eagerly in the singing at mass and other services (Jesús 1630a:100; B. López 1602; Pareja 1602). Various soldiers mentioned the inhabitants of the Mocama missions of San Pedro and San Juan del Puerto as being particularly active in singing at religious services (F. de Valdés 1602). There is no record of the instruments to which friars introduced Florida's natives. Menéndez de Avilés introduced them to the trumpet and other European instruments and provided a trumpeter to at least two Freshwater chiefs.

7.

TIMUCUA TRADITIONS
AND CUSTOMS

More is known about the Timucua's culture and customs than about those of any others among Spanish Florida's aboriginal peoples. The principal reasons are meticulous observations by the French in the 1560s and the writings of Fray Pareja, especially his *Confessionario*. French accounts are particularly informative about ceremonies and practices associated with warfare. The *Confessionario* is strong on Timucua religious ritual and practices friars regarded as superstitious.

Practices Associated with Warfare

Intertribal warfare was chronic but episodic. Surprise raids were the standard tactic. The goal was to kill as many men as possible and to capture women and children to be incorporated with the warriors' own people or held as slaves. When the element of surprise was lost, a raid might be aborted to avoid casualties among the attackers that a forewarning might portend. Warriors brought back the scalps of enemy dead as trophies and as evidence of their exploits. De Bry's mention of arms and legs among the trophies brought back for display would normally be suspect because they are not mentioned by other sources' accounts of the postvictory celebrations. But the caption for plate 15 indicates that Le Moyne himself was the source for that caption (Faupel 1992:178; Lawson 1992:99; Lorant 1965:65, 67, pl. 15, 16; Lussagnet 1958:43, 109–10).

Before setting out on an expedition, Saturiwa held a ceremony to invoke the sun-god's blessing on the warriors who were to participate in the attack. With the expedition's more than 500 warriors assembled near the river, Saturiwa went to the river's edge surrounded by 10 other paracousis who were to join him on the expedition. Taking a container of water in his hands, he looked up to the sky and began to gesticulate and shake his head back and forth with great anger, turning eventually toward the land of the enemy Thimagona to threaten them with death. He then looked toward the sun, asking for a glorious victory. After spending about half an hour in that exercise, he used his hands to pour some of the water over the heads of the 10 paracousis. Then, as if in furious anger, he threw the rest of the water on a fire prepared expressly for this function. After he had shouted, "He Thimagona" three times, all the warriors repeated the cry in unison. One of the Indians told Laudonnière that Saturiwa begged the sun-god in that ceremony to grant him a very successful victory so that he might scatter the blood of his enemies as he had scattered the water at the end and so that the chiefs whom he had sprinkled (*arrouez*) with it might return with the heads (*testes*) of their enemies (Lussagnet 1958:107–9).

In the account of the ensuing surprise attack at daybreak, scalps were the only trophies the warriors were mentioned as taking. To remove the scalps, Indians grasped the heads of the dead enemies and cut all around the circumference, taking a part of the bare skin (*taiz*) along with the scalp.[1] They also took 24 prisoners.

As soon as Saturiwa's victorious warriors reached their pirogues, they chanted praises to the sun for their victory, and those who had scalps attached them to the tips of their spears (*javelots*). On stopping for the night at Omoloa's village, the prisoners were distributed among the leaders, with Saturiwa receiving 13. He dispatched one of his people at once to take the good news to his village so that its people might begin the usual lamentations and celebrations that marked such events. The people began lamentations on receiving the news, while at night they began to dance and frolic in honor of the victory. When Saturiwa arrived on the next morning, he had all the enemy scalps set up in front of his door and encircled with branches of bay laurel. That set off another round of lamentations and moanings that lasted until nightfall, when they gave way again to celebrations and dances (Lussagnet 1958:107–10). As Lussagnet (1958:110n.3) observed, the lamentations were probably a manifestation of a custom a Spaniard observed at San Pedro in 1595: ceremonial wailing to welcome back an absent chief on his return.

In western Timucua at least, when scalps were taken by individuals in unplanned encounters with enemy Indians, the victorious scalper presented in the council house the scalp and any prizes he had taken from the victim. There he received the congratulations of his fellow villagers (A. García 1695:276, 279, 281, 288).

Speaking of Timucua warfare in general, Laudonnière noted that such victory celebrations lasted for three days and nights, consisting of singing and dancing. The Indians again sang praises to the sun for the victory while they were dancing. They required even the oldest women to dance while holding the scalps in their hands (Lussagnet 1958:43).

Ceremonial Wailing

Relative to the ceremonial wailing that took place, a Spaniard visiting San Pedro in 1595 reported that, whenever its head chief returned to his village after having been away for a time in a place as distant as St. Augustine, all the people in the village flocked to receive him. As soon as he landed and headed for his council house, all those assembled began to wail in a high voice. As the Spaniard remarked, it was "as if he had died before their eyes." The crowd continued their wailing as they followed the chief to the council house and went to the benches. They stopped only when the chief ultimately got up and left. Villagers who missed the first reception and people from distant villages subject to that chief took part in the procedure at later assemblies until the chief again rose up and left. The ceremony was repeated for days as new people arrived. This ceremony also was observed for the return of lesser chiefs of the subject villages.

The same Spaniard recorded that, while he was in St. Augustine, on every afternoon when he went to the river to fish, he would hear someone begin to cry in a high voice and that the whole village would soon follow in the same tone. On asking the reason, he learned that the chief had died and that they were obliged to wail for an entire year because of that (G. García 1902:200).

Burial Practices

Laudonnière commented at length on the burials of chiefs and priests but said nothing about the burials of ordinary Indians. The reliability of de Bry's brief allusions to burials is open to serious question. In 1630 a friar provided the only other description of the Timucua's pre-Christian practices. Unfortunately, he spoke only of the mission territory in general, which comprised all the Timucua provinces and Guale in 1630. And there is a possibility that some of his allusions refer to the Apalachee as well, as he seems to have traveled widely. In noting that practices differed from province to province, he failed to identify the provinces that departed from the norm. That lack of precision should be kept in mind in using the data that he provided.

In contrast to the yearlong wailing for a deceased chief cited for the vicinity of St. Augustine in 1595, Laudonnière gave six moons as the period during which certain women were delegated to do so each day in the morning, at noon, and in the evening. Chiefs were interred with great solemnity three days after their death. The people fasted during those three days and nights and wailed continuously. Upon burying a chief, they placed the vessel (*hanap*) from which he usually drank on top of the grave[2] and stuck many arrows in the ground around the grave. A friar indicated that chief's graves were "kept separate from the rest and all on the highest hills (*montes*), distanced (*apartados*) from the settlements." He noted that it was the custom in some provinces to bury children from the common people with a deceased principal chief. All the chiefs who were friends of the deceased commemorated his death in the same way.

All the rest of the people beyond those who offered children to accompany the chief offered a portion of their hair. Laudonnière specified that they cut off half of their hair. Fray Pareja indicated that it was customary for people to cut their hair upon the death of a relative as well. People also offered their most precious adornments (*alhajas*) for the deceased chief. Fray Jesús noted that in some provinces all the relatives, men and women, cut themselves on the upper parts of their arms and thighs with sharp flints until they had shed a great deal of blood for the deceased. In some provinces women wailed for deceased relatives for 30 days, while men cried in silence without having a set time.

Upon a chief's death all his possessions other than his drinking cup were placed in his house, which was then set afire so that none of them would ever be seen again. Laudonnière noted that the Timucua observed a priest's passage in the same way except that they buried a priest within his house before setting it afire.

For disposition of the remains of ordinary dead people, Fray Jesús noted that the Indians maintained charnel houses at some distance from their dwellings where the corpse remained until the flesh separated from the bones. The bones were then purified by fire and placed in small leather trunks (*petaquillas*), which were placed in little houses set on raised platforms (*barbacoas*). The Indians visited the bones every day with an offering of a small amount of everything that they ate. The friar observed that on becoming Christians, the Indians with great ease abandoned all their "diverse ceremonies and superstitions" related to treatment of the deceased (Jesús 1630a:99; Lorant 1965:115, pl.40; Lussagnet 1958:46–47; Milanich and Sturtevant 1972:25).

Little is known about the Timucua's beliefs about survival after death.

The attention given to remains of the deceased suggests that they had some concept of a life beyond death of the body. Olotocara, a nephew of Saturiwa, gave us one of the few inklings about their beliefs in this matter while marching at the side of Gourgues to attack San Mateo. Remarking that he expected to die in the assault but would not let that deter him, he asked the French leader, if he were killed, to give any gifts he meant to give him after the battle to his wife, to be buried with him in order that he might receive a better welcome to the village of the spirits. Lussagnet (1958:195, 195n.4) observed of this passage that it provides a precise meaning to the practice of burying personal objects with the dead. Fray Pareja and the findings of archaeologists attest to the continued inclusion of grave goods even after Christianization (Milanich and Sturtevant 1972:25, 45n.11).

Games

The French had relatively little to say about games that the Timucua played. Laudonnière mentioned running, archery, and a ball game. One of de Bry's engravings, based on Laudonnière's text, depicts all three activities. Laudonnière noted that the Timucua trained their young men to run well and awarded a prize to the one with the strongest wind. Of archery, he noted only that they practiced often. He briefly described a ball game that the eastern Timucua played that differed from the game played by the Apalachee and the western Timucua. The eastern game's goalpost was a tree eight or nine arm lengths' high, surmounted by splints or strips of wood linked to form a small square. The object of the game was to hit the square by throwing the ball (Lussagnet 1958:42–43). The engraving de-picts four men each throwing a ball and a fifth man sitting at the foot of the pole beside a basketful of balls. Lorant's (1965:107, pl. 36) does not reproduce all of de Bry's original Latin caption. The Latin caption placed the height of the post at twice the height given by Laudonnière. Faupel (1992:162) concluded that this engraving may have been entirely the work of de Bry.

A friar described dances as the natives' most usual form of entertain-ment, noting that they were held only in the council houses (*bohíos*) and community houses (*casas de comunidad*). It is not clear whether the two terms referring to structures represent seventeenth-century Spaniards' love of tautology or mean that dances were held in two distinct buildings. Men and women always danced separately. The friar remarked that the major-ity of the dances were decent. At times at least, dances were accompanied by singing and the use of little rattles (*atavales*) to set the rhythm. The musicians and the men played and sang in complete unison, while the women, "placed in a crescent and standing up, dancing, respond with the same rhythm (*el mismo concierto*)." De Bry's engraving, "The Sacrifice of First Born Children," depicts a dance that may well be similar to the one the friar described. The friar remarked that the dances were very lengthy and drawn out before the Indians became Christians, lasting for entire days and nights. Once they became Christians, their dances became shorter in duration, doubtless because of the greater attention to work demanded by the Spaniards. The friar noted that, in many areas, the Indians had abandoned their dances "despite their being decent and licit." That doubtless resulted from pressure from the more puritanically inclined among the friars (Jesús 1630a:97). Natives' complaints about friars banning such licit dances appeared perennially.

The so-called "Apalachee ball game" may be identified as closely with the western Timucua as it was with the Apalachee. The title for the manuscript on that ball game suggests such a possibility for the Yustaga at least. The title is "Origin and Beginning of the Game of Ball that the Apalachee and Yustagan Indians Have Been Playing since Pagan Times until the Year of 1676" (Hann 1988a:331). The game's deep roots among the western Timucua is reflected in the intensity of their resistance to abolition of the game. Apalachee's leaders appear to have acquiesced readily to arguments of the visitor, Domingo de Leturiondo, in 1677 for the game's abolition. He found the Yustaga far less compliant when he met with them at Potohiriba. He suggested that, as the game had been proscribed in Apalachee, it would be fitting that the Yustaga abandon the game as well. He argued that, because they played the same game, the Timucua's game could be presumed to contain the same evils that prompted prohibition of the Apalachee's game. Yustaga's leaders promptly informed him that their version of the game was not tainted by the superstitions that surrounded the one played in Apalachee. Ignoring their reply, he appealed to them as people who had been Christians longer than the Apalachee. He urged them to set an example, lest their continuing to play the game weaken the Apalachee's resolve to abandon the game and sow discord. The Yustaga held firm, arguing that they had no other games or entertainment to fill the void that would result from extinction of an institution so deeply rooted in their past. They insisted that they played the game without the contentions, violence, or frauds associated with Apalachee's game. Bowing to their persistence, the visitor agreed to leave resolution of the matter to the political and ecclesiastical authorities at St. Augustine. The Yustaga, in turn, pledged to suspend playing of the game until they heard from those authorities. The visitor met similar resistance when he introduced the same issue at a general assembly he held at San Francisco de Potano. Again both sides agreed to leave the matter to the authorities at St. Augustine (A. Bushnell 1978b:16–18; Hann 1988a:91–92; D. de Leturiondo 1678:127–28, 139). The authorities' decision is not known, but it is likely they would have sustained the visitor, if he pressed the point. However, a subsequent governor's renewed prohibition of the game in the 1680s indicates that it was still being played somewhere (Hann 1988a:90–91).

The game's basic components were a tall goalpost surmounted by an eagle's nest containing a stuffed eagle and a few shells; a small hard buckskin ball, slightly larger than a musket ball, filled with dried mud into which human hair was occasionally mixed; and two teams of varying size. The number varied with the size of the village, but 40 or 50 men to a team was typical. Feet were used exclusively for hurling the ball at the post. Players painted their bodies in colors associated with the dominant clans of the village they represented. A team gained one point each time it struck the post with the ball and two when it placed the ball in the eagle's nest. Eleven points brought victory.

Natives played the game only during the summer growing season, as one of its functions was to honor the sun-god, rain-god, and god of thunder, Nicoguadca, to whom the goalpost was dedicated. The aim was to assure the favor of those forces of nature so vital for good crops. There is no evidence that the game spread eastward beyond western Timucua.

In the functions it served, the game has a number of resemblances to the Mesoamerican ball game from which it presumably developed. Absence of a stick instrument differentiates it from other southeastern games and makes it resemble both Mesoamerican and southwestern games. Stephen Williams (1990) has suggested ties between details associated with the Apalachee game and prehistoric figurative drawings from Spiro that may indicate the route by which such outside influences may have reached Florida. The Apalachee-Timucua game was at once a sport, an act of worship, and a means of projecting a village's power and enjoyment of divine favor. It provided a substitute for war in the competition between polities within a tribe and for settling disputes between villages and their rulers. It offered warriors an opportunity to achieve status somewhat akin to that achieved by prowess in warfare. And like the Mesoamerican game and games of other native peoples throughout the Southeast and Southwest, it whetted the appetite for wagering (Hann 1988a:74–76, 86; Scarborough and Wilcox 1991:passim).[3]

It is not known whether the Timucua played the game against any Apalachee villages. That is unlikely to have occurred prior to their Christianization, as the two peoples seem to have been chronically at war prior to coming under Spanish influence. Within western Timucua even, there is no indication of the villages that played each other, in contrast to Apalachee, where Inihayca and Ivitachuco, head villages for western and eastern Apalachee, are known to have been rivals in the ball game and chunkey (Hann 1991c:154).

In 1630, before Spaniards had formally moved into Apalachee, a friar provided a novel detail about the Timucua game not mentioned in the 1676 ball-game manuscript. He observed that, because the game was attractive to watch, a great multitude assembled in the plazas where they played the game. "For this purpose only," he remarked, the plaza "is very large, level (*llana*), and hardened *empedrada*. There is a thick and tall log (*madero*) in the middle of it in this form [graphic design]." *Empedrada*'s primary meaning is "paved with stones." But it is very unlikely that this is what the friar meant, otherwise someone would have found such paving long before now. Other meanings of *empedrado* are "flecked with clouds (sky)," "dappled (horses)," "pitted with smallpox (face)." It is conceivable that a dappled effect was achieved by use of multicolored clays. But the friar is more likely to have used *empedrado* in a metaphoric sense to indicate that the field's clay surface was packed or hardened in some way to make it stone-like.

The upper limit of the number of players the friar stipulated in 1630 is considerably higher than the one mentioned in 1676. The difference probably reflects the much larger village populations of 1630 vis-à-vis those of 1676. The friar stated, "it is played 50 against 50 and 100 against 100 in conformity with the people who show up." He was more specific with respect to wagering than was the 1676 document, noting that "they wager everything [on it] that they are accustomed to have in the way of adornments (*alhajas*)." In contrast to the authors of the 1676 manuscript, the friar expressed no criticism of the game. That may indicate that the Timucua game was a tamer exercise and freer of religious implications than its Apalachee equivalent, as its Timucua defenders argued in 1677. Fray Pareja's questions for confessors of game-players in general, written almost a generation earlier, do not imply that the games that he had in mind had overtones of native religious beliefs from pre-Christian times. All but one of his questions are those a priest might address to a modern confessant recognized as an ardent sportsperson or gambler. Did you cheat or lie to win the game? Have you played with the intention of not paying what you bet if you should lose? Have you kept something you won, knowing it was stolen? Have you played so long that you lost everything that you had in your house? Have you become angry at someone over losing, or insulted a person with offensive words, or fought with someone because of the game? Even a last doubtful question has a potentially modern ring to it, if one substitutes "steroid" for "herb." Have you taken some herb and rubbed your hands with it with the desire of winning because of it? (Milanich and Sturtevant 1972:32–33). Most of those questions, of course, could refer exclusively to "other games" men played, which the friar identified in 1630 as "in the manner of our dice."

The same friar observed that it was rare for "women alone (*Mujeres solas*)" to play the ball game and that dancing was their only form of entertainment. He noted that they spent all the rest of their time and energy on housework.

He recorded that the natives still engaged in the races and leaping contests similar to those of the Spaniards, which the French were the first to note. Judges appointed for that purpose awarded the various established prizes to the winners (Jesús 1630a:97–98).

Although chunkey-playing is recorded in the origin myth of the Apalachee-Timucua ball game, there appears to be no specific documentation for chunkey-playing in Timucua territory. Chunkey is documented for the Apalachee and the Guale, two of the Timucua's closest neighbors and the ones to whom they were most closely related culturally. It is likely, therefore, that Timucua also played chunkey, but Timucua sites have not yielded any chunkey-stones to date (Jerald Milanich, personal communication 1993).[4]

Marriage

French and Spanish sources say little directly about marriage customs or sexual mores among the Timucua. Laudonnière and Le Challeux affirmed that monogamy was the general rule, but Laudonnière noted that chiefs were allowed two or three wives. His conclusion that only the first wife was recognized as queen is of very doubtful validity. It probably stems from his imposing a European view on native behavior, as it is coupled with a definitely erroneous statement, his assertion that only the queen's children inherited the goods and authority of the father (Lussagnet 1958:44, 212). Spanish sources establish clearly that the Timucua in general, like their Guale and Apalachee neighbors, were matrilineal. A chief's heirs were the children of his eldest sister, his nephews and nieces (Jesús 1630a:96). In some circumstances, rule passed first to a brother of the deceased chief (Machado 1597). That occurred probably when the eldest sister's children were too young to assume the chieftainship or not yet schooled in the things that a chief was supposed to know when he assumed the position.

Relative to Laudonnière's statement about the queen's rights, the pre-cariousness of a chief's wife's position is reflected in a comment by Fray Jesús (1630a:96–97). He noted that, if the new chief wished to take the houses and flocks (*casas y cabañas*) from the old chief's widow, "he does so, and if he does not, he gives orders to dig it [*la manda cabar*][5] so that she may be sustained until she finds someone with whom to marry." But the possibility that a chief's widow's status may not always have evaporated in that fashion is suggested by Laudonnière's tale of King Hioacaia's widow's generosity in supplying food to the French. She then ruled a Timucua territory on the Satilla River 12 leagues from the Frenchmen's fort (Lussagnet 1958:135–36). She, of course, could have been the proprietary ruler and Hioacaia only a prince consort. Or possibly the heirs were too young and she was serving as a regent.

Le Challeux remarked that the Timucua observed the sanctity of the marriage bond with full rigor. However, Spanish sources suggest obliquely that the rigor observed was not the same as that inculcated by European Christian mores or by the anti-incest taboos of many non-Christian societ-ies on the same cultural level as the Timucua. Fray Pareja's *Confessionario* as well as Fray Movilla's *Breve* (ritual) suggest that marriage conferred rights to sexual intercourse between the man and other women of his wife's family, such as her sisters and mother, and between the wife and her husband's brothers or other blood kin. Pareja's questions suggest that among Christianized natives such license was broadened to include even those related to them by the spiritual bond created by godparenthood.

Pareja's questions also suggest that there probably was no taboo against sexual relations prior to marriage. But children conceived outside wedlock were aborted. The intensity of the questions dealing with intercourse be-tween relatives indicates that such practices survived into Christian times. Questions indicate that both sodomy and pederasty were practiced (Milanich and Sturtevant 1972:29, 37–39, 43, 72–76; Movilla 1635b).

If de Bry's caption for his plate 8 is reliable, Chief Athore, a reputed son of Saturiwa, married his own mother and had children by her. However, the statement could easily be a product of French misunderstanding of the breadth of native kinship terms. Some southeastern Indians used the same term for a number of distinct kin (Hudson 1976:199–200; Lorant 1965:51, pl. 8; Movilla 1635b:13–14v.). The instructions that Movilla formulated for publishing the banns of marriage and for explaining the impediments to marriage observed among Catholics make it clear that the Timucua understood kinship terms such as mother, father, brother, sister, son, daughter, niece, nephew, and so forth to refer to others in their lineage even though their relationship by blood with those individuals was far removed. Movilla stressed the need, in discussing the impediments to marriage, to make it clear that Christians did not call anyone father except the one who sired them, nor brother or sister any but people whom their father sired or their mother bore, and so on for sons, daughters, nieces, nephews, and all other close blood relatives as far as first cousins. His instructions also suggest that incestuous marriages such as the one attributed to Chief Athore were possible. The friar considered it necessary to make it clear that "no Christian can marry his mother, grandmother, daughter, granddaughter, sister, or niece, aunt, or cousin." He also indicated that the Timucua viewed the marriage bond as having ceased to exist when the partners lived far away from each other for a time.

One source suggests that Timucua may have been matrilocal as well as matrilineal. A leading man, Antonio López, whose house was the only one that the Guale assaulted during their attack on San Pedro at the beginning of their 1597 revolt, was then living with his wife's family (Antonio López 1597).

Shamans officiated at the marriage ceremony during pre-Christian times and, in some instances, during early Christian times as well. When shamans were not properly compensated, they apparently were not above using their powers to harm the newly married couple. Shaman-wizards were to be questioned on using their powers "to entice a woman out of her house and on using herbs to attract a woman to themselves" (Milanich and Sturtevant 1972:31, 63).

Nothing is known about the circumstances under which the marriage bond could be dissolved other than the case of living far from one's spouse previously noted. Among other southeastern peoples who permitted dissolution of marriage, divorce usually occurred during the annual busk, or new corn ceremony. There is no mention of the busk for any of Florida's Indians, although they must have had something similar to it. Individual instances are mentioned of men leaving or putting aside their wives and of women leaving their husbands or living apart from them without mention of formal dissolution of the bond. One such case involved a Potano woman who became a *cimarrona,* or runaway. Six years after her marriage she ran away to the woods with a black slave. When they parted not long afterward, she continued to live in the woods. But she returned to her village of San Francisco Potano each year to make her Easter duty and during such intervals she resumed living with her husband while he was alive (Hann 1992a:460–62). The possibility of divorce would have been eliminated in Christian times, of course.

Husbands' abandonment of their wives even in Christian times is reflected in two of Pareja's questions for women about resort to superstitious practices to prevent a husband from leaving or to regain one who had left. The first asked, "Your husband having abandoned you, did you bathe with herbs, believing that because of this he would return to you?" The preventive measure involved wearing a Spanish-moss skirt after perfuming or smoking it with a herb (Milanich and Sturtevant 1972:58).

The Timucua prohibited intermarriage between certain lineages. On mentioning the lineages of the chiefs and the various levels of their counselors, Pareja (1612b:66) observed that all of these lineages did not marry with one another. He recorded that observance of the taboo persisted even after the people had been Christianized. But he remarked of the common lineages that they were able to marry with one another.

Despite the influence of Christianization, chiefs apparently maintained black slaves or servants as mistresses commonly enough to justify a question on that topic in the *Confessionario* (Milanich and Sturtevant 1972:185). Chiefs were to be asked as well whether they allowed their slaves to sleep together.

Laudonnière mentioned in passing a group he referred to as "daughters of the Sun." In contrast to the Inca's "Virgins of the Sun," who were sworn to perpetual chastity, "daughters of the Sun" served a sexual function as well as the religious one possibly suggested by their name. They may have been more akin to the rest of the Inca's "Chosen Women," from whom the "Virgins of the Sun" were set apart. Laudonnière attributed a prevalence of syphilis among Timucua men to "their too great love for women and the maidens whom they call daughters of the Sun" (Lussagnet 1958:43–44; Mason 1957:181).

Religion

Knowledge about the Timucua's religious practices is very scanty. The French recorded the coastal Timucua's worship of the sun and the moon and their attribution of victories they achieved to the sun-god. Laudonnière believed that they had no knowledge of God or religion in the European sense. But in view of the language barrier and the Indians' tendency to consider such knowledge as something to be held as a closely guarded secret from outsiders, or even from their own common people, the reliability of such assessments is questionable. Friars had little to say about the Timucua's religious beliefs and practices. The friar who initiated the mission at Timucua Province's head village burned 12 images there and six in each of its four satellite settlements. He gave no inkling of the identity of any of the images. The ball-game manuscript provides insights into the religious functions of that exercise designed to win the favor of the sun-god and gods of rain and thunder to assure a bountiful crop (Hann 1988a:331–50; Lussagnet 1958:43; Oré 1936:114).

Somewhat more is known about the priests or shamans who represented the native religious establishment. Head chiefs likely were the supreme religious authorities. They probably claimed special ties with the sun-god as did those of other southeastern groups. Timucua Province's head chief identified himself as leader in all of his Indians' ceremonies. His authorization of destruction of the idols suggests that he held supreme authority in religious matters (Oré 1936:114–15).

Laudonnière described the shamans as "great magicians, great diviners, invokers of devils, and healers who used herbs and drugs" (Lussagnet 1958:43). The groupings of Pareja's questions for confessors suggest distinct categories of shamans represented by those he categorized as sorcerers, doctors, herbalists, and midwives. But Milanich and Sturtevant (1972:42) noted that it is not clear how sharply herbalists or doctors were distinguished from those whom Pareja labeled as sorcerers. Sorcerers used herbs on occasion and herbalists were capable of bewitching. And herbs were used for purposes other than curing.

Rituals and Taboos for Mundane Activities

Timucua mores prescribed various rituals to facilitate success and taboos that were to be observed to avoid mishap and failure in such mundane activities as planting crops, gathering of wild produce, hunting, fishing, securing fish in a weir, removing the first stored maize from the village granary, and converting that first maize to flour. Most rituals required the presence of a shaman. Many of the taboos involved first fruits or natural phenomena affecting crops. At the initiation of all the subsistence activities mentioned, prayers were called for, made either by the individual engaged in the activity or by a shaman. Milanich and Sturtevant (1972:40) suggested that the prayers were more likely formulae or charms.

Rituals and taboos for planting and gathering were among the least numerous and least complicated. At planting time the chief ordered six old men to eat a specially prepared pot of porridge. A shaman-sorcerer was to pray to the first new maize. He was also to be the first to taste it and other new produce. The first maize from a new field and maize from a field or storage structure struck by lightning were not to be eaten. The first maize from a new clearing was not to be eaten by the one who planted it. The first produce from gathering activities was not to be eaten. A special ceremony involving use of bay laurel was prescribed before gathering nuts and palm berries.

Chiefs and leading men ordered that fishermen pray to a lake before beginning to fish in it and that the first catch be prayed to and then thrown on the grill (barbacoa), possibly as an offering. The leaders also ordered that the sorcerer pray over the rest of the fish caught in the lake and that he be given one-half of the catch.

Other rituals applied to the taking of fish from a new weir. Prayers were said over a newly built weir in the belief that many more fish would then enter it. The first to enter was taken out and placed next to the weir in the belief that this would bring a copious harvest. It was taboo to place the first fish caught in hot water because no more would then be taken in that weir. A man who had recently had intercourse was not to enter a weir as no fish would thenceforth enter a trap so contaminated.

The most numerous and complex rituals covered hunting, probably reflecting its greater difficulties and uncertainties. A chief or the leader of a hunting band made a prayer using tobacco before setting out. The band took deer antlers with them and prayed to them. Pareja's brief allusion to the bringing of antlers may also refer to a technique de Bry portrayed in which hunters approached their quarry covered with the skin, head, and antlers of a very large deer to get closer without spooking the deer. In what appears to be an allusion to the fire hunt technique or *hurimelas,* Pareja noted that "to go hunting deer, to hunt them, one had to burn some field with tall grass (*pajonal*) and make six arrows and six oaken splinters [that are] cleaved (*astillas de roble endidas*) and mixing a *yaquila* [an undefined Timucua word] all intertwined,[6] and this done, that they are to sing all through the night, and that they will go to hunt then and that they will catch many" (Milanich and Sturtevant 1972:53). When the hunters reached the forest, an old shaman said a prayer over all the arrows gathered together. The first deer killed went to the shaman. When the first arrow that hit a deer did not bring it down, the hunter prayed to the arrow so that the second one to hit would succeed. The hunter whose arrow killed the animal abstained from eating any of it; otherwise he would not have been able to kill another one. The same fate awaited hunters who threw a deer's liver and lungs into cold water to cook them or discarded its bones or those of other game that they caught. Instead the bones were hung up or placed in the roof thatch of the house. The Timucua believed that one who spilled broth made from a deer or quail would never snare another. There was a taboo on eating quail during the winter.

Taboos Involving Women

Women remained isolated and made a separate fire to prepare their food just after childbirth and during their periods. Presumably, they would have retired to a menstrual hut before Christianization. Pareja made no mention of such a structure, probably because the friars outlawed the practice as reflecting what they regarded as heathen superstition. During both pregnancy and menses, it was taboo for women to eat meat or fish. On some unspecified occasion when women anointed their hair with bear grease, they were required to abstain from fish for a certain number of moons. Milanich and Sturtevant (1972:43) suggested that this was probably done after childbirth. A taboo appears to have forbidden men from approaching a fire where a woman had given birth (Milanich and Sturtevant 1972:50, 57–58).

Observances Linked to Death and Burial

When a relative or one's spouse died, one was not supposed to eat food that the deceased had planted or that came from land that the deceased used to plant. After attending a burial, Timucua bathed and abstained from fish for an unspecified time. Pareja's questions about placement of grave goods inside the shroud of someone being buried and the cutting of one's hair upon the death of a relative indicate that both practices, in his mind, had religious or superstitious significance. Fray Alonso de Jesús (1630a:99) referred to the cutting of the hair as simply a sign of sorrow. Friars may have differed in their attitude toward such practices. That may account for the appearance of extensive grave goods associated with church burials in some places such as Santa Catalina de Guale. When chiefs and leaders were ill with diseases that they expected to be fatal, they had new houses built for themselves in which they might die.

Spells and Charms

The Timucua performed a number of forms of love magic. Women used various rituals to attract and/or hold a mate that involved bathing with herbs, perfuming the Spanish-moss skirts they wore, or fasting. Pareja noted that the women had many other practices of this nature that he omitted mentioning because women had abandoned using them or because they were practices confined to a specific province. It is likely that praying to the Franciscans' St. Anthony became a substitute for many of the practices for finding a husband. One of Pareja's questions for shaman-sorcerers was, "Have you drawn some woman out of her house with your spells by singing?" (Milanich and Sturtevant 1972: 57–58, 62–63).

Warriors believed that by bathing with juice from a certain herb when they were about to go to war, they could prevent arrows from wounding them. Whistling served as a charm for the traveler to stop a storm or to cross a patch of choppy water by canoe while passing over a sandbar or some other obstacle.

Portents and Omens

Timucua interpreted many phenomena as omens, both good and evil. Dreams presaged things that would come to pass. Trembling on hearing a blue jay's song meant that someone was coming or something important was about to happen. Twitching of the eyebrows could portend good or evil events. Trembling of the eyes forecast grief. Hearing an owl sing or encountering a snake in the path, fields, or house was a bad omen. Scaring a singing owl heightened the prospect of evil to come. But that bird's cry was not always a portent of evil. One of Pareja's questions for confessors asked, "When the owl hoots, have you believed that it will have pity on you?" As that question suggests, however, Timucua viewed the bird as an evil spirit or symbolic of one. The first part of the Timucua word for owl used in that question, *hitiquiry,* means "demon or evil spirit." Fittingly, one of the other synonyms is *hororo.* The owl totem depicted on the cover was recovered from a section of the St. Johns River believed to be in the land of Indians who bore the name Hororo or Jororo. Their name suggests that Timucua may have referred to those Indians as "people of the owl"

(Granberry 1989:216; Milanich and Sturtevant 1972:51, 54, 55). Making noise while hearing a woodpecker singing was believed to bring nose-bleed. Hearing a small goat baa also could lead to nosebleed unless one placed a certain herb in his nose, and death could follow if one did not return home to wash with the water of a certain herb. Seeing lightning meant the existence of war, while popping of the fire was a portent of war. Belching could mean either a future abundance of food or a wish to die. Similarly, trembling of the mouth could be either a good or a bad omen, portending that there would be food, or that someone was speaking ill of one, or that something bad would happen.

Curing Rituals

When a Timucua was ill, lighting of a new separate fire for cooking his or her food was believed to be a prerequisite to avoid death. The patient might secure a cure by offering maize to an unspecified god in the door of his or her house or by performing an unspecified ceremony in honor of one of the gods involving use of bay laurel. As one might expect, shamans played a major role in these rituals of curing as they did in many of the other rituals mentioned (Milanich and Sturtevant 1972: 49–51, 55–56).

Laudonnière was the first European observer to mention the Timucua's shamans. He noted that the priests served as doctors and surgeons and that they always carried a bagful of drugs and herbs with them (Lussagnet 1958:43). According to Milanich and Sturtevant (1972:42), it is not clear whether all the functions of seer, healer, magician, and herbalist were performed by a single individual or whether there was a degree of specialization. They noted that "herbalists could bewitch and that they knew the magic for making winners and losers in races" and that two curing techniques were attributed to the shamans whom Pareja characterized as "sorcerers." Pareja's devising of groups of questions to be addressed separately to "sorcerers," "doctors, herbalists, and sorcerers," "both herbalists and midwives," "sorcerers" alone, "herbalists" alone, and last to "both herbalists or midwives" suggests that there may have been a degree of specialization.

Laudonnière described an incident when some of his men observed the performance of a shaman-seer. As a consequence of Laudonnière's alliance with Paracousi Outina, some of the French soldiers participated in attacks Outina made on his enemy, Potano. On their second day's march, about three leagues away from Potano's village, a scouting party encountered three Potano fishing on a pond. The escape of two of them made it likely the attackers would lose the element of surprise Outina had counted on. Fearful that Potano might be strongly placed to receive them, Outina turned to his shaman (called an *Iarva* according to Laudonnière) for advice on the disposition of the enemy that he could expect. After performing ceremonies the French described as "hideous signs and frightful to see," the shaman advised against continuing the expedition, warning that Potano would be waiting for him in a certain place with a full 2,000 warriors, who carried cords for tying up the prisoners they were assured of capturing. At that, Outina suggested that the expedition turn back, but the French commander's anger and contempt shamed him into going forward (Lussagnet 1958:138–41).

One of de Bry's engravings purports to depict Outina's consultation of his shaman. Its caption provides additional details about the ceremony. For his divination, the shaman allegedly borrowed the French commander's shield, placing it on the ground and drawing a circle around it, within which he inscribed the signs the French found so hideous. They are nothing more appalling than sequences of geometric figures such as stars, squares, circles, and intersecting semicircles. Kneeling on the shield, the shaman whispered unintelligible words and gestured as though engaged in an animated conversation. After about 15 minutes he looked scarcely human, with his limbs twisted until the bones snapped out of place. After many other unspecified actions referred to as unnatural, the shaman suddenly became calm and stepped out of his circle to salute Outina and reveal the intelligence he had gleaned from his exercise (Lorant 1965:59, pl.12).

The shamans' repertoire, as detailed by Pareja, included finding lost things by divination, bewitching people for various purposes including death or threats of it to extort payment, causing rain and thunderstorms, preventing rain and stopping the clouds when it thundered by blowing toward the heavens, and curing people of their maladies. Many of the cures doubtless were based on use of herbs that had genuine medicinal properties. Others proceeded from the placebo effect or a process akin to faith healing. Milanich and Sturtevant (1972:42) remarked that "a sorcerer might place before a patient white feathers, new buckskin, owl 'ears,' and arrows stuck into the ground, saying that he was removing evil and sickness. He also removed intrusive objects from the patient's body, sucking out a piece of charcoal, a small lump of dirt, or a bit of matter that seemed to be alive, without rupturing the skin even when he operated on such spots as the forehead, the back of the neck, or the spine." For casting a spell on some-one, shamans used the skin of a poisonous snake (*ibora*) or a black snake along with black Spanish moss and other plants. While casting such a spell to kill someone, the sorcerer abstained from fish, from painting himself, and from sleeping with his wife. Upon the death of his victim, he bathed before resuming those activities. If the spell failed, the sorcerer believed that his own life would be forfeit.

Abortion

Abortion was standard practice for unmarried women who became preg-nant. Some used herbs to provoke the miscarriage. Others used physical means to injure or strangle the fetus and thereby induce a miscarriage. The practice continued to some degree long after the Timucua had been Christianized. In 1694 the visitor, Joaquín de Florencia, passed judgment on a woman of Yustaga's San Matheo mission, who was living apart from her husband and had been denounced for having terminated several preg-nancies by swallowing a substance called *verudises* (J. de Florencia 1695:198–99; Milanich and Sturtevant 1972:passim).

Geophagy

Two sources attest to the practice of geophagy among the Timucua, but it included more than the usual clays associated with that practice. It was prevalent enough to be noticed by Laudonnière, who recorded that "in need they eat a thousand vile things, even to swallowing charcoal and to the putting of sand (*sable*) in the porridge [made] from this flour [corn meal]" (Lussagnet 1958:45). Laudonnière gave no indication that the prac-tice he observed was sex-specific. The mixing of the sand with the porridge suggests that the usage was generalized to both sexes. Pareja, however, implies that the practices that he mentioned were restricted to women. He included among his questions for women in his *Confessionario,* "Have you eaten charcoal or earth (*tierra*) or pieces of clay pot (*olla*) or fleas or lice?" (Milanich and Sturtevant 1972:28, 58). The friar condemned ingestion of the first three items as damaging to the women's health. Swanton (1922:362), however, suggested that women consumed some of those sub-stances as remedies rather than as food.

8.
THE TIMUCUA
LANGUAGE

In comparison with that of Spanish Florida's other aboriginal peoples, the surviving literature in the Timucua language represents a cornucopia. Nine pieces survive, many of them lengthy published works, compared with a single letter and a few isolated words for Apalachee. Timucua is the only other aboriginal language of the mission territories or Florida proper of which any trace has survived other than place-names and people's names. In part this abundance may reflect interest shown by the Timucua-speaking people. Friars' remarks indicate that many Timucua showed interest in learning to read and write during the early days of the missions among them. One friar recorded that many knew how to read and write, noting that it was something to which they were all inclined, men as well as women, and that, consequently, they learned with great ease. Some even acquired the skill easily by themselves, once they had been taught the alphabet (Jesús 1630a:100; Oré 1936:103–4, 129).

The literature that friars prepared for this audience was more extensive than what has been found. It included childrens' primers (*cartillas*), catechisms, vocabularies, a grammar, a *confessionario*, and devotional booklets (*librillos*) (Jesús 1630a:95). The extant writings include three catechisms in Timucuan and Castilian, a confessionario, and a grammar, all written by Fray Pareja; two works by Fray Gregorio de Movilla, and two letters by Timucua leaders, one to a king and the other to a governor. Friars may have had a hand in writing the two letters, for they were accompanied by translations into Spanish done by friars. All the friars' surviving published works were written in the Mocama (maritime) dialect. The two letters reportedly are in the Potano dialect, even though the chief who allegedly wrote one of them, Cacique Manuel of Asile, was Yustaga. That letter may be the basis for Granberry's (1989:15; 1993:xvii, 7) identification of Potano as the dialect that the Yustaga spoke.

The following are translations of the titles of the friars' works. *Catechism in the Castilian and Timucuan Tongue in Which Is Contained That Which Can Be Taught to the Adults Who Are to Be Baptized,* published in Mexico in 1612; *Catechism and Brief Exposition of the Christian Doctrine, Very Useful and Necessary, Alike for Spaniards as Well as Natives in the Castilian and Timucuan Language, in the Manner of Questions and Replies,* published in Mexico in 1612; *Confessor's Manual in the Castilian and Timucuan Tongue with Some Counsels to Encourage the Penitent,* published in Mexico in 1613; *Rules and Pronunciation in the Timucuan Language and Castilian,* published in Mexico in 1614; *Catechism and Examination for Those Going to Communion, in the Castilian and Timucuan Language,* published in Mexico in 1627; *Brief Ritual for Administering the Sacraments to the Indians and to Spaniards Who Live among Them,* published in Mexico in 1635; and *Explanation of the Doctrine that Cardinal Bellarmine Composed by Order of Pope Clement VIII,* published in Mexico in 1635. The first five titles belong to Pareja. Lucien Adam and Julian Vinson published Pareja's grammar in Paris in 1886 under the title *Arte de la Lengva Timvqvana,* with a 26-page introduction in French by Julien Vinson.

The two extant letters date from the 1650s and the 1680s. Chief Manuel is credited with writing the earlier one, possibly at the prompting of friars opposed to continuance of a wheat and cattle hacienda that a governor had established on lands belonging to the village of Asile in the latter half of the 1640s. But the deed drawn up late in 1650, portraying Chief Manuel and Chief Luis Ivitachuco as donating the lands to the governor's son, Luis de Salazar Vallecilla (1651), states that Chief Manuel did not sign it because he did not know how. Chief Luis Ivitachuco, by contrast, did sign thus: "Luis Holatta ybittachuco." After the death of the governor in 1651, his interim successor and friend purchased the hacienda for the Crown from the governor's son. When the interim governor in turn died shortly after that transaction, friars persuaded his interim successor to close down the hacienda and auction off its stock, tools, and other effects. The chief's writing of this letter may have been part of the friars' campaign, which involved chiefs of neighboring Apalachee as well. Some of the documentation indicates that the hacienda extended into Apalachee. The second letter, dated 1688, was written conjointly by western Timucua's chiefs and addressed to the king at the request of a newly installed governor, Diego de Quiroga y Losada, attesting to the steps that he had taken to improve conditions and to counter the bad feelings left by his predecessor (Quiroga y Losada 1688; Rebolledo 1657a).

Scholarly Attention to the Language

Despite the availability of that grammar and of the many pages of Timucua text in the other sources, scholars have devoted relatively little attention to the language. Buckingham Smith began the modern study of the language in the middle of the nineteenth century after locating three of Pareja's publications while he was attached to the American legation in Madrid. He wrote an article, "The Timucua Language." He donated the documents and publications that he brought back to the New-York Historical Society. Before their appearance, Daniel G. Brinton (1859:134–37) lamented that none of Pareja's works was available in the United States and that the only knowledge of their content came from a few extracts in Hervas's *Catálogo de las Lenguas de las Naciones Conocidas*. Brinton, at that time, cautiously suggested the possibility of a relationship between Timucua and the Carib family of languages, based on Hervas's bolder assertion that abundant proof existed of such a connection. In his opening paragraph on the language of Florida's natives, Brinton characterized the few extracts that Hervas gave as hardly warranting a guess as to the classification of any of the area's languages. Thirty-two years later, on the strength of the French republication of Pareja's grammar and work by Albert S. Gatschet, Brinton concluded that Timucua was an independent stock (Brinton 1891:90).

Gatschet initiated the preliminary formal study of the language. Working with the Pareja publications brought back by Smith, Gatschet (1877, 1878, 1880) presented two papers on the Timucua language before the American Philosophical Society in April of 1877 and 1878 and a third paper in 1880. The Adam-Vinson republication of Pareja's grammar followed in 1886. Using the grammar and Gatschet's work, Raoul de la Grasserie, a French linguist, published four short studies on Timucua phonology, grammar, and vocabulary. John R. Swanton devoted much attention to the language during the first half of the twentieth century without achieving his goal of completing a lexicon of the language. The only publication in which he devoted some attention to the language was his 1929 article on the Tawasa language, occasioned by the discovery of a short vocabulary supposedly in the Tawasa tongue in association with the Lamhatty document. When Julian Granberry published an article on Timucuan prosodics and phonemics in 1956, Swanton, later that same year, passed on to him the fruits of his many years of research on the language. Thirty-one years later Granberry published the first edition of his *Grammar and Dictionary of the Timucua Language*, based on his own research and the notes and copies of the sources that he inherited from Swanton. He published a revised edition in 1989. Both the first and second editions were published privately and apparently have not circulated very widely (Crawford 1975:66–67; Granberry 1987, 1989:7–8; Grasserie 1888, 1892; Haas 1971:50; Milanich and Sturtevant 1972:7). The University of Alabama Press's 1993 republication of Granberry's work, it is hoped, will draw the attention of more linguists. A substantial rearrangement of the third edition represents a great improvement over the two earlier editions. About midway through the period of Granberry's research, Jerald Milanich and William Sturtevant made portions of Pareja's *Confessionario* more accessible in a publication that the Florida Division of Archives, History, and Records Management issued in 1972. But they focused their attention on that document's ethnographic content rather than on linguistic issues. Granberry has been the first student of the language to advance a detailed and reasoned thesis, based on extensive linguistic study, about the origin and affinities of the Timucuan language.

Origin and Affinities of the Language

The friars and Spaniards in general had surprisingly little to say about ties between languages spoken by Spanish Florida's aboriginal peoples or the lack of them. Without identifying specific peoples, the governor in 1602 stated that there were "more than six differences of languages" among the people who had given obedience to Spanish rule. He noted that usually no more than a channel separated chiefdoms of differing languages that were distinct enough so that one did not understand the other (Méndez de Canzo 1602). The six-plus certainly included the Guale, Escamacu, Mayaca, and Timucua. Tulafina might be considered a fifth distinct one, as part of Tama (Machado 1597). A year earlier the same governor spoke of the provinces of Santa Elena, Guale, Apalachee, and Tocobaga, in addition to the Timucua-speakers, as having five different languages (Méndez de Canzo 1601). Friars deemed the languages of the Apalachee, Timucua, and Guale to be sufficiently distinct to require friars skilled in all three to meet the religious needs of natives brought to St. Augustine to work. The Timucua-speakers recognized the linguistic distinctiveness of the Guale by referring to them as Ibaja-speakers.

In relatively modern times, as noted above, Brinton was the first scholar to hazard a judgment about Timucua's affiliation with other linguistic groups, flirting with the suggestion of a Carib tie. But Gatschet's work and republication of Pareja's grammar led Brinton to conclude that Timucua was an independent stock, as had Gatschet (1880:465) himself. Gatschet's position as a linguist for the U.S. Bureau of Ethnology under J. W. Powell facilitated his research on the topic. But Pareja's grammar had not yet been republished when Gatschet wrote, prompting him to observe that his "attempt to compare the Timucua language with other linguistic families in regard to lexical affinity may be called premature, for we do not know over two hundred vocables of it with some degree of certitude" (Gatschet 1880:477).

Despite Swanton's (1922:11; 1946:table 1 opp. 10, 193) extensive work on the language and access to all the extant writings in Timucua, he had almost nothing to say on the topic of the language's affiliation in either of his classic works on Indians of the Southeast in general. In the earlier work, probably influenced by Powell and Gatschet, he categorized Timucua as a distinct stock. In 1946, however, he listed Timucua as one of three divisions of the Muskogean stock, along with a Muskogean division and a Natchez division. Noting that Powell had given Timucua the status of an independent family, Swanton then affirmed that it "was undoubtedly a branch of the great Muskogean stock." Although Swanton by 1925 had completed in rough draft a 35-page manuscript, "A Sketch of the Timucua Language," and had accumulated by circa 1945 a 3,500-card lexical file, his only publication related to Timucua linguistics was his 1929 article on the Tawasa language. And it alluded only briefly to Timucua's overall affiliation. By that time, as Mary Haas (1971:46) phrased it, Swanton was at least suggesting that Timucua "might be an outlying relative of Muskogean." But Swanton's concluding paragraphs in the 1929 article indicate that in that year his stance on the issue was already much stronger than a mere suggestion.

In a paragraph bearing the heading "Relationship Between the Timuquanan and Muskhogean Stocks," Swanton (1929:452–53) wrote:

> The number of correspondences between the Muskhogean tongues and Timucua had, previous to the discovery of this Tawasa vocabulary, led the writer to believe in the genetic relationship of the two varieties of speech. The following examples may be given and at the same time they illustrate the number of resemblances in the grammatical processes. As in the case of the Natchez, it appears that the

resemblances are closest in the processes and the structure generally than in the vocabulary.

V. Timucua-Muskhogean Correspondences

English	Timucua	Muskhogean
I	-a	-a (M),-ya (N),-la (C)
me	ni-	ni-(N), tca (M, H, A), sa-(C)
you	tci-	tci
he	oqe	ak, akka, akko (A)
plural suffix	-bo	-bi (N),-pi (K)
negative suffix	-ti	-ti (H),-hat (N),-ti (it's noth'g) (A)
causative suffix	-si,-so	-tci (M),-tsi (N)
noun-forming prefix	na-	na-(C)
reflexive prefix	s-	c-(N)
this	ka	ka (N), ya (M)
that (remote)	ma (also article)	ma (passim)
up, above	abo	aba (C)
tree	aye	ahi (H)
to walk	aliho	aya, ala (A)
snake	yyola	ula (N)
Mother	isa	iy shki (C), itski (M)

In his closing paragraph under the heading "Conclusions," Swanton wrote:

The following conclusions seem inescapable:
   1. If Lamhatty's language is actually Tawasa the latter was a dialect belonging primarily to the so-called Timuquanan stock.
   2. It was intermediate between the dialects of that family hitherto known to us and the tongues of the Muskhogean group.
   3. Taken in conjunction with the numerous recognized points of resemblance between the languages of these two assumed stocks, including a virtual structural identity, it seems practically impossible to maintain longer the separate position of the latter. While there is a considerable body of material in Timucua, which cannot as yet be identified in the Muskhogean languages, the nature of the resemblances given in table V, which contains merely a selection, shows the vital character of those that are known.

Since Swanton avowed a Muskogean affiliation for Timucua, linguists have muddied the water considerably, suggesting Arawakian, Warao, Macro-Chibchan, Siouan, and various other affinities that can possibly be discerned in Timucua. Moved by the apparent Babel-like confusion of tongues reflected in the genesis of Timucua, Mary Haas (1971:50) listed it as "(of doubtful affiliation, Muskogean? Siouan? Arawakian?)." She observed in a note that in addition to Swanton's 1929 suggestion of a Muskogean affiliation, Morris Swadesh in 1964 had "noted a small number of Arawakian resemblances," but she countered that "Siouan resemblances of a similar nature can also be found." By the time Haas wrote in 1971, Granberry had taken a firm stance in favor of a Warao connection for Timucua. James M. Crawford observed that Granberry, after an exhaustive comparison of Timucua with other languages of the Gulf and circum-Caribbean areas, "reported that it can be stated with at least moderate confidence that Timucua seems to show closest genetic relationship with Warao, of the Orinoco Delta region of Venezuela and Guyana" (Crawford 1975:67, 102). The statement may not have fully reflected Granberry's views at that time, as he had made the statement in the abstract that he submitted to the American Philosophical Society in connection with a grant received from the society. More recently, as noted here in chapter 1, Granberry (1987, 1989:45, 46, 48) has portrayed Timucua's genesis and its affiliations as much more complex. While characterizing Timucua as a lexical isolate, he observed that "it nonetheless contains a fairly large number of lexical items stemming from" various sources, "one or more Waroid languages, Northwestern Chibchan, Northern Maipuran, Arawakan, and Muskogean." He did not believe that any of the lexical contributors could be considered dominant. He maintained that Timucua's basic grammar patterns closely resemble those of Macro-Chibchan, but again showing multiple influences from within that family from Warao in the east to Cuna in the west.

Only Granberry's fellow-linguists can adequately assess the validity of his thesis. One of the readers of my manuscript commented that Swanton's 1929 statement quoted here "is essentially what modern Muskogean language linguists told me it looked like to them. But they've never published on it." The only review I have seen to date, Crawford (1988), eschewed assessing the validity of Granberry's thesis. The reviewer limited himself to congratulating Granberry "for having produced an easy-to-use dictionary and a well-written grammatical sketch of Timucua." He closed with the comment that "interested scholars can examine the evidence and make their own judgment as to its Merit." Crawford commented on the first edition.

Between 1979 and 1988, Crawford (n.d.) wrote a paper on Timucua's relationship to Muskogean in which he reflected on ideas Granberry outlined in his 1979 abstract. Crawford noted that Granberry then held that Timucua, in addition to being closely related to Warao, shared cognates with Proto-Arawak, Proto-Gulf, Proto-Muskogean, and late Muskogean. Crawford commented that Granberry seemed to be using "cognates" rather loosely, observing, "It would appear that 'cognate' for Granberry, as 'affinity' for Gatschet, means merely a form in one language with some phonological resemblance to a form in another language." Crawford explained that he used cognate "to refer to forms in two or more languages which derive from a form in a common ancestral language" as "this usage allows only genetically related languages to share cognate forms." Of the structural similarities between Timucua and Warao that Granberry posited, Crawford noted that they were not in themselves "proof of genetic relationship, but do increase this possibility when combined with a reasonable number of lexical similarities." In a brief search for Timucua-Warao lexical similarities, Crawford found only two good sets but presumed that Granberry had found many others "to back up his claim."

Granberry himself (1989:47) confessed that the number of resemblances was small, in responding to a suggestion that Floyd Lounsbury made that Timucua's similarities, "particularly to Warao, 'are neither numerous nor strong enough to eliminate independent invention or the transmission of linguistic norms from one local population through another through trade or other means of intercommunication.'"

Relative to a Timucua-Muskogean relationship, Crawford presented 23 sets of words grouped into separate categories of borrowings and cognates, but conceded that "should Granberry produce convincing evidence of a Timucua-Warao genetic relationship, I would be willing to treat all these Timucua-Muskogean resemblances as borrowings—provided that no evidence can be found for a Timucua-Warao-Muskogean genetic relationship." It is lamentable that Granberry did not publish the articles on the structure and genetic affiliations of Timucua that he spoke of in 1970 as being in progress and that he did not present some of his ideas to colleagues in the field of linguistics for their reaction.

T. Dale Nicklas (1994:5) gave Granberry's thesis a cautious conditional approval, thus, in a passing allusion: "Julian Granberry (1987) asserts that Timucua is a South American immigrant. If he is correct, and he appears to be. . . ." Nicklas (1994:3, 4, 5) made this allusion in a context in which he argued that linguistic traits peculiar to "the Lower Mississippi Valley core area" (Natchez, Tunica, Atakapa, and Chitimaka) "appear to have spread along the Gulf and Atlantic coasts, with demonstrable effects on Biloxi, Timucua, and Catawba, the only documented coastal languages." He argued that traits shared by Lower Valley languages and Timucua indicate contact.

Comments made by Spaniards and the Portuguese Gentleman of Elvas may suggest a direct Taino influence on at least a few words Timucua allegedly used. Spaniards gave Taino names such as *barbacoa, buhío,* cacique, *guano, macana,* and *sabana* to items that they saw in Florida, at times saying or implying that such words were ones the Timucua themselves used. In most cases, however, one cannot be sure that the Spaniards' usage was not one they had acquired from their experience in the Caribbean. One less suspicious instance is Elvas's use of barbacoa for the food-storage structure at Napituca and his attribution of the name to the Timucua. He apparently had no prior experience in the New World (Clayton et al. 1993:1:69; García-Arévalo 1990:272–73).

Characteristics and Structure of the Language

The letters for the language, as transcribed by Pareja, generally parallel the Castilian alphabet. All of Timucua's words except *unam* end in one of the five vowels. The vowels also form syllables with the letter *i. G* and *x* appear only rarely, according to Pareja, being represented usually by *h.* In Granberry's dictionary *g* is represented only by two borrowings from Spanish, and *x* does not appear at all. The Timucua *l* is not doubled as it is in Castilian and neither is *r.* Timucua's possession of *r* sets it apart from its Muskogean neighbors. Timucua words often interchange *t* and *d* without that changing the meaning of the word. Similarly *u* can be added after *b* without affecting meaning. But when *u* is sounded after a *q,* the meaning of the word changes totally from the word that lacks the *u.*

Pareja presents words such as *nijo* or *nijomota,* meaning "a thing on fire," or "the color of fire," or "with a heart on fire," but Granberry changed the spelling to *niho* in his dictionary. However, he preserved the *nijo* spelling in his English-Timucua index. Similarly, Granberry changed Pareja's spelling of words such as *viro* for "man" to *biro.* Granberry placed a note under *V* indicating that all words beginning with *v* and a vowel should be considered to begin with *b* and a vowel and looked for under *B.* But he then listed *vichubi,* meaning "break," under *V.* He also has no listings under *J, K, W,* or *Z.* There appear to be very few words that begin with *r.* Granberry listed only four: one the suffix "-re"; a particle, *reqe;* the word *rey,* borrowed from Spanish; and *ruqui* from the Tawasa dialect, which is *aruqui* in the Mocama dialect. Pareja listed at least one other, *requiem,* borrowed from the Latin (Granberry 1989:157–89, 205; Pareja 1614).

Words with one, two, or three vowels are accented on the first vowel. But when the suffixed particle "co" is a sign of interrogation or a conjunction, it receives the accent as last vowel, as do some other conjunctive forms. Pareja showed accent marks on words in a few instances.

Suffixes are a major feature of the language, performing a myriad of functions. The same particles often serve many different functions, although Granberry (1989:118) observed that "the majority of Timucua suffixes are verbal in nature." Suffixes are used with verbs as indicators of tense, mode, voice, person, repeated action, and other functions. Suffixes attached to nouns indicate plural and possession and provide inflections equivalent to Latin's declensions. Pareja used a Latin framework in composing his grammar but noted that there was no declension of nouns as in Latin. Suffixed particles accomplished the purpose of Latin's case-endings (Granberry 1989:235–37; Pareja 1614).

Prefixes were limited in number and function. Timucua used only five. "Na-," one of them, was used with verbs to indicate the instrument by which something was done (Granberry 1989:116; Pareja 1614).

Adjectives remained the same in form whether they modified a male or female noun.

Tawasa's Timucua Connection

Prior to the 1928 discovery of a previously unnoticed Indian-English vocabulary of 60 words on the back of the Walker version of the Lamhatty account, it was assumed on the best of grounds that the Tawasa language "differed in no respect from standard Alabama, and this impression was actually strengthened by the discovery of the first Lamhatty manuscript and accompanying map" (Swanton 1929:436, 446–47, 453). After studying the new vocabulary, Swanton felt compelled to revise his conclusions and align Tawasa with the Timucua stock.

Briefly, the Lamhatty account records the travails of a native named Lamhatty, who appeared in Virginia in 1708, allegedly identifying himself as a Towasa who had been enslaved nine months earlier, allegedly by a Tuscarora raiding party. The Tuscarora are supposed to have attacked a number of villages shown on an accompanying map as located near what is believed to be the Gulf of Mexico, designated by the native name

Ouquodky. The 26-year-old Lamhatty had just endured nine months of privation and traumatic experience as a slave of his fellow natives or as a fugitive from that enslavement, the marks of which he still bore. There apparently was no interviewer available in Virginia who understood Lamhatty's language. Most disturbingly, the main text of Robert Beverly's version of the account, the first to be published, closed with the remark "but nobody can yet be found that understands his language." In his version, Walker noted similarly that, after Lamhatty had been in his house for a few days, "I got y[e] Interpreter and a tuscarora Indian to talk with him; he at all times seemed very inclinable to be understood, and was verey forward to talk, but neither of them could understand him." The main text of the Beverly version was followed by "Postscript [torn] after some of his Country folks were found servants [torn] he was sometimes ill used by Walker, became very melancholy after fasting and crying several days together sometimes using little Conjuration & when warme weather came he went away & was never more heard of." Despite this enigmatic postscript, the Tuscarora seems to have been the vehicle for the "intelligence" gained from Lamhatty.

Many of the words and, in particular, the numbers in the account identify Lamhatty as a Timucua-speaker, whatever his tribal identity was. The following list matches numbers derived from Pareja's grammar with their counterparts from the Lamhatty account.

Number	Pareja	Lamhatty
1	yaha	yánkiah[1]
2	yuca	Eúksah
3	hapu	Hóp-ho
4	ceketa	Checúttah
5	marua	Márouah
6	mareka	Mareékah
7	pikica	pekétchah
8	pikinahu	pekénnahough
9	pekecaketa[2]	pekétchcuttah
10	tuma	toómah
11	yahagala	toomayaúkfa
20	tumayuca	tomoeúcha

Granberry (1989:59) remarked that numbers and pronouns are often used as indicators of the extent of outside influence on a language. Their very high frequency of use makes them normally very resistant to change. Consequently, he noted, they "tend to maintain an overall patterning inherited from genetic forebears." Most of the other words on the list also resemble their Mocama dialect counterparts closely enough for the Timucua origin of the word to be obvious. The following examples are typical.

	Pareja	*Lamhatty*
woman	nia	Néah
man	viro	wiedōō
door	ucuchua	ocut-soúa
fire	taca	Tútcah
tobacco	hinino	hewéenou
dog	efa	Effallàh
bread	pesolo	písso
drink	ucu	ocoòl

One that, surprisingly, is quite different is the word for maize, given as *tapola* by Pareja and the French. Maize is *Chesapà* on Lamhatty's list (Swanton 1929:447–48).

Granberry (1989:37) observed that Lamhatty's vocabulary indicates that Tawasa-speakers "had been in close contact with the Muskogean Alabama for a considerable period of time" because "a blend of both Timucua and Alabama lexical stems and grammatical affixes occurs even in that short word list."

It is not clear what conclusions can be drawn from the Lamhatty document other than the ones that Lamhatty's language was basically Timucua and that he was from a town named Towasa. Except for its linguistic content, the Lamhatty account overall leaves much to be desired as a reliable historical source. It should, therefore, be used with great caution when it is not corroborated by other sources. As there is no other source that corroborates or even suggests that the people known historically as Tawasa or Toasi were indeed Timucua-speakers, this writer is hesitant to conclude that those Tawasa in general spoke a dialect of Timucua. Swanton himself (1929:443), after analyzing the names of the "Ten 'Tawasa' Towns" identified on the map that accompanied the Beverly version, concluded that the facts "show that the so-called 'Tawasa Nation' of Lamhatty, if indeed it was not rather a construct of the minds of his white auditors, was nothing more than a group of towns of Muskhogean, Timucua, and Yuchi affiliations." If the Tawasa were Timucua-speakers, it seems likely that someone among the Spaniards who had contact with the Tawasa during the last quarter of the seventeenth century would have commented on the Timucua connection, especially Marcos Delgado. His 1686 expedition northwestward from Apalachee took him as far as the Tawasa towns then located in northern Alabama. In reporting on his reception in the "Province of Tabasa," Delgado identified Ogchay as "of the Chacato nation"; four unnamed villages as speaking a Choctaw dialect; and Qusate as "of an unknown nation." The following year Tawasa's chief's visit to Apalachee's San Luis was mentioned by the province's deputy-governor (Boyd 1937:2–32, passim; Hann 1988b:92–103). The problem needs more research, as does the issue of the origin and affiliation of the Timucua language itself, particularly the nature and extent of Timucua's linguistic ties to its Muskogean neighbors.

Timucua's Ties with Muskogean Languages

Swanton (1929:453) was convinced by 1929 that Timucua bore sufficient resemblances to Muskogean languages in its structure to abandon his earlier stand that it was an isolate. At the same time he conceded that there was much material in Timucua "which cannot yet be identified in the Muskhogean languages." On the other hand, Granberry (1989:59, 72), the heir to Swanton's research, maintained that "there is only one structural similarity between Timucua and any of the Muskogean languages" and that the monosyllabicity of the form made comparison meaningless. He considered the small number of lexical similarities to be "loan words" derived either from Proto-Muskogean as reconstructed by Haas or from the Muskogean languages of the historic era, especially Alabama and Koasati. It is worthy of note that Alabama and Koasati are the two languages to which Apalachee is most closely related. In his latest edition Granberry (1993:56–60) has added Apalachee as a third important source, noting that it is interesting that Timucua's closest Muskogean ties are with those "westernmost of the Eastern Muskogean languages" rather than with "Eastern Muskogean languages" such as Creek or Hitchiti as one might expect.

To explain this, Granberry suggests that "at the 1,800–1,000 B.C. time-level Creek and Hitchiti speakers may have been located farther to the north and west than in later times" with "ancestral Alabama, Koasati, and Apalachee speakers forming a 'layer' of population to the south of them and spreading farther east than we now realize." His argument presumes that the Guale were then in place and that the Guale language was most closely related to Apalachee, Alabama, and Koasati rather than to Hitchiti and Creek. But Spanish sources indicate that Guale was very closely related to Hitchiti (see Hann 1992b:202–3).

The Timucua and Muskogeans shared various leadership titles. The Timucua's *holata* appeared among the Apalachee and other Muskogean groups as *holahta.* It was used among the Timucua and Apalachee to designate head chiefs and as the equivalent of *cacique* in the abstract sense. *Holahta* was used for lesser chiefs outside Florida while upper-level chiefs usually bore the title *mico. Holata* is generally believed to be of Muskogean origin, but the linguist Crawford (n.d.) held it to be "undoubtedly a Timucua word borrowed by Apalachee and Seminole" (Hann 1992b:198–201; Hudson 1990:62, 211–49, passim; Milanich 1972; Milanich and Sturtevant 1972:45n.13, 67, 68).

Other shared leadership titles were *iniha* and *chacal.* The title for the official interpreter in the forms *atequi, atiqui, athequi,* and *yatiqui* was widely dispersed, appearing even in the northern non-Muskogean territories that Pardo and Moyano traversed.

The names of three of Apalachee's largest and most important villages contain lexical forms found in the Timucua language. The villages are Ivitachuco, home of Apalachee's paramount; Anhayca, seat of the second most important chief; and Cupahica. Anhayca appeared in variant forms in Apalachee such as Inihayca, Inhayca, Iviahica, Iniahico, and Inatafum, forms that clarify the Timucua connection. Inatafum, in particular, shows that the *Yca* and *hica* of the variants were meant to be Timucua's *hica,* meaning "village." *Tafum* or *tafun* is the Apalachee equivalent of *hica.* The Inatafum form appeared in a 1676 friars' listing of missions. Western Timucua also had a village named Anhaica in the mid-seventeenth century. Similarly, the name Ivitachuco has strong Timucua ties in whole or at least in part. The *Ivita* portion of the name was attached to a number of arroyos in western Timucua, beginning just one-half day's journey west of the Pupo crossing on the St. Johns. The name of the first arroyo, Desiana ybitta, was followed successively by ajano ybitta, apixa yvitta, ajano yvitta chirico, ajano yvitta, apepa yvitta and usiybitta (Palacios 1675; Peña 1717). Ajano yvitta chirico means "river of little acorns," with *yvitta* meaning "river" and *ajano* meaning "acorns." Late in the seventeenth century *yvita* appeared in the name of a Timucua village, Yvitanayo.

Chuco was the Apalachee word for great or principal and appears in slightly variant forms in other Muskogean languages. *Iste-puc-cau-chau thlucco,* Hawkins (1982:70, 72) noted, was the Creek term for "Great Leader" and *Tustunnuggee thlucco* their term for "Great Warrior." It appeared again in Bartram's title of "*Mico Chlucco*" for the Long Warrior, king of the Seminoles. Timucua is not known to have had the *chuco* form. But it has the word *chucu*, meaning "blackness," "darkness," "dirt," "dark-colored," and "gourd," "pumpkin," or "squash" (Granberry 1989:162). Ivitachuco's chief used the *chucu* form in 1657 while signing his name as "Don Luis Ybitachucu" (Hann 1986b:102).

Granberry's Hypothesis on Timucua's Origin

Granberry (1989:73–85; 1993:15–17, 40–47) believes that both structural and lexical data indicate that Timucua "probably originated as a native language of northwestern Amazonia." He believes that its grammar "is quite clearly Waroid-based" and "conforms rather closely to Macro-Chibchan," with the nearest similarities found in "the Warao isolate of the Orinoco delta" and in "Cuna, a member of the Chibchan stock proper within the macro-phylum." He observed that some lexemes show a "striking resemblance to languages of the Vaupés-Caquetá-Inírida-Guaviare branch of Northern Maipuran Arawakan." He believes Timucua shows a long intercourse with Arawak-speakers in the Rio Negro region from Proto-Arawakan times (ca. 3500 B.C.) until about 1700 B.C. when the various Maipuran branches had developed. Timucua's similarities to Proto-Tucano suggest a Timucua presence in the Vaupés region by 2500 B.C. Peaceful long-term contact in which no party was culturally dominant produced a "mixing or interpenetration" of linguistic elements without any extensive relexification. Granberry suggests that the language's own original structures must have been very close indeed to the borrowed ones—perhaps resulting from panareal structural similarities. A role as a special trading class would provide the Timucua with such widespread contacts on that basis in a milieu where multilingualism was the norm. The Timucua-speakers' forebears made the move from northern South America directly to the north Florida-Georgia coast with no intermediate stops except possibly in western Cuba.

The unanswered question is what the Florida-Georgia coast or its hinterland had to offer to induce traders to venture such a voyage. The only potential material tie found to date that could link the two regions is the Orange and Stallings Island ceramics. Granberry (1989:45) presented his ideas as a hypothesis that can be tested in the light of current linguistic and archaeological data.

9.

BEGINNINGS OF MISSIONIZATION

Although priests accompanied Narváez and de Soto, no record indicates that they attempted to proselytize among the Timucua through whose territory they passed. Those expeditions' brutality toward the natives except for Mocoso would have undermined any attempts the priests might have contemplated. Menéndez de Avilés detailed some of his soldiers to serve as lay catechists among the Guale and Freshwater Timucua. But one of two recorded instances involving Chief Calabay was short lived. Nothing is known about the success of six men whom Menéndez left with Hotina as catechists (Solís de Merás 1923:206–8).

The Jesuits

Three Jesuits were the first missionaries Menéndez de Avilés secured specifically to work among Florida's natives. The Tacatacuru's killing of one of them before they could even begin to work among the natives, as well as the increasing hostility toward the Spaniards of most of the Saltwater Timucua and of Freshwater Timucua of the coast south of St. Augustine, precluded work of consequence by the Jesuits among the physically most accessible of the Timucua-speakers in the vicinity of St. Augustine and Forts San Matheo and San Pedro. Menéndez appears to have given scant attention to the Saltwater Timucua compared with that which he lavished on the Calusa, Guale, and Escamacu-Orista.

The Jesuits' voluminous records do not mention their having worked among any Timucua-speakers. Their work during their brief stays in Timucua territory appears to have been restricted to hearing soldiers' confessions during Easter season (Zubillaga 1946:324, 471–75, 511). When the Jesuits withdrew from their missions in Guale and Escamacu-Orista in 1570, arrangements appear to have been made with Saturiwa and

Tacatacuru for Saltwater Timucua children to be entrusted to the Jesuits to be educated at a school that they planned to establish in Havana. Father Juan Rogel (1570:307) reported that the vice-provincial had ordered Father Antonio Sedeño to accompany the others south as far as St. Augustine and to remain there to collect the children that Saturiwa and Tacatacuru had ordered their subordinates to provide. Rogel noted, however, that "we found the forts in such a bad state and the Indians giving so many indications of being on the warpath . . . it did not seem safe for him to remain there and thus he came to Havana with me."

Somehow, the Saltwater chief of Chinica and another chief named Sarabay were Christianized prior to the 1568 destruction of Fort San Matheo by Gourgues and his Indian allies. At that time, apparently, pro-French Indians attacked Chinica and Sarabay, killing some of their people and forcing the rest to scatter to the woods and hinterland. The two Christian chiefs appealed to the Crown later for support to restore them to possession of their villages and to reassemble their people (Cedulario of Florida 1573:69–71).

Chinica revived prior to 1602. It was then a visita with a church, served by the friar from San Juan del Puerto, which was a league and one-quarter away. Probably Christianized Sarabay also was located near the mouth of the St. Johns. But three distinct villages or chiefs bore that name. The most likely Sarabay was located one-fourth of a league from San Juan, which was a visita in 1602. It may have been farther from San Juan earlier, associated with the bar of Sarabay, one of the lesser channels for the river located about a league and one-half south of the main channel (Hann 1990b:40). But the 1560s' Christian Sarabay could well have been a Freshwater chief, known also as Calabay or Çarabay, who lived on the river 12 leagues from St. Augustine (Barrientos 1965:118). The third Sarabay or Saravay, located on the coast north of the St. Johns River, is an unlikely candidate as a subject of Tacatacuru (Lowery 1911:453).

Harder to account for is the Jesuits' apparent failure to attempt to work among the friendlier Freshwater Timucua who allied with the Spaniards in the 1560s. The insecurity of such a mission because of the hostility of Saturiwa and Potano may have been the reason. However, it could have been simply a concomitant of Menéndez's benign neglect of the Timucua.

The First Franciscans

Continued hostility of most of the Saltwater Timucua when the first Franciscans arrived in 1573 probably led them to confine their work in

Timucua territory to Spaniards, as had the Jesuits. Even after all the Salt-water Timucua had made peace, a governor lamented as late as 1579 that they showed no interest in abandoning their ancestral religion (P. Menéndez Márquez 1579:225–27). But prior to that year and possibly as early as the era of Menéndez de Avilés, two other leaders and their Indians began to show interest in Christianity. Their villages were the closest to St. Augustine, Nombre de Dios just to the north of it and San Sebastian just back of it or to the west on "the arm of the sea bearing that name" (A. de las Alas 1600).

Doña María, cacica at Nombre de Dios in 1600, claimed that her mother was the first leader who was Christian and one "who served and favored the Spaniards without wavering" even at the time of Francis Drake's attack in 1586, when some Timucua joined the English in looting the city. Doña María noted that she had been a Christian since infancy (Deagan 1979:21; María 1600). Gaspar Márques, San Sebastian's chief at the turn of the century, claimed that his father, don Pedro Márques, "was among the first caciques who harkened to the friendship of the Spaniards and to give obedience to his majesty" at the time of Menéndez de Avilés's arrival. His father's village was some distance from St. Augustine at that time. His father had moved his people to San Sebastian to be closer to the Spaniards and better able to serve them. They had probably moved from Tocoy on the east bank of the St. Johns, almost directly west of St. Augustine, for Gaspar Márques (1606) styled himself "principal cacique of San Sebastian and Tocoy." He described his parents, Pedro and Catalina, as "both caciques" and as among the first Christians.

At an unspecified time Nombre de Dios and San Sebastian became visitas or outstations served from St. Augustine. Work at both places had such success after Fray Alonso de Reinoso's arrival with new friars in 1577 that converts were soon attending mass regularly in St. Augustine. Further information on the early Timucua converts is not available because of a lack of parish records for the city prior to 1594 (Gannon 1983:191; Geiger 1937:55; Shea 1886:151).

First Formal Missions

The first formal missions among the Timucua date from Fray Reinoso's return with new friars late in 1587. Juan Menéndez Márques reported the friars' assignment "to the new villages that there are from the Island of San Pedro to this presidio and in that of San Sebastian and more belonging to the Rio Dulce, subject to Cacique Pedro Márques." The friars' work bore fruit before long, especially that of Baltasar López at San Pedro and that of the friar at San Juan del Puerto. Juan Menéndez Márques recalled that he had seen Fray López bring many leading Indians from San Pedro to St. Augustine to be baptized in the city's principal church, "among them Cacique Caçacolo, one of the most renowned and feared chiefs of this land, and, with him, his wife and the children he had at the time." Cazacolo had been allied with the French at the time of Gourgues's attack (Cedulario of Florida 1573). His village was on an island named Cazacolo located between San Pedro and San Matheo, north of the St. Johns River (J. Menéndez Márquez and A. de las Alas 1595).

Cazacolo was mentioned in accounts of the death of Governor Domingo de Martínez Avendaño. The governor went to San Pedro and Guale in mid-October 1595 to conduct a visitation there and disembark some friars from a newly arrived band. A cold-like illness (rromadizo) afflicted him while he was in Guale. On returning to San Pedro indisposed, he spent some days there in bed. While returning to St. Augustine by land from San Pedro, "on the way, in Caçacolo, he began to cough up a great deal of blood (hechar mucha sangre por la boca) and the soldiers brought him more than twelve leagues in a chair (silla), much in a concave shape (muy al cavo) by way of the beach of San Mateo." He suffered the bleeding periodically from Cazacolo on and died about nine in the morning of November 24 during another attack of bleeding 16 hours after his return to the city (J. Menéndez Márquez and A. de las Alas 1595; Ruidíaz y Caravia 1893:2:498).

Even Nombre de Dios mission appears to date only from 1587, when the recently arrived Fray Alonso de Escobedo was assigned there. Juan Menéndez Márques made it clear that San Sebastian was part of the first group of Florida missions that the Franciscans established in the latter half of the 1580s. And Chief Gaspar Márques (1606) noted that, once priests became available, his father had asked for one and built him a church. Yet San Sebastian does not appear on Maynard Geiger's list of places that had resident friars in 1587. Geiger observed, nonetheless, that the mission at San Sebastian appears to have been established in 1587 by one of the friars who arrived that year (Geiger 1937:55; 1940:114). The settlement's proximity to St. Augustine may be the reason for its absence from the 1587 list. The friar probably resided in St. Augustine's convent, which was only two pistol shots' distance from the city.

Before the end of 1588, San Pedro already had a number of Christians, whom Juan Menéndez Márques reported as attending mass and religious

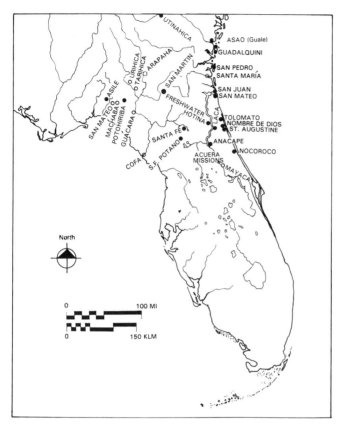

Timucua missions and sites to 1655

instruction with evident affection and devotion. Many of its natives had already been baptized when he stopped there in 1588. Mission work may have begun at San Pedro as early as 1585. Fray B. López (1602) claimed in 1602 that he had been working among the natives for 17 years. San Juan del Puerto is likely to have been established in some form by 1587, although it does not appear on Geiger's 1587 list of places with resident friars, and Fray Pareja, whose name is associated most closely with the early days of that mission, began his work there only in 1595. It is probable that a friar from St. Augustine or San Pedro served it at the start on an occasional basis, just as Pareja filled in at San Pedro in 1597 while Fray López was away in the head village of Timucua Province (Pareja 1602).

Antonico or San Antonio Anacape was the other Freshwater mission that Menéndez Márques mentioned without identifying it. It appears on

Geiger's list for 1587 and was a mission in 1602 as well. By then Antonico's chief was paramount for the upriver Freshwater Timucua rather than Nyaautina, the presumed successor to the Outina of the 1560s (Geiger 1940:119; F. de Valdés 1602).

There is no explicit evidence as to the cause of the change of attitude among the natives that permitted expansion of the missions to places such as San Juan and San Pedro. The change was probably partly a consequence of the first successes with Freshwater natives and several Saltwater chiefs, which broke the ice, as it were. The giving of imported Spanish clothing and tools to chiefs who aligned themselves thus with the Spaniards undoubtedly was a factor. Such exotic goods provided by the governor and the esoteric knowledge and skills such as reading and writing that friars made available enhanced chiefs' prestige and relegitimized the authority and rank they claimed when their inability to halt epidemics or to cope effectively with Spanish power was eroding their authority. Once a few chiefs took the step of accepting Christianity, it behooved their neighbors to do the same, especially those who were head chiefs, lest one of their subordinates do so and thereby possibly supplant them by becoming the chiefdom's broker with the new power source. But evidence is elusive for the first formal missions of the latter half of the 1580s.

The evidence is more substantial, although still fragmentary, as to factors that made additional leaders amenable to alliance with the Spaniards and to conversion beginning in the latter 1590s. By then the influence and good offices of already converted Saltwater Timucua leaders were an element, as was expansion of the gifts distributed by the governor. Gift-giving began earlier, but the Crown officially approved the practice only in 1593 (Prado 1654; Worth 1992a:35). The Crown's sanction and funding undoubtedly increased the scope and attractiveness of the gifts distributed. The influence of the already converted is documented for the turning around of Timucua Province's head chief. The successful overture of 1597 was made through Juan de Junco, a leading Indian from Nombre de Dios described as "an interpreter for Timucua [Utina] and aguaduce [Freshwater]." Fray Baltasar López's influence may have played a role as well. He appears to have been at the village of Timucua Province's head chief when that chief's brother and his entourage of 19 mandadores and leading men arrived in St. Augustine to see the governor on July 20, 1597. Fray López had been working in Timucua Province three months when the Guale Revolt broke out in late September of that year (Albárez de Castrillón 1597; Geiger 1937:234–35; B. López 1602; Machado 1597). War weariness was a factor in Potano's chief's decision to make peace. A series of Spanish successes against French intruders along the coast may have enhanced the Spaniards' image in the natives' eyes (Ross 1923:251–81; 1924:167–94). The rapidity with which such news traveled even across linguistic frontiers and the impact it had are reflected in a governor's report from 1605. Only weeks after an appearance of the French on Guale's coast, news of it and of Spanish preparations to confront the French reached the Ais and Surruque, who immediately sent a small force of warriors to St. Augustine to assist the governor in his campaign against the intruders (Ybarra 1605d). For some, such as Timucua Province's head chief, the change of heart may have been influenced by loss of faith in the native religious system, which no longer served as a bulwark for the leader's power. The attraction of items such as the horse possessed by San Pedro's Cacique don Juan in 1597 may also have been influential (Jusefe 1597:25).

During the 10-day stay in St. Augustine of the Timucua Province head chief's brother and his entourage, they were given a ration of 30 pounds of flour each day. The governor provided materials for suits (*vestidos*) for the visiting heir, his brother the head chief, other relatives of the head chief, and four mandadores, who probably were inijas. The material included eleven and two-thirds yards of diezocheno cloth (cloth with a warp consisting of 1,800 threads) for suits for four of the most important natives and 20 yards of coarse woolen cloth for the mandadores' suits. To finish and line the suits, the governor provided twenty and one-third yards of crimson calico (*bocacín*), six yards of stuff of the natural color of wool (*sinabafa*), two-thirds of a yard of taffeta of China, and 12 ounces of silk thread (*caiero*) for the caciques' suits. The suits were readied before the Indians' departure. The chief and his heir also received red hats and other items that included a shirt of Rouen linen, a doublet of Dutch linen, and a pair of double-soled shoes made of cordovan leather. The governor sent the chief two axes and a hoe to build a church and house for the friar who was to be stationed in the chief's village.

Although other major chiefs were treated with similar generosity, none received quite as much as Timucua Province's head chief and his heir. The suits given to the four mandadores seem to indicate that the friendship of the province was viewed as particularly valuable. Ibi's chief, who came with 10 Indians, received a fine white blanket, a common blanket, and other gifts. By contrast, four principal mandadores and three chiefs from Guale or near Guale (Ufalegue, Guale [St. Catherines Island's chief], and Tulafina) were given a common blanket (*fresada mestiza*) and a hoe. Some chiefs did not fare even that well. Potano's chief received only a hoe and his heir and two leading men received blankets. Puturiba and Tocoaya's chiefs gained blankets as did one of the five leading men with them, who was also a *fiscal* at Puturiba. Mosquito's chief's gift was only a blanket. His mandador received a hoe. Acuera's cacica, her husband, and her mandador each gained a blanket and a hoe. Don Francisco, Guale's *mico mayor*, along with don Alonso de Argüelles, who was cacique of Tupiqui, and Pedro de Castillo, cacique of an unidentified Guale village, who also served as an interpreter, received the usual suit, hat, and shirt awarded to those esteemed most highly. Don Juan, the Tolomato mico's heir, who would lead the Guale's revolt soon thereafter, received a shirt and a hat for his services in having accompanied Fray Pedro de Chosas and another friar to and from Tama. Cacique don Juan of San Pedro and his wife also were among the most favored. He received a fancy suit and she gained a dress skirt. Two dozen silk buttons were among other items awarded to them. For his services, Juan de Junco received three yards of diezocheno cloth and six yards of crimson calico among other things (Machado 1597).

For the greater part, those receiving the most valuable gifts were paramounts or leading chiefs. Pedro de Castillo is an unknown quantity, as his village was not identified. His role as an interpreter may have made the governor more generous toward him than his status justified. The low status of the gifts to Potano's leaders may reflect continued Spanish coolness toward Potano because of the soldiers killed there in the past. It is conceivable also that Potano did not have a dominant chief.

The relatively low-status utilitarian goods given to the Ufalegue, Tulafina, Puturiba, Tocaya, and St. Catherines Island chiefs and to the chieftainness of Acuera contrast sharply with the gifts suitable for ostentatious display awarded to paramounts and other important chiefs. The governor's choices may have reflected a desire to enhance the status of those "natural lords" and to avoid putting lesser lords on the same exalted level as the head chiefs. It is possible also, as some have suggested, that those whom the Spaniards chose to exalt were not always the "natural lords." But such conduct would have been inconsistent with the reverence for "legitimacy" that marked the age.

The process in which chiefs abandoned their earlier hostility to welcome the Spaniards and their friars did not always go forward smoothly. The chiefs who first invited friars to Apalachee beginning in 1608 were not always able to curb opposition to the friars' presence. Friars were twice forced to leave between 1608 and 1612, abandoning their efforts in that province for a generation (Hann 1988a:11–12). Fray López appears to have had similar experiences during his first efforts among the Tacatacuru. Gerónimo de Oré (1936:71) remarked that Fray López "suffered much among the Indians" and that "they had condemned him to death three times but God miraculously delivered him from them."

For the Tacatacuru, chronic warfare between their old enemies, the Guale, and the Spaniards, beginning in the first half of the 1570s, may have inclined them to take a kinder view of Spaniards as potentially valuable allies. In any event, at least five doctrinas, or mission centers, and an undetermined number of visitas were established among Fresh- and Saltwater Timucua by 1588.

The two treasury officers made the following turbid comment in 1595 on those beginnings of the conversions and their sudden acceleration. "The natives, with the good beginning in their conversion that they had during the time that Pedro Menéndez Márques governed [1571–94], and because of being set right to a greater degree now, and because of having become acquainted with the error of their way, are now being reduced to our holy Catholic faith all at once (de golpe)" (J. Menéndez Márquez and A. de las Alas 1595).

Missionization was not without drawbacks for the natives. One was a probable increase in epidemics. A report of a great number of deaths among the natives in 1595 suggests an epidemic. Its severity is indicated in a remark that it caused a food shortage in St. Augustine, as it coincided with a failure of the situado to arrive (B. de Argüelles 1596).

An increase in the demand for native labor and imposition of formal tribute payments were other negative consequences. Governor Martínez de Avendaño introduced the formal tribute of one arroba of maize for every married man during his visitation in 1595. He had established a precedent for it by persuading Nombre de Dios's Cacica doña María to accede to that demand for her village. It contributed 48 arrobas that year, which sold at auction for four reales per arroba. The two treasury officials criticized the move as a heavy burden on the natives and as counterproductive in view of doña María's and her mother's loyalty toward the Spaniards and their status as the first chiefs who received the gospel. They noted that the only tribute collected in Menéndez de Avilés's time was a demand that the Indians feed his people when they traveled among the tribes (J. Menéndez Márquez and A. de las Alas 1595).

Tribute was also being collected informally in the form of labor in the years prior to the Guale Revolt. In the revolt's wake, Bartolomé de Argüelles

(1598b) accused Governor Gonzalo Méndez de Canzo of wasting royal funds by paying a daily wage to Indians who worked on the fort. Argüelles reported that it had been customary until then to provide only some maize for those working on the fort and, when the work was completed, to give their chief some iron tools. The governor was providing red cloth directly to the workers.

Fear that the friars instilled in the natives facilitated the spiritual conquests they made at some point in the missionization process. One of the treasury officials reported in 1599 that the friars were disconsolate because the incumbent governor had stripped them of their weapon of fear by failing to support them in their conflicts with native leaders. He also undermined their influence by telling the tribal leaders that the governor was the only Spaniard whom they had to respect and that the friars could not hurt them. The treasury officer noted that, as the Indians were a people moved by fear, their ardor for conversion had cooled greatly because of the governor's words, and they no longer obeyed the friars unquestioningly. He cited as an example an experience of Fray López in 1598 with San Pedro's Cacique don Juan. He noted that until then the San Pedro natives had always done whatever López ordered during the more than 12 years that he had been teaching them. On Ascension Day 1598, when López saw natives going to work with axes in their hands, he told them not to work because it was a holy day. The chief then confronted the friar angrily and told him not to meddle by giving orders to his Indians in that way. The treasury officer reported that the Indians had consequently lost respect for the friars and that all the friars were saying that they would be wasting their time in working among the Indians unless the situation was reversed (B. de Argüelles 1599a).

A Spaniard who visited San Pedro in 1595 described the village as located "on the bank of the river or arm of the sea." He noted that the governor stationed a number of Spaniards there but did not indicate the function they served. One of the soldiers testified later that he had been placed there with his family to set a good example for the natives of how a Christian should live. The others probably fulfilled the same role. The soldiers also provided a pool of godparents for the new converts (F. de Valdés 1602).

Don Juan, San Pedro's chief in 1595, and his wife doña María were rather thoroughly acculturated, in that they spoke Castilian very well and dressed in the Spanish manner. But shipwrecked Spaniards who stopped there for a time were given atole as their daily ration. One of them noted that there were other villages on the island close to San Pedro. San Pedro's friar was absent during those Spaniards' two-week stay (G. García 1902:200; F. de Valdés 1602).

Although the year 1597 is known best for the Guale Revolt, it was also a time of notable expansion of Spanish contact with the Timucua, especially with the western Timucua. Three western chiefs rendered obedience to the Spanish monarch, two of them identified as having done so for the first time. They were the head chief of Timucua Province and the chiefs of Ocale and Potano. Timucua Province's chief was spoken of in 1597 as having "refused to come before now despite the many times he has been summoned by petitions or by threats." Acuera's cacica was another identified as having come for the first time. The same was undoubtedly true of Potano's chief, who had been at war with the Spaniards since the time of Menéndez de Avilés (Machado 1597).

Guale Revolt and San Pedro

The Spaniards' ability to capitalize on the new openings in Timucua territory diminished precipitately beginning in late September 1597 because of revolt among the Guale. They killed five of the six friars working among them and made a slave of the sixth one, young Fray Francisco de Avila. When the governor finally secured his release, Avila was allowed to return to Spain. Fray Pedro Fernández de Chozas, who was stationed at Puturiba on Cumberland Island's northern end at the time of the revolt, was sent to Spain by his superior to report directly to the Crown about the friars' deaths. The superior sent him despite the objection of Governor Méndez de Canzo, with some of whose policies the friars were at odds. The 80-year-old superior soon left for Cuba, and Fray Blas de Montes replaced him. At least two of the remaining friars were in ill health by the turn of the century. Two other friars left in disgust over the governor's lack of support and the insults he allegedly inflicted on the friars (A. de las Alas 1599; Ynclan 1600). Consequently, the Franciscans were too under-staffed until 1606 to undertake any new missions or even to reactivate many of the Guale missions once their natives had been brought back under submission.

A debate that raged for at least six years after 1597 over the Florida settlement's viability also probably would have curbed any expansion had friars been available for that purpose. In response to many complaints about conditions in Florida, authorities in Spain ordered a formal inquiry into the matter, which was held in 1602. Complete abandonment of the Florida outpost and the moving of the St. Augustine settlement to better and more populous lands farther north beyond Timucua-speaking territory were among the topics considered (F. de Valdés 1602).

There was no indication of unrest among the Christianized Timucua in 1597. The attempted Guale attack on San Pedro soon after the killing of the friars probably would have sufficed to keep the Christian Timucua allied to the Spaniards, even if there had been dissatisfaction with the mission regime. Whether consciously or not, the Guale chose the feast day of St. Francis, October 4, for their assault on the San Pedro mission, possibly calculating that whatever guard might have been maintained routinely would have been relaxed because of the holiday.

For the attack on Cumberland Island, 26 canoes with about 400 warriors headed directly for San Pedro on the Puturiba River, arriving a little before daybreak. Two, which seem to have arrived ahead of the other 24, landed near the house of an Indian named Antonio López, who was a leading man of the village. They set up an ambush around the house while waiting for dawn and the arrival of the rest of the canoes. The other canoes went to the village marina. On seeing a Spanish brig there, which had brought food for the friars, they abandoned the plan of attacking the island, fearing that the brig had brought Spanish soldiers.

In the meantime, a dog's barking at the invading Indians awakened Antonio López's father-in-law, named Jusepe. When Jusepe went out to investigate, thinking the dog might have been barking at the chief's horse, five arrows thudding into him knocked him to the ground, four hitting him in the upper back and one in an arm. He was able to get back into the house to sound the alarm and grab his bow and arrows despite his wounds, but they prevented him from bending the bow. On hearing his shouts, López grabbed his bow and arrows and flew out of the house, running to hide in his field (sabana). He went from there to look for his chief. The shouts also awakened other villagers. Fray Pareja (filling in for the absent Fray López) heard the hubbub while standing at the church door as Indians ran by shouting, "War, war!" The Guale from the two canoes hastily crossed the Puturiba River to the mainland. Shortly thereafter, Cacique don Juan and some of his Indians took two canoes in pursuit of them.

The chief's men overtook, killed, and scalped two of the Guale, even though their hair was short, indicating that they were Christians. One of those killed was mandador of Asao. When Indians from San Pedro went back for the two abandoned Guale canoes, they found the habit and cowl of Fray Francisco de Verascola, who had been stationed at Asao on the

Altamaha River a short distance inland from its mouth. The Timucua chased another lone canoe they encountered. The next day Indians from the village of Ayacamale brought in the scalp of another Guale, even though don Juan had charged his Indians that they should bring the Guale to him alive if they caught any.

The attack force's main contingent landed briefly above the village of San Pedro at a little beach where there was a cross. They shot five arrows into the cross and reembarked. When Fray Pareja asked his Indian informants what that gesture might mean, they told him that it signified that the Guale had killed five priests.

The force then went on northward toward Bejessi, a village at the island's end, without attempting to land elsewhere on that island, even though one contingent passed within sight of Puturiba. Neither did they attack a group of Mocama at Bejessi (here spelled Bejesse), who went out onto a shoal area and spoke with the chief of Asao, who was with the main contingent as it passed northward. A Mocama interpreter named Nysiscas reprehended Asao's chief and challenged him to land. The chief contented himself with displaying Fray Verascola's hat and the harquebus the friar used to hail passing canoes when he needed a ride to visit one of the villages under his jurisdiction (Choças n.d. [1597]).

The passing of this Guale force alerted Fray Chozas to the trouble a little after sunrise when his people, greatly disturbed, called him out of the friary. He reported that "on coming out of the house, he saw and counted eleven canoes of enemy Indians and natives of Ybaha, who are called Guale among the Spaniards." He observed that, as he had no other arms, he donned those of the church and began to celebrate the mass of St. Francis, whose feast day it was. A messenger from Fray Pareja brought news of the attempted attack on San Pedro by the time he had finished. Bejessi's cacique and Puturiba's fiscal arrived in Puturiba shortly thereafter along with three interpreters for the Guale language. They told of having been at the point of the island and of having counted 23 canoes containing between 300 and 400 Guale warriors. Asao's chief had told them about the killing of the five friars and had waved Verascola's hat as if it were a great trophy. The Guale had promised to return to kill all the Christian Indians.

With that threat in mind, Fray Chozas sent a letter to the governor, asking him to send six or more old soldiers to help defend the island's people. He suggested that the soldiers be divided between Bejessi, San Pedro, and Puturiba, possibly indicating that they were the main settlements. He proposed that the soldiers do sentinel duty with the Indians if they would be content with what the Indians had: cakes (*tortas*), *hacha* (probably meant to be *gacha*, a thin porridge or stew), and fish when it was available, but nothing else.

Bejessi's chief and some Spaniards went to Talaxe on the Altamaha, the site where the British later built Fort King George. They found many cudgels there in an abandoned canoe and caught and killed an Indian from that canoe.

On the evening of October 4, San Pedro's chief sent a messenger to St. Augustine on the Spanish brig with a bundle of letters that included the one that Fray Chozas wrote. The governor dispatched a 12-man force posthaste under Sergeant Juan de Santiago. They reached San Pedro on the morning of October 10 after traveling night and day by land, channel, and swamps. The sergeant carried instructions to set up a good guard and sentinel system that would assure the friars' safety should any new hostile incident occur. He was to help don Juan in any way he could in view of his having been so faithful. The Spanish force was not to go out from San Pedro for any reason, and Santiago was not to give don Juan permission to go out. Santiago was to see to it that his men did not harm don Juan's Indians and that they remained content with whatever food don Juan provided in response to the governor's request that he feed them (Méndez de Canzo 1597c; J. de Santiago 1597).

The governor followed Santiago as quickly as he was able, arriving on October 17. He used several vessels to carry 150 soldiers and a number of warriors identified only as friends of Cacique don Juan (B. de Argüelles 1600). The governor's objectives were to punish the Guale, capture any that he could for questioning, rescue any of the friars' effects they could find, and hold an inquiry at San Pedro into the attack on San Pedro and the causes for the killing of the friars. San Pedro became his base of operations for expeditions into Guale territory.

The governor began the inquiry on October 18 with San Pedro's 26-year-old chief, whose command of Spanish was so perfect that no interpreter was used either for questioning him or for taking down his statement. Antonio López and Jusepe, whose house the Guale had surrounded, followed the chief in testifying. Frays Chozas and Pareja then presented statements certifying what had occurred during the attack and in its aftermath (Juan [cacique] 1597; Jusefe 1597; Antonio López 1597).

The governor issued instructions the next day to Captain Vicente Gonsálves, who was to lead the first forces into Guale territory to establish contact with its people if he could. González left at once for Tolomato, where the revolt had begun, traveling 16 leagues to a point two leagues short of that village where they overtook a lone Guale in a canoe. They returned to San Pedro with him after questioning him. In formal questioning there, the Indian stated that all the friars were dead, that the cacique of each village that had a friar had killed the friar, and that those who told them to kill the friars were Indians from Cosahue, Tulafina, and Santa Elena, along with the Salchiche (Gonçales 1597; Guale Indian 1597; Méndez de Canzo 1597d).

The Spaniards' Attack on Guale

The governor set out for Guale on October 24 accompanied by four canoes containing the 70 Indian friends of Cacique don Juan who had accompanied the governor from St. Augustine. After having learned that the Guale were assembled at Ospo, the governor headed there on October 27 with the intention of arriving before dawn. A league and one-half from Ospo the governor discovered that the four canoes of 70 Indians and two Spaniards were missing. The size of that loss made the governor consult the more experienced soldiers as to whether the force was still adequate for confronting the Guale massed on Ospo. When they unanimously replied yes, they resumed the voyage at a fast rowing stroke through fog and a heavy shower, reaching Ospo at the crack of dawn. The Indians received them with a shower of arrows when they landed, wounding some soldiers. They entered the village, nonetheless, and burned it, including the principal houses (*buxios principales*) and corncribs, leaving only the church standing. The Indians attacked again while they were setting the fires. When the Spaniards drove them off and pursued them, the Indians escaped into the woods. The Spaniards found a missal, breviary, hat, chalice cloth, and a friar's scalp in the village.

Having done all the damage they could, the Spaniards withdrew to their supply ships at a rendezvous point referred to as the wood of Asao (*monte de Asao*).[1] They met the missing canoes two leagues out. The governor chastised the Indians and the two Spaniards verbally on reaching the supply ships. The documentation provides no information on the reason for their having fallen behind (Méndez de Canzo 1597d).

The governor set out again from the wood of Asao on November 2 and burned Sapala and its food supply on that day. He proceeded from there to Tolomato. There he found the church, principal houses, and houses of the friars already burned. The governor tarried there for two days because it was the principal village of the land, sending interpreters into the treetops to shout a request that the Guale come to speak with him about their motives for killing the friars. The Guale's only response was to sneak in close enough to wound two of the Indians allied to the Spanish. On November 4 the governor burned the rest of Tolomato's houses. His forces found an altar (*ara*)[2] and a statue of St. Anthony of Padua there in some thickets (*matas*) and handed them over to Fray Montes.

On that same day, November 4, the governor sent a force to St. Catherines Island. The soldiers returned at nightfall with the news that they had seen no Indians on the island but had found the charred remains of the church, friary, large council house, and chief's house. They had disinterred the bodies of the two friars but then reburied them on seeing the state they were in. The friars' arms and legs had each been broken in four places and their feet tied. Fray Miguel de Auñon's head had been separated from the body. The Spaniards brought back his head along with some small bones from his body. They burned the rest of the village before retiring.

When a force went to Tupiqui the following day to burn the village, it found church, friary, council house, and chief's house burned and Fray Blas Rodrígues's corpse with the head split into three or four pieces (Méndez de Canzo 1597d).

Evacuation of Cumberland Island

On returning to San Pedro, the governor informed its chief and some of the chief's leading men and relatives on November 11 that he was withdrawing the friars. He suggested that the chief and his Indians move to places such as "San Juan del Puerto, Socochono, and other villages of his land" where friars would be able to serve them without fear for their lives. He also met with Puturiba and Tocoaya's chiefs on the same day to urge them to evacuate as well. When the Indians at San Pedro agreed to move, the governor reduced the yearly maize tribute to a symbolic six ears of maize in recompense for their cooperation. He noted on this occasion that their subsistence "consisted of shellfish and acorns and other maizes from grasses for the greater part of the year." He remained on the island until November 16, possibly to give the Indians time to put their belongings on Spanish vessels (B. de Argüelles 1600; Choças n.d. [1597]; Méndez de Canzo 1598a).

There is no indication how soon the Indians abandoned the island, how complete the evacuation was, or how quickly they returned, but the with-drawal was a short one. Don Juan, his Indians, and Fray López had re-turned to the island before Ascension Day of 1598, probably for spring planting. They were still there on August 3, 1598 (B. de Argüelles 1598a; 1599a). Guale came to the island around October 11, 1598, burning three villages and killing some people. Don Juan asked for soldiers in the wake of this attack to assist him in repelling the Guale. The governor sent 16 soldiers but left it to the Indians to provide their food. A treasury official again criticized that niggardly policy (B. de Argüelles 1598b). At some point the governor sent 50 soldiers to San Pedro on two sloops and supplied them with munitions and food for a protracted stay. They used the sloops for frequent sorties against the Guale, running along the coast and rivers to seize canoes and supplies of food, burning the villages they found, cut-ting down their maize and other crops, and capturing some Indians. The hunger created by those raids eventually forced the Guale to sue for mercy (B. de Argüelles 1600).

Despite that success, friars and others criticized the governor's overall handling of the revolt. In 1600 a treasury official adjudged the initial effort to punish the rebels as having had little effect. He faulted the governor for his trade with the rebels once the second wave of reprisals forced the Indi-ans to sue for peace. He alleged that those dealings caused the governor to lose what reputation he had gained through his use of force. He noted that the minor trade with the rebels during those contacts had given rise to murmuring among some friendly Indians and that even the rest consid-ered it to be a vile action (B. de Argüelles 1600).

First Moves into the Hinterland

Friars had begun to work in the hinterland province known as Ibi or Yui some time prior to the Guale Revolt. Fray B. López (1602) had traveled 14 leagues from his base at San Pedro to preach at Ibi for some days. Ibi's chief had gone to St. Augustine in the wake of his visit to ask that it be made a doctrina. Fray Pareja (1602) also had visited five villages in the land of Ibi. Fray Pedro Ruiz was in Ibi to open a mission when the Guale Revolt forced his recall to St. Augustine (Geiger 1937:87; Pareja 1602). A shortage of friars apparently precluded regular work there until after 1612. The infu-sion of many new friars beginning in 1612 probably soon led to establish-ment of the Ibi mission, but the mission was first cited only in a 1630 petition by Fray Alonso de Jesús (1630b). He mentioned a San Lorenzo

Ibiica as one of seven hardship missions for which he requested horses to ease the workload of friars who struggled against age or illness or the swampy terrain of the land where they worked. The name San Lorenzo suggests a circa-1612 foundation date, assuming the mission was thus named as a tribute to the Franciscans' superior in that period, Lorenzo Martínez (1612; Pareja et al. 1617). Ibi's chief had five villages in 1602, which contained 700 or 800 Indians (B. López 1602). Ibiica did not appear on the 1655 listing of missions that had friars then.

Fray López's incipient work in the village of Timucua Province's head chief was also interrupted by the Guale Revolt. B. López (1602) stated that his experience during his three-month stay there in 1597 made him feel that there would be few problems blocking the Timucua's acceptance of the Christian law. That village was 50 leagues from San Pedro and more than 50 leagues from St. Augustine. The chief's head village and four others under his immediate jurisdiction then contained more than 1,500 adults and children (Méndez de Canzo 1601). Another friar described the chief as "the great cacique of Timucua who is greatly esteemed and feared in the whole land of Florida," having more than 20 places under his command (Oré 1936:114).

As was the case with Ibi, lack of friars delayed renewal of the work at the Timucua Province's head chief's village. Despite the chief's importance and the signal recognition the governor had given him in 1597, the village was not awarded a friar in 1606, when the first few new ones arrived. One reason apparently was its head chief's reluctance to accept baptism immediately. That delay highlights the importance of the chief's example in facilitating the friars' work. Two of the new friars went instead to the neighboring province of Potano, whose chief had already been baptized in St. Augustine earlier in the decade. However, one of the Potano friars, Martín Prieto, went to the Timucua chief's village frequently during 1607, exhorting the chief many times to become a Christian. Apparently as a result of Prieto's efforts the chief went to St. Augustine to ask anew for a friar for his village. The Franciscan superior ordered Prieto to accompany the chief back to his village and Prieto began his work there on May 1, 1608, even though the chief put off accepting baptism himself (Oré 1936:114).

Fray López had also visited the village of Potano twice in 1597 while he was in Timucua Province, as Potano's chief had requested a friar. The two villages were only 10 leagues apart. The friar referred to Potano's chief as "head chief of the land of Potano," providing the sole reference that he enjoyed that status. Potano consisted then of five villages containing well over 1,000 people (B. López 1602; Oré 1936:114). A young chief who assumed power in 1601 asked for the governor's permission to return his people to the site that had remained abandoned since the Spaniards burned it in 1584. He pointed out that its greater proximity to St. Augustine would facilitate his people's assisting the Spaniards. The governor approved of the move (Méndez de Canzo 1601; Worth 1992a:40–42).

Fray B. López (1602) described the three mainland provinces of Ibi, Timucua, and Potano as having good trails and lands that looked to be fertile "because they are clayey and not sandy." Their chiefs were independent and not subject to the chief of San Pedro. In the Spaniards' eyes the latter was head chief for all the Saltwater Timucua and for other groups on mainland Georgia.

In addition to Ibi, Timucua, and Potano, López had visited other places on the mainland that were closer to San Pedro and tributary to its chief. He referred to them initially as "Cascangue and eight villages that are called land of Ycafui." Later in the same letter he referred to "eight villages of Cascangue." Pareja (1602) gave the number of Cascangue villages as seven. López visited the Cascangue villages many times, remarking that he always found the people very well disposed toward his teaching. He catechized them extensively, but despite the clamor of many of them for baptism, he refrained from beginning to baptize them because no friar was available to maintain contact and because his own infirmities prevented him from doing so. The eight villages had about 1,100 adults and children.

Another hinterland area in Georgia with which Spaniards were in contact at this time was a land of Ocone (or Ocony) three days by trail from San Juan del Puerto and two from San Pedro. Worth (1992a:155–58) placed Ocone on the eastern edge of the Okefenokee Swamp, noting that it was considered part of the province of Mocama in 1655. Fray Pareja (1602) observed that Ocone's chief desired to become a Christian. The chief and his village had made crosses, as had other settlements that were neighbors. Pareja remarked that the inhabitants of Potano, Ocone, Cascangue, and Ibi all spoke the same language and that they had kinsmen and friends in the already Christianized Timucua-speaking villages, whom they visited frequently. Prior to the missions' spread into the hinterland, some of the visitors eventually moved to Christian villages, "turning out well like those from here [San Juan del Puerto]," in Pareja's words.

Friars established a mission among the Ocone at an undefined time, naming it Santiago de Ocone. It was described in 1655 as an island 30 leagues from St. Augustine and referred to earlier as *laguna* (lake, pond, or lagoon) of Ocone (Ruíz de Salazar Vallecilla 1646; Serrano y Sanz 1912:132). Those allusions make one think immediately of a coastal location. But Ocone's placement on the 1655 list and other factors suggest that it was not a coastal mission and that Worth's placement of it is correct. The coastal missions were mentioned in an order of increasing distance proceeding northward from Nombre de Dios to Chatuache, the farthest north at 60 leagues from St. Augustine. If Ocone were on the coast, one would expect it to be listed between San Pedro at 20 leagues and Guadalquini at 32. But, Ocone follows Chatuache and heads the listing of the hinterland missions of Timucua Province. References to Ocone's remoteness also do not accord with a coastal location. An allusion to the Ocone's dependence on wild roots rather than agriculture for their starch suggests the staple ache, which grew in swampy land away from the coastal islands (Hann 1986b:92–93; Pueyo 1695:235).

Nothing is known about the formal establishment of the Ocone mission. It was first mentioned in 1646 by Governor Benito Ruíz de Salazar Vallecilla. "Inasmuch as I have communicated with . . . Fray Juan de Hinestrosa, provincial, . . . that the Indians who are congregated at the place called Laguna de Oconi, who are fugitive Indians from the villages of the province of Timuqua and other parts—in order not to work, for they have roots, fish, and other produce in the said place—and so that they do not live as barbarians, they have been given a religious . . . [who is] very dispirited by the said place being, as it is, more than twenty leagues distant from the nearest doctrina." Because of that, the governor ordered the removal of Ocone's inhabitants to San Diego de Elaca to compensate for the latter's "lack of people." He described Elaca as the main gateway to the provinces of Timucua and Apalachee. Force was to be used if necessary to compel removal of the Indians to Elaca (Ruíz de Salazar Vallecilla 1646; Worth 1992a:156). If those orders were carried out, not all of the Indians were removed from Ocone in view of Ocone's appearance on the 1655 list and another governor's issuance of similar orders later for removal of Ocone's people to Nombre de Dios, which was then depopulated.

The second governor was no more successful than his predecessor. When asked to relocate, Ocone's chief agreed, but asked for time to harvest the year's crops. The governor imprisoned the chief and sent soldiers to remove the Indians and burn their houses. Most fled to the woods and never came back under Spanish rule except for a few who went to San Pedro (Mocama), from which they had originally come. Ocone was described again at this time as "remote," "between two lakes," and composed of "little towns (*pueblecillos pequeños*)," of which Santiago was the largest. It still had a friar at this time. There are no subsequent references to Ocone (Alcayde de Córdoba 1660:404–5; Worth 1992a:156–57).

The above information on friars' early contacts with hinterland provinces resulted from a full-scale inquiry (mentioned briefly earlier) held at St. Augustine in 1602 to look into reports about the city's unsuitability as capital of Spanish Florida and questions even about Florida's viability. Relating directly to the Indians, Madrid asked for data on the number of Indians, broken down by districts and the villages within those districts, assessments of the sincerity of the converts and of the likelihood of their perseverance in the faith. The inquiry produced the only detailed picture of the settlement pattern for the Salt- and Freshwater Timucua during the mission era and the only basis for comparison with the roster of villages mentioned for those peoples during the 1560s, although the results fell short of what the king had requested. It was the last mention of many of those two provinces's lesser villages (F. de Valdés 1602).

The Fresh- and Saltwater Timucua in 1602

The inquiry and other sources reveal three missions among the Saltwater Timucua in 1602 and a possible fourth one. Nombre de Dios, served by Pedro Vermejo; San Juan del Puerto, served by Pareja; and San Pedro, served by Fray López were identified definitively. Soldier-witnesses mentioned a San Antonio in San Pedro's district (presumably San Antonio de Aratabo) as having a friar, but they did not identify him. Lanning (1935:136, 147) seemed to indicate that Pedro Viniegra, who was a lay brother in 1602, resided at San Antonio. Puturiba was yet another mission in 1597, but it was reduced to visita status after the Guale Revolt. Strangely, Fray B. López (1602) did not mention Puturiba in his command report on the villages with Christians that were under his jurisdiction at San Pedro. Possibly, it was one of the villages destroyed in the post-1597 Guale attacks. But Andrés, "cacique of Potoriba," was present at San Pedro in 1604 for the governor's visitation and he was among those whom the bishop confirmed in 1606 (Dávila 1606; Serrano y Sanz 1912:171). Such mention, however, does not necessarily mean continued existence of the village. Chiefs continued to identify themselves as chief of village such-and-such long after the village ceased to exist. There was no mention of Mocama's Puturiba or its chief after 1606. Lack of mention of a mission associated with Saturiwa's village and passage of the paramountcy to Tacatacuru's

San Pedro suggests that its leadership disappeared or declined in status.

The inquiry produced two disparate listings of villages in which there were Christians. One is based on friars' reports. The other derives from soldiers' testimony except for several village names from San Pedro's jurisdiction drawn from reports on the Guale Revolt. The lists differ most strikingly in assigning certain villages, such as San Mateo and San Pablo, to different jurisdictions. Soldiers reported more places than did the friars and presented San Juan del Puerto as a subprovince under San Pedro's chief's jurisdiction. The soldiers' listing represents the native political organization's lines of jurisdiction. The friars' listing represents parish lines of jurisdiction. The latter apparently was based on geographic propinquity without regard to the political affiliation of the chiefs of the respective villages. Population is cited when that statistic was provided.

Nombre de Dios, under Cacica Doña María

Friars' List	Soldiers' List	
Soloy	Solo	San Pablo
Capuaca	Capuaca	San Mateo
Palica	Palica	Nombre de Dios Chiquito
	Caherico	Mose

Fray Vermejo (1602) put the combined population of Nombre de Dios, Soloy, Capuaca, and Palica at 200. Soloy was two leagues from Nombre de Dios. Capuaca was a league away (from Soloy presumably), and Palica an additional two leagues distant. Palica's distance from St. Augustine was given elsewhere as five leagues. San Mateo, San Pablo, Caherico, and Nombre de Dios Chiquito had churches. All were mentioned specifically as having Christians except Mose. San Mateo's Cacique Francisco was a nephew of doña María and subject to her, as were all the villages on the soldiers' list. She was married to Clemente Vernal, a Spanish soldier, and had three children by him.

San Juan del Puerto under Cacica Doña Inés

Friars' List			
La Veracruz	1/2 league	Ratobo	2-1/2 leagues
Molo	5 leagues	Potayo	4 leagues
San Mateo	2 leagues	San Pablo	1-1/2 leagues
Hicachirico	1 league	Chinysca	1-1/2 leagues
Carabay	1/4 league		

Distances refer to each place's distance from San Juan. San Juan and the nine places that were part of the parish had a Christian population of 500. All the places except Ratobo had churches, to which San Juan's priest went occasionally to celebrate mass, administer sacraments, and teach. But on most Sundays and holy days the villagers were expected to go to San Juan to attend mass and receive the sacraments once they were admitted to them. Pareja was conservative in admitting converts to communion, observing that some men and women of his mission had progressed sufficiently in their knowledge of Christianity to receive communion, but that the number whom he admitted was not large.

There is no soldiers' list per se for San Juan. Except for the accountant Alonso Sancho Sáez de Mercado, the lay witnesses mentioned San Juan and its subject villages in conjunction with those of San Pedro proper because San Juan was subject to Cacica Doña Ana, who had succeeded to San Pedro's chieftainship upon the death of her uncle don Juan. Only Sáez de Mercado identified doña Inés as San Juan's cacica. He mentioned that there were "churches in the district of the said cacica and its villages of La Vera Cruz, Chirica, and San Antonio de Aratabo because all the Indians who reside in them are Christians." A number of soldiers spoke explicitly of doña Ana as cacica of San Pedro and San Juan. In doing so, they may have been referring only to her paramountcy. Fray B. López (1602) described her as "head chief and head of all the rest of the maritime villages down to St. Augustine."

San Pedro under Doña Ana

Friars' List		*List from Soldiers and Others*	
Santo Domingo (Napoyca)	180	Napuyca	Vera Cruz
Santa María de la Sena	112	Santa María de la Sena	Moloa
San Antonio	30	Sto. Antonio	Chinica
Chica Faya La Madelena	40	Chicasa	Socochuno
Pitano	10	Puturiba	Aratabo
Utichine	3	Tocoaya	Ayacamale*
Ycapacano 2 houses	9	San Juan	Bejessi*
		Olatayco	

The numbers in the San Pedro friar's list refer to Christians in the village; names derived from the Guale Revolt reports have asterisks. Fray López spoke of the "island and village of San Pedro" as having 300 Christians. He may have been speaking of the village of San Pedro alone rather than the entire island, as 300 would have been a small number for the whole island. Puturiba, Bejessi, and Ayacamale were on the island and there probably were others. The shipwrecked Spaniard of 1595 spoke of wandering over to other villages that were close to San Pedro (G. García 1902:200).

Fray López spoke of Napoyca as an island "which is a tongue (*lengua*) from this one [San Pedro]." The context suggests that lengua could be a copyist's error for *legua*, or league. Santo Domingo and Santa María were on that island. The name Sena suggests that Santa María was located at the mouth of the St. Marys River. Sena was probably a carryover from Seine, the French name for the St. Marys.

Pitano and Utichine had non-Christian inhabitants who wanted to become Christians. Those in Pitano were "newly arrived," probably some of the immigrants from the mainland mentioned earlier. All the little places were a league and a half from a settlement that had a church.

Olatayco lay between San Juan and Cumberland Island. Governor Ibarra's stop there during his visitation and its possession of a principal council house suggest that it was a village of some importance (Serrano y Sanz 1912:170). Chica Faya and San Antonio were side by side. This San Antonio, belonging to San Pedro per se, was distinct from San Antonio Aratabo, which was affiliated with San Juan.

The 792 Christians whom Fray B. López (1602) gave as the total under his jurisdiction is greater than the sum of the Christians he listed for the individual places that he named. The 792 figure probably includes Christians from places López did not mention, such as Puturiba and Bejessi. The two treasury officials who participated in the 1602 inquiry described the coastal villages as small, having 20 to 30 or 30 to 40 houses at most, together with a community house where the people assembled to take cacina and tobacco and to receive orders from the chief. They depicted the settlement pattern as dispersed. Most of the houses were scattered through the woods next to the inhabitants' fields of maize, beans, and squash and close to the deer and rabbits that they hunted (F. de Valdés 1602).

The churches became other places of assembly on Sundays and holy days after Christianization. Holy Week appears to have been celebrated with particular solemnity at San Pedro and San Juan del Puerto, each of which had a Confraternity of the True Cross. The confraternities mounted two processions (referred to as processions of blood) each year during Holy Week. Indians had purchased the confraternities' banners and the candles used during the procession. They performed their flagellation and procession on Holy Thursday in accord with Spanish custom and assisted the priest in making the monument in which the Eucharist was enclosed. Warriors with their arms stood guard before it until it was opened on Good Friday. Friars and soldiers described the Indians as "officiating" at the masses and singing them.

Most soldiers evaded answering the question in the inquiry about the solidity of the Indians' Christianization and about whether they would persevere. Martín Gutiérrez de Utrera, however, commented that he had heard soldiers who had spent time among the Indians say that, although the natives were Christians, not many of them acted like Christians (no hacen muchos delles obras de xpianos). Evidence indicates that the process of conversion did not always proceed as smoothly as Fray López suggested in his remarks that, after spending four years catechizing San Pedro's people, "he found so good a disposition that, without any other intervention than the declaration of the law of God, they came asking for baptism. . . . And they have accepted our faith so well . . . it always seems to me to be on the increase and that they embrace what is taught to them with more devotion. For, laying aside that they come to mass very willingly and take part in the sung divine services and some . . . make their confessions with devotion, . . . it has seemed the right thing to me not to deny communion to them when they ask for it."

The existence of native fiscales indicates a degree of pressure or even of compulsion exerted on natives by friars. A soldier testified that he knew two Indian fiscales for San Pedro's church "who are placed by the friars so that they may make the rest of the Indians live as Christians." Another soldier noted that the fiscales saw to it that people attended church. Complaints by López and other friars about Governor Méndez de Canzo's lack of support also reveal the element of compulsion that marked the missionization process at times. López attributed his holding back from baptizing those whom he had catechized at Ibi and other places in part to the governor's lack of support. By support, López meant punishment or the threat of it to restrain Indians whom he referred to as "mischief-makers" and to secure the return to their villages of Christianized Indians who fled to non-Christian settlements to escape peer pressure to conform to Christian rules. Fray Vermejo (1602) blamed the governors in general for not correcting and punishing fugitive Indians, for not ordering the natives to respect the priests, and for not threatening punishment for Indians who became troublesome (B. López 1602; Pareja 1602; F. de Valdés 1602).

By 1602 a trade in sassafras root had become a source of income for

Cumberland Island's natives that undoubtedly contributed to the lavishness of religious services there. On December 23, 1602, a frigate that had brought provisions to St. Augustine from Havana received permission from the governor to go on to San Pedro to pick up 500 arrobas (12,500 pounds) of the sassafras for which the ship's master had already contracted. The trade had flourished for at least three years prior to 1602 (B. de Argüelles 1603; B. de Argüelles and J. Menéndez Márques 1603).

Planting of maize seems to have increased considerably in the territory of San Pedro not long after its missionization began. Spaniards mentioned its head chief's supplying maize to St. Augustine during times of need. The magnitude of such transactions is suggested by one from 1592 that Eugene Lyon (1992a:14) described. In a single sale Chief Cazacolo provided more than three tons of maize (263 arrobas) for "fifty silver ducats, six axes, three hoes, fifty varas of burlap cloth and some thread." The volume of such trade is indicated by the 350 ducats that San Pedro's natives provided for the rebuilding of their church (Ybarra 1603).

Many of the villages subject to San Pedro had churches. They include Olatayco (known also as Alatico), Santo Domingo, Santa María de la Sena, San Antonio (on Cumberland Island), Chica Faya la Madelena, Veracruz, Moloa, Potayo, Hicachirico (meaning "little village"), Chinica, Socochuno, San Juan, San Antonio Aratabo, and Puturiba. When San Pedro's church was rebuilt early in the seventeenth century under the governor's direction, he claimed that it was as large as the one in St. Augustine and would have cost 2,000 ducats if he had not provided soldier labor. He also contributed funds. Its church floor is recorded as having served as cemetery. Indians probably were buried in other mission churches, but that of San Pedro and those of Nombre de Dios and San Sebastian are the only ones for which burials are mentioned (F. de Valdés 1602; Ybarra 1603).

Rio Dulce or Freshwater villages, part under Chief Antonico

Friars' List	Soldiers' List (F. de Valdés 1602)
Tocoy	Tocoy
San Julian	San Julian
Filache	Filache
Antonico	Antonico
Eguale	Moloa
Anacabile	Calabay
Mayaca	Mayaca
	Nyaautina
	San Sebastian

Soldiers noted that there were other Freshwater villages than those they named, with two observing that there were many other villages that had many Christians. But Fray Blas de Montes put the number of Christians in the first six that he named at 200. He noted that 100 natives in Mayaca had not yet been baptized and that it was eight leagues distant from the nearest Freshwater village. All the caciques were Christian. San Sebastian, Tocoy, San Julian, Antonico, Calabay, Nyaautina, and Mayaca had churches. Soldiers noted that San Sebastian and Antonico had had friars for many years. Neither had a resident friar in 1602 or 1605. One soldier indicated that the friar's stay at Antonico had been intermittent, remarking that friars had gone there many times. Lanning (1935:239n.3) identified Vermejo as the friar working among the Rio Dulce.

The political structure was not defined as clearly for the Freshwater Timucua as it was for the Saltwater natives. Most soldiers identified Antonico as head chief and treated San Sebastian as a settlement apart, while mentioning it in conjunction with the Freshwater Timucua. But the first two soldiers to testify implied that its chief was head chief for the Rio Dulce, the second one doing so clearly in speaking of the "Indians of the Rio Dulce" as "vassals of Gaspar, cacique of San Sevastian and its district."

The largely ill-defined position of Mayaca adds to the turbidity. Some soldiers seemingly viewed Mayaca as part of the province of Rio Dulce, while others mentioned it separately in ways that could be interpreted as meaning that Mayaca was not part of the province. It is likely that the former were thinking of the riverine settlements only in geographical terms. They may not have intended to imply that Mayaca shared a common tribal affiliation with the other villages referred to as Rio Dulce, particularly in view of Mayaca's having joined Saturiwa and Potano in their war against Chief Hotina in Menéndez's time. Fray Pareja stated clearly that they were distinct, noting that there were six or more villages of Christians "in the land of the Agua Dulce" and that there were "other Indians whom they call of Mayaca."

Lack of friars did not hinder the governor's plans for developing economic contact with the peoples who gave obedience in 1597. Soldiers testified that they had seen Indians come in daily from the provinces of Timucua, Potano, and Acuera and from the Rio Dulce region and other areas 40 leagues or more distant to work in Spaniards' fields or to trade. Trade items included deerskins, chestnuts, and pots (ollas) (F de Valdés 1602). The governor had communications with the hinterland more than 60 leagues away. When he requested workers from chiefs such as those of Potano and Timucua, the chiefs sent them. Governor Méndez de Canzo made ample use of the increase in labor available. He boasted that he encouraged the soldiers to plant and that, as a result, the more than 12,000 arrobas of maize harvested in 1602 far exceeded the largest yield since St. Augustine's establishment, which he put at about 2,000. He observed that without the Indians' help, the soldiers would harvest little maize because of the great work involved "both in the hoeing and processing as well as in the protecting it from the jays and other birds and animals that eat it" (Méndez de Canzo 1602). Forty chiefs came to render obedience to a new governor, Pedro de Ibarra, in 1603. They included Guale as well as Timucua (Ybarra 1604a).

That governor's visitation in 1604 and one conducted by Cuba's bishop in 1606 provide the last substantial glimpse of the eastern Timucua until well into the second half of the century. The bishop's secretary reported the population of the Saltwater villages under the jurisdiction of Nombre de Dios's doña María at more than 3,000. He noted that the majority were non-Christian. He confirmed only 216 natives at Nombre de Dios and about 20 Spaniards. The latter figure probably indicates the number of soldiers who had married Indians and were living in the mission village rather than in St. Augustine. The bishop confirmed two of doña María's children. A Fray Romero was then the pastor at Nombre de Dios.

The bishop confirmed 488 people at San Juan del Puerto. The leaders included a doña María and don Alonso, who probably were San Juan's leaders as they were mentioned first. Other leaders confirmed were doña Francisca, cacica of San Mateo; the caciques of San Pablo and Chirica, and Chief Francisco of Veracruz. Others mentioned by name as having met the bishop in the council house were Chinica's Chief Felipe; a Melchor identified as capitanexo; don Diego de Belasco, a leading Indian; and Miguel, a local interpreter. Juan Junco served as official interpreter for the governor in 1604. The governor mentioned having met a mandador and a *fiscal mayor* of San Juan and a mandador for Moloa without identifying them by name.

The governor stopped briefly at Olatayco to greet its leaders and order them to attend the visitation at San Pedro, as he was headed there from San Juan. He visited the church and went from there to the council house, where the chief, mandador, and nonranking Indians gave him the salute. This salute, tendered to him also in the other places he visited, was probably akin to the one the Indians gave their chief.

Doña Ana, the cacica at San Pedro in 1602, had died by November of 1604. Doña María Meléndez, cacica of Nombre de Dios in 1602, had assumed the paramountcy at San Pedro when the governor arrived. She was still the ruler in 1606 and also held the title of cacica of Nombre de Dios. The bishop confirmed her at Nombre de Dios, but his secretary remarked that she usually lived at San Pedro. Her eldest son and heir was confirmed at San Pedro. Nothing is known about what claim, if any, she had to the San Pedro chieftainship or about the circumstances of her accession. There may be something to Deagan's (1978:103) suggestion of Spanish influence in view of her marriage to a Spanish soldier and partiality toward Spaniards.[3]

First Formal Western Timucuan Missions

Arrival of a few new friars in 1605 permitted launching of the first western Timucua missions in April of 1606 in Potano Province. Fray Martín Prieto and a second friar began their work in a village they named San Francisco de Potano, first of the Florida missions to bear the Franciscans' founder's name. After building a church, Prieto left his companion in charge there and went to work in three nearby Potano villages containing 1,200 people. If San Francisco's chief was the recently baptized young chief of the village of Potano, which seems to be the case, his abandonment of native religious beliefs, and possibly his youth, seemed to have weakened his control. The people of San Francisco rose up against the friar only 20 days after he began to teach catechism there. In fear for his life, the friar sought refuge with Prieto in a village named San Miguel, where Prieto had established his residence. Prieto mercifully sent the friar back to St. Augustine. It is likely that the friar stirred up the opposition when he began to speak disrespectfully of the natives' idols and gods, describing them as evil and devils in disguise. Jesuits at Calus and in Guale met similar opposition in the 1560s when they did the same (Hann 1991a:221–22; Zubillaga 1946:308).

Prieto worked alone for the next six months, enduring with more fortitude the hostility that had cowed his companion. Prieto had established a routine of saying mass at San Miguel and teaching its natives and then visiting the other two villages, Santa Ana and San Buenaventura, before returning to San Miguel at nightfall. Upon his companion's departure, Prieto substituted a daily visit to San Francisco for the one he had been making to San Buenaventura. San Francisco was one and one-half leagues from San Miguel. Prieto soon won attentive audiences at San Miguel and San Francisco. Before long he had baptized 200 people at each of those two missions. At Santa Ana, however, he endured jeers from most of his audience and physical intimidation as well. Santa Ana's elderly chief and some of his men had suffered at the hands of de Soto as boys. Because of this the chief had told his people they should not become Christians. On learning of this, Prieto visited the chief, who was bedridden by age. When the chief commanded his leading men to give the friar a beating and throw him out of the house, a fortuitous clap of thunder and a powerful wind and storm flattened much of the village. The incident convinced the natives that Prieto was a powerful shaman. After that he was able to instruct and baptize all 400 of Santa Ana's people, including the old chief. After Prieto had worked alone for six months, another friar took over his work at San Francisco and baptized the other 200 people who lived there. A third friar who took up the work at San Buenaventura baptized all of its people (Oré 1936:112–14). The various friars baptized more than 1,000 adult Potano between November 1606 and October 1607 (Pareja and Peñaranda 1607). Oré (1936:114) identified San Buenaventura as site of the earlier Potano village that Spaniards destroyed in the sixteenth century.

Archaeologists have found probable sites for two of these early Potano missions. They identify San Buenaventura and de Soto's village of Potano with the Richardson site on the northwest shore of Orange Lake just north of Evinston (Milanich and Hudson 1993:176). The other three missions probably were associated with the Fox Pond site, a cluster of sites near it, and a cluster just to the south around Moon Lake. San Miguel and San Buenaventura probably disappeared early because of epidemics. San Buenaventura was last mentioned in 1613 and Spanish artifacts found at its presumed site suggest an early demise. San Francisco became the principal Potano mission and survived until the beginning of the eighteenth century, although most of its inhabitants in the late 1670s were from Santa Ana and it may have had infusions of Yustaga or Utina earlier (Hann 1992a:460; D. de Leturiondo 1678:134–36; Worth 1992a:55–56, 74n.5, 6).

Apalachee asked for friars within a month or so of Prieto's initiation of his work in Potano Province. The friars that reported that request described Apalachee as near the province of Potano. They may have been speaking of the village of Cofa at the mouth of the Suwannee. Cofa's missionization began not long after Prieto started work in the Potano villages in the vicinity of Gainesville (Pareja and Peñaranda 1607; Worth 1992a:59–60).

When Prieto was beginning his work, the friar at San Pedro resumed catechization at Icafi and Yui on the Georgia mainland. A friar reported at the beginning of 1608 that more than 4,000 Indians had been Christianized during the previous year and one-half and that early in 1608 more than an additional 1,000 were receiving instruction (Peñaranda 1608).

Prieto also laid a foundation for the missionization of Timucua Province during 1607 by visiting its head chief's village, only 10 leagues distant, many times. He described the chief as having more than 20 places under his command. That number probably included only principal villages, but may have embraced those of Yustaga as well. Most of those principal villages probably had satellite settlements under their jurisdiction, as did the village of the head chief, who had four such satellites under his immediate jurisdiction. The pattern resembles the better known one that prevailed in Apalachee (Hann 1968a:374–75, 385–86; B. López 1602; Oré 1936:114).

At Prieto's urging, Timucua's chief went to St. Augustine in the spring of 1608 to ask for friars for his territory. The Franciscan superior ordered Prieto and at least one other friar to return to Timucua Province with its chief. They arrived on May 1, 1608. After Prieto had preached to the Indians for some days, the chief gave the friar his support for the burning of the village's idols. The chief explained that he was the leader in all the Indians' ceremonies, a statement that suggests that he held supreme religious authority as well as political authority. The friars burned 12 images in the head village and six in each of four other villages. The four other places probably were satellites of the chief's own village. It is worthy of note that no mention was made of destruction of any religious structures. That suggests that the images may have been displayed out of doors. Prieto then addressed the people, and the chief confirmed his approval of what they had done, informing them that they should put aside their traditional religious beliefs and become Christians. Prieto baptized about 100 boys and girls there. Another friar baptized the rest because Prieto became ill before he completed their catechization. The mission's Christian name of San Martín was first mentioned only in 1616 by Fray Oré (1936:114–16, 128).

Prieto subsequently visited all of Timucua Province, accompanied by the head chief. In the course of the tour Prieto came to view the province's chronic warfare with the Apalachee as an obstacle to the friars' work. He eventually overcame the chief's opposition to ending the war. Prieto and the chief set out for Apalachee in mid-July 1608 accompanied by 150 Indians from Potano and Timucua provinces. Starting presumably from San Martín they traveled six days to a large settlement named Cotocochuni, located in Yustaga Province 12 leagues east of Apalachee. From Cotocochuni Prieto dispatched two Apalachee held prisoner there to advise the Apalachee of his coming on a mission of peace. Most of Apalachee's people and 70 chiefs welcomed them to Ivitachuco, easternmost of Apalachee's principal villages and seat of its paramount. The negotiations went smoothly and, at the end, the assembled Apalachee chiefs delegated the chief of Inihayca, their other most important chief, to go to St. Augustine to give the province's obedience to the governor (Oré 1936:114–17).

Prieto's success in this venture cleared the way for the advance of the mission frontier to almost the full extent it would achieve later in the century. Friars could now move freely through Timucua territory to Apalachee's border and beyond it. Fray Alonso Serrano and four or five other friars worked informally in Apalachee on several occasions between 1608 and 1612. In the latter year political and religious authorities decided to defer the evangelization of Apalachee because of the problems it entailed, one being Apalachee's distance, which raised problems of supplies for the friars. Opposition of some Apalachee to their presence required military support that was not available. And, most important perhaps, the magnitude of the task of Christianizing the western Timucua, the Acuera, and Timucua of Georgia's coastal hinterland would require the effort of all the friars available for a generation to come (Hann 1988a:11–13; Oré 1936:118–19). But a watershed had been crossed. Missionization of the Timucua peoples had passed beyond its period of beginnings. By November 1607 there were more than 6,000 Christian Indians (Pareja and Peñaranda 1607).

As far as is known, Florida's friars did not follow a policy of forceful reduction, or *congregación,* in establishing their first missions among Timucua-speakers. All were established in existing villages. Because soldiers did not accompany the friars and because friars had no herds of cattle or supplies of maize or other foodstuffs to attract natives to settle at a point the friars found desirable, the religious had no choice but to go where the natives were living, beginning usually with the village of the head chief of a district. The friars and the Spanish community as a whole in Florida were net takers rather than givers from the beginning (B. López 1602).

The only phenomenon resembling congregación involved migrants from the hinterland who came to coastal villages so that they might become Christians. But this was a spontaneous voluntary phenomenon, distinct from the more or less coerced migrations that constituted congregación in places such as California. The only reference to the Florida migrants being reduced to new villages occurred in two friars' response to a query from Spain about relocating Florida's Christianized natives to Española if the Spanish presence were to be reduced drastically or ended. The friars replied that there was no way the natives could be induced to make such a move. They observed instead that in many cases even the voluntary migrations from the interior were a failure, remarking, "We see on reducing them to created villages (*pueblos formados*), this does not succeed, as they return to their lands" (Pareja and Peñaranda 1607).

Dispersed as were the natives' houses within principal settlements and as were those settlements' satellite villages and hamlets, most of the horticultural Timucua were still sufficiently concentrated and sedentary to make missions among them feasible without imposing too much strain on the friars. Only by the turn of the century, because of a sharp decline in the friars available and a shrinking of the native populations, did friars like Fray Vermejo recommend that hamlets of three to five houses be amalgamated with other settlements so that they might be instructed more effectively and so that friars could visit them more easily when the Indians were ill. The villages he had in mind were subject to Nombre de Dios. It is not known whether this was done.

Other friars advocated a different form of reduction, forcible return of Christianized coastal natives who migrated to the hinterland to escape the obligation of weekly mass attendance, other religious obligations that were at odds with native customs, or the secular labor obligations that accompanied entry into the Christian ecumene. Pareja maintained that this reduction could be achieved with nothing more than a threatening word from the governor indicating that he was ready to use force to bring back the few who went to the hinterland (B. López 1602; Pareja 1602; Vermejo 1602). There is no evidence that governors were amenable to that policy. When governors moved people about, it was for secular purposes.

The Freshwater Timucua and Reduction

A group for whom a reduction approach probably would have been necessary were Timucua living on freshwater inlets along the coast south of St. Augustine. That reality is probably one of the reasons friars appear to have made no effort to Christianize natives of that region. As a consequence little is known about the region's inhabitants after Menéndez de Avilés's brief contacts with them upon his arrival. In 1605 a governor's interest in establishing good relations with the Ais of the Indian River region shed a little light on the southernmost of those coastal Timucua-speakers in the village and district known as Nocoroco. The village was in the present Tomoka State Park just north of Ormond Beach.

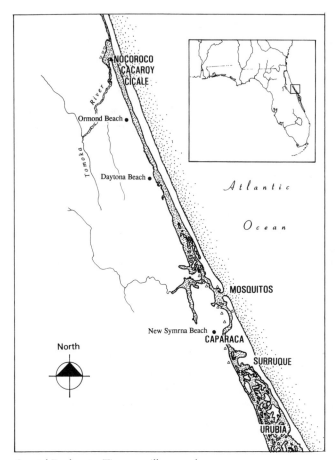

Coastal Freshwater Timucua villages and surruque

Alvaro Mexía, one of that governor's emissaries, described his itinerary from St. Augustine southward. Nocoroco was the northernmost village he mentioned. He placed it on the south side of the Tomoka Basin between the Halifax River and the mouth of the Tomoka River. A league and one-half farther south on the east side of the Halifax River was a village named Caçaroy and at a distance of three leagues the village of Cicale. Nocoroco's district continued southward to a little beyond Ponce de Leon Inlet, known to Spaniards as the bar of Mosquitos. Caparaca, one of the last villages of Nocoroco's district, occupied the site of present New Smyrna Beach. Midway between the bar and Caparaca, a small freshwater river that descended from the hinterland in the vicinity of Mayaca entered the Halifax River.

That stream, probably Turnbull's Creek, had many hamlets (rancherías) around its mouth, which were a day's journey from Mayaca. Beyond Caparaca one passed to Mosquitos and then entered the territory of the Surruque, a people probably related to the Ais like the Mayaca, although some authorities list them among the Timucua-speakers. The Surruque's territory began at Turtle Mound at least, at the beginning of the Canaveral National Seashore. Spaniards referred to the mound as the buhío of Surruque because it resembled a council house when seen from the sea. Mexía noted that Indians from Surruque launched their canoes from the foot of the hillock to go out to sea (Griffin and Smith 1949:340–43; Mexía 1605a, 1605b, 1605c, 1605d; Rouse 1951:34–39, 270; Ybarra 1605b).

Governor Pedro de Ibarra's interest in the southern coastal zone was stirred overall by a desire to assure the safety of survivors from Spanish shipwrecks along the coast from Cape Canaveral southward, much of which was subject to Ais's head chief to one degree or another. The presence of two escaped black slaves from St. Augustine among the Ais was a more immediate motive for the governor's diplomatic activity. Seven or eight slaves had sought refuge in Surruque territory in December of 1603. Spanish pressure on the Surruque brought the return of five. Two of the blacks were in Ais territory and had married Indian women there. The governor considered their presence there a security risk if European enemies of Spain were to land on those shores to parley with the Indians. He feared as well that in the case of new Spanish shipwrecks, the blacks would be even crueler than the Indians in killing survivors (Ybarra 1605a, 1605b, 1605c, 1605d, 1605e).

It is probable that Caparaca, as a frontier Timucua outpost, maintained intercourse with the Surruque that made it a good listening post. To safeguard the lives of shipwreck survivors and to prevent pirates from having dealings with those Indians, the governor included Caparaca's chief with the chiefs of Mosquito, Surruque, Ais, and Oribia (also spelled Urubia) as being important to cultivate (Ybarra 1605b, 1605h). Urubia was in the district of Nocoroco.

Little is known about the methods Spaniards used to avail themselves of the Caparaca listening post. The interpreter who accompanied Mexía to assist him in his contacts with the Surruque was an Indian named Francisco whom Mexía identified variously as being from Cicale and Nocoroco. It is likely he was from Cicale and that when Mexía spoke of him as being from Nocoroco he was referring to the district. This district probably included Mosquitos as well, although there is no clear evidence about the

Mosquitos' tribal identity beyond a statement that Nocoroco's district extended a little beyond the bar of Mosquitos (Mexía 1605c; Ybarra 1605d).

Relations between the Nocoroco and the Surruque were not entirely friendly. A Surruque leader known as "the little captain (*capitan chico*)" blamed the death of an Indian named Seguequeda, whom Mexía identified as the little captain's "cousin-brother," on the Nocoroco's having cast a spell on him. The little captain said that his people wished to exterminate the Nocoroco in reprisal and had desisted from doing so only because the Nocoroco were friends of the Spanish governor (Mexía 1605a, 1605b).

Mexía's interpreter's Christian name suggests that he had been baptized. There is no evidence that a mission ever was established in the Nocoroco district. Friars may have visited there from Mayaca or there could have been a mission whose existence was not recorded. John W. Griffin and Hale G. Smith (1949), in their work at the Nocoroco site, found no sign of a mission there, but noted that tidal action had eroded much of the site. It is possible that the interpreter lived in St. Augustine as a youth in the governors' school for interpreters.

The governor's efforts to win friends along the southern coast all the way to the Keys paid dividends shortly. A ship bringing a new band of nine friars in September of 1605 went aground in a storm in a mangrove thicket on Matecumbe Key. The Indians there assisted in unloading the supplies and refloating the vessel and brought everything back "without anything at all being missing," as the governor phrased it in a tone of surprise. After refitting in Havana, the ship encountered bad weather again and sought refuge at the bar of Mosquitos, where it received a friendly reception from the Indians (Arroyo 1605; Díaz 1605; Pereyra 1605; Ybarra 1605f, 1605h).

Little is known about the precise disposition of the nine new friars of 1605. The governor informed Fray Vermejo that the chiefs of Guale (St. Catherines Island), Asao, Xapuica, Antonico, Tocoy and Potano had asked for priests. He ordered Vermejo to station the seven priests among the newcomers in those six villages and Nombre de Dios. He wanted the two lay brothers sent to Santa María and Moloa. He indicated that an Indian interpreter would accompany each friar to transmit the friar's catechetical instruction until he became conversant with the native language. A soldier was to accompany the friars sent to work among the Guale and Freshwater Timucua to ensure a friendly reception and to see that the Indians gave their friar everything he needed. When the other three members of the band arrived, who had remained in Havana, the governor intended to specify where they should work. The friars do not seem to have followed the governor's orders entirely. Two friars went to Potano in 1606 to formally open missions there and at least two apparently were serving in Freshwater territory when Cuba's bishop visited there in 1606. Two of the new friars, one a lay brother, went to the Santa María mission, believed to have been on Amelia Island. One of them probably served Napuica, undoubtedly the governor's Xapuica. A Fray Romero served at Nombre de Dios in 1606, but Tocoy apparently still lacked a friar when the bishop visited there. Moloa likely received a friar as it had one by 1610. Fray Vermejo was then guardian of the convent of San Francisco de Moloa. San Juan and San Pedro of course still had friars (Dávila 1606; Hann 1990b:37, 39; Serrano y Sanz 1912:167, 171; Ybarra 1605g).

During his 1604 visitation at San Pedro the governor summoned 11 chiefs from the "pine barrens (*pinales*) in the hinterlands" to San Pedro to render obedience. All were Christians and vassals of San Pedro's doña María: a chief named Xatalano and the chiefs of Exangue, Lamale, Acahono, Tahupa, Punhuri, Talax, Panara, Utayne, and Huara (Serrano y Sanz 1912:173). Logic suggests that they belonged to the land of Cascangue or Ycafui except that neither Cascangue nor Ycafui were mentioned. The names of the 11 places do not appear in any subsequent documentation.

10.

THE ADVANCE OF

MISSIONIZATION, 1609–1655

In less than a decade after the start in 1607–8, friars carried the mission frontier westward through Timucua Province to a village on or near the Suwannee River, southwestward to the Gulf at the mouth of that river, and northward into central Georgia to the Altamaha. They established San Juan de Guacara on or near the Suwannee and Cofa at its mouth by 1612. By 1616 there were missions also at Santa Fé de Toloco in northern Alachua County; Santa Isabel de Utinahica on the Altamaha; Avino in the Acuera's territory; Apalo, which lay between the Freshwater mission of San Antonio de Anacape and the Potano missions; and at Santa Cruz de Tarihica in western Timucua Province (Oré 1936:127–30; Worth 1992a:60, 76nn.11, 13, 14).

Friars carried disease into the hinterland during those years along with the Gospel. A series of epidemics between 1612 and the end of 1616 killed half the natives in the villages being missionized. Presumably Indians living at mission centers or under chiefs who supplied laborers to St. Augustine were the hardest hit. That is the implication of a remark by Florida's Franciscan leaders. They told the king in an upbeat tone that "a very great harvest of souls has been made in these mortalities" with the help of 22 friars he had sent to Florida in 1612. They noted that more than 8,000 Christians survived (Pareja et al. 1617:13). Friars said nothing about the epidemics' toll in areas not in contact with Spaniards on a day-to-day basis. It is likely to have been substantial. By the onset of the epidemics, friars' repeated visits to Apalachee between 1608 and 1612 had brought them into contact with most of western Timucua, except perhaps some of its northern reaches in Georgia.

Little is known about the life of the natives, the rise of new missions, and the disappearance of established ones during the 1609–55 period. Until recently, the only major sources on the missions for that period were Oré's brief account of his 1616 visitation and a bare-bones listing of the missions that had friars in 1655. The material on the rebellion of 1656 that John Worth presented in his dissertation (1992a) and the many isolated fragments of information it contains on the missions in the first half of the seventeenth century have made his dissertation a third major source. Beyond those three sources, information on the Timucua missions for that period is very scattered and fragmentary.

The Guadalquini Coastal Mission

The dearth of information is greatest for eastern Timucua and above all for the Saltwater missions. Oré did not mention any of the Saltwater missions known to have existed in 1602 or earlier. Yet Nombre de Dios, San Juan del Puerto, San Pedro Mocama, and Santiago de Ocone of that earlier period appear on the 1655 list. San Buenaventura de Guadalquini was the only Saltwater Timucua mission that Oré mentioned visiting in 1616.

Guadalquini was first mentioned as a mission site on a 1587 list of dubious reliability that Geiger (1940:119) presented. Geiger offered no evidence for the existence of the convents mentioned on the list. Hard evidence from other sources indicates that a number of the list's alleged missions existed only on paper (Hann 1987:8–9). Juan Menéndez Márques noted that Cumberland Island was the northern limit of the missions in 1588 when he stopped at San Pedro (Ruidíaz y Caravia 1893:II, 498). Guadalquini's alliance with the French in 1580 and the lack of mention of Guadalquini in the extensive documentation for the Guale Revolt suggest that the mission began only sometime after 1597.

The Guadalquini mission was established by 1609. It appeared on three lists between 1609 and 1616. Lists for 1610 and 1616 name Frays Bartolomé Romero and Alonso de Nabos, respectively, as the mission's friar in those years. Oré chose the Guadalquini friary as site for the Franciscans' provincial chapter meeting in 1616, which he oversaw. He chose the site because food for the assembled friars and the Indians who accompanied them was less costly there than it would have been for a meeting held in St. Augustine. Also, the site's location permitted friars from coastal Timucua and Guale territories and from the St. Johns River valley to travel there by canoe. The Guadalquini mission, located 32 leagues from St. Augustine, still existed in 1655. The native portion of the name was rendered as Boadalquivi on the 1655 list and on some subsequent lists (Oré 1936:128; Serrano y Sanz 1912:132).

Confusion has existed about Guadalquini's location and the identity of its inhabitants. Swanton (1922:89) identified Guadalquini as a Guale mission and placed it on Jekyll Island. Most scholars have accepted his judgment unquestioningly, although there seems to be no Spanish source that identifies the inhabitants as Guale. It is worthy of note that Guadalquini never appears as the name of a Guale village in documentation for the 1597 revolt, in visitation records of that era, or in earlier documents on Guale. Herbert E. Bolton (1925:15) and John Tate Lanning (1935:71, 90) confused the issue further in extending Guale territory south to Jekyll Island. They placed Fray Francisco Dávila's Guale mission of 1597 on the island of Ospo and identified Ospo as Jekyll Island. The first identification of San Buenaventura's inhabitants' tribal affinity in 1648 implicitly links them with the Mocama. The 1677–78 visitation explicitly identifies them as Mocama-speakers. In 1648 one passed "on to the province of Guale" from Guadalquini. The visitor in the 1670s replaced his Guale interpreter with a Mocama interpreter in passing from Santo Domingo de Asao to Guadalquini (Antonio de Argüelles 1678:90–92; Ruíz de Salazar Vallecilla 1648).

Dávila's mission was farther north than Jekyll Island. The name Tulapo that Lanning gave to Dávila's mission village is clearly the Talapo of other sources, which was in the northern constellation of Guale villages. Lanning himself acknowledged "Tulapo's" northern affiliation during the bishop's 1606 visitation. The bishop confirmed Talapo's chief at Santa Catalina mission, his northernmost stop, rather than at either of his two stops farther south in Guale territory. The governor's 1604 visitation manifests Talapo's northern ties even more clearly. At Santa Catalina, Aluete's chief complained that the chiefs of Talapo, Ufaleque, and Orista, who were his vassals (and Orista his heir as well), had thrown off their allegiance to him and withdrawn to the territory of the *mico* of Asao, southernmost of Guale's major chiefdoms (Dávila 1606; Lanning 1935:90, 157; Serrano y Sanz 1912:188–89, 191).

The route the Spaniards took in their first move against the Guale rebels indicates that the Ospo mission was farther north than Jekyll Island. Vicente Gonsálves moved 16 leagues directly north from his base at San Pedro, capturing a lone Indian in a canoe two leagues from Tolomato. Guadalquini, on St. Simons Island, was only 12 leagues from San Pedro. If Jekyll Island were then the site of a Guale mission, one would expect it to have been the first place visited because of its proximity to San Pedro. The Spaniards learned from their lone captive that the rebels had assembled at Ospo. If Ospo were Jekyll Island, it would have been too vulnerable to be chosen as an assembly point. The ease of the rebels' withdrawal after the battle points to a mainland location for Ospo or at least easy access to the mainland through tidal marshes, as does Fray Dávila's account of his travails while he was being carried into captivity at Tulafina, a village some distance inland (Geiger 1937:103; Gonçáles 1597; Oré 1936:87–88).

John E. Worth (1995:app. A, 195–96) produced convincing evidence for Guadalquini's having been located on the southern tip of St. Simons Island. He presented a 1681 census that identified Guadalquini as southernmost of four settlements on an island that corresponds with modern-day St. Simons Island. The census placed the village directly on the bar of Guadalquini. Worth noted as well that in the Arcos mission itinerary of 1675, in passing from Guadalquini to San Phelipe on Cumberland Island, one crossed two bars (Guadalquini and Ballenas or Whales), "corresponding to St. Simons Sound and St. Andrews Sound respectively on either side of Jekyll Island." A 1683 census also placed the Asao (spelled as Asaho) mission and Guadalquini on the same island, noting that Guadalquini was four leagues by land from Asaho and six by water (Barbosa 1683). The Solana map of 1683 also supports his thesis, showing four villages on the island of Guadalquini and none on the unnamed feature that is obviously Jekyll Island.

Nothing is known about the circumstances of the establishment of the mission. Lanning (1935:8, 203) noted only that it was established on St. Simons Island between 1606 and 1655, as did Bolton (1925:21, 39), but without presenting any evidence to support that placement. Lanning then contradicted himself, speculating that "between Brunswick and St. Simon Island one may sometime come upon the remains of the mission San Buenaventura de Guadalquini, although the evidence is good that this mission was located on Jekyl Island."

Freshwater Timucua Missions

Friars returned to the St. Johns River valley prior to 1616. Oré began his visitation by traveling on foot from St. Augustine to the river. His calling it the river of Tocoy suggests that the village of Tocoy still existed and that it was the point from which he headed 20 leagues upriver by canoe to San Antonio de Anacape (rendered as Enacape by Oré). Anacape probably was the Antonico of 1602. Oré met at Anacape with friars from another convent he alluded to as Avino. Avino probably belonged to Acuera Province. Anacape and Avino's convents together apparently held at least five friars.

Oré (1936:126, 133–34) spoke of the guardian of each convent "as well as the religious of both guardianates and a definitor" as coming together at Anacape. The three extra friars undoubtedly served other villages along the river and in Acuera Province. Mayaca is likely to have been one of the other villages. It appeared on the 1655 list as San Salbador de Mayaca at 36 leagues from St. Augustine, 16 leagues beyond Anacape, which was referred to in 1655 as San Antonio de Nacape. Acuera's two 1655 missions of Santa Lucia and San Luis, at 34 and 32 leagues, respectively, from St. Augustine, are likely to have been the posts of the other two friars in 1616 (Díez de la Calle 1655).

Oré set out by foot from Anacape to go to San Francisco de Potano, reaching a new mission station known as Apalo after two and one-half days. Apalo was not mentioned again during the mission era. However, the French mentioned it in the 1560s. Le Moyne's map shows an Appalou a little to the northeast of Potano. Geiger's placement of Apalo south of Lake Orange seems more probable because of Oré's starting point at Anacape, which was near Welatka (Hann 1990b: 23–24; Oré 1936:127, 134n.12, 13).

Potano

San Francisco was the only one of the Potano settlements of 1607 that had a friar in 1616, although San Buenaventura had had one as late as 1613. Prieto was there in that year. Oré had nothing to say about Potano other than that he had stopped at San Francisco's convent and passed from there to the one at Santa Fé de Teleco and from it to "San Martín in Timucua" (Milanich and Sturtevant 1972:21; Oré 1936:127–28). San Francisco and Santa Fé were 25 and 30 leagues, respectively, from St. Augustine in 1655. Nothing is known about those two missions between Oré's visit and 1655.

Timucua Province

The province's head village of San Martín de Ayacutu (or Ayaocuto) was first mentioned as the site of a formal mission in 1610 with Fray Juan Gómez de Palma as its friar (Geiger 1937:234–35). He was still there in 1613 (Milanich and Sturtevant 1972:21). Oré assembled all the friars working in western Timucua at San Martín. In addition to the friars from Potano's two missions, friars came from Tarihica, Guacara, and Cofa.

Cofa was among the earliest of the new missions to be established in western Timucua after the start in Potano Province. In 1611 17 Indians were murdered on the "River of Cofa" while bringing supplies to a friar. Little else is known about the Cofa mission except that it had disappeared by 1635. Governor Luis de Horruytiner alluded to it in that year as a former village of Christian Indians that had been located at the mouth of the San Martín River (the Spanish name for the Suwannee). An earlier governor spoke of it in 1630, alluding to the River of Cofa and placing the village 20 leagues south of Apalachee and 30 leagues north of Pohoy (or Pojoy), a village on Tampa Bay's south shore (Worth 1992a:59–60, 76n.11).

Western Timucua's non-Christian neighbors created trouble for the newly converted Potano as early as 1608. Governor Ibarra reported on August 20 of that year that the Potano were being threatened by non-Christian neighbors, probably the Tocobaga and Pojoy, and he dispatched soldiers to assist the Potano in defending themselves. Tocobaga and Pojoy definitely were the perpetrators of the 1611 attack previously alluded to. Ibarra's successor sent soldiers to retaliate, who beheaded all the hostile Indians whom they captured. Tocobaga's and Pojoy's chiefs appear to have been among the casualties. The leader of a 1612 expedition that descended the Suwannee on its way to contact the Calusa reported that, when he had everything prepared for his expedition, he sent word to the heirs of the chiefs of Tocobaga and Pojoy that they should not harm the Christian settlements from that time forward. He informed them that the Spaniards wanted peace with them and that the punishment inflicted on them the previous year was for their predecessors' attack on the Christians. The launch and canoes he used for the expedition to Calus had been built on that river for the 1611 expedition (Fernández de Olivera 1612; Hann 1988a:10; 1991a:9; Worth 1992a:150–52).

Friars first went to Tarihica in 1611. Oré affirmed that at that time "there were not four Christian Indians, but now there were 712 living Christian Indians." His mention of "living" Indians probably alludes to the epidemics of 1616 and the years before it that halved the Christian population. Oré placed Tarihica eight leagues from the Guacara mission. The 1655 list placed Tarihica 54 leagues from St. Augustine as compared with 34 for the known point of San Martín (Oré 1936:129; Serrano y Sanz 1912:132). Worth (1992a:59, 75–76n.10) identified Tarihica with the Indian Pond site, believing that it was not on the main trail westward from San Martín to Guacara. Its being off the regular trail may be reflected in its inclusion on a 1630 list of seven missions where the friar needed a horse to serve his people more effectively because of the difficulty of the terrain and/or the age and infirmity of the priest (Jesús 1630b). Milanich (1978:71n.3) placed Tarihica "probably near O'Brien" in Suwannee County. Tarihica probably means "strong village," a likely characteristic for a place on the province's frontier (Granberry 1989:184).

San Juan de Guacara was the other of the early missions known with certainty to have been part of Timucua Province. It had been established by 1612 at least. Oré (1936:129) placed it at a point eight leagues equidistant from San Martín and Tarihica. Authorities have placed it variously at the Baptizing Spring site and at Charles Spring on the Suwannee River (Milanich 1978:71n.3; Worth 1992a:59, 75n.9). There are documentary indications that the Guacara mission occupied two distinct sites on or close to the Suwannee River in different epochs. B. Calvin Jones (personal communication 1986) identified a third site for Guacara on the river some distance north of the Charles Spring site. Guacara is known to have been on the river by 1675. Apalachee's lieutenant then gave its coordinates as nine leagues from San Pedro de Potohiriba (a Yustaga mission) and eight from Tarihica (Fernández de Florencia 1675a). If Guacara was initially at the Baptizing Spring site, a governor might well have ordered its removal to a site directly on the river, where its residents would be more available for ferrying people across. Guacara's inhabitants are known to have been obligated to perform that function. Suwannee is believed to have been derived from Guacara. Guacara does not appear on the 1655 list, but its participation in the 1656 revolt testifies to its continued existence.

Utinahica

Santa Isabel de Utinahica was the last of the interior missions Oré visited in 1616. He traveled 50 leagues to reach it from his starting point of Tarihica, presumably going in a northeasterly direction. It was deep in southern Georgia on or close to the Altamaha River, probably near its confluence with the Oconee. From Utinahica Oré descended a very large river that he described as larger than Portugal's Tagus, on which Lisbon is situated. The river brought Oré to the Guale mission on Sapelo Island at the mouth of the Altamaha. On his way to Utinahica he passed through a number of towns of non-Christian Indians who expressed interest in being Christianized. Oré sent a message to Tarihica's friar to send a Christian Indian to one of those villages, Tarraco, to instruct its people. Oré gave Tarraco the Christian name of Santa Barbara at the inhabitants' request. But there is no subsequent mention of a mission or visita of that name. The villages in the vicinity formed a fairly large district. Beyond Tarraco, Oré passed through three or four other small settlements before reaching Utinahica. Utinahica's name, meaning "lord's village," identifies the inhabitants as Timucua-speakers (Oré 1936:129–30).

A Spanish soldier made the last known mention of the Utinahica mission in 1630. He described it as bordering on Tama, a Hitchiti-speaking province, which he placed 30 leagues from Utinahica. Archaeologists have identified Tama with the Shinholser site in the upper Oconee River valley near Milledgeville. Utinahica also lay 30 leagues east of Arapaha, site of a later Timucua mission, 70 leagues from St. Augustine, that is believed to have been on the Alapaha River (Fernández de San Agustín 1630; Hann 1989:188; Hudson, Smith, and DePratter 1984:70; Serrano y Sanz 1912:132; Worth 1992a:68–69). Omission of Utinahica from the 1655 list indicates that either it lacked a friar in that year or the mission had disappeared.

Utinahica's location would have made it a likely early target for predator-peoples Spaniards referred to as Chiscas and Chichimecos when they began to attack the missions. The Chichimeco threat in Georgia emerged at least as early as the late 1640s (Ruíz de Salazar Vallecilla 1648). Chiscas became a problem in Timucua Province as early as the 1618–24 period, when Spanish authorities sent a punitive expedition against them. Chiscas were causing problems again in Timucua territory in the second half of the 1640s. They killed and carried off many men, women, and children from one or more Utina Province missions during that time. A small Spanish force the governor sent out killed many of the Chisca and forced the rest to flee (Worth 1992a:153–54, 257). Chisca were allied to the Apalachee who rebelled in 1647, killing Apalachee's first deputy-governor and his family and three friars. They would continue to be a thorn in the Spaniards' side into the 1670s at least in Timucua, Apalachee, and Chacato territory, and they would maintain that tradition into the eighteenth century, when they are believed to have metamorphosed into the people whom Spaniards then identified as Yuchi (Hann 1988a:16–19, 182–85, 232; 1988b:75–79; Swanton 1922:119, 288–89).

Other Western Timucua Missions

The records do not permit establishment of the time of foundation of the remaining missions believed to be part of Timucua Province as precisely as is the case for the missions that Oré visited. Two missions that postdate Oré's visit, San Agustín de Urica, or Urihica, and Santa María de los Angeles de Arapaha, were first mentioned in 1630 as among the missions whose friars needed horses (Jesús 1630b). Three others, San Ildefonso de Chamini (or Chamile), Santa Cruz de Cachipile, and San Francisco de Chuaquin, were 70 leagues from St. Augustine, like Arapaha, and were associated with Arapaha. The three with their satellite villages and Arapaha may have constituted a province or subprovince distinct from Timucua Province. A soldier, Juan Fernández de San Agustín (1630), referred explicitly to Arapaha as the "province of Harapaha," noting that it was 70 leagues northwest of St. Augustine. Although Governor Diego de Rebolledo included the villages as part of what he termed the province of Timucua, he used their isolation from the other settlements as an excuse for not holding an individual visitation for them, observing that the places of the province of Timucua were far apart from one another along crosswise paths (*caminos trasbersales*) and did not follow the royal road (Hann 1986b:104). Arapaha was 15 leagues east of Apalachee (Fernández de San Agustín 1630:69).

Paha means "house" or "dwelling." *Ara* can mean "much" or "many"; or the verb "help," "intercede," or "favor"; or the noun "bear." "Many houses" or "Beartown" seems a likely rendition for Arapaha. The form *hara* used by Fernandez San Agustín gives the town's name a less complimentary meaning. *Hara* is the verb "despise" and means prostitute in the form *haraca* (Granberry 1989:158, 161, 179). At 60 leagues from St. Augustine as compared with Tarihica's 54, Chuaquin was a northern Utinan mission but at some distance from the other three, Arapaha, Chamile, and Cachipile. Yet it was described in 1657 as being within Chamile's jurisdiction, as was Cachipile (Hann 1986b:104). The *chua* in Chuaquin, which means "sinkhole or pit," suggests that the village was associated with a sinkhole. *Cachi* means "bitter" and *pile* can mean "hut," "shed," "cabin," or "field" (Granberry 1989:158, 167, 179). There was no other mention of the Timucua Province missions between 1616 and 1655.

Yustaga Province

Yustaga's leaders did not follow the Utina's example of welcoming Christianization, although they had cooperated with Prieto's peace mission in 1608. Yustaga's head chief, Cotocochuni, rebuffed the initial moves to extend the mission effort into his territory a few years after Oré's 1616 visitation. Even after the first two friars, Alonso de Pesquera and Gregorio de Movilla, began work there in 1623, Cotocochuni forbade them to baptize anyone and attempted to force them out by denying them access to food. But he relented eventually, accepting baptism himself along with a daughter. More than 13,000 Yustaga had been baptized by 1635. The friar who reported the problems and the ultimate success referred to Yustaga as "the province and nation Cotocochono," but the name never reappeared after 1635 except possibly in an abbreviated form, Ocochunos. The friars' success there began some time prior to 1630 (Worth 1992a:65–66).

The relationship between Cotocochuni and Potohiriba is not clear. The Yustaga mission of San Pedro y San Pablo de Potohiriba or Poturiba existed by 1630, prior to the disappearance of the name Cotocochuni. Potohiriba's chief's leadership position in later times, together with Potohiriba's status as most populous of the Yustaga missions, suggests that Potohiriba and Cotocochuni could be one and the same. But Potohiriba's 1655 location of 60 leagues from St. Augustine is not entirely compatible with Prieto's placement of the Cotocochuni of 1608 at 12 leagues from Apalachee. Ivitachuco was 15 leagues farther from St. Augustine than Potohiriba in 1655 (Oré 1936:116; Serrano y Sanz 1912:132). The two fit together roughly, however, and Potohiriba's location as easternmost of the Yustaga missions also suggests their identity. There is a precedent for one village being known by two or more names. The most obvious example is Apalachee's Anhayca of the de Soto era, known also then as Iviahica. Those dual names reappeared in 1657 as San Luis de Xinayca and San Luis de Nijajipa and later as Talimali (Hann 1986b:93, 95). The documented existence of a new and an old Potohiriba and a new and an old Ivitachuco also provides some leeway for explaining the discrepancy in distances. Archaeologists have located a site for Potohiriba at Lake Sampala in Madison County. The lake's name could be a corruption of San Pablo.

Some have suggested that the Potohiriba name may indicate that Yustaga's Potohiriba was founded by migrating Mocama from Cumberland Island's Puturiba. The presence of a María Meléndez in 1657 as cacica of the Yustaga Potohiriba's satellite village of Santa Ana lends a certain credence to the suggestion, as the Meléndez name and female rule were associated with San Pedro Mocama. But there is no solid indication that Yustaga Potohiriba were other than genuine Yustaga. Yustaga was a supplier rather than a receiver of migrants. In view of the prominence of the Menéndez name, it is surprising that it did not appear more often.

The 1655 list contains the earliest mention of two of the other three Yustaga missions, San Miguel de Asile and Santa Elena de Machava, rendered at times as Machaba. However, their missionization probably began before 1630. In promoting abolition of the ball game, Domingo de

Leturiondo (1678:127–28) argued that the Yustaga as people older in the faith than the Apalachee should set an example for the Apalachee. Asile appeared in the de Soto chronicles under the variants Axile and Agile and was described as on the border with Apalachee. Ranjel described it as a "subject of Apalache" (Fernández de Oviedo y Valdés 1851:I, 554). The visitor in 1657, similarly, treated it as part of Apalachee and its chief was identified as an uncle of Ivitachuco's chief (Hann 1986b:101–2). Asile's 75-league distance from St. Augustine in 1655 was the same as that for Ivitachuco. Machava was 64 leagues away (Serrano y Sanz 1912:132). Later, Machaba moved farther east than the site it occupied in 1655. Its name means "swamp" in Timucua, possibly a clue to the nature of the land around the original site (Granberry 1989:173).

A fourth mission, San Matheo de Tolapatafi, did not appear on the 1655 list, probably because of not having had a friar at the time. It was mentioned two years later along with nine satellite villages bearing saints' names that suggest that it had been Christianized for some time. It should be noted, however, that there was no mention of San Matheo or of any of its satellites in the documentation for the 1656 revolt, either as rebels or as allies of the Spaniards. As late as 1656 a presumably Yustaga village named Pachala, located near Machaba, remained non-Christian (Hann 1986b:104–5; Worth 1992a:260). The native component of San Matheo's name, first mentioned only in the 1670s, possibly means "under the laurel tree." *Tola* means "in the air," "up," "oar," "paddle," or "laurel." *Patafi* means "below" or "obedience" (Granberry 1989:179, 185).

Except for Asile, nothing more is known about the Yustaga missions before 1655 beyond mention of Potohiriba in 1630 as one of the missions where a horse was needed. Asile drew attention only because of a governor's having established a hacienda on its lands.

Cotocochuni's initial resistance to Christianization of his province is a measure of Yustaga's autonomy vis-à-vis the head chief of Timucua Province. That autonomy suggests that the province's relationship with Timucua Province in the war against Apalachee earlier in the century was one of alliance rather than subjection. Cotocochuni's power or influence over all of Yustaga's people was demonstrated by their respect for his prohibition of their receiving baptism after he had permitted friars to begin instructing his people. It is not known what pressure or inducement led to his permitting the friars to preach or to his eventual acceptance of baptism, thereby opening the way for conversion of most of the rest of the province. The friar who revealed the difficulties his brethren had faced attributed their success to their perseverance and "the power of the divine word." When the chief sought to force the friars out by starvation, one of his women subjects had the courage to flout his will by bringing the friars a daily ration of pumpkin (Worth 1992a:65–66). The chief's opposition to the friars' work even after he admitted them suggests that duress was exerted from some quarter to gain their entry.

Another possible indicator of the separateness of the Yustaga from their Utina neighbors and other Timucua-speaking provinces is the absence of the words *utina* and *hica* from the names of Yustaga villages, in contrast to those of Utina Province, Potano, and coastal provinces. Of course that could simply be happenstance. But the absence is interesting in the light of indications that the Yustaga had certain cultural ties with their Apalachee neighbors. The most striking of those ties is reflected in the manuscript describing the Apalachee's ball game and the myths and ceremonies associated with it. Its title begins, "Origin and Beginning of the Game of Ball that the Apalachee and Yustaga Indians Have Been Playing since Pagan Times" (Hann 1988a:331). The title suggests that the game and its myths had been common to both people for a long time, perhaps time immemorial.

Not enough archaeological research has been done to assess Yustaga's ceramic relationship to Utina in protohistoric times. The ubiquitous Leon-Jefferson ceramics were dominant at Yustaga sites in the mission period, as they were in Apalachee and Utina (Milanich 1978:62, fig. 1). The Yustaga are supposed to have spoken the same dialect as the Potano (Granberry 1989:37, table 3). But if Onatheaqua is Utina Province or part of it, Yustaga and Utina chiefs in the 1560s shared a bond in that both painted their faces black (Lussagnet 1958:103).

Other Missions

Mission progress during this period was not confined to Utina and Yustaga. Friars had established a mission in Ibi by 1630, known as San Lorenzo de Ibiica. Ibiica undoubtedly is a variant of Ibihica meaning "Ibi village." It makes sense that this hinterland of the Georgia coast, to which a friar had gone as early as 1597, should be evangelized as early as the much more remote hinterland of northern Utina Province. The San Lorenzo mission was never mentioned again after 1630 (Jesús 1630b).

Friars also had established a mission in Ocale Province by 1630 known as San Luis de Eloquale. Eloquale first appeared on the Le Moyne map, which located it a little to the south of the Freshwater Chief Outina's village and somewhat to the west of it, but far south of Potanou, its nearest Timucua neighbor in reality. Eloquale is evidently a variant of the Etocale of the Biedma account, which is the Ocale of the other de Soto chroniclers. Eloquale may mean "song" or "singer of admiration or glorification." *Elo* by itself means "to sing or whistle," or "singer" or "song." *Qua* means "to glorify, honor, or venerate." *Quale* means "exclamation of wonder," "enough," or "admiration" (Granberry 1989:164, 182).

A mission named Urihica had been established by 1630. It is undoubtedly the San Agustín de Urica of the 1655 list, which was 60 leagues from St. Augustine. Its appearance on that list between Tarihica and Arapaha suggests that it was a Utina mission, although Worth (1992a:343) identified it as Yustaga. Urica's sharing of that 60-league distance from St. Augustine with Utina's Chuaquin and Yustaga's Potohiriba suggests that it was northeast of Potohiriba and located probably just over the Georgia border. The 60-league distance rules out Lana Jill Loucks's (1993:195) tentative association of the Urica mission with the Baptizing Spring site. Urihica means "sweeping village" (Granberry 1989:186).

Supply Problems

The missions' extension so deep into the hinterland created supply problems for the friars and for the Indians whom they served. That problem was responsible in part for the requests for horses mentioned earlier for places such as Arapaha, Tarihica, and Potohiriba. Sending supplies to the friars from St. Augustine was the crux of the problem. Water transport was lacking because the rivers that drained most of that remote mission territory flowed toward the Gulf coast. Consequently, provisions and other supplies the Crown provided to the friars for their sustenance and other needs and for the building and maintenance of the churches had to be hauled overland on the backs of the Indians. Fray Jesús (1630b) reported that because of the distances of 30 to more than 70 leagues, the weight of the burdens, the harshness of the terrain, and the miserable condition of the Indians, the cargo bearers arrived "so worn out and vexed" that they usually were no longer fit for regular work and that some even died from the strain. Moved by this affliction suffered by their "sons in Christ," many friars declined to send for all the provisions allotted to them. As a result friars lost their health, becoming unfit within a short time to carry out their work adequately. To remedy this situation, Fray Jesús requested six horses specifically for transporting friars' supplies, beyond the seven destined for the ministry of individual friars. The governor and his council informed the Crown that they could provide eight horses if it approved the request. They suggested that the horses for individual friars do double duty. Madrid authorized 13 horses for the friars from those available in Florida (Santander 1630). There is no indication whether the missions received those horses.

Mission Statistics

The missions' problems by 1630 flowed in part from a too rapid expansion of mission posts in the hinterland, in which the friars were clearly overextended. There were more missions and outposts to care for than there were friars available, not to mention an unspecified number of still almost completely non-Christian provinces that were reportedly clamoring for friars. Those provinces included Apalachee, Tama, Escamacu, Machaqua, and Cayagua, among others. At least the first three named had been asking for friars for many years. A spokesman for the friars informed the king in 1629 that 24 new friars were needed to staff places that lacked friars, to provide assistance for aged or infirm friars, and to open missions in the unserved provinces requesting them. The king sent only 12, one of whom died during the voyage from Spain. Two became ill in Havana while awaiting transport to Florida. Some of the original 27 friars in Florida already were ill from the toil and the harsh conditions they endured, particularly the winters' great cold spells and freezes that caught them on the trail afoot.

A 1630 memorial by Fray Jesús (1630a:99–101) reveals the magnitude of the problem. The 27 friars staffed 32 doctrinas, which in turn served over 200 places and congregated villages, more than 60 of which had churches. It is likely some abler friars were making forays into the closer non-Christian provinces as Frays López, Pareja, and Prieto had done earlier. There were reportedly 20,000 baptized natives in 1630 and more than 50,000 who had been catechized without having been baptized. The withholding of baptism was probably a consequence of the lack of friars to station among the newly catechized in outlying places to continue their instruction in the new faith, supervise fidelity to baptismal vows, and rebuke backsliders. The proportion of those 70,000-plus baptized or catechized Indians who were Timucua-speakers is not known. A substantial portion of the 50,000 catechumens must have been Timucua, as most of the new missions established during the preceding years were in the western Timucua hinterland. The disproportionate number of catechumens suggests that some may have been Apalachee who had been instructed by friars based in Asile or other Yustaga missions. The move into Apalachee only three years later was likely in part a response to that situation. Prior contact with the Apalachee is reflected in the knowledge of their language possessed by the two friars who launched the formal mission effort in 1633.

The number of baptized Christians topped 30,000 by 1635, distributed among 44 doctrinas served by 37 friars. More than 5,000 were newly baptized Apalachee. The shortage of friars was still so severe in 1633 and the clamor from Apalachee so strong that a friar who was guardian of the St. Augustine convent volunteered for the assignment (Hann 1988a:13–14; Jesús 1630a:99–101; 1635). The 70,000-plus natives of 1630 must have suffered a catastrophic mortality over the next 25 years. There were only 26,000 Christian Indians in 1655, who included a considerable number of Apalachee. Governor Rebolledo remarked in 1657 that there were few Indians left in Guale and Timucua because so many had died in the preceding years "with the sickness of the plague and of small pox." Those epidemics had affected Apalachee less drastically (Hann 1986a:111). Much of the loss occurred between 1649 and 1655 when a series of epidemics swept Florida, killing Spaniards and blacks as well as Indians. A measles epidemic in 1659 reportedly killed 10,000 natives (Hann 1988a:175–77).

Natives' Literacy

One of the factors that may have stimulated the Timucua's interest in being Christianized, especially among leadership elements, was the emphasis friars placed during that period on teaching natives to read and write. Many had learned the art of writing by the time of Oré's 1616 visitation (Gannon 1983:52). Oré (1936:129) reported of Tarihica, "There were some Indian men and women who knew how to read and write, being already 30 or 40 years of age. They have learned these things within four years." Fray Jesús (1630a:100) reported that many among the 70,000-plus catechized or baptized natives knew how to read and write, observing that women as well as men were so inclined to it that some even learned to read by themselves easily, once they had learned the alphabet. Fray Jesús recorded that the reading matter in the Timucua language included children's primers (*cartillos*), devotional books (*librillos*), and dictionaries (*vocabularios*) in addition to the catechisms, confessionario, grammar, and ritual that have survived. All the friars maintained schools for the children, in those early years of the century, having found education to be the most efficacious means "for imprinting the Christian discipline and doctrine in those hearts and lands with letters." That custom seems to have faded in the second half of the century. The visitor in 1677–78 found it necessary to order that schools be provided at many of the missions (D. de Leturiondo 1678:124–29, passim).

The Indians were particularly devoted to music and, accordingly, participated in singing the masses on Sundays, feast days, and Saturdays when the mass was celebrated in honor of Mary. Fray Jesús (1630a:100–101) observed that they were particularly devoted to her rosary and always wore it around their necks as did the friars. Confessing their sins was one Catholic practice that native men found particularly difficult and burdensome, although the friar stated that they adjusted to it. He revealed that when the natives first attempted the Catholic practice of kneeling during church services, they fell over when they doubled their knees. Possibly this was only a problem in the hinterland, as kneeling during a wailing ceremony was recorded for San Pedro Mocama in 1595. Men and women occupied separate sides of the church, as was the practice in the early days of Christianity. Women stood on the Epistle, or right, side and men on the Gospel, or left, side (Díaz Vara Calderón 1675a; Jesús 1630a:100–101). It is not clear whether friars introduced this separation of the sexes in church or whether it was an adjustment to native preference. In raising a new pole for the ball game, men and women pulled on the grape vines from opposite sides in a ceremony with religious connotations (Hann 1988a:339).

Mission Stability

Despite a sharp decline of the population during the 1609–55 period, the number of Timucua missions remained remarkably stable once it peaked—by 1630, or perhaps earlier. The 1655 listing includes 21 Timucua missions. At least two others, Guacara and Tolapatafi, were omitted because they did not then have friars. The village of Ahoica, associated later with a mission some believe to have been founded only after 1655, also was in existence in 1655. Among the missions known to have existed in 1609 or to have been established between 1609 and 1655, only Cofa, Eloquale, Ibiica, Utinahica, and Potano's San Buenaventura seem to have disappeared by 1655; at least, they were not mentioned in 1655 or thereafter. The following is a listing of missions known to have existed in 1655, grouped by province.

Saturiwa
Nombre de Dios

Potano
San Francisco Potano
Santa Fé de Toloco

Yustaga
San Pedro y San
    Pablo de Potohiriba
Santa Elena de Machaba
San Miguel de Asile
San Matheo de Tolapatafi*

Freshwater
San Antonio de Nacape
San Diego de Laca

Acuera
San Luis de Acuera
Santa Lucia de Acuera

Mocama
San Pedro Mocama
San Juan del Puerto
San Buenaventura de Guadalquini

Timucua or Utina
San Martín de Ayaocuto
Santa Cruz de Tarica
San Agustín de Urica
Santa María de los Angeles de Arapaja
San Ildefonso de Chamin
Santa Cruz de Cachipile
San Francisco de Chuaquin
San Juan Guacara*

Ocone
Santiago de Ocone, island

The two missions with asterisks do not appear on the 1655 list. I have not followed the spelling in the native component of the names used in the 1655 list when the spelling is clearly erroneous or substantially different from the usual one. The list is not a primary source in the sense of having been compiled in Florida by someone with firsthand knowledge of the missions. Its author, Juan Díez de la Calle, lived in Mexico and compiled the list in the course of his work for the *cronista mayor*. The most commonly used version of the list, published by Manuel Serrano y Sanz, has a number of divergences from Díez de la Calle's text.

Ocone, San Pedro Mocama, the two Acuera missions, and San Diego de Laca last appeared on that 1655 listing. Nothing is known of the circumstances of their demise, although the epidemics of the 1650s are a likely cause. Oré (1936:48) implied that by 1616 Cumberland Island had lost much of the large population it had in 1588. Laca, of course, metamorphosed, reappearing as San Diego de Salamototo on the next listings of the missions in 1675. The Salamototo were Timucua-speakers, not relocated Guale as at least one source has identified them. The only Acuera mentioned after 1655 were non-Christians (Hann 1992a). All or most of Anacape's original Freshwater Timucua inhabitants had disappeared by 1675 as the mission is not mentioned on that year's lists. It reappeared in 1679–80 with a largely or completely Yamasee population (Hann 1990b:23, 88–89; l991b:169).

Eastern Timucua

Little else is known about developments among the eastern Timucua during the 1609–55 period except that there was trouble in Mocama territory during the 1620s, including disturbances at Santa María and San Juan del Puerto in 1627. While Spaniards were bringing Santa María's chief to St. Augustine under custody, a cacica of San Juan del Puerto and an unspecified number of other Indians attempted to take the arrested chief from the Spaniards. The governor hanged the cacica for that attempt. He sentenced two youths (*moços*), who were close relatives of the cacica, to perpetual exile and detention in the fortress at Havana and had their ears cut off. The little known about this incident comes from a petition for pardon by the two youths in 1636, seven years after their sentencing. Both youths were literate. Three other Indians sent to Havana with them had died there. All the rest most involved in the resistance, who apparently had remained in Florida, also were dead. One of the petitioners, Juan Agustín, had two young daughters and a wife still living (López and Orata 1636). Three friars supported the petition, testifying that they had educated the two Indians (Martínez, Hernández, and Cruz 1636).

Other resistance in the 1620s involving Saltwater Timucua occurred in the village of Veracruz at about the same time as the trouble at Santa María and San Juan, and the unrest at all three places was probably linked. All that is known is that Governor Luis de Rojas y Borja sent soldiers and Indians to apprehend the Veracruz cacica because she had rebelled and denied obedience to the king (Caniçares Osorio 1635). There had been discontent earlier in the 1620s among other Mocama living farther north, as recalled by a soldier in 1635. He had been sent to the province of San Pedro in 1622 and 1623 to return fugitives, whom he characterized as "*Indios Simarrones,*" to missions from which they had fled (San Martín 1635). Another soldier who participated in one of those expeditions noted that Christian Indians had fled to the woods in both Guale and San Pedro provinces during the term of Governor Juan de Salinas (1618–24). The expedition brought the fugitives back to their villages (Caniçares Osorio 1635).

Later in the decade, a mineral-prospecting expedition that Governor Rojas y Borja sent into the northern interior found Mocama Province in rebellion and all the canoes removed from the usual crossing points (Terrazas 1678).

It is likely that eastern Timucua bore the full brunt of the 1614–17 series of epidemics because of being much more intimately in contact with Spaniards and blacks than were the western Timucua. Disappearance of most of the population of the eastern provinces and substantial losses among at least some of the western Timucua were important motivators for extension of the missions into Apalachee in 1633. Apalachee apparently was relatively unaffected by epidemics until the 1650s. The Apalachee's nonparticipation in the labor-*repartimiento* until after their 1647 revolt probably lessened the impact on them. Compared with the rest of Timucua, Yustaga also appears to have retained more of its population or to have had a much larger pool of inhabitants at contact (Hann 1990b:10). Some of the decline may have occurred during the 1620s. Rojas y Borja expressed mystification over the population's steady decline, remarking that Florida's natives were better treated than those elsewhere in Spanish America because of the absence of *encomiendas, obrajes,* and the draft labor for mines, an abusive exploitation of native labor.

Spanish Ranching

Disappearance of most of the Indians permitted the growth of Spanish ranching without significant opposition, as far as is known, from natives whose lands ranchers appropriated. The coastal Timucua in the vicinity of St. Augustine and Fort San Matheo reacted with great hostility toward cattle that Menéndez de Avilés introduced in the 1560s. To protect the cattle, Spaniards adopted the stratagem of isolating them on a garrisoned island. At night they loosed dogs trained to run down Indians. Isolation of the cattle in that fashion continued even after the Indians had been pacified, in part probably to avoid damage to the crops of natives and Spaniards (Barrientos 1965:134–35; A. Bushnell 1978a:409, 409n. 6).

Little is known about ranching's spread beyond the coastal islands through the first half of the seventeenth century. Charles Arnade (1965:5) dismissed the sixteenth-century attempts as "insignificant because of many adverse conditions." His judgment is validated by the 1602 Valdés report's failure to mention cattle-raising in the responses to a question about Florida's economic wealth. Arnade limited ranching to the 1655–1702 period, although he speculated that "its emergence may go back from about 1605, but probably a date closer to 1655." He saw 1680 to 1702 as the boom period for cattle-raising. The likely disappearance of most of the Saltwater and Freshwater Timucua by the end of the 1614–17 epidemics must have created an opportunity for cattle-raising to spread to abandoned Indian fields near St. Augustine. The expanses of open land and nearby water sources made abandoned village sites a good habitat for cattle. A number of Apalachee ranches were established on such sites (Hann 1988a:138–39). By the end of the seventeenth century, ranches occupied much of the coastal region from the mouth of the St. Johns River southward to the Mosquitos territory, westward beyond the St. Johns River, and southward along its banks into Mayaca-Jororo territory. But documentary evidence for most of them appears to date from the second half of the century. The earliest mainland ranch mentioned was established in Potano territory, possibly as early as the mid-1620s. It seems likely, however, that ranches appeared prior to that in the region between Potano and St. Augustine.

Choice of the Potano region was logical. It had some of the best natural pastures in Florida, characterized by treeless, seasonally flooded savannahs such as Paynes Prairie, one of the largest in the region. Potano was the location of the best known of Spanish Florida's ranches, the La Chua Hacienda, which had the largest herd in Florida by the century's end. It paid a tax of 77 calves in 1698, 35 percent of the total for all of Florida. The second-largest ranch paid only 13 calves, and the third largest, nine. Apalachee's largest paid only 15 head (Arnade 1965:6–9; Boniface 1971:140, 143–44). La Chua and a number of other ranches belonged to the well-connected Menéndez Márquez family, who were related to Pedro Menéndez de Avilés and frequently held positions in the royal treasury at St. Augustine. La Chua's founder, Francisco Menéndez Márquez, who was royal treasurer at his death in 1649, had held that post as early as the 1630s and probably used royal funds to some degree in establishing the operation (A. Bushnell 1978a:418–19). Worth (1992a:101–3, 116nn.6, 7) revealed that Francisco Menéndez had established La Chua by 1637, when he was arrested for fraud in collecting the situados for 1631 and 1632. Worth noted that, although the date of La Chua's founding remains unknown, Menéndez Márquez at some time during the 1620s or early 1630s "established an hacienda within the largely decimated province of Potano." A friar alluded in 1630 to horses, cows, young bulls, and heifers being brought to St. Augustine from Timucua.

Little is known of the La Chua Hacienda's early days down to the Timucua revolt of 1656. A mid-1630s foundation date would be compatible with Arnade's (1965:9) speculation that Luis Horruytiner, governor from 1633 to 1638, made the first major spate of land grants that led to important ranching activities. Horruytiner settled down in Florida after his term ended, as did Pablo de Hita Salazar, the other governor most closely identified with issuing land grants for ranching. The Horruytiners owned cattle ranches along the St. Johns River (C. de Florencia 1709; J. de Florencia 1695:164, 166, 182–84). La Chua's owners maintained good relations with Timucua Province's head chief. That chief's friendly feelings in 1656 toward the owner and his deceased father led him to spare the owner's life at his hacienda at the beginning of the 1656 revolt (Worth 1992a:101–3, 224).

The Alachua Sink site on the northern rim of Paynes Prairie is believed to be the location of La Chua Hacienda's headquarters. The ranch structures stood on a high bluff above the sinkhole and are only one set of many components that evidence human occupation of the site over thousands of years. The bluff dominates the countryside, and Alachua Sink is the drain for a lake that has periodically covered much of Paynes Prairie. The sink is located at the base of the Cody Scarp in that region. Henry Baker (1993:83–97), who has done archaeological work at the site, has demonstrated that it was the ranch's headquarters.

Twenty-five ranches are recorded as having been established in Timucua-speaking territory on a relatively permanent basis, in comparison with nine for Apalachee. The 25 do not include the short-lived Asile ranch. The visitor in 1694 deemed La Chua Hacienda and another ranch in the vicinity of San Francisco Potano sufficiently important to conduct visitation sessions for their personnel at that nearby mission. The second hacienda belonged to Captain Juan Antonio de Hita Salazar. The visitor held sessions at Salamototo for two other haciendas along the St. Johns River, San Joseph de Puibeta and the hacienda Piquilaco. The visitor admonished Piquilaco's owner for preventing the Indians from gathering wild fruits on the hacienda as they were accustomed to do, "such as bitter acorns (*bellota*), *ache*, and the rest that the aforesaid use for their sustenance." Indians complained that cattle from Puibeta, which was only one league from Salamototo, were destroying their crops and asked that the owner be required to build a fence around their village at his own expense. The visitor granted their request. In his regulations for the village, the visitor ruled that hacienda owners were to give natives free access as well for the harvesting of grapes, Spanish moss (*guano*), and chinquapins (*pinoco*) (J. de Florencia 1695:208–12).

In contrast to Apalachee, where cattle are known to have been owned by chiefs, villages, and ordinary Indians, little is known about Timucuan participation in cattle-raising. It is possible that Timucua were similarly attracted to this economic activity, which had resemblances to hunting, one of the Indian male's principal economic activities. But the high price for cattle cited by Amy Bushnell (1978a:418) for the early period when Timucua society was still vigorous would have made native entry into cattle-raising more difficult than it was for the Apalachee. The price of cattle fell drastically in Apalachee toward the end of the century (Hann 1988a:137–39). Santa Fé's chief was raising horses by the 1670s and, contemporaneously, Ahoica's chief, possibly under pressure from the governor, entered a partnership with a Spaniard to establish a cattle ranch on the abandoned lands of the village of Ahoica. The governor's involvement is suggested by the circumstance that the Spanish partner, Nicolás Suárez, held a land grant in the vicinity of Ivitanayo that he was being asked to surrender to make possible establishment of a native village there that would serve as a way station on the long trek between Salamototo and San Francisco Potano (D. de Leturiondo 1678:128, 129–30, 132–33).

Little is known about the western Timucua's reaction to the introduction of cattle-raising in their midst. Asile's chief objected to a governor's plans at mid-century to introduce cattle on lands belonging to that village. When the governor's agent, Agustín Pérez, broached the idea of running cattle on land toward the sea, the chief rejected the idea unequivocally because cattle would be a threat to the acorns and fruit of the palm that the Indians gathered there. He objected as well to the use of uplands for cattle but apparently made concessions allowing use of land to the north, away from the settlements' fields (Medina 1651; Ystasa 1651). The Timucua rebels' destruction of the La Chua ranch's headquarters and killing of its cattle and some of its workers in 1656 is the only other action that could be interpreted as an expression of their sentiments toward ranching activity in their midst. There is no evidence of lasting cattle ranches anywhere in western Timucua other than in Potano.

Data on the use of animals for food in western Timucua is very limited, being available for two sites only, Baptizing Springs and San Martín. The data consist of a Spanish and a native component at the Baptizing Springs site and a native component at San Martín. Interpretation is complicated by the small size of the three components, the limited range of species, a difference in recovery techniques, and uncertainty about the time of occupation of the Springs site. With those caveats, Elizabeth J. Reitz concluded that the "data may suggest that European animals did not replace wild animals in the subsistence strategy at Western Timucuan missions but were incorporated into a pattern that made extensive use of locally available wild foods. Domestic animals may have been rarely used by either Spaniards or Native Americans at Western Timucuan missions, although Spaniards may have had somewhat greater access to pigs and cattle than did Native Americans. Chickens may have been uncommonly consumed or else absent in the diet. . . . Both Spaniards and Native Americans appear to have made extensive use of two wild species: deer and gopher tortoises." Gopher tortoises represented 46 percent of the individuals in the Spanish component. Only one fish, a mullet, was found at Baptizing Springs and it was in the native component. Freshwater fish constituted most of the individuals at San Martín. Those results contrast sharply with the ones found at Apalachee's San Luis, where pork and especially beef "dominated the meat-based portion of the diet in Spanish components" (Reitz 1993:383–86, 390–91). The findings at San Luis may represent a later period, of course, when cattle were more plentiful, than the time of the findings at Baptizing Springs.

Data are available for eastern Timucua from the Fountain of Youth site associated with the natives belonging to the Nombre de Dios mission. Its large samples recovered using fine-screen techniques "indicate that in spite of the proximity to St. Augustine, the pre-Hispanic focus on marine resources remained intact throughout the first Spanish period." The reliance on marine resources was overwhelming and no domestic animals of any species were found (Reitz 1993:386–87).

The Asile Farm

Much more is known about one fledgling cattle ranch and wheat farm than about any other such Spanish enterprise, even though the farm and ranch were short lived. Soon after assuming office in 1645, Benito Ruíz de Salazar Vallecilla made arrangements with Asile's Chief Manuel Ystasa for the use of six leagues of land to raise livestock and wheat. To extort that concession from the chief, he used his position as governor and a pretense that use of the land was required for the king's service. The first governor known to have visited the north Florida hinterland, he made the preliminary arrangements for the use of the land on a trip that took him all the way to the Apalachicola country on the lower Chattahoochee in the vicinity of Columbus, Georgia. His interest in Spanish development of that hinterland is reflected as well in his 1645 appointment of the first deputy-governor for that region. His choice, Captain Claudio Luis de Florencia, went to Apalachee to serve as the governor's lieutenant there, bringing members of his family with the intention of beginning Spanish settlement in that province (C. de Florencia 1709; F. Menéndez Márquez and P. B. Horruytiner 1645; San Antonio et alia 1657:8).

Establishment of the Asile farm represented four years of heavy unrecompensed labor for Asile's inhabitants and for many Apalachee as well. Asile's chief remarked of that labor that it had involved not just "one or two, it was all the men and the women, boys and girls. And what we gained from all this work was solely fatigue and nothing else." He complained that even the hoes given to them to use as field hands were taken from them when the governor died and his son sold the operation and the land to the Crown. Discontent arising from agricultural labor and the work of transporting supplies to the farm was one of the factors that precipitated an Apalachee revolt early in 1647. The violence directed against Apalachee's deputy-governor and all his family, down even to a grandson still in the womb, indicates the intensity of the animosity it aroused. The rebels tied the youngest of his two daughters, who was in her early teens, to a pillar of a belfry and cut out her tongue and breasts, apparently in retribution for her preaching of the law of God to them during the torments they inflicted on other members of her family whom they killed.

Among the Timucua discontent with the Spaniards was not then sufficiently strong to outweigh the desire to strike a blow at their old enemy, the Apalachee. Despite the revolt's having begun at the beginning of the planting season, a Spanish force of 32 soldiers sent from St. Augustine recruited 500 Timucua as allies. A rebel force reputed at from 5,000 to more than 8,000 met them in a day-long battle on Timucua soil, at the end of which the rebels withdrew (Charles II 1682; Hann 1988a:16–20, 134, 140, 196, 320–21). There is no information about the casualties the Timucua and Spanish suffered during the engagement.

Upon Governor Ruíz de Salazar Vallecilla's death in 1651, his son and heir sold the Asile ranch to the Crown together with its equipment, improvements, stock, and two slaves, as the friars phrased it, "as if they [the lands] belonged to him and not to the cacique of Asile." An acting governor, who was a friend of his deceased predecessor, paid 500 pesos for the land in the king's name and 500 pesos more for improvements that included several structures and a corral. He gave the heir several thousand additional pesos out of royal funds for the slaves, stock, and equipment. Friars misrepresented the sale to a degree in saying that the 500 pesos for the structures were paid for one house alone, which they denigrated as having "four logs for a door and a little bit of mud covered with palm straw, which could be built for less than one hundred and sixty pesos at the most." The description was apt for one of the buildings but not for the more valuable principal one meant to be the headquarters residence. The structures included "a tall residence (*cassa de vibienda alta*) with good lumber with a cookhouse (*cossina*) belonging to the same house with its oven and two upright millstones (*molinos de pie*) covered (*soberadada*) with boards and another large house of straw where wheat is prepared (?) and a good corral (*potrero*), where the big cattle (*ganado grande*) are collected, and another new house with its walls of mud covered with straw." (For descriptions of the stock and equipment see Hann [1988a:157].)

The acting governor's death not long after his purchase of the farm brought a new acting governor to power. He proved more amenable to the joint protests of the friars, Asile's chief, and all the chiefs of Apalachee, who called for dismantling of the farm and return of its land to the rightful owners. Asile's chief insisted that in his conversations with the governor's agent in the final transaction for the use of the land, he had made it clear that he was only lending the land and not selling it. The chief stressed that he alone among the native leaders had been involved in the transaction, noting that he shared ownership in the land with his brothers and nephew and the other chiefs (*olatas*) and leading men. Asile had four other chiefs, whose minuscule satellite villages had 10, 12, 10, and 8 inhabitants, respectively. The chief asserted that he alone, therefore, could not alienate the lands in question even if that had been his intention (San Antonio et al. 1657:8–9; Ystasa 1651). The chief added that, as an inducement for his cooperation, the governor had made promises that he failed to keep, including a pledge to see that Indians from Asile who had moved to Apalachee were returned to their home village. Instead, the new demands for labor led to the flight of more of Asile's Indians. The Franciscan provincial observed that, as a consequence of those uncompensated, and excessive demands, most of the non-Christian natives obstinately refused to consider becoming Christians, whose lot was rigorous labor. He suggested that if those evils were not remedied, revolt could be the consequence, noting that the Apalachee had rebelled not long before with far less justification (Medina 1651; San Antonio et al. 1657:8).

The farm was one-half league equidistant from Asile and Ivitachuco. During an inquiry held to consider the farm's dismantling, soldiers who had lived on it testified that the farm occupied lands belonging to Ivitachuco's chief as well as lands under Asile's jurisdiction. That no doubt was one of the reasons for the Apalachee leaders' involvement in the campaign for abolition of the farm (Medina 1651; J. Menéndez Márqucz 1652; Sánchez 1651; Villareal 1651).

The 46 years between 1609 and 1655 saw great expansion of the missions among the Timucuans, especially in western Timucua, but the period does not deserve the encomium of "Golden Age of the Missions" often bestowed on it. The hollowness of such tributes is reflected dramatically in a comparison of the 26,000 Christians of 1655 with the 70,000-plus catechumens and baptized of 1630. The period saw relentless depletion of the native population, growing exploitation of the survivors for the benefit of Spaniards, and destruction or disruption of many aspects of the natives' traditional way of life. Discontent was growing steadily. Yet, in comparison with what the next 45 to 50 years were to bring, the temptation to view the years preceding 1655 as a halcyon period is understandable.

11.

THE TIMUCUA REVOLT

OF 1656

The period of Timucua history beginning in 1656 opened with revolt in western Timucua involving the Potano, Utina, and Yustaga. The revolt was anomalous in that it involved no fighting between Indians and Spaniards; friars were not a target of the rebels, and the rebellion's leaders professed continued allegiance to Spain's king, although the head chief suggested that all Spaniards except the friars return to their homeland for at least six years (Worth 1992a:231).

Causes of the Revolt

The revolt's immediate cause was Governor Rebolledo's summons of native militia from the interior provinces for the defense of St. Augustine in a manner that ignored social distinctions between the native ruling class and ordinary Indians. Fears that forces from Oliver Cromwell's England were about to attempt to seize Florida were the origin of that summons. England had recently made an unsuccessful effort to capture Española and had then seized Jamaica. Intelligence suggested that the English might strike elsewhere in the Caribbean and that Florida, in particular, was a likely target.

A group of friars gave the following account of the revolt's genesis:

> Around the month of April of the said year of fifty-six, the said governor received [the reports] about that [news] which came from Havana that your majesty sent to all his governors of the ports of the Indies that they should be on alert and look to the defense of their plazas lest the enemy who was roaming along the coasts of the Indies, should occupy them. Upon [the receipt] of this warning the governor assembled people at this presidio, and for this purpose he or-

dered that all the chiefs and leading men of the provinces of Timuqua and Apalachee should come in, carrying the provisions that they would need for the eight or ten days on the road and for the month that they would need to spend in this presidio: the said caciques and leading men did not question their being ordered to come, and responded at once that they were prepared to do so, [but that] what they did take issue with was his wanting to oblige each one of them to bring at least three *arrobas* of maize on his back. They were deeply offended, because of viewing themselves as natural lords in their lands and that they should be obliged to bear loads, something [to which] they have never been accustomed and which is done only by the plebeians among their vassals [and, the friar might have added, associated with women and in pre-Christian days reserved especially for the despised *berdaches*]. They remonstrated [with him] about this, and, notwithstanding that protest, the said governor dispatched an order . . . that the order that he had given [earlier] should be carried out. The said caciques and leading men were so offended by this decision that they did not hesitate, refusing obedience and killing the soldier and inflicting the other six killings that the province of Timuqua carried out. (Moral et al. 1657:11)

The revolt's genesis was more complex than the friars' account suggests. The governor's insensitivity toward the native elites' status was merely a spark for tinder piled high by earlier acts and omissions by Rebolledo in particular and to a degree by some of his immediate predecessors. The exasperation of at least one of the chiefs, Timucua Province's paramount, was fueled also by elements beyond the governors' control, particularly the loss of population to epidemics, which apparently left the chief virtually without vassals in the villages under his immediate control. Since assuming office, Rebolledo had ignored the long-established tradition that led Christian chiefs to expect gifts proportional to their status when they went to render obedience to a new governor. It was also traditional for governors to provide food and hospitality to native leaders and their retinue during their stay in St. Augustine and for their days on the trail while they returned home. Rebolledo ignored this tradition as well to some degree, but selectively, as he seems to have done also in the matter of gift-giving. Timucua Province's paramount and at least one other important chief, Tarihica's head chief, had experienced the governor's neglect in those matters (Alcayde de Córdoba 1660:404; Antonio Menéndez Márquez 1660:437–39; Pérez de Villareal 1660:382; Rocha 1660:420; Sotomayor

1660:414). It was that selectivity, perhaps, that made the governor's slights all the more galling. The consequences of such neglect for chiefs was highlighted by Patricia Galloway (1994:529). She noted that a Frenchman serving as interpreter for the English in their dealings with the Choctaw in 1765 sought to convince the English of the Choctaw leaders' need of "continuing to receive presents, stressing how without them they would fall from being 'dominant chiefs and the most respected of their nation' to 'objects of contempt in that Nation of which they had been the oracles.'"

The chief's disgust is epitomized in a soldier's testimony about the Timucua paramount's bitter feelings in this regard. The soldier reported that the paramount had complained to him that when he came to render obedience to Rebolledo, he had to eat at the house of a soldier who served as a Timucua interpreter. When the soldier testifying had asked the chief why the governor himself had not fed him, San Martín's chief replied "that if he were cacique of Ays or another heathen, that the governor would give it to him." The soldier had counseled patience in reply and the chief agreed that he would have patience "because he was a Christian" (Alcayde de Córdoba 1660:404).

The chief's reference to Rebolledo's benevolence toward Ais's cacique touches on a major reason for the governor's tightfistedness and lack of attention to chiefs whose favor and trade did not offer him prospects for substantial personal profit. The leading friars remarked that "unbounded greed" had been the lodestone that governed the policies of Rebolledo and three of his four immediate predecessors back to the late 1630s. The friars charged that those governors' principal guide in setting policy had been their private interest and convenience rather than interests pertaining to the king's service and the welfare of the Indians (Moral et al. 1657:8–11). Gift-giving on the usual scale would have lessened the royal funds that Rebolledo apparently contemplated embezzling from the time of his appointment. To obtain amber from the non-Christian Ais, he bartered away iron tools and other merchandise normally given as gifts to Christian chiefs. Rebolledo was accused of melting down cannon to obtain iron for more such tools to use in his trade for amber. St. Augustine's relative shortage of food provided him an excuse for not feeding the chiefs whom he chose not to entertain at his table (A. Menéndez Márquez 1660:437). When Rebolledo's immediate predecessor, Pedro Benedit Horruytiner, advised the new governor against any change in the policy of gift-giving because it served to maintain the devotion of the leading Indians to the Spanish cause, Rebolledo justified his departure from the policy by saying that the king's decree authorizing the gifts spoke only of heathen Indians. He ignored Horruytiner's response that the decree mentioned heathens because it was issued at a time (the 1590s) when most of the Indians were non-Christians (P. B. Horruytiner 1660:476).

That legal scruple did not prevent Rebolledo from generously entertaining and rewarding Apalachee's Christian paramount, Ivitachuco's principal chief. The reason again was in part private interest: the governor's trade in Apalachee's maize and other commodities. And Apalachee's continued ability to supply labor for St. Augustine gave the governor good reason to cultivate that chief's favor in the service of the king. The governor's purchases from Apalachee probably diverted additional items that normally would have been given as gifts. Fundamentally, the governor's policy of neglect toward Timucua and Guale may simply have reflected those peoples' declining importance demographically and, consequently, in the economic and military spheres (Sotomayor 1660:414).

Western Timucua's standing probably was low in the governor's eyes because it could no longer supply labor in quantity, as Apalachee still did, and it had neither the large surplus of provisions nor the amber that Rebolledo coveted. Even La Chua Hacienda relied on Apalachee for maize. Two of the first victims of the Timucua revolt were workers from the hacienda returning from Apalachee with maize for the ranch. Timucua Province's leaders' fall in status is reflected vividly in a complaint San Martín's chief made to his friend, the owner of La Chua, that "after your father died, no attention is paid to us now" (A. Menéndez Márquez 1660:438).

Another grievance of the province's head chief was Rebolledo's stiffening of his labor demands despite the province's having lost half its population to the mid-1650s epidemic. He demanded 50 or 60 laborers in 1656 when the previous year's quota had been 32. Reflecting on the deaths of so many at work in St. Augustine, San Martín's Chief Lucas Menéndez and another Indian had hinted darkly that "if they had to perish, it was better to rise up" (A. Menéndez Márquez 1660:438; Worth 1992a:191).

The Indians' complaints reflected a general discontent that had existed for a considerable time before it found expression early in 1656. Some of the soldiers were aware of it, possibly because they were married to Indian women or fraternized sufficiently with native workers or warriors to sense that something was amiss. Shortly before the revolt began, a soldier working on defensive trenches at St. Augustine's bar remarked to a comrade that the enemy they should be fearful of was not the one who might come against them from the sea but rather the Timucua, as "according to what he understood they had not been sure for many days" (Alonso de Argüelles 1660a:403). Another soldier reported in 1660 that the Timucua had wished to rise up more than six years earlier, which would have been prior to Rebolledo's assumption of the governorship (Puerta 1660:403). Other soldiers reported that the unrest extended back even earlier. One recorded that it had surfaced during an earlier reported enemy threat from without. The Timucua had favored rising up then and had built raised structures for firing arrows (*garitas de flechas*) (Rocha 1660:425; Worth 1992a:480n.7).

On April 19, 1656, Governor Rebolledo issued the orders that soon triggered the revolt. He asked Apalachee and Timucua Provinces to send 500 men to St. Augustine with bows and arrows to assist in defense of the city from an anticipated attack. He stipulated that the warriors be chosen from the most valorous leading men, men who would not be needed for labor in the fields, which was then under way. Two men, Agustín Pérez de Villareal and the interpreter Esteban Solana, set out that same day to deliver the orders. The governor also asked Guale for warriors without specifying a number but stipulating that the warriors sent include all the Indians who knew how to manage firearms. They were to bring all Guale's firearms along with its maize. He offered nothing more for the maize than a promise that he would pay for it as soon as possible. He sent additional orders on April 20 to Apalachee's deputy-governor, Antonio de Sartucha, asking for 500 warriors without delay, selected from the caciques, norocos, and leading men, who were the ones who did not work in the fields. They were to bring all the firearms, many bows and arrows, and food for the road and for one month in the city. He did not set a time limit for the warriors' stay in St. Augustine in the orders he gave to Pérez a day earlier (Worth 1992a:202–4).

In the light of the prior slights and insults Rebolledo had inflicted on Timucua's chiefs, his summoning of the Indian militia when food supplies were short at St. Augustine could not do otherwise than inflict a final culminating insult on the chiefs of Timucua Province and Apalachee and on other members of the leadership. The insult was inherent in his stipulation that only those exempt from labor in the fields should come. As Worth (1992a:197–201) noted, Rebolledo faced a fatal dilemma in his "urgent need for Indian warriors whom he could not feed." As it was planting time, most of the common Indians were needed at home and thus could not be spared to carry supplies for the warriors as they normally would have done. The governor was asking the leadership class to do something that was completely without precedent—alien to their society of sharp social distinctions between the leadership and the commonality. It amounted to stripping them of their special status. And Rebolledo was voiding another precedent in failing to provide the food himself for those he was summoning.

The tone Pérez used in delivering the governor's order may have stiffened resistance, for friars remarked that "the inclination of the said chiefs was strengthened further by the offensive words that they heard from the said Captain Agustín Pérez" (Moral et al. 1657:14). Pérez himself claimed that he had perceived no sign of antipathy when he delivered the governor's orders, asserting that otherwise he would have suspended their execution if he had and informed the governor of the problem. The validity of Pérez's claim is questionable. When the interpreter Solana reached Potohiriba, that mission's friar, Alonso Escudero, must have sent Pérez a warning through the interpreter, for Escudero sent letters of warning to Rebolledo and to his provincial. They accompanied a letter written to the governor by the chiefs of Potohiriba and San Martín, protesting the governor's order that Timucua's leaders should come to St. Augustine bearing cargo (Alejo 1660:469–70).

The insolence of some of the soldiers in their treatment of the Indians was another factor in building up Timucua resentment (Antonio de Argüelles 1660:393). One of the first soldiers to die was killed by a Potohiriba whom he had once mistreated (Pérez de Villareal 1660:387; Sotomayor 1660:417). San Martín's chief had involved himself on hearing of one such incident even though the mistreated Indian was part of an Apalachee labor detail, remarking to a soldier that such conduct was not proper. The soldier whom the chief had queried about the incident replied that "the soldier who had done it had not walked among them, and thus had done it ignorantly" (Biana 1660:478–79). Most of the western Timucua who remained loyal were from the northern tier of mission villages that were not on the Spanish trail to Apalachee and consequently had probably had less contact with soldiers than inhabitants of villages on the trail.

Pérez's Passage through Timucua with the Governor's Order

When Agustín Pérez reached San Martín with the governor's orders, its chief was away, consulting with Potohiriba's Cacique Diego. Chief Lucas seemingly had learned of the contents of the governor's orders before Pérez's arrival. Pérez's likely earlier stops at San Francisco Potano or Santa Fé seem the most likely source of San Martín's chief's advance information. Pérez and Solana then proceeded to Tarihica and Niayca in succession. Tarihica's Cacique Benito Ruíz and Niayca's Cacica María both reportedly promised to comply with the governor's orders. Pérez then sent Solana to Potohiriba to present the orders to its chief and to San Martín's chief, after which Solana was to go on to Machava to await Pérez's arrival. Pérez meanwhile was traveling to Arapaha to present the orders to its chief, Alonso Pastrana, who agreed to go to St. Augustine with his people. Because Pastrana was too old to travel such a distance, Pérez eventually persuaded him to name one of Arapaha's leading men to assume that duty. Pérez then headed for Machava with the contingent from Arapaha. Presumably it included people from Chamile and Cachipile, the other two northernmost missions, as Pérez made no mention of visiting them.

Solana did not find either Cacique Diego or Chief Lucas Menéndez at Potohiriba but sent word of the order to them. They replied that they would meet Pérez and Solana at Ivitachuco, where all the warriors and their supplies for the journey were to be assembled. Accordingly, Pérez and Solana finally met the two elusive chiefs at Ivitachuco. Pérez formally read the governor's orders to the warriors assembled at Ivitachuco in the presence of Apalachee's deputy-governor, who apparently was based in Ivitachuco at this time. Esteban Solana and Diego Salvador translated the orders into Timucua and Apalachee. Both interpreters knew both native languages. Salvador was a native of Mocoso in the province of Diminiyuti, but he had been raised in Apalachee and was serving there as royal interpreter. All present replied that they were ready to comply with the governor's order.

Pérez then dispatched the Timucua contingent in the charge of Solana, suspecting nothing of what was about to occur. Pérez remained behind to accompany the Apalachee contingent on the recommendation of Sartucha. The deputy-governor had advised keeping the two groups apart because they would steal from each other and cause trouble if they traveled together and because sending them at distinct times would ease congestion at the river crossings. While Pérez was waiting to set out, he sent Bartolomé Pérez, one of the two soldiers then stationed in Apalachee with Sartucha, to Asile to ready some maize to bring along on the trip. On the very day of the Timucua warriors' departure at about two in the afternoon, Fray Joseph Bamba of Asile galloped into Ivitachuco with news that Timucua had risen in revolt and that the Indians had killed Solana as soon as the Timucua in his charge reached Potohiriba. There San Martín's cacique issued orders to the assembled warriors to kill any Spaniards on whom they could lay their hands. Bamba also revealed that Bartolomé Pérez had been killed as soon as he arrived in Asile and entered its council house.

On hearing the order to kill Spaniards, a Potohiriba whom Bartolomé Pérez had once abused set out for Asile to seek revenge. Arriving at Asile before Pérez, the Indian killed the soldier with a hatchet blow to the head, struck from behind. (At some earlier time while the Potohiriba was in an Apalachee council house stretched out next to the fire to warm himself, Pérez had ordered him out with a kick, after calling him a dog.) The Indian then dragged Pérez outside and scalped him. At his trial the killer confessed that he had known that he would have to pay for what he had done sooner or later, but that he was satisfied because until then "he had not been a man, and with that action he was a *noroco* of God and the King, and he was very content" (Pérez de Villareal 1660:383–87; Sotomayor 1660:417–18; Worth 1992a:207–10).

That development effectively isolated the few Spaniards remaining in Ivitachuco. Sartucha and Pérez's first move was to dismiss the assembled Apalachee warriors, telling them to return to their villages. Apparently, the ones from Ivitachuco's immediate jurisdiction sufficed to guarantee the Spaniards' safety. The jurisdiction had 2,500 doctrina Indians in 1655. A problem, however, was the absence of Ivitachuco's principal chief, Apalachee's paramount. He had gone to St. Augustine earlier with other leading men from his village to accompany the labor contingent from Apalachee. Sartucha dispatched his one remaining soldier, Bartolomé Francisco, with two Apalachee Indians to bring news of the revolt to the governor. He instructed them to avoid the roads and to give the settled portion of Timucua a wide enough berth to avoid being captured (Pérez de Villareal 1660:387).

The Revolt

Despite Tarihica's chief's pledge to Pérez of compliance with the governor's orders, he was allegedly the first of Timucua's leaders to voice opposition to the governor's orders in refusing to send any of his leading men to St. Augustine bearing cargo like ordinary Indians. But the only source for that statement is a friar who was in Havana at the time he made it (Gómez de Engraba 1657b:128). None of the witnesses during Rebolledo's residencia mentioned any such primary leadership role for Tarihica's chief. San Martín and Potohiriba's chiefs emerge in that testimony as the principal organizers of the rebellion once they had learned of the governor's plans. If anybody played a catalyzing role at the start, it would seem to have been the chief of San Francisco Potano or that of Santa Fé or both, who presumably gave San Martín's chief the information that sent him hurrying off to enlist the support of Potohiriba's chief, the most important of Yustaga's leaders. All the evidence points to San Martín's chief as the principal leader of the movement, as befitted his position as paramount for Timucua Province. The friar who credited the chief of Tarihica (rendered here as Tari) with being the first to oppose the governor's order spoke of the role of San Martín's chief in the following terms. "On seeing these outrages and the evil treatment that they were subjected to and that they subject them to [still], one chief started a rebellion, like the emperor and absolute lord that he was formerly when they were pagans. And at the present time, while being Christians, they [still] recognize him as such an absolute lord, and, as a result, many other chiefs and leading men followed him" (Gómez de Engraba 1657a:127). That chief's dominant role was highlighted as well in the residencia testimony (Alonso de Argüelles 1660a:403–4; Calderón 1660:433).

Potohiriba was the principal scene of activity for the organization of the revolt. San Martín's chief summoned a number of Timucua leaders to meet there with him and Potohiriba's chief to rally support for his stand against the governor's orders. It is not clear how early the two chiefs revealed the full extent of their plans to the other leaders. As Worth (1992a:211) noted, San Martín's chief had already made his decision to rebel when he and Potohiriba's chief wrote to Rebolledo protesting the governor's order. Potohiriba's Fray Escudero sought in his letter to the governor to persuade him to drop his order requiring the leaders to carry their own provisions. Escudero alerted his provincial to the problem of a revolt in the making (Moral et al. 1657:13–14). Worth speculated that the friar was aware that the natives were planning to revolt but hoped to forestall the event by persuading the governor to suspend his order relative to the leaders' carrying their own provisions.

Worth went beyond that postulation to suggest that Escudero may have unwittingly played a role in sparking the revolt in possibly approving of the resistance to the governor's orders relative to cargo-bearing. A friar, José de Urrutia, made that accusation against Escudero. The charge brought stiff condemnation of Urrutia by Florida's Franciscan leaders, remarking that it made them blush that the order held such a man (Moral et al. 1657:13). Worth (1992a:214) noted that "rumor among the soldiers held that a friar had told the cacique Lucas Menéndez that Rebolledo wished to make slaves of the Indians and that he should rise up against the Spaniards." Chief Lucas used precisely that argument in his appeals to other natives for support for the rebellion, alleging that Rebolledo's goal in summoning the natives to St. Augustine was to enslave them (Alonso de Argüelles 1660a:396–98; Monzón 1660:412–13). It is unlikely that a friar would have encouraged such violence. At most, the friar may have expressed solidarity with the native leaders' objections to the governor's order and encouraged them to protest the cargo-carrying.

To deliver the three letters to the governor and the provincial, the chiefs enlisted two Indians, Juan Alejo, a native from the Santa Lucia mission in Diminiyuti Province (Acuera), and Antonio, son of Cacique Lázaro Chamile of San Ildefonso de Chamile (Alejo 1660:470). All that is known specifically about the contents of the three letters is reflected in the testimony of a soldier to whom the governor read Escudero's letter and in the leading friars' comments in a letter to the king. The soldier mentioned only "how . . . Pérez had given the order . . . to the caciques of that province, and they said that they did not wish to carry burdens" (Alonso de Argüelles 1660a:396–97). The friars said of the chiefs' letter to Rebolledo that the chiefs "did not question their being ordered to come, and responded at once that they were prepared to do so, [but that] what they did take issue with was his wanting to oblige each one of them to bring at least three *arrobas* of maize on his back" (Moral et al. 1657:11).

The friars in general placed full blame for the revolt on the governor for his intransigent response to the Timucua chiefs. Fray Gómez de Engraba (1657b:128) wrote that "the governor, like a man of little experience, made such an issue of this that he forced them to revolt, as they stated that they were not slaves, that they had become Christians to obey the holy Gospel and the law of God and that which the priests had taught them." Governor Rebolledo insisted, in his reply to the chiefs, on the native leaders' carrying their own provisions, reminding them that, on occasion, Spanish officers such as sergeant-majors and captains did the same.

The leading friars explained to the king in the natives' defense that they (the friars) were aware that governors' orders in matters of the royal service were to be carried out without any objections. But they observed that "Rebolledo should have chosen more appropriate measures rather than exciting passions with rash orders, taking into account the capacity of these natives and that it is a very different matter to give orders to a Spaniard, who knows what it is to obey, than [to give them] to one who does not know how to accept such orders; and that he should also have considered that it is a people that is subject to obedience to your majesty only because of the preaching of the gospel" (Moral et al. 1657:11).

Much as Rebolledo bore some of the responsibility for the revolt, his reply to the two caciques' letter of protest did not trigger the revolt in the manner the friars suggested. San Martín's chief issued his authorization and order to his people to kill all Spaniards before the two couriers returned to Potohiriba with the governor's response. The couriers learned of the revolt and the killings of the first two Spaniards at Asile and Potohiriba while the couriers were on the trail between San Martín and San Juan Guacara. Their informants were five Indians heading east on the trail, two men and a woman from Santa Fé and two men from San Martín. The informants also told them of Chief Lucas Menéndez's order that they should kill all Spaniards they met with the exception of friars.

As the couriers proceeded westward, at a place named Calacala in the forest of Ayaxeriva between the San Martín mission and the Suwannee they met two workers from La Chua Hacienda who had bedded down there for the night. The workers were Francisco Vásquez, a Spaniard, and Gerónimo, a Tabasca Indian. They became the revolt's third and fourth victims when the couriers killed them with several blows to the head with clubs. Antonio, Lázaro Chamile's son, then removed the Tabasca Indian's scalp, wrapping it in a cloth. The killing site was near the original mission of San Juan Guacara, about two leagues from the Suwannee River. The couriers finally encountered Chief Lucas Menéndez on the trail west of the river. The chief read one of the two letters they brought before putting them in his pouch (faldriquera). He approved of the killings they had done, but informed Antonio that he had not ordered the taking of scalps and directed him to bury the one he carried.

Chief Lucas then wrote a letter to Potohiriba's chief, informing him that he was headed for La Chua Hacienda looking for people to kill and asking for volunteers from Potohiriba to assist him in that enterprise. He ordered the couriers to deliver his letter to Potohiriba's chief and to report their killings to that chief. Upon Alejo's delivery of the letter, three Potohiriba responded to Lucas Menéndez's appeal and left to look for him (Alejo 1660:470–72; Alonso de Argüelles 1660a:397; Puerta 1660:373).

San Martín's chief perpetrated the last three killings of the revolt on the native side during his visit to La Chua Hacienda. He and a force of 23 Indians arrived at the hacienda's ranch house at nightfall. The 23 included the chiefs of San Francisco Potano and Santa Fé and an ordinary Indian named Francisco Pasqua, better known as Juan Pasqua. He was a Christian from San Luis in the province of Diminiyuti. Chief Lucas was very much surprised, on entering the ranch house, to find its owner, Juan Menéndez, there. When the chief resolved on the uprising, he wrote to Menéndez warning him not to return to his ranch. Menéndez, having received the letter as he was about to set out for his ranch and being unable to read Timucua, brought the letter with him. A Spanish-speaking Indian who read the letter to Menéndez upon his arrival omitted the part containing Chief Lucas's warning. Chief Lucas pulled Menéndez outside, holding him there while the other Indians killed a soldier named Juan de Osuna, who had accompanied Menéndez from St. Augustine, and two black slaves. Two Indian servants managed to flee. The Indians also killed the livestock they found at the ranch.

Chief Lucas told Menéndez that he was being spared because of the benefits the Indians had received from him and his father. He gave Menéndez a horse and some of his clothing for the 24-league journey to St. Augustine, advising him to go to Spain from there and explain to the king why the Indians had revolted. He informed Menéndez that he might return after six years, as by that time the chief expected to have "a good heart" once more toward the Spaniards. The chief sent two Indians to accompany Menéndez for his safety for the three leagues until he passed through San Francisco Potano. The Indians then all headed for San Martín and went from there to Santa Elena de Machava (Alonso de Argüelles 1660a:397; Calderón 1660:426; Antonio Menéndez Márquez 1660:440–41; Monzón 1660:409; Pasqua 1660:473–74). Juan Menéndez brought the first word of the revolt to St. Augustine, arriving before the soldier whom Sartucha had sent from Apalachee.

Francisco Pasqua, an Indian responsible for one of the killings at La Chua, appears to have been a prime example of a man who was in the wrong place at the wrong time. He was in St. Augustine under the labor draft working for Magdalena de Urisa when the revolt began to unfold. He had headed for the interior when his time was up, stopping in San Francisco Potano. He arrived there while its chief and Lucas Menéndez were planning the sortie to La Chua. Chief Lucas ordered Pasqua to accompany them to La Chua and at the ranch he sent Pasqua to kill one of the blacks, who lived in a hut apart from the ranch house. After Pasqua was handed over to the Spaniards, the governor tried him for that murder. Like Juan Alejo, Pasqua was sentenced to forced labor rather than death, presumably because he had acted under orders like Alejo rather than as a completely free agent. If the examples of Alejo and Pasqua are at all typical, they suggest that the labor draft's uprooting of natives from their home villages led to numbers of Acuera and members of other tribes moving about through the Spanish ecumene and possibly settling down eventually in a province other than the one in which they were born (Alejo 1660:469; Pasqua 1660:467–68).

The rebels' activity, after this brief spate of killings, appears to have been concentrated on building and manning a palisaded stronghold in a woods one-half league from Machava. They also attempted to enlist support from other Indians in western Timucua and Apalachee. Within the palisade were structures the Spaniards referred to as "fort," possibly modeled on Spanish blockhouses or possibly the protected firing platforms referred to as *garitas de flechas*. To enlist the Apalachee, the rebels spread rumors in their territory that the governor had imprisoned Ivitachuco's head chief along with the workers he had brought to St. Augustine. Yustagans served as the rebels' agents in Apalachee. The unrest they stirred up was sufficient to prompt the flight of five of Apalachee's friars on a ship sailing for Cuba. They perished when the vessel sank en route. When Spaniards moved forces into place to deal with the rebellion after many months of delay, the rebels spread false rumors among the western Timucua that the Spaniards had imprisoned the people of Pachala, a village of non-Christian Timucua near Machava, who had remained loyal to the Spaniards, and that Spaniards had assaulted the rebel palisade. The latter rumor led Chief Chamile's people to put pressure on their leader to end his neutrality, as many of them had kinsmen in the palisade (Alonso de Argüelles 1660a:398; Moral et al. 1657:13; Hann 1988a:22; Pérez de Villareal 1660:388; Rebolledo 1657b:112).

Spanish Reaction

Governor Rebolledo appears to have made no move to deal with the crisis when Juan Menéndez Márquez brought news of the revolt, thus complicating his plans for improving St. Augustine's defenses against a feared English attack. When Bartolomé Francisco arrived from Apalachee, the governor sent word to Sartucha and Pérez to sit tight in Ivitachuco, remaining alert until he came in person or sent someone to deal with the trouble among the Timucua. Before the governor dispatched that reply, more alarming news arrived. Apalachee leaders had sent several Indians to investigate Rebolledo's rumored imprisonment of don Luis Ivitachuco and the Apalachee labor-draft workers with the intention of enslaving them. To deal with this new potential crisis, the governor prevailed upon don Luis to dispatch his heir and several of his leading men, including his iniha, to assure the Apalachee that the rumored imprisonments were a lie and to bear his orders for the province to remain calm. The Ivitachuco leaders accompanied Bartolomé Francisco and three other soldiers who carried the governor's reply to Sartucha. The couriers again skirted Timucua territory for the trip back to Ivitachuco.

Three or four months passed before the governor sent the promised assistance to Sartucha to deal with the revolt. That delay accounts for much of the eight months that friars spoke of as the duration of the revolt. Worth has noted that little is known about Rebolledo's activity from the time he first learned of the revolt, probably early in May, until he dispatched a Spanish force early in September to quell the revolt. The reason for the delay was the English threat behind the governor's ill-conceived orders that created the crisis in St. Augustine's hinterland. The threat of English attack abated considerably after the beginning of September because of the stormy seas that mark the fall season along Florida's Atlantic coast (Alonso de Argüelles 1660a:398–99; Calderón 1660:427; Texeda 1660:464–65; Worth 1992a:233–36).

On September 4, 1656, the governor ordered Sergeant-Major Adrián de Canizares y Osorio to proceed with 60 soldiers to the place he judged most suitable for establishing communications with the rebels. He was to inform the rebels that he had not come to make war on them or to inflict punishment but to urge them to disperse peacefully and withdraw to their own villages. But if the rebels steadfastly refused to disperse, he was to threaten them with war without quarter in which he would not spare even women and children. The governor's emphasis, however, was on achieving a peaceful resolution by separating the leadership from the commonality. Once that had been achieved, Canizares was to apprehend the chiefs responsible for launching the uprising and the Indians who had done the killings and hold them in Apalachee in a secure place until the governor might decide their fate (Worth 1992a:253–57). The governor named Juan Menéndez Márquez as Canizares's second-in-command, with authorization to succeed him if Canizares were killed or incapacitated. Don Luis de Ivitachuco accompanied the Spanish force along with all the Apalachee workers who were in St. Augustine.

To provide firearms to the Apalachee, the governor confiscated those the Guale warriors brought, promising that he would pay for them when he received money from the king. He dismissed the Guale warriors at this time. A witness testified that the Guale understandably left very annoyed, amid reports that, if things later went poorly for the Spaniards in Timucua or Apalachee, the Guale were ready to revolt. Some of the Guale arms went to Spaniards, as harquebuses were then in short supply. In justifying the confiscation, Rebolledo remarked to Alonso de Argüelles in an aside that it was not just that the Indians should have firearms (Alonso de Argüelles 1660a:399; 1660b:454–55; Entonado 1660:445; Sánchez de Uriza 1660:366; Santiago 1660:374).

Canizares proceeded to San Martín and went on from there to Ivitachuco through what was described as an unpopulated region. He found about 2,000 Apalachee assembled at Ivitachuco as well as several loyal Timucua leaders. Among them were Francisco Hiriba, iniha of Potohiriba, and Diego Heva, cacique of Santa Catalina de Ayepacano. Cupaica's Cacique don Juan and another Apalachee chief named Benito (probably Ocuya's Benito Ruíz) were among the many chiefs of that tribe present. Five hundred Apalachee warriors were selected to accompany the Spanish force when it should move into Timucua territory to confront the rebels.

The sequence of events in Canizares's dealings with the rebels is somewhat confused in the records available. There are minor discrepancies between some of the accounts and major omissions in others. This is understandable in that the major source, the testimony from Rebolledo's residencia, was recorded three years after the events described. We do not have Canizares's report to Rebolledo after he captured most of the rebel leaders. He was not a witness at the residencia, having died in Apalachee in 1657. His second-in-command also did not testify because he was in Mexico to collect the situado. The following account, accordingly, is a composite, incorporating jigsaw-puzzle-like pieces of information provided by various witnesses and placed where they seem to fit together to form a coherent whole.

Canizares learned upon his arrival that the rebels were concentrated in a newly built stronghold a little over a mile from Machava, then the first major Timucua village east of Ivitachuco. Lázaro Chamile, whose northern village was four leagues from Machava, sent Canizares a message expressing his contentment over the Spaniards' arrival. He remarked that he had feared until then that the rebels might kill him because he refused to join them. He promised to be at the service of the Spaniards if they should come through Chamile or Machava (Cruz 1660:457).

Congregation of many of the rebels at their stronghold facilitated

Canizares's task of establishing contact and ultimately of apprehending most of the leaders. He initially sent several letters written in Timucua by Fray Umanes, expressing the governor's desire for a peaceful resolution of the conflict. He explained that he carried orders not to make war on them if that could be avoided, but rather to calm them and secure their peaceful return to their villages without any harm being done to them beyond the apprehension of the principal leaders and the individuals directly responsible for the killings. Francisco Hiriba and another Indian carried the first letter to the rebels.

When the letters brought no positive response, Canizares sent Hiriba several more times. Hiriba then delivered orally the messages the letters had contained: that Canizares would not make war on the Timucua unless they took up arms against him and that they should hand over any among them who were guilty, along with a request that some of the rebel leaders go to talk with Canizares to explain why they had rebelled. On the last of those missions, Machava's Chief Dionisio replied that he could not go alone to where Canizares was any more than that San Martín's chief should go with him. It is likely that Machava's chief became the spokesman because the rebel palisade was on land under his jurisdiction. Canizares decided to force the issue at that point by confronting the rebels at their palisade (Alonso de Argüelles 1660a:399–400; Calderón 1660:428–29; Cruz 1660:457; Monzón 1660:409; Pedrosa 1660:378; Rocha 1660:423).

One of the Spanish interpreters testified that, for the verbal communications, Hiriba passed through Chamile on each of his trips and that Chief Chamile was involved in those communications (Cruz 1660:458). None of the other witnesses gave a hint of Chamile's involvement at this stage. The interpreter's account indicates that Canizares's communications with the rebels consumed many more days than the other witnesses' accounts suggest.

The Spaniards' principal objective from the start of these contacts appears to have been to separate the rebel leaders physically from their followers or to induce all the rebels to disperse to their individual villages in order to facilitate apprehension of the leaders without bloody and destructive combat. The rebels apparently had a somewhat similar strategy for defeating the Spaniards. Spaniards, Timucua loyal to them, and Apalachee all heard rumors that the rebels' plan was to feign peace so that the Spaniards would dismiss the Apalachee warriors and Timucua loyal to the Spaniards, and at that point the rebels would attack the relatively small force of soldiers. But there is no evidence of rebel attempts to implement that strategy during Canizares's communications with them. Instead, the rebels tried several ploys during the progress of the communications to enhance their position by bringing the Christian Timucua northern villages into the rebel camp and by securing more recruits from villages already committed to their cause.

In response to Canizares's urgings that the rebels return to their villages, the leaders replied that they would comply. But those who went to their villages did so with the aim of summoning more chiefs and other Indians among those loyal to the rebel cause to join them at the palisade. It was during these contacts that the rebels falsely reported to Chamile that Canizares had imprisoned Pachala's inhabitants despite their loyalty to the Spaniards and that he had assaulted the palisade. Both reports were calculated to sow mistrust of the Spaniards among the northerners. The latter report in particular inflamed Chamile's and Arapaha's people, who had many kinsmen among the rebels.

The false report about Pachala's fate moved Chamile to send two Indians to investigate its truthfulness, and the rebel ploy then proved counterproductive. When Chamile learned that it was a lie, he went to meet Canizares along with Cachipile's Chief Francisco and Arapaha's Chief Pastrana. They then committed themselves more completely to the Spanish cause (Cruz 1660:460; Worth 1992a:266).

Events at the Palisade and in Machava

The months of inaction in the palisade and the rebel leaders' failure to galvanize support from the Apalachee or even from all of western Timucua's chiefs probably weakened the resolve of many of those who had joined the movement and made them begin to question the wisdom of the policies of San Martín's chief and those who supported him most avidly. The chief of San Martín and his two chiefly accomplices in the killings at La Chua may already have abandoned the palisade when Canizares began his march toward it. None of the three was present a few days later when rebel leaders went to Machava's council house for the meeting with the Spaniards and Apalachee that Canizares had requested insistently.

As Canizares approached the palisade and divided his forces into two units to invest it from two sides, the Indians within briefly sounded a call to arms. But they did nothing when the Spaniards and Apalachee halted at a distance of a harquebus's shot and sent Hiriba forward to present the usual explanations about the Spaniards' objectives and to ask the chiefs to come out so that Canizares might speak with them. Machava's chief and

San Juan Evanjelista's cacica came out to speak with him. They declared themselves friends of the Spaniards, promising obedience, and then asked Canizares to withdraw his forces to Machava. They promised that the chiefs would come to see Canizares the next day and that Indians from the palisade would bring firewood for them at Machava's council house that same day. They did not keep their promises. Canizares waited in vain for at least two or three days. It was doubtless during that delay that the rebels sent out their false report of an attack on the palisade. Then Canizares sent Chief Chamile to the palisade with what amounted to an ultimatum. Chamile returned with various rebel chiefs in tow, along with several heirs to chiefdoms, some leading men, and two Indians identified as servants of the chiefs.

Neither the residencia testimony nor the friars' critical comments about Canizares's procedure indicate what pledges of safe-conduct, if any, Canizares had given to the chiefs to persuade them to come to Machava to talk with him. The testimony suggests that Canizares to some degree had revealed earlier the orders he carried for apprehension of the revolt's leaders and those directly involved in the killings. Before the chiefs' arrival, Canizares detailed a number of soldiers and Apalachee leaders to sit beside specific rebel chieftains for the purpose of apprehending them and holding them so that they might be shackled. They were to make that move in accord with a prearranged signal he would give them. That circumstance indicates that Canizares practiced a degree of deception in luring the chiefs to Machava.

The leaders who walked into his trap included Diego, Dionisio, and Benito Ruíz, principal caciques, respectively, of Potohiriba, Machava, and Tarihica; Molina, cacica of San Juan (presumably de Guacara); María, cacica of San Juan Evanjelista; the cacica of Niaxica (doubtless the same as Niayca); Pedro, cacique of San Pablo; and the caciques of San Lucas (probably a satellite of Machava), of Santa Ana, and of San Francisco (Alonso de Argüelles 1660a:400–401; Calderón 1660:430–31; Cruz 1660:455; Gómez de Engraba 1657b:129; Hann 1986a:375; Antonio Menéndez Márquez 1660:444; Monzón 1660:411; Pedrosa 1660:380–81; Worth 1992a:268).

The identity of villages referred to only by saints' names is difficult to establish with certainty as some such names were attached to more than one western Timucua village. Inasmuch as Guacara's chief was identified as being among the rebels, it is likely that the cacica of San Juan whom Canizares captured was from Guacara. But the failure to identify her as principal cacica leaves some doubt. And Arapaha–Santa Fé had a satellite village named San Juan in 1657. The cacique of San Francisco was probably from Chuaquin, whose chief was among the rebels. But San Matheo had two satellite hamlets bearing that name. It is odd that none of the residencia witnesses mentioned San Matheo's participation in the revolt. Fray Gómez de Engraba (1986b:129) identified its chief as one of the rebels. The cacique of Santa Ana could have been from Potano's Santa Ana or a Potohiriba satellite village (Hann 1986a:374–75). Neither San Agustín de Urica nor San Agustín de Ahoica were mentioned by residencia witnesses or friars who commented on the revolt except for Martín Alcayde de Córdoba (1660:406–7). He mentioned San Agustín de Ahoica in conjunction with the rebel villages of San Francisco, Santa Fé, and San Juan de Guacara as depopulated settlements that Rebolledo had ordered revived by dismantling the northern villages of Chamile, Cachipile, Chuaquine, and Arapaha and its satellites. He described the latter's satellites as "three or four little villages (*lugarzitos*) of few people."

Canizares initially greeted the rebel chiefs in a friendly fashion and then directed them into the council house, seating them on its benches. After reprehending them for their rebellion, he asked the chiefs why they had rebelled and why they had killed the Spaniards. All but one of the residencia witnesses who referred to this episode said that the chiefs made no response and spoke only among themselves and that after Canizares repeated his questions several times, he gave the signal for apprehension of the chiefs. But the interpreter, Cruz (1660:462), testified that one of the chiefs (whose identity he did not recall) had replied that their only reason for rebelling was the order to them from San Martín's chief, who told them that the Spaniards intended to enslave them and to present most of them to the king as slaves. The chief who spoke added that, after the chiefs had conferred on the matter of revolt in Potohiriba, which he described as being "next to the village of Santa Catalina," two young men (*mozuelos*) had gone to kill Esteban Solana and that those assembled there had then gone to the forest where the palisade was built. In reply to a further question from Canizares, the rebel spokesman identified Solana's killer by name and reported that he was still in the palisade. At that point, according to Cruz, Canizares gave the signal for detention of the chiefs.

Soon thereafter, Canizares sent Santa Catalina's chief, Diego Heva (identified as Egua by Cruz) to apprehend the killers known to be in the palisade. Heva returned with Pérez's killer and an Indian who had helped kill one of La Chua's blacks. Canizares sent word to those still in the palisade that they should return to their villages, promising that he would not take any action against them. A soldier sent to the palisade later verified its abandonment. It is doubtful that all of its occupants returned to their villages in view of the settlements previously alluded to that were spoken of later as being depopulated and in need of resuscitation (Alonso de Argüelles 1660a:401–2; Alcayde de Córdoba 1660:406–7; Calderón 1660:431; Pérez de Villareal 1660:389).

Canizares held a trial the next day for Bartolomé Pérez's killer. The Indian confessed readily, without remorse, explaining his motive as revenge for earlier mistreatment at Pérez's hands. In a blending of the mores of the two worlds to which he belonged, he maintained in effect that San Martín's chief's order for the killing of the Spaniards had given him the authorization for the act in accord with the native code, although he admitted his awareness that he would eventually have to pay for that act under the Spanish code. Canizares ordered him garroted (Alonso de Argüelles 1660a:401–2; Calderón 1660:431; Cruz 1660:462–63; Sotomayor 1660:417–18).

Canizares set out for Ivitachuco that same day with the rest of his prisoners and placed them in its council house under secure guard. He sent word to Rebolledo, from there apparently, of his apprehension of most of the rebel chiefs and dispersal of their supporters without provoking an armed conflict, as the governor had ordered. Only Head Chief Lucas Menéndez and the chiefs of San Francisco Potano and Santa Fé had not been captured. Having received reports that San Martín's chief might be in Potohiriba or in Aramuqua, a ranchería alongside the Suwannee River, Canizares soon set out to search for him and to travel through a number of the former rebel villages to reassure their people about his peaceful intentions. On not finding Chief Lucas at Potohiriba or Aramuqua, Canizares traveled on to San Martín, whence he retraced the 18 leagues to San Pedro. From San Martín he had sent part of his force on to St. Augustine to give more detailed and updated reports to the governor. Sometime after Canizares's return to Ivitachuco, Diego Heva sent Francisco Hiriba with word that he had captured Lucas Menéndez. Heva asked Canizares to send a squad of soldiers to meet the natives who were bringing the captive to Ivitachuco. Alonso Argüelles took possession of the captive between Asile and Ivitachuco (Alonso de Argüelles 1660a:402; Calderón 1660:432; Cruz 1660:463; Monzón 1660:412; Pedrosa 1660:380; Worth 1992a:274, 285n.23).

Denouement under Governor Rebolledo

Receipt of Canizares's latest reports in November moved the governor to go to Ivitachuco to impose justice on the rebellion's leaders and to install new leaders to replace them. He also aimed to revive villages on the Spanish trail that were vital to St. Augustine's overland communications with Apalachee. He set out on November 27, 1656, seven fateful months after he had issued the orders to the hinterland chiefs that sparked the revolt. At San Francisco Potano and Santa Fé he apprehended their chiefs. But a subsequent search at San Francisco and Santa Ana for some ordinary Indians from those villages who were involved in the killings at La Chua was unsuccessful (Alonso de Argüelles 1660a:403; Entonado 1660:448; Ponce de León 1660:359; Puerta 1660:373; Worth 1992a:275–77). Upon his arrival in Ivitachuco, the governor began the trials of the rebel leaders and ordinary Indians who had been detained. He had brought San Juan del Puerto's 70-year-old principal chief, Clemente Bernal, to serve as interpreter. Bernal's Spanish name and his age suggest that he may have been a son of Nombre de Dios's Cacica doña María, who married a soldier named Clemente Vernal (Bernal 1660:467).

Little is known about the trials, as the *autos,* or records, for them have not been found. The residencia witnesses' testimony indicates that Rebolledo executed six of the chiefs and four ordinary Indians directly involved in the killings. The executed chiefs included the ones from San Martín, Potohiriba, Tarihica, Machava, San Francisco (presumably de Potano), and San Lucas. The bodies of the first three were left on display in Potohiriba, where the rebellion was hatched. Machava's chief was hanged on the road to his village. Rebolledo hanged San Francisco's chief and two ordinary Indians on the road to San Francisco. He hanged San Lucas's chief and the other two ordinary Indians in Asile. As Worth (1992a:279) noted, the places chosen for the display of the bodies coincided with the locations of the major activity by the rebels in a general fashion, with San Francisco standing in for La Chua because of its proximity to the hacienda and because of its chief's role in the killings. There is no mention of Santa Fé's chief's fate beyond the fact that he was replaced.

The number of leaders executed conceivably was higher. Rebolledo put the number of Indians he executed at 11 in a letter of September 1657. The 11 probably included the native Canizares executed. One residencia witness gave the number as 10 or 12. In the first of Fray Gómez de Engraba's letters cited here, he stated that "according to what they say, he hung six or seven chiefs." But the friar upped the number of chiefs hanged to 11 a little more than two weeks later. As the friar was in Havana, he possibly garbled the information he had received. In addition to the death sentences, Rebolledo handed down 10 or 12 sentences for limited terms at forced labor, some longer than others. Two of the native witnesses who testified at the residencia were still serving their terms in 1660 (Alejo 1660:469; Calderón 1660:432–33; Pasqua 1660:473–74; Ponce de León 1660:359; Rebolledo 1657b:3; Worth 1992a:278–79).

Uniqueness of the Timucua Revolt

The 1656 Timucua revolt stands apart for its relative absence of nativism as a motive or manifestation of the movement, at least on the part of its leaders. The most striking illustration of the absence of nativism is the rebels' sparing of the friars and church structures even though the friars were the primordial destroyers of the native culture. In the other three known mission-era revolts—in Guale, Apalachee, and Chacato territory—friars were prime targets of the rebels, as were their churches in at least two of those revolts. San Martín's chief's reprehension of the scalping of the Tabasca Indian also reflects the absence of nativism. It is exemplified above all in that chief's statement that he was not throwing off his allegiance to the king or abandoning the law of God. Some of the friars remained at their posts during the eight months that the rebellion endured. Immediately after the killings, a leader among the friars set out at night with a companion to speak to San Martín's chief. On locating the chief at Machava, the friar explained to him and others in a long speech the evil they had done in ordering the killing of innocent people (San Antonio et al. 1657:13).

In a masterful conclusion to his study of the revolt, Worth (1992a:320–29) portrayed the movement as primarily "the culmination of a power struggle between the Republic of Indians and the Republic of Spaniards." In the revolt the native leaders "were resisting the usurpation of their political authority and the complete integration of their aboriginal society into the colonial system of Spanish Florida." Worth argued that an inherent instability in Spanish Florida's political structure made such a revolt inevitable. The instability arose from the paradox of trying to maintain an autonomous Indian society under conditions that also encouraged assimilation of converted and acculturated Indians into a Spanish economic system based on aboriginal labor. "Optimally," Worth argued, Timucua's inhabitants "would have become a functioning part of the Spanish colonial society. Nevertheless, Timucua remained a mission province long after it should have been assimilated, leaving its caciques in the unenviable position of ruling an increasingly disfunctional society." Worth concluded that "in the final analysis, the Timucuan rebellion represented a decision by Lucas Menéndez and his fellow caciques to take up arms against the inevitable assimilation of their society into the colonial system of Spanish Florida." Their resistance only accelerated the process it was designed to halt.

The survival of all of Timucua's friars should not be overemphasized as an indication of a lack of hostility and nativism among the Indian rank and file who joined the movement. Some friars were sufficiently fearful to abandon their stations. A group of friars in Apalachee who had been designated to attend a provincial chapter in St. Augustine feared to travel without protection from a squad of soldiers. They delayed their journey until they could accompany Canizares when he traveled through the province in his search for San Martín's chief. A residencia witness attributed the survival of some of the friars who remained in Timucua territory to their having sought refuge in the northern villages that remained loyal. The difficulties some friars experienced are reflected in their leaders' account of that time of troubles. They noted the anguish those friars endured in finding themselves "reviled by the majority of the Indians, deprived of the necessary provisions, and many times forsaken and alone in their convents because the Indians gave their attention solely to their preparations for war and to their dances to which they devoted their time, living like heathens during that period." The friars' account of the mission to Machava of two of their number to talk to the chiefs reflects a certain fear and uncertainty about the reception they would receive and whether they would return alive (San Antonio et al. 1657:13).

There is no indication that the revolt spread beyond western Timucua. Because many other Timucua missions such as those in Acuera or Agua Dulce were last mentioned on the 1655 list, that supposition has sometimes been made. Those missions' disappearance undoubtedly resulted from the impact of epidemics, flight of the inhabitants, or other such causes. Only for Santiago de Ocone are there data on the cause of disappearance, which will be treated in the next chapter. The oft-repeated statement that Apalachee joined the rebels is plainly unfounded (see Hann 1988a:22). Worth (1992a:passim) presented clear evidence that the Apalachee resisted Timucua efforts to ensnare them in the revolt and that they played a prominent role in conjunction with the Spaniards in apprehending many of the rebel chiefs. Fifteen western Timucua villages are the only ones identified as having participated in the revolt, although individuals from several other villages were involved.

12.

THE TIMUCUA MISSIONS, 1657–1678

Except for the years 1657 and 1675–1678, developments during the 21 years from 1657 through 1678 are even less known than the ones for the 1616–1655 period. The only substantial sources are visitations at the beginning and end of this period. Two listings of the missions in 1675 also are of significance for locating the missions and one of them for its demographic information.

Aftermath of the Revolt

Rebolledo's execution of six western Timucua chiefs and the presumed sentencing of the remaining rebel chiefs to terms at hard labor left all of the villages whose leaders had joined the revolt essentially leaderless. Additionally, many of the villages had little or no population as those who survived fled or continued to live in the woods out of easy reach of Spanish authorities. There is no record of what action Rebolledo took immediately following the trials to remedy the situation created by his removal of so many of the leaders. He probably had several weeks to attend to that problem before beginning his visitation of Apalachee on January 15, 1657 (Hann 1986b:86). In contrast to Apalachee, where the governor held a meeting at each mission, Rebolledo conducted only a brief general visitation of what was left of western Timucua after convoking its chiefs to a meeting at Potohiriba.

That general visitation, held on February 13, 1657, is our best source for the consequences of the revolt, as much for what it does not say as for what it says. Based on the subjects brought up at the single meeting, the political and demographic restructuring of the province to guarantee continued viability of the *camino real* through western Timucua seems to have been the governor's principal objective. The following list records the villages represented at this meeting, and their leaders.

> *San Pedro de Potohiriba*—Diego Heba, principal chief
>   1. Santa Ana—María Meléndez, chieftainness
> *Chamile and San Martín*—Lázaro, principal chief
>   1. Cachipile—Francisco, chief
>   2. Chuaquin—Lorenzo, chief
> *Arapaja and Santa Fée*—Alonso Pastrana, principal chief
>   1. San Francisco Potano—Domingo, chief
>   2. San Pablo—Francisco Alonso, chief
>   3. San Juan—Juan Bautista, chief
> *Santa Elena de Machaba*—Pedro Meléndez, principal chief
>   1. San Joseph—Sebastian, chief
>   2. San Lorenzo—Dionisio, chief
> *San Matheo*—Sebastian, principal chief
>   1. San Francisco—Francisco, chief
>   2. San Miguel—Francisco Alonso, chief
>   3. Santa Lucia—Francisco, chief
>   4. San Diego—Francisco, chief
>   5. Santa Fée—Antonio, chief
>   6. San Pablo—Bernabé, chief
>   7. San Francisco—Francisco, chief
>   8. San Lucas—Lucas, chief
> *San Agustín* [de Urica? or Ahoica?]—Domingo, chief
> *Nihayca*—Lucia, principal chieftainness
> *Tari*—No leader in attendance
>   1. San Pedro de Aqualiro—Martín, chief
> *Santa María*—Alexo, chief, and Alonso, leading man
>   (Hann 1986b:104–6)

The italic names were principal villages; those preceded by Arabic numerals were satellite villages. The position of San Agustín and Santa María is anomalous in that neither of their chiefs was titled principal chief and neither was said to belong to the jurisdiction of a principal chief or to have other villages under its jurisdiction. Just prior to this time, two of western Timucua's villages, Urihica and Ahoica, bore the name San Agustín.

Comparison of the 29 villages listed with those on the 1655 list or with those whose existence during the years 1655–56 is known from other sources reveals the absence of a number of villages in 1657. Two principal villages, Asile and Guacara, were omitted in 1657. One of the San Agustíns also was omitted, as was Santa Catalina Ayepacano, the satellite of Potohiriba, and the Santa Ana in Potano. It is not clear whether Arapaha's San Juan of the visitation list is the San Juan Evangelista whose Cacica María was involved in the revolt.

Asile's absence from the list resulted simply from Rebolledo's inclusion of it in his visitation of Apalachee, possibly because it had an Apalachee as chief in 1657. Gaspar, its principal chief in 1657, was an uncle of Ivitachuco's chief (Hann 1986b:101, 102). Nothing is known of the circumstances of Gaspar's accession to that chieftainship. Asile's chief was a Timucua named Manuel in 1651. It is possible that Rebolledo gave Gaspar the position as a reward to the family of Apalachee's paramount for his resistance to the entreaties of the Timucua rebels to join the revolt. But Asile may have had special ties with Apalachee despite being Timucua-speaking. The village was described in de Soto's time as subject to Apalachee (Fernández de Oviedo y Valdés 1851:I, 534). Asile's proximity to Ivitachuco and the extensive buffer between Asile and the next Yustaga settlement to the east suggest that Asile must have had an understanding with Ivitachuco in order to have survived or, at least, to have had a tolerable existence. There is no indication of Asile's involvement in the revolt other than the killing of a soldier in its council house by a Potohiriba.

Guacara's absence from the 1657 list is likely to have resulted from the flight of its remaining population in the wake of the revolt's collapse and apprehension of its chief, Molina. It was identified as late as 1659 as one of the vital communication links still in need of being resurrected. If it had been repopulated before that date, the 1659 measles epidemic may have decimated the population anew. Its people's ferrying of travelers across the Suwannee would have given them a more-than-average exposure to traveler-borne pathogens. Yustaga recruited by Spanish authorities eventually repopulated it.

Santa Catalina de Ayepacano's disappearance doubtless resulted from the promotion of its Chief Diego Heva to the principal chieftainship of Potohiriba. His promotion probably was a reward for his service to the Spanish cause during the revolt, but it is conceivable that he was next in line to succeed to the chieftainship. Nothing is known about the procedure that Rebolledo followed in installing new chiefs to succeed those whom he executed or sentenced to forced labor except for the arrangements that he made for San Martín and Santa Fé.

San Martín emerged from the revolt leaderless and with little or no population. Rebolledo pressured Chief Lázaro Chamile to move the inhabitants of his village and those of two of its satellites to San Martín and its district to solve both problems. In acquiescing, the chief asked the governor to prohibit other natives from encroaching on the lands that he was leaving so that his people might hunt and gather fruit there. The request may also have been a subliminal reflection of his and his people's reluctance to leave the splendid isolation of their villages' northern locations far from the royal road.

The evidence is equivocal whether any or all of Chamile's people made the moves Rebolledo demanded of them during 1657. An order by the governor at the beginning of 1658 implies that they had moved in that it speaks of San Martín and other villages as though they were then in existence. The order was addressed in part "to all the caciques of the towns of the Camino Real, which are those of Salamototo, San Francisco, Santa Fé, San Martín, San Juan de Guacara, and San Pedro" (Worth 1992a:298). Yet Worth (1992a:299–300) noted that, probably at about the same time, the governor instructed his lieutenant for western Timucua to dismantle the villages of Chamile, Cachipile, and Chuaquin as well as the other northern village of Arapaha and its three or four small satellites. The lieutenant was to resettle those villages' people in San Francisco Potano, Santa Fé, San Martín, Guacara, and San Agustín de Ahoica. The lieutenant described the latter five villages as depopulated at that time because some inhabitants had died and others had fled (Alcayde de Córdoba 1660:406–7; Worth 1992a:299).

Worth's assumption that the governor dispatched his new lieutenant later in 1658 probably is correct. But the vagueness of the lieutenant's statement vis-à-vis the time frame he was speaking of, combined with Worth's uncertainty about the time of the lieutenant's appointment to the post, leaves open the possibility that the lieutenant was talking about the initial depopulation of those settlements in 1657 and that he was simply being ordered to continue the pressure that Rebolledo had applied when he first asked the chiefs to move. The lieutenant gave the same justification for the resettlement as the one Rebolledo gave during the visitation: the northern villages' distance from the royal road and that road's need for villages to maintain communication and commerce with Apalachee (Hann 1986b:104). Worth (1992a:295) aptly described the aim of Rebolledo's policy of resettlement as "the reorganization of a geographically dispersed and demographically imbalanced aboriginal society into a more or less linear series of populated way stations along the Camino Real between St. Augustine and Apalachee," noting that Rebolledo's policy "seems to have largely persisted throughout the final decades of the seventeenth century."

The policy failed, particularly in the phase launched by Rebolledo. His successor issued orders in November 1659 for recruitment of Yustaga to repopulate San Martín and three other missions along the royal road. The villages' depopulation at that time was attributed to some natives having died in an epidemic and to others having fled to the woods (D. de Leturiondo 1671). Some friars noted in 1662 that most of the Indians Rebolledo had transplanted had since fled to the woods to live with heathen natives. Observing that some had died there in apostasy, the friars asked that the survivors be allowed to return to their former homes (Spellman 1963:355). The lack of any further mention of Chamile, Chuaquin, Cachipile or Arapaha suggests that the people did not return. San Martín was last mentioned as a settled village and way station on the royal road in 1660.

The friars were prescient indeed in writing in September of 1657 that they saw Florida's native provinces and St. Augustine itself as "headed for extinction at full tilt" because of the greed-motivated policies Rebolledo and most of his immediate predecessors had pursued (Hann 1993a:7–8). But that they were not entirely impartial observers is reflected in one of their number's characterization of Rebolledo as "this criollo governor from Cartagena" in describing his oppressive treatment of the natives (Gómez de Engraba 1657a:127).

The move may have involved a downgrading in status for two of the northern villages. When Cachipile and Chuaquin were first mentioned in 1655, it was not clear whether their chiefs were then principal chiefs. But the villages' status as mission centers suggests that the chiefs were principal ones. Both became satellite villages under Rebolledo's reorganization. Chuaquin's downgrading may have been punishment for its participation in the revolt. There is no record of Cachipile's having been involved in the revolt.

The Potano region's demographic desolation was one of the motives for the coupling of Arapaha and Santa Fé. As had Chief Chamile, Arapaha's Chief Alonso Pastrana requested that the northern lands he was abandoning be reserved to him and his people so that they might hunt and gather there exclusively. Mention of Santa Fé among the missions in need of resuscitation in 1659 indicates that the moving of the Arapaha to Santa Fé was also unsuccessful. But the infusion of new people in 1659 appears to have succeeded, as Santa Fé appeared on subsequent mission lists and

survived until almost the end of the mission period. San Francisco's decline or punishment is seemingly reflected in its reduction to the status of
a satellite subordinate to Arapaha–Santa Fé.

Tarihica's inclusion among the villages that were to be summoned to
the visitation indicates that some of its people were believed to be there.
But no leader from it was mentioned as having participated in the visitation. Tarihica was represented through Chief Martín, leader of Tarihica's
satellite village, San Pedro de Aqualiro. Tarihica reappeared on later mission lists.

Little is known about Niayca, rendered here as Nihayca, whose Cacica
Lucia was identified during the visitation as a principal cacica. The only
other mention of the village stems from its involvement in the revolt. Its
cacica at that time, not identified by name, was among the rebel leaders
captured.

The status and identity of several leaders who attended the visitation
remains uncertain. The village of San Agustín represented by a Chief
Domingo (not a principal chief) could have been San Agustín de Urica or
San Agustín de Ahoica. Urica was a mission in 1655. Its 60-league distance
from St. Augustine suggests that it may have been in Yustaga. It was not
mentioned as involved in the revolt, but does not appear after 1655. Ahoica,
by contrast, was mentioned as in need of repopulation (Alcayde de Córdoba
1660:406). It had been resuscitated by 1675, when it was mentioned under the name Ajohica. The coordinates given for it in 1675 place it in Utina
Province, eliminating any pretext for arguing that Urihica and Ajohica are
variant names for the same settlement. Ajohica was fused with a mission
of Santa Catalina, three leagues distant from it, in 1675, when that Santa
Catalina appeared in the records for the first time. Subsequently Santa
Catalina was known as Santa Catalina de Ahoica or Afuica until its destruction in the mid-1680s. The survivors reemerged in 1689 in a village
named San Agustín de Ajoica (Díaz Vara Calderón 1675a; Ebelino de
Compostela 1689; Fernández de Florencia 1675a; D. de Leturiondo 1678).
Neither of the San Agustíns seems to have been involved in the revolt.

Chief Alexo of Santa María was the other unknown leader who attended the visitation. He was accompanied by a leading man named Alonso.
This village of Santa María was not mentioned elsewhere. Chief Alexo and
the chief of San Pedro de Aqualiro appear to have arrived late for the
visitation. They were mentioned apart from the rest of those attending,
after the record had been signed by the Spaniards officiating and the lone
literate western Timucua leader who was still in power after the revolt. He

was Chief Chamile, who signed his name as "Lazaro Chamile Holatama" (Hann 1986b:104–6).

Except for Urica, Yustaga's mission villages appear to have survived the revolt and the epidemics relatively intact. Yustaga was sufficiently fit demographically to supply people in 1659 to resuscitate villages in Utina and Potano territory. Potohiriba retained its position demographically and politically thereafter as Yustaga's leading village. Some Yustaga and Timucua took refuge in Apalachee during the revolt rather than fleeing to the woods or to heathen territory as others did. In a proclamation prior to his departure from Apalachee, the governor ordered that, except for those domiciled in Apalachee for two years, all Indian men and women then in Apalachee who belonged to the provinces of Timucua and Yustaga should return to their native villages within 15 days under stiff penalties for failure to comply (Hann 1986b:102–3).

Some rebel Timucua may have remained in Apalachee months after the governor's proclamation and some Yustaga may still have been trying to incite the Apalachee to revolt. As late as July 1657 a soldier conducting an investigation in Cupaica spoke of putting an Indian man and woman from San Pedro in chains. It is not clear whether they were Timucua or Apalachee or why they were being apprehended. But a few days later Apalachee's lieutenant wrote to the governor that Apalachee was very calm as far as he could see, even though its leaders had recently convened in a junta. The lieutenant observed about that meeting "that from this the Timucuan gossips have assumed that they [the Apalachee] are ready to revolt because they ask them to." The lieutenant had written in a similar vein two months earlier about warnings by the friars that there was a danger of revolt in Apalachee. He dismissed the reports, telling the governor that he "should understand that it has all been a hoax and invention of Ustacans and it is to put this cacique of San Luis in trouble because he does not welcome [them?], and, so that the Spaniards will look on him with suspicion, for it appears that even the chiefs of Apalachee have some envy toward him that he welcomes the Spaniards and esteems them" (Hann 1986b:117, 118). The latter alludes to that chief's having agreed to expansion of the Spanish garrison from 2 to 12 soldiers.

The fate of the Yustaga chief of San Matheo Tolapatafi after the revolt is another unknown. He was among the leaders who joined the revolt, but nothing is known about the role he played during it. He was not mentioned as being among the chiefs assembled at the stronghold near Machava nor as being among the ones captured. As he was not identified by name prior to the 1657 visitation, we cannot be sure he was not the Principal Chief Sebastian who represented San Matheo at the visitation, although it is unlikely that he was.

The eight satellite villages that San Matheo then had is surprising. The mission had a reputed population of only 300 in 1675. That suggests that the eight villages were very small unless San Matheo had many more people in 1657.

The settlement pattern for Utina and Yustaga, revealed by the 1657 visitation and other documents, closely parallels that of Apalachee. The pattern was one of principal villages surrounded by satellite settlements that had their own chiefs, each under the jurisdiction of the principal village's chief. But for these two western Timucua provinces there is no indication of dual centers of power that match Apalachee's rivals, San Lorenzo de Ivitachuco and San Luis de Inihayca, known later as San Luis de Talimali. San Martín's chief appears to have had no such rival. Neither did Yustaga's most important chief, the one at Potohiriba. In mission times the evidence is not as conclusive of primacy being exercised by any of the Yustaga centers as it is of San Martín's paramountcy for Utina Province and to some degree for Yustaga as well. A degree of primacy is clearer in the 1620s for Cotocochuni, which is believed to be a variant name for Potohiriba (Worth 1992a:64–67). French accounts from the 1560s definitely suggest paramount status for a chief identified only generically as Houstaqua (Lussagnet 1958:102). A case for head chieftainship could be made as well for the de Soto era's Usachile.

Chiefly positions held by women also distinguished the western Timucua politically from their Apalachee neighbors. It is not clear whether that was always the case. There was no evidence of female leadership in the de Soto era, and the meagre evidence suggests an exclusively male leadership when western Timucua's missionization began early in the seventeenth century. The epidemics' elimination of all potential male heirs could have been responsible for the change, if the appearance of female rulers indeed represents a change.

Besides attachment to their traditional lands, one of the possible reasons for the northern villages' resistance to moving to the settlements the governor had designated for them was continued abuse of native labor by soldiers traveling the royal road. The governor stipulated in article 1 of his regulatory code posted in Apalachee "that no Indian be obliged to go burdened to the presidio of St. Augustine, as has been the custom until now, unless there first precedes an order for it from the governor . . . except for the bedding and provisions of any soldier" sent on government business (Hann 1986b:89). A Timucua native's complaint about continued abusive demands by soldiers for burden-bearers prompted the governor to renew the order at the beginning of 1658. He then forbade the soldiers to de-mand more than one native bearer, and he instructed the chiefs of the six villages from Salamototo to Potohiriba through which the road passed not to grant more than one cargo-bearer unless the soldier carried an explicit written authorization signed by the governor. Even then chiefs were not to act in response to such an authorization before having the signature authenticated by the nearest friar (Worth 1992a:298–99).

Demography and Leon-Jefferson Ceramics

In summary, the 1650s were marked by a massive depopulation of the villages of western Timucua resulting from epidemics, exploitative labor practices, coerced movement of peoples from one village to another to serve Spanish purposes, and flight by many of those who were so moved and by others who were fearful of punishment for their part in the 1656 revolt or disappointed over its collapse. This was true particularly of the Utina missions that were stations along the Spanish trail to Apalachee and of the northern tier of villages when they were asked to move southward. Failure of Rebolledo's plan to move the northerners southward led to a new coerced migration of Yustaga eastward to repopulate the way stations on the trail left uninhabited or nearly so. It is not known whether any of those migrants in their turn resorted to flight as did those involved in a 1670s migration of Yustaga to create a new way station between Salamototo and San Francisco Potano.

For almost a generation after the 1657 visitation, there is another great hole in the fabric of documentation for all of Spanish Florida except St. Augustine. Not until 1675 was there another listing of the Timucua mis-sions. Many of those mentioned between 1655 and 1657 had disappeared by 1675. Apalachee constituted three-fourths or more of the total mission population by then, while most of the people living at the surviving west-ern Timucua missions were Yustaga.

Seemingly reflective of that demographic cataclysm and the demographic dislocations that accompanied it, archaeologists have found changes in ceramics in the interior mission provinces, including Apalachee, that seem in many cases to coincide temporally in a rough fashion with those demo-graphic developments recorded in the documents. Archaeologists have suggested that the pottery changes in Utina and Potano are reflective in part of a movement into those areas of natives from Apalachee, Yustaga, and northern Utina. But, in addition to those migrants from within the Spanish ecumene, they have suggested that the changes in ceramic types indicate that there was a movement of Creek into those areas of northern Florida during the middle of the seventeenth century (Milanich 1978:75).

More recently other archaeologists have proposed variants on those hypotheses that push both the ceramic changes and the in-migration supposedly responsible for the changes back to the early years of the seventeenth century. One of them, John Worth (1992a:171–82), maintained that sometime between 1606 and 1656 the aboriginal ceramics of Potano and Utina Provinces (Alachua and Suwannee Valley) gave way to "a radically different material culture known as the Jefferson culture." The change involved not only surface decoration "but also the entire range of vessel forms and the techniques of ceramic manufacture" such as "tempering materials, vessel wall thickness, vessel shape, and possibly firing temperatures." He believed that changes on that scale "argue for the presence of extra-local potters" and that "the rapid spread and eventual dominance of the introduced Jefferson culture suggests in-migration on a large scale." Worth remained a traditionalist in arguing that the migrants responsible for the change came from Apalachee and possibly Yustaga as well. He suggested that the changes they introduced may have included "subsistence strategies and other cultural phenomena associated with the Mississippian way of life." He recognized that documentation was lacking for such a massive migration, attributing its absence to the invisibility of the common Indian in the records.

Another archaeologist, Brent R. Weisman, in turn, seriously questioned the validity of the argument for an Apalachee-Yustaga origin for the Leon-Jefferson or Lamar-type ceramics found at the San Martín mission site at Fig Springs. Commenting on preliminary excavations there, Weisman (1988:7) recorded "the occurrence in unexpectedly large quantities of pottery types apparently with origins in central Georgia" that belong to the Lamar series. He noted further that "at Fig Springs, however, Lamar pottery is found in contexts that date to the early to mid-seventeenth century (if not slightly before), and is the most common decorated pottery found in and around the mission. The conclusion is certain that the mission Indians were the bearers of the Lamar ceramic tradition and must have in some way been related to Indians of central Georgia." He seemed to favor a direct migration from the Lamar area of central Georgia. His conclusion places Lamar-type ceramics at the San Martín site in significant quantity almost half a century before the type seems to have become predominant in Apalachee.

It should be recognized that part of the problem is the lack of securely dated information on the predominance of Lamar-type ceramics on Apalachee sites prior to 1656, the foundation date for that province's San Luis site, where Lamar-type ceramics predominate. John Scarry (1985:222) identified Lamar Complicated Stamped as "the major material culture marker" for his Velda Phase in Apalachee, which he dated variously as extending from 1450 or 1500 to 1633. Yet Lamar-type ceramics were not present at the 1540 de Soto winter campsite. And the relative absence of Lamar ceramics has been adjudged an indicator that the Patale site church belongs to the early period of the missionization of Apalachee (Jones and Scarry 1991:1; Jones, Scarry, and Williams 1991:59–61; Marrinan 1993:274).

In reporting his final conclusions on the excavations at Fig Springs, Weisman (1992:166–68) left the cultural identity of the mission population unresolved, observing that whether the evidence he adduced can be used to argue successfully for migration of Georgia peoples to San Martín and other Timucua missions and their replacement of the aboriginal Timucua population must await further research. But he went far beyond that hypothesis to raise a question about the identity of the entire mission population of Florida proper from eastern Timucua through Apalachee, noting that "not the least of the mysteries of the mission period is the cultural identity of the mission period Indians themselves. The uncertainty has arisen because the aboriginal pottery assemblages in the three best-studied mission provinces—Apalachee, Timucua, and St. Augustine—seem to reflect an almost complete replacement of indigenous types by complicated stamped pottery of apparent Georgia origin. Archaeologists have understandably interpreted the rather abrupt appearance of stamped pottery in the Florida mission provinces as evidence for the undocumented migration of peoples from areas of the Georgia piedmont and coastal plain, where unlike Florida, the well-developed stamping tradition persisted into late prehistoric times." Weisman seems to be suggesting the possibility that there were few or no Apalachee or Timucua by the mid-seventeenth century or earlier.

Mark Williams (personal communication 1989) believed that such a movement of Georgia peoples bearing the Lamar pottery style could well have taken place in the wake of the collapse of Mississippian societies that followed upon the de Soto intrusion. He felt that as massive a change as is seemingly reflected at Fig Springs would be difficult to explain by diffusion. Believing that native peoples were drawn toward points of power as to a magnet, Williams thought that the new Spanish center of power at St. Augustine could well have functioned thus, drawing in new peoples as north Florida's native peoples declined in numbers and the Georgians' own centers of power collapsed.

The hypotheses of a massive replacement of Timucua-speaking or Apalachee populations by Georgia natives are completely at odds with the extant documentation. The continued use of the Timucua language in eastern and western Timucua missions and of Apalachee at the Apalachee missions illustrates this reality most dramatically. Timucua and Apalachee interpreters were used for the two peoples' respective provinces as late as the 1695 visitation and even later for remnants of those peoples living in the vicinity of St. Augustine. For Timucua territory in 1695, the visitor chose Bartolo Péres, identified as a native of the province of Timucua and an interpreter of its language. For Apalachee, he chose Hubabaq Gaspar, identified as an Apalachee. The visitor in 1677 named Juan Bauptista de la Cruz as interpreter for Timucua, identifying him as having "an appointment in the language of Timucua from his majesty." He named the royal interpreter, Diego Salvador, for Apalachee in 1677. Salvador was Acueran by birth but grew up in Apalachee. He served as interpreter for both Apalachee and Timucua during the 1657 visitation.

Some migrants from the Lamar heartland had moved to Apalachee by 1675. They were Tama and Yamasee and clearly identified as such by Spaniards. Diego Salvador served as interpreter for them during the 1677 visitation in the Tama village of Candelaria in Apalachee. The use of Salvador suggests that the Tama-Yamasee's Hitchiti language, as a Muskogean language, was closely enough related to Apalachee to be understood by Apalachee-speakers or that the Tama-Yamasee had had sufficient contact with the Apalachee already to be familiar with their language. The Spaniards' conscientiousness in providing suitable interpreters is highlighted in the 1677 visitation of the Georgia coastal missions. When the visitor passed southward from the Guale mission of Santo Domingo de Asao on St. Simons Island to the same island's San Buenaventura de Guadalquini mission, he turned from his Guale interpreter, Diego Camuñas, to Juan Martín, identified as "interpreter of the language of Timuqua," in order to communicate with Guadalquini's Mocama-speakers. For his next two stops, at San Felipe and Santa María de los Yamases, he turned again to the Guale-speaking Camuñas. But for his subsequent stop at San Juan del Puerto, populated by Timucua-speakers, he relied instead on Juan Martín.

The record of the visitor's use of a Timucua interpreter at San Juan is particularly worthy of note because archaeologists have posited a Guale population for San Juan in the late mission period on the basis of Georgia-style ceramics found there. The explanation in this case possibly lies in those ceramics being those of the Mocama, who were Georgian in origin and identified documentarily as living at San Juan late in the mission period. On the visitor's last stop at Guadalupe de Tolomato, he turned again to Camuñas for the mission's Guale-speaking population living in Timucuan territory. The visitor further identified them as Guale and Georgian interlopers by identifying one of the mission's leaders as a mico, a chiefly title not found among the Timucua or even the Muskogean-related Apalachee (Antonio de Argüelles 1678:90–94; J. de Florencia 1695:154–55, 176; Hann 1986b:87, 105; D. de Leturiondo 1678:101–2). The clear documentation of the persistence of Timucua-speakers and Apalachee-speakers as the dominant element in the interior missions long after Leon-Jefferson or Lamar-style ceramics became prevalent at the inland missions makes the conclusion inescapable that an explanation other than massive migration of Lamar peoples must be found to explain this phenomenon.

There are still other considerations that rule out the migration thesis. There does not seem to be any documentary support for a substantial intrusion of Creek or any other peoples from beyond the Timucuan frontier in Georgia into western Timucua between 1570 and the mid-seventeenth century for the purposes of settlement. Indians whom Spaniards identified as Chichimeco came through Georgia as raiders at least as early as the 1620s, but they did not stay and would not have been a source of Lamar ceramics. From the 1670s on, limited numbers of Tama and Yamasee settled in Apalachee, as has been noted, but there is no evidence for even their limited presence in western Timucua except as raiders. Because Spaniards were careful generally to distinguish Indians by nation when writing about them, it is difficult to conceive of so massive an influx of newcomers over so wide an area not being recorded in some fashion in the documents. The Lamar peoples' use of the chiefly title of *mico* is a marker that almost certainly would have appeared in the records had they migrated in substantial numbers into western Timucua. Spaniards frequently recorded the title when writing of people who used *mico,* in contrast to their practice for the Timucua and Apalachee, for whom they used *cacique* rather than the indigenous *holata.*

For the 1650s, some archaeologists' belief in a mid-seventeenth century influx of Creek seems to be ruled out by Rebolledo's remark that
drastic decline of the Timucuan population removed the need for as many
friars as were then in western Timucua. The governor suggested that the
surplus might be better employed by being sent westward to launch the
Christianization of the Apalachicola (Creek) and Chacato. Had heathen
Creek then been moving into the abandoned or depopulated western
Timucua settlements, evangelization of them would seem to have provided ample work for the friars. In that event, the governor would have
been unlikely to have advanced such a proposal (Hann 1986a:384). An
alternate explanation needs to be found for the phenomena that have inspired those suggestions of migrations.

Another unanswered question is the ultimate fate of the rebel Timucua
who abandoned their villages and of the loyal Timucua from the northern
villages who were coerced into migrating southward, whom friars alluded
to as having fled to the wilderness to live with heathen natives. In view of
the apparent lack of documentary information on them, archaeology will
have to provide the solution. Close study of the ceramics of villages such as
San Martín, Guacara, Arapaha, and Santa Fé might provide a clue about
the regions in which the survivors among the fugitives eventually settled,
if distinctive features of the Lamar-type ceramics associated with each can
be established. Possible clues would be local variations in the application
of decoration, or site-specific chemical signatures or paste character, such
as the chemical signatures established for Jeddito Yellow ware that separate the one made at Kawaika-a from that made at Awatovi (Upham and
Reed 1989:60). For the Yustaga supposedly recruited in 1659 to revivify
settlements such as Guacara and Santa Fé, a similar close study of Yustaga
ceramics might provide evidence whether the appearance of Leon-Jefferson
ceramics at Santa Fé and San Francisco Potano during that era resulted
from a migration of Yustaga.

Santiago de Ocone

In 1655 Rebolledo also made an unsuccessful attempt to relocate the inhabitants of Santiago de Ocone and several other villages in its vicinity to
restore Nombre de Dios's depleted population. The Indians he sought to
move were described as fugitives from San Pedro Mocama. Ocone's chief
agreed to the migration but asked that it be delayed until his people had
harvested their crops. Infuriated, the governor imprisoned the chief in the

castillo to be held as a hostage for the coming of his people and the other chiefs from the Ocone district. The governor sent soldiers to Ocone to burn the Indians' houses and to remove the Indians to Nombre de Dios by force. Most fled into the forest and never returned to their villages or reestablished contact with Spaniards except for some who sought refuge at San Pedro. A soldier's recording of this incident was the last mention of the Ocone mission and its people (Alcayde de Córdoba 1660:404–5). Ocone was one more casualty of Governor Rebolledo's heavy hand in dealing with the Christian Indians.

Clemente Bernal and Eastern Timucua

Little else is known about eastern Timucua during this period. Nothing is known about their reaction to the 1656 revolt. There is no evidence that the rebels attempted to enlist the easterners' aid. Difficult as it is to believe, Clemente Bernal, principal chief at San Juan del Puerto, testified in 1660 that he first learned of the revolt in a letter from Rebolledo (probably in November 1656) asking him to serve as interpreter during the governor's trial of the rebel leaders and ordinary Indians involved in the killings (Bernal 1660:467).

   Chief Bernal's death around the beginning of 1665 created a power vacuum at San Juan as he had no direct heir there. The governor reported hearing that the rightful heir was Cacica Juana, then cacica at Santa María, because she was the most important (*mas principal*) leader of the district. He dispatched an experienced soldier to consult with San Juan's leaders and to install the cacica if they agreed to the validity of her claim. If she were unable to rule in person at San Juan, the soldier was to ask her to name someone to govern San Juan for her, making sure that her choice was someone with whom San Juan's leaders were content (Guerra y Vega 1665; Worth 1995:70–71). Worth (1995:35) indicated that Juana inherited Cacique Bernal's position and that she had passed it on to her niece, Merenciana, by the early 1680s. The recording of that line of succession occurred at the start of the 1680s when Yamasee living on Mocama lands on Cumberland Island complained to Governor Márquez Cabrera about tribute that Merenciana wanted from the products of their hunting and gathering on that land. She demanded a share of items such as bear fat, deerskins, acorns, and palmetto berries. The governor relieved them of the obligation of tribute but left the way open for a continued voluntary payment to Merenciana.

Earlier the three Mocama missions of San Juan, San Pedro, and Guadalquini were mentioned in passing in a 1648 order by Governor Ruíz de Salazar Vallecilla (1648). He dispatched Antonio de Argüelles by it to make sure of obedience to an earlier order in which he had stipulated that the Indians of those towns would be assembled "so that they might plant their fields and, with that, conserve the passages of the said towns." The "passages" probably referred to the towns' role in maintaining communications between St. Augustine and the Guale missions. Indians of the three Mocama missions ferried passengers from one Mocama mission to another and from Guadalquini on to the first Guale mission. The Indians were expected to provide food for the travelers even when, as was the case with Argüelles, they had their own transportation. The fields the governor ordered planted probably were devoted to meeting a communal obligation. Argüelles was also to conduct an informal visitation to learn what was going on in each village and to remedy any situation that required such action.

Chisca and Chichimeco

Chisca intruders became a problem anew for missions in Timucua Province at the beginning of the 1650s. Chisca attacked unidentified Timucua Province missions, killing some Indians and carrying off many men, women, and children. The governor instructed a soldier he sent to Guale in the first half of 1651 with supplies for its friars to inquire of the Guale leaders if they had any reports of Chisca Indians in or near their lands. If he heard any reliable reports of their presence, he was to assemble all the Guale warriors he felt were necessary and set out with them and the soldiers under his command to capture and kill the intruders and liberate their captives. Almost 30 years later Captain Matheo Luis de Florencia recalled having participated in a campaign against the Chisca in 1651 in which the soldiers endured many toils and risks until they had expelled the Chisca from the land (Charles II 1682). Another soldier, Juan Bauptista Terrazas, was sent as a scout with six soldiers and presumably with Indians as well to track down the same Chisca intruders. Terrazas reported that he had caught up with one of the Chisca bands, killing many of them, after which the rest fled, leaving the province free of them. The soldiers sent to Guale were to go in search of the Chisca even if they were two or three days distant from that province, in the hope that the Chisca would then give the Guale missions a wide berth. The governor's instructions suggest that he feared that Guale could well become a target, as it had been a little earlier for the Chisca's relatives, the Westo, whom the Spaniards called Chichimeco (Ponce de León 1651; Terrazas 1678)

Little is known about the origins of these predatory peoples whom Spaniards called Chisca and Chichimeco, and scholars differ about their identity. Spaniards' use of Chisca for questioning captured Chichimeco in the early 1660s suggests that the two groups spoke the same or closely related languages. U.S. history specialists generally identify the Spaniards' Chichimeco from the 1660s on with the Ricahecria who were driven from Virginia in 1656 and who were called Westo by the Carolinians (Crane 1956:5–6). There seems to be no doubt that the Carolinians' Westo are the Spaniards' Chichimeco. But the identification of the Ricahecria with the Chichimeco fails to account for the people whom Spaniards called Chichimeco in the 1640s or possibly earlier. Worth (personal communication 1994) believes that prior to the 1659–61 period Spaniards used the terms Chichimeco and Chisca interchangeably for predatory bands and that only from 1659 on did the name Chichimeco become associated exclusively with the Westo. He believes that the Chichimeco and Chisca were not related and that they probably became familiar with each other's languages in the course of their frontier raiding. But his identification of the Chichimeco with the Ricahecria leaves little time for such a learning process to have occurred by 1662, when two west Florida Chisca were recorded as having been employed as interpreters (Aranguíz y Cotes 1662; Hann 1988b:75–79).

Chichimeco became a threat again in 1661. Governor Alonso de Aranguíz y Cotes received word on Wednesday, June 29, 1661, that Chichimeco and other hostile tribes united with them were moving against the province of Guale "and that they were a half-day upon the road from the town of Obadalquini" (Mocama's Guadalquini). The governor sent Antonio de Argüelles northward, first to San Juan del Puerto to gather intelligence on the location, number, and intentions of the enemy force and to send back word at once. He was then to go on to Guadalquini to look for a frigate the governor had sent northward earlier with aid. The capture of Chichimeco at this time, mentioned earlier, indicates that there was an encounter between them and a Spanish force.

The governor's failure to mention San Pedro as a place where Argüelles should stop to gather intelligence suggests that it may have disappeared by 1661. By 1675 heathen Yamasee are the only natives mentioned as living on Cumberland Island. The last references to San Pedro are those of the

1655 mission list and Rebolledo's attempt to move the Ocone that same year (Alcayde de Córdoba 1660:404–5; Aranguíz y Cotes 1661). Appearance on that 1655 mission list may not be very meaningful for some of the mission villages. The smallpox epidemic of 1655 may have effectively eliminated the remaining population at some of the list's missions soon after the list was drawn up. Such appears to have been the case for Nombre de Dios in view of Rebolledo's order for coercing Ocone's inhabitants to move there. As some of Ocone's people sought refuge at San Pedro, it is conceivable that Rebolledo then turned to San Pedro for the repopulation of Nombre de Dios. In the early eighteenth century Nombre de Dios's inhabitants were identified as Mocama (Hann 1989:190).

In the late 1660s the first instance of what would soon become a significant threat to Florida's coastal native populations in general occurred at St. Augustine itself. *Repartimiento* laborers working there in 1668 were enslaved by the English pirate Robert Searles during his attack on the city. When St. Augustine's curate protested, the pirate responded that his patent from Jamaica's governor exempted only Spanish prisoners from enslavement and that it instructed him to sell any Indians, mulattoes, or blacks whom he captured as slaves without regard to their status at the time that he captured them (Sotolongo 1668). The tribal affiliation of the captured Indians was not indicated, but they are likely to have included Timucua-speakers.

Acuera

The two Acuera missions mentioned in 1655 may have effectively disappeared by early in that year. In March, Rebolledo, desperate for native labor to till St. Augustine's soldiers' fields, turned to Acuera's heathen population as a source. He had just received word from Apalachee that a great epidemic had so devastated the populations of western Timucua and Apalachee and had left so many others ill that the provinces could not send the usual contingent of repartimiento workers. The governor noted that he then resolved to send agents to the "province of Ybiniyutti [Acuera] and to others of that region so that from the heathen Indians who live in the said province and some fugitive Indians (*cimarrones*), who have fled from the word of the Gospel, they may be gathered together and brought to this city in order that some fields may begin to be worked with them, since the season is very far advanced—until further news can be had from the province of Apalachee." If San Luis and Santa Lucia de Acuera were still viable settlements at that date, one would expect that they would be tapped to some degree, even if they had already contributed an allotment of laborers, in preference to the dragooning of heathen Acuera and searching for fugitives from the missions. (It is unlikely that the two villages had already supplied laborers, for the governor's letter implies that no planting had yet been done.) The governor instructed his envoy to take out people from each heathen village proportional to its total population and to bring all the cimarrones whom he could find. He was to arrange for this as best he could with the heathen chiefs of those provinces, treating them kindly but firmly (Rebolledo 1655a). It is not known what success the governor had in this endeavor. The continued viability of the heathen villages suggests again that epidemics struck the mission centers more severely than other settlements in the same district.

Despite disappearance of the Acuera missions, heathen Acuera communities survived into the 1690s at least, two generations after Spanish interaction with them was believed possibly to have ended with the Timucua revolt of 1656 (Deagan 1978:112). Heathen Acuera reappeared first in a 1678 criminal case involving an Acuera murderer. It is not clear whether his killings represent a legacy of ill will toward Spaniards and Christian Indians allied with them, or an aberration of the natives' pursuit of warrior status, or simply the actions of a sociopath. In addition to the light it throws on the little known Acuera, the case is of interest as well for information it provides on the cimarrona phenomenon and Spanish reaction to it.

The principal actors in this drama were a young heathen Acuera warrior named Calesa, about 25 to 30 years old, and a Christian Potano woman named María Jacoba, about 35 years old. Two lesser figures were Cacique Jabahica (rendered also as Jabajica), uncle of Calesa and leader of Calesa's native village of Alisa, and an unnamed kindly Acuera inija, who seemingly was ultimately responsible for Calesa's detention by Christian Indian and Spanish authorities.

Calesa's crime was a series of killings that seem to portray him as a seventeenth-century Native American serial killer. He was accused of killing up to six people. When native authorities at San Francisco Potano first detained him, he allegedly admitted to having killed five people, all natives—four Christians and one heathen. In his formal testimony before the governor, Calesa admitted to only three killings. The first victim was a Christian Indian named Lorenzo, whom he took out to the woods of La Chua to hunt alligators. When the opportunity arose, he hit Lorenzo with a hatchet and returned to his village, leaving Lorenzo behind for dead. Lorenzo was only badly wounded, however, and made his way back to La Chua Hacienda, where he died of his wounds after several days. The second killing Calesa admitted to was that of a heathen Acuera. The third victim was a Christian Indian named Alonso, who was in the company of María Jacoba when Calesa and his band encountered the two near the banks of the Salamototo (St. Johns River). Calesa claimed that he killed Alonso at the specific orders of Chief Jabahica; that he had sought to dissuade Jabahica from that order because the Spaniards would punish the killer if he were captured; and that Jabahica had responded that Calesa's own life would be forfeit if he did not carry out the order. María Jacoba testified that she was to have been a fourth victim. She escaped death only through the intervention of the inija, who arrived at the head of a second band of Acuera before Calesa could kill her.

Calesa's public defender argued diminished responsibility for his client. He insisted that the governor should recognize that Calesa, as a heathen, did not acknowledge any authority in his land other than his uncle, Chief Jabahica; that the chief had given Calesa specific orders to kill Alonso despite Calesa's having objected to doing so three times; and that he had killed the other two in response to a general order by the chief to his people. Calesa's defender also propounded an argument suggesting that in the Spaniards' perception of the warrior ethos, a rather blurred line distinguished the killing of enemies in pursuit of noroco status, on the one hand, from simple murder, on the other. The defender noted that, "it being a general rule, as it is among the Indians, both heathen and Christian, [that] their greatest exploit (*valentía*) and trophy is to kill their enemies to obtain the name of *noroco*, he and the rest killed those whom they were able to in virtue of the said order both for the said [status] and to serve their chief. And as savages (*bárbaros*) ignorant of the evil that they were doing, if they knew that they would be punished for it, they would not have done it." (The same conclusion is suggested by aspects of a 1695 case involving a native of Yustaga's Potohiriba, which will be discussed later.) When he was captured, Calesa was wearing a headpiece called a *xadote*. Each time he killed someone, Calesa added a strip of deerskin (*gamuzita cortada*) to it to proclaim his exploits.

Calesa revealed in his testimony that his name as an adult was Yazah and that Calesa was the one he had received as a child. But the Spaniards persisted in calling him Calesa. A native witness described Calesa as a very evil name, but did not say what it signified. Calesa described his occupation as "hunter." Neither he nor María Jacoba was able to say how old he or she was. But Calesa was sufficiently acculturated that, in order to convince the governor that he had committed no more than three murders, he made the sign of the cross and, under it, repeated his statement. As a non-Christian, he had not been put under oath before his testimony. He was asked merely to promise to tell the truth in responding to the questions put to him.

María Jacoba's crime was her status as a cimarrona and her association with Calesa at the time of one of his murders. She identified herself as "native to the village of San Francisco de Potano, a vassal of the cacica of Santa Ana." She testified that she had lived with her husband for six years after their marriage, and after that "she went to the woods, from whence she came every year to go to confession at the proper time and she lived with her husband for some days while he was alive, and then she went back and forth to and from the woods and that this had been her style of living up until now." A runaway black slave had first brought her to the woods and kept her with him for some days 14 or 15 years before her trial. If accurate, that information suggests that she was married around 14 years of age. Some time prior to María Jacoba's encounter with Calesa, the owner of the La Chua Hacienda, Captain Tomás Menéndez, had captured her and sent her to his house in St. Augustine. There an Indian named Alonso, who worked for Menéndez, became enthralled with her and suggested that they run away together. She claimed that she had sought to dissuade him and that when she fled from Menéndez's house by herself, Alonso followed her and caught up with her on the trail of San Nicolás, which led to the St. Johns River crossing known to the English as the Cow Ford (site of the beginning of Jacksonville in 1822). After crossing the river on a raft that they built, they camped near an arroyo. On their fourth day there, while Alonso was hunting for deer and María Jacoba was pulling up ache in a thicket (*mata*) of it, Alonso encountered Calesa and his brother Pequatanalis and other Indians. Calesa killed Alonso at once, leaving him where he fell. They then carried her off to where they were camped. While they were making arrangements for killing her, another troop of heathen Acuera joined them and they suspended her execution and went off, leaving her alone with an iniha who was part of the second troop. He had been grieved over the killing of Alonso and had told the other Indians not to kill her. Later, he instructed Calesa and his brother to bring her safely to her village and told her secretly to have Potano's caciques apprehend the brothers as evil men. It was thus that Calesa was captured. The public defender argued in mitigation of María Jacoba's cimarrona status that, even though she lived in the woods as a runaway, she had done no harm to anyone while there and was an inhabitant of the woods by nature.

The severity with which Spanish authorities viewed the runaway's rejection of sedentism is reflected in the carrying out of her sentence of 100 lashes despite her defender's pleas for mercy. The officials were more receptive to his pleas for Calesa. His initial sentence of death was commuted to forced labor for life in Havana's Castillo del Morro.

It is not known whether the attempted apprehension of Chief Jabahica was successful. María Jacoba testified that he was in a little place called Biro Zebano that was close to Piriaco (Hann 1992a:451–74, passim).

Acuera appear in the records for the last time a generation later in association with a people having the Timucua-sounding name of Ayapaja, which means "forest-dwelling" or "forest-house." Ex-governor Diego de Quiroga y Losada reported in 1697 that while he was governor (1687–93) he had gathered the heathen Indians of Ayapaja and Acuera in the village of Ivitanayo. He served as godfather when the chief of the two bands was baptized. The Ayapaja's name, as well as their union with the Acuera under one chief, suggests that they may have been Timucua-speakers. But the evidence is equivocal. The name cropped up again in the form Aypaja in 1696 in the account of the killing of Fray Luis Sánchez at the Jororo mission of Atoyquime. A young chief living there, described as a "native of Aypaja," was killed when he opposed the Jororo's killing of their friar. In reporting the incident, Governor Laureano de Torres y Ayala (1697) identified Aypaja as one of the places of Jororo Province, noting that Aypaja's people had not joined the rebellion but had moved to San Antonio Anacape in the rebellion's wake. The Jororo were Mayaca-speakers rather than Timucua-speakers (Hann 1993a:111, 118).

The Acuera-Ayapaja presence at Ivitanayo ended soon after Quiroga completed his term as governor. Quiroga ([1697]) reported that they had gone to live in the woods, observing that Ivitanayo had been dismantled and that the Indians had left "because of the little attention that was given to supporting them and befriending them" as he had done during his term. Conceivably, the Aypaja cacique killed at Atoyquime was the cacique who was Governor Quiroga's godson. The Aypaja may be the heathens from the Rinconada de Carlos mentioned as belonging to the Piaja nation, who were living in a village near St. Augustine in 1726. The Piaja in that village consisted of 19 men, 11 women, and eight children (Hann 1991a:6, 146, 366–67; 1993a:126–28, 131–32). There does not appear to have been any mention of the Piaja or Aypaja after 1726.

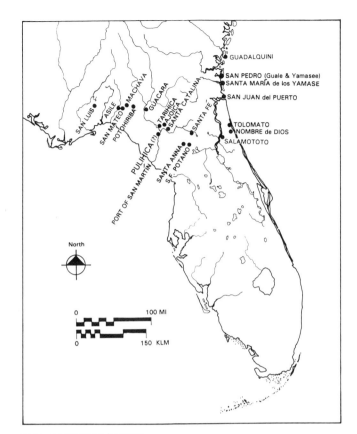

Timucua missions in 1675

Mission Lists of 1675

After almost 20 years marked by a dearth of information on the missions among Timucua-speakers, the years from 1675 to early 1678 provide a relative abundance of data, revealing the missions that were still extant and including the first general demographic information on individual missions since the first years of the seventeenth century. The two 1675 lists provide the first demographic information for most of the missions on them because few of them existed at the beginning of the century; the information includes minor discrepancies that involve the distances between villages, the number of places mentioned, and other concerns.

Most of the discrepancies can be accounted for. Many of the inconsistencies involving distances arose from one author's rounding off the figures. The six-month or more time difference that separates the 1675 lists accounts for other discrepancies. The bishop who composed one of the lists was in Apalachee in January of 1675, having set out for Nombre de Dios on October 18, 1674. The list by Apalachee's lieutenant, Juan Fernández de Florencia, dates from July 1675. The bishop described San Francisco Potano as unpopulated, while the lieutenant gave it a population of 60. The bishop's secretary, Palacios, supported the lieutenant in stating that the bishop confirmed people from Potano's San Francisco, Santa Ana, and the La Chua Hacienda while he was at Santa Fé. Santa Ana existed as a separate village when the bishop and his secretary traveled westward through Potano. Subsequently, Santa Ana's people moved to San Francisco because of the latter's small population, and in 1678 they constituted the majority of San Francisco's population. A similar explanation probably accounts for the lieutenant's failure to mention Ahoica. Its people had been moved to Santa Catalina by 1678 because of Ahoica's small population. In listing the coastal villages of what had been eastern Timucua territory in 1655, the bishop also mentioned more villages than did the governor's agent for that region, Pedro de Arcos. Not all the discrepancies between the bishop's list and the one by Arcos are so easily resolved.

List for 1675 by Bishop Díaz Vara Calderón

Doctrina of Nombre de Dios, 1/2 league north of St. Augustine, 30+ householders

Doctrina of la Natividad de Nra. Señora de Tolomato, 2 l. north of St. Augustine (Guale)

Doctrina of San Juan del Puerto, 10 l. from Tolomato (Timucua)

Doctrina of Santa María, 6 l. from San Juan del Puerto (Yamasee)

Doctrina of San Phelipe, 3 l. from Santa María (Guale)

Doctrina of San Buena Ventura de Guadalquini, 9 l. from San Phelipe (Timucua)

Doctrina of Sto. Domingo de Asahô (Guale), 6 l. from Guadalquini

Doctrina of San Diego de Salamototo, 10 l. from St. Augustine (Timucua)

Doctrina of Santa Fée, 20 l. from Salamototo

Doctrina of San Francisco, uninhabited, 3 l. from Santa Fée, to the south and to one side of it

Doctrina of Santa Catalina, 12 l. from Santa Fée

Doctrina of Ajohica, 3 l. away

Doctrina of Santa Cruz de Tarihica, 2 l. away

Doctrina of San Juan de Guacara, 7 l. away

Doctrina of San Pedro de Potohiriba, 10 l. away

Doctrina of Santa Helena de Machaba, 2 l. away

Doctrina of San Matheo, 4 l. away

Doctrina of San Miguel de Asyle, 2 l. away and 2 l. from Hibitachuco (Díaz Vara Calderón 1675a)

Combined List for 1675 Drawn from Those by the Governor's Agents

Doctrina of Guadalquini, 1-1/2 leagues from the place of Ocotonico, 40 persons, Fray Pedro de Luna

Doctrina of San Phelipe, 6 l. from Guadalquini, 36 persons, Fray Pedro de Lastra

First Village of the Isle of Mocama, 3 l. from San Phelipe, 60 heathen Yamasee

Place of Ocotoque, on Isle of Mocama, 1 l. from first village, 40 heathens

Place of La Tama, 2 l. from Ocotoque, 50 heathens

Place of Santa María, 1/2 l. from Tama, 40 heathens

Doctrina of San Juan del Puerto, 3 l. from Santa María, 30 persons, Fray Diego Bravo—last place of the province of Guale

Place of San Miguel de Asile, 1-1/2 l. from Yvitachuco, 40 persons

Doctrina of San Matheo, 2-1/2 l. from San Miguel, 300 persons

Doctrina of Santa Elena de Machava, 3 l. from San Matheo, 300 persons

Village of San Pedro, 1-1/2 l. from Machava, 300+ persons

Doctrina of San Juan Guacara, 9 l. from San Pedro, 80 persons

Santa Cruz de Tarigica, 8 l. from San Juan, 80 persons

Santa Catholina, 5 l. from Tarigica, 60 persons

Santa Fée, 9 l. from Santa Catholina, 110 persons

San Francisco, 4 l. from Santa Fée, 60 persons

Village of Salamototo, 16 uninhabited leagues from San Francisco, 40 persons (Arcos 1675; Fernández de Florencia 1675a)

The following is a translation of Pedro Palacios's (1675) notes on the bishop's journey as far as Tarihica. (The copy I used ends as it does here.)

We departed from Havana on Saturday, August 18, 1674 with the Fleet. We separated from it on Monday the 21st to reconnoiter Cape Canaveral. We arrived at the St. Augustine promontory (*punta*) at eight in the evening. We entered by way of the bar of the port on Wednesday the 23rd. The visitation began on the next day. There was no accusation (*delaccion*) against anyone. The bishop conferred minor orders on seven sons of honorable citizens and distributed a thousand pesos in alms to poor honest widows who were impoverished by the hurricane that struck that northern coast on the 17th of the aforesaid August, which flooded almost all the city.

We took our leave from them on October 18, going to the place of Nombre de Dios half a league away. And we went to sleep at country house (*quinta*) named La Rosa five leagues farther on. After traveling the same distance on the following day, we arrived at the place of San Diego de Salamototo, where we remained for two days. On Sunday the 22nd, we crossed the great river of Currents in two canoes tied together (*atados*), which has a width of a league and one-half and is very turbulent (*tormentosa*). We walked (*anduvimos*) 6 leagues on Monday to an arroyo named Ajano hibitachirico, which is [means] the same as river of Little Acorns. And on Tuesday [we traveled] another six [leagues] to another arroyo named Aquila, which means "stand of cane (*bejuco*)" or "grape arbor (*parra*)." After having endured three nights in an uninhabited area [exposed] to the inclemency of the skies, richly endowed with swamps, arroyos, and rains, after having walked for seven leagues, we arrived at the place of Santa Fée, where the sergeant-major don Tomás de Medina resides, [who is] head chief of all that Timuquana Province alias Ustana. We tarried there for four days. Those of the little places (*lugarcillos*) attached to this *doctrina* were confirmed, namely, San Francisco (S. F^{co}), Santa Ana, and those from the *quinta* of La Chua. From there [we went] 7 leagues to an arroyo where we slept. The next day we went two leagues from the arroyo to rest (*sestear*) at Santa Catalina and we went another three leagues farther on to sleep at the place of Ajoluca. From there we went three leagues to the place of Tarihica where we ate and to sleep.

It is not clear whether Salamototo occupied the site of the earlier river-crossing settlement of San Diego de Elaca, which it replaced. The 1655 list placed Elaca seven leagues from St. Augustine rather than the 10 leagues the bishop and his secretary posited as Salamototo's distance from St. Augustine.

For the coastal villages from San Juan del Puerto northward there are major discrepancies between the lists that the bishop and Arcos provided that involve distances between villages and other factors. But a 1683 document seems to resolve most of the problems. Juxtaposition of the two lists' data on distances highlights the problems.

	Bishop	*Arcos*
San Juan to Santa María	6 leagues	3 leagues
Santa María to San Phelipe	3 leagues	6-1/2 leagues
San Phelipe to Guadalquini	9 leagues	6 leagues
Guadalquini to Asaho	6 leagues	4-1/2 leagues

Arcos placed three settlements between Santa María and San Phelipe that the bishop omitted. The bishop described Santa María as a mission. Arcos characterized its inhabitants as 40 heathens and did not mention a resident friar. Arcos also mentioned two villages between Guadalquini and Asaho that the bishop omitted, probably because he never saw them, having taken the water route from Guadalquini to Asaho. Guale's lieutenant, Francisco Barbosa (1683), provided a clear solution to the discrepancy involving the distance between Asaho and Guadalquini. He indicated that Guadalquini and Asaho were four leagues apart if one took the land route between them but six leagues apart if one went by water. Barbosa's statement that San Phelipe was eight leagues from Guadalquini and that one crossed two bars to reach San Phelipe indicates that the bishop's nine leagues were closer to reality than Arcos's six. Barbosa clearly placed San Phelipe on Cumberland Island, noting that it was three leagues from San Phelipe "to the bar of San Pedro [the mouth of the St. Marys River] which comes to be the island of Santa María [Amelia Island]". But Barbosa's account supports Arcos in identifying a village of San Pedro on Amelia Island's northern tip as one the Yamasee had abandoned. Thus Arcos's placement of Santa María only three leagues from San Juan and the bishop's placement of Santa María only three leagues from San Phelipe are erroneous if both of them were talking about the village of Santa María on Amelia Island's southern end when they made those statements.

Barbosa's data, however, provide possibly plausible explanations for the bishop and Arcos's having made those statements. It is possible that the bishop was thinking of the island of Santa María when he gave Santa María's distance from San Phelipe as three leagues. When Barbosa alluded to the six-league passage from Santa María village to San Juan, he reported: "One crosses a bar, and once this bar, which they call of Santa María, is passed, there is an island which has three leagues that they call of Zarabay. It is possible to come by land down to in front of the landing place for San Juan, where one calls them by an harquebus-shot and they take one over." It is quite possibly that three-league walk that Arcos had in mind when he spoke of Santa María as being three leagues from San Juan.

It is worthy of note that Barbosa's total of 20 leagues as the distance between San Juan and Guadalquini coincides with the distance given on the 1655 mission list in contrast to the 15-1/2 and 18 leagues of the 1675 lists. If one adjusts for the bishop's one-league overstatement of the distance from San Phelipe to Guadalquini and Arcos's extra one-half league, both understate the distance by three leagues. As that is precisely the distance from Sarabay Island's northern tip to Santa María village and from that village to Santa María Island's northern tip and from that point to San Phelipe, there is reason for believing that Arcos and the bishop used the name Santa María loosely to refer to a village, island, and bar.

The correct listings by the bishop and Barbosa of six leagues as the distance between San Juan and Santa María village are confirmed also by listings from the 1690s and by archaeological findings. Data from the 1690s place the Santa Catalina de Guale mission of Amelia Island six leagues from San Juan, and both documents and archaeological research link that Santa Catalina site with the Yamasee Santa María of the 1670s. The church cemeteries of both have been found side by side.

But Arcos was not entirely in error. Documentation from the 1690s and archaeological research support his placement of other villages on Amelia Island. His La Tama, one league north of Santa María in 1675, was apparently the location of the 1690's San Felipe, while his unidentified first village "on the Isle of Mocama" was Barbosa's San Pedro. San Pedro became Santa Clara de Tupiqui in the 1690s, which was referred to occasionally as San Pedro de Tupiqui (Arcos 1675; Barbosa 1683; Bullen and Griffin 1952:37–64; Díaz Vara Calderón 1675a; Fernández de Florencia 1675a; Hann 1987:20–1; Palacios [1675]; Saunders 1992:139–81).

The lists from 1675 and the 1677 visitation record show that, except for San Juan del Puerto in the south and Guadalquini in the north, the numerous Timucua-speakers who earlier occupied the coastal zone between those two points had disappeared.

There has been confusion over the origin of the San Phelipe settlement of 1675 and the tribal affiliation of its inhabitants. Scholars have identified them variously as Timucua, Guale, and Yamasee. The majority were Guale and a few were Yamasee. There is no evidence that any were Timucua. The 1675 San Phelipe was probably a lineal descendant of one known earlier as San Pedro Atulteca or San Felipe de Athuluteca or simply San Felipe. Friars attested to the mission's Guale affiliation in 1676, identifying it by the name S^{cti} Philipi de Guale (Parete et al. 1676).

This mission first appeared on a 1616 list as San Pedro de Atulteca. Geiger (1937:247) classified it as Guale. It reappeared in a 1647 governor's

order identified as Guale (Menéndez Márquez and P. B. Horruytiner 1647c).
It was identified in 1655 simply as San Felipe, without the native component Tuluteca. Misled by the name change and seemingly following the
interpretation of Manuel Serrano y Sanz (1912:74, 87, 91, 95, 132), Bolton
and his student Lanning identified 1655's San Felipe mission with the sixteenth-century fort of that name at Santa Elena. Serrano y Sanz placed the
mission at Santa Elena as late as 1680 and seems to have found no problem in giving Santa Elena's distance from St. Augustine as 60 leagues while
reproducing the 1655 list placing San Felipe a mere 54 leagues away, only
four leagues farther north than Guale's Santa Catalina (Bolton 1925:21;
Lanning 1935:203). Swanton (1922:322, 324) first clearly established the
connection between the San Felipe name and the native name Tuluteca in
reproducing a 1680 list where the mission appeared as Señor San Felipe de
Athuluteca, with a note by Swanton that in 1643 its name was given as
San Pedro de Atuluteca. However, Swanton does not seem to have linked
Tuluteca with the San Felipe of 1655, which was clearly located in Guale
territory. He identified Athuluteca of the 1680 list as Timucua on the basis
of the 1675 San Felipe's presence in formerly Timucua territory. Deagan
(1978:101–2), however, noting a governor's remark that all of the Indians
on the Isle of Mocama were heathens, concluded that this meant a
repopulation of the area, observing that "it is probable that the new mission served the Yamasee rather than the Tacatacuru or other southeastern
Georgia eastern Timucua remnants." A more careful reading of Arcos's
statement that San Felipe "has thirty-six persons, between men, children,
and women and some pagans" (Boyd 1948:183) indicates that the 36 were
other than pagan and hence Christian. It is most likely the Christians would
be Guale. Their Guale identity was confirmed in the 1695 visitation. San
Felipe's 100 or so inhabitants at that time included Guale from Ajiluste,
Taljapu, Hospo, Aspogue, and Faxquis as well as Tuluteca (Pueyo 1695:229).

There are some distance discrepancies between the two 1675 lists for
western Timucua for which there seems to be no explanation. Fernández
de Florencia placed Santa Fé and Santa Catalina only nine leagues apart,
in contrast to the bishop's 12 leagues. But both agreed that Santa Catalina
and Tarihica were five leagues apart, with the bishop placing Ahoica between the two. There are also one-league discrepancies between the two
lists for the distances between Tarihica and Guacara and between Guacara
and Potohiriba. But both place Guacara on the bank of a large river that
the natives called Guacara. San Martín was the Spaniards' name for the
river (Díaz Vara Calderón 1675a; Fernández de Florencia 1675a).

Visitations of 1677–1678

Visitations of the coastal and hinterland missions held in 1677 and 1678 generated a third listing of the missions. It differs from the 1675 listings only in the elimination of Ajohica, which had become so depopulated by 1678 that the remnant of its people had moved to Santa Catalina. Beginning with the 1680 list, variants of Ahoica would be attached to the name Santa Catalina, although Ahoica's Christian name of San Agustín would resurface as well after Santa Catalina was attacked in 1685 (D. de Leturiondo 1678:122–45).

The 11 western Timucua missions mentioned on the three lists are considerably fewer than had been mentioned in the 1650s. Urica, Arapaja, Cachipile, Chuaquin, Chamini or Chamile, and San Martín had disappeared in the interim. By way of compensation Santa Catalina was mentioned for the first time in the 1670s, but that does not necessarily mean that it did not exist as early as 1655 or even earlier. Only the missions with resident friars were listed in 1655.

Spanish authorities as well as Ahoica's chief may have had an ulterior motive in permitting or promoting the fusion of Ahoica with Santa Catalina. During the visitation at Santa Catalina, Chief Lucas of Ahoica reported that he had struck a deal with Nicolás Suárez, a Spaniard, to establish a cattle ranch between the abandoned site of Ahoica and Santa Catalina. He claimed that the lands in question were his very own and that the cattle would pose no threat to the crops of neighboring places. It was probably not just a coincidence that Suárez was surrendering his claim to lands in a place he called Hivitanayo to permit establishment of a new native settlement there that would serve as a way station on the long uninhabited stretch between Salamototo and San Francisco Potano. Spanish interest in creating the new settlement probably led Leturiondo to broker the business deal between Chief Lucas and Suárez. Suárez was to live on the ranch at Ahoica (D. de Leturiondo 1678:129, 132–33).

To establish the new settlement, Spanish authorities moved to draw yet another draft from Yustaga's population pool. The visitor asked the leaders assembled for the general session at Potohiriba "whether there was some minor cacique among them who might be willing to go to . . . Hivitanayo with some families because of its being for their welfare, as it is, and for the welfare of those who come and go to and from these provinces." The natives' immediate reaction was negative; they alleged that it was too far away for carrying their household goods and that they lacked the wherewithal for sustaining themselves during the first year while they cleared land and built a village. The session concluded on that note. But Leturiondo apparently did some jawboning after the session. On the next day, Antonio, a chief from San Matheo, volunteered to establish the new settlement with some of his relatives and eight families selected from San Pedro, Machava, and San Matheo. His offer was conditioned on a pledge of assistance from the king in providing transport to carry them, their maize, and other possessions to Ivitanayo, and also axes for the work of clearing their new fields and opening the royal road to the new settlement. The visitor agreed to meet the chief's demands. He wrote at once to the deputy-governors, Juan Fernández de Florencia and Andrés Pérez, who were in charge of Apalachee and Timucua Provinces, respectively, "the one so that he might arrange for some canoes from the Tocopacas so that they might transport the maize and the rest of the goods that he spoke of through Basisa [Wacissa] to the River of St. Martin [the Suwannee] as far as Pulihica. And from there the cacique of Santa Fée obligated himself to transport them on horseback to the said region of Hivitanayo and to the Captain Andrés Pérez so that two soldiers might come escorting them to it and with his excellency promising to the families alluded to that he would petition the governor and royal officials about the need for the axes." Leturiondo assured the natives of his confidence that the royal officials would provide the axes and promised them that the lands of Ivitanayo would be deeded to them in the king's name. As an added inducement, he pledged that, "until the village should be well established and have plenty of people, digging Indians (*yndios de Caua*) would not be taken from it for some years." To the migrants' request for a friar he responded that, although the current shortage of friars ruled that out at the moment, he felt that, with arrival of an expected new band, the Franciscans' provincial would meet their need (D. de Leturiondo 1678:129–30).

The Spanish husband of the cacica of San Francisco Potano, Bartolomé Francisco, also had an interest in promoting the settlement of Ivitanayo. In November 1677, he requested of the royal officials that the people of his wife's village be relocated to the Ivitanayo site. Leturiondo found the natives definitely opposed to such a move, although Bartolomé had stated in his petition that both his wife and the Indians in her village were willing to move to the "woods of Bitanayo." The royal officials at St. Augustine took the position that the matter could be resolved only in Havana. But Leturiondo, during his visitation at Potano, assured the natives that they would not be required to move to Ivitanayo. The visitation record reveals that, except for San Francisco's cacica, all that village's people were subjects of Santa Ana's cacica who had been relocated there four or five years earlier because of the disappearance of San Francisco's own population (D. de Leturiondo 1678:134–36).

It is not known how quickly Ivitanayo was established or if a friar was assigned there. This was a time when a number of old established missions went without friars. Ivitanayo did not appear on a mission list composed late in 1680, but it had 20 families, or 100 people, in 1689. The visitor found the place deserted in 1695. Although he sent orders back to San Francisco that the fugitives were to be found and returned to Ivitanayo, the village does not appear on subsequent listings. Some of the fugitives settled eventually at Salamototo (Ebelino de Compostela 1689; J. de Florencia 1695:206–7).

Pulihica and the Port of San Martín

Little is known about the Pulihica alluded to during the Ivitanayo negotiations except that it was a landing place on the Suwannee. It is not clear whether there was a settlement there. It appears to have been distinct from another landing referred to as Port San Martín. Port San Martín conceivably served the anchorage off the mouth of the Suwannee where ships too large to navigate the river's shallow bar anchored while their cargo was lightered out to them on Tocobaga canoes. Amy Bushnell (1978:416, 424; 1988:2) identified Port San Martín with the Old Town Hammock and placed San Martín de Ayacutu there as well. Placement of the mission at Old Town is incompatible with Diego Peña's (1717) mention that the mission's ruins were only six leagues, or 15 and one-half miles, beyond the ruins of the Santa Fé mission.

The Western Timucua's Complaints in 1678

Because of a complaint made to the governor by Machava's friar, the visitation record reveals that Machava was then the seat of Timucua Province's deputy-governor and of a small garrison. That status probably reflects Yustaga's demographic primacy within the province, although the lieutenant and his garrison had moved to Santa Fé only seven years later. The friar had complained about the soldiers' causing losses to the natives, but the friar apparently had been no more specific than that in his complaint.

The visitor urged the Machava to speak freely about any injuries, losses, or harassment they had suffered from the soldiers. The village leaders expressed their embarrassment "over such complaints made in their name," remarking that they were capable of making such complaints themselves to the governor when there was a need. They assured Leturiondo that they had no occasion to do so and had nothing but praise for the lieutenant and the soldiers and gratitude for their protection, remarking that the place would have been depopulated by then were it not for the soldiers' presence. They suggested that the friar's complaint concerned an instance in which the Indians had divided a deer they brought back from a hunt, giving "one-half of it to the soldiery voluntarily and the other half to the religious," noting that the friar had scolded them for not bringing him the whole deer.

The Machava visitation record is exceptional in providing the only evidence during the entire seventeenth century of the natives' having access to alcoholic beverages on the missions. Leturiondo admonished the Machava "that they should extinguish the use of wine, both for the expense that it involves and for the offense to God that results from its use, not to mention that the same was ordered in the last visitation" (D. de Leturiondo 1678:125–27). Trade on the Suwannee to and from La Chua Hacienda was probably the source of the alcohol.

Guacara's natives asked the visitor to see to it that they were provided with a new canoe for the ferry service across the Suwannee, alleging that the one then in service was not of any real use. They also asked for food as compensation for the great amount of time they devoted to the ferry service, which kept them from providing adequate food for themselves. They noted that Indians had been deserting Guacara for that reason and that "at present only twenty people between young and old have remained in it." The visitor promised to present their request to the governor so that they might receive an annual subsidy (D. de Leturiondo 1678:131).

Santa Catalina's natives' only complaint was a perennial one about a puritanical incumbent friar who restricted and even prohibited some of their customary dances. They noted that he at times would not give permission or, when he gave permission, would ring the bell early for ending the dancing. Leturiondo gave them full permission, such as they had received earlier from the governor and the Franciscans' provincial, to hold any of the dances that they had approved on that occasion. Leturiondo remarked that there was no need for them to seek the friar's permission as this matter was not within the friar's competence. At some earlier date the Indians apparently had performed their repertoire of dances for the provincial, who had prohibited some and approved the rest (D. de Leturiondo 1678:132).

Leturiondo's instructions for Timucua Province's lieutenant as he wound up the visitation of the province reflect intolerance toward unregulated migration from village to village. He decreed "that no person from this province can move from one place to another without permission of the said lieutenant," to be given only after the lieutenant had looked into the reasons for the move and assured himself that it was not made to escape work or for some similar purpose. No vagabonds were to be allowed in the villages. Leturiondo decreed a fine of 12 deerskins per case for any chief and iniha who admitted an outsider into their village without the requisite permission from both the lieutenant and the chief of the migrant's village of origin. For the moment, however, Leturiondo exempted Ivitinayo from that regulation, authorizing unrestricted migration to it until it should become a village in due form. He also stipulated that, if the lieutenant had occasion to exile anyone for crimes or concubinage or other just causes, he might exile them to Ivitanayo to further augment its population (Leturiondo 1678:139–40).

13.

TIMUCUA DEMOGRAPHY

The village list prepared by the governor's agents in 1675 is one of only two such lists giving populations for all the individual missions after the missions had spread to the far hinterland of western Timucua. Unfortunately this list dates from a period when many Timucua missions had disappeared or become seriously depopulated. There are also reasons to believe that the 1675 list significantly understated the population for Timucua and Guale, as it is known to have done for Apalachee (Hann 1988a:165–66). It is equally unfortunate that, unlike the case for Apalachee, there are no early global estimates of the Timucua population as a whole or of most of its individual provinces against which to match the statistics from 1675.

There are various reasons for suspecting the reliability of the 1675 list as an indicator of the total mission population. The most immediate warning signal is the serious discrepancy between the total for the four peoples of Guale, Timucua, Apalachee, and Apalachicola and the 13,152 whom the bishop reported having confirmed earlier that same year. The bishop's total would not include young children as it is not customary to confirm young children under the age of 11 or 12. The 1675 list's understating of Apalachee's population is highlighted by another figure that the bishop provided. He reported that he found 4,081 women in the villages of Apalachee who were naked from the waist up. This figure has not previously drawn attention because Lucy Wenhold (1936:12) omitted the bishop's identification of the women as "Apalache" in her translation of the bishop's account. The reason for the bishop's having made so exact a count was his having provided a more ample garment made of Spanish moss for each of those 4,081 women. That number is almost half of the total population of 8,220 that Fernández de Florencia (1675a) reported for Apalachee's 14 missions. Apalachee's population must have been considerably higher than 8,220 if the total is to account for the women who were already fully clothed and a roughly equivalent male population, plus children. Another reason for suspecting the 1675 figures is a second general census from 1689. It showed an overall population about double that given for 1675, contrary to what one would expect (Ebelino de Compostela 1689). It is conceivable that the 1675 list was meant to indicate the pool of potential laborers available in each village for the labor draft.

The lists from 1675 combined indicate a total population of eastern and western Timucua of only 1,470-plus living at the missions. Seventy lived in the two surviving Mocama settlements. Thirty-plus of undesignated origin lived at Nombre de Dios. The missions from Salamototo through Utina Province contained 430 inhabitants. Yustaga's 940-plus were by far the largest single contingent. Their preponderance was probably even greater because it is likely that some inhabitants from Guacara eastward to San Francisco Potano were Yustaga. Either Yustaga started out with a far denser population than the rest of the Timucua-speaking provinces or it was protected to a degree from the epidemics by its greater distance from St. Augustine, as was Apalachee.

Yustaga is the only Timucua province for which there is a possibly reliable early global estimate of the population. A French source described Yustaga's ruler in the 1560s as so powerful that he could put 3,000 or 4,000 warriors in the field (Lussagnet 1958:137). Henry F. Dobyns (1983:186) and William R. Swagerty's postulation of a Yustaga population of 15,000 to 20,000 based on that estimated number of warriors is not unreasonable. A friar reported in 1635 that by then more than 13,000 people had been baptized in the Cotocochuni province and nation (Yustaga), implying that more remained to be baptized (Worth 1992a:65–66).

Beyond that single French source, there is only the most fragmentary demographic information from the de Soto chronicles and other French and Spanish sources from the sixteenth century. Garcilaso de la Vega, the most unreliable among the chroniclers, provided the most specific data. His account is particularly muddled for Potano and Utina Provinces. His high population figures are contradicted at times by the other more reliable de Soto sources. The three more reliable de Soto chroniclers provide the following demographic data.

Biedma described Ocale as "a small village," while Ranjel reported a good supply of maize in its countryside. Elvas described Itara, first village of Potano Province, as small and observed that Cholupaha (Santa Fé) had a great deal of maize. Two days' journey through uninhabited lands separated Cholupaha and Aguacaleyquen, first village of Utina. Ranjel noted that the land from Aguacaleyquen on seemed more populous and better provisioned. The greater population moved de Soto to send for his forces at Ocale lest he find himself outnumbered. Biedma described Aguaca-leyquen as "a moderately sized settlement (*razonable poblazon*)." On leaving Aguacaleyquen, de Soto slept the first night at a small settlement and then passed on to Uriutina, described by Ranjel as having a large council house and good population. On this stretch Elvas observed only that in five days' travel they passed some small settlements before reaching Napituca, where seven chiefs and 400 warriors confronted the Spaniards. Biedma put the number of warriors at 350. The force possibly was somewhat larger than 400 as, in addition to those killed during the battle with the Spaniards, Ranjel recorded that 300 Indians and five or six chiefs were captured from one of two ponds in which the warriors took refuge. But the number of warriors did not approach the vastly inflated figure of 10,000 that Garcilaso postulated. The Spaniards killed most of those captives after they staged a rebellion. After de Soto crossed into Yustaga territory, Ranjel noted that in one day "they passed through two little settlements and one very large one named Apalu" before they reached the head village of Usachile to sleep. Elvas concurred that Apalu, which he called Hapaluya, was a large settlement, adding that they found a great amount of food at Usachile (Biedma 1857:48; Elvas 1932:33–37; Fernández de Oviedo y Valdés 1851:I, 551–54; Vega 1723:59).

French accounts add little that is useful beyond the figures for Yustaga. Chief Outina took 300 bowmen for his attack on Potano, and his shaman-diviner predicted that Potano would meet him with at least 2,000 warriors. There is no indication whether the 2,000-man estimate was based on hard intelligence or the shaman's supposed powers of clairvoyance. Saturiwa assembled more than 500 warriors drawn from his own village and those of 10 of the chiefs subject to or allied with him for an attack on Chief Outina. Le Moyne described Saturiwa as approaching Fort Caroline with 1,200 or 1,500 warriors (Lorant 1965:42; Lussagnet 1958:109, 139–40).

With such a meager data base, much of it from questionable sources, Henry F. Dobyns (1983:passim) advanced a number of estimates of Florida's possible Timucua-speaking population that range from a minimum of 130,500 persons to about 800,000 or a little more. The heart of his work for Timucua is essay 4, "Timucua Population in the 1560s," which Dobyns coauthored with Swagerty. They designed the essay "to cross check the population estimates presented in earlier essays" (by Dobyns alone, estimating the potential population based on the land's carrying capacity) "against historical descriptions of the peoples of Florida" (Dobyns and Swagerty 1983:148, 204–8).

Dobyns and Swagerty have done scholarship a service in challenging views prevailing in the past that set Florida's prehistoric and early historic-era populations at very low levels, which, they noted, are still reflected in works such as "the standard state history" and articles published within the last quarter-century (Dobyns and Swagerty 1983:148–49). But most of their calculations for Timucua's population, particularly those for western Timucua, are open to serious question. David Weber's (1992:372n.57) remark, "Dobyns weakened his argument by his remarkably careless use of sources and cannot be taken seriously," expresses concisely what others like Sturtevant (1984:1381) have said more at length. Weber's criticism is particularly applicable to essay 4, in which Dobyns and Swagerty's conclusions for Utina, Potano, and Ocale are flawed fundamentally.

Their data for Utina Province derives from an uncritical identification of the Freshwater Chief Outina of the 1560s with the Utina Province of the de Soto chronicles and the mission era. Much of their data for Potano proceeds from uncritical and flawed use of Garcilaso's muddled account of de Soto's progress from Ochile-Aguacaleyquen to Vitachuco-Napituca. They treat the conflicts at Napituca as though they took place in Potano Province rather than in Utina Province. Their calculations for Ocale rely largely on data from Garcilaso's highly questionable account, which is contradicted by Biedma and is not corroborated by the other two accounts (Dobyns and Swagerty 1983:176–81).

The authors' use of the parity principle might be faulted for its assumption that, for the mutually hostile Timucua provinces to survive, their forces had to be at something approaching an equilibrium. That assumption seems to presume that the natives warred against each other in all-out struggles in the European fashion. Such a belief does not seem to reflect reality. Indian warfare throughout the Southeast seems to have consisted mainly of relatively small-scale surprise attacks on a single village for the taking of a few scalp-trophies and the capture of a few of the enemy to enslave or sacrifice. Just such a tactic among the Timucua was revealed in the disgust of the French auxiliaries who assisted Chief Outina in an attack on Potano (Lussagnet 1958:139–41).

Data simply do not exist to support what Dobyns attempted to do. With the possible exception of Yustaga, the data from the de Soto chronicles and French accounts permit nothing more than relative generalizations. As de

Soto's forces moved north of the Santa Fe River into Utina Province, they noted that the land was much more heavily populated than territories through which they had previously passed such as Potano and Ocale Provinces.

The seventeenth-century figures for Yustaga and Apalachee challenge another of Dobyns's theses, his belief that pandemics spread inexorably throughout the hemisphere with equal force from their points of origin in the Caribbean, Central Mexico, or Guatemala. Florida's data for 1675 and a mid-1650s statement by Florida's governor suggest that at times there was a degree of immunity proportionate to a settlement's distance from St. Augustine, the presumed entry point for most contagion for Florida. The 1675 data show an interesting spatial-temporal demographic pattern. Yustaga and Apalachee, which were farthest from St. Augustine among the mission provinces and the last to be missionized, held most of the mission population in 1675. Western Timucua as a whole (including Yustaga) held fewer people than did Apalachee's largest mission in 1675, San Luis de Talimali. It had 1,400 people to western Timucua's 1,330-plus. The four Yustaga missions contained 940-plus inhabitants, compared with 220 for three surviving Utina missions, 170 in Potano's two missions, and 40 at Salamototo. This phenomenon is somewhat surprising in view of Apalachee's occasional direct contact by sea with St. Augustine and above all with Havana, a major source of contagion as a staging area for the fleets returning to Europe.

The demographic results may have been skewed to some degree by the impact of the 1656 revolt and Rebolledo's relocation policy. Utina Province appears to have been hit particularly hard because of the flight of its natives from villages involved in the revolt and the later flight of people from its loyal villages after they were relocated. Even though most, if not all, of the Yustaga missions participated in the revolt, Yustaga was much more solidly represented at the 1657 general visitation than the rest of western Timucua (Fernández de Florencia 1675a; Hann 1986a:374–75, 378, 380–81; 1986b:102–6; 1990a:6–11).

There is limited demographic information for some provinces and individual settlements during the early years of the mission effort at the end of the sixteenth century and the beginning of the seventeenth, particularly for the eastern Timucua. Many of the data concern the number of Timucua who were Christians rather than the total population of a given jurisdiction or settlement. The earliest figure is a global estimate of 1,400 to 1,500 Christian Timucua in 1597, most of whom were Saltwater Timucua, although a few were Freshwater Timucua (Swanton 1946:194). Most of the rest of the data from that period from sources such as the 1602 Valdés inquiry is presented in chapter 9.

The first episcopal visit in Florida in 1606 produced additional demographic information on the eastern Timucua. The Saltwater Timucua from Nombre de Dios to San Pedro, who were all ruled then by Nombre de Dios's doña María, wife of Clemente Vernal, numbered more than 3,000. Not all of them were Christians. The following were the numbers the bishop confirmed at the five Timucua villages that he visited.

Nombre de Dios	216 natives; 20 Europeans
San Juan del Puerto	488 natives
San Pedro Mocama	314 and an unspecified number on a later stop
Tocoy	81
Antonico	230

It is probable that the 20 Europeans confirmed at Nombre de Dios were married to Indian women. Doña María was confirmed at Nombre de Dios, but it was noted that she usually lived in San Pedro, head village of the chiefdom.

A little over a year later Florida contained more than 6,000 Christian Indians. That 1607 figure included Guale as well as Timucua, but the vast majority undoubtedly were Timucua. The Timucua confirmed in 1606 were about double the number of Guale, and in 1607 the number of Christian Timucua had increased by well over 1,000 since the confirmations (Pareja and Peñaranda 1607). Over the next nine years 10,000 natives became Christians, most of whom probably were Timucua as those years saw a rapid spread of the friars' efforts into the Timucua hinterland. But a series of epidemics halved the Christian population from 1614 through 1616, leaving only slightly more than 8,000 Christian Indians by the beginning of 1617 (Pareja et al. 1617:13). Much of the previous expansion probably involved the populous province of Utina. Some of its missions may have been as populous then as the largest Apalachee mission was in 1675. The Franciscan visitor, Gerónimo de Oré, remarked that in 1616 Tarihica had 712 living Christian Indians as a result of the first five years of a friar's work there. If its Christian population had been halved by the epidemics, it would initially have contained over 1,400, assuming that it also still had some non-Christians (Oré 1936:129).

Data on missionized natives in 1630 suggests that that period, if not that exact year, may have been the high point demographically for the success of the mission effort among the Timucua if the figures are reliable. And there is no strong reason to doubt them. A leading friar reported in 1630 that Florida held more than 20,000 baptized natives and more than 50,000 others who had been catechized to some degree. There is no indication precisely how many were Timucua, but it is likely that a majority of them were, as the Timucua and the Guale were the only Florida peoples who had been formally evangelized at that date. The same friar reported that there were more than 203 places and congregated villages with more than 60 churches, belonging to 32 doctrinas, served by only 27 friars. The lack of friars to minister adequately to so many new converts was probably the reason for holding so many of the catechized in the status of catechumens. The only other global figure before 1675—the more than 26,000 Christians reported for 1655—indicates that there had been a considerable attrition of the missionized peoples over the 25 years that separate the two estimates. The loss of population among the Timucua-speakers must have been enormous, because Apalachee would be a major element of the Christian population by 1655 (Jesús 1630a:100; Serrano y Sanz 1912:133).

A 1681 partial census for the Mocama missions of Guadalquini and San Juan del Puerto provides another indication that the data from 1675 understated the population for most or all of the missions. Guadalquini and San Juan allegedly had 40 and 30 persons, respectively, in 1675. A 1681 census, which included only those 12 years old or more, gave Guadalquini's population as 45 men, 28 women who were wives of those men, and 14 unattached women. Thirteen of the men were chiefs. At San Juan, 17 men had wives and there were six unattached women (Worth 1995:100–3). Worth observed that the figures were broken down in that fashion in order to show how many men were available for the labor draft, as native leaders and married men were exempt from it. A 1683 census made in the wake of the pirate Agramont's raid showed the population of the two missions to be virtually unchanged from 1681.

A late-1685 visitation at Guadalquini identified the chiefs and cacicas living there at that time. In addition to the principal chief, Lorenzo Santiago, three other chiefs and two cacicas were living at Santa Cruz de Guadalquini. In the order of their mention, they were Marcos, chief of Utista; Santiago, chief of Pisocojolata; Manuel, chief of Samomo; Clara, cacica of Utinahica; and Francisca, cacica of Napofaie. Neither Samomo nor Utista appears to have been mentioned prior to this time. The only earlier mention of Pisocojolata, which occurred in 1684, concerned its chief being left in charge of Guadalquini when most of the inhabitants sought refuge on the mainland to escape an expected pirate attack. Napofaie probably is a variant of an early Mocama mission known as Napuica or Napoyca, located at the mouth of the St. Marys River (Worth 1995:111–13, 118–19). Juan Luis was principal chief at San Juan in 1685. His wife Merencia, identified as *cacica* of the village, was the cacica identified earlier as Merenciana. Three other chiefs lived there: Alonso, chief of Santa Lucia; Clemente, chief of Nebalasa; and Domingo, chief of Chololo. This was the first mention of Nebalasa and Chololo. The only Santa Lucia mentioned prior to this was an Acuera mission.

Mission List of 1689

The following are the Timucua-speaking missions listed in 1689 and their populations in terms of families, which totaled 2,796 for all the Florida missions. The list ends with the following note: "Which computed at five persons in each one of the families amounts to 13,980. And thus there are about fourteen thousand persons there."

San Juan del Puerto	25 families
Sta. Cruz de Obadalquini	60 families
Nombre de Dios	20 families
San Antonio de Mayaca	30 families
San Diego de Laca	40 families
Sta. Rosa de Hivitanayo	20 families
San Fran^{co} Potano	25 families
S^{to}. Thomás de Sta. Fée	36 families
S. Augustín de Ajojica	40 families
Sta. Cruz de Tarihica	20 families
S^{n}. Juan de Guacara	30 families
S^{n}. Pedro de Potoiriba	150 families
Sta. Elena de Machaba	100 families
San Matheo de Tocapatafe	50 families
San Miguel de Asile	30 families

San Juan and Obadalquini were listed as part of the province of Guale. All the rest, including Mayaca, were under the heading "Province of Timuqua." There is solid evidence that Mayaca's inhabitants were not Timucua-speakers, however. The Timucua-speaking missions contained 646 families, or about 3,230 individuals, more than double the population listed in 1675.

The proportion of Timucua to Apalachee had also increased significantly during that interval, from a little over 1:5 in 1675 to about 1:3 in 1689. Comparison of the 1689 and 1675 lists' figures shows that most Timucua villages had more people in 1689 than they were credited with having in 1675. Among the western Timucua villages, only San Matheo had fewer people in 1689 than it ostensibly had in 1675. San Matheo's contribution of people for creation of Ivitanayo provides a partial explanation for its population decline by 1689. The increase in population between the two dates is substantial for a number of the missions, representing a doubling or tripling of the number reported for 1675. The lack of uniformity in the increase lends verisimilitude to the figures for 1689, as does the compatibility of those figures with the number Bishop Calderón reported having confirmed in 1675.

Bishop Diego Ebelino de Compostela was the 1689 list's ostensible author, but he did not visit Florida and it is not known with certitude how he obtained the information the list contains. Florida's friars could be its source. But a more likely candidate is Juan Ferro Machado, whom the bishop sent to Florida from Cuba in the latter part of the 1680s to conduct a visitation of the missions (Ebelino de Compostela 1689; Hann l991a:126–27, 136).

The magnitude of the differences between the two lists, as well as the discrepancy in 1675 between the numbers of people whom the bishop confirmed and the total population reported by the governor's agents, are among the reasons scholars have suggested that the governor's agents understated the population in 1675. Conceivably the lists drawn up for the governor in 1675 excluded children under 12 or included only males subject to the labor draft as some population lists are known to have done, although the compilers of such incomplete lists made the limitation clear.

Demise of the Last of Utina Province's Missions

Utina Province's three remaining missions at Guacara, Tarihica, and Ahoica disappeared prior to the 1694–95 visitation, which began late in 1694. Nothing is known about the circumstances of the demise of Tarihica. Presumably it was swept away in attacks by Yamasee or Creek. Ahoica's people may have come under the jurisdiction of Santa Fé and disappeared from the records in that fashion. Both Tarihica and Ahoica survived as late as the beginning of 1691. The Santa Catalina name resurfaced at that time as well (Rios Henriques 1691). Indians from Apalachicola Province destroyed Guacara on August 30, 1691. The governor identified the attackers as Uchise and Yamasee. They killed many of the inhabitants and carried others off as prisoners, including men, women, and children. They burned the church, convent, and other parts of the village. The Franciscan provincial placed responsibility for the attack on the governor for having built a fort and placed a garrison in Apalachicola Province, forcing many of its inhabitants to abandon villages where they had earlier lived peacefully and traded with the Christian settlements of Apalachee. Shortly after Guacara's destruction, the governor made an ultimately unsuccessful effort to resurrect the settlement. In an *auto* of September 18, 1691, Governor Quiroga y Losada reported that a short while earlier he had sent five *reformados* as reinforcements to rebuild Guacara (Barreda [1692]; Quiroga y Losada 1691).

It is possible that Ahoica was not destroyed and that its inhabitants simply moved to the site Santa Fé occupied in 1690 or to an *ycapacha,* or abandoned site, of Santa Fé. Such a move was discussed in correspondence between the province's lieutenant and the governor and between the lieutenant and Ahoica's leaders. Santa Catalina de Ahoica was first mentioned during this period on September 2, 1690. The lieutenant reported that Marcos, chief of the Ocochunos, came to Santa Fé on August 25 to inquire whether Fray Pedro de la Lastra had been transferred from Santa Catalina. The chief and his people apparently had lived there earlier but had left because of the brutality of Fray Lastra, whom the lieutenant described as having the manners of a galley captain. The lieutenant noted on November 29, 1690, that he had received an order from the governor apparently approving the Ahoica's move to Santa Fé or to a former site of Santa Fé. The lieutenant then summoned Ahoica's leaders to propose the move because of the danger of enemy attack they faced at Ahoica. Only two of the chiefs and the leading men showed up, Fray Lastra having taken a third chief with him on a trip to San Pedro. The lieutenant proposed that they move to an apparently recently abandoned site of Santa Fé, promising that, if they chose to do so, he would leave its church, convent, council house, and ordinary houses standing. He also gave them the alternative of moving to Santa Fé's new site. The Ahoica said they would very much like to move but feared that Lastra would be angry with them because of the wheat that he had planted at Ahoica. The lieutenant replied that the wheat presented no problem as it was fenced in and that they could return to harvest it when it was ready.

When the lieutenant wrote his last letter on the subject on January 11, 1691, at least some of the Ahoica had moved to the ycapacha of Santa Fé. The lieutenant arrived at the ycapacha at about four o'clock that afternoon as an Indian man was arriving from Santa Catalina. The Indian had gone there to obtain maize, but Lastra would not let him have any and had sent him back with his shoulders dripping blood from a whipping the priest had ordered. On seeing that, all the other Ahoica there declared that they would not dare to go back to get their supply of maize and other possessions. The lieutenant asked the governor to remedy the matter, noting that Tarihica and Santa Catalina's chiefs had asked him to beg the governor to have mercy on them and replace Fray Lastra with Fray Joseph Pedrasa because "they were with a bad heart with Father Pedro." The lieutenant promised to go to Santa Catalina with the Indians and with Chief Riso to help them bring back their possessions and to prevent the priest from doing them any harm (Rios Henriques 1690a, 1690b, 1691).

The first of the lieutenant's letters mentioned here revealed that San Martín's church, council house, and chief's house were still standing. He mentioned in passing that he had ordered the cleaning of those structures and that this order raised the ire of Lastra against him once more because the priest inferred from the order that the governor had ordered the lieutenant to move Santa Catalina's people. The letter did not indicate for whom San Martín's structures were being readied. Possibly it was the Ocochunos, who were mentioned for the first time under that name in the lieutenant's letters. Conceivably, Ocochunos is a variant of Cotocochuni (Rios Henriques 1690a).

There were no further general censuses of the Timucua settlements prior to the attacks between 1702 and 1705 that effectively ended Spanish Florida's mission system. The surviving Timucua were reduced to a few villages or camps in the vicinity of St. Augustine. Eighteenth-century records contain a number of detailed censuses of those remnant populations. They will be discussed in chapter 15.

14.

THE EXTINCTION OF THE TIMUCUA MISSIONS, 1680–1704

A listing of the missions composed by incoming Governor Juan Márquez Cabrera in December 1680 indicates that the nine western Timucua missions that Leturiondo visited in 1678 and the two Mocama missions Argüelles inspected were still in existence. The new governor gave Santa Fé's name as Santo Thomás de Santa Fée—the first time "Santo Thomás" appeared as part of the mission's name. The apparent innovation may reflect a moving of the site of the mission. A new and an old Santa Fé were mentioned early in the 1690s. The mission's new name may be linked to the name of the mission's chief in 1680, don Tomás Medina. The name Ahoica was first attached to the Santa Catalina (rendered here as Cathalina) mission on this list. San Matheo's name appeared as San Matheo Tolapatafi, apparently the first mention of that mission's native name, which possibly means "below the laurel." Guadalquini appeared in the variant form Ovadalquini (Márquez Cabrera 1680a).

Attack on Guadalquini Island

Despite the stability reflected in the 1680 mission list, the decade began on an ominous note for two northern coastal missions. It was a presage of things to come and the first serious reflection of an English determination made as early as 1660 to eliminate the Spanish presence on the continent's Atlantic coast. Charles II's first grants of land claimed the coast for England to a point below St. Augustine. The grants violated the principle that English statesmen touted, that possession rather than prior discovery or earlier occupation should determine the validity of European claims of hegemony over Native American lands. Establishment of Charles Town in 1670 set the stage for implementation of that design and for removal of any Indians who remained loyal to the Spaniards. In the spring of 1680 a force of Chichimeco, Uchise, Chiluque, and possibly other nations attacked the island of Guadalquini (St. Simons Island). Their target was the settlement of heathen Colon in the middle of the island. Some of its inhabitants were killed. When the governor's lieutenant at the Guadalquini mission and that mission's natives sallied forth against the attackers, the latter withdrew, to reappear a few days later on St. Catherines Island. The attackers of the St. Catherines mission numbered more than 300 natives and some Englishmen described as instructors, presumably for the handling and repairing of firearms the English provided (Charles II 1681; Hita Salazar 1680a:216–17; Worth 1995:31).

The identity of the Chiluque among the attackers is a puzzle. Swanton (1922:90) identified them as Cherokee. Beginning at least as early as 1703, Spaniards used *Chiluque* to designate Mocama then living in the vicinity of St. Augustine (Benavides 1723:361; 1726:365; Nieto de Cabajal 1707). After Swanton (1946:119) became aware of the later Spanish usage, he identified the Chiluque of the 1720s as probably Mocama. There is no doubt about that assumption for the 1720s, as those Chiluque are identified as having been Christian for a long time. Although the *Chiluque* of the 1680 document could be a slip of the pen for *Chalaque,* the Spanish name for the Cherokee, even that identification is not without problems. Henry Woodward's 1674 description of the Cherokee as inveterate enemies of the Westo-Chichimeco seems to rule them out. The governor made a distinction between the Chiluque-Uchise component of the attacking forces and the Chichimeco segment. He noted that usually "the Chiluques and Uchizes were sociable (*comunicables*), dealing and trading with these provinces of Spanish Florida in fine friendship and that only the Chichumecos were always enemies" (Hita Salazar 1680a:216–17). The Chiluque of the 1680s, of course, could have been a Mocama faction that had fled from the missions earlier. The best evidence suggests that they were Yamasee, as will be seen in chapter 15.

Continued Pressure

French pirates, moving inland from the Gulf of Mexico in June of 1682, surprised La Chua Hacienda at two in the morning. They captured its owner, Thomás Menéndez Márquez; a son-in-law, Juan de Hita; and four servants, two of whom were women. The pirates set fire to the ranch's buildings and headed for the Rio Amajuro (the Withlacoochee), taking their captives with them for ransom. Menéndez Márquez escaped during a Timucua ambush of the retreating pirates (A. Bushnell 1978a:428). A 30-

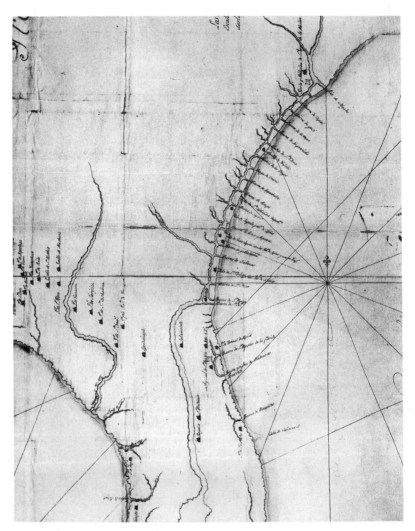

The Alonso Solana map of 1683

man force the governor sent pursued them as far as the Amajuro, where the soldiers learned that the pirates were already on the Gulf. They then concentrated attention on returning to their unidentified villages Indians who had fled out of fear of the pirates (Aranda y Abellaneda 1684).

In late spring of 1683, the French pirate Abraham Grammont (known to the Spaniards as Agramont), who was then leading a group of French and English vessels, attacked St. Augustine. After failure in that attack and loss of one vessel, the remainder, in need of provisions, sacked San Juan del Puerto and San Felipe as they sailed northward. They may also have struck the heathen Yamasee settlements of Santa María and San Pedro on Amelia Island.

Influenced by those events, Governor Márquez Cabrera began to plan a general withdrawal southward of the Georgia missions. Under his plan, Guadalquini's inhabitants were to move to San Juan del Puerto. Before his plan could be implemented fully, more pirate ships appeared in the latter half of 1684, putting men ashore who robbed and burned some of the remaining missions on the Georgia coast, including Guadalquini. Alerted to the pirates' presence, Guadalquini's Chief Santiago had moved to the mainland opposite St. Simons Island with most of his people. But he left 10 warriors at Guadalquini under his second-in-command, Chief Santiago of Pisocojolata. When a sloop from Jamaica, distinct from the pirates, landed at Guadalquini searching for provisions, Pisocojolata's chief captured its 11 unarmed English and Flemish passengers. When word of their capture brought Guale's lieutenant to Guadalquini, he ignored advice to move the prisoners and their sloop to the mainland at once to put them out of the reach of the pirates. When the pirates appeared the next day, the lieutenant abandoned the captives, retreating to the woods without attempting any resistance. Even when he received reinforcements from St. Augustine later that same day, he decided against challenging the pirates, who were still in Guadalquini. The pirates burned its church and convent before withdrawing (Bolton 1925:39, 41; Worth 1995:41–42, 127–45).

Guadalquini's inhabitants probably made the move southward in the wake of that incident, having transferred their maize and most of their other possessions to the mainland before the pirates arrived. However, they did not move to San Juan as the governor wished, but to a site on the north side of the St. Johns River on Fichinuica Strait about one league west of San Juan. The new mission took the name Santa Cruz de Guadalquini. Its location is shown on an undated Spanish map reproduced by Arnade (1959:18), which apparently was drawn early in 1703. Worth (1995:App. A, 198) demonstrated that Jonathan Dickinson's placement of Santa Cruz two or three leagues north of St. Augustine was a case of mistaken identity. Dickinson (1981:65–66) mistook Tolomato for Santa Cruz.

During the 1685 visitation Guadalquini's chief asked permission to incorporate Guale and Colon Indians who had expressed interest in coming to live at the new site. The Colon were the heathen inhabitants of San Simon, the first village to the north of the old Guadalquini site. Worth (1995:28, 111–12) identified the Colon as almost certainly from Colon, a

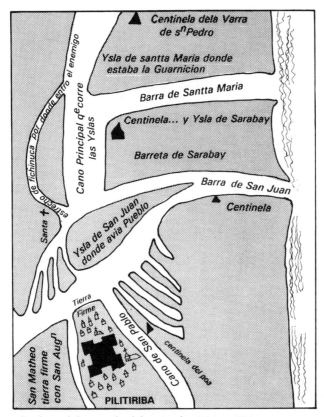

Pilitiriba and the mouth of the St. Johns River, 1703

town in Escamacu Province "described as a Yamasee town in 1663." The chief described the petitioners as then living distributed among the Yamasee and in "other forests." The visitor granted permission but cautioned the chief to assure himself that they were not coming just to cause trouble. It is not known whether any of the petitioners moved to Guadalquini at that time.

Attack on Santa Catalina de Ahoica

The British began their campaign for elimination of the hinterland missions early in 1685 with the destruction of Santa Cathalina de Ahoica. The attackers were about 60 Yamasee then living near Santa Elena, who had lived on Amelia Island a little earlier. Scots of Lord Cardross's colony, settled at Santa Elena, instigated the attack. About one-half of the Yamasee carried firearms described as large and small shotguns (*escopetas grandes y chiquitas*). The small ones probably were pistol-like fowling pieces, as the Yamasee carried them stuck in their belts. One-half of the Yamasee had bows and arrows and shields. They boasted to the Ahoica whom they captured that they would be received at Tama, their first destination, with a great reception and dances and that they would go on to Charles Town from there, where the English would receive them well and clothe them.

The Yamasee struck Ahoica at four in the morning, approaching in two bands, one moving in by the road from Tarihica and the other by the Santa Fé road. They killed 10 men and 8 women during the assault and carried off 7 men and 14 women to be sold as slaves to Cardross's Scots or to the English at Charles Town. Two of the captured women escaped during the first night on the trail after the moon went down. The Yamasee killed and scalped one of the women captives when she was unable to keep up the rapid pace her captors set. The Yamasee started out on the road to Santa Fé at eight in the morning, covering 14 leagues on the first day. While talking to their prisoners, the Yamasee tried to pass themselves off as Movila and Tiquepache, but the escaped captives judged them to be Yamasee.

A relief force sent from St. Augustine found the village burned, with no more than 10 houses left standing. They found about five or six people in the village, who had escaped into the woods during the assault. Still others remained in the woods. The chief and 16 of his men also escaped, having set out from the village on the day of the attack before the enemies' arrival. Ironically, Spanish authorities had received word of the planned attack from a friendly heathen Yamasee named Niquisaya. Although the governor hurried the intelligence to Timucua's lieutenant, the attackers struck Ahoica six hours before the warning reached there.

Marcos Delgado, who led the relief force of 16 men, set off on the trail of the Yamasee, walking for two days without overtaking them. But he met first one, then the other of the escaped women captives on his first night on the trail.

At some point during the year, a 153-man force set out from Timucua Province to track down the Yamasee who had attacked Ahoica. Timucua's lieutenant reported word from that force on November 10, 1685, that it had found no trace of the Yamasee and that they did not have a camp on the Georgia mainland. Guadalquini's chief told Mocama's lieutenant that the Yamasee had moved to the Guale Islands of Santa Catalina and Sapala (rendered here as Zapala). He maintained that he knew where to find them and promised to track them down with 50 men from Guadalquini and another 30 (Gómez 1685; Márquez Cabrera 1685a, 1685b, 1685c; Niquisaya 1685; Rodríguez Tiznado 1685). It is not known whether he undertook that mission.

Niquisaya's testimony, as well as that by a Guale Indian who was in Santa Elena during the genesis of the plans that led to the attack on Ahoica, suggests that the attack was far from being totally instigated by British authorities in South Carolina and that it was an initiative of the Indians to some degree. Niquisaya indicated that the Yamasee approached South Carolina's governor to express their desire to make war on the Indians of Timucua Province because they were their ancient enemies and because they were Christians. The governor then blessed the venture in providing 16 firearms and 11 cutlasses and in giving the Yamasee a letter to Cardross telling him that, if the venture appealed to him, he should supply the Yamasee with arms and munitions. The Guale witness reported hearsay that the Yamasee at Santa Elena reached agreement to attack Timucua in a meeting with the Cosapue, noting only that the English governor knew of it and that the British at Santa Elena provided 34 firearms and 12 cutlasses.

The Guale witness was a twenty-one-year-old Christian native of Sapala named Nicolás, literate enough to sign his name. He had fled to Charles Town with some Yamasee because he feared he was to be punished by an unnamed person. He said that he had intended to return to Sapala eventually, as he did. Guale's lieutenant encountered him there in 1685 and sent him to the governor.

Nicolás furnished information on the fate of the captive Ahoica and put their number at 22 Timucua women and three young men. He stated that 14 went to Cardross, who shipped them out on two vessels to a destination he was not aware of. Nine went to Charles Town, where three of the women and a man were shipped out to an unknown destination. The other five women remained at Charles Town until an English captain took them to his farm (Nicolás—Guale Indian 1686; Niquisaya 1685).

The records do not reveal whether Ahoica's survivors remained at Santa Catalina or went elsewhere immediately after the attack. The mission's presumed successor bore the name San Agustín de Ajojica on a 1689 list. That might suggest either that the survivors returned to the 1670s-era Ahoica site or that they were mainly Ahoica. But there is the matter of the Santa Catalina name in 1690–91 in the documents alluding to Fray Lastra's brutality at that mission. If the 1689 list's figures are reliable, Ajojica's population had been augmented from some source, possibly a satellite of Santa Catalina. Possibly the Ocochunos were living at the mission in 1689.

Mission Staffing

At this period staffing of the missions became a subject of controversy between the Franciscans' provincial, Fray Pedro de Luna, and the governor along with treasury officials. The matter came to a head in 1690 when Luna wanted to send 8 of 21 newly arrived friars to Havana or elsewhere in Cuba. The governor objected to the plan as a violation of royal decrees that friars sent as missionaries to the natives were not to be diverted to other work until they had served at least 10 years among the Indians. Eleven missions lacked friars prior to the arrival of that band of 21, and there was further need for friars to establish missions among the Jororo, Mayaca, Calusa, and other peoples of south Florida, which seemed a promising field for expansion at that time.

The Timucua missions that lacked friars were Ivitanayo, Guacara, and Asile in the hinterland and Nombre de Dios and Guadalquini on the coast. In a 1690 reassignment of the friars, Luna limited further the number of missions with resident friars. In western Timucua only Potohiriba and San Matheo, both in Yustaga territory, were to have friars, and on the coast only San Juan del Puerto. Each of those missions was to have two friars to facilitate teaching of the Indians' languages to the newly arrived friars. Although friars from nearby missions visited the unstaffed ones, the governor complained that under that regime weeks passed and, in some instances, even months without the natives hearing mass. He cited Ivitanayo specifically. Long gaps between visits also happened often at Nombre de Dios, whose people frequently had to go to St. Augustine's parish church for mass (Luna 1690; Quiroga y Losada 1690a, 1690b).

Two Prominent Timucua Chiefs of the Era

Two Timucua-speaking chiefs figured most prominently in Spanish records for the period following 1678. One was Guadalquini's chief, don Lorenzo Santiago, already mentioned earlier. Santa Fé's don Tomás Medina was the other, in part because he was called upon so often to perform missions for the Spaniards. One such assignment involved the 1677 troubles with Acuera natives. On concluding the case against Calesa, the governor gave Medina responsibility for tracking down and capturing Chief Jabajica, characterizing Medina as "the most prestigious defender of the Evangelical Law and of all those things that pertain to the service of his majesty" (Hann 1992a:470–71). Another mission involved an attempt at establishing contact with the Calusa of southwest Florida's coast.

Chief Medina maintained communications with Gulf Coast natives, probably through the Tocobaga living in Apalachee who handled riverine transport from La Chua Hacienda to and from the Gulf via the Suwannee and possibly via the Santa Fé River as well. Chief Medina's packhorses were employed in the transshipment of at least some of that commerce on to St. Augustine. Through Medina's contacts, the governor learned in 1679 that the Calusa allegedly were holding Spaniards as slaves. Medina supposedly offered his services in an attempt to ransom the captives. The governor accepted the offer and dispatched a small Spanish force to Calusa with Medina and a troop of his warriors. The effort was not successful. After receiving repeated warnings that they would not be welcome at Calus and that they should not go forward, Medina's warriors deserted the expedition at Tiquijagua, where the warnings were given much more insistently. The Spaniards decided to turn back after that development. The extent of the warnings, which had begun at Pojoy on Tampa Bay's southern side, suggest that all the territory covered was under the Calusa ruler's hegemony (Hann 1991a:23–26).

Friars' Brutality Toward the Indians

Reports of brutality by friars and excessive whipping of their parishioners resurfaced at the beginning of the 1680s. Governor Márquez Cabrera (1680b, 1683) made much of the issue in the wake of his visitation of the hinterland provinces at the beginning of his term. It became an issue also between the next regular governor and the Franciscan authorities in the early 1690s, indicating that the incidents involving Fray Lastra were not isolated ones. When the Franciscans named Fray Juan Angel to conduct a visitation of western Timucua and Apalachee, Governor Diego de Quiroga y Losada refused to allow him to leave St. Augustine on the grounds that he was not a suitable individual for correcting the abuses.

The friars' misconduct went beyond the excessive use of the whip. Three friars had to be withdrawn from their missions after terrifying their parishioners by firing shots at them. One of them, Fray Pedro Haze, while serving among the Chacato, was described as going about wearing a cutlass and pistols. He was transferred from there to San Juan del Puerto, presumably stripped of his weapons. The friars had justification for being armed while out on the trails in this era: the constant danger of an encounter with enemy Indians.

At some point in the struggle between the governors and the Franciscans, as the conflict intensified, Governor Quiroga involved the Indians themselves directly to block the travel of friars who did not carry a passport from the governor authorizing the travel. When Franciscan authorities transferred Fray Martín de Molina from San Juan del Puerto to Ivitanayo, the chiefs of San Juan and Santa Cruz blocked Molina's departure under orders from the governor (Barreda n.d. [1692]; Quiroga y Losada 1692b, 1692c). The issue appears to have been resolved before the 1694–95 visitation, as there is no mention of it in its records. The brutal Fray Lastra had been retired to St. Augustine by 1697.

Visitation of Western Timucua in 1695

All of Santa Catalina de Ahoica's people seem to have been moved to the vicinity of Santa Fé before the early 1695 visitations, as the visitor passed through Utina Province without stopping, going directly from Potohiriba to Santa Fé. Santa Fé's possession of two friars in 1697 suggests either that its population had been augmented directly by absorbing the Ahoica (and possibly the Ocochuno as well) or that the Ahoica had remained at the Santa Fé ycapacha and were being served by Santa Fé's second friar. It was then the only mission so endowed.

Despite disappearance of all the Utina missions and hostilities with the Apalachicola, the matters discussed during the visitation of western Timucua by and large do not reflect the air of crisis that obviously existed for the missions and their surviving populations. Western Timucua's relative air of tranquility contrasts with the foreboding reflected in a contemporary visitation of the Guale and Mocama missions. In western Timucua, only the topic of the manning of the Suwannee River crossing produced expressions of concern for the safety of those assigned to that task. It was recognized that reestablishment of a formal settlement at Guacara was out of the question. Even four years earlier, before the destruction of Guacara, the friars expressed concern as they traveled from their missions to St. Augustine. They asked for permission to take more than the usual two Indians with them on such occasions (Barreda 1690).

The only preoccupation reflected at Asile was the concern of the village's leading men that their chief, Bentura, was governing alone because he had not designated his principal heir, his son-in-law, Holata Lázaro, as his formal heir. Formal designation as heir would give Lázaro a voice in the government of the village. The leading men asked the visitor to declare Lázaro the designated heir so that he and the incumbent chief "might govern the village in unison and accord." On finding the move to be the general will of the natives, the visitor declared Lázaro the designated heir and instructed the villagers that "in consideration of this, they were to respect his preeminence as is customary among them."

The only concern Machava's leaders expressed pertained to the plight of a married woman whose husband had left her. They asked the visitor to search for him at Santa Fé.

The governing of the village appears to have been the Indians' only significant preoccupation at San Matheo as at Asile. For some time incapacitation had prevented San Matheo's cacica from governing. Her nephew, the legitimate heir to the chieftainship, was governing, but, as the leaders phrased it, "had preferred, nonetheless, not to take formal possession of the chieftainship until she dies because of the respect that he owes her." Here the visitor decided that there was no need to alter the status quo beyond transforming the nephew's position of "governor" de facto to one of "governor" de jure. Accordingly, he ordered that a title in due form be issued to the nephew so that he might rule with legitimacy.

At Potohiriba, where a situation partly similar to the one at San Matheo prevailed, the visitor accepted the leading men's position that there was no need to appoint a formal "governor," although Potohiriba's chief was incapacitated by old age and illness. The visitor initially proposed some means of replacing the old chief formally "so that the village would not be without a government both for the common good and for the service of his majesty." The leading men countered that such a provision had already been introduced de facto in that a group of the leading men was governing with the accord and support of all the leading men. They felt that their arrangement would be adequate until the legitimate heir should come of age. They assured the visitor that, if they ever saw a need for something more formal, they would ask the governor to appoint a "governor" for the village. The leaders at Santa Fé and San Francisco voiced no concerns at all to the visitor.

Only in the general session for the whole province, held at Potohiriba, did the danger of further attacks come up when the visitor raised the problem of the untended river crossing where the royal road intersected the Suwannee, the former site of the Guacara mission. He asked for a restoration of ferry service there. The Indians replied that they were agreeable to 11 men being stationed there regularly, with rotation of each crew after a month's service. They informed the visitor that, "even though they might wish to, they can no longer compose the group stationed there of families drawn from all the places as has been done on other occasions; they do not dare to because of the invasion that the enemy made in the said village." The visitor accepted their proposal at once.

General insecurity was reflected also in the leaders' reaction to a related proposal by the visitor and the visitor's subsequent remarks. He suggested that those manning the ferry service plant some crops at the river crossing in season to spare themselves the carrying of food from their home villages. The Indian leaders replied that, although it seemed like a good idea, "they feared that some vagrant Indians and Indians [who had] fled would disturb them so as to take away their produce, and that, accordingly, it was preferable to endure the burden of carrying in what they needed to eat." On agreeing with their reasoning, the visitor cautioned them to maintain the necessary vigilance, appointing sentinels at night.

One of the visitor's regulations, issued on his completion of his inspection, also indicated insecurity. The province's lieutenant was to make the rounds of its villages once every four months to see to it that the Indians had their arms ready and that each one had 50 arrows (J. de Florencia 1695:196–203, passim).

The common presence in the area of foreign enemy Indians and cimarrones is suggested by two other documents from the era. One is a 1695 inquiry into a murder charge lodged against a native of Potohiriba after he returned with a scalp from a Sunday afternoon's hunt. He claimed to have taken the scalp from one of four heathen enemy Indians who manifested hostile intent when he encountered them in the woods (A. García 1695:276). Although those particular enemy Indians may have been fictional, the scalp-taker's venturing of such a story suggests that such encounters were not uncommon. The second allusion appeared in a governor's instructions for an expedition he was sending into south-central Florida to apprehend the natives responsible for the deaths that occurred at two Jororo missions in 1696 and 1697. On the way, if possible, the expeditionaries, consisting of Spanish soldiers and 60 Apalachee and Chacato warriors, were to explore the woods and general environs of La Chua Hacienda to clear the land of the "*yndios cimarrones*" known to be wandering about in them (Zúñiga y Zerda 1701a).

Spanish authorities were most interested by 1695 in preserving San

Francisco Potano, Santa Fé, and Potohiriba among western Timucua's surviving missions. Article 14 of the visitor's regulations stipulated that Indians of Santa Fé, San Francisco, and even more so those of Potohiriba were
not to be permitted to move to other villages. But the lieutenant could
permit migrations from Machava or San Matheo to one of the other three
places. The regulation implies that the authorities were willing to sacrifice
Machava and San Matheo and that they were not on the main royal road
to Apalachee. The headquarters of the lieutenant of Timucua Province
had been moved to Santa Fé by 1685 from its 1678 location at Machava. It
remained at Santa Fé until August 1702 at least, despite Santa Fé's virtual
destruction in 1702 (Boyd et al. 1951:36–38; J. de Florencia 1695:206; A.
García 1695:276; Xaen 1703).

By the 1690s a number of Apalachee males were working on ranches
and farms in western Timucua and Timucua territory farther east toward
St. Augustine, some of them as contract laborers rather than as workers
brought in for short stints under the labor draft. The native workforce on
two of the Potano area haciendas was apparently large enough to justify
visitation sessions for them at San Francisco Potano. Two married Apalachee
were laboring under contract at Juan Antonio de Hita Salazar's hacienda.
The visitor renewed the prohibition on hiring such men to work at places
distant from their wives' homes, setting a fine of 25 ducats for chiefs and
lieutenants who consented to it. The visitor's article 19 indicates that the
number of unmarried Apalachee working in the region may have been
significant. Article 19 ordered the lieutenants to assemble all the Apalachee
in their territory during Lent in order to send them to their home province, where they might make their Easter duty with a friar who understood their language. Afterward the unmarried might return to their place
of employment if they wanted. His mention solely of the Apalachee suggests that they represented a large proportion of the ranch hands in the
region. But there is no indication that the presence of Apalachee or other
non-Timucua-speakers was significant enough to call for other than a
Timucua interpreter. A native named Bartolo Péres served as interpreter
for all the western Timucua villages and for Salamototo (J. de Florencia
1695:204).

San Francisco Potano's chief asked for permission to move his village
half a league toward the south because of the land's sterility at the existing
site. He observed that his people had already built a church and convent at
the new site, where lands were fertile. The visitor consented with the pro-
viso that the people agree to care for the poor widows and orphans and
other needy persons in their midst.

The visitor found Ivitanayo deserted and its council house dismantled. The rest of the houses apparently were intact. He ordered San Francisco's Chief Miguel to round up the fugitives and require that they reside at San Francisco or Salamototo so that their spiritual needs might be met. In effect, he abandoned the maintenance of Ivitanayo, which did not appear on subsequent village lists.

Salamototo's principal chief complained that his people suffered great hunger because neighboring haciendas prevented them from gathering bitter acorns, ache, and other wild plants on their lands. The visitor ordered an end to such prohibitions, observing that the wild plants were common property not included in the sale of the lands deeded to the haciendas's owners. He expanded the items the chief mentioned to include specifically grapes, Spanish moss, chinquapin (*pinoco*), and other such wild products.

The leading men complained of the great imposition that ferrying people across the river represented for the village's few common Indians. They asked the visitor to appeal to the governor to send some men to reside in the village to ease the burden. They suggested that the fugitives from Ivitanayo be recruited to live at Salamototo to assist in that work.

Four cacicas living at the village complained that the lieutenant there was not respecting their privileged position in requiring them to grind maize and assist in chores in the council house. The visitor ordered their privileges to be respected as was customary.

The principal chief concluded the requests in asking that a fence be built around the village to protect its crops from damage by cattle from Juan de Pueyo's hacienda, which was only one league from the village, and that it be done at Pueyo's expense. The visitor acceded, ordering the hacienda's foreman to build such a fence and to check it annually at planting time to see that it was still secure. He held visitations at Salamototo for Pueyo's Hacienda San Joseph de Puibeta and for the Hacienda de Piquilaco belonging to Bentura González, which was located on the river. The visitor ordered González specifically not to hinder the Indians' gathering of wild plants on his hacienda (J. de Florencia 1695:206–10).

The visitor's regulations stipulated that six of the village's Indians were always to be available for ferrying people across the river so that the mails would never be detained. The Indians were to be provided with rations while engaged in such duty. Soldiers on the king's business were to be ferried without charge. Those on private business were to pay each Indian who worked at ferrying one real for each crossing. The payment was to be given to the chief so that he might distribute it to those who did the work.

The Indians who provided passage across the river had the obligation of loading and unloading the passengers' bundles and delivering the bundles to the principal council house. The visitor forbade any regulation that obliged natives from neighboring places, who came to Salamototo in canoes, to tie up at the principal landing place. His regulations for Salamototo and for western Timucua provided that travelers who were Spaniards, blacks, or mulattoes were to sleep only in the council house. They were not to remain in an Indian village more than three days unless a legitimate impediment forced them to do so. The penalty for violators of that regulation was a 10-ducat fine for Spaniards and 50 lashes for blacks and mulattoes (J. de Florencia 1695:211–12).

The Santiago Murder Case, Potohiriba

An inquiry into a 1695 killing by a native of Potohiriba sheds light on aspects of daily life at that Yustaga mission and on the interest in and participation in the inquiry by leaders of neighboring villages as far away as Apalachee's Ivitachuco. Unfortunately, we do not have records of other such inquiries to indicate whether such widespread interest was typical. The Spanish process was initiated when western Timucua's lieutenant, based at Santa Fé, received word that an Indian of Potohiriba named Santiago had returned from a Sunday afternoon hunting expedition bearing a scalp. Santiago claimed that he took the scalp from one of four heathen enemy Apalachicola he had killed with a musket after they had attempted to kill him.

After summoning Santiago to Santa Fé to hear his story, the lieutenant placed Santiago in the village stocks and set out for Potohiriba to hold an inquiry there. But he went first to Machava, which lay beyond Potohiriba, to question an Apalachee named Lázaro, who had already begun an investigation of the case at the orders of his chief, don Patricio Hinachuba of Ivitachuco, Apalachee's paramount. That ongoing inquiry suggests that the first report of the alleged crime may have come from Lázaro or his chief.

When Lázaro asked Santiago to show him the place where the killing occurred so that he might see the body, Santiago replied that there was no need to do so, as wolves had already eaten the body but that he would show him the scalp. Lázaro claimed that, prior to confronting Santiago, he had learned from some young men of Potohiriba that a Chacato woman who had arrived on the preceding evening had disappeared after spending part of the night at the house of an Apalachee man just outside Potohiriba. Lázaro had then questioned that Apalachee, a man about 50 years old named Chucuta Antonio. Chucuta claimed to have met the woman on the trail leaving Potohiriba as he was returning from Saturday evening prayers at Potohiriba's church, lighting his way with a torch. She had been captured by Yamasee marauders, but had escaped from them. He gave her a little food on reaching home and invited her to spend the night there, promising to take her to mass the next morning. When he awoke before midnight, he found that she had left.

The lieutenant, Andrés García, proceeded from Machava to San Matheo, where native authorities had also commissioned an inquiry into the killing, sending one of their leading men named Diego to Potohiriba with several companions to look into the matter. At San Matheo the lieutenant questioned Diego and Chucuta Antonio. Diego testified that when he went to Asila Chua, where Santiago said he had killed the Apalachicola, he found no trace of the body, although Potohiriba who accompanied him to the spot tried to persuade him to tell San Matheo's leaders that he had seen traces of a body there. Then, when returning to San Matheo, about a league out from San Pedro, Diego found remains of a body in an arroyo named Ygiuiura Yvita. Only a shoulder blade and the ribs remained, as wolves had eaten the rest. The location was definitely not Asila Chua. The size of the body appeared to have been small, and there was long hair nearby that had probably been cut from the victim's head—both indications that the victim had been a woman.

Chucuta Antonio testified that he had met the Chacato woman a short distance from San Pedro, dressed in a small bearskin and carrying a little cup of unhusked nuts. When he awoke and found that she had left his house, he presumed that she had gone on to San Pedro, as its dogs then were barking. When he went to mass the next morning and did not see her there, he claimed that he had given no further thought to the matter.

The record does not indicate that the lieutenant went on to Potohiriba at that time. Instead he wound up his preliminary inquiry with the questioning of Chucuta Antonio and returned to Santa Fé, whence he sent Santiago to St. Augustine in irons on February 24, 1695, together with the evidence he had gathered. Santiago accompanied Timucua Province's labor contingent for the city's spring planting, which had been about to depart.

The governor took a statement from the prisoner in St. Augustine. Santiago gave his age as 58 and his work as tending his fields, carpentering, and hunting. His public defender portrayed him as a notable warrior holding the rank of noroco for three killings he had done in the heat of battle. In arguing for his acquittal, the defender claimed he would be sorely missed in the village as its only carpenter. The claim suggests the possibility that Santiago held a post similar to that of master carpenter, a known position in each village of neighboring Apalachee, having responsibility for all building projects. Santiago reaffirmed his claim that the one whom he had killed was a man from Apalachicola Province. He stated that, in accord with custom, he had presented the scalp in the council house of his village, along with a buffalo horn filled with powder that he had taken from his victim. The public defender seized on the powder horn as solid evidence for the veracity of his client, as such powder horns were found only in the Apalachicola region.

The defender attributed the filing of the charges against his client to a vendetta instigated by Ivitachuco's chief, who allegedly had been thwarted earlier by Santiago in an incident involving two Ivitachuco natives' poaching bear on Potohiriba lands. On finding the two Apalachee in Potohiriba territory, Santiago had allegedly taken the skins and lard from two bears as belonging to Potohiriba's chief. Offended by that action, Ivitachuco'c chief had then allegedly gone to Potohiriba with 12 of his norocos intent on taking goods from Santiago equivalent to the value of the confiscated skins and lard. But the chief was forced to return empty-handed when he met resistance in Potohiriba. The public defender claimed that Ivitachuco's chief had sworn vengeance for that rebuff.

After taking Santiago's statement, the governor ordered a trial. In preparation for the trial, the defender went to Potohiriba to take testimony from its 82-year-old principal iniha and two of its leading men. The iniha's testimony revealed that he had sent word to the lieutenant at Santa Fé about Santiago's having killed an Apalachicola while out hunting. All three witnesses told basically the same story as Santiago about the killing and made no mention of the Chacato women. The iniha and one of the leading men mentioned that, when Santiago came back to the village with the scalp to proclaim his feat, he had given the war cry. The testimony also revealed that Santiago allegedly was hunting on a former site of Potohiriba when he encountered the Apalachicola.

Another curious aspect of this case is a charge the defender made that, as soon as Santiago had been sent to St. Augustine, the lieutenant had used his power to evict Santiago's wife from the houses in which she lived and that he took them as a residence for himself and his family. The lieutenant did not dispute the charge that he had lived in Santiago's wife's houses while he was in Potohiriba, but he maintained that she had been moved to a better house and that the entire arrangement had been made by Potohiriba's chief and leading men acting on their own. Their object had been to free him from the distraction of having to build a house for his residence while he was there in connection with the inquiry. He produced a sworn statement from Potohiriba's leaders to substantiate his claim. When the governor learned that his lieutenant was living in Santiago's wife's house, he ordered him to move to the council house, the usual residence for such visitors.

Testimony given in 1700 for the residencia of the governor who conducted the trial shows that the governor was not swayed by the public defender's ingenious arguments for Santiago's acquittal. Santiago was found guilty and sentenced to forced labor in the royal works in St. Augustine. He was still serving his sentence in shackles in 1700 (A. García 1695:276–92, passim; Zúñiga y Zerda 1700).

Comparison of Mission Locations, 1675 and 1695–1697

Comparison of the order in which Joaquín de Florencia visited the western Timucua missions in 1695 with the two mission lists from 1675 suggests that in the interim there had been a drastic relocation of two of Yustaga's missions, Machava and San Matheo. Both 1675 lists show the order of visitation to have been, moving from west to east, Asile, San Matheo, Machava, and Potohiriba. That order was still reflected as late as 1689. In 1695, however, Florencia proceeded from Asile to Machava to San Matheo to Potohiriba. The 1697 list, in giving the distances between the missions, shows that there was more to the matter than a simple change in sequence: both San Matheo and Machava were closer to Asile in 1697 than San Matheo had been in 1675, when it was closest to Asile at two and one-half leagues' distance. In 1675, Machava was three leagues east from San Matheo and only one and one-half leagues west from Potohiriba. There is no overt indication of the reason for the relocation of the two villages. The move doubtless had a connection with the visitor's giving permission for the inhabitants of San Matheo and Machava to move to other villages, in contrast to his prohibition of any such moving about for the inhabitants of the rest of western Timucua's villages. The following is the 1697 mission list composed from the books of the Counting Office by the two treasury officers, Thomás Menéndez Márquez and Joaquín de Florencia.

Asile, 2 leagues from Vitachuco, no friar

Machava, 1 league from Asile, Fr. Manuel de Uriza

San Matheo, less than 1 league from Machava, Fr. Marcos de Soto

San Pedro, 5 leagues from San Matheo, Fr. León de Lara

Santa Fée, 22 leagues from San Pedro, Fr. Blas de Robles and Fr.
   Agustín Ponce

San Francisco, 3 leagues from Santa Fée, Fr. Martín de Molina

Salamototo, 18 leagues from San Francisco, Fr. Antonio de Vera

Nombre de Dios, 10 leagues from Salamototo and a cannon shot
   from St. Augustine, Fray Pedro de Luna (T. Menéndez Márquez
   and J. de Florencia 1697)

That this listing was up to date is indicated by the remark that Fray Luna had been assigned to Nombre de Dios only 20 days prior to the date of the list, which was April 20, 1697.

There are other differences as well in the distances between missions given for 1697 and those given for 1675. In 1675 the distance between Potohiriba and Santa Fé was between 31 and 34 leagues, in contrast to the 22 leagues for 1697. The 1697 figure represents a relatively direct-line passage between the two points. The 1675 figures reflect the route that went from Potohiriba to Guacara to Tarihica to Santa Catalina to Santa Fé and, for Bishop Calderón's list, with a trip to Ajohica thrown in as well. The other differences between the lists for 1697 and 1675 are minor ones. They involve the distance between Santa Fé and San Francisco and the distances between Salamototo and those two. They merely reflect the San Francisco move requested during the 1695 visitation and an earlier move by Santa Fé.

The revised sequence in the locations of the missions reflected in the 1697 list reappears in a visitation list from 1698. The 1698 list, reproduced as follows, identifies some of the village leaders.

Visitation List for 1698

Salamototo: don Alonso, chief

San Francisco Potano: Miguel, chief

Santa Fée: Captain Francisco Rizo, chief; Yaquialanayo, headman

San Pedro de Potohiriba: Thomás Plata, principal chief

San Mateo: Julian, principal chief; Santiago, headman

Machaba: Francisco, chief; Antonio Holata, headman

Asile: Bentura, chief; don Pedro, headman (Ayala Escobar 1698)

The 1698 visitation was prompted by complaints natives made against the governor's deputy in Apalachee. The visitation produced no results because the man whom the governor chose to conduct it was related to the powerful Florencia family whose actions were a major cause of the complaints. Apalachee's lieutenant at the time was a Florencia by marriage—the husband of the infamous doña Catalina de Florencia. The only substantive information in the record is the naming of the places where the visitor stopped and their leaders.

Visitation of Mocama in 1695

At the beginning of the visitation, Juan de Pueyo, the visitor, identified Santa Cruz de Guadalquini and San Juan del Puerto as constituting the province of Mocama. Mocama may also have been living then at Nombre de Dios and other settlements in the vicinity of St. Augustine. Early in the eighteenth century the inhabitants of Nombre de Dios and Palica were largely Mocama. Because of its location, Santa Cruz was allegedly considered to be at risk in 1695 and a few years earlier, despite a relatively robust population of about 300 attributed to it in 1689. The preceding governor, Quiroga y Losada (1687–93), probably early in his term, had ordered the people of Santa Cruz to move to San Juan del Puerto. That order, of course, probably had been inspired in part at least by the governor's desire to have more people available at San Juan for the ferrying of travelers across the St. Johns River and on to Santa María. That was part of the work that Spanish authorities assigned to San Juan's people. San Juan's leaders' only major complaint to the visitor involved the excessive drain on their time imposed by that obligation. They claimed that the frequent demand for ferry service kept them from their farm work. San Juan's leaders alleged that they had only nine vassal Indians between young and old, available for that work, five of whom were assigned to it regularly. If their claim was true, San Juan must have had a large number of Indians who were exempt from such labor. When the shipwrecked Englishman Jonathan Dickinson visited San Juan less than two years later, he described it as a large town with many people. He characterized its people as "very industrious, having plenty of hogs and fowls and large crops of corn, as we could tell by their corn-houses" (Dickinson 1981:66).

When the visitor asked Santa Cruz's leaders why they had not made the move to San Juan, they blamed demands made on their time by farming and work they did in the service of the king. Cacique Lorenzo de

Santiago stated that he had done his best to facilitate the move, even going so far as to build a council house for his people at San Juan. The other leading Indians assured the visitor that they were amenable to the move but explained that they could not do it at that time (February 15) because it would interfere with their field preparation. Omission of Santa Cruz on a 1697 mission list suggests that amalgamation of Santa Cruz with San Juan del Puerto had occurred before that time (T. Menéndez Márquez and J. de Florencia 1697). The first positive documentation of the fusion, however, appears in a 1701 letter by Governor Joseph de Zúñiga y Zerda (1701b). By 1701 Santa Cruz's Cacique Lorenzo Santiago was the cacique at San Juan (Worth 1995:45). Contrary to past practice, Dickinson's account cannot be used as a temporal parameter for the move because of his erroneous identification of the Tolomato mission as Santa Cruz.

During the visitation in February 1695, Santa Cruz housed five caciques and two inihas in addition to Cacique Lorenzo Santiago, who governed the village. The number of caciques and inihas suggests that Santa Cruz's inhabitants were drawn from several preexisting settlements. That was definitely so in the case of Pantaleon, cacique of Colon. His presence indicates that the Colon followed through on their desire expressed earlier to move south to settle with their former neighbors on St. Simons Island. Santa Cruz's people presented no complaints to the visitor, in contrast to the inhabitants of the three Guale missions, who asked for removal of the lieutenant, Diego de Xaen. The leaders at Guadalquini noted only that soldiers owed their people money for commodities they had given to the soldiers. The visitor added those debts to a list that his notary had begun when the visitation opened at Santa Clara de Tupiqui. Out of the four chiefs and two cacicas identified as residents in 1685 none had survived except the head chief, Lorenzo, and possibly a chief named Alonso Marcos.

San Juan del Puerto held three chiefs and two cacicas in 1695, compared with four chiefs and one cacica in 1685. None of the chiefs of 1685 survived. Chief Andrés, described as "cacique and governor," had replaced the head chief, Juan Luis, of 1685. But Juan Luis's wife, Merencia, appears to have survived. One of the 1695 cacicas was identified as María Merenziana. A 1695 chief, who was named Santiago, could have been the Chief Santiago of Pisocojolata, who was Guadalquini's second-in-command when that village was destroyed in 1684. San Juan had an iniha named Joseph in 1695.

The visitor's regulations contained the usual injunctions to sow two community fields and to have arms ready for war, as well as prohibitions against employing natives without paying for their work and against meddling in matters of royal jurisdiction. One of the community fields was destined for support of the king's service and of the needy. The lieutenant and the principal chief held the separate keys to the two locks protecting that reserve. The second field was for purchase of church ornaments. The friar and the chief held the keys to its produce. In a new order, chiefs and individual Indians were enjoined to raise livestock of all sorts. Another new regulation prohibited chiefs and Indians from purchasing trade goods on credit by pledging payment at harvest time in produce that might not cover their debts. It apparently had become the natives' practice in such situations to return used trade goods they could not pay for, no matter how marred or spoiled (Pueyo 1695:241–48).

Jonathan Dickinson (1981:65–67) passed through San Juan about a year after Pueyo's visitation. But he had much less to say about it than about Tolomato and Santa María, particularly their council houses. Of San Juan's council house he remarked only that it was larger than the one at Santa Cruz, misidentifying Tolomato as Santa Cruz. The Tolomato structure was about 50 feet in diameter and contained 16 eight-foot-wide compartments or cabins. Its roof opening formed a 15-foot square over the open space in the center where dances were held around the main fire. He described San Juan's village as being in the middle of an island about a mile from landing places on the north and south sides of the island. Indians provided Dickinson's party with food on the evening of their arrival and on the following morning. This suggests that the Saltwater Timucua may have abandoned their earlier practice of eating only once a day, in the evening. But the material used for the women's clothing had not changed much despite more than a century of contact with Spaniards. Dickinson observed that "the women natives of these towns clothe themselves with the moss of trees, making gowns and petticoats thereof which at a distance or in the night look very neat."

Visitation of 1701

During a mid-1701 visitation the governor confirmed that Santa Cruz's people had been incorporated with the San Juan mission, remarking, "This is the people whom they call, of the Mocama." Despite that identification and a clear statement by the same governor in reporting the visitation, "that the whole province of Guale is composed of three villages, which are Santa María, where the soldiery and the lieutenant lives, San Phelipe, and San Pedro de Tupiqui, all . . . on the island of Santa María," historian John Jay TePaske (1964:195–96) identified San Juan's inhabitants as Guale. His misstatement merits attention because it is probably the source that has led some archaeologists to misidentify San Juan's inhabitants of this era as Guale. TePaske's misinterpretation is in part probably a product of the traditional misidentification of Guadalquini's inhabitants as Guale. By mid-1701 the majority of San Juan's inhabitants seem to have been from Guadalquini. By then Guadalquini's inhabitants did in fact include some non-Timucuans: their Colon neighbors from St. Simons Island (Zúñiga y Zerda 1701e).

By the time of the 1701 visitation all of San Juan's inhabitants wished to move from Fort George Island to a place called Piritiriba or Pilitiriba, on the south side of the St. Johns River, that reputedly had good soil. The governor attributed their desire to move to a determination to free themselves from the work of ferrying people back and forth across the river and on to Santa María on Amelia Island without compensation. San Juan's leaders complained during the visitation that Guale from Amelia Island's three settlements insisted on being ferried across the river without paying the toll that Spaniards did when they were traveling on their own business. The Guale maintained that they were entitled to free service because of the burden they bore in providing seafood for the garrison at Santa María, an obligation not imposed on San Juan's people. However, San Juan was expected to provide 60 lots (*vezes*) per month of cacina for the soldiers at Santa María. The Guale complained that the Mocama did not always deliver it, thereby forcing them to send canoes to San Juan to bring it to the soldiers themselves. The Guale apparently had been making frequent trips to St. Augustine in repeated attempts to collect debts owed them by Spaniards there or to have their firearms repaired.

The governor insisted that a settlement had to be maintained at San Juan for security reasons, to provide a prompt warning of any hostile move by the English or native enemies to the north. In the face of the Mocama's firm stand, he permitted part of San Juan's inhabitants to move to Piritiriba, which was three leagues from San Juan. He also agreed that some of those who remained at San Juan might have plantings at Piritiriba. He noted that, at the time he was writing (June 22, 1701), plantings had already been made there and houses and storage huts (garitas) built. On feast days San Juan's friar went over to say mass for the migrants after having said mass in San Juan. The governor had petitioned the provincial for a resident friar for Piritiriba. To lessen the press of travelers desiring passage across the river, the governor issued a regulation that no Indian could go to St. Augustine "on the pretext of collecting debts or on any other one that is not very necessary" without permission from the lieutenant. To gain passage, travelers would be required to present a passport authorizing the trip. In the same vein, he forbade sending Indians as messengers unless it was for something urgent. Similarly, soldiers on sentry duty were not to cross over to San Juan unless the occasion was urgent enough to justify the bother to the Indians and their absence from their post.

The natives' dances were still a point of contention after somewhat more than a century of missionization in this coastal zone. Natives still performed dances at times that Spanish authorities had prohibited, and some puritanical friars were still prohibiting dances that their own and secular authorities had approved. In 1701 the governor again ordered that prohibited dances were not to be permitted and those that had been authorized were not to be forbidden. A new twist, however, was his provision that Indian women were not to be obliged to dance or to be punished or penalized for their failure to attend the dances. He also ruled that those performing war dances were not to carry firearms while doing so (Zúñiga y Zerda 1701a, 1701b, 1701d, 1701e). TePaske (1964:194) misconstrued the governor's order about war dances as a stipulation that "no Indians could take part in war dances or possess firearms."

The governor estimated San Juan's population at "very few less" than the 200 or so inhabitants of the three Guale missions on Amelia Island. He described these coastal natives as "all wretched (*miserable*) people, of little spirit, very poor and humble," noting that "they maintain themselves with their plantings of maize, beans, and other seeds, fishing and hunting, and other shell-fish, which the women harvest, all with excessive labor" (Zúñiga y Zerda 1701e).

Destruction of the Coastal Missions, 1702

Florida's governor remarked in June 1701 that "now, by virtue of the peace with England, we live with some security because of not having to fear that the English from St. George (the Spaniards' name for Charles Town) along with some Yamasee Indians will launch some harassment" (Zúñiga y Zerda 1701e). St. Augustine's pastor, Alonso de Leturiondo, was more perceptive a year earlier when he warned the king that "this peace and friendship is nothing more than a clever fiction under which, by acquiring vassals, they have people for the time of war, while we go on considering as friends those who in reality are hidden and concealed enemies, thieves within the house in whom one cannot trust" (Hann 1986b:176). The start of the War of the Spanish Succession in Europe, aimed at thwarting the accession of the French prince to whom the deceased Charles II had left his throne, provided the pretext for British aggression against Spanish Florida, even though Britain was allied to and supported the Austrian pretender to Spain's throne.

Less than a year and a half after the Florida governor made his hopeful remarks, the British of Charles Town and their native allies struck the final blow to the coastal missions, initiating a war that would sweep away the remaining hinterland missions as well within three years. Hostile forces landed on the north end of Amelia Island, beginning an advance southward that culminated with a British occupation of St. Augustine. But British failure to take its castillo before arrival from Cuba of Spanish relief forces obliged the invaders to withdraw after torching the city.

The governor received a forewarning of the invasion from his lieutenant in Apalachee in late October. A Christian Chacato woman, who had moved to Achito with her Savacola husband, witnessed an assembly of leaders of the Apalachicola towns in which they discussed an upcoming attack on Apalachee in conjunction with an English maritime force that was to move against St. Augustine. She hurried to Apalachee to alert Spanish authorities, arriving on the afternoon of October 21, 1702, just after the Apalachee's disastrous rout on the Flint River. Apalachee's lieutenant sent word to the governor on the following day by rapid courier, which reached St. Augustine on October 27. The governor put St. Augustine's forces on alert but does not seem to have warned his northern coastal outposts. The sentinels at San Pedro were surprised and killed by the invaders, who also caught Santa Clara de Tupiqui by surprise.

Fugitives from Tupiqui brought news of what Charles Arnade (1959:14) described as "the unexpected English invasion" to Santa María at one o'clock in the morning of November 4, 1702. With the Guale fleeing the island or seeking refuge in the woods in panic, Guale's lieutenant ordered evacuation of the island. The Spaniards and their Indian allies withdrew to San Juan del Puerto just ahead of the attack on Santa María. San Juan and Piritiriba in their turn fell to the English in short order. Again the Spaniards and natives withdrew from those points before the enemy arrived. But the English eventually captured Guale's lieutenant, his pregnant wife, and two friars who were with him. They took the prisoners to Charles Town when they abandoned St. Augustine. Salamototo's lieutenant and its people moved upriver before the invaders arrived there.

A relief force under Joseph Horruytiner, which the governor sent to bolster San Juan's defenses, never reached its destination, but it captured two Englishmen and a Chiluque Indian who had landed from a sloop. The three provided early intelligence on the size of Governor James Moore's forces and their intentions. The questioning of that Chiluque Indian suggests that he may have belonged to one of the numerous bands of Yamasee, as he understood the Guale language. He gave his name as Manuel Agramon and said that he was native to one of the places of the Chiluque, to whose nation he belonged. He was knowledgeable about the Yamasee attack on Santa Fé earlier in the year. He earned 10 pesos a month as a sailor on the English sloop (Agramon [Chiluque Indian] 1702; Arnade 1959:14–34; Fuentes 1702a, 1702b; Zúñiga y Zerda 1702a, 1702b, 1702c, 1702d, 1702e).

Arnade (1959:15, 16–18) spoke of and portrayed Santa Cruz on his maps for 1702 as though it were still a settlement distinct from San Juan, located at the mainland site it occupied prior to Governor Zúñiga's mention of its incorporation with San Juan. Arnade's source appears to be an anonymous undated Spanish map, which he reproduced in a line drawing. Events described in documents from early 1703 indicate clearly that the map was contemporaneous, drawn after Moore's invasion. The early 1703 map is particularly valuable for its portrayal of Piritiriba's location on the south bank of the river, between San Pablo and Isara Channels. Piritiriba (spelled Pilitiriba on the map) consisted in early 1703 of a sizable castillo or stockade with distinct settlements north and south of the defensive structure, each with its own church.

Destruction of Western Timucua's Surviving Missions

The first blow in the final struggle for western Timucua fell on Santa Fé in 1702, almost six months prior to Moore's invasion on the coast. An Apalachicola force attacked by surprise at dawn on May 20, burning much of the village, including its church, although villagers somehow saved the church's statues or paintings. A Chacato woman saw the attackers depart from Achito and return with many scalps, saucers (*platillos*), some silver jewelry (*algunas prendas de plata*), tacks, and a little box of clothing. She stated that all the attackers were Apalachicola.

The battle for the village lasted for three hours as western Timucua's lieutenant rallied his forces behind a stockade that served as a fence for the convent's garden. They checked the attackers' advance there and the invaders eventually withdrew. The battle left killed and wounded on both sides. But, as the governor remarked, the Spaniards' casualties would not have been large if the lieutenant, Adjutant Juan Ruíz de Canizares, had not imprudently set out with few men in pursuit of an enemy whose num-

ber had swelled after the battle. The small Spanish and Timucua force pursued the enemy for six leagues, or about 15 miles, before overtaking them
after dusk that same day. The lieutenant was mounted. It is not clear
whether the others with him also were. Ruíz de Canizares, his horse, another soldier, and about 10 of the Timucua died in the ensuing skirmish as
they blundered into the center of a crescent-shaped formation the enemy
natives had established. They were trapped as the crescent closed on them
(Zúñiga y Zerda 1702a).

The attack on Santa Fé set the stage for the Apalachee's disastrous rout
on the Flint River in mid-October of that same year. The Apalachee, fearful that more attacks would follow if Christians did not avenge the assault
on Santa Fé, pressed Spanish authorities to permit a reprisal. The
Apalachee's fears, based on their familiarity with their Indian neighbors'
war practices, were indeed justified. In the days prior to the encounter on
the Flint, the Apalachicola and other groups allied with the British were
meeting at Achito and targeting Apalachee's Bacuqua and Escambé. While
the Apalachicola were planning their attack, they received a forewarning
of the planned Apalachee reprisal, apparently from dissidents within
Apalachee ranks. With that knowledge, they prepared an ambush for the
Apalachee along the trail. A second troop set out from Achito at the same
time, headed for an unidentified target in Timucua. But it turned back
when some of its members dreamed that they would fare badly in Timucua.

The force allied to the English consisted of about 400 Chisca and
Apalachicola warriors, 10 Chichimeco men and three Chichimeco women,
one Apalachicola woman, two blacks, and three Englishmen. An Englishman known as Captain Antonio was squad leader. Captain Francisco Romo
de Urisa led a largely Apalachee force of 800 warriors, who included an
unspecified number of Timucua and Chacato, into the enemies' trap. More
than half of his warriors were killed or captured. Many of the 300 or so
who escaped left their arms behind on the battlefield. That blow and the
demoralization it induced facilitated the destruction of the last of the hinterland missions, which began early in 1704. In eliminating all the missions in Apalachee by the end of July 1704, the Apalachicola's campaign
left the surviving western Timucua missions, particularly the Yustaga missions, much more vulnerable (Boyd 1953:468–72; Hann 1988a: 233–34).[1]

Little is known about the impact that Moore's 1702 attack had on western Timucua. Santa Fé seems to have survived the blow it suffered in May
of 1702. For a time it apparently remained the residence of the new deputy-
governor, who succeeded the deceased Canizares. The new lieutenant,
Diego de Xaen, wrote to the governor from Santa Fé on November 14,

1702, noting that he had dispatched the two soldiers with the governor's second letter for Manuel Solana in Apalachee. He had charged the soldiers not to say anything (presumably about the English attack on St. Augustine) in the rest of the places at which they stopped or through which they passed. Xaen stated that he would go to San Francisco Potano that same day and withdraw the soldiers and that they would go together to Apalachee (Xaen 1702).

Destruction of the Yustaga missions occurred within weeks of the Spanish withdrawal from Apalachee. The governor reported on September 10 that heathen Indians led by the English had depopulated Apalachee "together with the greater part of Timuqua that had remained of some consequence." Five days later he added more specifically that the enemy had "defeated, laid waste, and burned alive the caciques of San Pedro and San Matheo and their vassals" and that they had killed a black and captured four others at the La Chua Hacienda, only four leagues from San Francisco Potano (Boyd et al. 1951:67–68). The only Christian Indians left in western Timucua by then were the inhabitants of Santa Fé and San Francisco Potano, along with the Apalachee who accompanied Ivitachuco's chief in the withdrawal from Apalachee.

The Apalachee, under don Patricio de Hinachuba, settled in Potano territory at a place called Abosaya, one day's journey from San Francisco. An enlarged Spanish garrison to protect what was left of western Timucua had been moved to San Francisco sometime in 1703. The governor described Abosaya as a land of many wild fruits and roots that would maintain the Apalachee migrants until they could harvest the crops they planted the following year. He had wanted the Apalachee to settle just south of St. Augustine, where he would be better able to assist them (Zúñiga y Zerda 1704b). The Apalachee had time to build their new village and erect a stockade around it before their enemies renewed their attacks in earnest. Except for the remnant populations from the coastal missions huddled in camps around St. Augustine, Florida's once-vaunted mission chain was reduced by the end of 1704 to San Francisco Potano, Ivitachuco at Abosaya, and Salamototo. Santa Fé's inhabitants had been moved to San Francisco Potano by then.

15.

THE TIMUCUA'S LAST YEARS IN FLORIDA

The dominant reality of the last 60 years of the Timucua-speakers' presence in Florida was persistent insecurity that kept them in the immediate vicinity of St. Augustine and relegated them to minority status among the natives living in that narrow zone. Few if any descendants of the original Saturiwa inhabitants of that region remained by the beginning of the eighteenth century. The neighboring Freshwater Timucua also seem to have disappeared by that time or even earlier. The largest element among the surviving Timucua-speakers was the Mocama, or Chiluque, the name Spaniards began to use for them almost exclusively from the 1720s on.

Intrusion of non-Timucua natives into Timucua territory was not new, of course. Back in the 1620s Spanish authorities moved the Guale of Tolomato to a site only three leagues north of St. Augustine to compensate for the disappearing Saturiwa. In a poorly understood process, Yamasee and the people of Athuluteca had appropriated the former Mocama territory of Cumberland and Amelia Islands by the 1670s. Yamasee also had moved up the St. Johns River to the former Freshwater mission site of Anacape. But Moore's 1702 destruction of the remaining coastal missions initiated a much more substantial influx of natives as the surviving Guale and Mocama moved to sites south of the St. Johns River. Moore's attack on Apalachee in 1704 and the continuing raids that followed it brought some Apalachee and the surviving hinterland Timucua to the vicinity of St. Augustine. By 1711 English-inspired raids into central and south Florida drove the first heathen native immigrants to the St. Augustine area from that region. But the largest influx was to come in the wake of the 1715 general uprising of the natives against the Carolinians that is known as the Yamasee War. A massive influx of Yamasee in particular made the Timucua-speakers from then on a definite minority in their own land.

Little is known about the fate of the Indians who fled from the coastal missions during the weeks that Moore's forces remained at St. Augustine. It is not clear how many found security in the castillo. Those from Nombre de Dios certainly did, and it is likely that those from Tolomato and Piritiriba or Pirihiriba joined them as well. In view of Moore's capture of Guale's lieutenant and his family and two of the friars despite their initial escapes, it seems probable that some of the Indians from San Juan and the Amelia Island missions were captured or killed, particularly if they remained with the Spaniards. There is no explicit indication that any Timucua-speakers joined the invaders, as many Apalachee did during Moore's invasion of their province in 1704, although Diego Peña (1717) recorded the presence of Mocama among the Creek on the Chattahoochee in 1716.

Revitalization of Spanish Defenses

After Moore abandoned his siege of St. Augustine's castillo, the governor's expectation that the English and their native allies would soon renew their attacks led him to make extensive preparations at once to deal with that eventuality as best he could. He raised a fortification with four bastions and two cannons around the church in Nombre de Dios and he placed a garrison there. He built a defense line from the Nombre de Dios marsh to the St. Sebastian River to close off the route by which Moore's forces had advanced on the city. He ordered his lieutenants to make stockades for defense of the native villages. He built a four-bastioned fort at Piritiriba, ten leagues to the north of St. Augustine, that included barracks, living quarters, and warehouses for supplies. It was to provide refuge for two villages located just to the north and south of the fort. Yguaja or Guale, undoubtedly from the Amelia Island missions, and Chiluque (Mocama), undoubtedly from Santa Cruz and San Juan del Puerto, lived in those two villages, each of which had its own church. Resettlement at Piritiriba took place very quickly after Moore's departure. In April 1703 the Indians there complained of bad treatment by the stockade's squad leader and asked for permission to leave (Nieto de Carbajal 1707). The soldiers there were equally unhappy with him. In response the governor reassigned him to Cañuelos. Sometime before Moore attacked Apalachee in January 1704, hostile Indians attacked Piritiriba and San Francisco Potano, possibly at the same time as the attack on Apalachee's Ocuia (Zúñiga y Zerda 1704a). During their attacks on those three settlements, the enemy killed many Christian Indians and carried off more than 500 as prisoners. After living at the two Piritiriba settlements for a year and one-half, their inhabitants moved to Palica and Nombre de Dios Chiquito. The Mocama moved to Palica. The

Guale moved on later to a place called the Point of Monzón and were still there early in 1707.

It is the account of those moves that dates the anonymous and undated map depicting the Piritiriba castillo and its two settlements. Governor Zúñiga y Zerda ordered it drawn up to show the paths, channels, estuaries, sandbars, and *vocainas* in the vicinity of Piritiriba. The legend on its depiction of Fort George Island, "Island of San Juan where there was a village," indicates that the map postdates Moore's 1702 attack and that San Juan was not reoccupied. The name "Santa +" appears at that mission's former mainland site just west of Fort George Island, suggesting that a lookout post had been established there. In contrast to the villages near Piritiriba, no houses or church are shown on the map for Santa Cruz, and Santa Cruz was not mentioned in the listings of native villages in the vicinity of St. Augustine in the years immediately following Moore's attack.

As part of his revitalized defense against the expected renewed English attack, Governor Zúñiga y Zerda also built a four-bastioned stockade in San Francisco Potano that enclosed the church. He placed the deputy-governor there and increased the garrison to 30 men. Santa Fé's remaining population was incorporated with that of San Francisco. But Timucua's lieutenant, Diego de Jaen, was still based at Santa Fé as late as August 11, 1703 (Xaen 1703). Similarly, La Chua received a garrison to defend its blockhouse because of the ranch's strategic role in supplying meat to the city. When Ivitachuco's inhabitants resettled at Abosaya, the governor posted six soldiers there to help defend the stockade that don Patricio Hinachuba had built. The governor added a stockade at Salamototo and put soldiers there to defend the river crossing.

A number of native villages were established south of St. Augustine prior to September 1705. One of them, occupied by Chiluque, may have housed the Mocama reported as having settled at Piritiriba in April of 1703, who moved to Palica later. Conceivably, a Mocama village of September 1705, described as three leagues south of St. Augustine, might have been Palica, although Palica was described elsewhere (Hann 1991a:378) as four leagues from the city.

Renewed Attacks on Native Villages

The governor's defensive measures were seriously tested early in the second half of 1705 by a new wave of attacks that began in August and reached their full fury in September. Three distinct troops of heathen enemy Indians from settlements under Charles Town's jurisdiction, who were armed and instigated by the English, arrived in Florida beginning in August. The governor's lieutenant in Potano received a forewarning of the attacks as early as May. Ivitachuco's chief reported at the end of May that he had had word from the lieutenant that the enemy was coming to destroy both Ivitachuco and San Francisco. Don Patricio asked the governor for a dozen more soldiers, provisions, munitions, and six muskets (Hinachuba 1705).

The first of the enemy forces apparently arrived in Potano just after mid-August 1705. They laid siege to Ivitachuco at Abosaya on August 20, 1705. Francisco de Florencia, who then headed the Spanish soldiers stationed at Ivitachuco, appealed to the governor for relief. He reported that the enemy numbered about 200, made up of "heathens and rebels," the latter apparently apostate Christian Apalachee. At that time Ivitachuco's chief was in St. Augustine with a few of his warriors making a personal appeal to the governor for more aid. By then the enemy was active also in the vicinity of San Francisco and the La Chua blockhouse. Florencia reported on August 27 that the scanty aid sent to him from San Francisco had been seized by the enemy nearly at the gate of the blockhouse (F. de Florencia 1705a, 1705b). The enemy lifted its siege of Ivitachuco after 20 days.[1]

As soon as word of the siege reached St. Augustine, the governor dispatched Captain Joseph de Beganbre with soldiers and two bands of native warriors whom he identified as Yguaja (Guale) and Chiluque (Mocama), from separate villages three leagues south of St. Augustine. Don Patricio accompanied them with his warriors. While that force was crossing the St. Johns River, word reached it that a second band from South Carolina had Salamototo under siege. Beganbre diverted his force and put Salamototo's attackers to flight. As he was about to resume his march to Abosaya, Beganbre learned that a third enemy troop had attacked the Chiluque village three leagues south of St. Augustine that had sent most of its warriors along with Beganbre. The enemy's intelligence apparently was as good as that of the Spaniards. That third enemy troop had captured 70 to 80 people, mostly Mocama women and children but also including black slaves and other people from St. Augustine, who happened to be in the village or in its environs on the day of the attack. After turning back, Beganbre's force intercepted that third enemy band in a marsh five leagues north of St. Augustine. Beganbre, up to 16 or 18 of his soldiers, and six of his Indians died in the encounter.[2] More than 70 of the enemy's captives managed to flee to their rescuers during the skirmish.

Beganbre's forces failed to free only the captives held in stocks (*cepos*), whose captors killed them during the battle.

When Beganbre diverted his force for the second time after lifting the siege of Salamototo, Ivitachuco's chief had gone on alone with his few warriors to La Chua and from there to Abosaya, where he penetrated the siege and entered his village. There he found many of his people ill (Nieto de Carbajal 1707; Zúñiga y Zerda 1706).

Late in September 1705 an enemy force reported to number 2,000 again attacked La Chua Hacienda. In the wake of that attack, the Apalachee abandoned Abosaya during the winter of 1705–6 for the vicinity of St. Augustine. They were distributed among several of the existing native villages south of the city, but they found no more security there than they had in the hinterland. Prior to the end of April 1706 many heathen Indians attacked those villages in conjunction with rebel Apalachee, killing don Patricio and most of the Apalachee who were with him and forcing the friars at those mission settlements and their surviving natives to seek refuge in or very close to the city within range of its castillo's cannon (A. Bushnell 1979:16; F. de Florencia and Pueyo 1706a).

Abandonment of the Hinterland, 1706

San Francisco Potano, earliest of the formal hinterland missions, was the last to be abandoned. After the Apalachee's withdrawal from Abosaya, the only Spanish outposts west of St. Augustine appear to have been the San Francisco mission, the nearby La Chua Hacienda, Salamototo, and the Afafa Hacienda upriver from Salamototo, on which at least twenty Christian and heathen Jororo were living. San Francisco contained something over 200 Indians led by Field-master don Francisco Rizo, identified as principal holata of Santa Fé, and Captain don Miguel, principal holata of San Francisco. It also housed a Spanish garrison of 22 men under Timucua Province's last lieutenant, Andrés García. Seven soldiers manned the blockhouse of the La Chua Hacienda. Only seven or eight Salamototo remained at the river-crossing village, protected by its small Spanish garrison (A. García 1706a, 1706b).

When Francisco de Córcoles y Martínez assumed the governorship on April 9, 1706, the hinterland outposts were coming under attack once again and enemy forces were operating freely east of the St. Johns River as well. San Francisco was under siege; its supply line from Salamototo had been cut for over a month by enemy activity on the St. Johns River opposite

Salamototo. When San Francisco's messengers made it safely to the river's west bank, neither their smoke signals nor shots brought a canoe across to pick them up. An April 15 attack ended the Spanish presence at La Chua. Enemy forces struck the blockhouse at two o'clock in the morning, killing one soldier and wounding another. The other five soldiers held them off for the three hours that the attack lasted. Three times attackers set fire to the kitchen made of straw, but each time the soldiers put it out. Their concern for the kitchen in the heat of battle suggests that it was attached to or very close to the blockhouse. García ordered abandonment of La Chua when its squad leader asked for a reinforcement of six soldiers. The withdrawing soldiers brought the remaining munitions and arms with them to San Francisco. Prior to April 23 García dispatched 10 soldiers to burn the La Chua blockhouse (Córcoles y Martínez 1706g; A. García 1706a, 1706b).

The new governor moved promptly to reestablish communications with San Francisco, to assess the viability of the Spanish presence there and the native leaders' willingness to abandon their village if the Spaniards withdrew. The air of crisis was heightened at St. Augustine on April 11, when Juan Alonso de Esquivel brought news at five in the afternoon that enemy Indians had killed his two brothers and up to 20 Jororo at the Afafa Hacienda, 20 leagues from St. Augustine. At nine that evening the squad leader for the five soldiers on sentinel duty at the mouth of the St. Johns River reported that about 20 enemy natives had killed or captured his men. He had escaped because he was outside the sentinel house when the attack occurred.

Córcoles y Martínez dispatched Juan Benedit Horruytiner with 80 soldiers in a fleet of pirogues led by the presidio's large launch to clear the St. Johns of enemy forces. The large launch was a pirogue armed with wall guns and bearing the native name of Mayman Yoha. Although the governor inclined from the beginning toward abandonment of San Francisco, he did not initially give Horruytiner, García, or the two chiefs unequivocal orders to that effect. Horruytiner, on arriving at Salamototo and hearing from García of the San Francisco garrison's dire straits, asked the governor for quick orders on the withdrawal of the soldiers and the course of action if the native leaders did not wish to leave with them. García reported that the Indians lacked maize to supply the garrison and that for some time his men had been subsisting largely on smoked beef from a bull after exhausting nine arrobas of maize San Francisco's friar had supplied. The natives apparently were subsisting largely on roots. In the governor's letter to the chiefs he spoke merely about the advisability of a move to Salamototo, St.

Augustine, or some other point agreeable to the natives that would lessen the problem of sending supplies to the garrison (Córcoles y Martínez 1706a, 1706b, 1706c, 1706g; F. de Florencia et al. 1706; A. García 1706b; J. B. Horruytiner 1706).

The two chiefs and their leading men initially resisted the idea of moving, thanking the governor for his offer of shelter but noting that the enemy was not of as much concern as the planted fields that they hoped to harvest. García reported on April 24 that the Indians' fields were doing well, as they spent their entire days in the fields with hoes in their hands and arms at the ready. He noted that, although some had been captured by the enemy, they escaped later. García recommended that the Indians be allowed to stay long enough to harvest their crops so they would have seed to take with them (A. García 1706b).

Not long thereafter, voluntarily or not, the Indians did abandon San Francisco, agreeing to move to Salamototo, where they arrived around May 9, 1706. A threat of imminent attack by a large enemy force may have led the Indians to acquiesce in the move. They had no sooner moved across the St. Johns River into Salamototo than 300 enemy Indians who had been looking for them appeared on the river's west bank. The enemy fired a few shots across the river and skirmished with the Spanish pirogues. Illness among the Indians may have been a factor as well. The governor spoke of them as getting better (*remediendo*) during twelve days they spent at Salamototo, sustained by food the governor had sent. Alleging a problem of supply even for Salamototo and the danger for the Indians at Salamototo when they went out into the countryside for firewood, edible roots, and other necessities, the governor ordered the natives to move on in to St. Augustine, where they arrived on May 23, 1707 (Córcoles y Martínez 1706e). Most, if not all, of those last Christian natives from the hinterland were Timucua-speakers. A Timucua interpreter explained the governor's letter to the two chiefs, in which he first broached their abandonment of the Potano region (A. García 1706b).

In reporting this denouement, the two treasury officials stated that over the preceding few years 29 Christian missions had thus been extinguished and that most of their Christian natives had been killed or sold into slavery (F. de Florencia and Pueyo 1706b:477–79). From a different perspective, the Englishman Thomas Nairne, one of the perpetrators of that destruction, boasted "that the garrison of St. Augustine is by this warr reduced to the bare walls their cattle and Indian towns all consumed Either by us In our Invasion of that place or by our Indian subjects . . . [who] have brought in and sold many hundreds of them and dayly now continue that trade so that in some few years thay'le reduce these Barbarians to a far less number" (Nairne 1708:(5) 196–97).

Retreat within the Defense Line

Spanish authorities' reports reflect the continuation of those attacks with particular intensity throughout 1706 and 1707. The villages south of St. Augustine came under attack beginning early in 1706. The enemy natives, including rebel Apalachee, made the Apalachee loyal to Spain a particular target, but the groups with whom the Apalachee were living suffered as well. Moved by the losses the Christian natives were suffering, Governor Francisco de Córcoles y Martínez brought all the villagers to places secured by the cannon of the castillo and the defensive line that Governor Zúñiga y Zerda had established, running east to west "from the marsh that surrounded the little fort of the village of Macariz called Nombre de Dios to the bank of the River of San Sebastian." The move was made prior to November 30, 1706. The new governor found the features of Zúñiga's line in an advanced state of decay, especially the palisades of Zúñiga's six little forts along that line. Córcoles y Martínez replaced them with three halfmoons containing artillery. So troubling were the attacks that the new governor, who assumed his post on April 8, 1706, found it necessary to delay the residencia for his predecessor until early in 1707.

The new governor described the native villages as five in 1706, noting in 1711 that they were not properly villages, but mere camps (rancherias). The following are the settlements he identified in 1706 and 1711.

1706	*1711*
Abosaya (Apalachee)	San Luis de Talimali alias Abosaya
San Francisco	Santo Tomás de Santa Fé alias Esperanza
Salamototo	Salamototo
Santa María (Guale)	Santa Catarina de Guale
Tolomato (Guale)	Tolomato
Nombre de Dios Macariz	Nombre de Dios
	San Juan del Puerto
	Indians de la Costa (Ais)

San Francisco–Santa Fé, Salamototo, Nombre de Dios Macariz, and San Juan del Puerto were Timucua-speaking settlements. Fray Alonso Santurro, who compiled the censuses for both Santa Fé and Tolomato, specifically identified the Santa Fé mission's inhabitants as Timucua-speakers. San Francisco–Santa Fé and Salamototo obviously held the migrants from the hinterland, and both settlements were served by the same friar in 1711. The change of San Francisco's name to Santo Tomás de Santa Fé by 1711 may indicate that a majority of the inhabitants were from Santa Fé by then, or it may be a consequence of leadership changes. San Francisco's Holata don Miguel of 1706 does not appear on the census for 1711. Juan Aruquetega (spelled on a later list as Arucatessa) rather than Holata don Francisco Rizo of 1706 was Santa Fé's chief in 1711. A man identified simply as Rizo was listed as fourth among the men of the village. Either the governor failed to mention all the Timucua settlements in 1706 or all the Mocama of San Juan del Puerto were then concentrated at Nombre de Dios with their fellow Mocama or were attached to one of the other settlements. By the 1720s the inhabitants of both Nombre de Dios and San Juan del Puerto de Palica were being identified regularly as Chiluque rather than as Mocama, as the use of the name Mocama disappeared. But the name Chiluque also appeared in 1706 and earlier, applied to Palica's inhabitants. The Indians de la Costa (of the Coast) of the eighth village of 1711 apparently were Ais, as the report for their village noted that 17 men had joined the village on February 26, 1711, one of whom was the cacique of Ais. From this point on, those Indians were identified simply as Costa (Benavides 1723:361–62, 1726:365; Córcoles y Martínez 1706f, 1707a, 1709, 1711; F. de Florencia and Pueyo 1706a, 1706b; J. López 1711; Santurro 1711; J. Solana 1706; Zúñiga y Zerda 1706).

Nature added to the woes of the inhabitants of St. Augustine and the native settlements on September 30, 1707, when a 48-hour hurricane struck the city and the settlements, inundating them and destroying most of the houses. The constant danger of Indian attack prevented the inhabitants even from going out to cut lumber to repair their houses (Córcoles y Martínez 1707b). During most or all of this period, the natives lived on the royal dole because of the constant hostilities.

The 1711 censuses, drawn up at the governor's orders by the friars who served the various settlements, give the population of each broken down by men, women, boys, and girls, with all the natives listed by name except for the heathen Costas. In contrast to the names given for the Apalachee, the names given for the Timucua and Guale are almost exclusively European, consisting in most cases solely of a first name such as Juan or María. The Timucua-speakers' contingent of 142 individuals, representing about one-third of the total of 432, were the largest single linguistic contingent, but just barely. There were 137 Costa, 105 Guale, and 48 Apalachee. Santa Fé, largest of the Timucua settlements, with 51 people, was surpassed by the Costa's settlement and by Santa Catalina, which held 61 people.

The following is the distribution of the population in the four Timucua settlements.

Santa Fé	Salamototo	San Juan	Nombre de Dios
16 men	5 men	11 men	16 men
19 women	7 women	14 women	11 women
5 boys		6 boys	5 boys
11 girls		9 girls	7 girls

The following are the names of Santa Fé's inhabitants as a sample of the names in currency.

Men	Women	Boys	Girls
Juan Aruquetega, chief	María Salomé	Marcos	Cathalina Lorenza
Juan Antonio	María Salomé	Pedro	María Magdalena
Martín Lasso	María Salomé	Marcos	Helena
Pedro Caule	María Pasqua	Antonio	María Juana
Rizo	María de la Cruz	Juan Alonso	Candelaria
Antonio Vtina (?)	María Cathalina		Antonia
Francisco	María de la Cruz		Luiza
Pedro Hiriva	Elena Cathalina		María Espíritu Santo
Antonio Gabriel	Luiza		Rossa
Lucas	María Cruz		María Josebe
Juan Baptista	María Azención		Rossa María
Andrés	María Cruz		
Miguel	María Cathalina		
Bartolomé Cruz	Dominga		
Pedro	María Espíritu Santo		
Juan	María Pasqua		
	María Yñéz		
	María Espíritu		
	María Magdalena		

The plenitude of María Salomés is atypical. Nombre de Dios had the only other María Salomé and she also appeared at the head of the list, a likely indication that she was of high status. On the Apalachee list, people whose native names reveal them to have been high in status headed the list. A woman named Merenciana, who headed the list at San Juan del Puerto, was probably the same Merenciana who was wife of San Juan's principal chief in 1685.

The 1711 census for Santa Fé–San Francisco reflects a drastic decline in that village's population after its departure from San Francisco in mid-spring of 1706. San Francisco held about 200 people at the time of the 1706 exodus. The governor described all the settlements as being within a pistol shot of the principal body of men on guard, presumably the castillo's on-duty garrison (Córcoles y Martínez 1711). Neither the 1706 list nor that for 1711 seems to account for the Guale who migrated from Piritiriba to Nombre de Dios Chiquito and then on to Monzón.

Consequences of the Yamasee War

The general Indian rebellion in South Carolina in 1715, known as the Yamasee War, had two important consequences for the Spaniards in Florida and for their native allies. It brought a new wave of native refugees to St. Augustine and a temporary relaxation of the constant assaults that terrorized the Spaniards and the natives allied to them. The so-called Yamasee War involved far more than that one nation. Verner W. Crane (1956:162) noted that the war constituted "a far-reaching revolt against the Carolinian trading regime, involving the Creek, the Choctaw and to a less extent the Cherokee, as well as the tribes of the piedmont and of the Savannah River and Port Royal districts." The Apalachee who went to South Carolina with Colonel Moore in the wake of his 1704 attack and the Apalachicola were among the Savannah River district Indians involved in the uprising. Although the Yamasee played a leading role, Crane believed that the Creek were the probable authors of the conspiracy, sharing with the Yamasee "and with other interior tribes a greater resentment of the tyrannies of the Charles Town traders." Crane concluded that because it led "as it did to the awakening of the English colonial authorities to the danger of French encirclement, to a constitutional revolution in South Carolina, to far-reaching migrations of the southern tribes, and to a reorientation of wilderness diplomacy in the South which altered seriously the prospects of English, French, and Spanish rivalry, it takes rank with the more famous Indian conspiracies of colonial times."

English defeat of the revolt more than doubled the native population at St. Augustine. The Yamasee, one of the major predator-peoples responsible for destruction of the missions and for the constant harassment of

"Spanish" Indians, constituted the majority of the rebels against the English who sought, among their former prey, refuge from English vengeance. Substantial elements among the various bodies that comprised the Creek, the other major predators, briefly moved toward a policy of neutrality and accommodation with the Spaniards, spearheaded by Lower Creek elements and a few Apalachee, who urged Creek alignment with the Spaniards. The turnabout permitted a momentary relaxation of the siege mentality that had held Spaniards and Indians under the protection of the castillo's cannon since 1706 (Crane 1956:254–55; Hann 1988a:312–14; 1989:181–82). Those consequences moved a new governor, Juan de Ayala y Escobar, to launch a resettlement of most, if not all, of the Indians of earlier settlements at the same time that the newcomers were assigned village sites. Some settlements were placed three to five or more leagues from St. Augustine. The change of name or disappearance of four settlements from the 1711 list is further indication of such reorganization and relocation.

The prime source on the changes in the settlement pattern is a detailed census of the new and old settlements taken in April 1717. Its author was Captain Joseph Primo de Rivera, a soldier with long experience in Florida. He visited each of 10 settlements to meet their people assembled in the principal council houses. This census provides the first mention of council houses since the destruction of the northern coastal and the interior missions.

Rivera gave the villages' names and specified the language of the main component of each and the identity of people of other linguistic groups living in the settlement. He also identifed the head chief of each one and indicated the number of the chief's leading men and the number of ordinary Indians residing in the village. Rivera recorded whether the leaders and the general population were heathen or Christian, whether the chief ruled de jure or de facto, and how many of the Indians were vassals of the ruling chief. He stated how many owed allegiance to other chiefs living in the village and, among those who had joined a particular village, how many lacked a chief. Rivera broke the tally down into categories of men, women, and children and listed the children by sex. He noted how many men were fit to be warriors and the number who were recent converts to Christianity.

The Timucua had become a distinct minority in their own land by 1717. Only three of the 10 villages were Timucua-speaking. Three Yamasee-speaking villages, two of Ibaja- or Guale-speakers, and one each of Apalachee- and Mayaca-speakers constituted the rest. Five of the camps mentioned in

1711 had disappeared or experienced a name change. They were San Luis de Talimali, Santo Tomás de Santa Fé, San Juan del Puerto, Salamototo, and the Costa's settlement. San Buena Bentura de Palica reappeared phoenix-like. The surviving Salamototo lived as "attached" inhabitants in San Buena Bentura. The Costa had disappeared, but they would return later. The other two Timucua-speaking settlements in 1717 were Our Lady of Sorrows and Nombre de Dios.[3]

Rivera described San Buena Bentura de Palica as of the Timucua language and Mocama nation. Two leading men assisted its Chief Juan Ximénez, who was identified as "cacique-governor." The presence of a doña Merenciana Martínez, identified as "principal chieftainness," indicates that San Buena Bentura was heir to the San Juan del Puerto of 1711. The village possessed a council house, church, and friary.

Primo de Rivera's Census of Native Villages, 1717

Santa Catharina de Guale (Ibaja language)
Don Alonso de la Cruz, principal chief, and 8 leading men
  34 Christian warriors and 6 attached heathen ones
  40 Christian women and 6 attached heathen ones
  24 Christian children (13 boys, 11 girls); 6 heathen children
    (5 boys, one girl)
  Fray Domingo Gaina
125 natives total

San Buena Bentura de Palica (Timucua language, Mocama nation)
Juan Ximénez, cacique-governor, and 2 leading men
Doña Merenciana Martínez, principal cacica
  51 warriors—23 Christian Mocama, 9 Christian Salamototo,
    19 heathen Chachise; Salamototo and Chachise attached
  44 women—26 Mocama, 4 Salamototo, 14 Chachise
  33 children—22 Mocama (11 boys, 11 girls), 1 attached heathen Yamasee child, 2 Salamototo girls, 8 heathen Chachise (5 boys, 3 girls)
  Fray Martín de Molina
132 natives total

Nuestra Señora de Candelaria de la Tamaja (Yamasee language and nation)
Don Antonio de Ayala, principal chief, and 8 leading men (5 Christian and 3 heathen)

10 warriors, Christian; 10 men, heathen
25 women—16 heathen, 9 Christian
18 boys—15 heathen, 3 Christian
18 girls—13 heathen, 5 Christian
Fray Marcos de Ita Salazar and fort with garrison
Cacique Tospe (Yamasee language), attached to Candelaria
    23 warriors—1 new Christian, 22 heathen
    23 heathen women
    14 heathen children (7 boys, 7 girls)
Cacique Alonso Ocute, cacique of Ocute, Christian (Yamasee
    language), attached to Candelaria
    8 men, his vassals, 7 heathen and one Christian
    3 heathen children, 2 boys and one girl
162 natives total

San Joseph de Jororo (Maiaca language)
Cacique Don Juan Romo; Christian, and 4 leading men,
    Christians
    11 warriors—9 heathen, 2 Christian
    13 women—10 heathen and 3 Christian
    4 children (2 boys, 2 girls), one girl Christian
    No friar
33 natives total

Our Lady of Sorrows (Timucuan language), all Christian
Don Juan de Arucatessa, cacique governor, and 5 leading men
    20 warriors, 2 of them attached Apalachee, vassals of this
    chief
    23 Christian women
    25 *doctrina* children (11 boys, 12 girls)
    Fray Joseph de Ita Salazar
74 natives total

Pocosapa (Yamasee language), heathen
Chief Langne Cap qui (or Langne Chap), heathen, and 7
    leading men (5 heathen, 2 Christian)
    34 heathen warriors and 11 Christian warriors, attached
    Apalachee and Timucua, who were under obedience to
    this chief
    31 heathen women and 10 Yamasee and Apalachee Chris-
    tian women

13 boys (12 heathen and one new Christian)
19 girls (14 heathen, 5 new Christians)
Attached heathen Casapuya (Casapuya language)
Cacique, unnamed, heathen
    14 warriors and one old man
    14 Casapuia women, heathen
    16 Casapuia children (7 boys, 9 girls)
    No friar, but a fort and garrison
172 natives total

Our Lady of the Rosary of Jabosaya (Apalachee language and nation)
Don Pedro Osunaca, principal chief, and one leading man
    10 warriors and one old man
    12 Christian women and 2 attached heathen women of the
        Chasta tongue and nation
    7 *doctrina* children (3 boys, 4 girls)
    Fray Phelipe Mandonado
34 natives total

Pocotalaca (Yamasee language and nation)
Don Francisco Ya (or La) Quisca and 6 leading men, 2 of them
    Christian
    35 men, vassals, 2 of them old, 4 Christians of the Oapa
        nation
    31 women, 6 of them new Christians
    25 heathen children (12 boys, 13 girls)
    No friar
96 natives total

Tolomato (Ibaja language and nation), Christians
Don Francisco Martín, principal chief, and 3 leading men
    14 men (12 strong, 2 old)
    21 women
    25 *doctrina* children (16 boys, 9 girls)
    Fray Pedro de ?
64 natives total

Nombre de Dios (Timucuan language), Christians
Don Juan Alonso, cacique governor, and 2 leading men
    12 strong men, 3 of them attached Apalachee

16 women, 4 of them attached from Salamototo, Timucuan
   language
19 *doctrina* children (10 boys, 9 girls)
50 natives total

Total number of natives for the ten villages, 942
(Primo de Rivera 1717)

The lineage of the other Timucua settlements that Primo de Rivera mentioned is not quite as clear as that of Palica. Our Lady of Sorrows of 1717 probably housed the surviving Timucua from Potano's San Francisco and Santa Fé. The name Our Lady of Sorrows did not appear on any subsequent list, but it is probably the village referred to later as "village of Timuqua" or as Santa Fé in the 1720s and 1730s. Survival of some of the people of Our Lady of Sorrows can be traced through its chief, don Juan de Arucatessa. His name reappeared on a 1736 list rendered as "El Cacique Alucatessa." He then headed a "village of Timucua." Another marker for Our Lady of Sorrows's later incarnations is the presence of Pojoy or Alafaes from Tampa Bay's south shore. Our Lady of Sorrows probably is the "village of Timuqua" of a listing of native baptisms that occurred between 1718 and the beginning of 1723. Twenty-eight Alafaes children and 134 Alafaes adults were baptized there during that five-year period. No Timucua children were baptized. That "village of Timuqua" is the Santa Fée of the 1726 census. It then had 25 "old Christians" (the Timucua) and 20 recent converts (the Alafaes). Its inhabitants consisted of 20 men, 17 women, and eight children. It was identified then as a "settlement of the Timucua and Pojoi nation, attached to . . . Nombre de Dios" (Benavides 1723:361, 1726:366; Hann 1989:193; Swanton 1922:105). This joining together of the Potano and Pojoy was logical as they had been in contact since the beginning of the seventeenth century at least, although their contact was not always friendly.

The Timucua contingent had declined by almost 50 since 1717, probably due to deaths. Deaths probably were not responsible completely for the sharp decline of the Pojoy-Alafaes from 162 in the 1718–23 period to 20 by 1726. The Pojoy-Alafaes, like other south and central Florida peoples who were not horticulturists who settled near St. Augustine during the first half of the eighteenth century, were inclined to come and go as whim struck them in the continued pursuit of their fisher-hunter-gatherer lifestyle. When the Pojoy reappeared, however, they were living with other groups more like themselves, the Amacapira and the Jororo.

A minor source of uncertainty about the identification of Our Lady of Sorrows with Santa Fée and the "village of Timuqua" of later lists is Fray Joseph de Bullones's retrospective account of the earlier vicissitudes of the native villages in St. Augustine's vicinity. He does not seem to have mentioned the Santa Fée of 1726 or its earlier incarnations such as Our Lady of Sorrows, possibly because of their having been attached to the Nombre de Dios mission in 1726. Bullones (1728:376–77) muddied the water further in mentioning a "village of Timuqua" that seemingly antedated the Potano's migration to the vicinity of St. Augustine. The inhabitants of his "village of Timuqua" appear to have been Mocama from the consolidated village of San Juan del Puerto–Santa Cruz de Guadalquini, who settled at Piritiriba in 1703. The following is Bullones's account of this "village of Timucua."

> After the invasion [of 1702] the village of Timuqua had its seat in an area that is called *los Varaderos* (the shipyards), twelve leagues distant from the presidio. And a short while ago it moved and, fearful of the enemy, passed over to [a place] six leagues distant. It had very few Indians, because in being loyal to the Spaniards, they died in their defense and thus came to remain with no more than fifteen men, eight women, and some children. From there they made another withdrawal, approaching to about a cannon's shot of the presidio, camping in a place called Abosaya and after having suffered a plague, no one was left except for a cacique and two Indians. (Bullones 1728:376)

Abosaya was probably the site known also as Moze, where later there was located a village of free blacks.

Bullones's account must be used with caution, especially its population statistics. It was a consequence of the collation controversy, occasioned by a move by the king and Cuba's bishop to convert the Indian doctrinas from missions to ordinary parishes staffed by beneficed secular clergy. While arguing that Florida's doctrinas were not prepared in any way to support such an elevation in status, the friar may have painted a darker picture than was justified in some instances. That seems to be the case for his portrayal of Nombre de Dios Macariz. Its stone church and friary, proximity to St. Augustine, income from alms left by devotees of the cult of Nuestra Señora de la Leche, and mission status going back to the sixteenth century would have made it the doctrina most likely to be considered ready for such a change. Bullones's statement that "Macariz, alias Nombre de Dios

. . . never surpassed ten Indians and a like number of women" contradicts the data from the 1711, 1717, and 1726 censuses. It had 50 inhabitants in 1717 and 62 by 1726.

The inhabitants were described in 1717 and in the 1718–23 baptismal count simply as of the Timucua language, with no indication of the tribe to which they belonged. Most probably were Mocama in 1717 as they were described as belonging to the "Chiluca nation" in 1726 and 25 of them "old Christians." Four of the women of 1717 were Salamototo and three of the men then were Apalachee. All 50 were Christian. By 1723, Nombre de Dios had gained at least four adults who had been baptized during the 1718–23 period. The recent converts had risen to seven by 1726 (Benavides 1723:362, 1726:365–66; Primo de Rivera 1717).

Bullones (1728:377–79) gave no population for Nombre de Dios in 1728, noting instead that it had been attacked in March 1728 by 200 Englishmen and an unspecified number of their Indian allies, led by Colonel John Palmer. The attackers set fire to the village, robbed its church and convent, and desecrated the statues. They killed a number of the fleeing inhabitants and carried others away as prisoners to be used or sold as slaves. After the enemies' withdrawal, Governor Benavides blew up Nombre de Dios's stone church and convent. Bullones remarked that nothing was left other than the ruins.

Nombre de Dios Macariz does not appear among eight settlements mentioned on a list from 1736 (Swanton 1922:105). It reappeared, however, on two mission lists from 1738. It is likely that Nombre de Dios was simply overlooked by the author of the 1736 list because the author of the earliest of the 1738 lists, the knowledgeable Governor Benavides, who had stepped down only in 1734 after 16 years in that post, spoke of Nombre de Dios's friar as having been there for four years (Benavides 1738). Prior to 1734, whatever inhabitants survived the Palmer raid probably lived in one of the two Timucua missions mentioned for 1736 or in St. Augustine itself.

The presence of an Indian community within St. Augustine itself was noted on the list of baptisms for the 1718–23 period, but the tribal identity of the community was not indicated, the only such omission on the list. Most, if not all, of its members were initially heathen, as 23 of the newly baptized were adults and only seven were children (Benavides 1723:361). One of those identified as living in St. Augustine at a later date is Chief Tospe or Hospo, a Yamasee, who was living in a settlement attached to Candelaria de la Tamaja in 1717 (Parker 1993:6–8; Primo de Rivera 1717). One of the 1738 mission lists mentioned that St. Augustine then contained about 10 houses of Indians who were served by one of the friars from the city's *convento* (Montiano 1738a). Chief Hospo may well have first considered making such a move in the wake of a Uchise attack on Candelaria on November 1, 1725, in which many of its Yamasee inhabitants were killed and others were carried off as prisoners (Bullones 1728:376).

The following are the listings of the native villages for the 1720s and 1730s. In the 1718–23 listing of baptisms, the first number represents children baptized. Where there is a second number, it represents adults baptized.

1718–23 baptisms

St. Augustine's native residents	7 and 23
Village of Costa Nation Guasacara	15 and 19
Nombre de Dios Chiquito—Yamasee	21 and 26
Casipuia Village	7 and 8
Palica—Chiluque	15
Village of Timucua—Alafaes	28 and 134
Poco Talaqua—Yamasee	4 and 13
Village of Hororo—Jororo	4 and 26
La Tama—Yamasee	23 and 82
Nombre de Dios Amacarisa—Timucua	18 and 4
Village of Moze—Apalachee	6
Tolomato—Ibaja	26 and 13

(Benavides 1723:361–62)

1726

San Antonio—Yamasee (recent converts); palm-thatch church and convent; 22 men, 16 women, 11 children

San Antonio—Yamasee (recent converts and 4 heathen); palm-thatch church and convent; 21 men, 12 women, 16 children, 4 heathens

San Diego—Yamasee (recent converts); palm-thatch church and convent; 26 men, 27 women, 12 children

Santta Cathalina—Iguaja (old Christians and attached recent converts); palm-thatch church and convent; 35 men, 47 women, 22 children

Our Lady of Guadalupe—Yguaja (old Christians and 6 attached recent converts); board church, palm convent; 11 men, 16 women, 18 children

San Joseph—Yguaja (10 old Christians, 5 recent converts, 2 women attached); settlement attached to Guadalupe; 15 men, 18 women, 5 children

San Buena Bentura—Chiluca (70 old Christians); palm-thatch church and convent; 19 men, 24 women, 27 children

Nombre de Dios—Chiluca (55 old Christians, 7 recent converts); stone church and convent; 19 men, 23 women, 20 children

Santa Fée—Timucua and Pojoi (25 old Christians, 20 recent converts); attached to Nombre de Dios; 20 men, 17 women, 8 children

San Luis—Apalachee (78 old Christians, 9 recent converts); palm-thatch church and convent; 36 men, 27 women, 24 children

San Anttonio—Cosapuya nation and other nations (43 recent converts, 12 heathen); palm-thatch church and convent; 24 men, 13 women, 18 children

San Anttonio—Costa nation (38 recent converts, 50 heathen); palm-thatch church and convent; 55 men, 13 women, 20 children

Indians from the *rinconada* of the Macapiras nation (18 recent converts, 6 heathens); attached to San Buena Bentura; 17 men, 6 women, 1 child

Indians of the *rinconada* of Carlos—Piaja nation (38 heathen); no church; 19 men, 11 women, 8 children

(Benavides 1726:364–67)

1728

Palica: 5 men, 5 women, 3 or 4 children

Nombre de Dios Chiquito: 30 men, 19 women, some children (*párbulos*)

Village of Timuqua: a cacique and 2 Indians

Thama—Yamasee: moved to Moze

Village of Jororo—Jororo, united with Pojoy and Amacapira: all gone

Costa Indians—most heathen: 20 men, 18 women, about 14 (?) children

Tholomato: 2 chiefs, 16 men, 16 women

Nombre de Dios Macariz

Moze: 3 men, 3 women

Casapuyas—most heathen: 15 men, 15 women, 5 children

Pocotalaca—some heathen: 14 men, 14 women, 5 or 6 children

(Bullones 1728:375–78)

1736 (lists only men 11 and above)

Pocotalaca: Cacique Clospo and 22 other men

Nombre de Dios Chiquito: Cacique Yuta and 14 other men

San Nicolás: Cacique Manuel and 9 other men
Tolomato: Cacique Bernardo and 12 other men; 2 communities
La Costa: Cacique Costa and 9 other men
Palica: Cacique Lorenzo and 17 other men, 2 of them chiefs, 1
    Apalachee
La Punta: Cacique Juan and 16 men, 1 of them Apalachee
Village of Timucua: Cacique Alucatesa and 16 men

(Swanton 1922:105)

1738, April 21
Chapter house (St. Augustine): about 10 houses, number of
    individuals not given
Macharis: 49 people, 15 of them warriors
La Costa: 6 or 7 after depopulation
Tolomato: 64 people, 14 of them warriors
Palica: 61 people, 17 of them warriors
Pocotalaca: 62 people, 23 of them warriors
La Punta: 41 people, 15 of them warriors
Nombre de Dios Chiquito: 56 people, 16 of them warriors
San Nicolás: number of people not given, nine of them warriors
Total of 350 people, of whom 215 were confirmed

(Benavides 1738)

1738, June 4
Chapter house: 24 people in 6 houses plus those working as ser-
    vants
Macaris: 46 people (16 men, 16 women, 13 children)
La Costa: 19 people
Tholomato: 30 people (7 men, 12 women, 11 children)
Palica: 53 people (18 men, 21 women, 14 children)
Pocotalaca: 47 people (14 men, 20 women, 13 children)
La Punta: 43 people (10 men, 13 women, 20 children)
Nombre de Dios Chiquito: 40 people
San Nicolás—Casapullas and Jororo: 32 people (8 men, 10 women,
    14 children)
Pojoy and Amacapiras: 38 people and 5 heathens

(Montiano 1738)

Late 1738	*Families*	*Persons*
Nombre de Dios Macaris	13	23
San Antonio de la Costa	7	29

N. Señora de Guadalupe, Tolomato	8	29
N. Señora de La Assumpción, Palica	11	48
N. Señora de la Concepción, Pocotalaca	14	44
N. Señora del Rosario, Punta	14	51
Santo Domingo de Chiquitos	18	55
San Nicolás de Casapullos	19	61

(Güemes y Horcasitas 1739)

1739, June 23
Nombre de Dios de Macaris
Nuestra Señora de Rosario de la Punta
Nuestra Señora de Guadalupe de Tolomato
Santo Domingo de Chiquito
Nuestra Señora de la Assunción, de Palica
Nuestra Señora de la Concepción de Pocotalaca
Pueblo de San Nicolás de Casapullos
Pueblo de San Antonio de la Costa

(Montiano 1739)

If one looks superficially at the population data reflected in the censuses from 1717 through 1738 presented on the preceding pages, the year 1726 appears to be the high point demographically for the native villages in the vicinity of St. Augustine for the period since the beginning of the century. The villages of 1726 held 1,011 people as compared with 942 in 1717. But the high point probably occurred at least several years earlier if one takes into consideration the losses suffered by the Yamasee and Timucua by 1726 and the disappearance of most of the influx of 162 Alafaes reported in 1723 as having been baptized since 1718. Only 20 of them, identified as Pojoy, remained at Santa Fé by 1726. The 385 people, exclusive of the Casapuias, who resided in the Yamasee villages in 1717 had fallen to 167 by 1726. The Timucua villages fell from 256 people to 177 over that nine-year span. Among the major groups represented in the 1717 census only the Guale held their own at 193 in 1726, a gain of four over 1717. The Apalachee village was the sole substantial winner, going from 34 to 87. Much of the decline for the Yamasee probably resulted from a special effort the English and their Indian allies made to exterminate that people. In recording their fate at Tamaja in a 1723 attack, Bullones noted that they were "hated by the rest of the nations. And they made war on them so much that they were being exterminated little by little" (Bullones 1728:376). But, although 1726 may not have been the peak year, it still represents something of a demographic watershed. Even though the decline for the Indians in general was probably not as precipitous as that posited by Bullones, it was a sharp one nonetheless. The inexact data he provided suggest a population of something over 244. It was probably considerably more than that in view of remarks by friars in 1738 that the population had been considerably higher in 1731. The first two censuses from 1738 put the population at 350 and 372, respectively (Benavides 1738; Montiano 1738).

For some tribes such as the Apalachee, the precipitous decline Bullones portrayed may indeed be reliable. His reference to Moze as having been left with only six people after an epidemic in 1727 was the last mention of an Apalachee village in the vicinity of St. Augustine. Guale's Santa Catalina was last mentioned on the 1726 list. Bullones, who gave no population for Tamaja after the 1725 attack, was the last person to mention that village.

The Timucua's Palica was one of the more stable villages during this period. Its Friar Joseph de Hita certified that 15 Chiluque children were baptized there between 1718 and the start of 1723. The village was referred to simply as San Buena Bentura in 1726 and identified as a "settlement of the Chiluca nation [containing] seventy old Christians" (Benavides 1723:361, 1726:365). Bullones (1728:378) said little about Palica's antecedents. He noted only Palica's original four-league distance from the city and the later withdrawal of its people to within a rifle shot of the presidio. He gave the population as "up to five men and a like number of women and about three or four children." If his figures were accurate, Palica received an infusion of new people from some quarter before 1736, when it reportedly had 18 males aged 11 and above and an unspecifed number of women and children. The men were identified by name and age as

Cacique Lorenzo	80	Manuel	12
Cacique Juan Ximénez	60	Juan Pufe	14
Ygnacio	80	Tomás	40
Joseph	80	Juan	11
Andrés	45	Pedro de la Cruz	35
Juan Bautista	18	Cacique Marcos	60
Lorenzo	20	Juan Melchor	11
Juan Savina	25	Juan the Apalachee	80
Miguel	20	Francisco del Maral	50
		(Swanton 1922:105)	

Ex-governor Benavides gave Palica's total population as 61 in his listing dated April 21, 1738, of whom 17 were warriors. He described Palica as right on (*imediata á*) the defense line and served by two friars from Spain, Pablo Rodrígues and Antonio Navarro, both of whom had been stationed there for four years. As Benavides was in Veracruz, Mexico, when he dispatched his report on the Florida missions, it is likely that it reflects conditions somewhat earlier than the date of April 21, 1738, that the document bears. The king had asked him in 1736 to provide that report along with his opinion about a suggestion by Cuba's auxiliary bishop, who was then living in St. Augustine, that all Florida's mission Indians be joined together in one consolidated village.

During the 1730s at least, nothing came of the bishop's suggestion for uniting all the native settlements. Benavides observed that, if the idea were to go forward, "the establishment of this united village should be in the territory that they call of Mose, which is half a league distant from the plaza of Florida. This spot and its environs have fertile and rich lands for cultivation; and, notwithstanding the fact that there are two villages among the nine mentioned, which are the Alafaes,[4] who are inclined to live always on the banks of the rivers for the shellfish, palmetto, and other edible roots, with these and other circumstances providing further reasons to choose the mentioned site of Mose, which is no more than a fourth of a league distant from the sea and overlooks (*interviene*) a saltwater river in which there is an abundance of shellfish and every type of fish." Shortly after his suggestion Mose became the site of a celebrated settlement of free blacks. The site, of course, had already been the location of a number of native villages going back at least as far as the early seventeenth century (Benavides 1738).

It is fortunate that Governor Benavides clearly identified Palica's Chiluca inhabitants of 1726 as "old Christians," because that identification indicates that they were the same people whom Primo de Rivera identified in 1717 as "of the Timucua language and Mocama nation." Palica's Fray Joseph de Hita muddied the water a bit as to the Chiluca's identity in a 1738 report to Governor Manuel Montiano in describing himself as an interpreter (*atequi*) of the Timucuan and Chiluque languages. Presumably, he was indulging seventeenth- and eighteenth-century Spaniards' love for tautology or using the word "languages" in the sense of dialects. But it is conceivable he was alluding to the Yamasee who bore the name Chiluque.

A "pueblo de Timucua" that seems to have been the successor of the Santa Fée of 1726 was the second Timucua village mentioned on the 1736 list. The following are the names and ages of its 17 men aged 12 and older.

Cacique Alucatesa	80	Miguel Mototo	60
Riso	60	Manuel Mototo	60
Crisóstomo	50	Miguel	12
Juan Bautista	50	Benito	12
Gaspar	25	Antonio	12
Santiago Baquero	40	Juan Chirico	50
Juan Alonso	20	Santiago	30
Bartolo	40	Solana	20
Miguel	25		

(Swanton 1922:105)

This "village of Timucua" does not appear on any of the subsequent lists for 1738 and 1739. It is likely that its survivors, if any, became part of Palica or of Nombre de Dios Macaris, which reappeared on the lists for 1738.

Benavides (1738) reported Nombre de Dios as having "forty-nine big and little persons, of whom fifteen were men of arms." During the two and one-half years the friar who composed the June 1738 report for Governor Montiano had served at Nombre de Dios, four of its inhabitants had died. Twelve of its 16 men were Timucua. Two were Apalachee and two were Yamasee. Only seven of its women were Timucua. Eight were Yamasee and one was Uchise. The friar reported that some of the ornaments used for religious services lost during Palmer's raid had not been replaced and that the church was using items borrowed from other churches. It also did not have a proper convent. The statue of Nuestra Señora de la Leche had been replaced or saved, as the friar noted that it was still a place of pilgrimage. By late in 1738 the 46 people of the June list had been reduced to 23. During the same interval, Palica's inhabitants had declined only by five.

The friars who composed the reports from which Governor Montiano composed his mission list of June 4, 1738, had nothing good to say about the people whom they served. They implied that the natives' conduct had left much to be desired for a long time but noted a particularly marked deterioration in their conduct since the accession of Governor Francisco del Moral in 1734. They alleged that before then the natives made greater efforts to restrain their evil inclinations, showed some obedience to their priests, and came to church with some regularity. Now they gave no heed to the friars and little obedience, either, to their chiefs and leading men. The friars reported that all of the adults were badly addicted to alcohol and that from their drunkenness resulted a great looseness of customs, lack of obedience to their chiefs, and loss of their fear of God. Drunkenness in some cases led men to abuse their wives and even to kill them. A friar who worked with various groups from south and central Florida described them as Christians only in name. The friar at Nombre de Dios conceded that the Timucua and Apalachee were a cut above the rest, considering themselves to be Christians at least, and people of their word. He remarked of them that they were only a little worse in their behavior than the Gypsies of Spain except in the matter of stealing, blasphemy, and cursing. The friars blamed much of the problem with alcohol on their settlements' proximity to St. Augustine, where it was available.

In a joint report three friars noted that in the 1731–33 period, when they first arrived in Florida, the native population had been larger. They attributed the decline to policies adopted by Governor Moral after he assumed office in 1734, which led to flight by Pojoy, Alafae, and Amacapira living together in one village at some distance from the city and by the Jororo of a village near the one of the other three tribes. The governor had forced some of them to move to a site close to the castillo and had placed others of them among the Casapuia, one league from the presidio. The governor failed to keep promises that he had made to them at the time of their moves and burdened them with much unrecompensed labor. The friars remarked that the aggrieved natives had withdrawn furtively to the southern coast, returning to their heathen ways and to their wars with one another, observing that they had shrunk in numbers as a consequence. Eight of them had returned and were lodged with the Casapuia shortly before the friars composed their report. Because of this flight, they noted, the mission villages' population scarcely amounted to 400, including men, women, and children. The actual count drawn from the various friars' reports and including those living in St. Augustine itself was 372-plus. The increment represented an unspecified number working in the city as servants.

Some of the decline in fervor among the Indians may be attributable to the friars themselves. Enmity between *criollos* and *peninsulares* among the friars seems to have been particularly strong during this period. A concomitant of the resultant struggle was a constant shifting of friars from mission to mission that gave newcomers from Spain no opportunity to learn any of the native languages properly. The frequent changing of the saints' names for a number of the missions may reflect this struggle and fluidity of assignments. The mid-1720s plethora of San Antonios gave way in the 1730s to a multiplicity of missions bearing various titles of the Blessed Virgin.

Friars' lack of empathy with their charges, particularly those from central and south Florida who were fisher-hunter-gatherers, may have been partly responsible for the aloofness of the natives. It is epitomized in Fray Bullones's (1728:377) remarks about the "uselessness" of the Costa and about the wandering life-style they and the Jororo, Pojoy, and Amacapira maintained in harvesting palm berries and in "searching for the marine life with which they sustain themselves, killing alligators and other un-clean animals, which is delectable sustenance for them."

Friars' desire for control over the Indians was probably another source of native alienation as the natives' proximity to St. Augustine highlighted for them the difference in their status as Christians and that of the Span-iards. That tension is reflected best in friars' attempts to keep the Indians residing in St. Augustine itself in subjugation. A friar at the chapter house in 1738, who was designated to serve the city's native community, com-plained that its members most of the time refused to recognize that they were under the convent's jurisdiction or that they were Indians. He attrib-uted this behavior to conceit arising from their frequent contact and famil-iarity with Spaniards and, in some women's cases, to pride in the posts that their husbands held as soldiers, thinking, as the friar put it, that with this they ceased to be Indians (Montiano 1738).

The Last Remnants

In contrast to the relative abundance of population data from 1717 through the 1730s, there is seemingly no information at all through the 1740s to 1752 and, for Nombre de Dios Macariz, to 1759. A 1752 listing provides data for the five settlements of Tolomato, Pocotalaca, the Costa, Punta, and Palica but omits Nombre de Dios. The lists identify all the individuals in each village. Palica, the sole Timucua village mentioned, contained 12 men, seven women, and 10 children (seven boys, three girls). Juan Ximénez was then Palica's chief (Franciscan friars 1752). He had been 60 years old in 1736, when his name appeared in the list reproduced by Swanton (1922:105).

The following were the remainder of Palica's inhabitants in 1752.

Men	Women
Joseph Anayo	Asenisia
Miguel Hicapuca	Guadalupe
Antonio Espinosa	Lusia
Marzelo	Gertrudis
Francisco	Cruz

Antonio	Thereza
Miguel de los Santos	Lusia
Lorenzo Anayo	
Benito	
Patricio Anayo	

Boys	*Girls*
Pablo de Lozo	María
Manuel Leonar	María
Joseph Antonio	Francisca Mauiela
Juan Paisqua	
Joseph Espinosa	
Antonio Espinosa	
Francisco	

The Guale's Tolomato had 12 men, 14 women, and no children. Ana María, one of its women, was Chiluque. The Yamasee's Pocotalaca contained eight men, 13 women, six boys, and six girls. One of the girls was identified as Magdalena la Mestiza (the Mixed Blood). Only three men and five women were listed as present in the Costa village, but three other men were listed as alive but absent. One bore the name Francisco Cosapuya, and one of Pocotalaca's women was identified as María Cosapuya. La Punta was the largest village: 25 men and 34 women, but no children listed. Antonio Juta, their chief, bore a name that appeared on the 1736 list (Swanton 1922:105). The Chief Yuta of 1736 was then chief of the village of Chiquito and was 40 years old. Pocotalaca had a 25-year-old Antonio Yuta in 1736. The name Yuta of La Punta's chief in 1752 suggests that its inhabitants were Yamasee, as those of Nombre de Dios Chiquito had been earlier (Friars 1752).

By 1759 the people of 1752's six settlements had been consolidated into two, Nombre de Dios and Tolomato. Nombre de Dios's 11 households represented Yamasee, Timucua, Ibaja, Chiluque, Costa, Casipuya, and Chickasaw. Yamasee had the largest contingent, 23 people. Only six Timucua and one Chiluque remained, but five children were half Timucua and half Yamasee. There were 10 Ibaja, 9 Costa in the one household, two Chickasaw, and one Casipuya. Nombre de Dios's Chief Juan Sánchez, who was Yamasee, had been Pocotalaca's chief in 1752. He was 32 and married to 25-year-old Josepha Domínguez. They had three children: Leocadia, seven; Manuel de Jesús, six; and Juana Luisa, one.

The surviving Timucua at Nombre de Dios were Manuel Riso, 90 years old and sole occupant of the second household; Juan Alonso Cavale, 50; María Gertrudis Soto, 30; María Paisqua, 20; and Marselo Matheo, 27. The latter two were attached to María Gertrudis's household. Two other Timucua, Juan Puje, 50, and Lucia, 70, were attached to a Yamasee household along with the lone Chiluque, Margarita Sosa, 30. It is worthy of note that Palica had a Juan Pufe in 1736, who was 14 at that time. Likewise, the "Village of Timucua" of 1736 had a 60-year-old named Riso. Cavale, who was married to a Yamasee named Rosa María, had sons aged 14 and 16. Another Yamasee woman was attached to his household. María Gertrudis, who was married to a 30-year-old Yamasee, had sons aged four, six, and 12. She could be the Gertrudis listed for Palica in 1752. Juan Puje had a 60-year-old Yamasee wife.

The village's name appeared on this census as Nuestra Señora de la Leche rather than as Nombre de Dios (Ruís 1759).

Tolomato, originally a Guale village, contained nine adult Chiluque and three Chiluque children in its eight houses in 1759. The Chiluque adults outnumbered the adult Ibaja by three. Five of the Chiluque adults bore the surname Uriza and two others were spouses of Urizas. The Spanish name Uriza did not appear in the censuses for 1752, but some of the Urizas of 1759 seem to be the Anayos of 1752. Tolomato's lone Chiluque of 1752, identified simply as Ana María, probably was the Ana María Uriza of 1759. Others among Tolomato's Chiluque of 1759 have possible counterparts in 1752's Palica, but the matches are not clearcut.

Tolomato's Chiluque in 1759 were Lucia Uriza, 40; Joseph Uriza, 78, who was married to a 70-year-old Chiluque named María Asenisia; their 23-year-old son, Patrizio; Lorenzo Uriza, a 32-year-old widower; Ana María Uríza, 30; Francisco Vicente, 28, who was married to María de la Cruz Uriza, a 33-year-old Chiluque; and María de los Santos, 23. María Asenisia has a likely counterpart in 1752's Palica, one of whose women was identified simply as Asenisia, a rather unusual name. The only Joseph in 1752's Palica to match her 1759 husband, Joseph Uriza, was identified as Joseph Anayo. Interestingly, there was a Patricio Anayo in 1752 who matched these Urizas' son Patrizio of 1759, and there was also a Lorenzo Anayo in 1752's Palica who matched 1759's Lorenzo Uriza. The conclusion is inescapable that the Anayos of 1752 were transformed into Urizas by 1759. A Palica woman identified simply as Cruz in 1752 was probably 1759's María de la Cruz Uriza. Palica had a Francisco in 1752 who could have been her husband. Palica in 1752 had a girl named María and a man named Miguel de los Santos to provide a counterpart for 1759's María de los Santos. Consequently, Palica was the likely source for Tolomato's influx of Chiluque between 1752 and 1759.

The Spaniards' precision in identifying the Mocama-Chiluque as Chiluque in this period rather than characterizing them simply as "Timucua" is worthy of note. Their exactness stands out particularly in the 1759 census for Nombre de Dios, which identified six as "Timuquana" and one as "Chiluque." The specificity undoubtedly reflects their recognition of the cultural distinctiveness of the Mocama vis-à-vis other Timucua-speakers that archaeologists recognize today.

Among Tolomato's Chiluque in 1759, Lucia Uriza was married to a 42-year-old Ibaja, Miguel de los Santos. They had a daughter, María de los Angeles, 17. The widower, Lorenzo Uriza, had a three-year-old son, Manuel. Ana María Uriza was married to an Ibaja named Juan Christóval, aged 33. María de la Cruz Uriza and Francisco Vicente had three children: Francisco, nine; Yñés, six; and Juan, two. María de los Santos shared a house with an 80-year-old Yamasee widow, María de Grazia (Truxillo 1759).

All the surviving inhabitants of those two villages, along with the natives residing in St. Augustine itself, accompanied the Spaniards in their withdrawal to Cuba when Florida was surrendered to Britain in exchange for Britain's return of Havana, which it had captured when Spain entered the Seven Years War in its closing days. Robert L. Gold's study of the transfer does not provide a tribal breakdown for the 89 Indians involved. The Indian departees numbered only six fewer than the 95 recorded by the 1759 census. If the same standards were used in 1763 as in 1759 for the dividing line between child and adult, the proportion of children increased considerably over the four-year interval. Thirty-seven of the 89 exiles were children, compared with the 22 of 1759. The 29 men and 38 women of 1759 declined to 20 men and 32 women by 1763. At least two Timucua-speakers, Manuel Riso and Juan Alonso Cavale, were among the emigrants.

The exiles' departure ended the Timucua experience in Florida. The émigrés did not fare well in Cuba, as lack of subsistence and disease or, in Riso's case, old age took their toll. By 1766 their number had shrunk to 53. More than one-half of the adult males had become casualties (Gold 1969:67, 76, 81). Marselo Matheo, Lucia Uriza, and Juan Alonso Cavale were among the early casualties. Cavale died in 1767 (Lyon 1992b). Most of the Indian émigrés settled in Guanabacoa, a haven not far from Havana that had traditionally been a village for Cuba's surviving native population. The disappearance in Cuba of those last survivors of the Timucua-speakers ended the memories passed down by their ancestors of traditions developed over 12,000 years of adaptation to the world they found in Florida (Landers 1992).

16♦

TIMUCUA ACCULTURATION

The small Timucua-speaking remnant population living in the vicinity of St. Augustine and at San Francisco Potano and Salamototo in the first years of the eighteenth century differed in many ways from their ancestors, who first came into contact with Europeans between the late 1520s and the mid-1560s. Compared with our knowledge of their Apalachee neighbors, little is known about the acculturation of the Timucua or their interaction with and influence on the Spaniards, from either documentary or archaeological sources. In certain respects, Timucua-speakers seem to have been quicker to adopt European ways than were the Apalachee, although that judgment may be warped by the documentation available and the Timucua-speakers' longer sustained contact with Spaniards. A striking example is the Timucua's early and extensive abandonment of their native names for completely Christian and/or Spanish ones. Few of the Christian Timucua leaders whose names are known retained a native component. After the initial hostility toward the Spaniards of most Timucua-speakers in the 1560s and early 1570s, there is little evidence of a nativist reaction among the Timucua to match the one represented by the 1647 Apalachee revolt. Again, this may be a document-based bias. There was trouble among the Saltwater Timucua in the 1620s, but nothing is known of the basic issues involved. The 1656 revolt was more a protest against a governor's ignoring of the chiefs' status and prerogatives than a throwing off of Spanish ways. There is no evidence of Timucua disaffection from the Spaniards to match that among substantial elements of Apalachee's population during the final cataclysmic years of the missions' destruction.

In many other respects, nonetheless, Timucua-speakers remained as much as or more attached to native ways than were their Apalachee counterparts. The western Timucua's greater resistance to the Spaniards' campaign to abolish the ball game is one indication of their traditionalism. But the scope of that traditionalism vis-à-vis the game is diminished by the Timucua's arguments in support of continuing to play it, for they maintained that their playing of the game did not involve the "abuses" that led to the Spaniards' call for banning of the Apalachee version. Customs such as scalping and inheritance through the matrilineal line remained strongly rooted in general except for instances of inheritance in which ruling cacicas married Spaniards. The Apalachee did not confront that problem, as no Apalachee women are known to have held positions as ruling chiefs or as heirs to chieftainships. The strength of some Timucua's adherence to scalping as late as 1701 is reflected in an incident in the Mayaca country during an expedition by Spanish soldiers and Timucua and Guale warriors to bring fugitives back to their missions in that area. The governor had instructed the members of the expedition to exercise moderation even if hostilities broke out and not to initiate hostilities under any circumstances. Despite those cautions, some of the Timucua killed and scalped some natives of the Mayaca region, whom they encountered by chance wandering in the woods, who had not given obedience to Spain's king (Zúñiga y Zerda 1701d).

Timucua adopted the raising of hogs and chickens, but there is no evidence one way or the other relative to cattle-raising. But European animals did not replace wild animals or, in the case of the coastal people, marine resources in the Timucua's subsistence strategy (Reitz 1993:384–87). Santa Fé's Chief don Thomás Medina had a supply of packhorses by the beginning of the last quarter of the seventeenth century. As early as 1597 the Mocama paramount at San Pedro had a horse at a time when horses seem to have been a luxury even for most Spaniards in Florida. Adherence to traditional healing practices as late as the 1690s is reflected in the documents.

On the other hand, Timucua appear to have taken the lead among Spanish Florida's Indians in taking advantage of the opportunity to learn to read and write when it was made available to them early in the seventeenth century. Spaniards' remarks suggest that many Timucua showed a spontaneous interest in acquiring those skills (Jesús 1630a:100). A friar claimed that on becoming Christians they abandoned with ease their traditional ceremonies and "superstitions" involved in the disposition of the remains of their deceased (Jesús 1630a:99).

The council house remained a most important focus of village life until the end of the mission era. It retained most of the functions it had housed prior to the Timucua's Christianization. For the Indians at least, preparation and consumption of cacina remained restricted to its confines.

The Timucua's profession of Catholicism doubtless brought some of the most profound changes in their customs and outlook. But there is little documentary evidence concerning those changes, particularly for the late seventeenth century, when the change must have been greatest after successive generations had lived under the mission regime. As few Timucua left the Spanish ecumene, we do not have observations by outsiders as to the fervor of the Timucua's practice of their new faith such as we have for the Apalachee who migrated to Mobile in 1704 and then on to the Louisiana territory's Red River in 1763.

Timucua retained their tribal identification until the exodus in 1763 and continued to live in communities of their own kind to a considerable degree at least as late as 1752. They preserved even their subgroup identities such as Salamototo and Chiluque-Mocama. But in view of the steady decline in their numbers and the Catholic Church's prohibition of marriage between close relatives, the Timucua had begun to intermarry with members of other Indian tribes. That intermixture and the chaotic life all the "Spanish" Indians endured for most of the 1702 to 1763 period, when they were chronically harassed by Spain's enemies, together with the incidence of alcoholism, led to a serious decline in their adherence to native traditions during that era. A strong indication of the degree of change that had occurred since the early seventeenth century was their decision to abandon their homeland in 1763. They had become sufficiently attuned to Spanish society by 1763 to identify their interests with those of Spain and to face the uncertainties of the move to Cuba in preference to remaining in their land and facing the uncertainties of dealing with its new English masters. At the beginning of the seventeenth century, when the king was considering abandonment of Florida and asked about the possibility of moving its Christianized Indians to Cuba, a friar testified that nothing could persuade the Indians at that time to make such a move.

NOTES

Chapter 2. The Timucua People at Contact

1. I have modernized the spelling where I felt that Hakluyt's sixteenth-century spelling might hinder easy comprehension.

2. Lucy L. Wenhold (1936:12) omitted the identity of the topless women in her translation of the bishop's letter.

3. Another source definitely linked use of shell money to the Guale. It is probable that it existed as well among the coastal Timucua at least.

4. *Traen* could be rendered in other senses that fit this context. One among them is "collect." *Arrecades* does not appear in modern dictionaries but undoubtedly is a type of adornment.

Chapter 3. First Contacts with Europeans

1. *Apiladas* could be rendered as "peeled" as well as "dried."

2. Menéndez de Avilés (1965a:75) gave the time and place as August 25, Sunday, at midday above (*sobre*) Cape Canaveral at 28 degrees. As Solís de Merás, Barrientos, and López de Mendoza all agree on August 28, Menéndez's August 25 may be a scribe's mistake. Spanish sources contain a number of such discrepancies. López de Mendoza, in particular, diverges from other contemporary accounts on a number of points.

3. Solís de Merás (1923:82) said the Indians informed them the French were 20 leagues to the north. It is unlikely that data that specific would be communicated by sign language. His remark is probably an interpolation made from knowledge gained by hindsight. López de Mendoza Grajales's account of this episode differs considerably from the ones presented by Menéndez de Avilés and Solís de Merás. According to Grajales, Menéndez put 50 armed men on land and their captains lit many fires to attract Indian attention. When the fires brought no response, the soldiers went inland four leagues, where they found a village in which they were well received.

4. *Quilate* was also the name of an ancient coin. López de Mendoza Grajales described the gold as "two pieces of gold, although not very good in the way of carats."

Chapter 5. Timucua Political Organization

1. *Yvita* or *ivi* means water in a lake, pond, or river (Granberry 1989:169). *Yvita* appears frequently as a place name for a number of arroyos or streams westward from the St. Johns River on the mission trail. They include such names as *ajano ybitta, apixa yvitta,* and *ajano ybitta chirico* (Palacios 1675; Peña 1717). Pedro Palacios, Bishop Díaz Vara Calderón's secretary, defined the last of those names as meaning "river of little acorns."

2. I omitted the *ytorimitono* because Pareja, after mentioning him as the last of the counselors, added that they then paid no attention to him (*de que ya no hazen caso*).

Chapter 6. The Timucua's Material World

1. *Jacal* is a Mexican term for hut or house derived from the word *xacalli.*

Chapter 7. Timucua Traditions and Customs

1. Bennett (1975:85) rendered the passage somewhat freely as "the Aggressors took the heads of their slain enemies and cut the hair off, taking a piece of skull with each scalp." Nothing resembling *taiz* appears in modern French dictionaries. I suspect that it is a cognate of the Spanish *tez,* which means "skin."

2. Archaeologists have found busycon shells to be the drinking vessel placed on such graves.

3. For more details on the Timucua game and the rituals and myths associated with it, see Hann (1988a), where a translation of the Apalachee-Yustaga ball-game manuscript is also presented.

4. One of the manuscript's readers identified a limestone disk found at Fig Springs in recent excavations as possibly a chunkey-stone, but Weisman's illustration and data for the disk (1992:141, fig. 68, 143) (11 cm diameter and 1 cm thick) do not seem compatible with such an identification.

5. This refers to the preparing of a field or savanna for support of the widow.

6. Milanich and Sturtevant's (1972:25) translator rendered this passage differently: "To go hunting deer and to burn a pile of straw to hunt them have you made six arrows and six splinters of oak and mixing a *yaquila* all between a woven cloth?" Pareja's Timucua text and his Spanish translation of it do not seem to correspond entirely. The Timucua text begins with *Huri melaso,* which means "to fire-hunt." Unless Timucua has a word meaning "deer" in addition

to *honoso,* the Timucua text does not contain the word "deer." A number of the words in the Timucua text do not seem to appear in the Spanish text, namely *pahama,* meaning "house," and *aya,* meaning "forest," which immediately precedes *pahama.*

Chapter 8. The Timucua Language

1. Granberry (1989:40) rendered this as *yaukfa.*

2. Granberry (1989:40) rendered Pareja's words for 2, 4, 7, 8, and 9 respectively as *yucha, cheqeta, piqicha, piqinaho,* and *peqecheqeta.*

Chapter 9. Beginnings of Missionization

1. *Monte* could be rendered also as "hill." In this context that rendering could possibly be more appropriate.

2. Maynard Geiger (1937:103) rendered *ara* as "altar-stone."

3. To avoid confusion, note should be made of the existence of a second María Meléndez living at St. Augustine or Nombre de Dios at this time. She was an Escamacu princess, sister of María Ruíz del Castillo, a *cacica* from Escamacu. This María Meléndez also was married to a soldier. She had been brought up in the house of Governor Menéndez Márques who gave her his name. Menéndez Márques had high regard for María Ruís, who had served as an interpreter and used her influence to bring the Escamacu into obedience to Spain's King and secure the conversion of Escamacu's leaders. María Ruíz had a natural daughter by a Spanish soldier, Joan de Valdés (C. de Valdés 1616).

Chapter 14. The Timucua Missions' Extinction, 1680–1704

1. Mark Boyd's translations of Romo de Urisa's and Manuel Solana's letters telling of the debacle on the Flint leave something to be desired. In his translation of the Chacato woman's account of the natives who made up the attack force that set out from Achito (Chisca, Chichimeco, Apalachicola, Chata, and Uchisi), Boyd rendered Chata as Chacato and Uchisi as Yuchi. The Chata in this instance probably were Choctaw. Elsewhere in his letter, Romo de Uriza used the spelling "Chacato" when he had Chacato in mind. The Uchisi were a Muskogean people with no relation to the Yuchi, as far as is known. Uchisi were the probable ancestors of today's Mikasuki.

Chapter 15. The Timucua's Last Years in Florida

1. Another less reliable source gave 30 days as the length of the enemy's siege of Ivitachuco (Nieto de Carbajal 1707).

2. Nieto de Carbajal (1707) gave the number of captives as more than 80. He put the number of soldiers killed at 18. He identified the village from which the captives had come as an Yguaja village. The governor's account is probably the more reliable, as Carbajal's account was a later one and may have been given off the cuff.

3. For greater detail on the non-Timucua settlements of 1717, see Ayala y Escobar (1717) or Hann (1989:183–95).

4. The meaning of this reference is unclear. The two villages could be La Costa and San Nicolás or it could be that Benavides considered the Alafaes and Pojoy as distinct peoples. Some Alafaes were living with the Costa at that time. A chief identified himself in 1735 as "Don Antonio Pojoy, head as I am of the Alafaia Costas nation" (Hann 1991a:358). It is also possible that he was referring to San Nicolás alone. It contained two distinct settlements in June 1738.

GLOSSARY

Some Spanish and Indian terms in this glossary have meanings peculiar to Florida or to the Antilles, especially Cuba, from which some of them derived.

Ache: an unidentified starchy tuber that grew in water in swampy habitats, used by Indians and Spaniards, described as being similar to *yuca,* probably meaning manioc; it requires grinding and purification with water to remove poison and pungency; erroneously identified, at times, as a Zamia.

Adelantado: a person to whom the king granted authority to lead an overseas expedition of discovery and conquest, bestowing on him beforehand powers of government in the lands that he might discover and conquer.

Arroba: for Spanish Florida and for some Spanish American countries today, an old Spanish unit of weight equal to about 25 pounds.

Atequi (rendered also as *atiqui, athequi,* and *yatiqui*): a native name for the official interpreter, a position of importance that could only be held by members of the chiefly class; found among Muskogean peoples as well as among the Timucua and in the northern non-Muskogean territories that Juan Pardo and Hernando Moyano traversed in the 1560s.

Atole: a gruel made of maize flour and boiling water or, in Cuba, milk.

Auto: as used here, embraces a wide range of judicial processes, inquiries, reports, taking of testimony, pleadings, and records of proceedings; usually done under oath unless the witness was non-Christian, in which case the witness was asked to promise to tell the truth.

Barbacoa: of Antillian origin, applied in Spanish Florida to a number of raised, often grill-like structures that included grates used in the open air for smoking, drying, or roasting meat, fish, and fruit; benches in houses and in the council house on which people sat and slept; and elevated, enclosed sheds in which maize and other foodstuffs were stored.

Berdache: used for Indians whom the French described as having adopted the role and clothing of women in native society as an alternative to becoming warriors.

Cabildo: the municipal council or the structure in which it met; or a cathedral chapter, the meeting of such a body, or the place where it met.

Cacica: of Antillian origin, denoting either the wife of an Indian chief or a native woman who was a chieftainness in her own right.

Cacina: a native tea made from the toasted powdered leaves of the yaupon holly (*Ilex vomitoria*), which anthropologists refer to as black drink.

Camino real: a principal road or trail linking St. Augustine with the native provinces of the hinterland that acknowledged the Spanish governor's jurisdiction over them.

Chacal: title for native officials who were deputies of the *iniha,* used at times to refer to the *iniha* himself; found among the Apalachee and Chacato as well as among the Timucua.

Chichimeco: a name of Mexican origin that Spaniards in Florida applied to some predatory groups of Indians who harassed the inhabitants of the missions, one group of whom were the native called Westo by the English of Charles Town.

Cimarron and *cimarrona:* used in Spanish Florida to refer to Indians who abandoned the regimented life of the mission village or of the non-Christian native villages to live in the woods beyond the control of native authorities; used at times to refer seemingly to intrusive Indians of unknown origin, living in the woods near missions or Spanish ranches. The name Seminole is believed to have derived from this Spanish word and usage.

Confessionario: a guide written by Fray Francisco de Pareja containing questions and counsel in Spanish and Timucua, side by side, to serve as an aid to friars who were less skilled than he in the Timucua language to enable them to hear the confessions of natives who did not speak Spanish.

Congregación: one of several names for forms of directed settlement used in the establishment and maintenance of some missions in order to bring in natives from remote or small settlements and assemble them at a more accessible site, usually one chosen by a friar.

Cronista mayor: an official employed by the Crown in Mexico to assemble information on developments in the territories under the Mexican viceroy's jurisdiction and to record such data in an official chronicle.

Doctrina: the term used most frequently in Florida to refer to a mission center that possessed a resident friar or at times one that had possessed one. The name reflects the indoctrination or instruction of the natives that was a major activity at mission centers. Unlike *congregación* and *reducción,* the name does not necessarily imply the drawing in or settling down of natives at the mission center.

Encomienda: a system developed to exploit the labor of the Indians under which private individuals or the Crown collected tribute from designated groups of Indians in exchange for protection and instruction in Christian doctrine and European ways.

Fiscal: a native official in the mission villages who served as the eyes and ears of the friar, reporting on Christian natives who did not live in accord with Christian mores or missed mass regularly on Sundays. He also probably supervised the planting, harvesting, and disbursement of the produce from fields planted for support of the church and the needy.

Gacha: a thin watery mass or stew; in the plural, porridge or pap.

Garita: in Spanish Florida, the elevated structure or barbacoa in which the natives stored their maize and other provisions, so-called because of those structures' resemblance to the little towers on the salients of forts to shelter the sentinels or the little houses of sentry posts, the more typical meanings of this Spanish term.

Gobernador: a title meaning governor usually bestowed in Spanish Florida on de facto native rulers who were governing a village in lieu of the legitimate chief or chieftainness when the legitimate ruler was incapable of doing so because of age or infirmity. At times the title also was given to legitimate chiefs when they were officially installed or recognized by Spanish authorities, possibly to forestall any challenge to the chief's right to rule without a recourse to Spanish authorities.

Guano: generally used elsewhere to denote dried bird dung, but in Spanish Florida designated Spanish moss and palm straw used to make clothing; probably of Cuban origin as it was used there as a generic name for various species of palms.

Holata: a title for chief used by the Timucua, Apalachee, and many other peoples throughout the Southeast. Timucua usage of the title most closely resembles that of the Apalachee, used for head chiefs and for the word chief or cacique in general.

Iniha: a title designating the second in command among the Timucua, Apalachee, and many other peoples throughout the Southeast; handled most of the village's day-to-day administrative functions and served as the Timucua chief's foremost counselor.

Lengua: Florida Spaniards used this word meaning tongue in the anatomical and linguistic senses often to designate an interpreter or translator for communications with non-Spanish-speaking natives. Spaniards used the term also as a synonym for tribal territory, particularly in referring to Guale territory as the lengua de Guale.

Mandador: a Spanish word meaning order giver; used in Florida as a synonym for iniha.

Mica: a term for chieftainness among Muskogean peoples such as the Guale that Spaniards probably derived from Mico.

Mico: title designating first-rank chiefs found among Muskogean peoples, such as the Guale, Tama-Yamasee, and Apalachicola, but not among the Apalachee.

Mil: a French term meaning millet, which French sources on Florida used for maize. Translators of these sources have rendered it erroneously at times as millet. The sixteenth-century Florida French usage was possibly influenced by *milho,* the Portuguese word for maize.

Noroco: a title that Timucua and Apalachee conferred on warriors who had killed three enemies in battle. It gave such warriors special rank and prestige.

Obrajes: as used here, designates large textile-manufacturing operations in Mexico and South America based on exploited native labor, which manufactured cloth and finished products.

Parucusi: a Timucua title for chiefs. Its use may have been confined to the Timucua, as was *utina.*

Reducción: a term for mission center more or less synonymous with *doctrina,* but usually denoting a directed settlement, as does *congregación.*

Repartimiento: as used here, designates a system for recruiting native labor by requiring villages to supply quotas of workers proportional to their adult male population available for labor to serve in rotation for a limited period on Spanish projects, public and private. Such workers were to receive a daily wage of one-half *real* and sustenance.

Residencia: a judicial inquiry into the propriety with which officials such as Florida's governors fulfilled the duties of their office. It was held at the end of the official's term, and, in the case of governors, it was usually conducted by the governor chosen to succeed the outgoing governor. During the inquiry the people over whom the outgoing official had exercised jurisdiction could present complaints about the official's fulfillment of his duties or about unjust treatment they believed they had received at his hands.

Rinconada: a Spanish term denoting a sheltered or remote place that constituted a distinct unit because it was surrounded by woods or river or a box canyon that could be isolated easily as a corral for cattle.

Situado: the royal subsidy paid from surplus funds generated by the viceroyalty of Mexico, which provided the salaries for the royal officials and soldiers and the stipends given to the friars as well as most of the other expenses linked to maintenance of the Spanish presence in Florida. The small amount of revenue the Crown received from Florida made the situado a necessity.

Utina: a chiefly title found only among the Timucua, applied to paramount chiefs of so exalted a status that non-Christian Timucua used the title for the Christian's God. It appeared as part of the name of a number of hinterland villages and was and is used as a name for the hinterland province that Spaniards usually referred to as Timucua Province.

Vara: the Spanish yard, which is divided into three feet or four palms and which is equivalent to about 33 inches or 835 millimeters and nine-tenths.

Visita: the Spanish term for a missionized village that did not have a resident friar, which friars visited occasionally to say mass and to catechize the inhabitants. When a *visita* was within a reasonable distance of a mission center or *doctrina,* the inhabitants usually went to the mission center for Sunday mass.

Vocainas: although this term does not appear in modern dictionaries in this form or as *bocainas,* it is probably a diminutive of *boca* used to refer to a minor mouth or entrance to a river.

Ycapacha: a Timucua term meaning abandoned village site, equivalent to the Apalachee term *chicasa.* Ycapacha probably represents a Spanish corruption of the Timucua word *hicapacha* in which *hica* means village and *pacha* signifies ancient or old.

ABBREVIATIONS

The abbreviations are used in designating the source of documents consulted in the preparation of this work.

ACNL	Ayer Collection, Newberry Library, Chicago.
AGI	Archivo General de Indias, Sevilla.
BAR	Bureau of Archaeological Research, Tallahassee.
EC	Escribanía de Cámara.
JGSC	John Gilmary Shea Collection, Special Collections Library, Georgetown University, Washington, D.C.
JTCC	Jeannette Thurber Connor Collection, Library of Congress. Consulted in a microfilm copy at the P.K. Yonge Library of Florida History, University of Florida, Gainesville.
JTLC	John Tate Lanning Collection, Thomas Jefferson Library, University of Missouri, St. Louis.
PKYLFH	P.K. Yonge Library of Florida History, University of Florida, Gainesville.
SC	Stetson Collection, P.K. Yonge Library of Florida History, University of Florida, Gainesville.
SD	Santo Domingo.
WLC	Woodbury Lowery Collection, Library of Congress.

Microfilm copies at the P.K. Yonge Library of Florida History, Gainesville, and Florida State University's Strozier Library, Tallahassee, differ in the number of reels; my citations reflect the reel division at the Strozier Library.

BIBLIOGRAPHY

Adam, Lucien, and Julian Vinson
  1886   *Arte de la Lengva Timvqvana Compuesto en 1614 por el P^e Francisco Pareja* (Grammar of the Timuquan language composed by Fr. Francisco Pareja). Paris: Maisonneuve Frères et Ch. Leclerc.
Agramon [Chiluque Indian]
  1702   Statement, November 8, 1702. In Zúñiga y Zerda 1702e, q.v.
Alas, Alonso de las
  1599   Letter to the King, March 20, 1599. AGI, SD 229, JTCC, reel 3.
  1600   Letter to the King, January 12, 1600. AGI, SD 229, JTCC, reel 3.
Alas, Esteban de las
  1569a   Bill of Exchange on Juan Junco to G. Camacho, January 12, 1569. AGI, Justicia 1, 001, no. 2, RI, A, pieces 1, 2. Summary by Eugene Lyon.
  1569b   Case against Captain Francisco Núñez, Ensign Diego de Castillón, and Sergeant Navarro over the loss of the fort of San Matheo. AGI, Justicia 998. Microfilm copy made available by Eugene Lyon.
Albárez de Castrillón, Pedro
  1597   Testimony, September 17, 1597. AGI, SD 231, SC.
Alcayde de Córdoba, Martín
  1660   Testimony, Ivitachuco, May 2, 1660. In Worth 1992a:404–7, q.v.
Alegre, Francisco Javier, S.J.
  1956   *Historia de la Provincia de la Compania de Jesús de Nueva España* (History of the province of the Company of Jesus of New Spain). Vol. 1. New edition, introduction by Ernest J. Burrus, S.J., and Felipe Zubillaga, S.J. Rome: Institutum Historicum, S.J.
Alejo, Juan
  1660   Testimony, Ivitachuco, May 17, 1660. In Worth 1992a:392–93, q.v.
Aranda y Abellaneda, Pedro de
  1684   Petition to Juan Márquez Cabrera, November 11, 1684. AGI, EC, leg. 3 of the residencia, tome C, JTCC, reel 1.

Aranguíz y Cotes, Alonso de
    1659   Letter to the King, November 1, 1659. AGI, SD 852, SC.
    1661   Order to Antonio de Argüelles, June 29, 1661. AGI, SD 23. Translation by Eugene Lyon in the possession of John H. Hann.
    1662   Letter to the King, September 8, 1662. AGI, SD 225, WLC, reel 3.
Arcos, Pedro de
    1675   Report to Pablo de Hita Salazar, 1675. In Hita Salazar 1675b, q.v.
Argüelles, Alonso de
    1660a Testimony, May 2, 1660. In Worth 1992a:393–404, q.v.
    1660b Testimony, May 11, 1660. In Worth 1992a:454–55, q.v.
Argüelles, Antonio de
    1660   Testimony, May 1, 1660. In Worth 1992a:392–93, q.v.
    1678   Visitation of Guale and Mocama, November 29, 1677–January 10, 1678. In Hann 1993b:83–94, q.v.
Argüelles, Bartolomé de
    1596   Letter to the King, May 12, 1596. AGI, SD 229, JTCC, reel 3.
    1598a Letter to the King, August 3, 1598. AGI, SD 229, JTCC, reel 3.
    1598b Letter to the King, October 31, 1598. AGI, SD 229, JTCC, reel 3.
    1599a Letter to the King, March 20, 1599. AGI, SD 229, JTCC, reel 3.
    1599b Letter to the King, March 20, 1599. AGI, SD 229, JTCC, reel 3.
    1600   Letter to the King, February 20, 1600. AGI, SD 229, JTCC, reel 3.
    1603   Letter to the King, April 20, 1603. AGI, SD 229, JTCC, reel 3.
Argüelles, Bartolomé de, and Joan Menéndez Márques
    1603   Letter to the King, April 20, 1603. AGI, SD 229, JTCC, reel 3.
Arnade, Charles W.
    1959a *The Siege of St. Auqustine in 1702.* Gainesville: University of Florida Press.
    1959b *Florida on Trial, 1593–1602.* Coral Gables: University of Miami Press.
    1965   *Cattle Raising in Spanish Florida, 1513–1763.* St. Augustine: St. Augustine Historical Society, publication no. 21. Reprint from *Agricultural History* 35 (1961).
Arroyo, Pedro de
    1605   Testimony, December 12, 1605. AGI, Patronato 19, JTCC, reel 1.
Ashley, Keith H.
    1994   Late Prehistoric Occupations near the Mouth of the St. Johns River, Florida: St. Johns or St. Marys? Paper presented at the 51st Annual Meeting of the Southeastern Archaeological Conference, Lexington, Kentucky.
Atanacio [Apalachee Indian]
    1676   Testimony, June 26, 1676. In Jones, Hann, and Scarry 1991:154–58, q.v.

Ayala y Escobar, Juan de
  1698   Visitation of the provinces of Apalachee and Timuqua, February
          18, 1698. AGI, EC, leg. 157A, microfilm 27-P (residencia series),
          PKYLFH.
  1717   Letter to the King, April 18, 1717. AGI, SD 843, SC. Translation by
          John H. Hann on file at BAR.
Ayeta, Francisco de
  1691   Deposition, February 5, 1691. AGI, SD 864, JTCC, reel 6.
Baker, Henry
  1993   Spanish Ranching and the Alachua Sink Site: A Preliminary
          Report. *Florida Anthropologist* 46 (June 1993):82–100.
Baldés, Miguel de
  1608   Certification, January 1, 1608. In Sánchez Judrero 1608, q.v.
Barbosa, Francisco
  1683   List of the number of Indians that the province of Guale has and
          the padres *doctrineros* that there are, San Juan del Puerto, June 7,
          1683. AGI, SD 839, JTCC, reel 5.
Barreda, Jazinto de
  [1692] Petition, n.d. [second half of April 1692]. In Quiroga y Losada
          1692c, q.v.
Barrera, Rodrigo de
  1675a   Letter to Andrés Pérez, San Carlos, July 26, 1675. In Hann
          1993b:38–39, q.v.
  1675b   Letter to Andrés Pérez, Santa Cruz, July 31, 1675. In Hann
          1993b:40, q.v.
Barrientos, Bartolomé
  1902   Los Naturales de America bajo la Dominación Española: Vida y
          Hechos de Pero Menéndez de Avilés (The natives of America
          under the Spanish domination: Life and exploits of Pedro Menéndez
          de Avilés). In G. García 1902:1–152.
  1965   *Pedro Menéndez de Avilés, Founder of Florida.* Translated by Anthony
          Kerrigan. Gainesville: University of Florida Press.
Basanier, M., ed.
  1853   *L'Histoire Notable de la Floride Située en Indes Occidentales. Contenant
          les Trois Voyages Faits en Icelle par Certaines Capitaines et Pilotes
          François, Descrit par le Capitaine Laudonnière, Qui Y A Commandé
          L'Espace d'un An Trois Moys: a la Quella A Esté Adiousté un Quatresme
          Voyage Fait par le Capitaine Gourgues* (The notable history of Florida
          located in the West Indies. It contains the three voyages made to
          it by certain French captains and pilots, described by Captain
          Laudonnière, who commanded it for the space of one year three

months, to which a fourth voyage has been added made by Captain Gourgues). Paris: Cley P. Jannct.

Benavides, Antonio de

1723   Register of Baptisms between 1718 and 1723 by Fray Joseph del Castillo, February 25, 1723. In Hann l991a:361–62, q.v.

1726   Visitation of Settlements near St. Augustine and San Marcos de Apalachee, December 1–11, 1726. In Hann l991a:363–68, q.v.

1738   Letter to the King, Veracruz, Mexico, April 21, 1738. AGI, SD 265, SC.

Bennett, Charles E.

1964   *Laudonnière and Fort Caroline*. Gainesville: University of Florida Press.

Bennett, Charles E., trans.

1975   *Three Voyages: René Laudonnière*. Gainesville: University Presses of Florida.

Bernal, Clemente, Chief

1660   Testimony, May 16, 1660. In Worth 1992a:467–69, q.v.

Bianna, Luis de

1660   Testimony, Ivitachuco, May 20, 1660. In Worth 1992a:478–80, q.v.

Biedma, Luys Hernández de

1857   Relación del Suceso de la Jornada Que Hizo Hernando de Soto, y de la Calidad de la Tierra por Donde Anduvo (Report concerning the outcome of the expedition that Hernando de Soto made and the nature of the land through which he traveled). In Smith 1857:47–64, q.v.

Bolton, Herbert E., ed.

1925   *Arredondo's Historical Proof of Spain's Title to Georgia*. Berkeley: University of California Press.

Boniface, Brian George

1971   A Historical Geography of Spanish Florida, Circa 1700. Master's thesis, University of Georgia.

Booker, Karen M., Charles M. Hudson, and Robert L. Rankin

1992   Place Name Identification in the Sixteenth-Century Southeast. *Ethnohistory* 39 (Fall):399–451.

Bourne, Edward G., ed. and trans.

1904   *Narratives of the Career of Hernando de Soto in the Conquest of Florida*. 2 vols. New York: A. S. Barnes.

Boyd, Mark F.

1937   The Expedition of Marcos Delgado from Apalache to the Upper Creek Country in 1686. *Florida Historical Quarterly* 16 (July):2–32.

1948   Enumeration of Florida Spanish Missions in 1675. *Florida Historical Quarterly* 27 (October):181–88.

1953   Further Considerations of the Apalachee Missions, Documents. *The Americas* 9 (April):459–79.

Boyd, Mark F., Hale G. Smith, and John W. Griffin.

1951   *Here They Once Stood: The Tragic End of the Apalachee Missions.* Gainesville: University of Florida Press.

Boyrie Moya, Emile de, et al.

1957   Zamia Starch in Santo Domingo: A Contribution to the Ethnobotany of the Dominican Republic. *Florida Anthropologist* 10 (March):17–40.

Brinton, Daniel G.

1859   *Notes on the Floridian Peninsula, Its Literary History, Indian Tribes, and Antiquities.* Philadelphia: Joseph Sabin. Reprint. New York: Paladin Press, 1969.

1891   *The American Race: A Linguistic Classification and Ethnographic Description of the Native Tribes of North and South America.* New York: N. C. C. Hodges.

Buarque de Holanda, Sérgio

1963–   *História Geral da Civilização Brasileira* (General history of Brazilian
1967   civilization). 2d ed. 5 vols. São Paulo: Difusão Européia do Livro.

Bullen, Ripley P., and John W. Griffin

1952   An Archaeological Survey of Amelia Island, Florida. *Florida Anthropologist* 5 (September):37–64.

Bullones, Joseph de

1728   Letter to the King, Havana, October 5, 1728. In Hann 1991a:371–80, q.v.

Bushnell, Amy

1978a   The Menéndez Márquez Cattle Barony at La Chua and the Determinants of Economic Expansion in Seventeenth-Century Florida. *Florida Historical Quarterly* 56 (April):407–31.

1978b   That Demonic Game: The Campaign to Stop Indian Pelota Playing in Spanish Florida, 1675–84. *The Americas* 35 (April):1–19.

1979   Patricio de Hinachuba: Defender of the Word of God, the Crown of the King, and the Little Children of Ivitachuco. *American Indian Culture and Research Journal* 3:1–21.

1981   *The King's Coffer: Proprietors of the Spanish Florida Treasury, 1565–1702.* Gainesville: University Presses of Florida.

Bushnell, David I., Jr.

1908   The Account of Lamhatty. *American Anthropologist,* n.s., 10:568–74.

1919   *Native Villages and Village Sites East of the Mississippi.* Bureau of American Ethnology Bulletin no. 69. Washington, D.C.: Smithsonian Institution.

Calderón, Manuel
  1660   Testimony, Ivitachuco, May 7, 1660. In Worth 1992a:426–33, q.v.
Cañiçares Osorio, Adrián de
  1635   Report. In San Martín 1635, q.v.
Castilla, Juan de
  1740   Letter to Joseph de la Quintana, January 6, 1740. AGI, SD 2565, SC.
Cedulario of Florida
  1570–   AGI, SD 2528, SC.
  1604
Charles II
  1681   Decree to the Governor of Florida, Madrid, November 8, 1681. AGI, SD 834, SC.
  1682   Order to Juan Márques Cabrera, Madrid, August 31, 1682. AGI, SD 834, SC.
Choças, Pedro Fernández
  n.d.   Letter to Gonzalo Méndez de Canzo, Puturiba, today,
  [1597]   Saturday, day of the revolt. In Méndez de Canzo 1598a, q.v.
Clayton, Lawrence A., Vernon James Knight, Jr., and Edward C. Moore, eds.
  1993   *The De Soto Chronicles: The Expedition of Hernando de Soto to North America in 1539–1543.* 2 vols. Tuscaloosa: University of Alabama Press.
Connor, Jeannette Thurber, trans. and ed.
  1925   *Colonial Records of Spanish Florida.* Vol. 1, *Letters and Reports of Governors and Secular Persons, 1570–1577.* Deland: Florida State Historical Society.
  1930   *Colonial Records of Spanish Florida.* Vol. 2 *Letters and Reports of Governors, Deliberations, Decrees, and Other Documents, 1577–1580.* Deland: Florida State Historical Society.
Córcoles y Martínez, Francisco de
  1706a   *Auto,* April 11, 1706. In Córcoles y Martínez 1706g, q.v.
  1706b   Letter to Andrés García, April 18, 1706. In Córcoles y Martínez 1706g, q.v.
  1706c   Letter to don Francisco Rizo and don Miguel, April 18, 1706. In Córcoles y Martínez 1706g, q.v.
  1706d   Letter to the King, May 3, 1706. In Boyd 1953:476–77, q.v.
  1706e   *Auto,* May 23, 1706. In Córcoles y Martínez 1706g, q.v.
  1706f   Letter to the King, September 30, 1706. AGI, SD 858, ACNL (residencia for Joseph de Zúñiga y Zerda, Quaderno I). Translation by F. Wayne Childers, in the possession of John H. Hann.
  1706g   Letter to the King, November 30, 1706. AGI SD 841, SC.

1707a   *Auto,* January 12, 1707. AGI, SD 858, AGNL (*residencia* for Joseph de Zúñiga y Zerda, Quaderno I). Translation by F. Wayne Childers, in the possession of John H. Hann.

1707b   Charges against Joseph de Zúñiga y Zerda, February 11, 1707. AGI, SD 858, ACNL (residencia for Joseph de Zúñiga y Zerda, Quaderno I). Translation by F. Wayne Childers, in the possession of John H. Hann.

1707c   Letter to the King, November 12, 1707. AGI, SD 840, JTCC, reel 5.

1709   Letter to the King, July 20, 1709. AGI, SD 843, SC. Translation by John H. Hann on file at BAR.

1711   Letter to the King, April 9, 1711. AGI, SD 843, SC. Translation by John H. Hann on file at BAR.

Cordell, Ann S.

1993   Chronological Variability in Ceramic Paste: A Comparison of Deptford and Savannah Period Pottery in the St. Marys River Region of Northeast Florida and Southeast Georgia. *Southeastern Archaeology* 12 (Summer) 1993:33–58.

Crane, Verner W.

1956   *The Southern Frontier, 1670–1732.* Ann Arbor: University of Michigan Press.

Crawford, James M.

1988   Review of *A Grammar and Dictionary of the Timucua Language,* by Julian Granberry. *American Anthropology and Linquistics Newsletter* (University of Georgia) 5, no. 2 (March).

n.d.   On the Relationship of Timucua to Muskogean. Typescript furnished by Charles Hudson. Written (post-1979).

Crawford, James M., ed.

1975   *Studies in Southeastern Indian Languages.* Athens: University of Georgia Press.

Cruz, Juan Bauptista

1660   Testimony, May 13, 1660. In Worth 1992a:455–64, q.v.

Dávila, Diego

1606   Report Concerning the Pastoral Visitation Which the Bishop of Cuba Made to the Province of Florida, presented to H. M. in the Council of the Indies, June 27, 1606. AGI, SD 235, WLC, reel 2. Translation by John H. Hann on file at BAR.

Deagan, Kathleen A.

1978   Cultures in Transition: Fusion and Assimilation among the Eastern Timucua. In Milanich and Proctor 1978:89–119, q.v.

1979   Timucua 1580. Research paper submitted to the St. Augustine Restoration Foundation, St. Augustine, Fla.

Díaz, Diego
  1605   Testimony, December 12, 1605. AGI, Patronato 19, JTCC, reel 1.
Díaz Vara Calderón, Gabriel
  1675a Letter to the Queen, Havana, 1675. AGI, SD 151. Microfilm copy
          furnished by William H. Marquardt.
  1675b Letter to Juan de Mendoza Escalante, Havana, June 8, 1675.
          JGSC.
Dickinson, Jonathan
  1981   *Jonathan Dickinson's Journal or, God's Protecting Providence: Being the
          Narrative of a Journey from Port Royal in Jamaica to Philadelphia
          between August 23, 1696 and April 1, 1697.* Edited by Evangeline
          Walker Andrews and Charles McLean Andrews. Stuart, Fla.:
          Florida Classics Library.
Díez de la Calle, Juan
  1659   Noticias Sacras i Reales De Los Dos Ymperios De Las Indias
          Occidentales de la Nueva España (Sacred and royal reports con-
          cerning the two empires of the West Indies of New Spain). 2 vols.
          Manuscript 2023–24, Biblioteca Nacional, Madrid. Photocopy
          furnished by Mary L. Mitchell, Madrid.
Dobyns, Henry F.
  1983   *Their Number Become Thinned: Native American Population Dynamics
          in Eastern North America.* Knoxville: University of Tennessee Press.
Dobyns, Henry F., and William R. Swagerty
  1983   Timucuan Population in the 1560s. In Dobyns 1983:147–211, q.v.
Ebelino de Compostela, Diego
  1689   Letter to the King, Havana, September 28, 1689. AGI SD 151, SC.
Elvas, Gentleman of
  1932–   *True Relation of the Hardships Suffered by Governor Fernando de Soto*
  1933   *& Certain Portuguese Gentlemen during the Discovery of the Province of
          Florida.* Translated and edited by James Alexander Robertson. 2
          vols. Deland: Florida State Historical Society.
Entonado, Bartolomé
  1660   Testimony, May 10, 1660. In Worth 1992a:445–50, q.v.
Faupel, W. John
  1992   Appendix I, An Appraisal of the Illustrations. In Lawson 1992:150–
          78, q.v.
Fernández de Florencia, Juan
  1675a Letter to Pablo de Hita Salazar, San Luis de Apalachee, July 15,
          1675. In Hita Salazar 1675b, q.v.
  1675b *Auto* Concerning the Rebellion of the Chacatos, San Carlos,
          October 3–12, 1675. In Hann 1993b:43–53, q.v.
Fernández de Olivera, Juan
  1612   Letter to the King, October 13, 1612. AGI, SD 229, WLC, reel 3.

Fernández de Oviedo y Valdés, Gonzalo
1851–   *Historia General y Natural de los Indios, Islas y Tierra-Firme del Mar*
1855   *Oceano* (General and natural history of the Indians, islands, and mainland of the ocean sea). 4 vols. Madrid: Imprenta de la Real Academia de la Historia.
Fernández de San Agustín, Juan
1630   Testimony, April 1630. In Worth 1992a:68–69, q.v.
Florencia, Claudio
1709   Report about the services performed for his majesty by the Captain don Jasito Roque Perez, deceased, and by the grandparents and great grandparents of doña Juana Cathalina de Florencia, her father, and various others among her brothers, and the political and military positions that they have held since the foundation of this presidio, 1709. In Córcoles y Martínez 1709, q.v. Translation by John H. Hann on file at BAR.
Florencia, Claudio, et al.
1707   Letter to the King, May 7, 1707. AGI, SD 863, JTCC, reel 6.
Florencia, Francisco de
1705a   Letter to Andrés García, Bitachuco [at Abosaya], August 23, 1705. In Boyd 1953:474, q.v.
1705b   Letter to the commander at [Hacienda] La Chua, Bitachuco, August 27, 1705. In Boyd 1953:474, q.v.
Florencia, Francisco de, and Juan de Pueyo
1706a   Letter to the King, April 30, 1706. In Boyd 1953:475–76, q.v.
1706b   Letter to the King, August 13, 1706. In Boyd 1953:477–78, q.v.
Florencia, Francisco de, et al.
1706   Junta, April 12, 1706. In Córcoles y Martínez 1706g, q.v.
Florencia, Joaquín de
1695   General Visitation that the Captain Joaquín de Florencia, Interim Treasurer of the Presidio of St. Augustine of Florida, made of the provinces of [illegible], Apalachee and Timuqua [several illegible words] by title of the Señor Don Laureano de Torres y Ayala, Knight of the Order of Santiago, governor and captain general of the said presidio and provinces by His Majesty, November 5, 1694–January 2, 1695. In Hann 1993b:152–219, q.v.
Ford, James A.
1969   *A Comparison of Formative Cultures in the Americas: Diffusion or the Psychic Unity of Man.* Smithsonian Contributions to Anthropology, no. 11. Washington, D.C.: Smithsonian Institution Press.
Friars
1664   Letter to the King, June 16, 1664. AGI, SD 848, WLC, reel 3.
1752   Indians who reside in the village of Palica, 1752; Native Indians, residents of the village of Nuestra Señora de Guadelupe de

Tolomato, 1752. AGI, SD 2604. Photocopy furnished by Jane Landers.

Fuentes de Galarza, Francisco de

1702a   Letter to Joseph de Zúñiga y Zerda, San Juan del Puerto, November 4, 1702, 4 o'clock in the afternoon. AGI, SD 858, JTCC, reel 6.

1702b   Letter to Joseph de Zúñiga y Zerda, n.d. [written before November 29, 1702]. AGI, SD 858, JTCC, reel 6.

Galloway, Patricia

1991   Where Have All the Menstrual Huts Gone? Paper presented at the 48th Annual Meeting of the Southeastern Archaeological Conference, Jackson, Miss.

1994   Confederacy as a Solution to Chiefdom Dissolution: Historical Evidence in the Choctaw Case. In Hudson and Tesser 1994:393–420, q.v.

Gannon, Michael V.

1983   *The Cross in the Sand: The Early Catholic Church in Florida 1513–1870.* Paperback edition. Gainesville: University Presses of Florida.

García, Andrés

1695   *Autos* from the Chamber of Justice made officially by the Adjutant Andrés García, Lieutenant of the Province of Timuqua against Santiago, native of the village of San Pedro, Year of 1695, Santa Elena de Machava and elsewhere in Timucua Province, February 19 to September 23, 1695. In Hann 1993b:276–96, q.v.

1706a   Letter to Francisco de Córcoles y Martínez, April 23, 1706. In Córcoles y Martínez 1706g, q.v.

1706b   Letter to Francisco de Córcoles y Martínez, April 24, 1706. In Córcoles y Martínez 1706g, q.v.

García, Genaro

1902   *Dos Antiquas Relaciones de la Florida* (Two ancient reports about Florida). Mexico: Tip. y Lit. de J. Aguilar Vera y Comp.

García-Arévalo, Manuel

1990   Transculturation in Contact Period and Contemporary Hispaniola. In Thomas 1990:269–80, q.v.

Gatschet, Albert S.

1877–   The Timucua Language. *Proceedings of the American Philosophical*
1880   *Society* 16:1–17; 17:490–504; 18:465–502.

Geiger, Maynard

1937   *The Franciscan Conquest of Florida, 1573–1618.* Washington, D.C.: The Catholic University of America.

1940   *Biographical Dictionary of the Franciscans in Spanish Florida and Cuba (1528–1841).* Franciscan Studies, vol. 21. Paterson, N.J.: St. Anthony Guild Press.

Gilbert, William Harlen, Jr.

  1943   *The Eastern Cherokees.* Anthropology Paper no. 23. Bureau of American Ethnology Bulletin 133:169–413.

Gold, Robert L.

  1969   *Borderland Empires in Transition: The Triple-Nation Transfer of Florida.* Carbondale: Southern Illinois University Press.

Gómes, Manuel

  1685   Letter to Juan Márques Cabrera, Santa Fé, November 12, 1685. AGI, SD 639, JTLC, vol. 3 of "Misiones Guale," doc. dd, pp. 47–48.

Gómez de Engraba, Juan

  1657a   Letter to Francisco Martínez, Havana, March 13, 1657. In Hann 1986b:127–28, q.v.

  1657b   Letter to Francisco Martínez, Havana, April 4, 1657. In Hann 1986b:128–29, q.v.

Gonçales, Vicente

  1597   Statement, San Pedro [Mocama], October 22, 1597. In Méndez de Canzo 1598a, q.v.

González de Barcia Carballido y Zúñiga, Andrés

  1723   *La Florida del Inca: Historia del Adelantado Hernando de Soto, Governador y Capitan General del Reino de la Florida, y de Otros Heróicos Caballeros, Españoles, e Indios* (The Florida of the Inca. History of the adelantado Hernando de Soto, governor and captain general of the kingdom of Florida, and of other heroic gentlemen, Spaniards and Indians). Madrid: En la Oficina Real y á Costa de Nicolás Rodríguez Franco, Impresor de Libros.

  1951   *Barcia's Chronological History of the Continent of Florida.* Translated by Anthony Kerrigan. Gainesville: University of Florida Press.

Gourges, Dominique

  1964   *A Notable History Containing Four Voyages Made by Certain French Captains unto Florida by Rene Laudonnière.* Edited by Thomas R. Adams. Facsimile of the 1587 edition, London. Farnham, Surrey, Eng.: Henry Stevens, Sons, & Stiles.

Granberry, Julian

  1987   *A Grammar and Dictionary of the Timucua Language.* Anthropological Notes, no. 1. N.p.

  1989   *A Grammar and Dictionary of the Timucua Language.* 2d ed. Anthropological Notes, no. 1. Horsehoe Beach, Fla.: Island Archaeological Museum.

  1993   *A Grammar and Dictionary of the Timucua Language.* 3d ed. Tuscaloosa: University of Alabama Press.

Grasserie, Raoul de la

  1890   Textes Analysés et Vocabulaire de la langue Timucua. *Congrès*

International des Américanistes, Comte-rendu de la Septième Session (Analyzed texts and vocabulary of the Timucua language. International Congress of Americanists, account delivered for the seventh session), Berlin 1888. Berlin: Librairie W. H. Kohl.

1892   *Vocabulaire Timucua* (Timucua vocabulary). Orleans: Imp. Georges Jacob.

Griffin, John W., and Hale G. Smith

1949   Nocoroco, a Timucua Village of 1605. *Florida Historical Quarterly* 27 (April):340–61.

Guale Indian [unnamed captive]

1597   Testimony, San Pedro [Mocama], October 22, 1597. In Méndez de Canzo 1598a, q.v.

Güemes y Horcasitas, Juan Francisco

1739   Letter to the King, Havana, May 21, 1739. AGI, SD 866, SC.

Guerra y de la Vega, Francisco de la

1665   Order to Martín Alcayde de Córdoba, January 17, 1665. In Worth 1995:70, doc. 5, q.v.

Gutiérrez de Palomar, Juan

1571   The Captain Juan Gutiérrez de Palomar, being in this court, with the señor *Fiscal* about being paid the salary that is owed to him for the service that he did in Florida, 1571. AGI, Justicia, leg. 906, no. 6.

Haas, Mary J.

1971   Southeastern Indian Linguistics. In Hudson 1971:44–54, q.v.

Hakluyt, Richard, trans.

1964   *A Notable History Containing Four Voyages Made by Certain French Captains unto Florida by Rene Laudonnière.* Edited by Martin Basanier. Facsimile of original edition of 1587, with "a Survey of the Sixteenth-Century Printed French Accounts of the attempts to establish a French Colony in Florida," by Thomas R. Adams. Farnham, Surrey, Eng.: Henry Stevens, Sons & Stiles.

Hann, John H.

1986a   Demographic Patterns and Changes in Mid-Seventeenth-Century Timucua and Apalachee. *Florida Historical Quarterly* 64 (April):371–92.

1986b   Translation of Governor Rebolledo's 1657 Visitation of Three Florida Provinces and Related Documents; AGI, EC, leg. 155B, SC and WLC, reel 3. *Florida Archaeology* 2:81–146.

1986c   Church Furnishings, Sacred Vessels and Vestments Held by the Missions of Florida: Translation of Two Inventories. AGI, SD 235, WLC, reel 4. *Florida Archaeology* 2:147–64.

1986d   Translation of Alonso de Leturiondo's Memorial to the King of Spain; AGI, SD 853, SC. *Florida Archaeology* 2:165–225.

1986e   The Use and Processing of Plants by Indians of Spanish Florida. *Southeastern Archaeology* 5 (Winter):91–102.

1987   Twilight of the Mocamo and Guale Aborigines as Portrayed in the 1695 Spanish Visitation. *Florida Historical Quarterly* 66 (July):1–24.

1988a   *Apalachee: The Land between the Rivers.* Gainesville: University Presses of Florida.

1988b   Florida's Terra Incognita: West Florida's Natives in the Sixteenth and Seventeenth Century. *Florida Anthropologist* 41 (March):61–107.

1989   St. Augustine's Fallout from the Yamasee War. *Florida Historical Quarterly* 68 (October):180–200.

1990a   De Soto, Dobyns, and Demography in Western Timucua. *Florida Anthropologist* 43 (March):3–12.

1990b   *Summary Guide to Spanish Florida Missions and Visitas with Churches in the Sixteenth and Seventeenth Centuries.* Washington, D.C.: Academy of American Franciscan History. Reprint (with illustrations added) of article published in *The Americas* 46 (April):417–513.

1991a   *Missions to the Calusa.* Gainesville: University of Florida Press.

1991b   The Mayaca and Jororo and Missions to Them. *Florida Anthropologist* 44 (June–December):164–75.

1991c   Murder of the Tama-Yamasee 1675. In Jones, Hann, and Scarry 1991:152–58, q.v.

1992a   Heathen Acuera, Murder, and a Potano Cimarrona: The St. Johns River and the Alachua Prairie in the 1670s. *Florida Historical Quarterly* 70 (April):451–74.

1992b   Political Leadership among the Natives of Spanish Florida. *Florida Historical Quarterly* 71 (October):188–208.

1993a   The Mayaca and Jororo and Missions to Them. Revised. In McEwan 1993:111–40, q.v.

1993b   Visitations and Revolts in Florida, 1656–1695. *Florida Archaeology* 7:1–296.

Harper, Roland M.
1914   *Geography and Vegetation of Northern Florida.* Tallahassee: Florida State Geological Survey, Sixth Annual Report.

Hawkins, Benjamin
1982   *Letters of Benjamin Hawkins, 1796–1806.* Spartanburg, S.C.: Reprint Company. Originally published as vol. 9 of the *Collections of the Georgia Historical Society,* 1916.

Herrera, Antonio de
1720   *Historia General de los Hechos de los Castillanos en las Islas i Tierra Firme del Mar Oceano* (General history of the deeds of the Castilians on the islands and mainland of the ocean sea). 2 vols. Madrid: Imprenta Real de Nicolás Rodígues Franco, 1720, 1726.

Hinachuba, Patricio de
  1705   Letter to Joseph de Zúñiga y Zerda, Bitachuco at Abosaya, May 29,
          1705. In Boyd 1953:473–74, q.v.
Hita Salazar, Pablo de
  1675a   Convocation of Council of War, August 9, 1675. In Hann 1993b:36–
          37, q.v.
  1675b   Letter to the Queen, August 24, 1675. AGI, SD 839, SC.
  1680   Letter to the King, May 14, 1680. In Serrano y Sanz 1912:216–19,
          q.v.
Hoffman, Paul E.
  1990   *A New Andalucia and a Way to the Orient.* Baton Rouge: Louisiana
          State University Press.
Horruytiner, Juan Benedit
  1706   Letter to Francisco de Córcoles y Martínez, April 24, 1706. In
          Córcoles y Martínez 1706g, q.v.
Horruytiner, Pedro Benedit
  1660   Testimony, May 8, 1660. In Worth 1992a:475–77, q.v.
Hudson, Charles
  1976   *The Southeastern Indians.* Knoxville: University of Tennessee Press.
  1979   *Black Drink: A Native American Tea.* Athens: University of Georgia
          Press.
  1990   *The Juan Pardo Expeditions: Exploration of the Carolinas and Tennessee,
          1566–1568.* Washington, D.C.: Smithsonian Institution Press.
Hudson, Charles, ed.
  1971   *Red, White, and Black. Symposium on Indians in the Old South.* South-
          ern Anthropological Society Proceedings, no. 5.
Hudson, Charles, and Carmen Chaves Tesser, eds.
  1994   *The Forgotten Centuries: Indians and Europeans in the American South,
          1521–1704.* Athens: University of Georgia Press.
Hudson, Charles, Marvin T. Smith, and Chester B. DePratter.
  1984   The Hernando de Soto Expedition: From Apalachee to Chiaha.
          Southeastern Archaeology 3 (Summer):65–77.
Hulton, Paul, ed.
  1977   *The Work of Jacques Le Moyne de Morgues, a Huguenot Artist in France,
          Florida and England.* 2 vols. London: British Museum Publications.
Jesús, Francisco Alonso de
  1630a   1630 Memorial of Fray Francisco Alonso de Jesús on Spanish
          Florida's Missions and Natives. Translation by John H. Hann. *The
          Americas* 50 (July):85–105.
  1630b   Letter to the King, n.d. [1630]. AGI, SD 235, PKYLFH, microfilm
          28K, reel 36. Translation by John H. Hann on file at BAR.
  1635   Petition to the King, February 27, 1635. AGI, SD 235, SC.

Johnson, Kenneth W.
  1991   Mission Santa Fé de Toloca. *Florida Anthropologist* 44 (June–December):176–86.
Johnson, Kenneth W., and Bruce W. Nelson
  1990   The Utina: Seriation and Chronology. *Florida Anthropologist* 43 (March):48–62.
Jones, B. Calvin, and John F. Scarry
  1991   Introduction. In Jones, Hann, and Scarry 1991:1–9, q.v.
Jones, B. Calvin, John Hann, and John F. Scarry
  1991   San Pedro y San Pablo de Patale: A Sixteenth-Century Spanish Mission in Leon County, Florida. *Florida Archaeology* 5:1–201.
Jones, B. Calvin, John F. Scarry, and Mark Williams
  1991   Material Culture at Patale. In Jones, Hann, and Scarry 1991:59–108, q.v.
Juan, Don [cacique]
  1597   Testimony, San Pedro [Mocama], October 18, 1597. In Méndez de Canzo 1598a, q.v.
Jusefe [Mocama Indian]
  1597   Testimony, San Pedro, October 18, 1597. In Méndez de Canzo 1598a, q.v.
Kwachka, Patricia B., ed.
  1994   *Perspectives on the Southeast: Linguistics, Archaeology, and Ethnohistory.* Southern Anthropological Society Proceedings, no. 27. Athens: University of Georgia Press.
Landers, Jane
  1992   An Eighteenth-Century Community in Exile: The Floridanos in Cuba. Paper presented at the Conference on Latin American History, Washington, D.C., December.
Lanning, John Tate
  1935   *The Spanish Missions of Georgia.* Chapel Hill: University of North Carolina Press.
Larsen, Clark Spencer
  1990   *The Archaeology of Mission Santa Catalina de Guale: 2. Biocultural Interpretations of a Population in Transition.* New York: Anthropological Papers of the American Museum of Natural History, no. 68.
Larson, Lewis H.
  1980   *Aboriqinal Subsistence Technology on the Southeastern Coastal Plain during the Late Prehistoric Period.* Gainesville: University Presses of Florida.
Lawson, Sarah, trans.
  1992   *A Foothold in Florida. The Eye-Witness Account of Four Voyages Made by the French to That Region and Their Attempt at Colonisation, 1562–1568, Based on a New Translation of Laudonnière's L'Histoire Notable de la*

Floride. East Grinstead, West Sussex, Eng.: Antique Atlas Publications.

Leturiondo, Alonso de
1697 Letter to the King, April 29, 1697. AGI, SD 235, JTCC, reel 4.

Leturiondo, Domingo de
1671 Partial report of the service record of Captain Juan Francisco de Florencia, January 29, 1671. AGI, SD 225, WLC, reel 4.
1678 Visitation of the Provinces of Apalachee and Timucua, 1677–78. In Hann 1993b:95–146, q.v.

Long, Robert W., and Olga Lakela
1971 *A Flora of Tropical Florida. A Manual of the Seed Plants and Ferns of Southern Peninsular Florida.* Coral Gables, Fla.: University of Miami Press.

Lópes, Agustín, and Juan Orata [Timucua Indians]
1636 Letter to the King, Havana, July 6, 1636. AGI, SD 27, JTCC, reel 2.

López, Antonio [Mocama Indian]
1597 Testimony, San Pedro, October 18, 1597. In Méndez de Canzo 1598a, q.v.

López, Atanasio, OFM, ed.
1931 *Relación Histórica de la Florida Escrita en el Siglo XVII* (Historical report about Florida written in the 17th century). 2 vols. Madrid: Imprenta de Ramona Velasco, Viuda de P. Pírez.

López, Baltasar
1602 Letter to Blas de Montes, September 15, 1602. AGI, SD 235, WLC, reel 2. Translation by John H. Hann on file at BAR.

López, Joseph
1711 Report about the Indians of La Costa who live in this presidio of St. Augustine of Florida at present February. In Córcoles y Martínez 1711, q.v.

López de Mendoza Grajales, Francisco
1567 Letter to Pedro Menéndez de Avilés, August 6, 1567. Translated by Edward Lawson. Vol. 2, letter no. 52, PKYLFH.
n.d. Relación hecha por el Capellan de Armada francisco López de Mendoza Grajales del viaje que hizo el Adelantado Pedro Menéndez de Avilés a la Florida (Report made by the armada chaplain Francisco López de Mendoza about the voyage to Florida that the adelantado Pedro Menéndez de Avilés made). In Ruidíaz y Caravia 1893:2:431–65, q.v.

Lorant, Stefan
1965 *The New World: The First Pictures of America Made by John White and Jacques Le Moyne and Engraved by Theodore de Bry with Contemporary Narratives of the French Settlement in Florida, 1562–1565, and the*

English Colonies in Virginia, 1585–1590. Rev. ed. New York: Duell, Sloan, and Pearse.

Loucks, Lana Jill
1993   Spanish–Indian Interaction on the Florida Missions: The Archaeology of Baptizing Spring. In McEwan 1993:193–216, q.v.

Lowery, Woodbury
1911   *The Spanish Settlements within the Present Limits of the United States. Florida 1562–1574.* New York: G. P. Putnam's Sons.

Luna, Pedro de
1690   Memorial of the Distribution and Assignment of the Religious of the Mission with the Ministers of the Provinces who are going to learn the languages, August 1690. In Quiroga y Losada 1690b, q.v.

Lussagnet, Suzanne, ed.
1958   *Les Français en Amérique Pendant la Deuxième, Moitié du XVIe Siècle: Les Français en Floride, Textes de Jean Ribault, René de Laudonnière, Nicolas de Challeux et Dominique de Gourgues* (The French in America during the second half of the 16th century: The French in Florida, texts of Jean Ribault, René de Laudonnière, Nicolas de Challeux and Dominique de Gourgues). Paris: Presses Universitaires de France.

Lyon, Eugene
1976   *The Enterprise of Florida: Pedro Menéndez de Avilés and the Spanish Conquest of 1565–1568.* Gainesville: University Presses of Florida.
1988   Letter to Wallace Hibbard, March 16, 1988. Copy in the possession of John H. Hann.
1992a   Richer Than We Thought. The Material Culture of Sixteenth-Century St. Augustine. *El Escribano* 29:1–117.
1992b   Cuban Church Records Examined in June 1992. Typescript in the possession of John H. Hann.

McEwan, Bonnie G., ed.
1993   *The Spanish Missions of La Florida.* Gainesville: University Press of Florida.

Machado, Francisco
1597   Account of the clothing, flour, iron tools, and other things that have been given to the Indians by order of Gonzalo Méndez de Canço, governor and captain general of the provinces of Florida, 1597. AGI, SD 231, WLC, reel 2. [Machado's name may have been miscopied by Lowery; John E. Worth, who has used the original document, rendered the name as Mugado (Worth 1992a:494).]

Manrique de Rojas, Hernando
1564   Relación de los franceses que an ydo a Poblar a la costa de la florida (Report about the Frenchmen who have gone to settle the coast of Florida). Havana, year of 1564. AGI, SD 99, JTCC, reel 2.

María, Chieftainness of Nombre de Dios
    1600   Letter to the King, Nombre de Dios, February 20, 1600. AGI, SD
            231, JTCC, reel 4. Translation by John H. Hann on file at BAR.
Márques, Gaspar, Chief of San Sebastian
    n.d.   Letter to the King, n.d. AGI, SD 232, JTCC, reel
    [1606] 4. Translation by John H. Hann on file at BAR.
Márquez Cabrera, Juan
    1680a   Report on the religious existing in the missions of Florida and on
            the villages in which there are doctrinas, December 6, 1680. In
            Márquez Cabrera 1680b, q.v.
    1680b   Letter to the King, December 8, 1680. AGI, SD 226, WLC, reel 4.
    1683   Letter to the King, June 28, 1683. AGI, SD 226, SC.
    1685a   Letter to the King, March 22, 1685. AGI, SD 839, JTLC, vol. 3 of
            "Misiones Guale," doc. dd.
    1685b   March 22, 1685. In Márquez Cabrera 1685a, q.v.
    1685c   Letter to the King, April 15, 1685. AGI, SD 856, JTLC, vol. 3 of
            "Misiones Guale," doc. EE.
    1686   Letter to the King, March 22, 1686. AGI, SD 839, JTLC, vol. 5 of
            "Misiones Guale," doc. 10, pp. 1–3.
Marrinan, Rochelle A.
    1993   Archaeological Investigations at Mission Patale. In McEwan
            1993:244–94, q.v.
Martínez, Lorenzo
    1612   Letter to the King, September 14, 1612. AGI, SD 232, SC.
Martínez, Lorenzo, Francisco Hernández, and Francisco de la Cruz.
    1636   Petition to the King, Havana, 1636. AGI, SD 27.
Mason, J. Alden
    1957   The Ancient Civilization of Peru. Harmondsworth, Eng.: Penguin
            Books.
Matheos, Antonio
    1686   Letter to Juan Márquez Cabrera, San Luis, May 21, 1686. [Enclo-
            sure i] Viceroy of Mexico, Count Paredes and Marquis of Laguna
            to the King, July 19, 1686. AGI, Mexico 56, JTLC, vol. 5 of
            "Misiones Guale."
Medina, Juan de
    1651   Letter to Pedro Benedit Horruytiner, December 29, 1651. AGI, EC,
            leg. 155B, microfilm 27-F, reel 5, residencia series, PKYLFH. Folio
            355v. of the residencia of Benito Ruíz de Salazar Vallecilla.
            Translation by John H. Hann on file at BAR.
Méndez de Canzo, Gonzalo
    1597a   Instruction to Captain Juan de Santiago, October 15, 1597. In
            Méndez de Canzo 1598a, q.v.

1597b   Instruction to Captain Vicente Gonçáles, San Pedro, October 19, 1597. In Méndez de Canzo 1598a, q.v.

1597c   Statement, San Pedro, October 24, 1597. In Méndez de Canzo 1598a, q.v.

1597d   Statements, San Pedro, November 2, 4, 5, 1597. In Méndez de Canzo 1598a, q.v.

1598a   Testimony about what happened in the language of Guale on the trip that Gonzalo Méndez de Canzo, Governor and Captain General of the province by the King Our Lord, made to investigate and punish the deaths of the Religious whom they killed in the tongue, January 12, 1598. AGI, SD 224, JTLC, vol. 3 of "Misiones Guale," doc. AA.

1598b   Letter to the King, February 23, 1598. AGI, SD 224.

1600a   Letter to the King, January 28, 1600. AGI, SD 224, WLC, reel 2.

1600b   Letter to the King, February 28, 1600. AGI, SD 224, WLC, reel 2.

1601   Letter to the King, April 24, 1601. AGI, SD 224, WLC, reel 3.

1602   Letter to the King, September 22, 1602. AGI, SD 224, JTCC, reel 2. Translation by John H. Hann on file at BAR.

Menéndez, Juan

1584   Letter to the King, Florida, April 6, 1584. AGI, SD 231, SC.

Menéndez de Avilés, Pedro

1565a   Letter to the King, from these provinces of Florida, September 11, 1565. In Ruidíaz y Caravia 1893:2:74–84, q.v.

1565b   Letter to the King, from these provinces of Florida, from the strand (*ribera*) of Sant Pelayo and fort of St. Augustine, October 15, 1565. In Ruidíaz y Caravia 1893:2:84–105, q.v.

Menéndez Márquez, Antonio

1660   Testimony, Ivitachuco, May 9, 1660. In Worth 1992a:437–45, q.v.

Menéndez Márquez, Francisco, and Pedro Benedit Horruytiner

1645   Certification of the taking of power as governor of Benito Ruíz de Salazar Vallecilla, April 11, 1645. AGI, EC, leg. 155B, in microfilm 27-F, reel 5, residencia series, PKYLFH. Folio 322 of the residencia of Benito Ruíz de Salazar Vallecilla.

1647a   Letter to the King, March 18, 1647. AGI, SD 229, SC.

1647b   Letter to the King, July 27, 1647. AGI, SD 235, JTCC, reel 4.

1647c   Order to Antonio de Argüelles, December 1, 1647. AGI, SD 23. Translation by Eugene Lyon in the possession of John H. Hann.

Menéndez Márquez, Joan, and Alonso de las Alas

1595   Letter to the King, December 13, 1595. AGI, SD 229, JTLC, vol. 3 of "Misiones Guale," doc. rr.

Menéndez Márquez, Juan

1652   Testimony, March 11, 1652. AGI, EC, leg. 155B, microfilm 27-F, reel 5, residencia series of the PKYLFH. Fols. 371–78, residencia of Benito Ruíz de Salazar Vallecilla.

Menéndez Márquez, Pedro

1568   Letter to Pedro Menéndez de Avilés, Habana, March 28, 1568. AGI, SD 115, SC.

1578   Letter to the King, June 15, 1578. In Connor 1930:79, 81, q.v.

1579   Letter to the *Audiencia* of Santo Domingo, April 2, 1579. In Connor 1930:224–27, q.v.

1580   Letter to the King, January 3, 1580. In Connor 1930:252–57, q.v.

1593   Letter to the King, August 24, 1593. AGI, Patronato 258, SC.

Menéndez Márquez, Thomás, and Joachín de Florencia

1697   Letter to the King, April 20, 1697. AGI, SD 230, JTCC, reel 4.

Merrill, William L.

1979   The Beloved Tree: Ilex vomitoria among the Indians of the Southeast and Adjacent Regions. In Hudson 1979:40–82, q.v.

Mexía, Alvaro de

1605a   Letter to Pedro de Ibarra, Horruque, June 8, 1605. AGI, SD 224, JTCC, reel 1.

1605b   Letter to Pedro de Ybarra, Urubia, June 15, 1605. AGI, SD 224, JTCC, reel 1.

1605c   Statement, July 11, 1605. AGI, SD 224, JTCC, reel 1.

1605d   Rutter for the coast south to Ais [1605]. AGI, SD 224, JTCC, reel 1. Published in Rouse 1951:265–74, q.v.

Milanich, Jerald T.

1972   The Timucua (draft of chapter 43 of the volume on the Southeast, William C. Sturtevant, ed., *Handbook of North American Indians*). Copy in the possession of John H. Hann.

1978   The Western Timucua: Patterns of Acculturation and Change. In Milanich and Proctor 1978:59–88, q.v.

1979   Origins and Prehistoric Distribution of Black Drink and the Ceremonial Shell Drinking Cup. In Hudson 1979:83–119, q.v.

1994a   *Archaeology of Precolumbian Florida.* Gainesville: University Press of Florida.

1994b   Florida Indians and the European Invasion. Typescript.

Milanich, Jerald T., and Charles H. Fairbanks

1980   *Florida Archaeology.* New York: Academic Press.

Milanich, Jerald T., and Charles Hudson

1993   *Hernando de Soto and the Indians of Florida.* Gainesville: University Press of Florida.

Milanich, Jerald, and Samuel Proctor, eds.

1978   *Tacachale: Essays on the Indians of Florida and Southeastern Georgia during the Historic Period.* Gainesville: University Presses of Florida.

Milanich, Jerald T., and William C. Sturtevant

1972   *Francisco Pareja's 1613 Confessionario: A Documentary Source for Timucua Ethnography.* Translation by Emilio F. Moran. Tallahassee: Division of Archives, History, and Records Management.

Mitchem, Jeffrey M.

1989a   Ethnohistoric and Archaeological Evidence for a Protohistoric Provincial Boundary in West Peninsular Florida. Paper presented at the 46th Annual Meeting of the Southeastern Archaeological Conference, Tampa, Fla., November 8–11.

1989b   Redefining Safety Harbor: Late Prehistoric/Protohistoric Archaeology in West Peninsular Florida. Ph.D. dissertation, University of Florida.

Mitchem, Jeffrey M., and Dale L. Hutchinson

1986   *Interim Report on Excavations at the Tatham Mound, Citrus County, Florida, Season II.* Miscellaneous Project Report Series, no. 28, Florida State Museum, Department of Anthropology, Gainesville.

1987   *Interim Report on Archaeological Research at the Tatham Mound, Citrus County, Florida, Season III.* Miscellaneous Project Report Series, no. 30, Florida State Museum, Department of Anthropology, Gainesville.

Montiano, Manuel

1738   Letter to the King, June 4, 1738. AGI, SD 865, SC.

1739   Report of the number of missionaries that there are in this province of Santa Elena, June 13, 1739. AGI, SD 851, SC.

Monzón, Francisco de

1660   Testimony, Ivitachuco, May 4, 1660. In Worth 1992a:408–13, q.v.

Moral, Alonso del, et al.

1657   Letter to the King, September 10, 1657. In Hann 1993b:7–19, q.v.

Moreno Ponce de León, Pedro

1651   Letter to the King, September 7, 1651. AGI, SD 225, WLC, reel 3. Translation by John H. Hann on file at BAR.

Morton, Julia F.

1982   *Wild Plants for Survival in South Florida.* Miami: Fairchild Tropical Garden.

Movilla, Gregorio de

1635a   *Explicación de la Doctrina Qve Compvso El Cardenal Belarmino por mandado del Señor Papa Clemente 8* (Explanation of the doctrine which Cardinal Bellarmine composed by order of Pope Clement VIII). Translated into Floridana tongue by the priest fray Gregorio de Movilla. Mexico: Imprenta de Juan Rúyz.

1635b   *Forma Breve de Administrar los Sacramentos á los Indios e Españoles qve Viven entre Ellos* (Brief ritual for administering the sacraments to the Indians and Spaniards who live among them). Mexico: Imprenta de Juan Rúyz.

Nairne, Thomas
    1708   Letter to an unidentified Lord, July 10, 1708. In Salley 1947:5:193–202, q.v.

Nicklas, T. Dale
    1994   Linguistic Provinces of the Southeast at the Time of Columbus. In Kwachka 1994:1–13, q.v.

Nicolás [Guale Indian from Zapala]
    1685   Testimony, December 29, 1685. AGI, SD 839, JTLC, vol. 3 of "Misiones Guale," doc. dd, pp. 57–58.

Nieto de Carbajal, Bernardo
    1707   Defense against charges against Joseph de Zúñiga y Zerda, February 11, 1707. AGI, SD 858, ACNL (residencia for Joseph de Zúñiga y Zerda, Quaderno 4). Translation by F. Wayne Childers in the possession of John H. Hann.

Niquisaya [Yamasee head chief]
    1685   Testimony, March 22, 1685. In Márquez Cabrera 1685a, q.v.

Oré, Luis Gerónimo de
    1936   *The Martyrs of Florida (1513–1616).* Translation by Maynard Geiger. New York: Joseph F. Wagner.

Palacios, Pedro
    [1675]   Report about the voyage to Florida of Bishop Gabriel Díaz Vara Calderón, 1675. In Díaz Vara Calderón 1675b, q.v.

Pareja, Francisco de
    1597   Certification, San Pedro [Mocama], October 17, 1597. In Méndez de Canzo 1598a, q.v.
    1602   Letter to Blas de Montes, September 14, 1602. AGI, SD 235, WLC, reel 2.
    1612a   *Catechismo y Breve Exposición de la doctrina Christiana* (Catechism and brief exposition of Christian doctrine). Mexico: en casa de la Viuda de Pedro Balli.
    1612b   *Cathecismo en Lengva Castellana y Timuquana, en el Qual Se Contiene Lo Que Se les Puede Enseñar á los Adultos Que An de Ser Baptizados* (Catechism in the Castilian and Timuquan languages in which is contained what can be taught to the adults who are to be baptized). Mexico: en la Imprēta de la viuda de Pedro Balli.
    1613   *Confessionario en Lenqua Castellana y Timuquana con Alqunos Consejos para Animar al Penitente* (Confessionario in the Castilian and Timuquan languages with some counsels to encourage the penitent). Mexico: en la Imprenta de la viuda de Diego López Daualos.
    1614   *Arte y Pronunciación en Lengva Timvqvana y Castellana* (Grammar and pronunciation in the Timuquan and Castilian languages). Mexico: en la Imprenta de Juan Rúyz.

1627 *Cathecismo y Examen para Los Qve Comvlgan en Lengua Castellana y Timuquana* (Catechism and examination in the Castilian and Timuquan languages for those who go to communion). Mexico: en la Imprenta de Juan Rúyz.

Pareja, Francisco de, and Alonso de Peñaranda
1607 Letter to the King, November 20, 1607. AGI, SD 224, JTCC, reel 2.

Pareja, Francisco de, et al.
1617 Letter to the King, January 17, 1617. In Hann l991a:13–19, q.v.

Parker, Susan R.
1993 Spanish St. Augustine's "Urban" Indians. *El Escribano* 30 (1993):1– 15.

Parkman, Francis
1907 *Pioneers of France in the New World. Huguenots in Florida. Samuel de Champlain.* Boston: Little, Brown.

Pasqua, Francisco
1660 Testimony, Ivitachuco, May 17, 1660. In Worth 1992a:473–74, q.v.

Peck, Douglas D.
1992 Reconstruction and Analysis of the 1513 Discovery Voyage of Juan Ponce de León. *Florida Historical Quarterly* 71 (October):133– 54.

Pedrosa, Salvador
1660 Testimony, April, 1660. In Worth 1992a:376–81, q.v.

Peña, Diego de la
1717 Diary of this trip, of Apalache and of the province of Apalachecole ordered to be made by the Señor Governor and Captain General Don Pedro de Oliver y Fullana. AGI, SD 843, SC.

Peñaranda, Alonso de
1608 Letter to the King, January 1608. AGI, SD 224, WLC, reel 3.

Péres, Andrés
1675 Letter to Pablo de Hita Salazar, San Luis, July 29, 1675. In Hann 1993b:37–38, q.v.

Perete, Francisco, et al.
1676 Provincial chapter roster, St. Augustine, April 25, 1676. Document in the New York Historical Society Library. Copy furnished by F. Wayne Childers.

Pereyra, Juan
1605 Statement, December 12, 1605. AGI, Patronato 19, JTCC, reel 1.

Pérez de Villareal, Agustín
1660 Testimony, April 30, 1660. In Worth 1992a:382–91, q.v.

Ponce de León, Nicolás
1651 Order, June 30, 1651. AGI, SD 23. Translation by Eugene Lyon in the possession of John H. Hann.

Ponce de León, Nicolas
  1660   Testimony, April 26, 1660. In Worth 1992a:356–60, q.v.
Prado, Antonio de
  1569   Memorial on four forts of Florida presented to His Majesty by
         Captain Antonio de Prado. In Connor 1925:291–93, q.v.
Prado, José de
  1654   Letter to the King, December 30, 1654. AGI, SD 229, SC.
Primo de Rivera, Joseph
  1717   Census, April 1717. In Ayala y Escobar 1717, q.v.
Puerta, Pedro de la
  1660   Testimony, April 1660. In Worth 1992a:369–74, q.v.
Pueyo, Juan de
  1695   General Visitation of the Provinces of Guale and Mocama Made by
         the Captain Don Juan de Pueyo by Title and Nomination of the
         Señor Don Laureano de Torres y Ayala, Knight of the Order of
         Santiago, Governor and Captain General of the City, Presidio and
         Provinces of St. Augustine of Florida for His Majesty, January 25,
         1695. In Hann 1993b:220–48, q.v.
Quiroga y Losada, Diego de
  1688   Letter to the King, April 1688. AGI, SD 839, SC.
  1690a Letter to Pedro de Luna, August 15, 1690. In Quiroga y Losada
         1690c, q.v.
  1690b Auto, August 26, 1690. In Quiroga y Losada 1690c, q.v.
  1690c Letter to the King, August 31, 1690. AGI, SD 228, JTLC, vol. 4 of
         "Misiones Guale."
  1691   Auto, September 18, 1691. In Quiroga y Losada 1692a, q.v.
  1692a Letter to the King, April 10, 1692. AGI, SD 228, JTLC, vol. 4 of
         "Misiones Guale."
  1692b Auto, April 14, 1692. AGI, SD 228, JTLC, vol. 4 of "Misiones
         Guale."
  1692c Letter to the King, April 30, 1692. AGI, SD 228, JTLC, vol. 4 of
         "Misiones Guale".
  [1697] Memorial to the King, n.d. [1697]. AGI, SD 840, JTCC, reel 5.
         Translation by John H. Hann on file at BAR.
Rebolledo, Diego de
  1655a Order to Antonio de Argüelles, March 10, 1655. AGI, SD 23.
         Translation by Eugene Lyon in the possession of John H. Hann.
  1655b Letter to the King, October 7, 1655. AGI, SD 852, SC.
  1657a Residencia for Benito Ruíz de Salazar Vallecilla, 1657. AGI, EC,
         leg. 155B, microfilm 27-F, reel 5, residencia series, PKYLFH.
  1657b Letter to Fray Francisco de San Antonio et al., August 5, 1657. In
         Hann 1986b:109–15, q.v.
  1657c Letter to the King, September 18, 1657. In Serrano y Sanz
         1912:202–5, q.v.

Reitz, Elizabeth
  1993   Evidence for Animal Use at the Missions of Spanish Florida. In McEwan 1993:376–98, q.v.

Ribaut, Jean
  1927   *The Whole & True Discouery of Terra Florida.* Facsimile reprint of the London edition of 1563. Deland: Florida State Historical Society.

Rios Henriques, Dionisio de los
  1690a   Letter to Diego de Quiroga y Losada, Santa Fée, September 2, 1690. In Quiroga y Losada 1692c, q.v.
  1690b   Letter to Diego de Quiroga y Losada, Santa Fée, November 29, 1690. In Quiroga y Losada 1692c, q.v.
  1691   Letter to Diego de Quiroga y Losada, Santa Fée, January 11, 1691. In Quiroga y Losada 1692c, q.v.

Rocha, Francisco de la
  1660   Testimony, May 6, 1660. In Worth 1992a:420–26, q.v.

Rodríguez Tiznado, Juan
  1685   Letter to Juan Márquez Cabrera, Santa Fé, March 16, 1685. AGI, SD 838, JTCC, reel 5, and JTLC, vol. 3 of "Misiones Guale," doc. dd.

Rogel, Juan
  1568   Letter to Jerónimo Ruíz del Portillo, Havana, April 25, 1568. In Hann l991a:234–78, q.v.
  1570   Letter to Pedro Menéndez de Avilés, Havana, December 9, 1570. In Ruidíaz y Caravia 1893:II, 301–8, q.v.

Ross, Mary
  1923   French Intrusions and Indian Uprisings in Georgia and South Carolina, 1577–1580. *Georgia Historical Quarterly* 7 (September):251–81.
  1924   The French on the Savannah, 1605. *Georgia Historical Quarterly* 8 (September):167–94.
  1926   The Restoration of the Spanish Missions in Georgia, 1598–1606. *Georgia Historical Quarterly* 10 (September):171–99.

Rouse, Irving
  1951   *A Survey of Indian River Archeology.* Yale University Publications in Anthropology, no. 44. New Haven: Yale University Press.

Ruidíaz y Caravia, Eugenio
  1893   *La Florida, Su Conquista y Colonización por Pedro Menéndez de Avilés* (Florida, its conquest and colonization by Pedro Menéndez de Avilés). 2 vols. Madrid: Imp. Fund. y Fab. de Tintas de los Hijos de J. A. García.

Ruís, Alonso
  1759   Census of the Indian Village of Nuestra Señora de la Leche. AGI, SD 2604. Photocopy furnished by Jane Landers.

Ruíz de Salazar Vallecilla, Benito
  1645   Order to Alonso de Argüelles, September 9, 1645. AGI, SD 23.
          Translation by Eugene Lyon in the possession of John H. Hann.
  1646   Order to Alonso de Argüelles, January 27, 1646. AGI, SD 23.
          Translation by Eugene Lyon in the possession of John H. Hann.
  1648   Order to Antonio de Argüelles, April 22, 1648. AGI, SD 23.
          Translation by Eugene Lyon in the possession of John H. Hann.
  1650   Letter to the King, July 11, 1650. AGI, SD 225, WLC, reel 3.
Russo, Michael
  1992   Chronologies and Cultures of the St. Marys Region of Northeast
          Florida and Southeast Georgia. *Florida Anthropologist* 45 (June):107–
          26.
Salazar Vallezilla, Luis de
  1651   Deed of donation for Asile Hacienda lands, March 25, 1650, San
          Lorenso de Ybittachuco. AGI, EC, leg. 155B, microfilm 27–F, reel
          5, residencia series, Folios 445–47v. of the residencia of Benito
          Ruíz de Salazar Vallecilla.
Salley, Alexander S., ed.
  1947   *Records in the British Public Records Office Relating to South Carolina.* 5
          vols. Columbia: Historical Commision of South Carolina, 1928–
          47.
San Antonio, Francisco de, et al.
  1657   Letter to the King, September 10, 1657. In Hann 1993b:7–27, q.v.
Sánchez, Francisco
  1651   Testimony, December 10, 1651. AGI, EC, leg. 155B, microfilm 27-
          F, reel 5, residencia series, PKYLFH. Folios 367v.–70.
Sánchez de Uriza, Juan
  1660   Testimony, April 28, 1660. In Worth 1992a:366–68, q.v.
Sánchez Judrero, Juan
  1608   Petition to the King and testimonies, November 29, 1608. AGI, SD
          232, SC.
San Martín, Pedro de
  1635   Petition, 1635. AGI, SD 233, SC.
Santander, Juan de
  1630   Letter to the King, November 25, 1630. AGI, SD 235, JTLC, vol. 2
          of "Misiones Guale," doc. p.
Santiago, J. de
  1597   Certification, San Pedro [Mocama], October 22, 1598. AGI, SD
          224. In Méndez de Canzo 1598a, q.v.
Santiago, Phelipe de
  1660   Testimony, April 26, 1660. In Worth 1992a:374–76, q.v.
Santurro, Alonso
  1711   Report about the Indian men and women, boys and girls that the
          village of Santo Thomás de Santa Fée, alias Esperanza, of the

Timucua language, has up to today, the day of the date January 13, seventeen hundred and eleven. In Córcoles y Martínez 1711, q.v.

Sauer, Carl Ortwin

1971 *Sixteenth-Century North America: The Land and the People as Seen by the Europeans*. Berkeley: University of California Press.

Saunders, Rebecca A.

1992 Continuity and Change in Guale Indian Pottery, A.D. 1350–1702. Ph.D. dissertation, University of Florida.

Scarborough, Vernon L., and David R. Wilcox, eds.

1991 *The Mesoamerican Ballgame*. Tucson: University of Arizona Press.

Scarry, John F.

1985 A Proposed Revision of the Fort Walton Ceramic Typology: A Type-Variety System. *Florida Anthropologist* 38 (September):199–233.

Serrano y Sanz, Manuel

1912 *Documentos Históricos de la Florida y la Luisiana, Siglos XVI al XVIII* (Historical documents about Florida and Louisiana, 16th to the 18th Centuries). Madrid: Libreria General de Victoriano Suárez.

Shapiro, Gary N., and John H. Hann

1990 The Documentary Image of the Council Houses of Spanish Florida Tested by Excavations at the Mission of San Luis de Talimali. In Thomas 1990:511–26, q.v.

Shapiro, Gary, and Bonnie G. McEwan

1992 Archaeology at San Luis, Part One: The Apalachee Council House. *Florida Archaeology* 6:1–173.

Shea, John Gilmary

1886 *The Catholic Church in Colonial Days, 1521–1763*. New York: John G. Shea.

Smith, Buckingham

1857 *Colección de Varios Documentos para la Historia de la Florida y Tierras Adyacentes* (Collection of various documents for the history of Florida and adjacent lands). London: Casa de Trubner y Compañía.

Solana, Juan

1706 Testimony on the reason it has not been possible to take the residencia, September 23, 1706. AGI, SD 858, ACNL (residencia for Joseph de Zúñiga y Zerda, Quaderno I). Translation by F. Wayne Childers in the possession of John H. Hann.

Solís de Merás, Gonzalo

1923 *Pedro Menéndez de Avilés, Adelantado, Governor and Captain General of Florida, Memorial*. Translated by Jeannette Thurber Connor. Deland: Florida State Historical Society.

Sotolongo, Francisco

1668 Letter to the King, July 4, 1668. AGI, SD 235, JTLC, vol. 2 of "Misiones Guale," doc. x.

Sotomayor, Juan Joseph de
  1660   Testimony, May 1660. In Worth 1992a:414–19, q.v.
Spellman, Charles W.
  1965   The "Golden Age" of the Florida Missions, 1632–1674. *Catholic Historical Review* 51 (October):354–72.
Sturtevant, William C.
  1977   The Ethnological Evaluation of the Le Moyne–De Bry Illustrations. In Hulton 1977:69–74, q.v.
  1984   Review of *Their Number Become Thinned,* by Henry F. Dobyns. *American Historical Review* 1984:1380–81.
Swanton, John R.
  1922   *Early History of the Creek Indians and Their Neighbors.* Bureau of American Ethnology Bulletin 73. Washington, D.C.: Government Printing Office.
  1928   *Social Organization and Social Usages of the Indians of the Creek Confederacy.* Washington, D.C.: Bureau of American Ethnology 42d Annual Report, 23–472.
  1929   The Tawasa Language. *American Anthropologist,* n.s., 31 (1929):435–53.
  1946   *The Indians of the Southeastern United States.* Bureau of American Ethnology Bulletin 173. Reprint. New York: Green Press Publishers, 1969.
  n.d.   A Sketch of the Timucua Language, n.d. Typescript. National Anthropological Archives doc. 2446-g TIMUCUA. [I used a copy at the PKYLFH.]
TePaske, John Jay
  1964   *The Governorship of Spanish Florida.* Durham, N.C.: Duke University Press.
Terrazas, Juan Bauptista
  1678   Memorial, October 20, 1678. AGI, SD 234, SC.
Texeda, Pedro
  1660   Testimony, Ivitachuco, May 14, 1660. In Worth 1992a:464–66, q.v.
Thomas, David Hurst
  1987   *The Archaeology of Mission Santa Catalina de Guale:* I. *Search and Discovery.* New York: Anthropological Papers of the American Museum of Natural History, vol. 63, part 2.
Thomas, David Hurst, ed.
  1989   *Columbian Consequences:* I. *Archaeological and Historical Perspectives on the Spanish Borderlands West.* Washington, D.C.: Smithsonian Institution Press.
  1990   *Columbian Consequences:* II. *Archaeological and Historical Perspectives on the Spanish Borderlands East.* Washington, D.C.: Smithsonian Institution Press.

Torres y Ayala, Laureano de
    1697   Letter to the King, April 20, 1697. AGI, SD 230, JTCC, reel 4.
Truxillo, Agustín
    1759   Census of the Village of Nuestra Señora de Guadalupe de Tolomato.
            AGI, SD 2604. Photocopy furnished by Jane Landers.
Upham, Steadman, and Lori Stephens Reed
    1989   Regional Systems in the Central and Northern Southwest:
            Demography, Economy, and Socio-Politics Preceding Contact. In
            Thomas 1989:57–76, q.v.
Valdés, Catalina de
    1616   Petition to the King, 1616. AGI, SD 232, JTCC, reel 4.
Valdés, Fernando de
    1602   Florida, Government Matters, 1602. AGI, SD 2533, SC. Transla-
            tion by John H. Hann on file at BAR.
Valverde, Miguel de, and Rodrigo de la Barrera
    1674   Certification by the priests, Fray Miguel de Valverde and Fray
            Rodrigo de la Barrera, about the conduct of the Captain Juan
            Hernández de Florencia, San Nicolás, September 10, 1674. In
            Hann 1993b:34–35.
Van Horne, Wayne Williams
    1993   The Warclub: Weapon and Symbol in Southeastern Indian Soci-
            eties. Ph.D. dissertation, University of Georgia.
Vargas Ugarte, Ruben
    1935   The First Jesuit Missions in Florida. In *Historical Records and Studies
            of the United States Catholic Historical Society,* ed. Thomas F. Meehan,
            25:59–148.
Varner, John Grier, and Jeannette Johnson Varner, trans. and ed.
    1951   *The Florida of the Inca.* Austin: University of Texas Press.
Vega, Inca Garcilaso de la
    1723   *La Florida del Inca. Historia del Adelantado Hernando de Soto, Governador
            y Capitan General del Reino de la Florida y de Otros Heróicos Caballeros
            Españoles e Indios* (The Florida of the Inca. History of the adelantado
            Hernando de Soto, governor and captain general of the kingdom
            of Florida and of other heroic gentlemen, Spaniards and Indians).
            Madrid: Oficina Real á Costa de Nicolás Rodríguez Franco, Impresor
            de Libros.
Vermejo, Pedro
    1602   Letter to Blas de Montes, September 14, 1602. AGI, SD 235, SC.
            Translation by John H. Hann on file at BAR.
Villareal, Juan de
    1651   Testimony, December 10, 1651. AGI, EC, leg. 155B, microfilm 27-
            F, reel 5, residencia series, PKYLFH. Residencia for Benito Ruíz de
            Salazar Vallecilla. Folio 365.

Vinson, Julian
    1885   Introduction. In Adam and Vinson 1886:v–xxxi, q.v.
Weber, David J.
    1992   *The Spanish Frontier in North America.* New Haven: Yale University
            Press.
Weddle, Robert
    1985   *Spanish Sea: The Gulf of Mexico in North American Discovery, 1500–
            1685.* College Station: Texas A&M University Press.
Weisman, Brent Richards
    1988   Excavations at Fig Springs (8CO1), Season 2, July–December
            1988. Florida Archaeological Reports 4. Tallahassee: Bureau of
            Archaeological Research, Division of Historical Resources.
    1992   *Excavations on the Franciscan Frontier: Archaeology at the Fig Springs
            Mission.* Gainesville: University Press of Florida.
Wenhold, Lucy L., trans.
    1936   *A Seventeenth-Century Letter of Gabriel Díaz Vara Calderón, Bishop of
            Cuba, Describing the Indians and Indian Missions of Florida.* Smithsonian
            Miscellaneous Collections, vol. 95, no. 16.
    1959   Manrique de Rojas's Report on French Settlement in Florida,
            1564. *Florida Historical Quarterly* 38 (July):45–62.
Williams, Stephen
    1990   Some Old Questions with Some New Views. Paper presented at
            the 47th Annual Meeting of the Southeastern Archaeological
            Conference, Mobile, Ala., November.
Worth, John E.
    1992a   The Timucuan Missions of Spanish Florida and the Rebellion of
            1656. Ph.D. dissertation, University of Florida.
    1992b   Revised Aboriginal Ceramic Typology for the Timucuan Mission
            Province. In Weismann 1992:188–205, q.v.
    1995   The Struggle for the Georgia Coast: An Eighteenth-Century Span-
            ish Retrospective on Guale and Mocama. Athens: Anthropological
            Papers of the American Museum of Natural History, no. 25,
            distributed by the University of Georgia Press.
Xaen, Diego de
    1703   Certification, Santa Fée, August 11, 1703. AGI, SD 858, AGNL,
            residencia for Joseph de Zúñiga y Zerda, Quaderno I. Translation
            by F. Wayne Childers in the possession of John H. Hann.
Ybarra, Pedro de
    1603   Inquiry into the services rendered by Gonzalo Méndez de Canzo
            in Florida, year 1603. AGI, SD 232, JTCC, reel 4.
    1604a   Letter to the King, January 8, 1604. AGI, SD 224, SC.
    1604b   Letter to the King, April 12, 1604. AGI, SD 224, SC.

1604c   Report on the trip that the Señor Pedro de Ibarra, Governor and Captain General of Florida made to visit the Indian Villages of the Provinces of San Pedro and Guale, November and December of 1604. In Serrano y Sanz 1912:164–93, q.v.

1605a   Order to Alvaro Mexía, May 31, 1605. AGI, SD 224, JTCC, reel 1.

1605b   Letter to Alvaro Mexía, June 10, 1605. AGI, SD 224, JTCC, reel 1.

1605c   Order for Hernando Guillén, June 26, 1605. AGI, SD 224, JTCC, reel 1.

1605d   Letter to the King, July 10, 1605. AGI, SD 224, or Patronato 19, JTCC, reel 1.

1605e   *Auto,* September 2, 1605. AGI, SD 224, JTCC, reel 1.

1605f   *Auto,* December 12, 1605. AGI, SD 224, JTCC, reel 1.

1605g   Letter to Pedro Vermejo, December 13, 1605. AGI, SD 232, JTCC.

1605h   *Auto,* December 14, 1605. AGI, SD 224, JTCC, reel 1.

1609a   Letter to the King, September 1, 1609. AGI, SD 128, SC.

1609b   Letter to Fray Benito Blanco, December 7, 1609. AGI, SD 232, SC.

Ynclan, Sebastian de

1600   Letter to the King, February 24, 1600. AGI, SD 229, JTCC, reel 3.

Ystasa, Manuel

1651   Letter to Pedro Benedit Horruytiner, San Miguel de Asile, n.d. AGI, EC, leg. 155B, microfilm 27-F, reel 5 of the residencia series of the PKYLFH. Folios 382–83 of the residencia of Benito Ruíz de Salazar Vallecilla.

Zeitlin, Judith Francis, and Lillian Thomas

1992   Spanish Justice and the Indian Cacique: Disjunctive Political Systems in Sixteenth-Century Tehuantepec. *Ethnohistory* 39 (Summer):285–315.

Zubillaga, Felix, ed.

1946   *Monumenta Antiquae Floridae (1566–1572)* (Record of ancient Florida, 1566–1572). Rome: Monumenta Missionum Societatis Iesu, no. 3.

Zúñiga y Zerda, Joseph de

1700   Residencia for Laureano de Torres y Ayala, November 16, 1700. AGI, EC, leg. 157A, microfilm 27-P, residencia series, PKYLFH.

1701a   Order to Joachín de Florencia, January 20, 1701. AGI, SD 840, JTCC, reel 5.

1701b   General Visitation for Guale, Santa María, February 7, 1701. AGI, SD 858 (Quaderno 4), JTCC, reel 6.

1701c   *Auto* concluding visitation of Guale and Mocama, San Juan del Puerto, February 10, 1701. AGI, SD 858, JTCC, reel 6.

1701d   Letter to the King, March 14, 1701. AGI, SD 858, JTCC, reel 6.

1701e   Letter to the King, June 22, 1701. AGI, SD 840, JTCC, reel 5.

1702a   Letter to the King, September 30, 1702. AGI, SD 840, JTCC, reel 6.

1702b   *Auto*, November 5, 1702. AGI, SD 858, JTCC, reel 6.

1702c   Proclamation, November 5, 1702. AGI, SD 858, JTCC, reel 6.

1702d   *Auto*, November 6, 1702. AGI, SD 858, JTCC, reel 6.

1702e   *Auto*, November 8, 1702. AGI, SD 858, JTCC, reel 6.

1704a   Letter to the King, March 30, 1704. AGI, SD 840, JTCC, reel 5.

1704b   Letter to the King, October 6, 1704. AGI, SD 858, JTCC, reel 6.

1706   Letter to the King, January 30, 1706. AGI, SD 858, JTCC, reel 6.

Index

abortion, 112, 121

Abosaya village (near St. Augustine), 310, 312

Abosaya village (Potano Province), 294–95, 298–300

acculturation: and adoption of new foods, 99; differences in, 326; resistance to, 221–22, 326–28; symptoms of, 83

ache, 95, 156, 243, 333

Achito village, 293–94

acorns, 44, 96

Acuera (chief), 43, 144

Acuera people: alliances of, 4, 80, 147; classification of, 5; dialect of, 6–7; gifts for, 144; material culture of, 13; Spanish relations with, 72, 163; and trade goods, 43; traditions of, 101. *See also* Diminiyuti Province; Ibiniyuti people; Mocoso people, village

Acuera Province: disturbances in, 275–76; missionization of, 12, 168, 174, 177–78, 190–91, 240–44; murders in, 241–44; territory of, 12. *See also* Diminiyuti Province; Ibiniyuti people; Mocoso people, village

Acuera village, 12, 81

Adam, Lucian, 123, 124

adjectives, forms for, 131

adornment: and burial of chiefs, 106; description of, 21–22, 24–25; metals for, 22, 47, 49; shells as, 24; as wagers, 110. *See also* clothing; metals

Afafa Hacienda, 300–301

Africans: influence by, 99; as servants, 114; as threat, 171; Timucua contact with, 47–48; villages of, 312, 319

Agile village, 31–32, 34–35. *See also* Asile village; San Miguel de Asile

Agramon, Manuel, 293

Agramont. *See* Grammont

agriculture: description of, 94–95; importance of, 5, 12, 13–14; and livestock, 197, 289, 327; planting, 115–16, 238, 240–41; rituals for, 115–16; tools and techniques for, 99–100. *See also* fields; food; ranching; subsistence activities

Aguacaleyquen village, 31, 258–59. *See also* Caliquen village; Ochile village

Agua Dulce people: and chiefdom succession, 83; classification of, 5; dialect of, 7. *See also* Agua Fresca dialect; Freshwater people

Agua Fresca dialect, 6. *See also* Freshwater people

Agua Salada dialect, 6–7. *See also* Saltwater people

Ahoica village: location of, 251; migration from, 246; missionization of, 189; name of, 252, 268; ranch at, 195. *See also* Ajohica village; San Agustín de Ahoica; Santa Catalina de Ahoica

Ais (chief), 52, 58, 171, 202

Ais Indians: alliances of, 42, 143, 171; and missionization, 169; names for, 304; and Spanish, 54, 202; subsistence activities of, 100; territory of, 3. *See also* Costa Indians

Ajiluste village, 251

Ajohica village, 228, 252, 286. *See also* Ahoica village; San Agustín de Ahoica; Santa Catalina de Ahoica

Ajoluca village, 248

Alabama, Timucua territory in, 4, 13

Alabama language, 134–35

Alachua County: missions in, 17, 174; tribes in, 9, 10

Alachua Sink site, 194
Alachua tradition: characteristics of, 13–15; dominance of, 85–86; locale for, 3, 30. *See also* Ocale people; Potano people
Alafaes Indians, 311, 317, 319, 321
Alapaha River, 9, 181; origin of the name, 3
Alas, Estaban de las, 61, 66, 67
alcohol, 255, 320–21, 328
Alejo, Juan, 209–12
Alexo (chief), 228
Alimacani (chief): alliances of, 64; French visited by, 47; and missionization, 53; power of, 79; title for, 78
Alimacani village: blockhouses at, 62–63, 65–66; and Ribaut expedition, 36; and Saturiwa confederation, 81. *See also* San Juan del Puerto
Alisa village, 241
Alligator Lake, village near, 34
Alonso, 242–43
Alonso (chief of Santa Lucia), 264
Alonso, don (at San Juan), 164
Alonso, don Juan (chief), 310–11
alphabet, letters used in, 130–31
Altamaha River: as boundary, 3; and material culture, 87; missions near, 174, 180; and trade contacts, 28; villages along, 11, 89, 149–50. *See also* river of Santa Isabel
Aluete, chief of, 176
Amacapira Indians, 311, 321–22
amalachini, 77
amber, 202–3
Amelia Island: attack on, 292; ferries for, 290; missions on, 173; tribes on, 97, 272, 296; villages on, 249–50, 271
Ana, doña (chieftainness), 159–60, 164
Anacabile village, 162
Anacape village. *See* Encaque village; San Antonio de Anacape
anacotima, 77–78
Ana María, 323–24
Anayo family, 324
Andrada, Capt. Pedro de, 64
Andrés (chief of Potoriba), 157
Andrés (chief of San Juan del Puerto), 287
Angel, Fray Juan, 276

Anhaica (Timucua) village, 135
Anhayca (Apalachee) village, 35, 135, 183. *See also* Apalachee Indians; Inatafum
animals, 88, 195–96. *See also* livestock; ranching
ano paracusi holata yco, 76, 78
Antonico (chief), 78, 162–63
Antonico village: chief of, 142; confirmations at, 262; jurisdiction of, 78, 162–63; missionization of, 141–42, 172; subsistence activities of, 94. *See also* Encaque; San Antonio de Anacape
Antonio (chief of San Matheo), 253
Antonio (English captain), 294
Antonio, Chucuta, 283
Aotina. *See* Outina (chief)
Apalachee Indians: acculturation of, 326; alliances of, 181, 297, 303, 306; appearance of, 24; attack on, 292, 294, 297; chiefdom succession for, 112; and epidemics, 192, 318; and friars, 144–45, 187; games of, 107–11, 185; language of, 122, 125, 134–35; material culture of, 185, 231–33; and militia conscription, 204; models for, 184; and murder, 282–85; political organization of, 4, 77–78, 79–80, 167; and ranching, 193–95, 197; relocation of, 232, 295, 296, 300, 328; revolt by, 197–98, 229, 326; subsistence activities of, 196; terms used by, 75, 77, 101, 305–6; and Timucua Revolt, 206–7, 222, 229; visitation of, 223, 225; and warfare with Timucua, 167–68; workers from, 280
Apalachee Province: council houses in, 90; deputy-governor for, 197; expeditions to, 27–35; jurisdiction of, 31–32; missionization of, 166, 168, 174, 188, 192, 328; population of, 257–58, 261, 263–65, 317; settlement patterns in, 230; Spanish withdrawal from, 295; territory of, 5–6, 9, 18; Velda Phase of, 233; villages in, 32, 183–84, 234
Apalachicola Indians: alliances of, 292–95, 306; missionization of, 236; population of, 257; raids from, 265–66, 277; ranching in, 197
Apalo mission, 174, 178

Apalu village, 31–32, 259
Appalou (Apalo) mission, 174, 178
appearance: after baptism, 23, 24; of chiefs, 21–22, 24–25, 40, 185; and gender, 21–24; and hair, 21–23, 106, 117; and tattoos, 21; and warfare, 101. *See also* adornment; clothing
Aquila village, 248
ara, 182
Aramazaca, pigments from, 91
Aramuqua ranchería, 219
Arapaha, meanings of, 182
Arapaha Province: alliances of, 182; autonomy of, 9; isolation of, 9; location of, 5, 9; migration from, 85; missionization of, 181; name for Onatheaqua, 18
Arapaha village: disappearance of, 252; location of, 182, 186; name for, 3, 182; removal of, 218, 226–27; and Timucua Revolt, 206, 216. *See also* Santa María de los Angeles de Arapaha
Arawak language, 128–29, 136
Arcos, Pedro de (agent), 177, 246, 248–51
Argüelles, Antonio de, 238–39, 268
Argüelles, Bartolomé de, 145–46
Argüelles, don Alonso de (chief), 144, 214, 219
Arnade, Charles, 192–94, 271, 292, 293
arroba, 145, 333
arroyos, names for, 135
Arucatessa (or Aruquetega), Juan (chief), 304, 309, 311
Asaho village, 249. *See also* Asao people; Santo Domingo de Asao
Asao people: alliances of, 176; and domesticated animals, 99; and Guale Revolt, 148–49; location of, 177; material culture of, 29; missionization of, 172; tea consumed by, 97
Asenisia, 324
asetama, 77–78
Asila Chua village, 283
Asilepaja village, 90–91
Asile village: chief of, 76, 122–23, 225; jurisdiction of, 198–99; leadership for, 225, 277–78; location of, 225; missionization of, 188, 275; names for, 184; ranch at, 123, 184, 195–200; and Timucua Revolt, 206. *See*

also Agile village; San Miguel de Asile
Aspogue village, 251
assimilation. *See* acculturation
atequi, 333
Athore (chief), 64, 112–13
Athore village, 46, 81
Athuluteca village, 250–51, 296. *See also* San Felipe de Athuluteca; San Phelipe; S^{cti} Philipi de Guale
atole, 98, 146, 333. *See also* corn meal porridge
Atoyquime village, 4, 244
Aucilla River, as boundary, 3, 9
Auñon, Fray Miguel de, 152
Avila, Fray Francisco de, 147
Avino (mission): and Acuera, 7, 12–13; establishment of, 174, 177. *See also* Acuera people
axes, 101
Axile village. *See* Asile village
Ayacamale village, 149, 159–60
Ayacutu village, 94. *See also* San Martín de Ayacutu
Ayala, don Antonio de (chief), 308
Ayala y Escobar, Gov. Juan de, 307
Aypaja (Ayapaja) people/village, 4, 244. *See also* Piaja Indians

Bacuqua village, 294
Bad Peace village, 29
Baker, Henry, 194
ball field (*empedrado*), 110
ball game: description of, 107–11; and gender, 111, 189; manuscript on, 108, 110; and Mesoamerican game, 109; prohibitions on, 183–85, 326–27
Bamba, Fray Joseph, 206–7
baptisms: appearance after, 23, 24; by friars, 166–67, 183, 187–88; at Ivitanayo, 244; and village lists, 308–11, 314–17
Baptizing Spring site, 180, 186, 195–96
barbacoas, 87, 93, 130, 333
Barbosa, Francisco, 249–50
Barrientos, Bartolomé, 52, 81, 329n. 2
Bartram, William, 91, 136
Bauptista de la Cruz, Juan (interpreter), 218, 234
bay laurel, uses of, 36, 119
beads, as gifts, 65

Beganbre, Capt. Joseph de, 299–300
Bejessi village, 149–50, 159–60
Benavides, Gov. Antonio de, 313, 318–20
Bennett, Charles E., 45, 76, 81, 330n. 1
Bentura (chief), 277–78
berdaches, 24–25, 334
Bernal, Clemente (chief), 220, 237–38
berries, for food, 95–96
Beverly, Robert, 132–33
Biedma, Luys Hernández de, 28, 258–60
Biloxi language, 130
birds, as omens, 118–19
Biro Zebano village, 244
blacks, 282
Blessed Virgin name, 321
Boadalquivi village. *See* San Buenaventura de Guadalquini
body painting, 21–22, 185
Bolton, Herbert E., 176–77, 251
boucane, 98
bowls, for grinding maize, 28–29
bows and arrows, 40, 101, 116–17
brass, as adornment, 22
breechclouts, 1, 22–23
Brinton, Daniel G., 124, 126
buffalo horn, 284
buhío, 65
Bullones, Fray Joseph de, 312–13, 317–18, 322
burials: and acculturation, 327; of chiefs, 105–6; in churches, 162; customs for, 23, 89, 97, 105–7, 117–19; structures for, 13–14, 87
Bushnell, Amy, 195, 254
Bushnell, David I., 91

Cabeza de Vaca, Alvar Núñez, 16, 27–28
Caçaroy village, 170
Cachipile village. *See* Santa Cruz de Cachipile
cacina (tea): consumption of, 96–97; defined, 334; preparation of, 2, 26, 97; restrictions on, 90–92, 328
cacique, 76, 79, 135, 235
Caherico, 158
Calabay (chief): alliances of, 59, 78; and missionary efforts, 58, 137, 138
Calabay/Çarabay village, 58, 81, 162–63
Calacala, 210
Calanay (chief), 43, 78
Calesa (murderer), 241–44, 275. *See also* Yazah

Caliquen (chief), 33–34
Caliquen village, 31, 33
Calusa Indians: alliances of, 179; expeditions to, 54, 137; missionization of, 165, 275; political organization of, 4, 74; Spanish contacts with, 276; traditions of, 35
Camino Real: and Rebolledo visitation, 223–24; towns of, 226–27
Camuñas, Diego (interpreter), 234–35
Canaveral National Seashore, 10, 171
Candelaria village, 234. *See also* Nuestra Señora de Candelaria de la Tamaja
Canizares y Osorio, Sgt.-Maj. Adrían, 213–20
canoes, 100
Caparaca village, 38, 170–71
Cape Canaveral, 3, 27, 42, 48, 247. *See also* Canaveral National Seashore
Capuaca village, 158
Çarabay (chief), 138. *See also* Sarabay (chiefs)
Carabay village, 81. *See also* Calabay/Çarabay village
Cardross's colony, 272–74
Carib language, 126
Carlos (chief), 52
carpenter, master, 284
Casapuia Indians, 317, 321
Cascangue (Guale), 11
Cascangue (Timucua): classification of, 5–8, 11; jurisdiction of, 173; language of, 6, 12, 155; villages of, 11, 155; visitors to, 12, 155
cassinet, 96
Casti, 46, 47, 81
Castillo, Pedro de (chief), 144
Catawba language, 130
catechisms, language of, 17, 122, 123
Catholicism. *See* Christianization; missionization
cattle: fences for, 194–95, 281; and Indians, 60, 327; protection of, 62, 192–93; and subsistence, 195–96
Cautió peninsula, 1
Cavale, Juan Alonso, 324–25
Cavale, Rosa María, 324
Caxon Island, 61
Cayagua Province, 187
Cazacolo (chief), 68–69, 140, 162
Cazacolo Island, 140
ceramics: appearance of stamped, 233; as boundary markers, 31; and

cacina, 97; changes in, 85, 231–32; classification of, 13–15, 236; and gender of pottery-makers, 86; and migration, 231–35; for trade, 163; transition zone in, 14

ceremonies. *See* holy days; rituals

chacal, 78, 135, 334

Chacato Indians: alliances of, 292, 294; hostility of, 181; missionization of, 236, 276; and murder investigation, 282–83; political organization of, 78

Chamile, Antonio, 209–10

Chamile, Lázaro (chief): and Indian removal, 226–27; literacy of, 76; power of, 228–29; and Timucua Revolt, 209–10, 212, 214–17. *See also* San Ildefonso de Chamini

Chamile village. *See* San Ildefonso de Chamini

Channel of San Pablo, 38

Charles II (English), 268

Charles II (Spanish), 291–92

Charles Spring site, 180

Charles Town (English), 268, 273–74, 291–92, 299

charms, 118

charnel houses, 106

Chatuache mission, 156

Cherokee Indians, 77, 269, 306

chestnuts, 29, 163. *See also* chinquapins

Chibchan language, 128, 136

Chica Faya La Madelena village, 159–60, 162

Chichimeco Indians, 181, 235, 239, 269, 294, 334. *See also* Ricahecria Indians

chickens, 196

chiefs: alliances of, 78, 80, 142; appearance of, 21–22, 24–25, 40, 185; Christianization of, 138, 142, 154, 163, 166, 183–84; death of, 23, 34, 105–6; executions of, 220–21, 223; gender of, 26, 230; gifts for, 143–44; housing for, 87, 88, 106; illnesses of, 117–18; lists of, 224, 286; and missionization, 144–45; power of, 57–58, 78–80, 142, 167, 198, 201; privileges of, 25–26, 74, 90–92, 98–99, 111, 114, 281; religious functions of, 74–75; rivalries of, 80–82; and social structure, 25, 200–203; succession of, 45, 82–84, 112, 277–78; terms for, 16, 28, 38–39, 75–78, 135, 157,

235; wailing for, 104–6. *See also* warriors

childbirth, 87, 93, 117

children: literature for, 122; out-of-wedlock conception of, 112; with physical defects, 21; schooling for, 67, 137–38, 188–89

Chiluque (Mocama), 297, 299, 304, 314, 315, 319, 323,, 324–25. *See also* Mocama people

Chiluque (Yamasee), 269, 293

Chinica (chief), 68, 138

Chinica village, 138, 159, 162

chinquapins, 29, 44, 281. *See also* chestnuts

Chinysca village, 158

Chirica village, 164

Chisca Indians, 181, 238–40, 294. *See also* Yuchi

Choctaw Indians, 134, 202

Chololo village, 264

Cholupaha village: de Soto at, 29–30; location of, 9, 31; maize supply at, 258; material culture of, 30–31. *See also* Santa Fé de Toloco

Chosas (or Chozas), Fray Pedro Fernández de, 144, 147, 149–50

Christianization: of chiefs, 138, 142, 144–45, 154, 163, 183–84; and communion, 159; and confession, 103, 122, 189; and early converts, 71; effects of, 106–8, 114; and literacy, 188–89; and marriage, 112–14; and mass, 160–61, 169, 189, 320; and music, 101–2, 189; and population, 261–63; process of, 161, 167; and ranching activities, 198; response to, 58, 69; and rosaries, 189; solidity of, 161. *See also* missionization

chua, 182

Chuaquin village. *See* San Francisco de Chuaquin

chuco, 135

chucu, 136

chunkey (game), 110, 111

Cicale village, 38, 170, 171

cimarrona/cimarrones, 114, 191, 241, 243–44, 334

citizenship, and council houses, 91

clans, 83, 113–14. *See also* chiefs, succession of

Clara (chieftainness of Utinahica), 263

climate, 50–51, 56–57, 304–5
clothing: breechclouts, 22–23; deerskins
    as, 21–24; as gifts, 142–43; material
    for, 143, 257, 289. *See also* adornment
clubs, 101
Cody Scarp, 194
Cofatichiqui village, 35
Cofa village: location of, 9, 179; mission-
    ization of, 166, 174, 178–79, 189
cognate, definition of, 129
Colon Indians, 269, 271–72, 288, 290
commoners: and burials, 106; and
    citizenship, 91; and political
    organization, 74; and religious
    knowledge, 115; and social
    structure, 25
communion, restrictions on, 159
confederations, 81–82
confession, resistance to, 189
Confessionario, 103, 122, 334. *See also*
    Pareja, Fray Francisco de
confirmations: of chiefs, 164–65, 262;
    by friars, 164–67, 176, 187; and
    village lists, 308–11, 314–17; during
    visitations, 164, 176, 246, 248, 262
Confraternity of the True Cross, 160–61
congregación (reduction), 168–73, 334
copper, red, 22, 47
Córcoles y Martínez, Gov. Francisco de,
    300–301, 303
corn. *See* maize
corncribs (*garitas*), 89, 212
corn meal porridge (*migan*), 20, 98. *See
    also atole*
Cosahue village, 151
Cosapoy village, 69
Cosapue Indians, 274
Cosapuya, Francisco, 323
Cosapuya, María, 323
Costa Indians, 304–5, 308, 322–23,
    332n. 4. *See also* Ais Indians
Cotocochono. *See* Yustaga Province
Cotocochuni village: missionization of,
    167, 182–84; population of, 258;
    status of, 230. *See also* Potohiriba
    village
council houses: description of, 87, 89–
    90, 289; excavation of, 90; exclusion
    of women from, 90; importance of,
    327–28; property of chief, 91; and
    social stratification, 25–26; uses of,
    91–92, 285, 307
Cow Ford, 243

Crane, Verner W., 306
Crawford, James M., 128–29, 135
Creek Indians: alliances of, 297, 307;
    attacks by, 265; and ceramics
    changes, 232, 235–36; language of,
    134–36; moieties of, 77; practices of,
    36; and Yamasee War, 306–7. *See
    also* Apalachicola Indians
cronista mayor, 334
Cruz, don Alonso de la (chief), 308
Cuba: atole in, 98, 333; migration to,
    325; provisions from, 57; schools in,
    67, 138; as source of contagion, 261
Cubaconi (queen of Yufera), 11, 46, 112
cult of idols, 74
Cumberland Island: chiefs from, 40;
    depopulation of, 183, 190, 239–40;
    evacuation of, 152–53; fort on, 66;
    material culture of, 14; and
    missionization, 18, 69, 175; and
    trade goods, 161–62; tribes on, 10–
    11, 296; villages on, 5, 7–8, 147,
    149, 177, 249. *See also* San Pedro
    Mocama
Cuna language, 136
Cupahica village, 135, 214, 229. *See also*
    Apalachee Indians
customs. *See* rituals; traditions

dances: firearms in, 291; regulations on,
    255, 291; types of, 107–8, 291
d'Arlac, Lord, 43
daughters of the Sun, 114
Dávila, Fray Francisco, 176–77
Daytona Beach, as boundary, 3, 10
Deagan, Kathleen A.: on Acuera, 127;
    on doña María, 165; on mission
    locations, 251; on tribal identities, 7;
    on Yufera, 11
death, 106–7, 117–18. *See also* burials
de Bry, Theodore: accuracy of, 20–21,
    88–89, 92–93, 105, 112; on clothing,
    24; on customs, 97, 107–8; on
    shamans, 120; on subsistence
    activities, 99–100, 116; on tattoos,
    22; on village structures, 88; on
    warfare, 103
deer: and hunting rituals, 116–17; terms
    for, 330–31n. 6; uses of, 88, 196
deerskins: as clothing, 21–24; as gifts,
    36–37, 39, 65; symbolism of, 242;
    for trade, 163
Delgado, Marcos, 134, 273

demography: and Leon-Jefferson ceramics, 231–36; sources on, 257–67. *See also* population

de Soto, Hernando: and Acuera people, 12–13; and ceramics, 233; effects of, 36, 166, 234; expeditions of, 28–35, 94, 258–59; and Indian leadership, 79; interpreter for, 3; and tribal names, 16

De Soto Trail Project, 31, 34

dialects: Cascangue, 6, 12, 155; description of, 4, 6–8; Maritime (standard), 6–7; Ocone, 155; Potano, 155. *See also* language

Díaz Vara Calderón, Bishop Gabriel: on council houses, 90; on Indians' appearance, 23–24; missions listed by, 246–48, 286; on population, 265; on subsistence, 98; transportation for, 100

Dickinson, Jonathan: on council houses, 90–91, 289; error of, 271, 288; on fishing, 100; on population, 287; on rituals, 97

Diego (chief of Potohiriba), 205–8, 210, 217

diet. *See* food

Díez de la Calle, Juan, 190

diffusion versus migration, 233–34

Diminiyuti Province, 5, 206, 208, 211. *See also* Acuera Province; Mocoso people

Dionisio (chief of Machava), 215, 217

disease, 140, 302. *See also* epidemics

divorce, 113–14

Dobyns, Henry F., 35, 258–61

doctors, 115, 119

doctrinas, 71, 246–47, 335

Domingo (chief of Chololo), 264

Domingo (chief of San Agustín), 228

Domínguez, Josepha, 323

d'Otiggny (Lt.), 43–44

Dougherty Uplift, 13–15

Drake, Francis, 139

dreams, 118–19, 294

drinks. *See* alcohol; cacina (tea)

ear piercing, 24

Easter duty, 280

eastern division, 4–5, 35, 39, 73, 85–86, 107, 164, 175, 191–92

Ebelino de Compostela, Bishop Diego, 265

Eguale village, 162

Eloquale. *See* San Luis de Eloquale

eloquale, meaning of, 186

Elvas, Gentleman of: on food-storage structures, 93; on language, 130; on maize preparation, 29; on population, 258–59

Emoloa (chief), 46, 48, 60

Emoloa (son of chief), 60

Emoloa village, 81

Encaque village, 46, 81

encomiendas, absence of, 192, 335

Enehau Ulgee, 77

English: alliances of, 292–95, 296; attacks by, 200–201, 213, 240, 272–74, 292–95, 296–97, 312; Florida surrendered to, 325; and French threat, 306; and gift-giving, 202; goals of, 268, 302–3; Spanish peace with, 291–92

environment: and climate, 50–51, 56–57, 304–5; descriptions of, 11–13; and population, 32–33; and village locations, 14, 56–57, 81, 88

epidemics: effects of, 79, 166, 193, 201, 203, 227, 312; and labor shortage, 240–41; locations for, 192, 225, 241, 258; and missionization, 145, 174, 190, 262; origins of, 261; and political organization, 79, 230; timing of, 188, 240; types of, 188

Escamacu (chief), 52

Escamacu Province, 187, 271–72

Escamacu-Orista Indians, attacks on, 69–70; language of, 125; and Menéndez, 137; revolt of, 68

Escambé village, 294

Escobedo, Fray Alonso de, 71, 140

Escudero, Alonso, 205, 208–9

Española, English attack on, 200

Esquivel, Juan Alonso de, 301

Etocale village. *See* Ocale village; San Luis de Eloquale

Europeans: animals of, 195–96; first contacts with, 1–2; influence by, 99; sustained contact with, 39, 47–48; warfare defined by, 42, 44. *See also* English; French; Spanish

Evinston area, sites in, 30, 166

family, 113–14. *See also* chiefs, succession of; marriage

faunal remains, 88, 195–96

Faupel, W. John, 21, 107

Faxquis village, 251
Felipe (chief of Chinica), 164
Fernández de Florencia, Juan: missions listed by, 246, 251; on population, 257; and village establishment, 253
Fernando de Valdés Inquiry (1602), xii
ferries, regulations for, 281–82, 287, 290–91
fields: and attacks, 301–2; cultivation of, 92; harvesting, 115–16; location of, 88; planting of, 115–16, 238, 240–41; preparation of, 98–99, 288; protection for, 93
Fig Springs site, 15, 34, 232–34. *See also* Itchetucknee Springs; San Martín de Ayacutu
fire: and death of chief, 106; and gender, 117, 119; and hunting, 98–99, 116
firearms, and militia conscription, 204
fiscales, 161, 335
fish/fishing: as gifts, 36, 46; importance of, 94; rituals for, 115–16; techniques for, 100, 116; uses of, 88, 97–98
Flemings' ship, 59–60
Flint River, battle at, 292, 294–95, 331n. 1
Florencia, Capt. Claudio Luis de, 197
Florencia, Francisco de, 299
Florencia, Joaquín de, 121, 285
Florida: censuses in, 304–5, 307–11; consolidation of, 319, 323; Indians' departure from, 325; names for, 1; viability of, 147–48, 157
flutes, 101
food: availability of, 32–33; crops for, 95; influences on, 99; preparation of, 2, 28–29, 29, 88, 96–99; storage of, 92–93; taboos on, 117; and trading, 44–45. *See also* agriculture; foods; subsistence activities
foods: *ache,* 95, 156; acorns, 44, 96; berries, 95–96; chestnuts, 29, 163; chinquapins, 29, 44, 281; grapes, 281; hickory nuts, 96; mulberries, 36; nuts, 95–96; roots, 94–95; sand mixed with, 121; wheat, 196–97. *See also* maize
Fort Caroline: attack on, 48, 50–54; and d'Arlac expedition, 43–44; harassment of, 60; and Indian territory, 11; killings near, 10; renaming of, 53;

and village locations, 52, 81. *See also* San Mateo
Fort George Island, 10, 36, 290, 298. *See also* Alimacani village; San Juan del Puerto
Fort King George (British), 150
forts: attacks on, 48, 50–51, 53; construction of, 145–46, 212; establishment of, 40–41, 66; names of, 251; and palisades, 88, 212, 216–19
Fort San Mateo, 138
Fort San Pedro, 66–67
Fort Santa Elena. *See* Santa Elena de Machava
Fountain of Youth site, 196
Fox Pond site, 166
Francisca (chieftainness of Napofaie), 263
Francisca, doña (chieftainness of San Mateo, St. Johns River), 164
Franciscans: deaths of, 147, 152; duties of, 138–39; opposition to, 165; saints of, 118; success of, 139–40. *See also* friars; missionization
Francisco, Bartolomé, 207, 212–13, 253
Francisco (chief of Cachipile), 216
Francisco (chief of San Mateo, St. Johns River), 158
Francisco (interpreter), 171–72
Francisco (mico mayor of Guale), 144
French: alliances of, 40–44, 50–51, 54, 64, 68, 70; attacks by, 269–71; equipment of, 43; expeditions of, 35–41, 69–70; and Guale Revolt, 143; provisions for, 44–46; revenge of, 64; and search for precious metals, 39–43, 47; Spanish attacks on, 50–51, 54; Spanish control of, 53; terms used by, 18–19, 20; Timucua assistance for, 51–52. *See also* Huguenots; *names of specific people*
Freshwater people: appearance of, 22; battles of, 41–44, 47; classification of, 5; dialect of, 6; disappearance of, 193, 296; enemies of, 16, 63–64; gold of, 48–49; jurisdiction of, 10, 162–63; leadership for, 45, 78, 142; material culture of, 13, 86; and Menéndez's expedition, 57–59; missionization of, 137–41, 145, 157–65, 168, 169–73, 177–78, 190, 262; musical instruments of, 102; political

organization of, 73, 157, 163; and reduction, 169–73; rituals of, 94; Spanish contact with, 48; subsistence activities of, 94; terms used by, 16, 76; and trade goods, 43; villages of, 38, *170;* warriors of, 82. *See also* Agua Dulce people; Agua Fresca dialect; Outina (chief)

friars: assignments for, 172–73, 275, 286, 321; attitudes of, 322; authority of, 146; brutality by, 266–67, 274, 276–77; complaints of, 254–55, 320–21; conditions for, 154, 174, 186–87, 277–79; deaths of, 10, 59–60, 63, 137, 147, 152, 212; enmity among, 321–22; evacuation of, 152–53; and governors, 147, 161–62, 320–21; horses for, 179, 181–82, 184, 186–87; requests for, 154, 167, 172, 187, 236; resistance to, 184–85; shortage of, 154, 187–88, 263; on Timucua political organization, 73–74; and Timucuan revolt, 200–201, 209–10, 221–22

gacha, 98, 150, 335
Gainesville area, tribes in, 9, 166
Galloway, Patricia, 93, 202
games: ball game, description of, 107–11; chunkey, 110, 111; and gender, 189; prohibitions on, 183–85, 326–27; reasons for, 109, 115
García, Lt. Andrés, 282–83, 300–302
gardens. *See* fields
garitas, 89, 212, 224, 335
garitas de flechas, 204
Gaspar, Hubabaq (interpreter), 234
Gaspar (chief of Asile), 225
gathering: bay laurel, 36, 119; foods for, 29, 36, 44, 95–96, 163, 281; importance of, 94; and ranch expansion, 194–95, 281; rituals for, 115–16; Spanish moss, 23–24, 257, 281, 289
Gatschet, Albert S., 76, 124, 126, 129
Geiger, Maynard: on mission locations, 140–42, 175, 178; on tribal affiliations, 250
gender: and appearance, 21–24; of chiefs, 26, 230; and dances, 107; and games, 111; and geophagy, 121; and homosexuality, 25; and literacy, 188; and participation in mass,

189; of pottery-makers, 86; and separate fires, 117, 119; and warfare strategies, 42. *See also* men; women

geophagy, 121
Georgia: French presence in, 70; Indian territory in, 3–4, 8–9, 11–14, 55; migration from, 232–35; ranching in, 197; Spanish withdrawal from, 271; visitation to, 234–35
gifts: as bribe, 45–46; for chiefs, 142–43; differences in, 143–44; expanded distribution of, 142–43; importance of, 39–40, 201–3; in religious rituals, 94; types of, 36–37, 39–40, 43, 46, 65, 142–43
Gil, Capt. Gilberto, 69–71
God, names for, 76–77
godparenthood, 112, 146
gods (native), games to honor, 109, 115. *See also* sun-god
gold: as adornment, 22, 49; search for, 40–43, 47, 48
Gómez de Engraba, Fray Juan, 209, 220
Gonsálves, Capt. Vicente, 70, 150–51, 176
gopher tortoises, 196
Gourgues, Dominique de: alliances of, 64–65, 82, 107, 140; attacks by, 65–66, 138; expeditions of, 63, 68
governor (applied to native leaders), 83–84
governors: chiefs' treatment by, 201–10; death of, 140, 197; friars' relations with, 147, 161–62, 320–21; gifts of, 142–44; greed of, 202–3, 227; land grants by, 194–95; sentences by, 211–12, 285
grammar, preparation of, 122. *See also* language
Grammont, Abraham (pirate), 263, 270–71
Granberry, Julian: on Agua Salada dialect, 7; grammar published by, 124–25; hypothesis of, 136; on Lamhatty document, 133; on language, 128–34; on Mocama name, 18; on Potano dialect, 123
grapes, 281
Grasserie, Raoul de la, 124
grave goods, 107, 117
Guacara. *See* San Juan de Guacara
Guacara River, 251. *See also* Suwannee River

Guadalquini. *See* San Buenaventura de
     Guadalquini
Guadalquini Island, 268–72
Guadalquini people, 70
Guadalupe de Tolomato, 235. *See also*
     Tolomato village
Guale Indians: alliances of, 61, 63, 66,
     70, 299; appearance of, 23; attack on
     Strozzi, 69; attacks on, by Spanish
     (1570s), 69–70, (1597 and later),
     151–52, 176, 238–39, 292; com-
     plaints of, 97; enemies of, 10–11, 69,
     80; expeditions to, 55, 59, 137; and
     food preparation, 29, 97; games of,
     111; gifts for, 143–44; language of,
     125, 134–35, 234; material culture
     of, 29, 85–87; and matrilineal
     inheritance, 112; and militia
     conscription, 204; missionization of,
     58, 165, 172, 176, 180, 249–51, 262,
     264, 277; names for political
     organization of, 73–74; population
     of, 257, 317, 322–23; relocation of,
     271–72, 296, 298, 306; structures of,
     89–90; terms for, 76; territory of,
     176; and Timucua Revolt, 213–14;
     villages of, 251, 289–90. *See also*
     Guale Revolt (1597)
Guale revolt (1576), 68
Guale Revolt (1597): captives from, 11;
     conclusion of, 143; description of,
     113, 142, 147–51; effects of, 153–54,
     157; leadership for, 144
Guanabacoa (Cuba), Indians' resettle-
     ment in, 325
Guana River, sites along, 86
guano. See Spanish moss
Gutiérrez de Palomar, Capt. Juan, 66–
     67
Guyana, language of, 128

Haas, Mary, 126, 128, 134
haciendas: Afafa, 300–301; Aramuqua
     ranchería, 219; at Asile, 123, 184,
     195–200; establishment of, 123;
     Piquilaco, 194, 281; San Joseph de
     Puibeta, 194, 281. *See also* La Chua
     Hacienda
Haipaha/Harpaha (chief), 64
hair, 21–23, 106, 117
Halifax River, villages near, 170–71
Halmacanir (chief), 64
hanap, 97

Hapaluya village. *See* Apalu village
Harapaha, meaning of name for, 182
hassez, 95. *See also ache*
Hawkins, Benjamin, 77, 135
Hawkins, John, 46
Haze, Fray Pedro, 276–77
healing practices. *See* medicine
Heliocopile/Helycopile (chief), 64
Helmacope/Helmacape (chief), 64
herbalists, 115, 119
herbs, 121
Heva, Diego (chief), 214, 218–19, 225
hica, 135
Hicachirico village, 158–59, 162
hickory nuts, 96
Hinachuba, don Patricio (chief), 282,
     295, 298–99
Hiocaia (king of Yufera), 11, 46, 112
Hiriba, Francisco (chief), 214–16, 219
Hita Salazar, Gov. Pablo de, and
     ranching, 194
Hita Salazar, Juan Antonio de, 194, 269,
     280
Hitchiti language, 134–35, 234
hoes, 99
Hoffman, Paul, 70
holata, 16, 75, 76, 135, 235, 335
holatama, 75
holy days: Ascension Day, 146; Easter,
     280; labor on, 146
Holy Week celebration, 160–61
homosexuality, 25
Honosonayo (White Deer) clan, 83
Horruytiner, Gov. Luis de, 179, 194
Horruytiner, Gov. Pedro Benedit, need
     for gift-giving, 202
Horruytiner, Joseph, 292–93
Horruytiner, Juan Benedit, 301
horses: for friars, 179, 181–82, 184,
     186–87; influence of, 143; and
     mission locations, 179; raising of,
     195; uses of, 53–54, 154, 327
horticulture. *See* agriculture; fields
Hospo (or Tospe) (chief), 309, 313–14
Hospo village, 251
Hotina. *See* Outina (chief)
houses, 65, 86–88, 198
Houstaqua (chief): appearance of, 22;
     status of, 79, 230; title for, 76;
     wealth of, 43. *See also* Yustaga
     Province
Hudson, Charles, 12, 30, 32–33, 81
Huguenots, 20, 35–37, 52

hunting: fire used in, 98–99, 116; importance of, 14, 94; and poaching problems, 284; rituals for, 115–17; and tribal lands, 284; weapons for, 101

hurimelas, 98–99, 116, 330–31n. 6

hurricanes, effects of, 50–51, 304–5

Hutchinson, Dale L., 28

Ibaja speakers, 125, 308, 310, 314, 323, 325. *See also* Guale; Yguaja

Ibarra, Gov. Pedro de: on disorder among Indian groups, 179; interests of, 171; obedience of chiefs to, 164; terms used by, 77; visits by, 160

Ibiica, 185, 189

Ibiniyuti people, 5. *See also* Acuera Province; Diminiyuti Province

Ibi people: classification of, 5; dialect of, 6, 12, 155; gifts for, 143

Ibi Province: environment of, 155; missionization of, 153–54, 185; territory of, 12

Icafi dialect. *See* Itafi dialect

Icafi people, 5, 7–8, 166

Icafui people, 5–8, 11

illness. *See* disease; epidemics

Inatafum village, 135. *See also* Anhayca village; Inihayca village; San Luis de Talimali

Inca Indians, traditions of, 114

incest taboos, lack of, 112–13

Indian Pond site: and material culture, 15, 30; village near, 34, 179

Indian River: and fishing techniques, 100; Spanish garrison on, 54; villages along, 52, 169

Indians de la Costa, 304. *See also* Ais Indians; Costa Indians

Inés, doña (chieftainness), 158–59

iniha/inihama, 75, 77–78, 135, 335

Inihayca village, 110, 168. *See also* Anhayca village; Inatafum village; San Luis de Nijajipa

inija. See iniha/inihama

insects, and food storage, 93

interpreters: and language choices, 234; priests accompanied by, 172; reports of, 319; titles for, 135

Iracana River, 11, 46. *See also* Satilla River

Islands of Tacatacuru, attack on, 61. *See also* Cumberland Island

Isle of Mocama, 251

Itafi dialect, 6–7, 12

Itaraholata, 75. *See also* Itara village

Itara village, 29, 31. *See also* Itaraholata

Itchetucknee River, 31

Itchetucknee Springs, village at, 9, 31

Itchetucknee State Park, archaeolgy at, 15

Iufera (Yufera) dialect, 6–7, 12

ivi, 330n. 1

Iviahica village, 183. *See also* Anhayca village

Ivitachuco, Luis (chief): lands owned by, 123, 199; and Timucua Revolt, 207, 212–14, 225; title for, 123, 136

Ivitachuco village: alliances of, 225; attack on, 299–300; and games, 110; location of, 32, 183–84; mission at, 275; and murder investigation, 282, 284; Prieto's negotiations at, 168; relocation of, 298; status of, 135; survival of, 295; and Timucua Revolt, 203, 206–7, 212–14, 219, 220. *See also* Abosaya village; Apalachee Indians; San Lorenzo de Ivitachuco

Ivitanayo village: baptisms at, 244; disappearance of, 244, 281; establishment of, 252–54, 256, 265; friars at, 277; land grants at, 195

Jabahica (chief), 241–42, 244, 275–76

jacal, 89

Jacksonville area, Indian sites, 10

Jacoba, María, 241–44

Jaen (or Xaen), Lt. Diego de, 288, 294–95, 298

Jamaica, 200, 240

Jeddito Yellow ware, 236

Jefferson culture, 232

Jefferson Ware, 15. *See also* Leon-Jefferson complex

Jekyll Island, 11, 176–77

Jesuits: deaths of, 59–60, 137; duties of, 137–38; opposition to, 165; schools of, 67

Jésus, Francisco Alonso de: on burning of fields, 98–99; on council houses, 89–90; on customs, 82, 106, 112, 117; on food distribution, 92; on friars' conditions, 186–87; on houses, 87; on literacy, 188; on rosary, 189; on social stratification, 25–26

Johnson, Kenneth, 31
Jones, B. Calvin, 180
Jororo Indians: attack on, 301; dialect
  of, 3–4; and friar's death, 244;
  meaning of, 118; missionization of,
  275; Pojoy living with, 311
Jororo Province: deaths in, 279;
  territory of, 300; villages in, 244
Juan (chief of Cupaica), 214
Juan, don (San Pedro chief): accultura-
  tion of, 146, 150; gifts for, 144; and
  Guale Revolt, 148–51; horse of, 143;
  succession of, 159
Juan, don (Tolomato heir), 144
Juana (chieftainness), 237
Julian (heir to chiefdom), 84
Junco, Juan de, 142, 144, 164
Jusepe, 148, 150
Juta, Antonio (chief), 323

kinship, 113–14. See also chiefs,
  succession of
Koasati language, 134–35

labor: authority over, 146; and
  Christianization, 169; demands for,
  203; and epidemics, 192; forced,
  145–46, 230, 240–41, 321; and
  population counts, 258, 263; and
  ranch establishment, 197; sources
  for, 163, 203, 280
Laca. See San Diego de Elaca mission
la Caille, Françoise de, 39
La Chua Hacienda: attacks on, 195,
  210–11, 218, 220, 269–70, 295,
  298–301; cimarrones near, 279;
  garrisoned, 288, 300; location of,
  194; and missionization, 246, 248;
  murder near, 241–43; provisions for,
  203; size of, 193; as source of
  alcohol, 255; and Timucua Revolt,
  210
Lake Butler, villages near, 28
Lake County, sites in, 3
Lake George, and Indian territory, 10,
  58
Lake Grandin, and Indian territory, 16
Lake Harney, and Indian territory, 10
lake of Maymi (Lake Okeechobee), 58
Lake of Ocone, 5, 155–56
Lake Sampala, site near, 34–35, 183
Lake Weir, villages near, 12
Lamar complex: locale for, 14–15, 85;
  origins of, 232–35

Lamar Complicated Stamped, 15, 233
Lamhatty document, 6, 124, 127, 131–
  33
Langne Cap qui (chief), 309
language: characteristics of, 125, 128,
  130–33; difficulties with, 39–40;
  early writing on, 122–24;
  Granberry's hypothesis on, 136; and
  migration questions, 234; and
  Muskogean languages, 124–29, 134–
  36; origins of, 125–30, 136; and
  Tawasa language, 131–34; teaching
  of native, 275. See also glossary (333-
  37); languages; names
languages: Alabama, 134–35;
  Apalachee, 122, 125, 134–35;
  Arawak, 128–29, 136; Biloxi, 130;
  Caribbean, 126, 128; Catawba, 130;
  Chibchan, 128, 136; Choctaw, 134;
  Creek, 134–36; Cuna, 136;
  Escamacu-Orista, 125; Guale, 125,
  134–35, 234; Guyana, 128; Hitchiti,
  134–35, 234; Koasati, 134–35;
  Macro-Chibchan, 128, 136;
  Maipuran, 128, 136; Maritime
  (standard), 6–7; Mayaca, 3–4, 125;
  Mikasuki, 3; Mocoso, 3; Muskogean,
  126–29, 133–36, 234; Proto-Tucano,
  136; Seminole, 3, 135–36; sign, 36,
  38–39; Siouan, 128; Taino, 130;
  Tawasa, 6, 124, 126, 131–34, 133–
  34; Tocobaga, 125; Tucano, 136;
  Tulafina, 125; Uçita, 3; Warao, 128–
  29, 136; Yamasee, 319
Lanning, John Tate: on friars' locations,
  157, 163; on mission locations, 10,
  176–77, 251
Larando, Capt. Pedro de, death of, 63
Large Deer lineage, 83
Lastra, Fray Pedro de la, and brutality,
  266–67, 274, 276–77
Laudonnière, René de: alliances of, 40–
  44, 46, 50, 64, 119; attack on, 50–
  51; on council houses, 89; descriptions by, 20–24; expedition of, 38–
  41, 47; on foods, 91–92, 94–95; on
  games, 107; on geophagy, 121; on
  Indians' power, 79, 82; on marriage
  and sexuality, 111–12, 114; on
  material culture, 97; and Outina's
  detention, 45–47, 82; paracusi used
  by, 75–76, 78; provisions for, 46–47;
  on scapegoat ceremony, 80–81; on
  shamans, 115, 119; on traditions, 96,

105–6; and tribal names, 16, 18–19; on warfare, 42, 104–5; on Yufera, 11

Lawson, John, 93

Lázaro (chief), 278

Lázaro, investigation by, 282

Le Challeux, Nicolas: on appearance, 21, 23; on foods, 20, 97–98; on houses, 87; on marriage, 111–12

Le Moyne du Morgues, Jacques: accuracy of, 93; on communication with Indians, 39; descriptions by, 22; drawings by, 20–21; map by, 18, 30, 81, 178, 185; on musical instruments, 101; on warfare, 103, 259

Leon-Jefferson complex: and demography, 231–36; dominance of, 85–86, 185; influences on, 14–15; origins of, 232–33

letters (alphabet), functions of, 131

letters (in the language), 122–23, 191, 209–10, 215

Leturiondo, Alonso de, 95–96, 291–92

Leturiondo, Domingo de: on abolition of games, 108–9, 183–84; ranch deal brokered by, 252–53; visitation by, 255–56, 268

Le Vasseur, Capt. Thomas, 42

literacy: and acculturation, 327; and appeals for pardon, 191; of chiefs, 76; and Christianization, 188–89; and gender, 188; level of, 122, 188–89

literature: language of, 122; titles of, 123; types of, 188

Little Manatee River, de Soto's camp on, 28

livestock, 196–97, 289, 327. See also cattle

López, Antonio, 113, 148, 150

López, Fray Baltasar: assignments for, 153–55, 157; authority of, 146; on Christianization, 161; and Guale Revolt, 154; on jurisdictions, 159–60; problems faced by, 145; on San Pedro's neighbors, 11; success of, 140–41; on Timucua name, 17

López de Mendoza Grajales, Francisco, 48, 329n. 2–3

Lorant, Stefan, 81, 107

Lorenzo, 241–42

Louck, Lana Jill, 186

Lounsbury, Floyd, 129

Lower Mississippi Valley, and linguistic traits, 129–30

Lower Timucua, 17

Lucas (chief of Ahoica), 252

Lucayos (Bahamas and its population), 1

Lucia (chieftainness), 228

Luis, Juan (chief at San Juan), 264, 288

Luna, Fray Pedro de, 275, 286

Lussagnet, Suzanne: on cultivation and harvest, 91–92; on grave goods, 107; on scapegoat ceremony, 81; on wailing, 104

Lutherans (Huguenots), 20, 35–37, 52

Lyon, Eugene, 63–64, 162

Machaba/Machava. See Santa Elena de Machava

Machado, Juan Ferro, 265

Machaqua Province, friars requested by, 187

McKeithen site, 34

Macoya (chief), 58, 78

Macoya village, 81. See also Mayaca village

Macro-Chibchan language, 128, 136

Madison County, sites in, 183

Maipuran language, 128, 136

maize: abundance of, 12, 28–29, 40, 94, 258; cultivation of, 94, 164; description of, 98; distribution of, 91–92, 204; as gifts, 36, 46; preparation of, 2, 20, 28–29, 98, 281; rituals for, 116; source for, 202–3; storage of, 89, 92–93; terms for, 133; as trade good, 162; tributes of, 145, 152

mandador, 77. See also iniha

Mandonado, Fray Phelipe, 310

Manrique de Rojas, Hernando, 38

Manuel (chief of Asile), 76, 122, 123, 225

Manuel (chief of Samomo), 263

Marcos (chief of Ocochunos), 266

Marcos (chief of Utista), 263

Marcos, Alonso (chief), 288

María (chieftainness of Niayca), 206

María (chieftainness of San Juan Evangelista), 217

María, doña (at San Juan), 164. See also Meléndez, doña María (chieftainness)

Marion County, sites in, 3, 29

Maritime (standard) dialect, 6–7

Márques, Catalina (chief), 139

Márques, Gaspar (chief): alliances of, 71; jurisdiction of, 163; on missionary efforts, 139–40; and patrilineal succession, 82–83

Márques, don Pedro (chief): alliances of, 71–72, 139–40; successor to, 82–83
Márquez Cabrera, Gov. Juan, 237, 268, 271, 276
marriage: between tribes, 328; description of, 111–14, 278; and place of employment, 280
Martín (chief), 228
Martín, don Francisco (chief), 310
Martín, Juan (interpreter), 234–35
Martínez, Lorenzo, 154
Martínez, doña Merenciana (cacica), 308
Martínez, Father Pedro, 10, 60, 63
Martínez Avendaño, Gov. Domingo de, 140, 145
mass: Indians' participation in, 160–61, 169; music in, 189; ornaments for, 320
Matanzas Inlet, 39, 48, 51
Matanzas River: blockhouse constructed at, 62, 67–68; and shipwreck, 51
Matecumbe Key, shipwreck on, 172
material culture, 13–15. See also Alachua tradition; ceramics; Safety Harbor culture; St. Johns tradition; San Marcos tradition
Matheo, Marselo, 324, 325
matrilineal succession, 82, 112, 327. See also patrilineal system
Matthew, feast day of, 53
mattocks, 99
Mayaca people: alliances of, 42, 63–64, 81; language of, 3–4, 125; subsistence activities of, 94–95
Mayaca village: jurisdiction of, 162–63; language of, 309; location of, 58, 171; missionization of, 178, 275; population of, 264; and scalping incident, 327
Mayman Yoha (armed pirogue), 301
Mayrra (chief), 42–43
medicine: adherence to traditional, 327; and curing rituals, 119–21; herbs for, 121; practitioners of, 115, 119. See also epidemics
Medina, Sgt.-Maj. don Tomás de: assignments for, 268, 275–76; and horse-raising, 327; residence of, 248
Meléndez, doña María (chieftainness at Nombre de Dios): acculturation of, 145; Christianization of, 139, 165, 262; jurisdiction of, 158, 164–65,

173, 262; marriage of, 83, 220; possible migration of, 183
Meléndez, María (Escamacu princess), 331n. 3
men: adornment for, 24–25; appearance of, 21–23; meals for, 92; place in church of, 189
Méndez de Canzo, Gov. Gonzalo, 146–47, 161, 163
Menéndez, Lucas (chief), and Timucua Revolt, 201–2, 203, 205–11, 219
Menéndez, Capt. Tomás, 243
Menéndez de Avilés, Pedro: alliances of, 52, 68, 139; attacks by, 50–51; building of blockhouses by, 63, 65, 67–68; and cattle-raising, 62, 192–93; death of, 56; defensive plan of, 62–63; expeditions of, 38, 47–49, 50, 57–60, 169; Indian policies of, 53–54; meetings with Indians by, 52, 57–59, 61–62; missionary efforts by, 58, 137; musical instruments introduced by, 102; as rainmaker, 55, 57; and St. Augustine, 38, 54–57; and tributes, 145
Menéndez Márques, Francisco, and La Chua hacienda, 193
Menéndez Márques, Juan: on friars' assignments, 139–40; on mission locations, 140–41, 175; and Timucua Revolt, 211–14
Menéndez Márques, Pedro: attacks by, 70, 71–72; defenses constructed by, 68–69; and Indian attacks, 60–61, 67; and missionization, 145
Menéndez Márques family, 193
Menéndez Márquez, Thomás, 269, 285
menstrual huts, 87, 93, 117
Merenciana (chieftainness), 237, 264, 288, 306
metals: as gifts, 39–40, 65; search for, 40–43, 47, 48; types of, 22, 47, 49
Mexía, Alvaro, 170–72
Mexico, atole in, 98
mica/mico, 76, 135, 235
Micanopy area, tribes in, 9
micoo, 38
midwives, 115, 119
migan, 20, 98
migration: and ceramics changes, 231–35; and material culture, 85–86; and reduction, 168–69; regulation of, 226, 231, 256, 280; resistance to,

230–31; and village establishment,
252–53
Miguel (chief), 281
Miguel, Capt. don (chief), 300, 304
Mikasuki language, 3
Milanich, Jerald T.: on de Soto's
expedition, 30, 33; on hunting, 330–
31n. 6; on language, 125; on names,
18; on political organization, 77–78;
on St. Marys tradition, 10; on
shamans, 115–16, 119–20; on
taboos, 117; on territory, 3; on
village locations, 12, 32, 81
Milledgeville area, sites in, 181
mineral prospecting, 192
Miranda, Gutierre de, 72
missionization: and compulsory
attendance, 161; drawbacks of, 145;
effects of, 23–25, 166–67, 328; and
epidemics, 145, 174, 190, 262; high
point for, 262–63
missions: assemblies at, 160–61; attacks
on, 181, 265–66, 296–302; crisis in,
277–78; disappearance of, 257, 265–
67, 291–95, 302–3; establishment of,
71, 139–47; expansion of, 153–57,
174–86, 192; funds for, 275; lists of,
175, 224–25, 231, 245–52, 264–65,
268, 285–86, 319–20; locations of,
141, 158–63, 168–69, 175–79, 245,
285–87; population of, 258;
provisions for, 186–87; sources on,
137, 174–75, 231; stability of, 189–
91; statistics on, 187–88; status of,
312. See also friars
Mississippian society, collapse of, 233–
34
Mitchem, Jeffrey M., 28
Mocama people: alliances of, 297, 299;
attack by, 269; classification of, 5,
325; dialect of, 6–7, 17–18, 122, 176,
234; French relations with, 68; and
Guale Indians, 89, 149; leadership
for, 157; and material culture, 8, 86,
235; migration of, 183, 240, 313;
and music, 102; names for, 304;
relocation of, 297, 304; survival of,
296
Mocama Province: disturbances in, 191–
92; missionization of, 69, 190, 238,
263, 268, 277, 287; population of,
258; territory of, 5, 10, 155; villages
of, 298; visitation of, 287–89. See also

San Pedro Mocama; Tacatacuru
Province
Mocamo (misspelling of Mocama), 18
Mocoso people, 3, 80, 137. See also
Acuera Province; Diminiyuti
Province; Ibiniyuti people
Mocoso village, 29, 81, 206. See also
Acuera people, Province
Moiety system, 77–78
Molina (chief), 217, 225
Molina, Fray Martín de, 277, 308
Moloa, 60
Moloa village: jurisdiction of, 159, 162;
missionization of, 164, 172–73
Molona (Freshwater chief), 22, 43
Molona/Moloua (Saltwater chief), 64,
80
Molona villages, and confederation, 81
Montes, Fray Blas de, 147, 152, 163
Montiano, Gov. Manuel, 319–20
Moon Lake, sites near, 166
Moore, Gov. James, English force of,
293–94, 296–97, 306
Moquoso (chief), 43. See also Mocoso
people, village
Moral, Gov. Francisco de, 320–21
Mose village, 158, 312, 318–19
Mosquito Inlet, 38
Mosquito people, 171–72
Mosquitos, bar of, 170, 172. See also
Ponce de Leon Inlet
Mosquitos village, 144, 193
Movilla, Fray Gregorio de: assignment
for, 182; on marriage, 112–13; ritual
of, xii; writings by, 122
Moze. See Mose
mulberries, as gifts, 36
murals, on council houses, 91
murders, 241–44, 279, 282–85
music, 101–2, 108, 118, 189
Muskogean languages, Timucua's ties
with, 126–29, 133–36, 234

Nacape. See San Antonio de Anacape
Nairne, Thomas, 302–3
names: abandonment of native, 326;
Apalachee, 16; difficulties with, 217–
18; importance of, 185; influences
on, 20; lists of, 304–5, 322–23;
Mocama, 17–18; Onatheaqua, 18;
spellings of, xv–xvi; Tacatacuru, 18;
Timucua, 15–17. See also glossary
(333–37)

Napituca village: battle at, 31–34; de
    Soto at, 31, 259; food-storage
    structure at, 93; misidentified, 32;
    population of, 259
Napofaie, 263–64
Napoyca/Napuica village, 159–60, 264
Narváez, Pánfilo de, 27–28, 33
nativism, absence of, 221–22
Nebalasa village, 264
necklaces, 24
New Smyrna Beach area, sites in, 27,
    170
New-York Historical Society, documents
    in, 124
Niayca village, 206, 217, 228
Nicoguadca (god of thunder), 109, 115
Nicolás (Indian witness), 274
Niklas, T. Dale, 129–30
Niquisaya, 273–74
nobles: privileges of, 25; terms for, 77–
    78
Nocoroco village: archaeology at, 172;
    defense of, 68, jurisdiction of, 171–
    72; location of, 38, 169, 170; and
    missionization, 169
Nombre de Dios: census of, 310–11; and
    chiefdom succession, 83; defense of,
    297, 303; depopulation of, 156;
    jurisdiction of, 158, 164, 262;
    location of, 156; migration to, 156,
    304; missionization of, 71, 139, 140,
    157, 162, 172–73, 175, 190, 262,
    275; population of, 258, 305, 320–
    24; repopulation of, 236–37, 240;
    subsistence activities at, 196; tribal
    affiliation of, 287, 303–4; tributes
    from, 145; visitors to, 246, 248. See
    also Nombre de Dios Macariz
Nombre de Dios Chiquito: jurisdiction
    of, 158, 169; population of, 323;
    relocation to, 297
Nombre de Dios Macariz: attack on,
    313; description of, 312–13;
    population of, 322; tribal affiliation
    of, 303. See also Nombre de Dios
noroco, 101, 207, 242, 284, 336
Northern Maipuran area language, 128,
    136
nouns, compared with Lamhatty's, 133
Nuestra Señora de Candelaria de la
    Tamaja, 308–9, 313–14, 317–18
Nuestra Señora de la Leche cult, 312,
    320, 324
Nuestra Señora del Pinar (frigate), 61

numbers, compared with Lamhatty's,
    132
nuts, for food, 95–96
Nyaautina (chief), 76, 78, 142
Nyaautina village, 16, 78, 162–63
Nysiscas (interpreter), 149

Oathaqua (chief), 42
obrajes, 192, 336
Ocala area, sites in, 3
Ocala forest, 10
Ocale people: dialect of, 6; diet of, 28–
    29; material culture of, 13–14, 85–86
Ocale Province: alliances of, 147;
    missionization of, 185–86; popula-
    tion of, 258–61; territory of, 5, 10,
    28
Ocale village: and de Soto's expedition,
    12–13, 28; descriptions of, 28–29. See
    also San Luis de Eloquale
Ochile village, 32. See also
    Aguacaleyquen
Ochoa, Capt. Martín de, 60
Ocochuno Indians, 266, 275. See also
    Yustaga Province
Ocone people (Hitchiti-speaking), 4
Ocone people (Timucua-speaking):
    classification of, 4–5; language of, 6–
    7, 155; location of, 155–56;
    missionization of, 8, 155–56, 190;
    origin of, 156; relocation of, 236–37,
    239; removal of, 8, 156–57;
    subsistence activities of, 94, 156. See
    also Santiago de Ocone village
Oconee River, missions near, 180–81
Oconee Valley (Georgia), 4, 11
Ocuia village, 297
Ocute, Alonso (chief), 309
Ocute village, 11–12
Ogchay, 134
ojeo, 98
Okefenokee Swamp, and Indian
    territory, 3, 5, 9, 155
Oklawaha River, and Indian territory, 3,
    12
Olatayco village, 159–60, 162, 164
Old Town Hammock, 254
Olotocara, 65–66, 107
omens, 118–19
Omittaqua (chief), 43
Omittaqua village, 81
Omoloa (chief), 47, 104
Onachaquara (chief), 43
Onachaquara village, 81

Onatheaqua (chief): appearance of, 22, 185; power of, 79, 80; title for, 76; wealth of, 43

Onatheaqua people, 18–19

Onatheaqua Province, 5, 18. *See also* Arapaha Province; Utina Province

Orange and Stallings Island ceramics, 136

Orange Lake, sites near, 30, 166, 178

Oré, Fray Gerónimo de: on friars' problems, 145; on literacy, 188; on missions, 166–67, 174–75, 180, 190; on number of Christians, 179, 262; terms used by, 76–77; visitation of, 177–82

Oribia (chief), 171

Orinoco Delta region, language of, 128, 136

Orista village, chief of, 52, 176

Orlando area, sites in, 28

Ormond Beach area, sites in, 169

Ortiz, Juan, 3

Osachile village, 32

Ospo Island: and Guale Revolt, 176–77; village on, 151

Osuna, Juan de, 211

Osunaca, don Pedro (chief), 310

Ouquodky (Gulf of Mexico), 131–32

Our Lady of Sorrows (mission), 308–9, 311–12

Our Lady of the Rosary of Jabosaya (mission), 310

Outina (chief), 16; alliances of, 42–45, 47–48, 51, 71, 78, 81; battles of, 41–44, 47, 119–20; and Christianization, 137; enemies of, 63–64; as hostage, 45–47, 82; and Menéndez's expedition, 57–59; misidentification of, 19; power of, 78, 80, 81–82; and shamans, 44, 82, 120; successor to, 142; terms for, 16, 76, 78; and trade goods, 44–45, 49; warriors of, 82, 259

Outina confederation, villages or provinces in, 81

Outina village, 81, 94

Ovadalquini. *See* San Buenaventura de Guadalquini

owls, as omens, 118

Pachala village, 184, 212, 216

paha, 182, 330–31,n.6

painting: body, 21–22, 185; on council houses, 91

Palacios, Pedro, 246–48, 330n. 1

Palica Island, defense of, 62–63

Palica village: alliances of, 81; jurisdiction of, 158; migration to, 297–98; population of, 308, 318–20, 322–24; tribal affiliation of, 287, 304

palisades, 88, 212, 216–19

Palmer, Col. John, 313, 320

palm fiber, 1, 22

pandemics, spread of, 261

panpipes, 101

Pantaleon (chief of Colon), 288

paracousi/paraousti, 39, 75, 78

paracoxi, 28, 75

Pareja, Fray Francisco de: assignments for, 141, 157; on Cascangue villages, 155; on chiefdom succession, 83; on communion, 159; on customs, 103, 106–7, 112, 114, 117–18; on games, 110–11; on geophagy, 121; and Guale Revolt, 148–50; on hunting, 116; and language, 6–8, 130–31; numbers used by, 132; on Ocone people, 155; on political structure, 76–78, 163; on reduction, 169; on shamans, 115, 119–20; use of terms by, 17–18; writings by, xii, 17, 122–26

parity principle, problems with, 260

parucusi, 28, 75, 76, 336. *See also* *paracousi*

Pasqua, Francisco (Juan), 211–12

Pastrana, Alonso (chief of Arapaha), 206, 227

patafi, 184

Patale site church, 233

patrilineal system, 82–83. *See also* matrilineal succession

Paynes Prairie, 30, 193–94

pederasty, 112

Pedro (chief of San Pablo), 217

Peña, Diego, 254

Pequatanalis, 243

Péres, Bartolo (interpreter), 234, 280

Pérez, Andrés, 195

Pérez, Bartolomé, 206–7, 218–19

Pérez de Villareal, Agustín, 195, 204–7, 212

Pesquera, Alonso de, 182

Piaja Indians, 244. *See also* Ayapaja people

Picolata, Indian trail near, 16

Pilitiriba. *See* Piritiriba village

pine barrens or pinales villages, 173
Piquilaco Hacienda, 194, 281
pirate attacks, 263–64, 269–71
Piriaco village, 244
Piritiriba village: attack on, 292, 297–98; location of, 272, 293, 298; migration to, 290, 312
pirogues, 100
Pisocojolata village, 263, 271, 288
Pitano village, 159–60
plazas: absence of, 89; site of ball game, 110
poaching, 284
Pocosapa village, 309–10
Pocotalaca village, 310, 322–23
Point of Monzón, 298
Pojoy, don Antonio (chief), 332n. 4
Pojoy Indians: attacks by, 179; baptisms of, 317; flight by, 321; subsistence activities of, 322; villages of, 311; warnings received by, 276
political organization: description of, 4, 39, 73–74, 79; divisions in, 75–78; and epidemics, 79; gobernador, 83–85, 335; influences on, 83–84; and matrilineal succession, 82, 112; and moieties, 77–78; rankings in, 75–77; and religion, 74–75; and village jurisdictions, 158–59, 167; and village list, 224. See also chiefs; commoners; nobles
Ponce de León, Juan, 27
Ponce de León Inlet, 27, 170. See also Mosquitos, bar of
population: and Christianization, 261–63; concentrations of, 32–33; decline of, 192, 203; effects of hostilities on, 68; increase in, 265; and material culture, 231–36; methods for counting, 261; and parity principle, 260; sources on, 257–67; of villages, 246–47, 264, 304–5, 320
Port Royal (French), 38
Port San Martín, 254
postchildbirth huts, 87, 93, 117
Potano (chief): gifts to, 144; hostility of, 138; power of, 80–82; title for, 76. See also Potavou
Potano people: alliances of, 63, 147; attacks on, 72, 119–20, 179; classification of, 5; and divorce, 114; enemies of, 43, 71; gifts for, 144; and Guale Revolt, 143; hostility of, 71–

72; housing of, 87–88; language of, 6–7, 122–23, 155, 185; leadership for, 40, 144; material culture of, 13–14, 30–31, 85–86, 232; and warfare, 18–19, 41–44, 64
Potano Province: abandonment of, 302–3; and chiefdom succession, 83; depopulation of, 227; de Soto in, 29–30; environment of, 155, 193; merger with Utina, 5; missionization of, 30, 154, 165–66, 172–74, 178–79, 190, 246; name for, 17; overlooked, 32; population of, 258, 260–61; power of, 80–82; ranches in, 193; territory of, 5–6, 9, 15, 18, 30; villages in, 30–31, 75, 82, 154–55; workers in, 280. See also Timucua Revolt (1656)
Potavou (chief), 40, 42. See also Potano (chief)
Potayo village, 158, 162
Potohiriba village: games at, 108–9; leadership for, 278; location of, 183, 251; mission at, 275; and murder investigation, 279, 282–85; status of, 229–30; and Timucua Revolt, 205–8, 210, 217, 219–20. See also San Pedro y San Pablo de Potohiriba
Potoriba (chief of), 157. See also Puturiba village
pottery makers, gender of, 86. See also ceramics
powder horn, 284
Powell, John Wesley, 126
Prado, Capt. Antonio de, 66, 68
prefixes, functions of, 131
presents. See gifts
priest (Indian), burial of, 106
Prieto, Fray Martín: images burned by, 94, 167; on mission locations, 183; missionary efforts by, 30, 154, 165–68; and negotiations with Apalachee, 167–68
Primo de Rivera, Capt. Joseph, 307–8, 319
Proto-Tucano language, 136
provinces: description of, 4–6; locations of, 2. See also names of specific provinces
public house, 91–92
public works, leadership for, 77
"pueblo de Timucua," 319–20
Pueyo, Juan de, 281, 287–89
Pulihica village, 253–54

Punta village, 322–23
Putnam County, and Indian territory, 16
Puturiba River, and attack on Cumberland Island, 148
Puturiba village: gifts for, 144; and Guale Revolt, 149; jurisdiction of, 159–60, 162; migration from, 183; missionization of, 147, 152, 157. *See also* Potoriba

quail, taboos on, 117
quilates, 49
Quiroga y Losada, Gov. Diego de: and baptisms, 244; on friars, 276–77; policies of, 123–24, 287; and rebuilding mission, 266
Quisca, don Francisco Ya (chief), 310

rain-god, 109, 115
ranching: at Asile, 123, 184, 196–99; establishment of, 252; and landownership, 197–99; locations for, 192–95; structures for, 198; and wild food gathering, 194–95, 281; workers for, 280
Ranjel, Rodrigo: on council houses, 89; on de Soto's expedition, 32; on provisions, 258–59; on villages, 29–31, 184, 259
Ratobo village, 158–59
rattles, musical, 101, 108
rebels, palisade of, 212, 216–19
Rebolledo, Gov. Diego de: and cargo-bearing by chiefs, 200–210; chiefs promoted by, 225–26; on epidemics, 188; greed of, 202–3, 227; on population, 236; and reaction to revolts, 212–15, 219; records of, xi, 207; relocation policy of, 226–27, 231, 236–37, 261; sentences by, 220–21, 223; on village locations, 182, 225; visitation by, 223–29
red copper, 47
reduction (*congregación*), 168–73, 336
Reinoso, Fray Alonso, 71, 139
Reitz, Elizabeth J., 196
religion: and chief's power, 143, 167; description of, 114–15; loyalty to, 139, 165, 326–28. *See also* rituals; sun-god
repartimiento, 336
residencia, absence of, for native rulers, 83, 336

revolts. *See* Guale Revolt (1597); Timucua Revolt (1656)
Ribaut, Jean: alliances of, 40; attacks on, 50–51, 53; on council houses, 89; death of, 54; expeditions of, 35–37, 39, 47, 49, 79; on fishing, 100; on houses and gardens, 87–89; Indians described by, 21–23; on Satilla River, 11–12
Ribera de la Cruz (Shore of the Cross), 38
Ricahecria Indians, 129, 239. *See also* Chichimeco Indians
Richardson site, 30, 72, 88, 166
Rinconada, 337
Rio Amajuro. *See* Withlacoochee River
Rio Dulce. *See* Freshwater people
Rio Negro region, language of, 136
Riso, Manuel, 323, 324, 325
rituals: for curing, 119–21; for everyday activities, 115–17; gifts in, 94; musical instruments for, 101; for new corn, 113; scapegoat, 80–81; for taking possession of land, 50; vessels for, 97; and wailing, 104–6; for warfare, 41, 44, 80–81. *See also* cacina (tea); shamans
river of Cofa, 179. *See also* Suwannee River
river of Currents, 53, 248. *See also* St. Johns River
river of Little Acorns, 248
river of May, 53. *See also* St. Johns River
river of Salamototo, 53. *See also* St. Johns River
river of Santa Isabel, 3. *See also* Altamaha River
rivers: as boundaries, 31; and ferry regulations, 281–82, 287, 290–91; safety at crossings of, 31, 180, 225, 255, 277–79; transportation on, 100
Rizo, don Francisco (chief), 267, 300, 304
Robinson Sinks cluster, 30–31
Rodrígues, Fray Blas, death of, 152
Rogel, Father Juan, 67, 138
Rojas y Borja, Gov. Luis de, 191–92
Rollestown, 8, 10, 86
Romero, Fray Bartolomé, 164, 173, 175
Romo, don Juan (chief), 309
Romo de Urisa, Capt. Francisco, 294
roots, for food, 94–95
rosaries, 189

Ruíz, Benito (chief of Tarihica), 206–8, 214, 217
Ruiz, Fray Pedro, at Ibi, 153
Ruíz de Canizares, Adj. Juan, 293–94
Ruíz del Castillo, María (cacica from Escamacu), 331n. 3
Ruíz de Salazar Vallecilla, Gov. Benito, 156, 196–97, 238
rulers. *See* chiefs

Safety Harbor culture, 3, 28, 93
St. Anthony, prayers to, 118
St. Anthony of Padua, statue of, 152
St. Augustine: attacks on, 139, 240, 270–71, 292, 297–99; conditions in, 202–3, 261; defense of, 62, 68–69, 200–201, 204, 212, 297–98; as defensive line, 303, 319; destruction of, 55–56, 304–5; establishment of, 10, 38; Indian population of, 105–6, 313–14, 320–22; material culture of, 233; Menéndez at, 50–57; and Ponce de León's landing, 27; relocation to, 302–3, 306–7; school for interpreters in, 172; status of, 66–67, 157, 234; treasurers for, 193; trial at, 283–84; and village locations, 7, 11, 22, 48, 52, 69, 137; visitas of, 139; and Yamasee War, 306–8
St. Augustine Harbor, 50
St. Catherines Island, 144, 152, 269. *See also* Guale Indians
St. Francis feast day, 148–49
St. George. *See* Charles Town
St. Johns River: and bar of Sarabay, 138; blockhouses at, 62–63, 65–66; crossings on, 8, 135, 243, 248; enemy activity on, 300–301; and fishing weirs, 100; and French presence, 21, 35–39; and Indian territory, 3–5, 9–12, 14, 28, 52, 80, 296; Jesuit killed near, 60; and Menéndez's expedition, 47, 57; mouth of, 272; name of, 53; ranches near, 193–94; resources along, 40, 94; totems from, 118; villages along, 290. *See also* river of Currents; Salamototo River; San Mateo River
St. Johns tradition: characteristics of, 13, 14; locale for, 3, 8; successor to, 85
St. Marys River: attacks near, 60–61;

defense of, 66; Gourges's arrival at, 64; and Indian territory, 10, 11; names for, 10, 40; structures along, 87, 89; villages along, 36, 160, 249, 264
St. Marys tradition, 14, 86
St. Simons Island: attack on, 268–72; Indians on, 288, 290; languages on, 234–35; mission on, 10, 176–77. *See also* San Buenaventura de Guadalquini
Salamototo people, 5, 8, 86; identity, 190
Salamototo River, 242. *See also* St. Johns River
Salamototo village, 8. *See also* San Diego de Salamototo
Salchiche village, 151
Salinas, Gov. Juan de, 191
Salomé, María, 305
Saltwater people: alliances of, 51, 63–65; attacks on, 138; attitudes of, 52–53, 137–39, 289; descriptions of, 21, 157; dialect of, 6–7; disappearance of, 193, 250, 296; disturbances among, 191, 326; enemies of, 16, 71; European relations with, 35, 59–61, 64, 68–71, 83; leadership for, 155; material culture of, 86; missionization of, 142, 145, 157–65, 175, 190, 261; political organization of, 73, 163; population of, 164, 262; San Mateo attacked by, 64; schooling for, 67, 137–38; subsistence activities of, 95; warriors of, 59–61, 64. *See also* Mocama people, dialect of; Saturiwa (chief); Seloy (chief)
Salvador, Diego (interpreter), 206, 234
Samomo village, 263
San Agustín de Ahoica: disappearance of, 265–67; name of, 224–25, 252; relocation to, 226; and Timucua Revolt, 218; and visitation, 228
San Agustín de Ajoica/Ajojica, 228, 274. *See also* Ahoica village; Ajohica village; Santa Catalina de Ahoica
San Agustín de Urica: disappearance of, 252; location of, 181–82, 186; missionization of, 190; name of, 224–25; and Timucua Revolt, 218; and visitation, 228–29

San Antonio, use of name, 321
San Antonio (on Cumberland Island),
    159–60, 162
San Antonio de Anacape: location of,
    177–78; migration to, 244, 296;
    missionization of, 141–42, 174, 190–
    91. See also Antonico village
San Antonio de Aratabo, 157, 162
San Antonio de Nacape. See San
    Antonio de Anacape
San Buena Bentura de Palica, 308, 318–
    19. See also Palica village
San Buenaventura de Guadalquini:
    attacks on, 271; closing of, 189;
    council house at, 91; establishment
    of, 165–66, 175; French at, 70;
    governor's orders to, 238–39; and
    language, 234; leadership for, 275;
    location of, 10, 156, 175–77, 249–
    50; missionization of, 175–78, 190;
    name of, 268; tribal affiliation of,
    10–11, 176, 290; visitors to, 249–50.
    See also Santa Cruz de Guadalquini
Sánchez, Juan (chief), 323
Sánchez, Juana Luisa, 323
Sánchez, Leocadia, 323
Sánchez, Fray Luis, killing of, 244
San Diego de Elaca mission: and
    material culture, 86; missionization
    of, 190; relocation to, 8, 156;
    replacement of, 248. See also San
    Diego de Salamototo
San Diego de Salamototo: attack on,
    298–300; food shortage at, 281;
    location of, 53, 286; and material
    culture, 86; migration to, 254, 302;
    origins of, 8, 190; palisaded, 298;
    population of, 258, 261, 305, 308;
    ranches near, 194–95; survival of,
    295; tribal affiliation of, 303–4;
    visitors to, 248
San Felipe de Athuluteca: attack on,
    271; and language, 234–35; location
    of, 250–51. See also Athuluteca
    village; San Phelipe; Sᶜᵗⁱ Philipi de
    Guale
San Francisco de Chuaquin: disappear-
    ance of, 252; location of, 182, 186;
    material culture of, 236;
    missionization of, 190; removal of,
    218, 226–27; and Timucua Revolt,
    217–18

San Francisco de Moloa, friars at, 173
San Francisco de Potano: attack on, 295,
    297–301; and divorce, 114; fortified,
    298; games at, 109; Indians' removal
    to, 226; leadership for, 253; location
    of, 17, 286; missionization of, 165–
    66, 178, 190, 246; murderer's
    detention in, 241; population of,
    246, 253–54, 300, 306; ranches
    near, 194; relocation of, 280, 286,
    301–2; revolt in, 165; status of, 279–
    80; and Timucua Revolt, 206, 208,
    210–11, 219–20; tribal affiliation of,
    303–4; visitors to, 178. See also Santo
    Tomás de Santa Fé
San Ildefonso de Chamini: disappearance
    of, 252; location of, 182; mission-
    ization of, 190; removal of, 218,
    226–27; and Timucua Revolt, 209
San Joseph de Jororo, 309
San Joseph de Puibeta Hacienda, 194,
    281
San Juan (Mocama), 238
San Juan de Guacara: disappearance of,
    265–67; establishment of, 174;
    location of, 180, 251, 286;
    missionization of, 178, 189–90, 275;
    relocation to, 226; repopulation of,
    225, 236; requests from, 255;
    stability of, 189; and Timucua
    Revolt, 210, 217
San Juan del Puerto: attack on, 271,
    292; council house at, 289;
    disappearance of, 298; disturbances
    at, 191; establishment of, 53; friars
    at, 140, 157, 173, 275–77; holy days
    at, 160–61; Indian removal to, 91,
    271; jurisdiction of, 158–59, 162,
    248–50; and language, 235;
    leadership for, 237, 264, 288;
    location of, 36, 53; material culture
    of, 86, 235; missionization of, 141,
    159, 164, 175, 190, 262, 275; music
    at, 102; population of, 235, 263–64,
    280, 291, 293, 305, 308; relocation
    of, 290; royal demands on, 281–82,
    287–90; successor to, 308; and
    Timucua Revolt, 220; tribal
    affiliation of, 287, 303; visitas of, 138
San Juan Evangelista, 217
San Juan River, 53. See also St. Johns
    River

San Julian village, 162–63
San Lorenza Ibiica, 153–54, 185
San Lorenzo de Ivitachuco, 230
San Lucas, 217, 220
San Luis (Apalachee), subsistence at, 196
San Luis de Acuera: disappearance of, 240–41; location of, 178; missionization of, 190
San Luis de Eloquale: closing of, 189; location of, 185–86
San Luis de Inihayca, and settlement patterns, 230. See also Inatafum village; Inihayca village; San Luis (Apalachee); San Luis de Nijajipa; San Luis de Talimali
San Luis de Nijajipa, identification of, 183. See also Inatafum village; Inihayca village; San Luis (Apalachee); San Luis de Inihayca; San Luis de Talimali
San Luis de Talimali: council house at, 90; names for, 183; population of, 261, 308; and settlement patterns, 230. See also Inatafum village; Inihayca village; San Luis (Apalachee); San Luis de Inihayca; San Luis de Nijajipa
San Luis site (Apalachee), material culture at, 233
San Luis village (Diminiyuti), 211. See also Acuera Province; Ibiniyuti people; San Luis de Acuera
San Marcos tradition, 85–86
San Martín de Ayacutu: chief's power, 79; disappearance of, 252; and Freshwater village, 16–17; leadership for, 225–26; location of, 31, 167, 178, 232, 254; material culture of, 232–33; missionization of, 190; repopulation of, 226–27; status of, 230; structures at, 267; subsistence at, 195–96; and Timucua Revolt, 205–8, 210–11, 216, 219–21; tribal affiliation of, 79
San Martín River, 179, 251. See also river of Cofa; Suwannee River
San Mateo (Yustaga mission): investigation at, 281, 283; leadership for, 278; mission, 275; relocation of, 285; and Timucua Revolt, 218. See also San Matheo de Tolapatafi

San Mateo River, 53, 72
San Matheo (fort on St. Johns River): attacks on, 64–66, 69; cattle at, 192; Indian harassment of, 55, 56, 60; mutinous soldiers at, 55; naming of, 53; prisoners at, 61; Spaniards at, 52, 54, 59–60
San Matheo (village on St. Johns River): Christianization of, 164; French ships at, (1580), 69–70; jurisdiction of, 158–59
San Matheo de Tolapatafi: and abortion, 121; establishment of, 184; leadership for, 84, 229–30, 278; missionization of, 189–90; name of, 268; population of, 230
San Miguel de Asile: establishment of, 183–84; location of, 35; missionization of, 165, 190
San Nicolás (trail), 243
San Pablo (St. Johns River): chief confirmed, 164; jurisdiction of, 158
San Pedro (de Tupiqui) (on Amelia Island), 249–50, 271
San Pedro (fort on Cumberland Island), 66–67
San Pedro de Aqualiro, 228
San Pedro de Atulteca, 250–51
San Pedro de Tupiqui, 250, 289–90
San Pedro Mocama (mission): attack on, 89, 113, 148, 292; ceremonies at, 104–5, 189; Christians in, 159–61; council house at, 89; disappearance of, 239–40; disturbances at, 191; domesticated animals at, 99, 143, 327; establishment of, 175; governor's orders for, 238; and Guale Revolt, 147–51; holy days at, 160–61; and Indian neighbors, 7–8, 11, 137; and Indian removal, 236–37; jurisdiction of, 158–60, 262; leadership for, 164–65, 183; location of, 5, 8, 11, 156; missionization of, 139–40, 140–41, 152, 157, 162, 173, 190, 262; music at, 102; subsistence at, 94; and Timucuan name, 17–18; wealth of, 161–62
San Pedro y San Pablo de Potohiriba: location of, 35, 183, 186, 286; missionization of, 190; Spanish interest in, 280. See also Potohiriba village

San Phelipe: location of, 177, 249–50; tribal affiliations of, 250–51, 289–90. *See also* Athuluteca; San Felipe de Athuluteca; S^{cti} Philipi de Guale

San Salbador de Mayaca, 178. *See also* Mayaca

San Sebastian River, 10

San Sebastian village: establishment of, 10; jurisdiction of, 162–63; location of, 56; missionization of, 71, 139–40

San Simón. *See* Mosquitos, port of

Santa Ana: jurisdiction of, 253–54; leadership of, 183; missionization of, 30, 165–66, 246; and Timucua Revolt, 217–18, 220; and village lists, 225

Santa Barbara, 180

Santa Catalina (Utina): establishment of, 252; location of, 248, 251, 286; population of, 305; and Timucua Revolt, 216, 228. *See also* San Agustín de Ahoica; Santa Catalina de Ahoica

Santa Catalina de Ahoica: attack on, 272–75; complaints from, 255; disappearance of, 228, 277; establishment of, 252; migration to, 246, 252; name of, 266–67, 268. *See also* Santa Catalina

Santa Catalina de Ayepacano: disappearance of, 225; and Timucua Revolt, 214; and village lists, 225

Santa Catalina de Guale (Amelia Island): disappearance of, 318; location of, 250; missionization of, 176; population of, 308

Santa Catalina Island, 273

Santa Clara de Tupiqui, 250, 288, 292. *See also* San Pedro de Tupiqui; Tupiqui village

Santa Cruz de Cachipile: disappearance of, 252; location of, 182; missionization of, 190; removal of, 218, 226–27; and Timucua Revolt, 216

Santa Cruz de Guadalquini: disappearance of, 298; location of, 271; population of, 263–64, 271–72, 287–88; relocation of, 287–89, 293; staff for, 275

Santa Cruz de Tarihica: disappearance of, 265–67; establishment of, 174;

location of, 286; missionization of, 190. *See also* Tarihica village

Santa Elena de Machava: attack on, 70; customs of, 278; establishment of, 183; expeditions to, 55, 59; investigation at, 283; language of, 125; leadership for, 52; location of, 184; missionization of, 190; population of, 272–73; relocation of, 280, 285; status of, 66–67, 254–55; structures at, 68, 212, 251; and Timucua Revolt, 206, 211, 214–20; visitation to, 254–56

Santa Fé (post-1720), identification of, 311–12

Santa Fé de Toloco: attack on, 293–95; destruction of, 280; establishment of, 174; and horse-raising, 195, 327; leadership for, 225–26, 275; location of, 9, 17, 30–31, 178, 251, 286; material culture of, 30–31; migration to, 226–28, 266; missionization of, 190, 246, 277; murder trial at, 282; population of, 304; relocation of, 295; repopulation of, 236, 298; status of, 254; and Timucua Revolt, 206, 208, 210–11, 219–20; tribal alliances of, 30–31; visitors to, 248. *See also* Santo Tomás de Santa Fé

Santa Fe River, 9, 29–30, 32–33

Santa Isabel de Utinahica mission: as boundary, 3, 9; establishment of, 174; location of, 3, 180–81; name of, 76

Santa Lucia de Acuera: dialects at, 7; disappearance of, 240–41; leadership for, 264; location of, 12, 178; missionization of, 190; and Timucua Revolt, 209

Santa María (Guale and Yamasee): attack on, 271, 292; council house at, 289; location of, 249–50; soldiers at, 97; tribal affiliation of, 234–35, 289–90

Santa María (Mocama): cacica of, 237; disturbance at, 191; friars at, 172–73

Santa María de la Sena: church at, 162; and village lists, 159–60

Santa María de los Angeles de Arapaha: location of, 181–82; missionization of, 190. *See also* Arapaha village

Santa María Island, 250
Santa María village (western Timucua), 228
Santiago (chief of Pisocojolata), 263, 271, 288
Santiago (murderer), 282–85
Santiago, Sgt. Juan de, 150
Santiago, don Lorenzo de (chief): leadership of, 263, 275, 288; and pirate attacks, 271; and relocation, 287–88
Santiago de Ocone village: disappearance of, 222; establishment of, 155, 175; location of, 156–57; missionization of, 190; relocation of, 236–37, 239. See also Ocone people
Santo Domingo de Asao, 234. See also Asaho village; Asao people
Santo Domingo (Napoyca) village, 159–60, 162, 176
Santo Tomás de Santa Fé: origin of, 268, 304; population of, 305–6, 308, 317; successor to, 319–20. See also Santa Fé de Toloco
Santurro, Fray Alonso, 303–4
Sapala Island, tribes on, 273–74. See also Sapelo Island; Zapala village
Sapala village, 151. See also Zapala village
Sapelo Island, mission on, 180. See also Sapala Island; Zapala village
Sarabay (chief, mouth of St. Johns River), 68, 138
Sarabay, bar of, 138
Sarabay Island (Mocama), 249, 250, 272
Sarabay/Saravay (Mocama chief), 138
Sarabay village, 81, 138
Saranay (chief), 47
Sartucha, Antonio de, 204, 206–7, 211–13
sassafras root, trade in, 161–62
Satilla River, and Indian territory, 11, 40, 46, 112
Satouriona. See Saturiwa (chief)
Saturiba/Saturiva. See Saturiwa (chief)
Saturiwa (chief): alliances of, 44–45, 50, 52, 58, 63–65, 78–79; battles of, 41–43, 61; confederation of, 81; description of, 24, 36–37, 39; and French fort, 40–41, 50–51; and Gourgues, 64–65; and hostages, 45–46, 54, 65; hostility of, 54–57, 60–61, 137–38; and Jesuits, 67, 137–38; and Laudonnière, 39–40; maize

distribution by, 92; and Menéndez, 52, 61–62; musical instruments of, 101; and names, xvi, 16, 78; power of, 75, 78, 80, 81–82, 157; and Ribaut, 36–37; sons of, 60; and Thimagona people, 39–41; and warfare ceremonies, 103–4; warriors of, 22, 82, 259. See also Alimacani village; Saltwater people
Saturiwa confederation, 81
Saturiwa people: alliances of, 51; attacks on, 59; as captives, 60–62; classification of, 5; dialect of, 6, 18; enemies of, 39–42; and fast, 37; food patterns of, 92, 96; housing of, 87–88; material culture of, 13, 86; political organization of, 77–78; territory of, 10; and warfare strategies, 53–54
Saturiwa's village, blockhouses at, 62–63
scalping, 104–5, 327
Scarry, John F., 15, 233
Scots, settlements of, 272–73
S^cti Philipi de Guale, 250. See also Athuluteca village; San Felipe de Athuluteca; San Phelipe
Searles, Robert, 240
Sebastian (chief of Tolapatafi), 230
Sedeño, Father Antonio, 67, 138
Seine River, 40, 160. See also St. Marys River
Seloy (chief), 50–51
Seloy village: destruction of, 56; European landings at, 38, 48, 50; and Saturiwa confederation, 81. See also St. Augustine
Seminole Indians, 3, 95, 135–36
Serrano, Fray Alonso, 168
Serrano y Sanz, Manuel, 190, 251
settlement patterns, 14, 88, 230, 307. See also villages
sexual mores, 112–14
shamans: duties of, 115–17, 119–21; and marriage ceremonies, 113; predictions of, 44, 82; spells cast by, 121
shell middens, differences in, 13–14
shells, uses of, 24, 97, 106
Shinholser site, 181
Shore of the Cross (Ribera de la Cruz), 38
Sieroa Pira, 47. See also copper, red
sign language, 36, 38–39
silver: as adornment, 22; as gifts, 39–40, 65; search for, 39–43, 47

Siouan language, 128
Siquetoro, 60
situado, 337
slavers, 1
slavery, 147, 171, 240, 273–74, 302–3
slaves, black, 114
Smith, Buckingham, 124
Smith, Hale G., 38, 172
smoking of food, 2
social stratification: description of, 25–
    26; and food distribution, 99; and
    militia conscription, 200–202, 204–
    10; symbols of, 101. *See also* chiefs;
    commoners; nobles
Socochuno village, 159, 162
sodomy, 112
Solana, Alonso, map by, 177, 270
Solana, Esteban, and Timucua Revolt,
    204–6, 218
soldiers: abusiveness of, 205, 230–31,
    284–85, 288, 297; complaints about,
    254–55; diet of, 28; equipment for,
    67; and ferries, 290–91; instructions
    to, 63; maize planted by, 164;
    opinions of, 161, 203–4; provisions
    for, 97, 150, 290, 301–2; role of, 58–
    59, 146, 172; unauthorized attacks
    by, 59; villages listed by, 158–63
Solís de Merás, Gonzalo, 52, 55–56, 58,
    81, 329n. 2–3
Soloy village, 62–63, 81, 158
Somme River, 40. *See also* Satilla River
sorcerers, 115, 119–21
South Carolina, 38, 274, 306–8
spades, 99
Spanish: alliances of, 47, 50, 61, 64, 66–
    69, 71, 142, 147, 171, 197; battles
    of, 60–62, 64, 151–52, 296–300;
    brutality of, 137; cabildo govern-
    ment of, 83; and defense against
    British, 297–98; expeditions by, 11–
    12, 27–35, 38, 47–49, 50, 57–59,
    137, 191–92; informers for, 50–51;
    peace achieved by, 70–72, 291–92;
    and reduction of forces, 67; and
    succession to throne, 292; terms
    used by, 1, 15–18, 22–23, 29, 32, 53,
    75–77; and viability of settlement,
    147–48, 157; withdrawal by, 325.
    See also friars; ranching; *names of
    specific people*
Spanish moss: for clothing, 257, 289;
    gathering of, 281; women's use of,
    23–24, 335. *See also guano*

spells, 118, 121
Spiro village, games at, 109
stone, uses of, 37, 39, 92
Strozzi, Nicolas, 69–70
structures: on Asile farm, 198; *barbacoas,*
    87, 93, 130; blockhouses, 62–63, 65–
    68; charnel houses, 106; corncribs,
    89, 212; food-storage, 93; and
    furnishings, 64–65, 87, 90–91;
    houses, 65, 86–88, 198; palisades,
    88, 212, 216–19; for parleys, 36; and
    plazas, 89, 110; public house, 91–92.
    See also council houses; forts
Sturtevant, William C.: on hunting,
    330–31n. 6; on de Bry illustrations,
    20, 93; on language, 125; on
    population, 260; on shamans, 115–
    16, 119–20; on taboos, 117
Suárez, Nicolás, 195, 252
subsistence activities: animals for, 195–
    96, 327; attitudes toward, 322; as
    clue to locale, 156. *See also* agricul-
    ture; fish/fishing; gathering; hunting
suffixes, functions of, 131
sun-god, 41, 103–5, 115
superstitious practices: herbs for, 121;
    and husbands' abandonment, 114;
    love magic, 118; and omens, 118–19
Surruque people: alliances of, 143, 171–
    72; related to Ais, 3; territory of, 3,
    170, 171
Suwannee County, sites in, 180
Suwannee River: as border, 3, 9, 179;
    crossings of, 31, 180, 225, 255, 277–
    79; and Indian territory, 3, 9, 179;
    and migration, 253; missions near,
    166, 174, 180; trade on, 255; villages
    along, 254. *See also* river of Cofa; San
    Martín River
Suwannee Valley complex, 15
Swadesh, Morris, 128
Swagerty, William R., 258–60
Swanton, John R.: on geophagy, 121;
    on Indian tribes, 269; on language,
    6, 124–28, 131, 133–34; on mission
    locations, 176, 251; on tribal
    territory, 3; on village locations, 7,
    12
syphilis, 114

taboos, 114–17
Tacatacuru (chief): alliances of, 64, 68,
    78; death of, 63; and Jesuits, 138;
    power of, 40, 80; title for, 78

Tacatacuru Island, 10, 60, 61, 66
Tacatacuru people: alliances of, 51–52, 66–67; battles of, 60–61, 66; classification of, 5; dialect of, 6, 18; Jesuit killed by, 60, 137; leadership for, 78–79; material culture of, 13, 14; Spanish relations with, 63; subsistence activities of, 94. See also Mocama people
Tacatacuru Province: missionization of, 17, 251; power of, 157–58; and Saturiwa confederation, 81; territory of, 10
Tacatacuru River. See St. Marys River
Tacatacuru village, 61
Taino language, 130
Talaje, 11, 150
Talapo village, 176
Talimali. See San Luis de Talimali
Taljapu village, 251
Tamaja village, 308–9, 313–14, 317–18
Tama people, 234–35
Tama Province: expedition to, 11–12; friars requested by, 187; location of, 181; receptions at, 273
Tama village (Amelia Island), 250
tambourines, 101
Tampa Bay area: sites in, 3, 16, 27–28, 34, 52; as Timucua territory, 3
tapola, 133
Tarihica village: literacy in, 188; location of, 9, 179–80, 186, 251; missionization of, 178–79, 262; and Timucua Revolt, 206–8, 217, 220; visitors to, 228, 248. See also Santa Cruz de Tarihica
Tarraco village, 180
tattoos, 21
Tawasa Indians: language of, 6, 13, 124, 126, 131–34; territory of, 4, 6, 13, 134
temples/temple mounds, 93
TePaske, John Jay, 289–91
Terrazas, Juan Bauptista, 238
Thimagona people: attack on, 41–43; enemies of, 39–40; territory of, 16; and warfare, 80–81, 104
Thomas, Lillian, 74–75
thunder-god, 109, 115
Timucua Indians: acculturation of, 326–28; attitudes of, 142, 195; battles of, 33–35, 197, 291–95; characteristics of, 1–2, 21–25, 101, 307–8;

classification of, 4–8; complaints by, 254–56; demography of, 231–36, 257–67; disappearance of, 47–48, 296–325; literacy of, 122, 188–89, 327; names for, 15–19, 304–5; remnants of, 322–26; security concerns of, 277–80; subsistence activities of, 94–100; territory of, 2, 2–4, 8–13; traditionalism of, 326–28; writings by, 122–23, 191. See also language; political organization; religion; social stratification; Timucua Revolt (1656); traditions
Timucua Province: alliances of, 54, 69–70, 146, 148; attacks in, 238–40; enemies of, 181; environment of, 155; gifts for, 142–43; headquarters for, 280; missionization of, 115, 142–43, 154, 167–68, 174, 178–80, 190, 328; population of, 154, 256–57, 262–65; power of, 184, 203; ranching in, 194; territory of, 5–6, 154; and visitation, 256; warfare with Apalachee, 167–68. See also Utina Province
Timucua Revolt (1656): causes of, 200–205, 326; characteristics of, 200, 221–22; conclusion of, 219–21; effects of, 223–31, 241; events of, 207–13, 216–19; Pérez's part in, 205–7; reaction to, 212–16, 237
Timuqua, spelling of, xv, 16. See also Timucua Indians
tinaja, 97
Tinicua (chief), 68
Tiquijagua village, 276
Toalli village, 93
Tocoaya village, 144, 152, 159
Tocobaga (chief), 52
Tocobaga people, 3, 179
Tocobaga Province, 6, 125, 276
Tocoy village: chief of, 139; establishment of, 71; jurisdiction of, 162–63; missionization of, 172–73, 177, 262; subsistence activities of, 94
tola, 184
Tolapatafi. See San Matheo de Tolapatafi
Tolomato (chief): in 1560s, 52; in 1580, 70
Tolomato mission (Guana River), 86, 271
Tolomato people: in 1597, 144; Guana River, 297. See also Guale Indians

Tolomato village (in Guale): destruction of, 151–52; and Guale Revolt, 150–52

Tolomato village (in Timucua territory): council house at, 288; population of, 304, 310, 322–25

Tomoka Basin, 38, 68, 170

Tomoka River, villages near, 170

Tomoka State Park, sites in, 169

tools, 99–100, 142–43, 253

toponole, 77

Torres y Ayala, Gov. Laureano de, 244

Tospe (chief), 309, 313–14

totems, 118

Towasa village, 131, 133

trade: area for, 163–64; credit for, 289; of deerskins, 163; with French, 44; and governor's treatment, 202–3; of maize, 162; of sassafras root, 161–62

traditions: and abortion, 112, 121; adherence to, 326–28; curing, 119–21; death and burial, 23, 89, 97, 105–7, 117–18; and depopulation, 35; everyday activities, 115–17; games, 107–11; geophagy, 121; magic, 118–19; marriage, 111–14; parleys, 36–37; religious, 114–15; taboos, 115–17; transhumance, 13; wailing, 104–6; warfare, 41, 44, 80–81, 103–5. *See also* burials; rituals

transport, 100, 186–87, 253, 276

tributes, 145–46, 237

Troche, Ens. Rodrigo, 54–55

Tucano language, 136

Tucuru/Tucururu people, 5–7, 12

Tulafina language, 125

Tulafina village, 144, 151, 177

Tulapo. *See* Talapo

Tuluteca, 251. *See also* San Pedro de Atulteca

Tupiqui village, 70, 144, 152. *See also* San Pedro de Tupiqui; Santa Clara de Tupiqui

Turnbull's Creek, 171

Turtle Mound, as boundary, 171

turtles, use of, 88

Tuscarora Indians, 131–32

Uchise Indians, 265–66, 269

Uçita people, 3

Ufalegue village, 144, 176

Upper Timucua, 17

Uqueten village, 29

Urihica. *See* San Agustín de Urica

Uriutina (chief), 34

Uriutina village, 31, 34, 75, 89, 259

Uriza, María Asenisia, 324

Uriza, María de la Cruz, 324–25

Uriza family, 324–25. *See also* Anayo family

Urrutia, Fray José de, 208

Urubia people, 171

Usachile (chief), 33, 79, 230

Usachile village, 31–35, 259. *See also* San Pedro y San Pablo de Potohiriba

Utichine village, 159–60

utina (chiefly title), 75, 76, 337

Utinahica, meaning of, 181

Utinahica chieftainness, 263

Utinahica people, 5, 180–81, 189, 263

Utinahica Province, 9

utinama, 76–78

Utinama village, 29, 75

Utinamocharra village, 75

Utina people: alliances of, 30–31; dialect of, 6–7; material culture of, 13, 15, 85–86, 185, 232; musical instruments of, 101; political organization of, 74; Spanish relations with, 72

Utina Province: Alta, 17; attacks on, 181; and de Soto's expedition, 34; lower, xvi; migration from, 231–32; missionization of, 94, 182, 186, 190, 265–67, 277; names for, 16–19, 185; population of, 258–62; power of chief, 74; propriety of name, xvi; relocation to, 85; settlement patterns in, 230; structures in, 89, 93; territory of, 5, 9; upper, xvi, 17; villages in, 9, 32, 75, 228. *See also* Timucua Province; Timucua Revolt (1656)

Utista village, 263

Valdés, Fernando de, xii, 192, 262

Valdés, Joan de, 331n. 3

Vallecilla, Luis de Salazar, 123

Vásquez, Francisco, 210

Vaupés region, language of, 136

Vega, Garcilaso de la, Inca: on food, 28–29; on population, 258–60; reliability of, 32

Venezuela, language of, 128

Veracruz, 158–59, 162, 164, 191

Verascola, Fray Francisco de, 148–49

verudises, 121

Vermejo, Fray Pedro: assignments for, 157, 172–73; on consolidation, 169; on government support, 161; on population, 158

Vernal, Clemente, 83, 158, 220, 262

Villafarta (Rich City) village, 29

"village of Timuqua," 311–12, 320, 324

villages: complaints from, 254–56; demands on, 281–82, 287–90; depopulation of, 231; descriptions of, 88, 160; establishment of, 40–41, 195, 252–53; fences for, 281; fortification of, 88; of free blacks, 312, 319; French visits to, 37–38; layout of, 90, 169; leadership for, 223; lists of, 158–63, 224–25, 246–47, 303–4, 307–8, 314–17; locations for, 14, 56–57, 81, 88; names of, 135, 183, 217–18; number of, 303; plaza in, 89, 110; population of, 246–47, 264, 304–5, 320; regulations for, 281–82; relocation of, 307; repopulation of, 226; and settlement patterns, 14, 88, 230, 307; status of, 224–25, 227

Villaroel, Gonzalo de, 60

Viniegra, Pedro, 157

Vinson, Julian, 6, 123–24

visitas, 71, 337

Vitachuco village, 32. *See also* Napituca

vtina paracusi holata, 76

wagering, 110

wailing, 104–6, 189

Walker, John, 6, 131–32

Warao language, 128–29, 136

warfare: European ideas of, 42, 56; and missionization, 145; nature of Indian, 41–42, 56, 103, 260; preparation for, 40–41; rituals for, 41, 44, 80–81, 103–5, 118, 120; and scalping, 104–5, 327; strategies for, 33, 41–42, 44, 53–55, 101; weapons for, 40, 101, 116–17, 273

War of the Spanish Succession, 292

warriors: confederations of, 82; ethos of, 242; numbers of, 259; rituals for, 118; symbols for, 101; tactics of, 103

Weber, David, 260

Weisman, Brent R., 232–33

Welatka, and Indian territory, 10, 178

Wenhold, Lucy, 257, 329n. 2

western division, 4–6, 28, 32, 73, 104, 107, 196, 326

Westo Indians. *See* Chichimeco Indians

wheat, 196–97

whistling, 118

White Deer (Honosonayo) clan, 83

widow, status of, 112

Williams, Mark, 233–34

Williams, Stephen, 109

Withlacoochee River, 3, 10, 28, 269–70

women: abandonment of, 114; and abortion, 112, 121; activities of, 111; appearance of, 21–25, 257–58, 289; as captives, 273; and childbirth, 87, 93, 117; and dance regulations, 291; leadership by, 230; and matrilineal inheritance, 82, 112; meals for, 92; murder of, 283; and rituals, 106, 117–18; status of, 26, 189, 230, 322

wood of Asao, 151

Woodward, Henry, 269

words, pronunciation of, 131

Worth, John: on ceramics, 232; on Indian leadership, 237; on Indian names, 239; on mission locations, 179, 186, 271; on Ocone, 4, 155–56; on population, 263, 271–72; on ranching, 193; on resettlement, 226–27; on Salamototo, 8; on San Buenaventura, 10, 177; on Timucua Revolt, 175, 204–5, 208–9, 220–22

Wrights Landing site, 86

xadote, 242

Xaen, Diego de, 288, 294–95, 298

Xapuica village, 172–73

Ximénez, Juan (Palica's chief), 308

Yamasee Indians: attacks by, 265–66, 269, 271, 272, 293, 306–7; captives of, 273, 283; complaints of, 237; disappearance of, 317; language of, 308–10, 319; migration of, 234–35, 239, 296–97, 313–14; missionization of, 251; population of, 191, 322–23; villages of, 249–50, 272; weapons of, 273–74. *See also* Chiluqua (Yamasee); Yamasee War

Yamasee War, 296, 306–8

yaupon holly, 96

Yazah (Calesa) (murderer), 241–43

ycapacha, 337

Yguaja, 297, 314. *See also* Guale Indians; Ibaja speakers

ynihama, 77

Ystasa, Manuel (chief), 76, 122–23, 196–97

Ytara village, 75

ytorimitono, 78

Yuchi Indians, 181. *See also* Chisca Indians

Yufera people, 5–7, 12

Yufera Province, 11–12, 167

Yui people, 5, 166. *See also* Ibi Province

Yustaga (chief), 79, 80

Yustaga people: alliances of, 184–85; dialect of, 6, 122–23, 185; games of, 108–9, 183–85; leadership for, 79, 84; material culture of, 14–15, 85–86, 185, 236

Yustaga Province: abortion in, 121; attacks on, 293–95; de Soto's expedition through, 31–34; merger with Utina, 5–6; migration from, 183, 227, 229, 231–32, 236, 252–53; missionization of, 180, 182–86, 188, 190, 285; names for, 17–18, 185; population of, 192, 258–59, 261; settlement patterns in, 230; territory of, 5–6, 9; villages in, 31–32, 229. *See also* Timucua Revolt (1656); Usachile (chief); Utina Province

Yuta, Antonio, 323

yvita, 135, 330n. 1

Yvitanayo village, 135

yvitano, 77

Zamia integrifolia, 95

Zapala. *See* Sapala Island

Zapala village, 70

Zapotec, chiefs for, 74–75

Zarabay Island (Mocama). *See* Sarabay Island

Zeitlin, Judith Francis, 74–75

Zetrouer site, ceramics at, 86

Zúñiga y Zerda, Gov. Joseph de: defenses of, 298–300, 303; and Santa Cruz relocation, 288, 293

THE RIPLEY P. BULLEN SERIES

Jerald T. Milanich, General Editor

Tacachale: Essays on the Indians of Florida and Southeastern Georgia during the Historic Period, *edited by Jerald T. Milanich and Samuel Proctor (1978). First paperback edition, 1994.*

Aboriginal Subsistence Technology on the Southeastern Coastal Plain during the Late Prehistoric Period, *by Lewis H. Larson (1980).*

Cemochechobee: Archaeology of a Mississippian Ceremonial Center on the Chattahoochee River, *by Frank T. Schnell, Vernon J. Knight, Jr., and Gail S. Schnell (1981).*

Fort Center: An Archaeological Site in the Lake Okeechobee Basin, *by William H. Sears, with contributions by Elsie O'R. Sears and Karl T. Steinen (1982). First paperback edition, 1994.*

Perspectives on Gulf Coast Prehistory, *edited by Dave D. Davis (1984).*

Archaeology of Aboriginal Culture Change in the Interior Southeast: Depopulation during the Early Historic Period, *by Marvin T. Smith (1987).*

Apalachee: The Land between the Rivers, *by John H. Hann (1988).*

Key Marco's Buried Treasure: Archaeology and Adventure in the Nineteenth Century, *by Marion Spjut Gilliland (1989).*

First Encounters: Spanish Explorations in the Caribbean and the United States, 1492–1570, *edited by Jerald T. Milanich and Susan Milbrath (1989).*

Missions to the Calusa, *edited and translated by John H. Hann, with an Introduction by William H. Marquardt (1991).*

Excavations on the Franciscan Frontier: Archaeology at the Fig Springs Mission, *by Brent Richards Weisman (1992).*

The People Who Discovered Columbus: The Prehistory of the Bahamas, *by William F. Keegan (1992).*

Hernando de Soto and the Indians of Florida, *by Jerald T. Milanich and Charles Hudson (1993).*

Foraging and Farming in the Eastern Woodlands, *edited by C. Margaret Scarry (1993).*

Puerto Real: The Archaeology of a Sixteenth-Century Spanish Town in Hispaniola, *edited by Kathleen Deagan (1995).*

A History of the Timucua Indians and Missions, *by John H. Hann (1996).*